Capital Budgeting Techniques

F. M. Wilkes
University of Birmingham

A Wiley – Interscience Publication

JOHN WILEY & SONS
London · New York · Sydney · Toronto

Library of Congress Cataloging in Publication Data:
Wilkes, F. M.
Capital budgeting techniques.

'A Wiley–Interscience publication.'
Includes bibliographical references and indexes.
1. Capital budget. 2. Capital investments.
I. Title.
HG4028.C4W52 658.1'54 76–18280
ISBN 0 471 99416 2

Typeset in IBM Journal by
Preface Ltd, Salisbury, Wilts.
Printed and bound in Great Britain by
Pitman Press Ltd., Bath

For Mom and Dad

Preface

This book is concerned with the investment problems faced by the management of businesses in modern free enterprise and mixed economies. An investment may be defined as a set of changes in the income stream (or, more specifically, the cash flow) of a business. The 'business' may be, at the one extreme, a large conglomerate corporation or, at the other, the toolshed entrepreneur. The word 'investor' will be used to describe whatever decision making unit is faced with an investment problem. Of course, it will not be possible to include all the detailed considerations which will vary from case to case. The objective is to illustrate usable (and modifiable) approaches to the solution of some representative problems.

Investment problems can usually be divided into three parts:

(i) Finding investment opportunities and obtaining information relating to the cash flows that would be generated by these investments. Also, the obtaining of information about costs and sources of finance.

(iia) Deciding which projects to invest in and where there is a choice, the extent of the investment in each.

(iib) Deciding on the amounts to be raised from each source of finance and hence the total amount to be invested.

The second and third aspects of the problem are listed as (iia) and (iib) since decisions relating to them would, ideally, be made simultaneously. In general, the optimum amount of funds to raise from each source will depend upon the nature of returns from each of the investment opportunites available as well as the 'cost' of finance from that and the other sources. Typically, there will be constraints on the choices that can be made under (iia) and (iib). That is to say the investor will not be able to raise unlimited funds from any one given source; it may not be feasible to undertake investment two if investment one is not made; there will be limits given by productive capacity on the choice of investments. There may also be legal requirements to be met. Solvency is an obvious requirement. There may be others relating to design (safety aspects) and distribution (sales of strategic commodities). Also involved in (iia) and (iib) is the problem of deciding the firm's objectives. Usually it will be desired to make some measure of return and risk as favourable as possible, but there may be other objectives such as company size or market share. Some of the erstwhile objectives may be expressed as constraints; for instance the objective of securing at least a given return whilst minimizing risk.

The problems of (i) could, at least at an abstract level, be regarded as similar to (iia) and (iib) – viz, deciding in which areas to search for profitable investments, how much to spend in each area and how the expenditure should be financed. The returns from investments in search activity are especially uncertain and whilst it is obvious that search activity should be carried out to the point where the marginal costs of searching are equal to the marginal return from projects discovered; as Jaaskelainen points out 'The conversion of this general principle into operational rules of behaviour is, however, only at its beginning'.†

We shall not attempt here to set down an optimum approach to the entire problem (i), (iia) and (iib) but will focus on problems relating to the use of funds. An approach of suboptimization will therefore be adopted, concentrating upon the problems of (iia) for the most part and assuming that decisions relating to (i) and (iib) are given. However, discussion of (i) and (iib) will not be avoided altogether. It is often convenient to think of (i) as being completed before (iia) and (iib) are solved. The greater the size of the investments concerned the more likely this is to be the case. In fact the investor is sometimes constrained to do things in this order. If outside finance is to be raised, the suppliers of that finance will want to know for what purposes the finance is going to be used so that at this stage the firm must know the major parts of its investment programme. The sequence; search, evaluate, finance is often the most practicable one.

Chapter 1 introduces fundamental concepts in capital budgeting. Chapter 2 brings in some more advanced topics and introduces the notion of constraints on investor choice. Chapters 3 and 4 introduce linear programming within an investment context. Chapter 5 draws upon the capital budgeting concepts of chapters one and two and the programming methods of three and four to discuss capital rationing problems in greater depth. Chapter 6 extends the work on capital rationing to more ambitious financial planning models. Chapter 7 discusses problems raised by indivisible investments and gives two integer programming algorithms. Interpretation of dual variables and sensitivity analysis are also given. Chapters 8 and 9 introduce the techniques of critical path and modified distribution method to tackle problems at the planning and developmental phases of large scale investment projects. Chapter 10 tackles problems of non-linearity in an investment context. Requisite mathematics are developed and a quadratic programming algorithm is presented. Stochastic problems and advanced computational devices are surveyed. Chapter 11 is concerned with portfolio problems. The classic Markowitz model is discussed in detail, index models are presented and the quadratic programming material of chapter ten is drawn upon.

The prerequisites of the book are minimal. No previous acquaintance with the received theory of capital budgeting is assumed. On the mathematical side no calculus is assumed. Requisite maths is developed as required in an unsophisticated fashion. Any mathematical arguments used are supported by verbal and diagrammatic discussion. The rather technical and seemingly advanced material of

†Jaaskelainen, V., *Optimal Financing and Tax Policy of the Corporation.* Helsinki Research Institute for Business Economics. Publication No. 31. p. 36.

Chapters 5, 6, 7, 10 and 11 need not deter the student equipped with 'O level' mathematics and motivation.

I am obliged to J. M. Samuels, V. Srinivasan, V. Jaaskelainen, R. J. Deam, J. W. Bennet and J. Leather for permission to reproduce certain of their material. I should also like to thank Sam Pooley for checking the first draft and making helpful suggestions. Needless to say, remaining errors are my own fault. Of the numerous people who have contributed to the typing up I should particularly like to thank Kathy Major, Jenny Saxby, Marilyn Corne and Marci Creen. In conclusion I hope it will not seem too presumptuous or sanctimonious if I thank the writers and teachers in this area who have awakened and sustained my interest in this subject.

University of Birmingham
February, 1976

F. M. WILKES

Contents

CHAPTER 1

Fundamentals of Capital Budgeting

In the introduction three aspects of the investment decision problem were listed. These were first: the problems of searching out projects and obtaining information about them, second: deciding which projects to invest in and the extent of the investment in each and third: deciding upon the sources of finance upon which to draw and how much to obtain from each source. The second of these problems is the principal concern of this text, and we shall begin by introducing some of the concepts fundamental to capital budgeting.

1.1 Discounting

As it is ordinarily thought of, the making of an investment will require money to be outlayed at some times (usually including the present) whilst the 'returns' to the investment will be received at other times. Financially, the investment produces a set of changes in the investor's monetary position both at the time that the investment is made and in subsequent years.

Discounting methods make precise allowance for the distance (from the present) of receipts and payments and the notion of discounting is common to most methods of investment appraisal.[1] To illustrate the problem and the discounting approach to its solution consider a simple example. Most people would value a promissory note that can be exchanged for one pound tomorrow more highly than one which could be exchanged for one pound in a year's time. But how much more is the earlier dated note worth? This depends upon the objectives of the individual concerned (who we shall refer to as 'the investor') and the opportunities that are open to him. If upon receipt of a pound tomorrow the individual would wish to invest the pound for a year and earn 10% interest per annum, then the original pound would have become £1 + £0.1 = £1.1 after one year, and it is this sum that should be compared with the longer dated promissory note.[2] Clearly if the investor had received £1/1.1 immediately this would have become £(1/1.1) = £1 in one year's time. Thus, the guaranteed receipt of £1 in one year's time has a 'present value' of £1/1.1 = £0.9091. Equivalently with the same one year horizon and an interest rate of 10%, £0.9091 can be said to have a terminal value (sometimes called future value) of £1. In terms of the promissory note which 'matures' in a year's time, an individual whose best alternative was investment at 10% would just be prepared to pay £0.9091 for the note; it being assumed that there is no possibility of default. Also, transaction costs which can be important in building or revising portfolios have been ignored here. In other words, a receipt of £1 one year hence if discounted at 10% has a present value of £0.9091. The figure 0.9091 is referred to as the *discount factor* or present value factor and is obtained by reference to tables of such factors. 0.9091 will be seen to be the first entry (for $n = 1$) in the column headed $r = 0.1$ (the column) of table one in Appendix 1.

By a continuation of the argument £1 invested for two years at 10% with annual compounding, would become £1 x (1.1) x (1.1) = £1.21 and a receipt of £1 postponed for two years would have a present value of £1/1.21 = £0.8264. Figure 1.1 extends the results to apply to more general circumstances.

	Year 0	1	2	3	4	...	n
A	1	1.1	$(1.1)^2$	$(1.1)^3$	$(1.1)^4$	...	$(1.1)^n$
B	1	1.1	1.21	1.331	1.4641	...	
C	1	$(1 + r)$	$(1 + r)^2$	$(1 + r)^3$	$(1 + r)^4$	...	$(1 + r)^n$
D	S	$S(1 + r)$	$S(1 + r)^2$	$S(1 + r)^3$	$S(1 + r)^4$	...	$S(1 + r)^n$
E	S	$S/(1 + r)$	$S/(1 + r)^2$	$S/(1 + r)^3$	$S/(1 + r)^4$	...	$S/(1 + r)^n$

Figure 1.1 Compound amounts

Rows A and B show what one pound will amount to with annual compounding (at 10%) at the end of various numbers of years. Row C generalizes row A for an arbitrary rate of interest of $100r$% (e.g. for 25% $r = 0.25$). Row D shows what a sum of £S invested now would amount to and row E shows the present value of a receipt of £S for a rate of discount of $100r$%.

1.2 Assessment of Individual Projects by Present Value

Investment projects typically generate a series of returns rather than just one and we might label the returns to a hypothetical project S, as S_t where the t subscript gives the timing of the return. So that if where are n returns in all they could be written out in full as $S_1, S_2, S_3, S_4, \ldots,$ where S_1 is the return after one year, S_2 the return after two years and so on.

For the moment we shall think of 'returns' as accruing at equally spaced intervals of time and being the change in the cash flows in various years that are attributed to a particular investment.

The present value of the entire stream is the sum of the individual present values. Thus the present value of the entire n year stream is given by equation (1.1).

$$\text{Present value} = \frac{S_1}{(1 + r)} + \frac{S_2}{(1 + r)^2} + \frac{S_3}{(1 + r)^3} + \frac{S_4}{(1 + r)^4} \cdots \frac{S_n}{(1 + r)^n} \tag{1.1}$$

which can be written more concisely in summation or 'sigma' notation as

$$\text{Present value} = \sum_{t=1}^{n} S_t(1 + r)^{-t} \tag{1.2}$$

The symbol Σ in equation (1.2) is read as 'sigma' and tells us to sum all terms which follow it (the general form of these terms being $S_t\ (1 + r)^{-t}$) over the range of values t from $t = 1$ up to and including $t = n$. The terms S_t represent the returns to an investment project (although in general they might not all be positive) and in order to secure them it will usually have been necessary to invest money in one or more years. If an investment of £K now is required to secure the returns S_t then (1.2) is said to be the *gross present value* (GPV) of the investment and the GPV minus K (the initial outlay) is called the *net present value* (NPV) that is

$$\text{NPV} = \sum_{t=1}^{n} S_t(1+r)^{-t} - K \tag{1.3}$$

In relation to an individual investment opportunity the single project *NPV decision rule* R1, is as follows:

> (R1) Invest in the project if the NPV is positive. Do not invest if the NPV is negative.

It should be noted that if NPV = 0 it makes no difference to the investor, so far as present value is concerned, whether the project is accepted or rejected. The rationale of (R1) is that if for a particular investment opportunity (which we shall now call a 'project') NPV is positive this must mean that GPV $> K$. Now GPV is the present value of the returns – it is a sum of money which if received now is 'equivalent' to all the returns in the sense that if it was invested at $100r$% it would just generate the said stream, i.e. an amount S_t could be withdrawn from the investment of GPV in the tth year. £K is that sum of money which has to be parted with now in order to secure the returns. Thus if GPV $> K$ and therefore NPV > 0 this means that the present value of the stream of returns exceeds the present value of the money required to secure them. If on the other hand GPV $< K$ then the outlay required at the present moment exceeds the present value of the returns that it is expected to generate. Consequently the proposed investment should be rejected. The objective of the exercise is to compare like with like and this is achieved with present values. GPV is a single figure equivalent of the stream of returns.

As an illustration of the use of (R1) consider the following investment opportunity. A company has the opportunity to purchase a machine at the price of £2,200. It will have a productive lifetime of three years, and the net additions to cash flows (after tax and including scrap value at the end of the third year) at the end of each of three years are respectively £770, £968 and £1,331. The company has sufficient funds to buy the machine without recourse to borrowing and the best alternative is investment elsewhere at an annually compounded interest rate of 10%. Should the machine be bought? Insertion of the data given into equation (1.3) gives the NPV of the investment in the machine. It is

$$\frac{770}{1.1} + \frac{968}{(1.1)^2} + \frac{1{,}331}{(1.1)^3} - 2{,}200 = 300$$

So that by (R1) the investment is worthwhile, that is, the machine should be bought.

In reality of course projects may generate inconvenient patterns of cash flow, (discussed below) or give returns at monthly rather than yearly intervals and interest may be compounded half-yearly or even continuously. These are simple enough technical problems to resolve. Modifications would need to be made to the formulae but not the principles of the approach.[3]

The discount rate is clearly very important to the NPV decision rule. For example if the discount rate employed to evaluate the investment in the machine had been 20% ($r = 0.2$) instead of 10% ($r = 0.1$), then the NPV of the project would have been

$$770 \times 0.8333 + 968 \times 0.6944 + 1{,}331 \times 0.5787 - 2.200 = -115.9$$

where

$$0.8333 = \frac{1}{1.2}, \quad 0.6944 = \frac{1}{(1.2)^2} \quad \text{and} \quad 0.5787 = \frac{1}{(1.2)^3}$$

and the project should have been rejected. It should be noted that although the investment in the machine is profitable in its own right in the sense that the undiscounted sum of the returns that it would generate exceeds the cost of the machine, *it is not profitable enough* when there is the opportunity to earn 20% on the money that would be needed to buy the machine. In other words, the discount rate should reflect such foregone opportunities when an investment is accepted. It represents an *opportunity cost* of the investment. The problem of the choice of discount rate is discussed in section 1.6 below.

Normally a table of discount factors such as Appendix 1 is used in the calculation of present value. The following example illustrates a convenient layout for the use of such a table. Below is a schedule of the net receipts and outlays (including tax payments) that would arise if a particular project is undertaken. The receipt in year 5 uncludes the residual value of the project at that time.

	Year					
	0	1	2	3	4	5
Initial outlay	500					
Net Receipts		150	150	150	150	225

The net present value of the project is determined by discounting the receipts and outgoings arising from the project, (i.e. multiplying each figure by the appropriate discount factor) and summing the discounted figures.

Year	Receipt (outlay)	Present value factor 10%	20%	Present value at 10%	20%
0	(500)	1.00	1.00	(500)	(500)
1	150	0.9091	0.8333	136	125
2	150	0.8264	0.6944	124	104
3	150	0.7513	0.5787	113	87
4	150	0.6830	0.4823	102	72
5	225	0.6209	0.4019	140	90
			Net present value	£115	–£22

1.3 Net Terminal Value

In some circumstances net *terminal value* (NTV), or as it is sometimes called net future value, is a more convenient yardstick for projects than NPV. Both measures give the same accept or reject decision for a project if the same interest rate is used for both calculations. (Although there can be time-horizon problems when projects are being compared with each other but we shall come to this matter later on). NTV is that sum of money that the investor will have at the end of the project in excess of the amount that would have been obtained had the project not been undertaken. Suppose in the first case above the firm considering the purchase of the machine had had £3,000 available for investment. If the investment is undertaken £800 will remain and can therefore be invested at 10% becoming £880 after one year, when it is added to the first receipt from the project, £770, and carried forward at 10%. After three years of this reinvestment process, at the end of the project the investor will have

$$\{[(3{,}000 - 2{,}200)(1.1) + 770]\ (1.1) + 968\}(1.1) + 1{,}331 = 4392.3$$

Subtraction from this sum of the amount that would have been obtained had the project not been undertaken $3{,}000\ (1.1)^3 = 3{,}993$ gives the NTV of the project, that is

$$\text{NTV} = 4{,}392.3 - 3{,}993 = 399.3$$

Notice that this sum is $300\ (1.1)^3$, illustrating the relationship between NTV and NPV. In the single discount rate case and for an n period project this is given by equation (1.4)

$$\text{NTV} = \text{NPV}(1 + r)^n \tag{1.4}$$

The example illustrates a point in connection with NPV. If the NPV formula is to be appropriate, funds as they accrue must be reinvested at the rate of discount. This is valid in the case of finance by borrowing too; the returns being used to repay both capital and interest on the borrowed sum. This subject is discussed in some detail in chapter two. NTV was obtained assuming a reinvestment process, and NPV is obtained from NTV by dividing by $(1 + r)^n$. If the returns to an investment are held as cash and if the sum invested would also have been held as cash then the appropriate discount rate would also have been 0%.[4]

1.4 Yield

The yield of a project known also as the internal rate of return or DCF (Discounted Cash Flow) rate of return, or simply rate of return is defined as that rate of discount for which the NPV of a project would be zero. It is that rate of discount, which if appropriate, would cause the investor to be indifferent between investing in the project and not investing in it. In general yield is i or $100i$% where i is given by

$$\sum_{t=1}^{n} S_t(1 + i)^{-t} - K = 0 \tag{1.5}$$

If this approach to project evaluation is adopted, the yield when calculated is compared with an appropriate 'external' rate – the rate of discount that would have been used to determine NPV. The single project yield decision rule is:

> (R2) If the yield of the project exceeds the comparison rate then undertake the investment. If the yield is less than the comparison rate reject it.

It is not always a simple matter to determine the yield of a project since, as can be seen for (1.5), an nth order equation has to be solved. Discount tables can be employed to give an approximate answer, in which case trial values for i are used to discount the project and interpolation can be used between the adjacent rates of discount which give NPV either side of zero.[5] By this means the reader may verify that the yield for the project –2,200, 770, 968, 1,331 is a little under 17%. Figure 1.2 illustrates how (R2) is used.

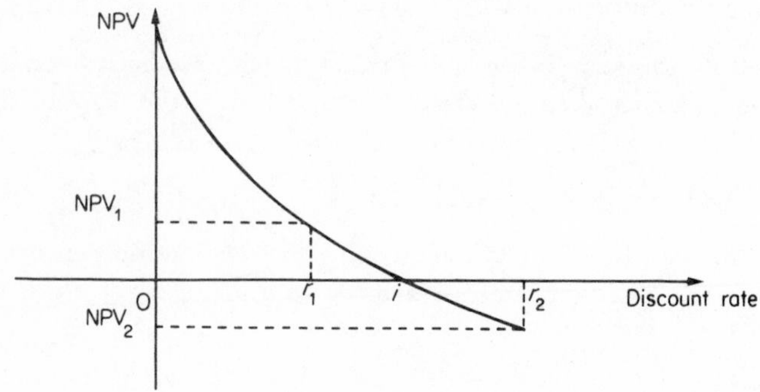

Figure 1.2 Present value graph

The NPV of a 'well behaved' project is graphed against the discount rate. The figure shows that the yield and present value (and also terminal value) decision rules (R1) and (R2) must be consistent in the one project case. If the rate used to determine NPV was $100r_1$%, then the project's NPV is NPV_1 which is positive, indicating acceptance by (R1). Also the yield of the project, $100i$%, exceeds the 'external' discount rate $100r_1$% so that the yield rule would also indicate acceptance of the project. If the NPV discount rate was $100r_2$% NPV would NPV_2 which being negative indicates rejection of the project. Since the project's yield is less than $100r_2$% the project would be rejected by (R2) also. The two rules, however, do not always give the same answers when several projects are being ranked, but detailed discussion of this point is deferred to section (1.8). We must now consider a much discussed problem of the yield method; multiple rates of return.

1.5 Multiple Rates of Return

It is possible that a project can have more than one IRR as defined by (1.5), if some of the returns S_t are negative. In such a case of 'multiple rates' it is necessary to obtain a 'modified' IRR for comparison with the external rate.

One method of approach to the problem would be to discount positive and negative terms separately. In formula (1.6) terms with subscript h refer to positive components of the stream of returns, and terms with subscript L are 'losses'. Thus NPV can be written as:

$$\sum_h S_h(1+r)^{-h} - \left\{K + \sum_L S_L(1+r)^{-L}\right\} \tag{1.6}$$

where the bracketed term is the initial outlay plus the present value of the losses. The expression (1.6) is the 'modified' project for which we determine the yield, i^*, from

$$\sum S_h(1+i^*)^{-h} - \left\{K + \sum_L S_L(1+r)^{-L}\right\} = 0 \tag{1.7}$$

Now if the expression (1.7) is positive, (1.6) and (1.7) together yield

$$\sum S_h[(1+r)^{-h} - (1+i^*)^{-h}] > 0 \tag{1.8}$$

Therefore $i^* > r$. The converse applies if expression (1.6) is negative.

Figure 1.3 illustrates this method. The vertical axes show net present value, the horizontal axes discount rate. The distance OA is:

$$\sum_h S_h - \left\{K + \sum_L S_L\right\}$$

and the distance OA′ is:

$$\sum S_h - \left\{K + \sum_L S_L(1+r)^{-L}\right\}$$

Note that the NPV of the stream at the external rate is unchanged and that since in this illustration NPV is positive at r then i^* exceeds r.

As an example of a case of multiple rates consider the project

−1,000   3,600   −4,310   1,716

where the term−1,000 represents an initial outlay of 1,000 to start the project; that is, $K = 1{,}000$. The term −4,310 is a 'negative return' – a loss year for the project. Yield for this project is found by solving the equation:

$$1{,}000 = \frac{3{,}600}{(1+i)} - \frac{4{,}310}{(1+i)^2} + \frac{1{,}716}{(1+i)^3}$$

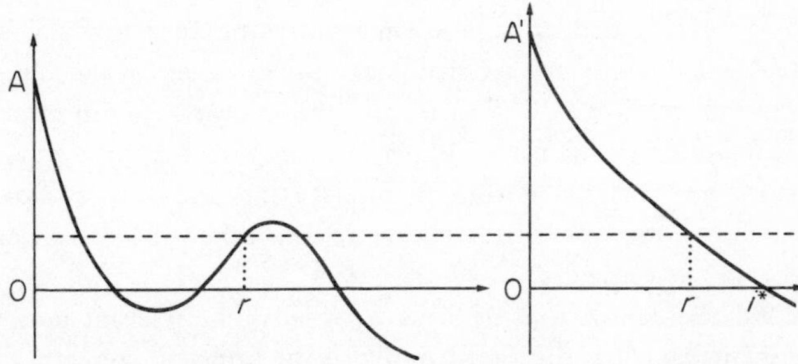

Figure 1.3 Multiple rates of return

Three values for yield emerge, 0.1, 0.2 and 0.3. Now suppose that the appropriate discount rate for determining NPV is 15%. The reader may verify that NPV is (slightly) negative at this rate. Equation (1.7) with $r = 0.15$ should now be solved for i^* which emerges as slightly less than 0.15. Thus the comparison of the single, modified IRR, i^*, with the NPV discount rate 0.15 tells us that the project is not worthwhile. The extended yield method discounts the negative returns back only as far as is necessary to obtain a modifed stream with no negative components.[6] This method also provides an IRR decision consistent with NPV. For instance consider the project:

−200 120 194 −55

(the initial outlay is 200) where the NPV discount rate is 10%. The extended yield method discounts the negative return in year 3 back to year 2 at 10%. Thus a revised stream

−200 120 144

is obtained, where $144 = 194 - (55/1.1)$. The IRR is found for the revised stream, which in this case is 20%. This exceeds the NPV discount rate so the project is worthwhile. Although valid in principle, both approaches become rather involved when more than one rate of interest has to be used, and add little extra valuable information to NPV.

1.6 Data for Calculations

There are two problems that could properly be considered under this heading. Firstly there is the problem of actually obtaining data by search, calculation and estimation and deciding how reliable the data is. The estimating of costs and revenues in future periods is a difficult and important problem and usually involves the use of statistical methods of forecasting. Within the limited objectives of this text it is not possible to expound these methods adequately and we do not attempt to do so.[7] However, two points may be made here. There is the question of uncertainty which as yet we have not explicitly introduced into the examples. This problem is discussed at some length in chapter ten and to a more limited extent in chapter two.

There is also the question of the costs involved in obtaining data. Information is not a free good and the quality as well as the quantity of information may depend upon the effort and money put into obtaining it. Although this problem could be formulated as a capital budgeting problem we do not believe that this is particularly useful to tackle it this way and we shall make things easier for ourselves and assume here that the information expenditure problem has been resolved prior to the other investment decisions being made. Experience may give a good guide to what is about the right level of expenditure in this area and, for some companies at least, the sums involved may be small relative to the other costs associated with the making of capital investments.

The second problem is that of deciding what is the relevant data to include in NPV calculations and it is this problem that is the principal concern of this section.

The two decision rules that have been examined so far are sometimes referred to as DCF (discounted cash flow) decision rules. The yield, as we have mentioned, is sometimes called the DCF rate of return. The principle of discounting has already been discussed. The cash flow part of DCF is important too. What this means is that the data employed in the NPV or yield calculation should ideally be all the receipts and outflows of money associated with a project, and the timing of each receipt and outflow will, given the discount rates, determine the discount factor to be employed for it. This is very much an ideal and in practice it is necessary to use annual or in some cases half-yearly or quarterly forecasts of the excess of revenues over costs associated with the proposed investments. There may be a good deal of doubt about the precision of such estimates (say for five years hence the most sensible estimate that could be made might be that net revenue (revenue minus costs) is expected to be ten per cent greater than in year 4), but they are nevertheless preferable to figures distorted by arbitrary non-cash flow items such as depreciation. The composition of 'costs' and 'revenues' is discussed further below. There is, however, nothing to stop the decision maker from working with annual profit data if he wishes as long as the 'profits' accruing from individual investments can be identified, but his data may not reflect the 'true' profitability of investments.

We shall not have a great deal to say about taxation and except where taxation is explicitly mentioned, it will be assumed in the examples employed that the data are net of tax. In reality 'netting the data of tax' may be an involved process. For instance consider just one of the returns to an investment – say S_3, the return in the third year – if the company as a whole is in a healthy profit-making situation then S_3 will be added to taxable earnings. There will then be a cash outflow of $t.S_3$ (where t is the rate of profits tax) when the tax is payable. If S_3 had represented a loss then if the company is earning a profit on other activities the tax bill in total will be reduced by $t.S_3$. On the other hand if the company was not making any taxable profits then, the project would add the full amount S_3 to earnings with no offsetting additions to tax. However, it is clear that at least in principle tax payments can be treated in the same way as other cash flows. The following example illustrates how taxation can be included in a DCF calculation. The data and the tax structure are artificial.[8] 

An investment project requires the purchase of a machine now at a cost of £10,000. The project will give net returns (revenues minus operating costs) of £5,000 in each of the next four years. The problem is to decide whether the investment is worthwhile after having made allowance for taxation and investment grant, and provision for working capital. By including working capital it is being assumed that there will be minor cash flow items that it is not possible to include in the original NPV calculation. The rate of discount employed is 12% ($r = 0.12$). As can be seen from Figure 1.4 the data that are eventually used for the DCF calculations are rather different from the original outlay and return figures.

The NPV of the project is therefore £7,000 x 0.8929 + 3,500 x 0.7972 + 3,500 x 0.7118 + 4,000 x 0.6355 – 1.500 x 0.5674 – 1.0 x 10,500 = £2722.7 and the investment in the machine is justified.

YEAR	0	1	2	3	4	5
Outlay and net returns	−10,000	5,000	5,000	5,000	5,000	
Working capital[a]	−500				+500	
Investment grant		+2,000				
Taxation[b]			−1,500	−1,500	−1,500	−1,500
Net Cash Flow	−10,500	+7,000	+3,500	+3,500	+4,000	−1,500
Discount Factor[c]		0.8929	0.7972	0.7118	0.6355	0.5674

Figure 1.4 Data for NPV calculation

Notes

[a]Throughout its lifetime the project needs a sum of £500 cash to be set aside for day-to-day contingencies. £500 is taken out of other uses in year zero and replaced at the end of the final year.

[b]The Government calculates the tax payable as follows: Although the investment grant is in fact received after one year, the Government assumes an immediate outlay by the Company of £8,000 and allows it, for the purposes of assessing taxation, 'straight line' depreciation of £2,000 in each of the four years of the project's life. Tax payable (lagged by one year) is 50% of net return minus depreciation, i.e. each year's tax will be £0.5 (5,000 minus 2,000) = £1,500. Thus depreciation is relevant to cash flow calculations in so far as it affects tax payments.

[c]In determining these weights the usual assumption is made that returns occur at year-ends, e.g. the £7,000 comes in one year after the project is started.

If the project is to be evaluated using (R2) then the yield, $100i\%$, would have to be found either by solving the fifth order polynomial equation (1.9) for i by numerical methods or by repeated trials and interpolation.

$$-10{,}500(1+i)^5 + 7{,}000(1+i)^4 + 3{,}500(1+i)^3 + 3{,}500(1+i)^2 + 4{,}000(1+i) - 1{,}500 = 0 \quad (1.9)$$

The reader may verify that the emergent value of i is 0.268 (to three decimal places). That is in percentage terms the yield of the investment is 26.8% which is well in excess of the discount rate, 12%, so that the project should be accepted.

The data employed in project evaluation should also allow for any 'external effects' that an investment may have elsewhere in the firm. For example, if a motor manufacturer established a new plant to produce a new model of a car, the annual net cash flows on which were estimated at £1 million, but the car competed somewhat with other models in the range consequently reducing cash flows elsewhere in the organization by £150,000 then the appropriate figure to use in an NPV assessment of the new plant is £850,000.

Opportunity costs should be included in the data for a project. The opportunity cost of a course of action is defined as the value of the best alternative that is foregone. For instance, if a firm could, with the resources at its disposal, manufacture either monochrome TV sets or colour TV sets, but to manufacture both was impracticable, then the opportunity cost of producing monochrome sets is the cash flows that would have resulted from in the manufacture of colour sets.

To illustrate how opportunity costs can be included in the data consider the case of a firm that has a building which can be either used to house extra machinery of its own or rented out for three years at £250 a year as storage space to an outsider. The machinery would cost £1,000 and last for three years and give net returns of £600 in each year. But if the machinery is installed the rental monies are foregone, so that the returns from the machinery each year over and above what would otherwise have been made are £350. The firm therefore should evaluate the single project (C).

	Year 0	Year 1	Year 2	Year 3
C:	−1,000	350	350	350

which comes to exactly the same thing as choosing between the original projects of

A:	−1,000	600	600	600

and

B:	0	250	250	250

If a 10% rate of discount is appropriate the firm is best advised to rent out the building since the NPV of C emerges as −129.6. This is not to say that the machinery will make an over-the-counter loss, in fact the NPV of A is +492.1. The point is that A is not profitable enough since if it is adopted then B is foregone and B has an NPV of +621.7.

To summarize: unless otherwise stated it will be assumed that estimates of the 'returns' to projects have been made and these returns will be regarded as:

(i) Certain in the sense that decisions will be based on them without explicit allowance for 'risk';
(ii) net of external effects, i.e. the external effects that projects might have, have been allowed for;
(iii) net of tax;
(iv) net of all opportunity costs except those represented by the discount rate.

It will also be assumed that the appropriate rate at which to discount the returns has been found prior to the evaluation of projects. As we have suggested, this itself is a difficult problem about which it is time to say a little more.

1.7 Choice of Discount Rate

A crucial datum for the evaluation of investments is the rate of discount to be used in NPV calculations. The discount rate needed depends upon the circumstances in which an investment decision is to be made and may also depend on the investment project itself.

At the beginning of the chapter the principle of discounting was introduced by way of an example where the potential investor already had money available for investment. The investor had the opportunity to earn a rate of return of 10% on his money and since we supposed that this was the only (and therefore the best) alternative available any project undertaken must show a positive NPV when discounted at this rate.

The determination of the appropriate discount rate is rarely so simple a matter and is frequently an extremely complex problem. The investor's own money (retained earnings) is seldom the only possible source of finance that can or may need to be drawn on, and each source will have its own costs and particular conditions attached to it. Gordon has defined the cost of capital to a firm as a discount rate with the property that an investment which has a yield above (below) this rate will raise (lower) the value of the firm.[9] This is an eminently plausible approach since one expects managers to be keenly aware of the position of the owners of the company, but there is no single agreed method by which a precise figure can be arrived at. However, alternative methods of arriving at the cost of funds for a company give answers that fall within a relatively narrow range. The difficulties are in obtaining figures for the costs of funds obtained from various sources (measuring the costs of equity and retained earnings is more of a problem than finding the cost of loan stock) and bringing the figures together. There are many complicating factors such as risk, taxation, inflation and distribution policy all of which can affect the cost of capital. We should note however that without the presence of risk it can be argued that the costs of all sources of funds should be the same – there would be no reason to invest in debentures at a lower expected return than equity because of their greater security. Provided *knowledge* of the predetermined figure is fully disseminated amongst all potential investors this is plausible and would greatly simplify the cost of capital problems.

But, not all would agree that it is always the value of a company's equity at a given moment that management wishes to maximize. Even two firms in identical circumstances considering identical investments could apply different rates of discount to the investments because the objectives of the firms are different. Managers and owners can be distinct groups and given 'adequate' share price behaviour management may go for long term growth (because they like to manage large companies) even though share prices may be depressed for a year or more, i.e. the NPV of the growth project is, according to the market, negative. The managers could still be viewed as behaving *as if* they used an NPV rule but along with a lower rate of discount. Certainly they do not discount the large returns later on as heavily as the market does.

There are undoubtedly instances of projects being undertaken which are known to have rates of return below the cost of capital. Apart from plausible divergences of interest between the management and the owners of the company, there are other reasons. For instance a bus company might be obliged (or wish to out of altruism) to provide unprofitable country services or an airline company might, for a number of reasons, purchase a plane of domestic manufacture rather than a more profitable foreign competitor. Such 'non-monetary' factors have sometimes to be taken into account when an investment decision is being made, but the calculation of present values at the cost of capital may help the company to determine the cost of its social obligations. We shall concentrate upon these decisions in which the investor has a real choice, and it will be assumed that projects with negative NPVs when discounted at the cost of capital will be rejected. This is not a restrictive assumption if the investor can include in the returns to a project monetary evaluations of the 'non-monetary' returns.

In practice a weighted average approach to the 'solution' of the cost of capital is frequently adopted. There are several sources of funds and the overall cost is obtained by weighting the cost from each source by the proportion of the total of funds that it constitutes. Briefly, there are three principal long term sources of funds for a company. Equity Capital (an issue of shares), Debt [the issue of debentures at given interest rate (or rates) and with a given interval in which the principal may be repaid] and Retained Earnings (profit from previous operations that can be 'ploughed back'). Debt is the cheapest source of long term funds, then comes retained earnings and then, most expensive of all is new equity. Very rarely can debt alone be employed. The firm is required to keep a balance between debt and equity, and there is usually a ceiling (one or less) to the debt/equity ratio for a company and retained earnings may not always be large enough to avoid issuing new equity. The cost of capital will be a weighted average of the costs from the three (or more) sources, but it is difficult to determine the individual costs or the best values of the weights.[10]

The discount rate employed should be (if the weighted average view is taken) the *average* marginal cost of funds, that is, the average cost of the next several increments of capital. This is because it may happen that a particular project could be financed entirely from an especially cheap source of funds (say debt), but the next project may as a result require the raising of more expensive funds (say new equity) as a result of which it may be possible to finance the next project by debt . . . and so on. However, on many occasions it is not possible to identify the source of funds that are used on a particular project. In such cases and where a project is a relatively small part of total investment, some overall cost of capital needs to be used. This cost should be the increase in costs that result from the next increment of capital the company will obtain. That is not the cost of just the next increase from one source – say loan funds – but the entire next round of capital, i.e. the equity, retained earnings plus loan capital. The project is being financed out of this next increment of funds, and it is the marginal cost resulting from this balanced increment that is appropriate.

A firm does not usually float issues of equity capital and debt capital simultaneously; usually one follows the other. Each issue of debt is dependent upon some equity base. The debt increases the risks of the equity shareholders, it increases the risks attached to both their capital and their income stream. Consequently an investment financed with funds from a debt issue needs to earn more than the interest rate attached to the debt. The equity holders need to receive some additional return to compensate for their higher risks. Similarly a new issue of equity increases the borrowing base, and so access to cheaper capital. It is the cost of the next package of capital and the effect on the costs of the existing capital of this new increment that is the appropriate cost.

Once it has been estimated, the cost of the capital is the discount rate that 'should' be used to determine present value of a project in non-capital rationing circumstances. The presence of limits on borrowing either in total or from individual sources complicates the discount rate problem still further. This is a problem which is taken up in a later chapter.

1.8 The Ranking of Projects

Introduction

Both the NPV and yield decision rules can be extended to apply to problems involving choices from amongst several projects, but they will no longer necessarily give the same answers. The problem of choice may be that of selecting all worthwhile projects or choosing from amongst mutually exclusive ones. Using an NPV rule in the former case, all projects with positive NPV are selected and in the latter case the projects with the greater NPVs are preferred. These rules can be stated formally as:

(R3) Accept all projects with positive NPV. Reject those with negative NPV.

(R4) If m projects are to be selected from a group of n, select those m projects which have the greatest NPVs.

In stating (R4) as above it is being assumed that the m projects selected all have positive (or at least non-negative NPVs). This assumption can be dropped in the case where m projects *must* be accepted. Using a yield approach all projects with yields greater than the NPV discount rate would be worthwhile; whilst from amongst a set of mutually exclusive projects the yield rule would prefer those projects with the greatest yields. The yield rules are:

(R5) Accept all projects with yields greater than the comparison discount rate. Reject projects with yields less than the comparison rate.

(R6) If m projects are to be selected from a group of n select those m projects with the greatest yields.

A similar qualification to that made to (R4) should be made in respect of (R6).

To illustrate the use of the rules (R3) to (R6) consider the four projects shown in Figure 1.5.

Project	Returns			NPV(10%)	NPV(25%)	NPV(30%)	NPV(35%)	IRR(%)
A	−100	80	60	22.3	2.4	−3	−7.8	27.2
B	−120	40	100	−1.0	−24.0	−30.1	−35.5	9.5
C	−60	40	50	17.7	4.0	0.4	−2.9	30.5
D	−30	30	20	13.8	6.8	4.9	3.2	45.7

Figure 1.5 Project ranking example

The first entry in each row of the 'Returns' column is the initial outlay in pounds for the project concerned and the two positive returns arrive after one and two years respectively. Recalling that the NPV discount rate is the comparison rate for the yields, both (R3) and (R5) would select A, C, and D and reject project B at either the 10% or 25% rates of discount. When the discount rate is 30% both would select C and D and at 35% both would choose only project D.

There is no conflict between the two rules when all worthwhile projects can be accepted but if two projects were to be selected from the four with the 10%

discount rate (R4) would select projects A and C whilst (R6) would select projects D and C.

Before the (R4) versus (R6) dilemma is discussed in more detail, in respect of (R4) it should be noted that in the case where there are *n* ways of performing a given task (the 'separate' projects are alternative ways of doing the same job) then (R4) will select the least cost method. For instance suppose that a contract gives revenues of 100 (thousands of pounds) in each of three years. Method A fulfils the contract with costs of 90, 80 and 70 in each of the three years respectively. Method B would incur costs of 60, 90 and 90. The *net* revenues from the two projects are 10, 20 and 30 for method A and 40, 10 and 10 for method B. (R4) would select whichever of the 'projects'

A: 10 20 30

and

B: 40 10 10

had the greater present value. That is, it would compare

A: 100 – 90 100 – 80 100 – 70

and

B: 100 – 60 100 – 90 100 – 90

Let PV100 represent the present value of the 'gross' returns 100, then (R4) is comparing

A: PV100 – PV(90, 80, 70)

and

B: PV100 – PV(60, 90, 90)

that is, the present values of the returns (which is the same in each case) minus the present value of the costs. So whichever method gives the lowest present value of costs will be preferred by (R4).

Irrespective of the discount rate the full ordering by yield is D, C, A, B. At the 10% discount rate the full ordering by NPV is A, C, D, B, whilst at the 25%, 30% and 35% rates the ordering in terms of NPV is D, C, A, B. That the NPV ordering changes does not discredit the NPV rule since conditions have changed. The changed discount rate affects different projects to different degrees. In general, projects with their greater returns in the more distant future will be affected more by a rise in the discount rate than projects with the larger returns near to the starts of the projects.

Conflict between the rules (R4) and (R6) often arises if there is mutual exclusion between the projects. Suppose for example that A and C were mutually exclusive and the discount rate was 10%. By 'mutually exclusive' it is meant that one or other project may be undertaken but not both – for example, A might be 'build the warehouse for the Midlands area in Nottingham' and C 'build the warehouse for the

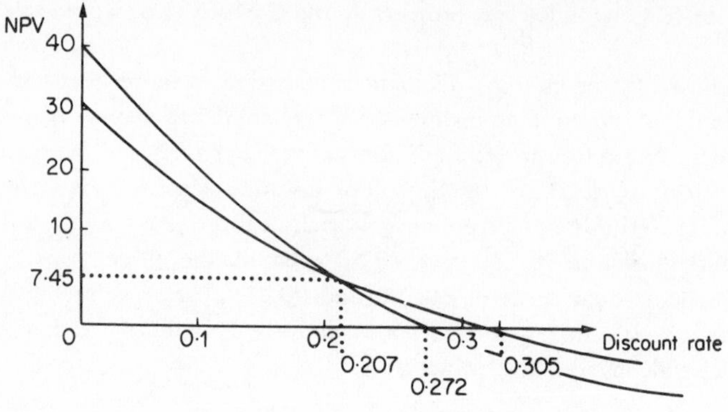

Figure 1.6 NPV and yield conflict

Midlands area in Leicester', only one warehouse being required. Consequently, if one project is to be chosen from the group comprising A and C then the (R4) would select A if the discount rate was 10%, whilst (R6) would prefer C. Figure 1.6 illustrates the choice situation. (R4) and (R6) will contradict each other if the NPV discount rate is below 20.7% but will be in agreement for greater rates. Which rule is to be preferred? Usually the NPV rule is taken to be correct and the yield rule has to be modified. The weakness of the yield rule is that it considers only the *rate* of return on projects and not the *scale* of profits to be made. For instance the projects −6, 4, 5 and −600, 400, 500 have equal yields although the second project gives much more profit in total.

The incremental yield method modifies the 'naive' yield rule (R6) to give decisions consistent with the NPV rule, by explicitly considering the scale of projects. Consider again the problem of choice between A and C with an external discount rate of 10%. A is the more expensive of the two in that it requires an extra £40 immediate investment. Define the incremental project as A *minus* C. Call this project I, that is

	A	−100	80	60
	C	−60	40	50
A − C =	I	−40	40	10

The yield of the incremental project is now determined and this rate is compared to the NPV discount rate. If the yield of I exceeds the discount rate the more expensive of the projects is preferred otherwise the cheaper project will be chosen. This, the incremental yield method, gives decisions consistent with the NPV rule. The rationale is that the extra money required to finance A rather than C (i.e. the 'outlay' for the incremental project) is worth spending if the return on it exceeds the discount rate. In the case above the yield of I is 20.7% so that A would be preferred any discount rate below this. If 10% was the cost of capital and therefore all projects had to earn this amount then the project I is worthwhile. In other words, if both I and C could be adopted they would be – but this would be the same as project A. (R7) is a decision rule based on the incremental yield method and therefore takes scale into account. It can be stated as:

> (R7) Of two projects, select the more expensive one if the yield of the incremental project exceeds the comparison discount rate. Select the less expensive one if the yield of the incremental project is less than the discount rate.

Quite apart from the fact that in some cases the extended yield method, or an equivalent device, may have to be applied to the incremental project, the incremental yield method itself can be time consuming if there are more than two projects to be considered. For instance in the four project situation shown in Figure 1.5 suppose two projects were to be chosen. Not only are the incremental yields of A, B and C over D required but also further applications of the method for A and B over C – all to get a result that would have been given by (R4) to begin with! However, the method is worth knowing since yields of projects rather than present values are still the language of discourse in many business circles.

The recommendation that is made here is that (R3) and (R4) should be used. That is, in the absence of financial or other constraints, between non-mutually exclusive projects those projects that have NPV > 0 are worthwhile and should be undertaken. When choosing between mutually exclusive projects those projects should be undertaken that have the greatest NPVs. (R3) and (R4) are widely used rules, or at least they form the basis of many capital budgeting decisions. We hasten to add that the rules do not, as yet, take account of risk. This will be introduced later on.

It is appropriate at this point to support the use of the word 'should' above. Mention was made in note 1 of the notion of 'Time preference'. Let us consider this subject briefly in relation to investment decisions and project ranking. The time preference structure for an individual is a statement of how that particular individual (person or institution) subjectively compares receipts of income at different times. For instance if I am much more interested in present consumption than possible consumption next year I should rate a current receipt of a given sum considerably superior to the same sum next year. Put another way I should discount next year's receipt using as the discount rate my subjectively decided rate of time preference. This may be quite different from the interest rate or rates that prevail in this year. It will, however, still be strictly correct to compare alternative projects on an NPV basis using the relevant interest rate (or rates) provided that a uniform rate of interest applies to both borrowing and investment in any one year. This is because if $NPV_A > NPV_B$ even though the original income stream from project B was preferred to that of project A discounting by time preference, after taking advantage of borrowing and lending possibilities the income stream from project A can be rearranged to dominate any possible rearrangement of the flows from project B.

Consider an example. Let the cash flows from the projects be:

A:	−100,	150
B:	100,	−105

Now, if an interest rate of 20% prevails, cash flows from B can be rearranged to:

$$B' \quad 100 - y, \quad -105 + y(1.2)$$

where y, representing inter-year transfer of funds, may be positive or negative. But A can be rearranged to:

$$A' -100 + 255(1.2)^{-1} - y, \quad -105 + y(1.2)$$

i.e.

$$112.5 - y, \quad -105 + y(1.2)$$

which is preferable to B′ for any value of y so that project A (NPV at 20% is 25) is preferred to project B (NPV at 20% is 12.5).

As between two n year projects with a uniform interest rate of $100r$% prevailing throughout, the possible cash flow patterns that can be generated in each case can be written as:

$$\sum_{t=1}^{n} (1 - y_t)\, N_A, y_1(1 + r)N_A, y_2(1 + r)^2 N_A \ldots y_n(1 + r)^n N_A$$

$$\sum_{t=1}^{n} (1 - z_t)N_B, z_1(1 + r)N_B, z_2(1 + r)^2 N_B \ldots z_n(1 + r)^n N_B$$

where N_A and N_B are the net present values of the two projects and the y_t and z_t are arbitrary numbers. Now clearly if $N_A > N_B$ for any set of z_t equal y_t could be chosen so that the investor's cash position in every one of the n years is better with project A than it is with project B.

An extension of this discussion to the non-uniform interest rate case (and mention of the subsequent difficulties) is postponed until chapter five when simultaneous consideration can be given to interest rates and constraints on investor behaviour.

1.9 Non-discounting Methods

Although the idea of discounting the income stream of an investment is centuries old, non-discounting methods of investment appraisal are still employed to-day. That the use of these methods should have persisted as long as it has in some business circles is perplexing but is presumably accounted for by reluctance to change and the fact that survival, or even a good living is possible with poor decisions if the quality of competition is low enough. It would be as well to point out some of the ideas and indicate their shortcomings, which in fact provide the justification for the rational methods of investment appraisal.

Firstly consider the *payback period* method. The payback period of an investment is the length of time required by the investment project to return its initial outlay. For evaluation of an individual project a predetermined maximum payback period (say p^* years) would be compared with the payback period of the project in question (say p_1 years). If $p_1 < p^*$ the project would be accepted and if $p_1 > p^*$ the project would be rejected. As between two mutually exclusive projects

Year	Project one Cash flow	Σ Cash flow	Project two Cash flow	Σ Cash flow
0	−20,000	−20,000	−20,000	−20,000
1	11,000	−9,000	1,000	−19,000
2	5,000	−4,000	3,000	−16,000
3	2,000	−2,000	5,000	−11,000
4	1,000	−1,000	11,000	0
5	2,000	+1,000	5,000	
6	7,000		3,000	
7	9,000		1,000	

Figure 1.7 Payback example

the project with the shorter payback period would be preferred. For an example consider the data of Figure 1.7. A choice is to be made between the two projects on the basis of payback period. The payback period for each project can be determined by accumulating the cash flow items. As soon as the cumulative cash flows becomes non-negative the project has 'paid back'. Thus project one pays back in five years ($p_1 = 5$), while project two pays back in four ($p_2 = 4$). Hence since $p_2 < p_1$ the second project would be preferred by the payback period criterion. Cash flows after the payback year are ignored. If the projects had been compared on the basis of NPV then project one, with NPV = £6,130 at 10% would have been selected. Indeed project two is not worthwhile at all having NPV = −£31 at 10%. It is worth noting that project one has greater NPV than project two at *any* discount rate and that project one has 'paid back' 80% of its capital outlay after only two years, whereas project two has paid back only 20% at this stage. The payback method is discredited by its two major characteristics, namely that the timing of cash flows within the payback period are ignored and that cash flows outside of what turns out to be the payback period are not considered. One justification for the use of payback method that has been forwarded is that in situations of considerable risk the project that returns its outlay sooner is to be preferred since there is less risk overall attached to it. This argument will not stand up. What justification is there for implicitly assuming that returns up to the payback period (itself an unknown quantity until calculations are made) are certain and that thereafter returns will be assumed to be zero (or rather have zero expectations in each year). Equally it will not do to argue on grounds of anticipated capital shortage within the next few years after a project has been undertaken. The argument carries no weight because payback ignores the timing of returns within the payback period and in any case a correctly employed NPV approach would take account of this fact *in the discount rate* (or rates) used or in more involved circumstances a capital rationing approach (chapter five) would be indicated. In this connection also the payback method takes no account of interest charges if the initial capital sum was borrowed. A veneer of respectability can be stuck on to the payback philosopy if the payback period is determined using the discounted cash flow items. Such a concession to commonsense would be welcomed, but many objections remain including that of the problem of how an appropriate value for payback period is to be determined.

It is concluded therefore that there is no justification for the use of payback methods in preference to an NPV approach.

A method of investment appraisal with some similarities to payback period but which employs discounting in the *Finite Horizon Method.* In this approach returns after a predetermined period are assumed to be negligible or rather to make negligible contributions to present value. Discounting is employed and individual projects are assessed and mutually exclusive projects compared within the same horizon. In assessing some hydroelectric projects in the United States the public authorities used a horizon of fifty years. With half-plausible interest rates the discount factors for greater than fifty years are zero to two or more decimal places so that with such a long horizon there will be no practical difference between finite horizon decisions and straightforward NPV decisions. If however, for some reason the horizon was 'short' (defined in relation to information quality, project lifetime, the inventor's preferences etc.) similar criticisms to those applied to payback period would apply.

The other category of non-discounting methods goes under the heading of 'return on captial'. The number of possible measures of this concept is the product of the number of possible definitions of 'return' and the number of possible definitions of 'capital'. Usually the 'rate' of return on capital is expressed as the ratio of average return to 'average' capital. For example in respect of the projects one and two of Figure 1.7 if average capital is taken to be one half of initial capital (the initial outlay) i.e. £10,000 in either case and average return is taken as the total of undiscounted returns divided by project duration then return on (average) capital for the two projects is:

$$\frac{100(5{,}286)\%}{10{,}000} = 52.86\% \quad \text{and} \quad \frac{100(4{,}143)\%}{10{,}000} = 41.43\%$$

respectively.

The decision rules based on returns on capital would accept an individual project if its return exceeded the target figure and of a mutually exclusive pair would select the project with the greater return on capital figure. Thus project one would be selected here. If initial capital is used in place of average capital the return figures are halved but the decision between the projects by return on capital is unaffected. Inclusion of scrap (non-zero terminal capital) in a measure of average capital would make no difference to the result if in each case scrap value was the same percentage of original capital.

Although return on capital does consider returns over the whole lifetime of projects it nevertheless, like payback period, ignores the timing of returns. The claim that once definitional problems are overcome, rate of return on capital has the advantage of simplicity of calculation seems rather pathetic when set against the substantial losses that may result from its use as a decision making tool. If the ratio of the total of discounted returns to initial outlay had been taken then a measure would have been produced which could be useful in a capital rationing context. This topic is discussed at the end of chapter two.

In summary the view is expressed in this digression from discounting that non-discounting methods such as payback period and return on capital have no points in their favour (apart from simplicity of calculation) that are not better met by present value methods. In addition non-discounting methods have such serious shortcomings that they should certainly never be used in decision making, their only conceivable use being as curiosities in some financial reporting.

1.10 Risk and Uncertainty

So far the returns to projects have been treated as if they were certain and the effects of risk having only been discussed peripherally in the context of the cost of capital problem. More detailed consideration of the treatment of the risks associated with projects and the effects (on overall risk) of inter-relationships between projects is deferred until portfolio analysis is considered. The purpose of the present section is to introduce some of the basic concepts involved in the consideration of risk in capital budgeting theory.

If the returns to a project are not known with certainty, but the probability distributions of possible outcomes are known then it is possible to calculate the *expected* present value (EPV) of a project. This can be a complicated procedure if the returns in one period depend upon (are jointly distributed with) returns in other periods. The following two period example outlines the Expected Net Present Value (ENPV) approach.

A project costs 150 to initiate – let us assume that this is known with certainty – but after one year could return 130 with probability 0.7 or 90 with probability 0.3. If the 130 return materializes then there is a 0.4 chance of a return of 120 and a 0.6 chance of a return of 70 after two years. If the return of 90 occurred in the first year then the probability distribution of returns in year 2 is 130 with a probability of 0.5 and 100 also with probability 0.5. The 'tree' of Figure 1.8 presents the information concisely. From the tree it can be seen that there is a 0.28 (= 0.4 x 0.7) chance of the project giving a return of 130 in the first year *and* 120 in the second so that assuming that a 10% rate of discount is employed there is a 0.28 chance of NPV being 67.4 (= $130/(1.1) + 120/(1.1)^2 - 150$). The other possible values of NPV are shown in Figure 1.8.

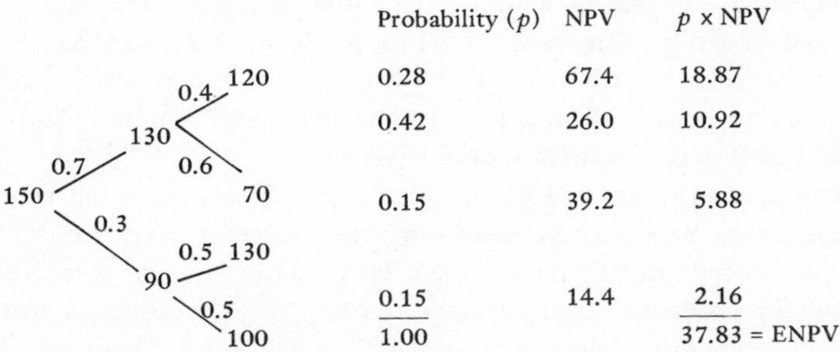

Probability (p)	NPV	p x NPV
0.28	67.4	18.87
0.42	26.0	10.92
0.15	39.2	5.88
0.15	14.4	2.16
1.00		37.83 = ENPV

Figure 1.8 ENPV example

The ENPV of the project is 38.25, being the sum of the products of each possible value of NPV and its chance of occurring. 38.25 is not 'expected' in the sense that we expect it to occur — it can never occur. It is expected in the statistical sense that if several 'trial runs' of the project were made the average value of the NPVs that emerged would be near to 38.25.

A plausible decision rule using ENPV would be based on (R1). It would be to accept the project if ENPV is positive and reject it if ENPV is negative. One would not have any qualms about using such a rule in the case of the project above but suppose there were just two possible values of NPV, +200 with a probability 0.9 and −1,000 with probability 0.1. The ENPV is +80 but there are good grounds for not preferring it to a project giving ENPV = 70 from possible NPVs of +80($p = 0.5$) and +60($p = 0.5$). Apart from the obvious desire to avoid ruinous losses it is generally accepted that investors are 'risk averse' which in the present context is interpreted to mean that as between two projects with equal ENPV that project would be preferred that had the narrower *spread* of possible returns. The dispersion of possible NPVs is taken to represent the riskiness of a project. If this is accepted, then for a quantitative decision rule it is necessary to measure the dispersion. There is debate as to what an appropriate measure would be, but the most widely used measures are the variance and standard deviation (s.d.) of NPV.[11] The standard deviation of the NPV of the project in Figure 1.8 is about 19.6 and is calculated from the formula

$$\text{s.d.} = \sqrt{\Sigma p \cdot (\text{NPV} - \text{ENPV})^2}$$

Variance is the square of standard deviation and is an alternative measure of dispersion. The first risk included decision rule that is being developed uses ENPV as a measure of central tendency and standard deviation as a measure of dispersion as a proxy for risk. It cannot be proved to be superior to other decision rules using different measures of central tendency (e.g. the mode) and different measures of dispersion (e.g. the range). The decision rule as stated for the two project case is:

> (R8) Select the project with the greater ENPV if it also has an equal or lower standard deviation of NPV.

There are three points to be made concerning (R8). Firstly in principle it applies (not very helpfully) to the evaluation of an individual project since this exercise can be regarded as a comparison with the null project (zero ENPV and zero s.d.). Secondly it does not give an answer in all cases (the project with the higher ENPV might have the higher s.d.). Thirdly (R8) is equivalent to the rule: select the project with the lower (or equal) s.d. if it also has the higher ENPV in the 'equal' s.d. case or an equal ENPV in the 'lower' s.d. case.

If (R8) is applied to all pairs of possible projects it will single out those which are 'mean-variance efficient'. A mean-variance efficient project has the highest ENPV of all projects with the same or smaller variance. Equally, it has the lowest variance of all projects with the same or greater ENPVs. A hypothetical 'frontier' of such efficient projects is shown by the line F F′ in Figure 1.9. There is no necessity for the frontier to be smooth but there are reasons to expect that the line

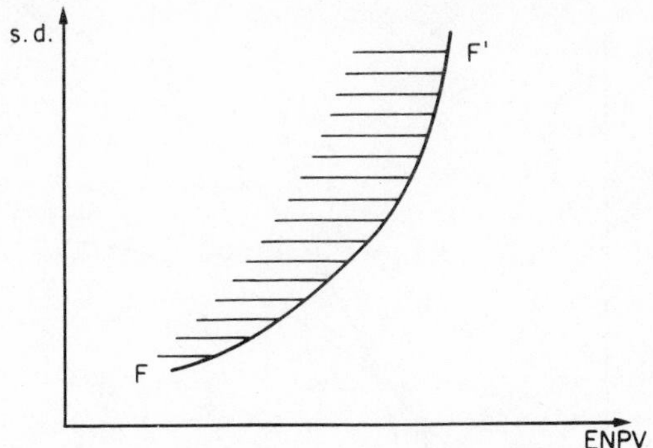

Figure 1.9 Risk-return efficiency frontier

connecting efficient points would have the curvature shown – eventually, greater returns are only achieved by the acceptance of increasingly greater risks. Points in the shaded area represent inefficient projects and points to the right of FF′ cannot be achieved. The investor's problem has been narrowed down to that of choosing from amongst the set of efficient projects represented by FF′, and in a sense this is the easiest part of our task.

The qualitative assumption of risk aversion enabled us to get as far as (R8) but in order to get to grips with choice situations where a higher ENPV also means a higher s.d. we must have more information regarding the degree of risk aversion of the investor. Is the investor a gambler or a play-safer? Figure 1.10 shows 'risk-return indifference curves' for two different people. Risk is measured by s.d. and returns by ENPV. An indifference curve is the locus of combinations of risk and return between which the individual is indifferent. Each combination of risk and return on any given curve is equally attractive (or unattractive) to the individual. Curves further to the right for any one individual represent superior risk-return

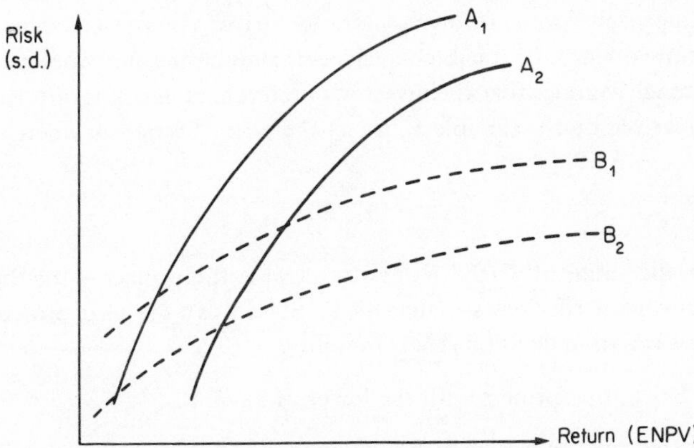

Figure 1.10 Investors' indifference curves

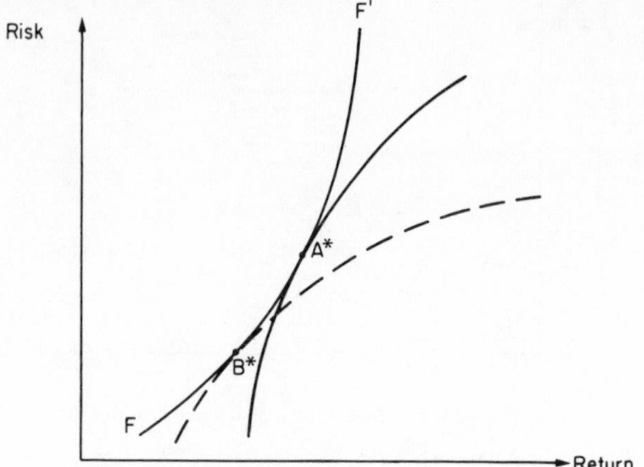

Figure 1.11 Optimal risk-return combinations

combinations. Thus for individual A all points on the curve A_2 are preferred to all points on A_1. Mr. A is clearly more of a gambler than Mr. B (dashed indifference curves); only a small increase in return is required to compensate for a large rise in risk.

Bringing together the information contained in Figures 1.9 and 1.10 gives the solution to the problem. Graphically, the problem is to choose a point on FF′ that is on the highest (i.e. furthest to the right) indifference curve. This is achieved at a point of tangency (for illustrative purposes we shall assume that there is a continuum of projects in risk-return space), and is illustrated in Figure 1.11. The conservative Mr. B is happiest with the project represented by B* whilst the uninsurable Mr. A selects a point, A*, much further up the efficiency frontier.

The use of indifference curves is a somewhat idealized solution procedure for many practical purposes, although if it is reasonable to assume that the indifference curves are straight lines then the procedure is practicable.[12] There are a number of alternative approaches some involving more restrictive assumptions than those made above and consequently (through no accident!) simplifying the problem.

One approach assumes that the investor's preferences in risk-return combinations can be summarized by the variable V, *the coefficient of variation* where

$$V = \frac{\text{s.d.}}{\text{ENPV}}$$

The smaller the value of V the more attractive is the project – the 'best' project being the one with the lowest value of V. Stated for the two project cases the coefficient of variation decision rule is therefore:

(R9) Select that project with the lower value of V.

The rationale for the use of such a decision rule based on V is plausible enough. The larger the ENPV of a project the larger is an acceptable range of variation about that mean. Clearly an s.d. of 50 is much more acceptable with an ENPV of 130 than with an ENPV of 30. The reader may verify that this approach is equivalent to assuming that the investor's indifference curves are straight lines through the origin in the risk-return diagrams.

We have been discussing cases in which the probability distribution of returns is known. Suppose now that although the investor is aware of the possible alternative outcomes of an investment he has no objective information regarding probabilities. This situation is usually described as *uncertainty*. How may the decision-process be formalized in such a case?

A number of criteria have their bases in *game* theory. For instance, a rather cautious investor might, from amongst several projects, choose that project for which the minimum value of NPV was the greatest. This is a *maximin* approach. Mr. A, of previous acquaintance, might be more attracted to a *maximax* policy and select that project with the greatest maximum present value. Maximin and maximax are extreme examples of the *Hurwicz-criterion* in which the investor attaches subjectively determined weights to the best and worst outcomes of projects – a pessimist weighing the worst outcome more heavily than an optimist would. The *minimax regret* criterion selects that investment which minimizes maximum opportunity loss.

In order to be able to illustrate these game-theoretic decision rules, a little basic knowledge of game theory is required. A game is defined as a competitive situation in which the gains of any one participant are affected by the actions of the others. The conflict situation may be tossing coins on a street corner or competition among firms for market share. A constant-sum game is one in which the same total kitty is distributed among the players whatever happens.

Each player has the choice of a number of strategies and a play of the game occurs when a strategy is chosen by each player. Strategies are selected simultaneously, there being no prior knowledge of opponents' choice of strategies, and the outcome of each play is a payoff – who pays who how much depending on the strategies chosen by each player.

Figure 1.12 shows payoff for a two-player game with a constant sum of four. The figures represent what player A receives, B receives four less whatever A obtains. Thus if both select their first strategies A receives 6 and B gets −2. If A selects his second strategy and B selects his first then A receives 1 and B receives 3. Which strategy should each player choose? Should the same strategy always be chosen?

The maximin-minimax criterion is a play-safe criterion – each player assumes

		B: Strategy one	B: Strategy two	B: Strategy three
A	Strategy one	6	3	4
A	Strategy two	1	2	7

Figure 1.12 Two-player game example

that whatever he does his opponent will optimize. For instance, if player B selected strategy one he would assume that player A would select his strategy one rather than his strategy two.

If A adopts the maximin criterion he will seek to maximize his minimum possible gain and inspect each row in the payoff matrix for its minimum value and select the strategy which gives the maximum of these minimum values (maximin). A thus selects stragegy one. B, also cautious, selects the strategy corresponding to the column in the payoff matrix with the lowest maximum value (minimax) – strategy two.

When the maximin equals the minimax an element of the payoff matrix is simultaneously the minimum of its row and the maximum of its column. The game is then said to have a saddle point, and neither player can improve things for himself by departing from his original strategy as long as his opponent retains the minimax strategy.

Not all payoff matrices have saddle points, for instance consider the payoff matrix

2	4
5	3

In such cases it turns out that the best policy (in the minimax sense) is for each player to be unpredictable and assign only probabilities to the selection of each of his strategies. Thus if at any play A attaches probabilities p and $(1-p)$ to the selection of his strategies one and two, then if B selects his strategy one, A has an expected payoff of

$$E_1 = 2p + 5(1-p)$$

but if B selected strategy two, A's expected payoff would be

$$E_2 = 4p + 3(1-p)$$

Now both E_1 and E_2 are functions of p, and A's caution would lead him to expect that B would adopt that strategy which produced the lower of the two values. A's problem then is to choose a value of p so as to maximize the minimum of values E_1 and E_2. In the 2 x 2 case this can be found by equating E_2 (which increases with increasing p) to E_1 (which decreases with increasing p).

Similarly player B can determine optimum probabilities to attach to the selection of each of his strategies. Thus A should allow an equiprobable selection of either of his strategies, ($p = ½$) while B should attach probabilities of ¼ and ¾ to the selection of his first and second strategies. Player A is said to adopt a *pure* strategy if $p = 1$ or 0 (A saddle point exists to begin with) or a *mixed* strategy if $0 < p < 1$.

The maximin criteria has much to commend it in a game against an active and knowledgeable adversary; but many would consider it an overcautious approach in a 'game against nature', where there is uncertainty but no specific active opponent who could reasonably be assumed to repeatedly select the *least favourable* strategy to 'our' player. Many investment decisions would have this character and other policies may be preferred. Return to the data of the original example where the outcomes for player A are as before but where 'player' B is, for want of a better description, 'nature' and the process by which nature selects strategies is unknown. Player A may still wish to employ the maximin criterion but the maximax criterion (foolish if B applies minimax) is now plausible. If player A adopted this policy he would select strategy two. In this case if the strategies represent mutually exclusive investment opportunities the one with the potentially greatest NPV is chosen – at the risk of a possible poor performance.

The Hurwicz criterion uses a weighted average of the maximum and minimum payoffs of each strategy, ignoring the intermediate possibilities (as do maximax and maximin). The player would choose weights that reflect his own psychology rather than probabilities of occurence of A's strategies. Suppose that a weight of $\frac{1}{3}$ was attached to the best possible outcome of each strategy and $\frac{2}{3}$ was attached to the worst outcome. The two strategies would be then evaluated as:

Strategy one: $6(\frac{1}{3}) + 3(\frac{2}{3}) = 4$
Strategy two: $7(\frac{1}{3}) + 1(\frac{2}{3}) = 3$

and strategy one would be selected.

Clearly the Hurwicz approach could be generalized so that weights were attached to each possible outcome. If all outcomes are given equal weights then the *Bayes criterion* is produced. The Bayes criterion is sometimes referred to as the 'equiprobability of the unknown' criterion for obvious reasons. At first acquaintance this procedure has intuitive appeal but it should be pointed out that the more that nature's strategies are sub-divided the lower is the weight attached to any possible outcome, so that the strategy finally selected by this criterion can be a function of the detail of classification of natures' strategies. Of course it is not necessary to assign each outcome an equal weight (or even to use the same weights for each strategy of player A). The unequal weights could be viewed as subjectively determined prior probabilities.

Finally we come to the minimax regret criterion. To employ this a regret matrix is formed. Elements in each column of the regret matrix are the difference between the maximum element in that column (the outcome of the best strategy that A could have played in the circumstances) and the individual payoff. Thus the regret matrix derived from Figure 1.11 is

Strategy one	0	0	3
Strategy two	5	1	0

and accordingly strategy one is selected when the minimax rule is applied to the regret matrix.

The reader may consider that these game theoretic decision rules are somewhat esoteric and whilst they may be of value at high levels of abstraction something more down to earth might find more regular application. One of the most widely used decision making aids in circumstances of risk that meets this criterion is known as *sensitivity analysis.*

It is an eminently practicable way of considering risk and represents a formalized version of the 'what would happen if . . . ' approach. For a given criterion say NPV, the calculations can be done, for example, for alternative values of the cost of capital – is the choice of project highly sensitive to the discount rate employed? If the answer is no the choice will be clear. If the answer is yes it may be worth studying the cost of capital problem more closely. The significance of variations in returns, probabilities and lifetimes can be deduced. There may, at a less detailed level, be only a few key factors on which the profitability of a project (or the choice amongst projects) depends. Market share, development costs, the pace of inflation and taxation policy are examples. Different assumptions can be made in respect of these factors and the consequences deduced. Sensitivity analysis presents derived information in a revealing way and can often prove to be a valuable exercise for a range of problems from those demanding large computational facilities down to 'bus-ticket' problems.

As an example of the use of sensitivity analysis consider the following situation (in which, for simplicity, taxation considerations are not included). A manufacturing project requires an outlay of £40,000 and would run for six years. Returns, R, result from the sales of a product and it is estimated that sales, q, would be two thousand units per year in each of the first two years, three thousand units per year in each of the next two years and one thousand five hundred units per year in each of the final years. Selling price, p, is estimated at £20 per unit throughout the lifetime of the project and unit costs, c, are expected to be £15. The appropriate discount rate is estimated to be 10%.

The return on the investment in any year t, is given by $R_t = (p - c)q_t$ so that anticipated cash flows over the six year life are:

−40,000 10,000 10,000 15,000 15,000 7,500 7,500

At the discount rate of 10% it emerges that GPV = £47,761 and therefore NPV = £7,761 so that the project is worthwhile. The question to be answered now is: for what range of variation in each of the estimated figures will the NPV of the project remain non-negative?

First consider the unit profit on the product. This is $p - c$ and is currently £5. Any variation in this figure would have equal proportionate effect on each return and hence on GPV as a whole so that so long as unit profit is not less than (40,000/47,761) (£5) = £4.19 with the other data unchanged NPV will not become negative. Thus with unchanged unit costs, so long as selling price is not less than £19.19, the project will still be viable. In other words price must not drop by more than 4.05%. On the other hand if unit costs remain below £15.81 then NPV will be positive, so that any increase must not exceed 5.4%. If unit profits are unchanged but sales are 83.75% [= (40,000/47,761) · (100)] of the original estimates in each year (i.e. do not fall by more than 16.25%) the project is viable.

For the remaining parameters, again considered individually, NPV will become zero for an initial outlay of £47,761 that is, 19.4% above the original figure. The yield of the project is 16.57% so that a 65.7% increase over the original value for discount rate is tolerable. Variation in project lifetime are somewhat more difficult to allow for, for two reasons. If lifetime was increased we should have to have estimates of returns beyond year six and if reductions are being considered we must recall the implicit assumption that returns occur at year end so that some approximating assumption will be necessary if reductions in life involving a fraction of a year are involved. If the projects life was four years, that is, if the last two returns of £7,500 are ignored the G.P.V. would be £38,870 a decrease of £8,891. To make GPV £40,000 the contribution to present value of returns in the fifth year needs to be £1,130. The present value of £7,500 after five years is £4,657 so that if we supposed that the project ran for (1,130/4,657) of the fifth year but that the hypothetical return of (£1,130/4,657) (7,500) = £1,820 was not received until the end of that year then G.P.V. would be £40,000. Clearly this is not the only assumption that could be made regarding happenings in a truncated fifth year, and other possibilities might be more appropriate in some cases. However in the case considered the minimum project lifetime works out at 4.243 years a reduction of 29.8% of the original figure.

Datum	% change
Price	4.05
Unit cost	5.40
Sales	16.25
Outlay	19.40
Discount rate	65.70
Lifetime	29.28

Figure 1.13 Sensitivity results

The data obtained is summarized in Figure 1.13. Entries in the % change column are unfavourable changes (decreases or increases as the case may be) which if occurring individually would reduce NPV to zero. It is evident that the present value is much more sensitive to sales price and unit cost than any other datum. What is indicated by this is that management efforts should be concentrated in these areas either before the event in obtaining more precise estimates of the figures, or, if it is decided to go ahead with the project, in controlling any unfavourable variations that may arise.

Sensitivity analysis does not make the decision for the investor, it merely provides useful information for him. The decision is still to be taken. Of course, the nature of the analysis does not have to be precisely as detailed above. It may be appropriate to consider groups of changes that are thought possible. For instance, in inflationary circumstances where selling price is expected to rise (starting at $t = 0$) at 20% per annum but unit costs are anticipated to rise at 25% per annum, other figures remaining unchanged then NPV works out at £6,044. This is perhaps larger than might have been expected but results from the fact that the selling price inflation is upon a larger base (20) than unit cost inflation and in fact it is not until year four that the difference between the two, unit profit, drops below the original value of five pounds.

It will have been noted that sensitivity analysis has the advantage of simplicity over some of the more sophisticated approaches to risk. It is also true, however, that sensitivity analysis does not include any information as to *how likely* possible changes are. If such probabilistic information is available the investor would, no doubt, wish to make use of it at least in respect of the larger decisions.

There are a number of older methods of attempting to allow for risk – the better known ones being the *payback period* approach and the *finite horizon method* already discussed and the *risk discount method.*

In the risk discount method or risk premium approach returns to a project are discounted using a rate in excess of the rate that would have been used had the project returns been assessed. The risk discounted present value could then be written as either:

$$\mathrm{NPV}^* = \sum_{t=1}^{n} R_t(1 + r^*)^{-t} - K \tag{1.10}$$

where $r^* > r$ the normal discount rate figure or:

$$\mathrm{NPV}^* = \sum_{t=1}^{n} R_t(1 + r)^{-t}(1 + \alpha)^{-t} - K \tag{1.11}$$

where $\alpha > 0$. Clearly the two formulations are equivalent since for any given r^* a value can be chosen for α such that:

$$\alpha = \frac{r^* - r}{(1 + r)}$$

The effect of $r^* > r$ or $\alpha > 0$ is to apply a higher discount factor to all returns, but the further away a return is from the present then the larger is the increase in the discount factor. The rationale for this is that risk also increases with t and distant returns should therefore be penalized more heavily.

Clearly the risk premium (which is $r^* - r$) approach does not pretend to great accuracy and will not be indicated when the nature of risks can be described quantitatively. The method would discriminate against 'growth' projects with returns increasing with time as compared with quick payback projects. The size of the risk premium used in a particular case would be decided on the basis of experience with similar projects in similar economic conditions, or subjectively.

It is evident that the investor has a wide choice of strategies and different strategies can be expected to give different choices of investments. This is as it should be – in most walks of life different people and institutions have different views of the same world. Partly the views reflect the uneven dispersion of information and computational ability and partly they reflect differences in values. A given decision rule will choose an investment but the investor must choose the decision rule!

In fact there is no reason why the investor should not employ a decision procedure which involves the use of several concepts. Projects can be subjected to a 'filter' comprising several criteria. For instance the decision rule might be: choose the project that has the highest NPV of those projects that have a 95% chance of having a postive NPV *and* an expected yield of at least 12%.[13]

In conclusion it is worth noting that it cannot actually be proved that modern methods are superior to the older ones in all instances. There is an element of fashion in respect of the style in which a problem is tackled (e.g. use of computers), and the apparent return of payback to respectability in some circles gives support to the pendulum as against the progress view of the history of the art.

Notes

1. The 'precise allowance' is in the financial sense discussed below rather than in the subjective sense of 'time preference'. This point is taken up later in the chapter. For a comprehensive introduction to the principles of discounting see Merrett, A. J., and Sykes, A., *The Finance and Analysis of Capital Projects,* Longmans, London, 1963, Chapter 1. See also Dewhurst, R. F. J., *Mathematics for Accountants and Managers*, Heinemann, London, 1968, Chapter 8.
2. Unless otherwise stated the sums of money and the interest rates mentioned are assumed to be known with certainty.
3. See Samuels, J. M., and Wilkes, F. M., *Management of Company Finance*, Nelson, London, 1971, pp. 225–226.
4. Assuming that the cash does not serve a cost saving purpose, on which there is an implied rate of return. See Samuels, J. M., and Wilkes, F. M., *Management of Company Finance*, Nelson, London, 1971, pp. 310–312.
5. For an illustration of this process see Samuels, J. M., and Wilkes, F. M., *Management of Company Finance*, Nelson, London, 1971, pp. 163–164.
6. See Merrett, A. J., and Sykes, A., *The Finance and Analysis of Capital Projects*, Longmans, London, 1963, pp. 163–165.
7. The interested reader is referred to Rowley, J. C. R., and Trivedi, P. T., *Econometrics of Investment*, Wiley, 1975.
8. Tax rates and structures change with time and can exert significant influences on the profitability of investments. For a more detailed discussion of taxation in relation to capital budgeting decisions, see Samuels, J. M., and Wilkes, F. M., *Management of Company Finance*, Nelson, London, 1971, pp. 215–223.
9. See Gordon, M. J., *The Investment, Financing and Valuation of the Corporation,* Irwin, Homewood, 1962, p. 218.
10. For examples of the use of the weighted average approach see Samuels, J. M., and Wilkes, F. M., *Management of Company Finance*, Nelson, London, 1971, pp. 128–133.
11. For an introduction to the use of these statistics in an investment context see Dewhurst, R. F. J., *Mathematics for Accountants and Managers,* Heinemann, London, 1965, Chapters 6, 7 and 8. It can, however, be argued that only those deviations producing NPV *below* the mean should be considered as risks.
12. This matter will be taken up again in Chapter 10.
13. For a presentation of more sophisticated screening procedures see Hertz, D. B., 'Investment policies that pay off', *Harvard Business Review,* January–February, 1968.

Additional References

1. Adelson, R. M., 'Criteria for capital investment: an approach through decision theory', *Operational Research Quarterly,* 1965.
2. Adelson, R. M., 'Discounted cash flow – Can we discount it? A critical examination', *Journal of Business Finance*, Summer 1970.
3. Bailey, M. J., 'Formal criteria for investment decisions', *Journal of Political Economy,* October 1969.
4. Baumol, W. J., *Economic Theory and Operations Analysis,* Second Edition, Prentice-Hall Inc., Englewood Cliffs, New Jersey, 1965.

5. Bierman, H., and Smidt, S., *The Capital Budgeting Decision*, Second Edition, Macmillan, 1966.
6. Bromwich, M., 'Capital budgeting – a survey', *Journal of Business Finance*, Autumn **1970.**
7. Fisher, I., *The Theory of Interest*, Macmillan, London, 1930.
8. Hertz, D. B., 'Risk analysis in capital investment', *Harvard Business Review*, **1964.**
9. Hirschleifer, J., 'On the theory of the optimal investment decision', *Journal of Political Economy*, **1958.**
10. Hirschleifer, J., 'Risk, the discount rate and investment decisions', *American Economic Review*, **1961.**
11. Hirschleifer, J., 'Investment decision under uncertainty: choice theoretic approaches', *Quarterly Journal of Economics*, **1965.**
12. Hirschleifer, J., 'Investment decision under uncertainty: applications of the state preference approach', *Quarterly Journal of Economics*, **1966.**
13. Hirschleifer, J., *Investment, Interest and Capital*, Prentice-Hall, Englewood Cliffs, N.J.; 1970.
14. Knight, F. H., *Risk, Uncertainty and Profit*, Houghton-Mifflin, 1921.
15. Luce, R. D., and Raiffa, H., *Games and Decisions, Introduction and Critical Survey*, Wiley, London, 1957.
16. Lutz, F., and Lutz, V., *The Theory of Investment of the Firm*, University Press, Princeton, N.J., 1951.
17. Mao, J. C. T., 'Survey of capital budgeting: theory and practice', *Journal of Finance*, May, **1970.**
18. Massé, P., *Optimal Investment Decisions*, Prentice-Hall, Englewood Cliffs, N.J., 1962.
19. Quirin, G. D., *The Capital Expenditure Decision*, Irwin, Homewood, Illinois, 1967.
20. Shackle, G., *Expectations in Economics*, 2nd. Ed., Cambridge University Press, 1962.
21. Solow, R. M., *Capital Theory and the Rate of Return*, North Holland, Amsterdam, 1963.
22. Teichroew, D., Robichek, A. A., and Montalbano, M., 'An analysis of criteria for investment and financing decisions under certainty', *Management Science*, November, **1965.**
23. Townsend, E. C., *Investment and Uncertainty – A Practical Guide*, Oliver and Boyd, Edinburgh, 1969.
24. Van-Horne, J., *Financial Management and Policy*, Prentice-Hall, Englewood Cliffs, N.J., 1971.
25. Williams, J. D., *The Compleat Strategist* (Revised Edition), McGraw-Hill, New York, 1966.

CHAPTER 2

Further Topics in Budgeting

In this chapter we shall examine some more complicated difficulties with basic discounting methods and look at some applications of the DCF approach to financial problems. The chapter concludes with some introductory concepts in capital rationing, a subject that is taken up at greater length in Chapter 5 after linear programming methods have been presented in Chapter 3 and 4.

2.1 Many Interest Rates

In Chapter 1 we examined problems in which it was presumed that the same rate of discount could be used for all projects in all time periods. This procedure will not always be appropriate. For example if it is known that the cost of capital to a firm is not constant over time, how can this be taken into account in the DCF calculations? The first point to make is that such changes in rates of interest are not *necessarily* relevant to all investment decisions. For instance if a small company finances a project yielding 15% by a loan raised at a *fixed* interest rate of 10% then the project could well be worthwhile even if the interest rate for new loans the following year became 20%. The project −100, 132.25 is an example. It is being assumed that borrowing at 10% is not the cause of the changed rate. The reinvestment problem has been deliberately avoided. It is clear however that only one rate of discount is appropriate to this project.

The changed rates may however, be relevant – as for instance when there is a uniform rate for borrowings/reinvestments. Where these changes are known in advance the NPV formula can be modified accordingly. If r_1 is the rate appropriate in the first year, r_2 in the second and so on, the NPV formula becomes:

$$\text{NPV} = \frac{S_1}{(1+r_1)} + \frac{S_2}{(1+r_1)(1+r_2)} + \frac{S_3}{(1+r_1)(1+r_2)(1+r_3)} + \ldots$$

$$\ldots + \frac{S_n}{\prod_{t=1}^{n}(1+r_t)} - K \qquad (2.1)$$

where

$$\prod_{t=1}^{n}(1+r_t)$$

in equation (2.1) represents the product of all discount factors. That is

$(1 + r_1).(1 + r_2).(1 + r_3) \ldots (1 + r_{n-1}).(1 + r_n)$. As an example, suppose it was required to calculate the NPV of the project −500, 300, 400, 200 where $r_1 = 0.10$ (first year discount rate of 10%) $r_2 = 0.13$ and $r_3 = 0.11$. Then, by substitution into equation (2.1)

$$\text{NPV} = \frac{300}{(1.10)} + \frac{400}{(1.10)(1.13)} + \frac{200}{(1.10)(1.13)(1.11)} - 500 = 239.5$$

Net terminal value is given by:

$$\begin{aligned} \text{NTV} &= 300(1.13)(1.11) + 400(1.11) + 200 - 500(1.10)(1.13)(1.11) \\ &= 330.4 = 239.5(1.10)(1.13)(1.11) \end{aligned}$$

It is noteworthy that if, somewhat arbitrarily, the project had been discounted at the arithmetic mean of the three rates, i.e. $[(1.10) + (1.13) + (1.11)] \div 3 = 1.113$ then the resulting NPV is 237.5, an error of 0.84%. The smallness of this error suggests that single interest rate approximations may be expected to give good enough approximations in practice, and since future interest rates are rarely known with precision this is just as well. However, it should be pointed out that the percentage error in estimation of NPV is heavily influenced by the size of the initial outlay. It is perhaps better to look at the percentage error in GPV which in the example cited here is 0.24% and might reasonably be expected to be below 1% for plausible variations in interest rates.

Another case where more than one interest rate may need to be used is the case where in any given time period several rates of interest may be relevant. As we have seen in section seven of chapter one there will be a cost of capital problem. Frequently an average rate would be employed, but sometimes it is possible to be more precise. The simplest case is where there are two distinct interest rates, referred to as the 'borrowing rate' and the 'lending rate'. An example will illustrate the complication that is brought about and how the problem may be tackled.

A company providing warehousing facilities has a lease on one particular warehouse with two years to run. It can either leave the warehouse as it is, or build a temporary extension at a cost of £17,000. The company estimates that the extension would add £10,000 to the excess of income over operating costs in each of the two years but would have zero residual value. It has £9,000 'cash' available for which the only alternative use would be investment in securities giving a yield of 7%, and any future surpluses may also be invested at 7%. If it decides on the extension, the other £8,000 required can be borrowed on bank overdraft at 9%. The company wishes to adopt that course of action which would cause it to have the most money after two years when it plans to purchase a replacement warehouse. Should the extension be adopted?

If the extension was *not* built the company would invest the £9,000 and obtain (in addition to its other monies) £9,000 $(1.07)^2$. On the other hand if the extension *was* built the company would obtain

$$[-8{,}000(1.09) + 10{,}000]\ (1.07) + 10{,}000 = 11{,}369.6 \tag{2.2}$$

The square bracketed terms in equation (2.2) is the cash position after one year.

The company has borrowed £8,000 at 9% but the first year's extra 'profit' of £10,000 enables both principal and interest to be repaid and leave some over (the contents of the square brackets) for investment in securities at 7% yield. The investment is clearly worthwhile, the NTV of the decision to invest being:

$$[-8{,}000(1.09) + 10{,}000]\ (1.07) + 10{,}000 - 9{,}000\ (1.07)^2 = 1{,}065.5 \qquad (2.3)$$

which means that the company ends up with £1,065.5 more than it would have done if it had not built the extension.

Two interest rates enter into the NTV expression (2.3) and strictly speaking, it would have been incorrect to assess the project using one or other rate alone. There *is* an interest rate which could be applied to the project −17,000, 10,000 10,000 to give an NTV of 1,065.5, but this cannot be known in advance of the calculation (2.3). This interest rate is about 7.65% but in general, this would not apply to other projects.

Using symbols, if the investment costs K and gives returns of S_1 and S_2; if the firm has M of its own resources and can borrow at $100i\%$ and invest surpluses at $100r\%$ where $i > r$; if $K > M$ and $S_1 \geqslant (K - M)(1 + i)$ then the NTV of the project would be

$$\text{NTV} = [(M - K)(1 + i) + S_1]\ (1 + r) + S_2 - M(I + r)^2 \qquad (2.4)$$

from which it can be seen that if $i \neq r$ the term in M does not cancel out if $M < K$. If $M > K$ only r would enter into (2.4) but there is no reason why this should always be the case. If however, either $i = r$ of $M > K$ the NTV would be given by

$$\text{NTV} = [(M - K)(1 + r) + S_1]\ (1 + r) + S_2 - M(1 + r)^2 \qquad (2.5)$$

and cancellation of the term in M and division through by $(1 + r)^2$ would give

$$-K + \frac{S_1}{(1 + r)} + \frac{S_2}{(1 + r)^2} = \text{NPV} \qquad (2.6)$$

The derivation of (2.6) from (2.5) serves to illustrate the point that the familiar NPV formula is strictly correct only if the projects returns are reinvested at the rate of discount used to determine NPV. The reinvestment may be repayment of borrowed funds which were obtained at an interest rate equal to the rate of discount.

In general the use of several discount rates in the calculation of NPV and NTV may be pretending a greater degree of precision than can be expected in reality. However, it is thought that for the smaller company, or the private individual for whom interest rates are more clearly defined, the exercise is practicable.

2.2 The Time Horizon

Over what period of time should projects be assessed or compared? The lifetimes of alternative investments may differ considerably and the investor may have a time horizon which is different from any of these. Should projects be compared over four years or five or ten or twenty-five? In general, what time horizon should be used in the decision rules? There is no one answer that would apply to all circumstances – indeed it is possible to construct artificial examples where no optimal time horizon can be determined. However, the problem can appear more serious on paper than it is for 'practical' purposes – for even if a 'wrong' choice of horizon is made the cost of this may be slight. In some cases, however, the choice of horizon may be important.

As an example consider the choice between the two mutually exclusive projects

A: −100 180 20

and

B: −100 180

It is clear that Project A will be preferred to B on either a yield or a present value basis at any discount rate. But suppose now that each project could be repeated – that is, project A could be replaced by another project A after two years and project B after one year. Assuming that project A is not to be cut short after one year then with a two year horizon the choice would be between A_2 and B_2:

t	0	1	2
A_2:	−100	180	20
B_2:	−100	80	180

since B can be started again after one year (the figure 80 is 180 minus the 100 reinvestment). B_2 will be preferred by (R6) and by (R4) developed in chapter one at any discount rate below 60%. If the time horizon was four years there would be time to repeat A once and B three times and the choice is between A_4 and B_4.

t	0	1	2	3	4
A_4:	−100	180	−80	180	20
B_4:	−100	80	80	80	180

and once again the 'B series' is preferable by (R6) and at any plausible discount rate by (R4).

The problem of reinvestment in 'lumpy' projects is taken up again later, but it is important that the same time horizon be chosen for both projects such that cycles of investments can be completed. The preceding statement should be qualified to the extent that the horizon chosen should be equal to or within that of the investor himself. Problems in which the investor has a predetermined horizon are simpler than those in which the horizon has to be decided upon. The question of how post-horizon returns are to be treated is crucial. The Finite Horizon method simply ignores post horizon returns. The more distant the horizon and the larger the discount rate the less this will matter, but a more attractive approach is to discount the post horizon returns back to the horizon itself. This is how the residual value of assets at the horizon may be determined. The discount rate to be applied in such a process can be important. For example, consider the two projects A and B below.

t	0	1	2
A:	−100	140	200
B:	−100	270	50

Suppose that both projects are financed by borrowing at 20% (to exaggerate the results) and reinvestment of returns not used to repay borrowing is at 10%. If the horizon is at $t = 1$, what are the post horizon returns of 200 or 50 worth? If they are worth that amount which may be borrowed in exchange for them (i.e. 200/1.2 and 50/1.2 respectively), then the 'terminal' values of the projects at $t = 1$ would be given by:

$$(\text{NTV A})_{t=1} = -100(1.2) + 140 + 200(1.2)^{-1} = 186.67$$

and

$$(\text{NTV B})_{t=1} = -100(1.2) + 270 + 50(1.2)^{-1} = 191.67$$

so that project B would be preferred by a 'terminal' value rule. B would also be preferred by (R4) at $t = 0$ (which is the horizon if the investor wants immediate cash and can borrow on the strength of the projects) since NPV A(at 20%) = 155.56 and NPV B(at 20%) = 159.72. But if the horizon is set at $t = 2$ then on the basis of our assumptions and the interest rate specified, project A would be selected by the appropriate (based on R4) terminal value rule since:

$$(\text{NTV A})_{t=2} = [-100(1.2) + 140]\ (1.1) + 200 = 222$$

whilst

$$(\text{NTV B})_{t=2} = [-100(1.2) + 270]\ (1.1) + 50 = 215$$

Unless further information is forthcoming in respect of the investor's preferences (and opportunities and constraints if not all are reflected in the data we have used) it is not possible to say what is the 'correct' horizon to take. The problem should be addressed case by case and one cannot escape the possibility that in some instances (especially likely in problems that are complicated in other respects) an arbitrary choice may be necessary.

The preceding discussion relates to the choice of a fixed rather than a 'rolling' horizon which may be adopted in a dynamic context. The problem of horizons will be revisited in chapter five.

2.3 Project Truncation and Replacement

Quite often it is possible and desirable to terminate a project even though it would have continued to yield some positive returns beyond the date of termination. This may be a possibility to be considered in advance, or may be considered at a point in time after the project has been undertaken, possibly in the light of revised estimates of returns to the project.

To begin with, it will be assumed that there is no replacement of the project and that 'scrap value' is zero at any time. Even so, the problem of determining the optimum cut-off time is not trivial. The optimum cut-off time will be defined as that time for which the NPV of the project is a maximum. Alternatively, we can define optimum time as that time starting from which there is no positive discounted stream of returns of any size. The latter definition can be restated in terms of NTVs and it is with this definition that we shall work. It should be noted, however, that the objective should not be to seek that point in time which maximizes NTV, for consider the project

−50	155	−5
$(t = 0)$	$(t = 1)$	$(t = 2)$

Obviously the best cut-off point is at $t = 1$, NPV is maximized here. But for some rates of discount NTV is not maximized at $t = 1$. For instance suppose that the appropriate discounting rate is 10%, then at $t = 1$, NTV is 100 $(= -50(1.1) + 155)$ and at $t = 2$ NTV is 105 $(= 100(1.1) - 5)$. The NTV would have been 110 at $t = 2$ had it not been for the return −5.

Turning now to less obvious cases consider the stream of returns

50 70 60 | −40 30 20 | −20 40 | −50 10 |
(cut-off points: 1, 2, 3, 4 at the successive bars)

Clearly, with the no-scrap-value and no-replacement assumptions, a project would not be truncated at a point where the next return is positive, so we can indicate possible cut-off points by dividing the project into segments beginning with a negative return and ending with a positive one. We can then determine that NTV of each segment, starting from the negative return. For example, if an interest rate of 10% was appropriate for the above stream of returns, then the NTV at point 2 of the segment 1–2 is

$$-40(1.1)^2 + 30(1.1) + 20 = 4.6 > 0$$

so it is worth continuing at least till point 2. Similarly the segment 2–3 has a positive NTV, but the segment 3–4 does not. Thus the optimum cut-off point is at 3 – immediately after the return 40 has been received. In a somewhat more difficult case, suppose a project was segmented as above, and the signs of the NTVs of each segment were as follows

+ | + | − | + | − | + | − |
(points: 1, 2, 3, 4, 5, 6, 7 at the successive bars)

Clearly here in the first instance we must proceed to at least the point 2. Points such as 3 and 5, at the end of negative segments can be ruled out, for obvious reasons. We must now decide whether it is worth carrying on beyond 2, to 4 say. We must now determine the NTV of the segment 2–4 at 4. If this is positive we must move at least to 4 and examine the segment 4–6. If, however, the segment 2–4 had been negative we should then have had to examine the larger segment 2–6. This procedure is continued until a point is arrived at, starting from which there are no positive segments of any size. This is then the optimum cut-off point. This procedure, written down as a systematized sequence of operations, can be adopted for projects of any size.

So far, scrap value has been ignored. It can be included of course, but considerably complicates the calculations – the TV of a segment depends on whether or not the project is scrapped at the end of the segment. But the inclusion of scrap values is best considered as a special case of the replacement problem, where the project is scrapped and replaced by the 'null' project. In replacement problems the return in any year may depend on the timing of decisions to scrap and replace. We shall think of replacement problems as capital-budgeting problems where a choice is to be made between a number of mutually exclusive 'projects', each of which is distinguished by different timing of replacement. As an example consider a project R which can run for up to four years and can be scrapped and replaced, at the end of the second, third, or fourth years, by a project S which runs for two years. The problem is, then, to choose between the three 'projects'

A	$-K_r$	R_1	R_2	R_3	$(R_4 + C_4 - K_s)$	S_1	S_2
B	$-K_r$	R_1	R_2	$(R_3 + C_3 - K_s)$	S_1	S_2	
C	$-K_r$	R_1	$(R_2 + C_2 - K_s)$	S_1	S_2		

where K_r and K_s are the costs of initiating the projects, the Rs and Ss the returns, and C_t indicates the scrap value of the project R at the end of year t. Clearly, whichever 'project' has the highest NPV is selected – thus determining the timing of replacement.

Where more projects are involved the number of possible choices can increase enormously, but where the timing of replacements is fixed and the decision problem is which project to replace with which and not when, then the number of possible choices is considerably diminished. Consider first the case of two existing projects either of which can be replaced by a third at time $t = 3$. If R and S are the existing projects and T the possible replacement then the choice is between the PVs of A, B and C where

a_1	$-K_r$	R_1	R_2	$(R_3 - K_t + C_r)$	T_1	T_2	etc.
A	+						
	$-K_s$	S_1	S_2	S_3	S_4	etc.	
B	$-K_r$	R_1	R_2	R_3	R_4	etc.	
	+						
b_2	$-K_s$	S_1	S_2	$(S_3 - K_t + C_s)$	T_1	T_2	etc.
C	$-K_r$	R_1	R_2	R_3	R_4	etc.	
	+						
	$-K_s$	S_1	S_2	S_3	S_4	etc.	

Case C is included to allow the possibility of no replacement at all. Notice of course that a simple comparison of the NPVs of only the replaced projects (that is, comparing a_1 with b_2) is incorrect – we are concerned with *overall* NPV including the project which is not replaced. Clearly, where the *timing* of replacement is not fixed a much greater number of choices exists, and with an enumerative selection procedure as above, computational time can become important when the number of projects is very large.

2.4 Timing the Start of a Project

Up to this point we have discussed only questions relating to the problem of deciding whether or not to undertake a project, but the question of *when* to initiate it also arises – the value of a project may increase if its start is postponed because postponement will (inflation aside) reduce the present value of the initial outlay, and this may more than offset the reduction in the present value of the returns. The influence of calendar time is particularly important in this connection. A numerical example will illustrate this point.

The Government is considering the construction of a nuclear power station. It can build the station in 1975 or 1985. The cost of construction will be £400 million if the station is built in 1975 or £500 million if it is built in 1985. In either case the station has a lifetime of twenty years from the date of construction. Demand and cost conditions are such that the net returns at the end of each of the ten years 1975 to 1985 would be £40 million, from 1985 to 1995 £60 million per annum, and from 1995 to 2005 £80 million per annum. The cost of capital is 10%. When should the Government build the station?

We shall assume that the choice of date will be determined by the net present values that would be obtained in each case. It is as if two mutually exclusive projects A_1 and A_2 were being considered. The cash flows in each case are:

Calendar date:	1975		1985		1995		2005
A_1:		−200 + 40 p.a.		+ 60 p.a.			
A_2:				−500 + 60 p.a.		+ 80 p.a.	

The present values of these projects at 1975 are −£12.08 million for A_1 and +£22.44 million for A_2. It is therefore preferable on financial grounds to construct the power station in 1985. Needless to say the result will not always be in favour of the later starting date, it will depend upon the particular demand and cost conditions that obtain. But illustrated above is a case where the NPV of a project not only changes in magnitude as a result of a changed starting date, but also changes in sign. The graph of NPV (1975) of a project against starting date may in general have any shape depending on the nature of the returns. One possibility is illustrated in Figure 2.1 where it can be seen the NPV of the project if started now (1975) is negative and that the optimum starting date is 1979. The graph of NPV

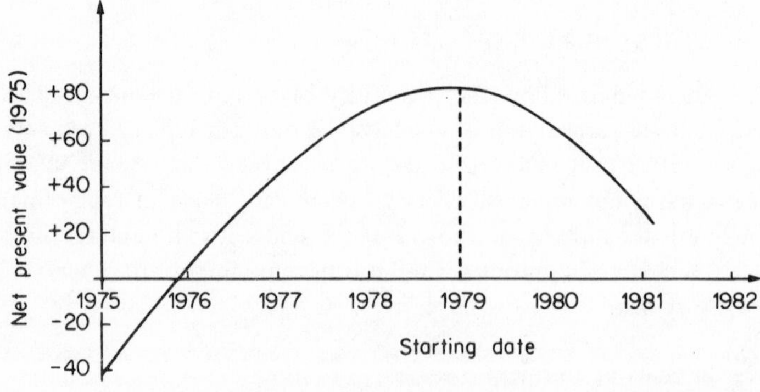

Figure 2.1 Optimal starting date

against starting date for a project with constant returns and constant outlay would tend monotonically to zero – that is, the earlier the starting date the better if NPV (1975) was positive and the later the better if NPV (1975) was negative.

2.5 Effects of Errors in Data

When using or considering the use of any decision making technique it is of value to know the possible effects of less than perfect information. Rarely will the data used be precisely accurate and in this section some of the effects of incorrect information are examined. In particular we shall consider the effects on estimates of gross present value, net present value, and the yield (IRR) of a project of incorrect information regarding:

(i) The discount rate.
(ii) The project lifetime.
(iii) The initial outlay.
(iv) The project's returns.

Each case will be treated separately but indications will be given about the changes in magnitude of the errors for qualitative changes in some of the other parameters.

(i) Incorrect Estimation of the Discount Rate

If all project returns are non-negative, underestimation of the discount rate leads to overestimation of NPV and this will be the larger in absolute terms the longer the project. If NPV and GPV refer to the supposed net and gross values, and RNPV and GRPV to the correct net and gross present values then GPV/RGPV will increase with increasing project length (n) provided the further returns are all positive, but NPV/RNPV could move either way. Figure 2.2 illustrates the proportionate overestimation of GPV for a project yielding equal returns in each period, where although s is the supposed rate of discount, the true rate is αs. Thus, if $s = 0.05$ and $\alpha = 1.2$ then the true rate $\alpha s = 0.06$.

In this constant-returns case the proportionate error in GPV is less than the corresponding proportionate error in the discount rate and unless the larger returns clustered towards the end of the project this would be the general case. For instance, the Figure 1.15 for $\alpha = 1.6$, $s = 0.05$, and $n = 10$ means that if the

α	$s = 0.05$† $n = 10$	$s = 0.05$ $n = 50$	$s = 0.2$ $n = 10$	$s = 0.2$ $n = 50$ (approx)
1.2	1.05	1.16	1.14	1.2
1.6	1.15	1.49	1.43	1.6
2.0	1.26	1.84	1.74	2.0

†s = estimated discount rate; n = project length.

Figure 2.2 Effect of errors in discount rate

discount rate assumed for the calculation of GPV was 5% but in fact it turned out to be 8% then the proportionate error in GPV would be 15%. That is to say GPV at a 5% discount rate exceeds GPV at an 8% discount rate by 15%.

If several projects are being evaluated, incorrect estimation of the discount rate can result in the wrong ordering. This applies to both present value and yield methods.

(ii) Incorrect Estimation of Project Lifetime

If n is the number of periods for which a project will run and if all returns are positive, if ΔNPV and ΔGPV represent the changes in NPV and GPV consequent upon a change in n of Δn then:

$$\frac{\Delta \text{NPV}}{\Delta n} = \frac{\Delta \text{GPV}}{\Delta n} > 0$$

and of course the larger is n (for all positive returns) the greater will be the yield of a project. That is:

$$\frac{\Delta \text{IRR}}{\Delta n} > 0$$

Less obviously it can be shown that the proportionate error in GPV consequent upon incorrect estimation of project lifetime gets smaller as the rate of discount for the project increases, but the proportionate error in NPV could move either way as the discount rate changes. Also, it can be shown that the proportionate error in yield diminishes as n increases in the case of equal returns.

The effect of incorrect estimation of project lifetime can be illustrated by reference to GPV, which is not affected by the size of the initial outlay. Letting GPV_2 correspond to the true project lifetime and GPV_1 correspond to the estimated lifetime, Figure 2.3 gives $\text{GPV}_2/\text{GPV}_1$ in some different circumstances for a project yielding equal returns in each period.

In the constant-returns case if a project has an estimated lifetime of five years and in fact runs for six with a discount rate of 5% then

$$\frac{\text{GPV}_2}{\text{GPV}_1} = 1.172$$

That is to say, GPV would be 17.2% greater than anticipated.

Estimated	n	r	True n 6	10	11	20	21	40
	5	0.05	1.172	1.783				
	5	0.2	1.112	1.402				
	10	0.05			1.076	1.614		
	10	0.2			1.032	1.161		
	20	0.05					1.029	1.377
	20	0.2					1.004	1.026

Figure 2.3 Effect of errors in project lifetime

As regards selection between several projects, since each in general may be affected differently by incorrect estimation of life, incorrect selection on the basis of any of the criteria is possible.

(iii) Incorrect Estimation of the Initial Outlay for a Project

Errors in estimation of initial outlay k affect NPV and IRR. Obviously $\Delta NPV/\Delta k = -1$ and the proportionate error in NPV is smaller for an extended project (as n increases to include further positive returns) and larger for a larger discount rate. However, the proportionate variation in yield would have to be determined numerically.

In the case of project ranking the nature of the errors in estimation of the initial outlays is important. If, for example, there is the same proportionate error in the estimate of the outlay in each case then both yield and NPV rules can give wrong orderings. If the error is the same absolutely in all cases, the yield rule may still given an incorrect ordering, but NPV will preserve the correct ordering. This point can be illustrated with a numerical example.

A choice is to be made of one or other of the two following projects. Both will cost the same amount k, to initiate, the first (A) runs for two periods yielding 1,000 at the end of each period and the second (B) for five periods yielding 500 at the end of each period and $r = 0.1$. Figure 2.4 gives the NPV and yield (approximately) of each project for different estimates of k. Project B always has the higher NPV, but the ordering by yield changes as the estimate of k nears 1,600. Thus, if k = 1,400 the yield method would rank project A above project B, but if k = 1,600 it would prefer B to A.

k	IRR_A	IRR_B	NPV_A	NPV_B
1,400	0.272	0.226	335	495
1,500	0.215	0.200	235	395
1,600	0.162	0.169	135	295
1,700	0.115	0.144	35	195
1,900	0.035	0.099	−165	−5

Figure 2.4 Effect of errors in initial outlay

(iv) Incorrect Estimation of Project Returns

The relative effects on GPV, NPV and yield of incorrect estimates of returns depend upon the nature of the errors.

The following notation will be used in this section:

$\overline{GPV}$ = Proportionate error in estimate of GPV
$\overline{NPV}$ = Proportionate error in estimate of NPV
$\overline{IRR}$ = Proportionate error in estimate of yield

If the errors are the same numerically in each year (say a constant overestimate), then $\overline{GPV}$ will be less than $\overline{NPV}$, but $\overline{IRR}$ could exceed or be less than either of these. But if several projects are involved GPV and NPV still preserve the true ordering when the projects concerned have the same lifetime, whereas yield in general does not. If the errors in returns are proportionately the same, then some more definite relationships exist between $\overline{\text{GPV}}$, $\overline{\text{NPV}}$ and $\overline{\text{IRR}}$, namely

(a) In the equal returns case $\overline{\text{NPV}} > \overline{\text{IRR}} > \overline{\text{GPV}}$.
(b) In the non-equal returns case $\overline{\text{NPV}} > \overline{\text{IRR}}$, $\overline{\text{NPV}} > \overline{\text{GPV}}$, but $\overline{\text{IRR}} \lesseqgtr \overline{\text{GPV}}$.

In all cases the proportionate error in GPV will be the same as the proportionate error in the returns. To illustrate the point that $\overline{\text{IRR}}$ can be less than $\overline{\text{GPV}}$ consider the case where the project -1, 0, 0, 3 is estimated as 1$-$, 0, 0, 6, then GPV is overestimated by 100% but yield is overestimated by less than 85%. It is therefore, apparent that if the larger returns are clustered towards the end of the project, $\overline{\text{IRR}}$ may be less than $\overline{\text{GPV}}$, but otherwise not.

It is difficult to find representative numerical illustrations of the results. However, Figure 2.5 gives some examples of the equal returns case. The project returns are actually R per period, but are estimated as $R(1 + p)$. A rate of interest of 5% is appropriate to the calculation of GVPs and NPVs, and the initial outlay is set so as to give a true yield of 10% in each case. Figure 2.5 gives $\overline{\text{GPV}}$, $\overline{\text{NPV}}$ and $\overline{\text{IRR}}$ for two values of p and three of n (length of project). As an example, for $p = 0.5$ (which is a 50% overestimate of all the returns) and for $n = 5$ (a five-year project) the 2.81 in the $\overline{\text{IRR}}$ column means that the estimated yield is 2.81 times the true yield, and the 5.02 in the $\overline{\text{NPV}}$ column means that estimated NPV is 5.02 times the true NPV. Figure 2.5 gives only a rough indication of the magnitudes of $\overline{\text{NPV}}$ and $\overline{\text{IRR}}$ for cases similar to that on which the table is based. $\overline{\text{NPV}}$ would diminish if the rate of discount was increased and $\overline{\text{IRR}}$ would fall as the true yield rose.

	$\overline{\text{GPV}}$	$\overline{\text{IRR}}$	$\overline{\text{NPV}}$	
p 0.1 p 0.5	1.1 1.5	1.38 2.81	1.80 5.02	$n = 5$
$p = 0.1$ $p = 0.5$	1.1 1.5	1.15 1.68	1.32 2.58	$n = 20$
$p = 0.1$ $p = 0.5$	1.1 1.5	1.1 1.5	1.2 2	$n \to \infty$

Figure 2.5 Effect of overestimated returns

In respect of all the above possible sources of error it is important to remember that the present value and yield decision making methods are not alone in being affected by data errors. Any quantitative procedure would be affected. Heuristic (intuitive) judgements also depend upon information input and it must be emphasized that the justification for the use of any procedure is simply that it improves on *what else would have been done* and does not depend on the finding of the precisely accurate 'true' solution. The word 'incorrect' has been used from time to time in this section but the context is important. An 'incorrect' decision (e.g.

choosing project A rather than project B) may mean only a marginal drop in profits – and a drop compared with the 'true' maximum at that. The profits made by a theoretically suboptimal project may be much greater than those that would have been made from projects selected by unscientific procedures for which the consequences of error cannot, in any case, be evaluated.

2.6 Yield and the Reinvestment Assumption

Where the opportunity exists to invest the returns from a project as they arise, the investor will take advantage of this, and can make a wrong decision (on the basis of DCF methods) if he does not. Consider the following example.

An investor has 20 units which he can invest in the project −10, 9, 5 and/or elsewhere at 20%. In general the NTV of the project for any investment rate $100r\%$ where there is reinvestment is:

$$(20 - 10)(1 + r)^2 + 9(1 + r) + 5 - 20(1 + r)^2$$

or

$$-10(1 + r)^2 + 9(1 + r) + 5$$

which in our case is

$$-10(1.44) + 9(1.2) + 5 = 1.4 > 0$$

so clearly the project is worthwhile. Suppose, however, that the return 9 had *not* been reinvested at 20%. NTV would have been

$$-10(1.44) + 9 + 5 = -0.4 < 0$$

and the project would not have been worthwhile. Now, if we calculate, using the familiar formula, the yield of the project, this is i where i is found from

$$-10(1 + i)^2 + 9(1 + i) + 5 = 0$$

which solves for $i \approx 0.288$ – a yield of 28.8%. This is greater than the outside investment rate of 20%, so the yield rule says the project should be invested in. But clearly this decision is correct if the return 9 is reinvested and is incorrect if it is not. Thus the yield rule will only necessarily give correct answers if returns are reinvested as they occur at the interest rate used to determine NTV.

Similarly, if a project is financed by borrowing, then repayment of capital and interest should be made as soon as possible out of the returns unless the outside investment rate exceeds the cost of capital. Logically these repayments represent investments – the returns to which are the savings in the repayments that would otherwise have had to be made.

For instance, consider the project which generates the following cash-flow pattern

Year	0	1	2	3
Cash in		1,000	1,000	1,000
Cash out	1,952			

The yield is 25%: therefore if it were financed by borrowing at a rate of 25%, the firm might appear to break even at the end of the project's life. But there are two possible financing situations. If only the interest due each year can be repaid from the £1,000 cash inflows (and there is no opportunity to invest elsewhere) and repayment of the principal is after three years, then the cash-flow pattern is:

Year	0	1	2	3
Cash in	1,952			
Cash out		488	488	2,440

combining the cash flows would give

Year	0	1	2	3
Cash in		512	512	
Cash out				1,440

If the net intermediate cash inflows of 512 in years 1 and 2 were reinvested at 25% then they would accumulate to 1,440 in year 3. If they were reinvested at any other rate, the firm would not break even. The assumption that inflowing funds can be reinvested at the rate of return of the project itself may be unrealistic, especially for investments with very high, or very low, rates of return. It is when the yield is used as a device for ranking investments that these assumptions are important.

2.7 Discount Calculations

Throughout the book the usual assumption is made that receipts occur and interest is compounded at the end of each time period. In some instances receipts may in fact be more or less continuous and interest may be compounded differently. Leaving aside simple interest it is possible to distinguish four separate cases according to the nature of receipts and the method of compounding interest.

If receipts and compounding are at period end, then the present value of £R per period for n periods with an interest rate of $100r$% is

$$\text{PV} = \frac{R}{r}\left(1 - \frac{1}{(1+r)^n}\right)$$

The second case is the limiting case of evenly spaced very frequent receipts with interest compounded at the time of each receipt. For instance if £R is received during the course of a year at four-monthly intervals rather than all at the end, it has a present value of

$$\text{PV} = \frac{\tfrac{1}{3}R}{(1+r)^{1/3}} + \frac{\tfrac{1}{3}R}{(1+r)^{2/3}} + \frac{\tfrac{1}{3}R}{(1+r)}$$

In the limit, if £R is received evenly throughout each of n years, the present value of these receipts is

$$\text{PV} = \frac{R}{\log_e(1+r)}\left(1 - \frac{1}{(1+r)^n}\right)$$

Thirdly, if interest is compounded continuously and receipts of £R occur at the end of each period for n periods the present value formula is

$$PV = \left(\frac{R(1 - e^{-nr})}{e^r - 1}\right)$$

Finally, if receipts are continuous and interest is compounded continuously, the present value formula is

$$PV = \frac{R}{r}(1 - e^{-nr})$$

To give an indication of the relative orders of magnitude in each case (numbered 1 to 4 as above, with $R = 1$), Figure 2.6 gives PV for various values of r and n.

In practice the investor would determine what the appropriate discounting formula was. The principle of the methods is not in question, and having drawn the reader's attention to this matter we shall continue to assume that it is appropriate to use the 'period end' formula.

	2	4	1	3
$r = 0.1$ $n = 8$	5.597	5.507	5.335	5.233
$r = 0.2$ $n = 4$	2.840	2.753	2.589	2.487
$r = 0.4$ $n \to \infty$	2.972	2.500	2.500	2.033

Figure 2.6 'Unusual' receipts and compounding

2.8 Capital Budgeting and Inflation

Inflation can increase the difficulty of the problem of the assessment or comparison of investment projects in several ways. Firstly, by adding one more exogenous factor to the problem, uncertainty is increased. Secondly, data difficulties are added to, in that future costs and revenues have to be calculated in terms of future prices as well as future technical processes and ambient economic conditions (unless we are prepared to make the simplifying, though substantially inaccurate, assumption that relative prices do not change). Thirdly 'conceptual' difficulties are increased in respect of any effects of inflation on the validity of decision rules formerly employed.

At the theoretical level these difficulties caused by inflation can appear formidable. The reader is referred to the papers by Bromwich; Foster; Schofield, McBain and Bagwell and Wilkes in respect of these matters. A comprehensive treatment of the subject would require a substantial part of a book and will not be attempted here. It is the author's view that some of the points are rather 'fine' when it comes down to practical application and the objective of the present sections is to give an idea of how inflation problems are approached by reference to selected examples.

There are two uses of the word inflation in the present context. The first describes (amongst other things) some general escalation of prices and the second the escalation of costs specific to particular projects. These are not usually entirely unrelated of course, although the latter could arise solely because of unforeseen technical problems.

The effects of 'inflation' will depend on:

(i) the type of 'inflation';
(ii) the investor's criteria;
(iii) the particular problem environment.

As has been suggested, the reader may find that he can specify circumstances other than those that will be discussed, but he will be able to apply some of the principles outlined to the analysis of such problems.

To begin with, consider the effects of the investor's own criteria; suppose an investor wishes to realize an investment at time t and has to choose between two projects A and B. Suppose also that there are no further returns to either project after time t, then ignoring any inflation the comparison is between $\mathrm{NTV_A}(t)$ and $\mathrm{NTV_B}(t)$ where the NTVs are expressed in nominal or 'face-value' monetary terms.

If, however, an appropriate index of prices has been rising at $100\alpha\%$ per year then the 'real' values (their actual 'purchasing power' allowing for the increase in the price index) of the two NTVs become

$$[\mathrm{NTV_A}(t)]\,(1+\alpha)^{-t} \text{ and } [\mathrm{NTV_B}(t)]\,(1+\alpha)^{-t}$$

giving the same choice. It is improbable of course that such inflation proceeds only outside of the two projects, for if steel prices are rising and steel is used in the projects then the face value of the NTVs will be affected, and a different choice may have to be made. Also, conceivably different rates of inflation may apply to each project – for instance if they were in different countries (with no transference of funds on realization) – then again a different choice may have to be made.

Let us examine now what might happen if the investor has to decide whether to 'spend' the returns as they come in or to (say) 'bank' them at some outside rate of interest, $100r\%$. Consider a situation where it is the investor's desire to maximize, by the time the project is completed, the number of shares he holds in a particular company and where these share prices are rising at $100\alpha\%$ per year. A return of R, received now and banked, becomes in face-value terms $R(1+r)$ next year, but the real comparison to be made is between the share-buying power of R now and $R(1+r)$ next year – that is, between R and $R(1+r)/(1+\alpha)$. Clearly in this case if $r > \alpha$, the investor should delay his purchases till the end of the project: if $r < \alpha$, he should spend the returns on receipt or borrow and spend at once if this is possible at a rate of interest less than $\alpha\%$. If a choice has to be made from among several projects and $r > \alpha$, the investor should spend at the end and a comparison can be made between the NTVs using r as the discount rate. If $r < \alpha$ and borrowing is not possible, spending should be on receipt and the 'NTVs' should be calculated using α as the discount rate.

Similar considerations apply in 'real-cost' minimization problems. Suppose a public concern borrows money to finance the construction and running of a public utility, then to minimize cost in 'real' terms, repayments should be made (extraneous considerations aside) as soon as possible if the cost of capital exceeds the appropriate rate of inflation and as late as possible in the converse case.

For example suppose that two companies tender for a construction contract. Company one proposes to spread the work over two years and company two would take three. The public authorities wish to choose that method for which real cost is minimized.

Charges made to the authorities by company one would be C_{10}, C_{11}, C_{12} and by company two C_{20}, C_{21}, C_{22}, C_{23}. The terms C_{10} and C_{20} represent payments due at the inception of the project, C_{11} and C_{21} after one year and so on; where these cost figures are known at the outset of the project.

The authority may pay these costs as they arise, or may defer payment for up to two years in which case the companies would charge them interest at a rate of i. Consider the cost C_{10}. If payment is postponed for two years, the 'real' payment then including the interest charges is $C_{10}(1+i)^2/(1+\alpha)^2$. Clearly if $i < \alpha$, the real cost is less and all payments should be deferred the full two years. The minimum total real cost for company one's tender, TC_1, would be given by

$$\mathrm{TC}_1 = \frac{C_{10}(1+i)^2}{(1+\alpha)^2} + \frac{C_{11}(1+i)^2}{(1+\alpha)^3} + \frac{C_{12}(1+i)^2}{(1+\alpha)^4}$$

that is

$$\mathrm{TC}_1 = \left[C_{10} + \frac{C_{11}}{(1+\alpha)} + \frac{C_{12}}{(1+\alpha)^2}\right]\frac{(1+i)^2}{(1+\alpha)^2}$$

and similarly for company two's tender

$$\mathrm{TC}_2 = \left[C_{20} + \frac{C_{21}}{(1+\alpha)} + \frac{C_{22}}{(1+\alpha)^2} + \frac{C_{33}}{(1+\alpha)^3}\right]\frac{(1+i)^2}{(1+\alpha)^2}$$

and the comparison can be made between the square-bracketed components of each expression – the real present values of the expenditure.

Note that as long as the deferment period is the same for each tender this leaves the choice unchanged. The real present values are what the total real cost would have been if all payments had been made as soon as the costs arose. The term $(1+i)^2/(1+\alpha)^2$ weights each term in each equation equally, and its size determines only the timing of payments and not the choice of tender.

For a numerical example let $C_{10} = 0.6$, $C_{11} = 0.5$, $C_{12} = 0.4$, $C_{20} = 0.5$, $C_{21} = 0.4$, $C_{22} = 0.4$, $C_{23} = 0.3$, $i = 0.1$ and $\alpha = 0.08$. The comparison is made between the square-bracketed parts of the expression above, and these emerge as about 1.4059 for the two-year tender and 1.4515 for the three-year tender. Thus company one would be awarded the contract, and payments would be made as soon as they become due.

Where the term 'inflation' refers to the escalation of costs associated with projects, two cases should be distinguished. Firstly, if prior to the investment decision inflation is unsuspected but subsequently occurs, then, clearly, an incorrect decision may have been made; efforts to redeem the situation might involve renegotiation of prices with customers, project truncation and so on. On the other hand, if the investor is aware of cost escalations prior to a decision he may include these (or estimates of them) in his calculations. As an illustration of this second case consider the following example.

A water board is to supply water to a large industrial enterprise in each of three years. The requirements of the enterprise in the three years are for three, four and five thousand million gallons respectively. There are two technically different ways the board can supply the water. Method one would imply costs (estimated on the basis of present prices) of £400,000, £500,000 and £650,000 occurring at the end of the three years respectively. Method two would imply costs of £600,000, £500,000 and £500,000. However, it is known that costs will inflate at 5% per year, and the board's cost of capital is 10%. Public policy decrees that the board should aim to 'break even' after the three years. The same price (expressed as per thousand gallons) is to be charged to the industrial concern in each of the three years. It is assumed that no further costs and revenues occur subsequently. Which method would enable the board to supply the water at the lowest price?

The 'break-even' condition here means zero NTV for the board after three years. Thus we shall express the NTVs for the board as functions of price for each of the two possible methods, equate the NTVs to zero, and solve for the prices.

For method one, with a price of P_1, we obtain

$$\begin{aligned}\text{NTV}_1 = {} & \{[-400{,}000(1.05) + 3{,}000{,}000\,P_1\,](1.1) - 500{,}000(1.05)^2 \\ & + 4{,}000{,}000\,P_1\}(1.1) - 650{,}000(1.05)^3 + 5{,}000{,}000\,P_1 = 0\end{aligned}$$

and for method two, where the price would be P_2, we obtain

$$\begin{aligned}\text{NTV}_2 = {} & \{[-600{,}000(1.05) + 3{,}000{,}000\,P_2\,](1.1) - 500{,}000(1.05)^2 \\ & + 4{,}000{,}000\,P_2\}(1.1) - 500{,}000(1.05)^3 + 5{,}000{,}000\,P_2 = 0\end{aligned}$$

Solving for P_1 and P_2 we obtain $P_1 \approx$ £0.143 and $P_2 \approx$ £0.149. Thus method one will supply the water at a lower price and would be preferred.

This section on inflation provides a transition from the essentially technical problems discussed up to this point and the subsequent sections illustrating applications. It is to the first of these that we now turn.

2.9 Make or Buy

Sometimes a firm may have the choice of making an item it needs or buying in supplies of the item manufactured elsewhere. The costs in each case usually have a different structure. The problem can often be formulated as a capital-budgeting problem, although there may be some important factors that are not readily quantifiable – for instance, the benefits of any extra security of supply if the 'make' decision is taken.

To illustrate the capital-budgeting approach consider the case where the 'make' decision would entail an outlay of K now for equipment which would last n years, and where $M_1, M_2, \ldots, M_n$ represent the costs of producing the requisite numbers of the item in each year and $B_1, B_2, \ldots, B_n$ are the alternative buying-in costs. Then the project to be evaluated is

$$-K, (B_1 - M_1), (B_2 - M_2), \ldots, (B_n - M_n + S_n)$$

where S_n represents scrap value of equipment at n.

Some of the usual complications can of course be worked into this basic framework. If funds tied up in the manufacturing process could have been invested profitably in other projects which can now not be undertaken, then the returns to these opportunities foregone, must be included in the figures $M_1, M_2, \ldots, M_n$.

As a numerical example, consider the case of a firm which is considering manufacturing for itself a component it needs in an assembly operation. In order to do the manufacturing it would need to buy a machine for £4,000 which would last for four years with (solely for simplicity) no scrap value. Manufacturing costs in each of the four years would be 6, 7, 8 and 10 thousand pounds respectively. If the firm obtained the components from a supplier the costs would be 9, 10, 11 and 14 thousand pounds respectively, in each of the four years. However, the machine would occupy floor space which could have been used for another machine which could be hired at no initial cost to manufacture an item, the sales of which would produce net cash flows in each of the four years of £2,000. It is impossible to find room for both machines and there are no other external effects. The cost of capital is 10%. Should the firm make the component or buy from the supplier?

The stream of costs (in £1,000s) associated with manufacture are

(i) 4 6 7 8 10

and those associated with buying are

(ii) 0 9 10 11 14

thus the savings in costs of making rather than buying (ii) – (i) are

(iii) −4 3 3 3 4

but if the firm manufactures the component, it foregoes a profit of £2,000 in each year, thus the true savings are

−4 1 1 1 2

so that we wish to find the value of

$$-4 + \frac{1}{1.1} + \frac{1}{(1.1)^2} + \frac{1}{(1.1)^3} + \frac{2}{(1.1)^4}$$

which is −0.15. Thus the firm should buy the component from the supplier and use the floor space for the other manufacturing process.

2.10 Credit and Debt

It was noted in the introduction that it is not only problems of investment in heavy plant and equipment that can be structured as 'capital budgeting' problems.

This and the following sections are intended to provide illustrations of such problems. One instance of a problem in the routine management of a business that can usefully be approached from a capital budgeting standpoint is the decision on credit and discount (and other incentives) extended to customers. The extension of credit represents an investment, the returns to which are increased profits resulting from greater sales. The investment is not normally risk free and different policies costing the same amount could generate differing patterns of expected returns. The preferred policy would, of course, be that which gave the greatest return on the sum invested. Whether or not credit is extended there is rarely certainty that payment will be received during any given time period. It is assumed that there is a probability p_t that payment will be received during period t. The actions of the creditor company may influence this probability distribution. Such actions would not as a rule be costless – they might be a scheme of progressively diminishing discounts or a less generous 'adjustment' procedure. The problem of what action to take or whether to introduce any scheme to speed payment can be viewed as a capital-budgeting problem. Consider a numerical illustration.

A company is owed £1,000 and previous experience leads it to believe that the probability of receiving this payment immediately or in one or other of the succeeding six quarterly periods is as given by column p_n in Figure 2.7. It is assumed that payment will be made in one lump sum rather than in instalments.

If the company introduces a discount/penalty scheme of 3% for immediate payment, 2% if payment after one month, and so on, it is believed that the estimated probabilities of payment are as given in column p_d (the amounts that would be received are shown in parentheses). Alternatively it can threaten legal action if payment is not made within a year, and column p_l gives the probabilities in this case. Costs are deducted from returns where they occur – for instance in column p_l quarter 0, there is cost of £10 for a threatening letter sent at the commencement of this policy (the probability 0 does not apply to this figure). The law suit, it is assumed, would be successful and costs incurred would be recouped in

	Probability of receiving payment:				Expected net present value:		
Q	With no action	With a discount scheme	After legal action	Discount factor	With no action	With a discount scheme	With legal action
	p_n	p_d	p_l				
0	0	0.2(970)	0*(−10)		0	194	−10
1	0.1	0.2(980)	0	0.970874	97.09	190.29	0
2	0.2	0.2(990)	0.21(1.000)	0.942956	188.59	186.71	188.59
3	0.3	0.2(1,000)	0.3 (990)	0.915142	274.54	183.03	271.80
4	0.2	0.2(1,010)	0.4 (980)	0.888487	177.70	179.47	348.29
5	0.1	0	0.1(1,040)	0.862609	86.26	0	89.71
6	0.1	0	0	0.837484	83.75	0	
Total					907.93	933.50	898.39

Figure 2.7 Adjustment procedures example

quarter five. The final column gives the discount factor for each quarter (3% cost of capital per quarter assumed). The lower half of the table gives the expected net present value from each quarter under each scheme. So, clearly, the discount scheme is preferred to no action, which is preferred to legal action.

2.11 Share Valuation

There are a number of schools of thought on the subject of share valuation and the subject is indeed a complex one. One of the more scientific approaches is as follows.[2] Ownership of a company share entitles the owner to a revenue stream – the future dividend payments of the company. The value of the share corresponds to the present value of this stream of dividend payments. Obviously there is considerable uncertainty surrounding the size of the future dividends; indeed it is frequently as a result of changing expectations about future dividends that share prices fluctuate.

Of course the owner of a share at any moment will usually consider his returns as accruing not just from dividend payments but from the possible additional gains resulting from any capital appreciation on the share. Normally, the owner does not intend to hold the share in perpetuity; he wishes to sell the share at some stage, but when he sells the share, the buyer is also simply purchasing a stream of future dividend payments, so once again, the price is determined by future dividend expectations.

This theory can be demonstrated. Suppose an investor buys a share expecting to hold it for two years: the value of the share to him is the present value of the two dividend payments, plus the discounted value of the price he expects to receive on selling the share. If P_0 = price of share today, P_2 = price of share at the end of the second year, D_1 = dividend per share to be received at the end of the first year, r = discount rate and D_2 = dividend per share at the end of the second year, then price is given by:

$$P_0 = \frac{D_1}{(1+r)} + \frac{D_2}{(1+r)^2} + \frac{P_2}{(1+r)^2}$$

The investor who buys the share at the end of the second year pays P_2 for it, and expects to hold it for two further years; so, looked at from time 0:

$$\frac{P_2}{(1+r)^2} = \frac{D_3}{(1+r)^3} + \frac{D_4}{(1+r)^4} + \frac{P_4}{(1+R)^4}$$

The price at the end of the fourth year and all future prices are determined in a similar manner. Therefore the equation for the price of the share at the present time can be rewritten as:

$$P_0 = \frac{D_1}{(1+r)} + \frac{D_2}{(1+r)^2} + \frac{D_3}{(1+r)^3} + \frac{D_4}{(1+r)^4} + \ldots = \sum_{t=1}^{\infty} \frac{D_t}{(1+r)^t} \qquad (2.7)$$

Of course, this simple picture is complicated by tax considerations, in particular differences in the rates of income and capital gains taxation, but the model (2.7) can be used as a starting point.

2.12 Cost–Benefit Ratios

Frequently in the public sector the approach to investment decision making that is adopted is cost–benefit analysis. Measurement of the benefits and costs of a public utility is both difficult and in practice imprecise. Much of the literature on cost-benefit analysis rightly dwells on the theoretical and practical difficulties of benefit and cost evaluation, but here we are concerned with the decision making tool itself – when the hard work has been done!

In principle, if B represents the present value of future revenues b_t and C represents the present value of future costs C_t, (including operating costs) associated with an n-year project, with a discount rate of $100r\%$ then, when the first 'benefit' occurs after one year;

$$B = \sum_{t=1}^{n} b_t(1 + r)^{-t}$$

and where the first cost is incurred immediately;

$$C = \sum_{t=0}^{n} c_t(1 + r)^{-t}$$

where c_0 is the initial outlay on the project, then the *aggregate benefit-cost ratio* is defined as $R_A = B/C.A$ project with $R_A > 1$ would be accepted. In public utilities especially, the terms c_t and b_t often include monetary estimates of 'social' benefits and 'social' costs – the external effects of the project on the community and the environment, as well as outflows and inflows of hard cash. Note that the net present value of the project is $B - C$.

In many cases, large projects require cash outlays for more than one year before inflows of cash occur. If such outlays are required during the first m of the n years we can write $C = C_1 + C_2$ where

$$C_1 = \sum_{t=0}^{m} c_t(1 + r)^{-t}$$

and, for the operating costs after m:

$$C_2 = \sum_{t=m+1}^{n} c_t(1 + r)^{-t}$$

The present value of the stream of benefits is

$$B = \sum_{t=m+1}^{n} b_t(1 + r)^{-t}$$

which is B defined as previously except that the first m of the b_t are zero. The *netted benefit–cost ratio*, R_N, is defined as:

$$R_N = \frac{B - C_2}{C_1}$$

By this criterion projects with $R_N > 1$ are accepted and those with $R_N < 1$ are rejected. In summary then, $\text{NPV} = B - C_1 - C_2$, $R_A = B/(C_1 + C_2)$, $R_N = (B - C_2)/C_1$. Where a single project is being assessed with the object of providing a 'yes' or 'no' answer to the question 'should we invest?', the three criteria will give the same answer, for clearly if $\text{NPV} > 0$ this is because $B > C_1 + C_2$ so that $R_A > 1$ and also $B - C_2 > C_1$ so that $R_N > 1$ as well. But when the projects are to be ranked, or a choice made between mutually exclusive projects the R_A and R_N rules can contradict each other and either may be at variance with the NPV rankings, a point which the reader may easily verify by appropriately choosing value for B, C_1 and C_2. Which rule is to be preferred?

Like yield, both benefit–cost ratios can be blind to the scale of profit to be made: they are, by definition, more concerned with the ratios of benefits received to costs outlayed rather than the magnitude of the excess of benefits over costs. For instance consider two projects I and II. For project I let $B = 3$ and $C_2 = C_1 = 1$ and for II let $B = 11$ and $C_2 = C_1 = 4$ (say, millions of pounds). Both benefit–cost ratios would indicate acceptance of the smaller project I which gives a profit (in present-value terms) of one million pounds rather than project II which gives a profit of three million pounds. This illustrates the crucial difference between the NPV and benefit–cost approach. A profit-minded organization should not decline a course of action leading to three million pounds profit in favour of one which yields one million. Costs of capital and/or opportunities for investment elsewhere are taken account of by the discount rates used. Also when risk is allowed for, as Schwab and Lusztig[3] show, claims for the superiority of the netted ratio over NPV cannot be supported, and that in any circumstances the aggregate benefit–cost ratio should be rejected. Thus the use of benefit–cost ratios is a questionable procedure and it would seem to be preferable to employ the NPV approach once the major problem of data collection has been overcome.

This section concludes the presentation for the time being, of illustrative applications of discounting methods. We turn now to consideration of constraints on choice of investment.

2.13 Project Selection under Constraints

In this section we introduce a type of problem the character of which is central to the remainder of this book and in Section 2.14 a simple problem structure is presented and examined. We begin with some generalities concerning project selection under constraints.

In the case of an already established company using buildings, materials and machinery and employing various categories of labour to manufacture one or several products, in any given period of time there are limits (upper bounds in particular) to the amounts of the factors of production such as materials, machine time, floor space, that it can call upon. Finance too is a scarce resource – unlimited amounts cannot be obtained at a given cost, there are conventional constraints on the mix of finance from various sources (debt/equity ratio) and some sources may impose conditions on the use of the money they supply (e.g. banks). Weingartner[4] doubts whether an upper limit on borrowing exists in the sense that if a firm has sufficiently attractive investment opportunities there will (or should be) some 'rational' source ready to provide finance – at a price. This would be true in a perfect (in respect of information) riskless world. Even if it is true in the real world it hardly makes the problem easier because there certainly are constraints on how much can be obtained from given sources at given costs even if there is no constraint on the total amount that can be raised.

Furthermore there are year to year (or more frequent) changes in the financial position of a firm and the financial positions and outlooks of the providers of finance. Large projects or continuing investment programmes will require capital inputs over long periods of time so that changes in the financial constraints that are faced by a firm may be expected.

If a company is establishing a new plant or if a completely new company is to be formed, we may expect fewer physical constraints (in the shape of plant size, number and types of machines) and more financial ones. In this case the investment projects are the first to be undertaken so that we need not be concerned with interactive effects with existing projects.

If 'the investor' is an individual person rather than a company, his problem may be that of selecting or building a portfolio of investments in the form of stocks and bonds. Apart from time it is unlikely that there will be effective physical constraints (e.g. on storage space for documents!) but there will be quite explicit financial constraints. Disinvestments and loans from financial institutions will be the main source of finance and no doubt the reader will verify the stringency of conditions applied to the latter!

Financial and physical constraints are part and parcel of the environment in which investment decisions are made so that technique of project selection must be able to take them into account. But before proceeding to the development of these techniques the character of programming problems should be introduced.

A programming problem is a problem in which there is an objective to be achieved but where there are constraints on the courses of action available which restrict the degree of achievement of the objective. Thus in this general sense many aspects of day to day behaviour can be viewed as programming problems. This is not to say that programming methods (the ways in which programming problems are solved) are necessarily of any value in such situations as crossing the road – where the objective is, presumably, to get to the other side and there are constraints determined by subjective assessments of the degree of risk in the traffic flow situation, the urgency of one's business and jaywalking laws.

Before programming methods can be of any help it is necessary to be able to measure (at least in an ordinal sense) the degree of achievement of the objective or objectives and to quantify the constraints. This is possible across a broad spectrum of business problems. For example the objective may be to choose the most profitable product range and the levels of production of these products subject to restrictions in the form of limits on floor space, machine time, labour time, raw materials supply and so on. Also of course there will be the requirement that no product is to be produced in a negative amount! In the investment context that concerns us here the objective will be to choose that investment programme which maximizes terminal value, present value, rate of growth or whatever is/are the objective/s subject to the physical and financial constraints already referred to and certain 'logical' constraints. These constraints may be that investments be made only in whole number units and in some problems the only whole numbers permitted may be zero (don't invest) and one (invest). In general there will also be constraints relating to mutual exclusion, to which we have already referred and contingency (only consider project C if project B is decided upon) and other such constraints.

A linear programming approach to the solution of some of these problems will be explained in the following chapter. To conclude the present chapter we shall examine a one constraint problem that has become something of a classic, but is also of current interest in that one constraint problems still exist today.

2.14 The Lorie–Savage Problem

One of the simplest (in terms of size) investment problems which is a programming problem is that where the net present value of investments is to be maximized subject to the choice of investments satisfying the condition that the initial outlays on the investments do not exceed a predetermined limit, where no investment may be undertaken at more than unit level or less than zero level and where the rate of discount used to determine the NPVs is known *a priori*. The earliest reference in the literature to this problem appears to be an article by J. H. Lorie and L. J. Savage,[5] and the problem has come to be known as a Lorie–Savage problem. To express the problem in symbolic terms suppose that there are n possible investments, the numbers of units taken of each investment being represented by the variables x_j for $j = 1, 2, \ldots, n$. Let N_j represent the NPV, per unit, of the jth investment and K_j represent the initial outlay, per unit, of the jth investment and let L represent the amount of money that is available for investment. The problem can be written as[6]

$$\text{Maximize } N = \sum_{j=1}^{n} N_j x_j \tag{2.8}$$

where

$$\sum_{j=1}^{n} K_j x_j \leqslant L \tag{2.9}$$

and

$$x_j \geqslant 0 \quad j = 1,2, \ldots, n \tag{2.10}$$

and

$$x_j \leqslant 1 \quad j = 1,2, \ldots, n \tag{2.11}$$

Expression (2.8) is called the *objective function* and (2.9) is referred to as a *constraint*. Conditions (2.10) are *sign requirements* which rule out the possibility of negative investments and (2.11) are constraints which impose the condition that no more than one unit of any project may be taken.

How is the best combination of projects to be determined? At first glance it might be thought that a modified version of (R4) of Chapter 1 would be appropriate, namely: rank projects by NPV and starting with the project with the greatest NPV work down the list accepting projects with progressively lower NPVs until available funds are exhausted. The fact that this rule does not generally lead to an optimal selection of projects can be seen from the following example involving three projects.

Project one: $K_1 = 5, N_1 = 9$

Project two: $K_2 = 10, N_2 = 17$

Project three: $K_3 = 6, N_3 = 12$

The sum available for investment is 11. The decision rule above would suggest one unit of project two and, if fractions are accepted, one sixth of a unit of project three (i.e. $x_1 = 0$, $x_2 = 1$, $x_3 = 1/6$) giving a total net present value of 19. If $x_3 = 1/6$ is not meaningful then the solution indicated would be $x_1 = 0$, $x_2 = 1$, $x_3 = 0$ giving a net present value of 18 if the unspent unit is added to N_2. In either case the answer is obviously incorrect and inspection quickly gives the optimal solution $x_1 = 1$, $x_2 = 0$, $x_3 = 1$. The trouble with the proposed decision rule in this case was that the outlay on project two used up so much of the budget that neither project one nor project three could be financed from the funds that remained. Reference to the projects' outlays was made only to check the feasibility of a solution.

The solution procedure that was proposed by Lorie and Savage took account of the outlays straight away. It was first to rank the projects by ratio of net present value to initial outlay and then 'once investment proposals have been ranked according to this criterion it is easy to select the best group by starting with the investment proposal having the highest present value per dollar of outlay and proceeding down the list until the fixed sum is exhausted'. That is, the procedure is to compute the numbers N_j/K_j – call the result R_j – and work down the list starting with the project with the greatest value of R until no funds remain. This procedure is seen to give the optimal solution to the three project problem above. The projects are ranked in the order three, one, two since $R_3 = 2$, $R_1 = 1.8$ and $R_2 = 1.7$. Hence project three is accepted first, then project one by which time the budget limit is reached. Fortunately the problem of fractions has not arisen.

Were it not for the constraints (2.11) the problem would be simpler, only one investment would be selected namely that project with the greatest R (say R_j) and set at the level L/K_j, which may not be a whole number, to give a value of N of $L.R_j$. However, in the presence of the constraints more than one x_j will be positive as long as $L > K_j$ for all values of j and one project, but no more than one – the last one taken – may be fractional. If fractions are permissible and there are no other interrelationships between the investments to be considered, then the Lorie–Savage procedure gives the correct answer.

R. N. Anthony[7] forms the ratio of Gross Present Value to outlay and calls the result a Profitability Index. The use of GPV/outlay ratio gives the same result as use of the NPV/outlay ratio, since as between two projects A and B the condition $NPV_A > NPV_B$ can be written

$$\frac{GPV_A - K_A}{K_A} > \frac{GPV_B - K_B}{K_B}$$

$$\frac{GPV_A}{K_A} - 1 > \frac{GPV_B}{K_B} - 1$$

and adding one to both sides gives

$$\frac{GPV_A}{K_A} > \frac{GPV_B}{K_B}$$

In examples below profitability index will be used to mean NPV/outlay. The idea of ranking projects by the ratio of present value to outlay is an intuitively appealing one and is apparently still being 'discovered'.

However, the profitability index approach runs into trouble when fractional investments are meaningless. In fact Lorie and Savage were aware of the problem but were unable to solve it. One technique that can be used to solve this problem will be presented in Chapter seven, but in some 'real world' situations it has been suggested that the indivisibility problem can be 'resolved' by cheating a little. The argument forwarded is that in practice budgetary limits are not hard and fast and can always be stretched a little; enough, hopefully, to enable the level of the last project to be 'rounded up' to one. If this is done it must be assumed that obtaining the extra money does not change the cost of capital and so affect the present values of the investments. The method avoids some unpleasant computational problems and should be used if circumstances permit. However, it is important to ensure that the budgetary limit can be stretched enough for the 'right' project to be rounded up. Possible pitfalls are illustrated in the case of the six investment problem data which are given in Figure 2.8. The row labelled PI gives the profitability index (NPV/outlay) in each case.

In detail, if fractional projects are meaningless, the selection procedure based on PI is to first select the project with the greatest PI (if its outlay does not exceed the limit) then take the project with next greatest PI (if the two outlays do not exceed the limit) and so on until a point is arrived at where the project with the next greatest PI would cause the budgetary limit to be exceeded. Projects with lower PIs are then examined and the one with the greatest PI *that can be afforded* is chosen.

Investment	A	B	C	D	E	F
NPV (£1,000)	42	36	27	23	19	12
Outlay (£1,000)	10	9	7	6	5	4
PI	4.20	4.00	3.86	3.83	3.80	3.00

Figure 2.8 PI example

The list is then searched for the project with the greatest PI that can be afforded from the funds which then remain. Selection is completed when the cheapest project (of those remaining) cannot be financed from the funds yet unused. For example, consider the projects in Figure 2.8 where there is an expenditure limit of 22 (£1,000), which for the moment we shall assume is rigid and that any money unspent is added to the NPVs of the projects selected, then the PI method would select A and B (leaving 3 unspent) giving a total NPV of 42 + 36 + 3 = 81. However, it is seen that investments A, C and E together give the maximum NPV of 42 + 27 + 19 = 88. If fractions had been meaningful 3/7 of project C would have been undertaken giving an NPV of 89 4/7. If the budget limit could be stretched to 26 then project C could be accepted in its entirety giving (in addition to projects A and B) an optimal total NPV of 105. C is the 'right' project to round up. But suppose expenditure could be stretched to 23 but no more then it would be possible to 'round up' project F to unit level (the inflexible level of 3/4 would have been preferred in conjunction with A and B in preference to an unspent balance of 3) and give a total NPV of 90. But the optimal solution in this case is A, C, D which gives an NPV of 92. It is only when the constraint is stretched at least to 24 that the PI method gives the correct answer (A, B and E if the limit is 24).

The example was chosen to show PI in a bad light. In favourable circumstances where the outlay on each project is small as a proportion of the budget limit or if there is in fact a good measure of flexibility in the 'limit' the PI method gives satisfactory results and is much to be preferred to casual inspection. The results can be expected to be satisfactory in the sense that even if the maximizing group of investments is not selected then the group actually selected will give a value of the objective function that is 'very close' to the maximum value. When there are many variables in the problem an inspection approach may not be computationally feasible. For instance if there were 20 possible investments there may be more than 100,000 different combinations of investments that could be afforded!

As alternatives to the PI method there are a number of programming algorithms available to solve the problem but it is not always worthwhile using these methods especially for problems involving only a small number of variables; the investor would have to decide whether the extra expense involved in the use of these more sophisticated methods was worthwhile. If calculations are performed by hand they may take much longer too although extra information of some value will be obtained.

In problems with two financial constraints programming methods begin to come into their own and there is no alternative to programming methods when there are several potentially binding constraints. If there are financial constraints this year we could not reasonably expect them all to have disappeared by next year. Nor should we expect all of the physical constraints to have vanished although perhaps both the financial and physical constraints may have changed. Equally it would be unusual if capital outlays were only required in one period on all projects and that the income from these investments was more than adequate as a source of finance for the outlays required on future investments. Although the PI method can be adapted to two constraint problems it can be computationally inefficient. In some cases, however, a cursory examination of the problem might suggest that it is worth trying – for example in a case where those projects that require the large outlays in the second year are the ones requiring the large outlays in the first year. PIs would be formed from one constraint alone and if the solution was feasible in terms of the second constraint it would be optimal (assuming that any necessary rounding up is possible). If the solution was not feasible then PIs would be formed using the second constraint and the solution obtained checked for feasibility with the first constraint. If this does not work it may be as well to begin the programming calculations there and then.

Notes

1. The reader will be aware that public utility projects normally run for many more than the three years (chosen for simplicity) in this example. The principles involved, however, would be unchanged.
2. For much more extensive discussions of this problem see Samuels, J. M. and Wilkes, F. M., *Management of Company Finance*, Nelson, London, 1971, Chapters 15 and 18, and Gordon, M. J., *The Investment Financing and Valuation of the Corporation*, Irwin, Homewood, Illinois, 1962.
3. See Schwab, B. and Luztig, P., 'A comparative analysis of the NPV and the benefit-cost ratio as measures of the economic desirability of investments', *Journal of Finance*, June, **1969**.
4. Weingartner, H. M., 'Criteria for programming investment project selection', *The Journal of Industrial Economics*, November, **1966**.
5. Lorie, J. H. and Savage, L. J., 'Three problems in rationing capital', *Journal of Business* **XXVIII**, No. 4., October, 1955, and reprinted in Solomon, E. (Ed.), *The Management of Corporate Capital*, The Free Press, Glencoe, Illinois, 1959.
6. An introduction to the Linear Programming notation that will be used here is given in Dewhurst, R. F. J., *Mathematics for Accountants and Managers*, Heinemann, London, 1968, pp. 55–64.
7. Anthony, R. N., *Management Accounting*, Revised Edition, Irwin, Homewood, Illinois, 1961, p. 154.

Additional References

1. Arditti, F. D., 'The re-investment assumption in the internal rate of return', *Journal of Business Finance*, Spring **1973**.
2. Bromwich, M., 'Inflation and the capital budgeting process', *Journal of Business Finance*, Autumn **1969**.
3. Foster, E. M., 'The impact of inflation on capital budgeting decisions', *The Quarterly Review of Economics and Business*', **10**, no. 3, Autumn 1970.
4. Lerner, E. M. and Carleton, W. T., 'The integration of capital budgeting and stock valuation', *American Economic Review*, **54**, September 1964.
5. Layard, R. (Ed.), *Cost–Benefit Analysis*, Penguin Modern Economic Readings, 1972.
6. Marglin, S. A., *Approaches to Dynamic Investment Planning*, North Holland Publishing Company, Amsterdam, 1963.
7. Nichols, D. A., 'A note on inflation and common stock values', *The Journal of Finance*, **23**, No. 4, September, 1968.
8. Scholefield, H. H., McBain, N. S. and Bagwell, J., 'The effects of inflation on investment appraisal', *Journal of Business Finance*, Summer **1973**.
9. Walters, A. A., 'A note on the choice of interest rates in cost–benefit analysis', *Economica*, February, **1970**.
10. Wilkes, F. M., 'Inflation and capital budgeting decisions', *Journal of Business Finance*, Autumn **1972**.

CHAPTER 3
Linear Programming

Many of the essential features of large programming problems can be illustrated in the context of quite small ones. The major part of this chapter examines a 'two by two' problem – one in which there are two constraints and, at the outset, two variables. The problem is one in which there is one 'physical' constraint and one financial constraint and a predetermined rate of discount. The chapter begins with examination of a 'one by two' problem which is later expanded.

3.1 A 'one by two' problem

The problem is to determine the numbers to be purchased of machines of two types so as to maximize the present value of the returns that the machines generate. Capital outlays on the machines are not to exceed a predetermined level. It is assumed that all relevant data is to hand. Call the machines type 1 and type 2, and let the numbers purchased of each type be represented by x_1 and x_2 respectively. Forecasts suggest that the NPV of each machine of type 1 is £6,000 and the NPV of each machine of type 2 is £4,000. Total net present value, N, is then given (in £1,000 units) by equation (3.1).

$$N = 6x_1 + 4x_2 \tag{3.1}$$

Equation (3.1) is called the *objective function*. Suppose that each machine of type 1 costs £4,000 and each machine of type 2 costs £2,000. The firm's budget for expenditure on these new machines is £16,000 so that the budget constraint is:

$$4x_1 + 2x_2 \leqslant 16 \tag{3.2}$$

It is being assumed in the formulation (3.1) of the objective function that any remainder from the amount 16 is not added to present value. This would be the case if 16 was an allocation from 'headquarters', any remainder being distributed elsewhere.

Also we shall assume that only purchases rather than sales of machines are being considered and that apart from (3.2) there is no restriction on the numbers that may be bought. Therefore the specification of the problem is completed by the sign requirements. It should be noted that the sign requirements are not of a different nature to the constraint (3.2). The sign requirement for x_1 could be written as:

$-x_1 + 0.x_2 \leqslant 0$. The complete problem is to

$$\begin{aligned} &\text{maximize} && N = 6x_1 + 4x_2 \\ &\text{subject to} && 4x_1 + 2x_2 \geqslant 16 \\ &\text{and} && x_1 \geqslant 0, x_2 \geqslant 0 \end{aligned}$$

The solution of this problem is rather obvious and it is unnecessary to devise a computational procedure to solve it. Incidentally, the word 'solution' can be employed in two senses. The problems can be said to be 'solved' when the maximum value of the objective function has been found. This is the sense in which the word is used in the immediate context. Below, 'solution' will also be used to refer to a set of values of the variables which satisfy both the constraint and the sign requirements, i.e. any point in OAB in Figure 3.1 can, in this sense, be said to be a 'solution'. The context should make clear the sense in which the word is being used. The very obviousness of the solution, however, may help in understanding the *simplex method* of computation. But before the simplex method is discussed, let us consider a graph of the problem.

The shaded region, OAB, in Figure 3.1 is called the *feasible area*. Other names for the feasible area are 'opportunity set', 'feasible production set' (in a production problem!) and 'set of attainable combinations'. The feasible area contains all combinations of x_1 and x_2 that satisfy (3.2) and the sign requirements and are therefore 'feasible'. Points on the line AB correspond to (3.2) holding as a strict equality whilst points below the line mean that a strict inequality holds in (3.2). The dashed lines in the Figure 3.1 are iso-present value (IPV) lines and represent combinations of the xs which give equal values of N. For example, the $N = 24$ line has end points $x_1 = 4$, $x_2 = 0$ and $x_1 = 0$, $x_2 = 6$, both of which clearly give $N = 24$ as does point C ($x_1 = 2$, $x_2 = 3$). The IPV lines all have the same slope, 6/4, since (3.1) can be rewritten as:

$$x_2 = \frac{N}{4} - \frac{6}{4} x_1 \tag{3.3}$$

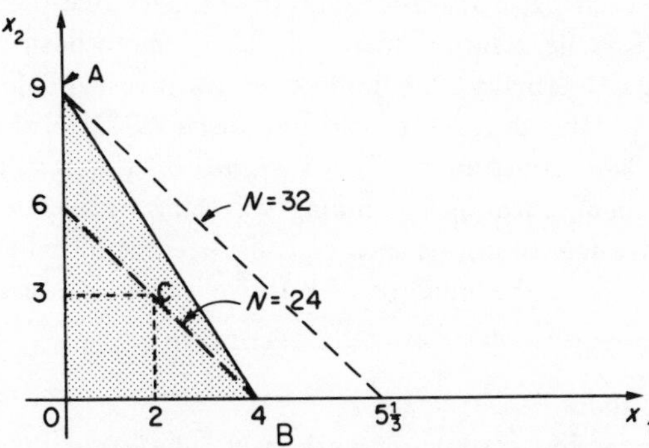

Figure 3.1 Graph of 'one by two' problem

A higher value of N corresponds to an IPV line further from the origin and the problem can be described as that of finding a point somewhere in the feasible area that is on the highest IPV line. This is clearly at point A where $x_1 = 0$, $x_2 = 8$ and $N = 32$. This is the *optimal solution* to the problem.

Whether point A or point B or somewhere in between is the optimal solution can be seen to depend upon the relative slopes of IPV lines and the constraint. The slope of the constraint is -2. The line AB is defined by $x_2 = (16/2) - (4/2)x_1$. If the IPV lines were steeper (in an absolute sense) than the constraint then point B would be optimal. This would correspond to the case where machine one had a substantially increased present value and/or reduced initial outlay *vis-à-vis* the current situation. It is evident that points between A and B can never be superior to both A and B. They can be equally good only in the case of a coincidence of slope between the IPV lines and constraint. In this case it does not matter what combination of purchases is made as long as the budget is exhausted. The optimal solution is said to be *non-unique*.

The investor can simplify matters for himself by considering only three points A, B and O. The origin would be optimal in the case where both present values were negative. These three points have the common characteristic of being corner points of the feasible area. They are referred to as *basic feasible solutions* to (3.2) and the sign requirements. A most important property of the basic feasible solutions can be shown if (3.2) is re-expressed as an equality. This is done by the addition of a *slack variable*, S_1, being the unused portion of the expenditure allowance and formally defined by:

$$S_1 = 16 - 4x_1 - 2x_2 \tag{3.4}$$

so that (3.2) can be rewritten as:

$$4x_1 + 2x_2 + S_1 = 16 \tag{3.5}$$

provided that $S_1 \geqslant 0$, a condition which is appended to the sign requirements. It can now be seen that at each of the basic feasible solutions one of the three variables is positive and two are zero. At O $x_1 = 0$, $x_2 = 0$, $S_1 > 0$. In a one constraint problem each basic feasible solution will have one positive variable. In general, at a basic feasible solution there will be no more positive variables than there are constraints. Normally the number of positive variables will equal the number of constraints. In a degenerate solution (discussed later) there will be fewer positive variables than constraints. For a proof of the result, which is the fundamental theorem of linear programming see Danø (reference 5). These facts, that only the basic feasible solutions need be considered, and that at these solutions there is an upper limit to the number of positive variables, are exploited by the simplex method.

3.2 The Simplex Method

An apparently naive but systematic method of solution of the problem can be based on the method of substitution. The objective function, including S_1 with a zero coefficient is:

$$N = 6x_1 + 4x_2 + 0S_1 \tag{3.6}$$

The first step is to solve the constraint (3.5) for S_1 [giving (3.4)] and substitute this expression for S_1 into (3.6). The result is

$$N = 6x_1 + 4x_2 + 0(16 - 4x_1 - 2x_2) = 0 + 6x_1 + 4x_2 \tag{3.7}$$

The value of the objective function is zero if both xs are zero (and consequently $S_1 = 16$ by 3.4) and the coefficients of the xs can be interpreted as meaning that if either were raised from zero level then the value of the objective function would increase by the coefficient of the variable. Since x_1 has the greater coefficient (each time x_1 is increased by one unit the objective function increases by six) let us repeat the above procedure for x_1, solving (3.5) for x_1 gives

$$x_1 = 4 - \frac{1}{2} x_2 - \frac{1}{4} S_1 \tag{3.8}$$

Notice that (3.8) can be obtained by changing the positions of $4x_1$ and S_1 in (3.4) and dividing by four. Now substitute (3.8) into (3.6). The result is

$$N = 6\left(4 - \frac{1}{2} x_2 - \frac{1}{4} S_1\right) + 4x_2 + 0S_1 = 24 + x_2 - \frac{6}{4} S_1 \tag{3.9}$$

which means that if x_2 and S_1 are zero and therefore x_1 is at its maximum level the value of the objective function is 24. If x_2 is raised to unit level then N will increase by the coefficient of x_2 in (3.9), i.e. by one. The important point is that this increase is *net* of the drop in the objective function caused by the necessary reduction in x_1. This is because the relationship between x_1 and x_2 in (3.8) has been incorporated into (3.9) and is implicit in the far right hand side (R.H.S.) of (3.9). The coefficient of S_1 in (3.9), 6/4, means that if S_1 was raised to unit level N would *decrease* by 6/4. The value of the solution $x_1 = 3¾$, $S_1 = 1$ [from (3.8)] is $24 - 6/4 = 22½$. It is clear that S_1 should be left at zero level and x_2 raised. Since the problem is entirely linear each and every unit by which x_2 is raised increases the objective function by one, so we clearly wish to 'introduce' x_2 to the maximum extent. Now, repeating the procedure above, changing the positions of $½x_2$ and x_1 in (3.8) and dividing through by one half [equivalent to solving (3.5) for x_2] gives:

$$x_2 = 8 - 2x_1 - ½S_1 \tag{3.10}$$

and substitution of (3.10) into (3.6) gives:

$$N = 6x_1 + 4(8 - 2x_1 - ½S_1) = 32 - 2x_1 - 2S_1 \tag{3.11}$$

If x_1 and S_1 are both zero [and therefore $x_2 = 8$ from (3.10)] then $N = 32$. The negative coefficients of x_1 and S_1 in (3.11) show that if they are raised from zero level then N will fall. Since x_1 and S_1 cannot be lowered because of the sign

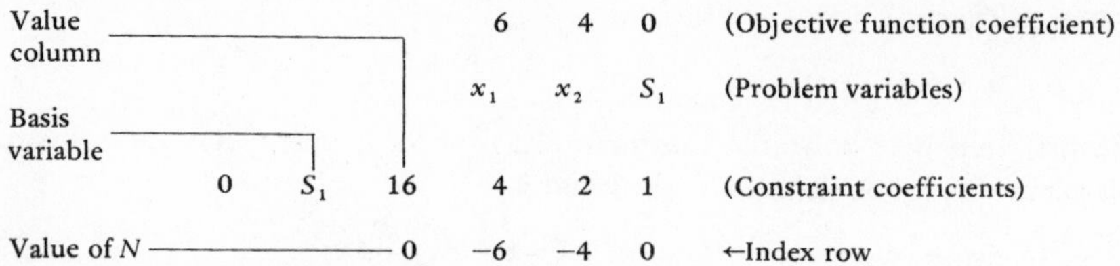

Figure 3.2 Simplex tableau for initial solution

requirements, 32 is the maximum value of N and the optimal solution ($x_1 = 0$, $x_2 = 8$, $S_1 = 0$) has been found.

We shall now repeat the foregoing calculations in the tableau format which will be the cornerstone of the computational sections of this book. Figure 3.2 describes the first solution that was tried above (with S_1 positive and x_1 and x_2 zero).

To form the tableau first write down the problem variables then, above each one, write its objective function coefficient and below each variable write its coefficient in the constraint equation. Then select the variable that is to be set at a positive level (the basis variable) and write this in to the left of the constraint coefficient row. To the right of the basis variable write in its value and to the left put the objective function coefficient of the basis variable. Before coming to the row 'index row' it should be noted that the constraint coefficients can be regarded as rates of exchange between the basis variable and the 'non-basis' variable in question. For example, 4, under x_1, means that each time x_1 is raised by one unit S_1 must be *lowered* by four units. Similarly each time x_2 is raised by one unit S_1 must be lowered by two units. The figure one, under S_1, can be considered a 'self with self' exchange rate. Now, since only the basis variable is positive the value of N can quickly be found by multiplying the figure to the right of the basis variable (its level, 16) by the figure to the left (the objective function coefficient). The result goes at the bottom of the value column. Numbers in the index row show how much the objective function would *decrease* by if the corresponding variable at the head of the column was raised to unit level. In some ways it is unfortunate that it is standard practice to form the index row and the rates of exchange so that the numbers are of the intuitively 'wrong' sign. For example, the figure −6 means that if x_1 was raised to unit level then N would increase by +6. Because of the one-for-one exchange rate with itself the basis variable will have a zero index row number. The index row numbers are calculated as follows. If x_1 is raised to unit level than S_1 must diminish by four each unit of which contributes zero to the objective function, whilst a unit of x_1 in its own right adds six. The excess of the drop in N due to reduction of S_1 over the increase in x_1 is $4 \times 0 - 6 = -6$ meaning that there is a net increase in N. As mentioned earlier this arrangement is not convenient for expository purposes but one rapidly gets used to it. By the same arguments the index row number for x_2 is $2 \times 0 - 4 = -4$ and for S_1 itself $1 \times 0 - 0 = 0$.

Each basic feasible solution that is arrived at will be described with the same tableau format as in Figure 3.2. An index row will be calculated and negative numbers in the index row will mean that the objective function can be increased by introducing a variable with a negative index row number. When a solution is obtained for which the index row is all non-negative the optimum has been reached. The next step in the procedure is to move from the solution described in the initial tableau to an improved solution.

As we have seen, in a one-constraint problem only solutions with one positive variable need be considered so that if x_1 or x_2 is raised to a positive level then this level must be such that S_1 falls to zero. But which variable should be introduced? The most frequently applied decision rule is that that variable should become a basis variable that has the 'most negative' index row number, i.e. shows the greatest per unit improvement in the objective function, x_1 in this case. Figure 3.3 extends the tableau of Figure 3.2 to show the first iteration.

The variable x_1 has become the basis variable and the lower half of Figure 3.3 is formed by first writing in x_1 in the position occupied by the basis variable. Then to the left of this is written its objective function coefficient. The elements of the 'main row' are the elements of the old constraint coefficient row divided by what is termed the *pivotal element*. The pivotal element is the rate of exchange between the variable leaving the basis and the variable entering it. Division of the constraint coefficient row by the pivotal element and changing the positions of x_1 and S_1 is equivalent to the formation of equation 3.8 above. The only difference is the change of sign – it should be remembered that in the tableau rates of exchange refer to *decreases* in the outgoing variable. The new index row is formed in the same way as before. For example the -1 under x_2 is $1/2 \times 6 - 4$ and the element $6/4$ is $1/4 \times 6 - 0$. The solution described in full is $x_1 = 6$, $x_2 = 0$, $S_1 = 0$ and $N = 24$ ($=6 \times 4$). Remember that all variables except the basis variable are at zero level.

Further improvement can be effected by the introduction of x_2. Figure 3.4 includes the next and final iteration. x_2 replaces x_1 as basis variable (since only x_2 has a negative index row number) and its objective function coefficient is 4 entered to the left of x_2. Main row elements in one-constraint problems are the old main row elements divided by the pivotal element, but in larger problems, with more than one constraint, it is not always the main row of a tableau that is divided by the pivotal element to form the new main row. We shall come to this presently. The new

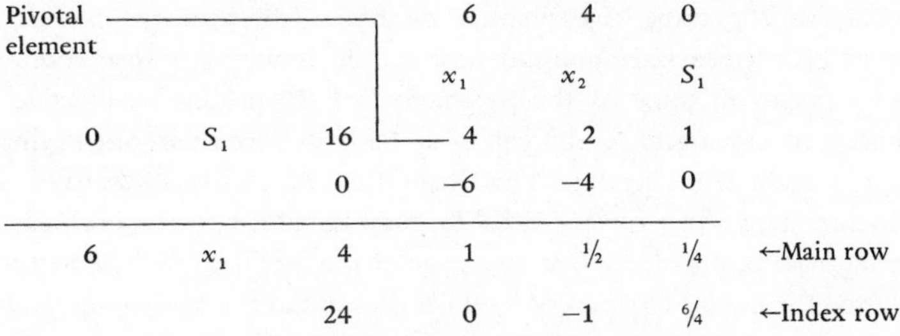

			6	4	0	
			x_1	x_2	S_1	
0	S_1	16	4	2	1	
		0	−6	−4	0	
6	x_1	4	1	½	¼	←Main row
		24	0	−1	6/4	←Index row

Figure 3.3 Simplex tableau: first iteration

			6	4	0	
			x_1	x_2	S_1	
0	S_1	16	4	2	1	
		0	−6	−4	0	
6	x_1	4	1	(½)	¼	Pivotal element
		24	0	−1	6/4	
4	x_2	8	2	1	½	←Main row
		32	2	0	2	←Index row

Figure 3.4 Simplex tableau: second iteration

index row is all non-negative indicating that the optimal solution has been reached. This solution in full is: $x_1 = 0$, $x_2 = 8$, $S_1 = 0$ and consequently $N = 32$.

It will, no doubt, have occurred to the reader that to begin by trying S_1 as basis variable was rather stupid. It consumes resources and contributes nothing to the objective function. The reason for starting with a 'slack variable solution' is that it is an easy one to find. The simplex method works by starting with a basic feasible solution (in principle *any* basic feasible solution will do) and subsequently moving to improved basic feasible solutions if such exist. It is therefore important to have a basic feasible solution to start with, and in somewhat larger problems it can be a lengthy task to find a starting solution including 'x' (structural) variables.

It will also have been noticed that the simplex procedure is apparently long winded and the 'obvious' solution with x_2 as basis variable was the last one to be arrived at. Why is such a procedure used to solve linear programming problems? The answer is that although a one-constant two-variable problem is much better solved by inspection, there is nothing at all obvious about larger problems. A systematic, automaton-like procedure is required to solve them. The simplex method guarantees that, if a finite optimum exists to a problem, this solution will be reached in a finite number of iterations. Some experience with the method will reveal that judgements (about which variable to bring in) overriding the most-negative-element decision rule can be effective. But there are important further reasons for using the simplex method. The principal one is that the calculations generate a large amount of valuable economic information. Also the effects of changes in some of the parameters of the problem (objective function coefficients and constraint levels) can be quickly deduced without having to start the problem again from scratch. This is the field of *sensitivity analysis* which we shall come to later. Also further variables may be added to the problem (perhaps representing new opportunities) at any stage of the calculations. The method is also ideally suited for use by computers – which is essential for really large problems.

More detailed examination of Figure 3.4 particularly in respect of the optimal solution, yields some potentially valuable information. The index rows are particularly useful for interpretative purposes. Consider the number in the final index row under S_1. We have already seen that it means that if S_1 was raised to unit level then N would drop by two units to 30. However, since the problem is linear it also means that if S_1 was *lowered* to a level of minus one then N would *increase* to 34. Now $S_1 = -1$ is not permitted but $S_1 = -1$ and an expenditure limit of 16 is equivalent to $S_1 = 0$ and an expenditure limit of 17. This is easily verified by reference to equation (3.5). So that setting $S_1 = -1$ tells us what would happen if the expenditure limit could be stretched by one (thousand pounds) and would enable the evaluation of borrowing opportunities. This possibility will be investigated further in an example later on. It should be noted that N can only increase by 2 if the constraint level goes up to 17 and x_2 can be set at the level of 8½. The rate of exchange between x_2 and S_1 tells us this – the figure ½ also operates both ways, if S_1 is *reduced* to -1 then x_2 *increases* by ½. Of course it might not be possible to buy a half share in a machine, in which case the index row number under S_1 would have to be interpreted in an avarage sense. If the expenditure limit could be raised by two units to 18 then x_2 would go up to 9 and N to 36. The extra two units of expenditure then have raised N by four. Equally, of course, a cutting back of the expenditure limit to 14 would cause a reduction of N by four. The index row allows the consequences of budget 'economies' to be quickly evaluated. The *shadow price* of funds at $t = 0$ (the present time) is two. This shadow price relates directly to the value (or cost) *to the investor* of extra (or decreased) funds at the margin.

It should be noted too that the value of the objective function at each solution is the shadow price of funds multiplied by the amount of funds – the index row number under the slack variable times the constraint level. In the optimal solution $32 = 2 \times 16$ in the previous solution, where less effective use is made of money available, $24 = (6/4) \times 16$. The shadow price can be thought of as a valuation of funds *on average* as well as at the margin – each and every unit decrease in money available (equivalent to raising S_1 by one unit) reduces N by two in the optimal solution.

The shadow price should be clearly distinguished from the 'over the counter' price that would have to be paid to secure extra funds. For instance if money over and above the original £16,000 could be borrowed from outside at 10% interest, if the discount rate used to determine the NPVs from the machines was 15% and if cash flow from the projects allowed repayment after one year then we can quickly compute the change in total net present value. It would be $2 - (1.1/1.15)$. Clearly it is worth the companies while to find a source of extra funds. In the extreme, in order to secure an extra £1,000 now it would be prepared to pay back after one year up to £2,300 (since $2 - (2.3/1.15) = 0$) – an implied maximum borrowing interest rate of 30%.

The index row number 2 under x_1 can also tell us quite a lot. For example if the company, because of a contract or to promote goodwill, felt that it was obliged to buy one machine of type one then present value would be reduced by 2 – this is the cost to the company of maintaining the goodwill. This is not to say that the company physically loses money when it buys a type one machine, the cost is an *opportunity cost:* it loses the opportunity to make an extra £2,000 profit (in present value terms). The index row number also shows what would happen if it was possible to disinvest in x_1. If the company had a stock of type one machines and could sell each one for £4,000 then this provides capital for the purchase of further type two machines with the net result that N increases by two. Of course, if the type one machines were sold for less than £4,000 the increase in N would be that much less than £2,000.

The *basis* of the solution to a linear programming problem is the matrix of coefficients in the original constraints of the variables which are positive. In the present one-constraint example the basis is the coefficient of the basis variable. In the first solution, with S_1 positive the basis is unity. In the second solution the basis is four and in the final solution the basis is two. The rate of exchange between the basis variable and the slack variable S_1 is the inverse of the basis. This is a valuable piece of information because the inverse of the basis, along with the constraint level, determines the level of the positive variable in the solution. For example, consider the solution with x_2 as basis variable. The constraint can be written as

$$2x_2 = 16 - 4x_1 - S_1$$

or

$$1x_2 = (½)16 - (½)4x_1 - (½)S_1$$

The inverse of the basis is ½ and the product of the basis inverse and constraint level gives the value of x_2. It is evident that since the coefficient of the slack variable in the original form of the constraint is unity, then the rate of exchange with x_2 must be the inverse of the basis. Using the inverse of the basis it is possible to calculate quickly the consequences of changes in the constraint level. If £20,000 were available initially the new level of x_2 would be (½)20 = 10.

With the existing alternatives there is no way of improving on the optimal solution to the example problem shown in Figure 3.4 $x_1 = 0$, $x_2 = 8$, $S_1 = 0$ is the equilibrium solution – provided that circumstances do not change. We shall be examining the effects of changing costs and constraint levels later on, but there is one other change to the problem that can conveniently be considered now. This is the case where additional investment opportunities are discovered after the original problem has been solved.[1] Suppose that two further investment possibilities arise – purchase of machines of type three and four. Each machine of type three costs £5,000 and the present value of the returns generated is £9,000. Each machine of type four costs £1,600 and the present value of returns generated is £3,500. Can the hitherto optimal investment programme be improved?

To answer this question it is not necessary to solve a new problem right from scratch. All that needs to be done is to add two extra columns, corresponding to the new investment opportunities, to Figure 3.4. In fact this need be done only for the last part of the tableau in respect of the optimal solution, but for completeness this has been done throughout in Figure 3.5. It is evident that x_3 is, in an opportunity sense, not a profitable investment. Each type three machine bought

			6	4	9	3.5	0
			x_1	x_2	x_3	x_4	S_1
0	S_1	16	4	2	5	1.6	1
		0	−6	−4	−9	−3.5	0
6	x_1	4	1	½	5/4	2/5	¼
		24	0	−1	−6/4	−11/10	6/4
4	x_2	8	2	1	5/2	4/5	½
		32	2	0	1	−3/10	2
3.5	x_4	10	5/2	5/4	25/8	1	5/8
		35	11/4	3/8	31/16	0	35/16

Figure 3.5 Additional investment opportunities

would, because of the necessary reduction in numbers of type two machines, cause N to fall by one unit. However, the type four machines are, in both an absolute and a relative sense, profitable. This is shown by the index row number −3/10. The solution with x_2 as basis variable is no longer optimal, but the new optimum with x_4 as basis variable is obtained in one iteration taking the original optimum as the starting point. It is not necessary to begin the problem again from scratch.

It will no doubt have been noticed that, rather conveniently, the answers to the above problems have been whole numbers. The problem of fractional answers will be addressed specifically at a later stage and is a complication that will be deliberately avoided for the time being.

3.3 A 'Two by Two' Problem

It has so far been assumed that there are sufficient physical resources, manpower, materials, space, etc., to meet the demands made by any machines that are purchased. We shall now drop this assumption and explicitly introduce a physical constraint – a limit on the floorspace available for the machines. With the original two alternative machine types, suppose that each machine of type one requires two hundred square feet (including working and access space) of floorspace and each machine of type two requires three hundred square feet. There are one thousand two hundred square feet of floorspace available. What is the optimal investment package? The floorspace constraint can be written as:

$$2x_1 + 3x_2 \leqslant 12 \tag{3.12}$$

or, with a slack variable, S_2 [defined as was S_1 in (3.4)] specific to this constraint as:

$$2x_1 + 3x_2 + S_2 = 12 \tag{3.13}$$

S_2 is, of course, required to be non-negative and has a zero objective function coefficient on the assumption that unused floorspace has no alternative use of

			6	4	0	0	
Pivot column → x₁ column; Pivot element → 4			x_1	x_2	S_1	S_2	
0	S_1	16	4	2	1	0	Pivot row
0	S_2	12	2	3	0	1	
		0	−6	−4	0	0	Index row
6	x_1	4	1	½	¼	0	Main row
0	S_2	4	0	2	−½	1	
		24	0	−1	6/4	0	

Figure 3.6 Two-constraint problem: first iteration

value. Recalling that the simplex procedure required as basic feasible solution to start with, and that the easiest one to find is the origin ($S_1 = 16$, $S_2 = 12$, $x_1 = 0$, $x_2 = 0$), Figure 3.6 presents this solution and the first iteration.

Variable x_1 has the 'most negative' index row number, and so will be a basis variable in the next solution. The x_1 rates of exchange form the *pivot column.* Now, in a two-constraint problem only two variables will be positive in any basic feasible solution, so that if x_1 is brought in either S_1 or S_2 must drop out. In other words there are now two alternative candidates for *pivot row*. The pivot row is selected by forming the ratios of elements in the value column and rates of exchange in the same row in the pivot column i.e. 16/4 and 12/2. Whichever of these is the smaller determines the pivot row. The reason for this procedure is clear when it is recalled that the rate of exchange, 4, between S_1 and x_1 means that each time x_1 is raised by one unit S_1 must diminish by four units. Since S_1 is at the level 16 and must not be negative in any solution, the maximum extent to which x_1 can be introduced on this account is 16/4. A similar argument applies in connection with S_2. To ensure that S_2 is non-negative x_1 must not be (in the next solution) greater than 12/2. Since both S_1 and S_2 are to be non-negative, the smaller ratio determines the variable that is 'leaving the basis.[2]

The next basic feasible solution will therefore have x_1 and S_2 as basis variables. We can begin by writing these in and to the left of them their objective function coefficients can be written. The main row in the new tableau is in the same position as the key row in the old one and, as was the case in the one-constraint problem, it is obtained by dividing the pivot row by the pivot element. The remaining rates of exchange are found in a different way. Suppose we are engaged in finding the new rate of exchange between x_2 and S_2. The effects of any change in value of x_2 in both constraint equations need to be considered. The rate of exchange between x_2 and S_2 was originally 3, this being determined from the second constraint alone. However, since x_1 also appears in the new solution the effects of the change in x_2 on x_1 have to be allowed for. If x_2 is set at unit level then, as can be seen from the main row, x_1 must be reduced by ½ and reference back to the original solution and the rate of exchange between x_1 and S_2 tells us that if x_1 is reduced by ½ then S_2 will *increase* by 1 on this account. So the net change in S_2 is $3 - ½ \times 2 = 2$ and this is the new rate of exchange. All remaining rates of exchange and the new level of S_2 can be found by a similar process of argument and it turns out that all the numbers are as given by the following formula:[3]

'new' number = 'old' number − corresponding main row number

x corresponding pivot column number

The 'new' number is the number in the new tableau in the same position as a given number in the previous tableau — the 'old' number. In the example above, 3 is the 'old' number and 2 is the 'new' number. The 'corresponding main row number' is the number in the main row of the new tableau in the same column as the new number, i.e. ½ in the example. The 'corresponding pivot column number' is the number in the pivot column of the old tableau in the same row as the old number, i.e. 2 in the example. The remaining numbers are: level of $S_2 = 12 - 4 \times 2 = 4$; x_1, S_2 rate of exchange $= 2 - 1 \times 2 = 0$; S_1, S_2 rate of exchange $= 0 - \frac{1}{4} \times 2 = -\frac{1}{2}$; S_2, S_2 rate of exchange $= 1 - 0 \times 2 = 1$. Three points should be noted. Firstly, for a basis variable (such as x_1 in the second tableau) the column of rates of exchange consists of unit for the 'self with self' exchange rate and zero elsewhere. Secondly, the rate of exchange −½ between S_1 and S_2 means that as S_1 is raised by one unit S_2 will *increase* by ½. Thirdly, the index row numbers may be calculated using the new/old number formula.

Clearly the x_1, S_2 solution is not optimal since introductions of x_2 would effect improvement. Figure 3.7 shows the next, and final iteration. The optimal solution of the problem is therefore $x_1 = 3$, $x_2 = 2$, $S_1 = 0$, $S_2 = 0$ and $N = 26$. This solution can now be compared with the one-constraint case. The optimal value of the objective function has, of course, diminished since adding extra constraints will, if they are not 'redundant',[4] cut down the feasible solution set and as is the case here cut out the original optimum. The situation is graphed in Figure 3.8. The original optimum (now labelled D) is 'cut off' by the addition of the floorspace constraint

			6	4	0	0	
			x_1	x_2	S_1	S_2	
0	S_1	16	4	2	1	0	
0	S_2	12	2	3	0	1	
		0	−6	−4	0	0	
6	x_1	4	1	½	¼	0	
0	S_2	4	0	2	−½	1	Pivot row
		24	0	−1	6/4	0	
6	x_1	3	1	0	3/8	−¼	
4	x_2	2	0	1	−¼	½	
		26	0	0	5/4	½	

Figure 3.7 Two-constraint problem: optimal solution

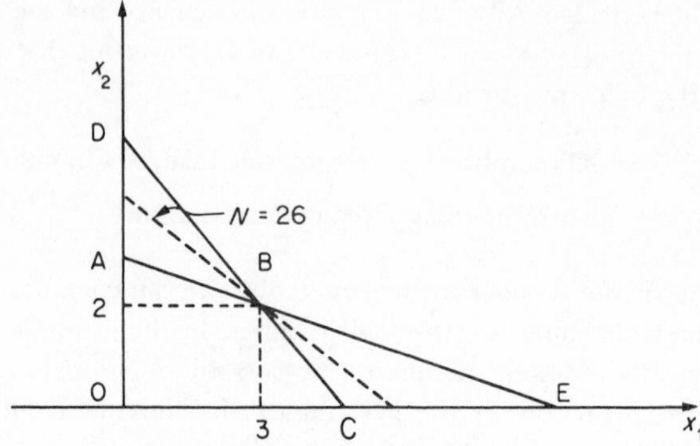

Figure 3.8 Graph of two-constraint problem

AE. The new feasible area is O A B C and the new optimum is B. Note that B is preferred to A, the solution where only type two machines are bought. Although type two machines are economical in their use of finance, they are relatively extravagant consumers of the new scarce resource: floorspace. Type one machines although costly to purchase are economical users of floorspace. The optimum represents levels of x_1 and x_2 such that economical use is made of *both* resources, although it should be pointed out here that two constraint problems do not, inevitably, have two structural variables positive at the optimum.

The Simplex method examined solutions O, C and B respectively. The reader may verify that solution A would be as described in Figure 3.9. With the presence of the floorspace requirement the opportunity cost of buying only as many 'profitable' type two machines as could be accommodated is $26 - 16 = 10$. It can be seen from the index row of Figure 3.9 that each type one machine would add 10/3 to N. This figure provides a check on the calculations since if x_1 can be set at $8 \pm 8/3 = 3$ the value of N in the next solution should be $16 + 3 \times 10/3 = 26$.

The final index row of Figure 3.7 gives optimal shadow prices for both resources. Provided that fractional values of the xs are meaningful an extra £1,000 expanded optimally would add £1,250 to present value, whilst an extra one hundred square feet of floorspace would add £500 to N. Note that if floorspace is fixed, but more money becomes available, x_1 goes up whilst x_2 decreases. With an extra £1,000 available the optimal value of x_1 is $3\frac{3}{8}$ and the optimal value of x_2 is $1\frac{3}{4}$. Because of the floorspace requirement, the extra finance could be put to work effectively only by buying type one machines. The requisite floorspace is obtained by having fewer type two machines. If more floorspace is available this is put to best use by having more type two machines. The requisite financial resources are freed by

0	S_1	8	$8/3$	0	1	$-2/3$
4	x_2	4	$2/3$	1	0	$1/3$
		16	$-10/3$	0	0	$4/3$

Figure 3.9 Two-constraint problem: sub-optimal solution

having fewer type one machines. With an additional 100 square feet of floorspace the optimal values of xs are $x_1 = 2\frac{3}{4}$ and $x_2 = 2\frac{1}{2}$. Variations in constraint levels are discussed in detail in chapter 4. As a further illustration of the use of Linear Programming in investment decision making we shall now state and solve a three-constraint problem.

3.4 A Three-Constraint example

A firm is considering the purchase of machines of two types. The new machines will work in conjunction with existing machines (on which there is some spare capacity) to produce components for sale to vehicle assemblers. Money for capital expenditure on the new machines is limited as is floorspace. Other essential inputs can be obtained in any desired quantities and costs associated with these inputs are allowed for in the net revenue figures. The firm has a five year horizon and post horizon returns (appropriately weighted) appear in the year 5 figures. Estimated net revenues for each machine of each type are:

Year	1	2	3	4	5
Type one	3,500	4,200	−2,000	5,600	5,000
Type two	1,100	3,500	2,500	1,600	4,700

Letting x_1 and x_2 represent the numbers of machines purchased the constraints that apply are, respectively, financial outlay (thousands of pounds), floorspace (hundreds of square feet), and time required on other machines (hours per period time). In algebraic form the constraints emerge as:

$$5x_1 + 3x_2 \leqslant 55$$

$$2x_1 + 3x_2 \leqslant 40$$

$$9x_1 + 4x_2 \leqslant 92$$

$$x_1, x_2 \geqslant 0$$

The cost of capital for the firm is thought to be 10% and this is to be employed for all exercises involving discounting. The objective is to maximize the present value of investment in the machines.

Discounting the returns we find that the GPV of each machine of type one is £12,080 and therefore, subtracting the outlay of £5,000 the NPV is £7,080. GPV for type two machines is £9,782 and so NPV is £6,782. The objective is therefore to

$$\text{maximize } N = 7.08x_1 + 6.782x_2$$

For ease of calculation, however, we shall work with the function

$$N^* = 7x_1 = 6.8x_2$$

and the final index row will be checked with the correct figures 7.08 and 6.782. The statement of the problem and its solution is given in tabular form in Figure 3.10.

The answer to the firm's investment problem is to purchase five type one

			7	6.8	0	0	0
			x_1	x_2	S_1	S_2	S_3
0	S_1	55	5	3	1	0	0
0	S_2	40	2	3	0	1	0
0	S_3	92	9	4	0	0	1
		0	−7	−6.8	0	0	0
0	S_1	35/9	0	7/9	1	0	−5/9
0	S_2	176/9	0	19/9	0	1	−2/9
7	x_1	92/9	1	4/9	0	0	1/9
		644/9	0	−33.2/9	0	0	7/9
6.8	x_2	5	0	1	9/7	0	−5/7
0	S_2	9	0	0	−19/7	1	9/7
7	x_1	8	1	0	−4/7	0	3/7
		90	0	0	33.2/7	0	−13/7
6.8	x_2	10	0	1	−2/9	5/9	0
0	S_3	7	0	0	−19/9	7/9	1
7	x_1	5	1	0	1/3	−1/3	0
		103	0	0	7.4/9	13/9	0

Figure 3.10 Three-constraint problem: simplex solution

machines and ten type two machines. There will be seven hours per day ($S_3 = 7$) slack time still remaining on the existing machines. This investment plan gives a total NPV of £103,000. There are several points to note from Figure 3.10. Firstly, in a three-constraint problem there will be three variables in the basis and since there are only two structural variables any basis must contain at least one slack variable so that no more than two constraints can be binding simultaneously. The firm must, therefore, end up with some of at least one resource unused. Secondly, calculating the index row with the exact (perhaps overly exact) objective function coefficients gives 103.22 as the value of the solution. The other elements in the index row are, respectively, 0, 0, 7.436/9 13.36/9, 0. Thirdly, the variable S_3 left the original basis only to re-enter the final basis. The fact that a variable leaves a solution therefore does not mean that it can be forgotten. Fourthly, the final index row gives the marginal valuations of the scarce resources.

Ignoring whole number problems, a further hundred square feet of floorspace would increase present value by 13/9, provided, of course, that it is made use of in an optimal manner. From the rates of exchange in the S_2 column it can be seen that a further nine hundred square feet of space would enable x_2 to be set at $15(= 10 + 9 \times 5/9)$, $S_3 = 14(7 + 9 \times 7/9)$, $x_1 = 2(= 5 - 9 \times 1/3)$ giving an increase in N of $13(= 9 \times 13/9)$. Whole number difficulties are not always so conveniently resolved in general, but the figure 13/9 would always provide an *upper bound* for the value per unit of additional space. This point will be developed in Chapter 7.

The S_1 index row number means that if a further thousand pounds were available then *net* present value would increase by £7,400/9. Note that this is less than the given NPV that could be achieved if one thousand pound's worth of a type one *or* a type two machine could be bought. This arises because of the tightness of the floorspace constraint. Room could not be found for the extra one fifth or one third of a machine as a net addition to the number of machines. If more units of one type of machine are installed then there must be fewer units of the other type. An extra one thousand pounds, optimally used would mean reducing x_2 by $\frac{2}{9}$ and increasing x_1 by $\frac{1}{3}$. The resultant increase in GPV would be 16.4/9 and NPV would be up by 7.4/9(= (16.4/9) – 1). Were it not for the lack of floorspace the extra one thousand would be best spent on $\frac{1}{3}$ of a type two machine increasing N by 6.8/3 and it is of interest to see that (7.4/9) + (13/9) = 6.8/3. In other words, the cost (in an opportunity loss sense) of not having the requisite floorspace to install the extra machinery is 13/9 {= (6.8/3) – (7.4/9)} which is precisely the valuation of floorspace at the margin given by the optimal solution. The figures 7.4/9 and 13/9 can also be interpreted as average (i.e. per unit) valuations of the scarce financial and space resources in that (55 x 7.4/9) + (40 x 13/9) = 103. This is the way things always work out in linear problems – profit is divided between the resources which create the bottlenecks. The 'average' interpretation can, however, be misleading since although it is correct to say that a marginal unit of resource three (other machine time) has zero value the resource is far from worthless on average. In fact no profit at all could be made without this resource. It so happens that there is a little more than is needed at the optimum. The problem is graphed in Figure 3.11. The feasible area is O A B C D and the simplex method successively tried basic solutions O D C and B. the optimum position B is below the line for constraint three although this resource is fully used at points C and D.

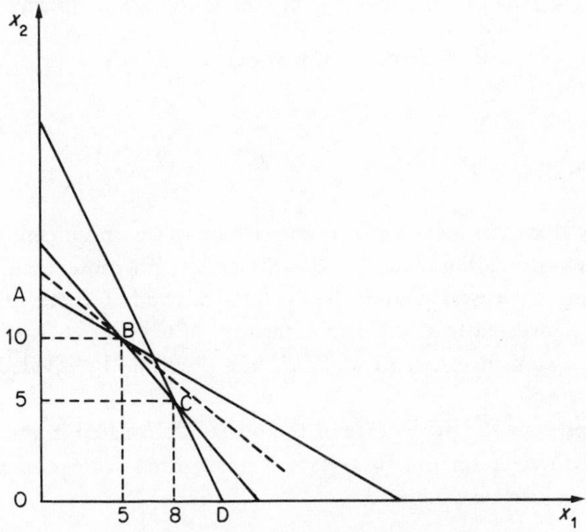

Figure 3.11 Three-constraint example graphed

The solution of the problem required three iterations. One iteration could have been saved if x_2 had been introduced in the first instance instead of x_1. The choice of pivot column is normally determined by the non-basic variable with the 'most negative' index row number. This will effect the greatest improvement *per unit* of the variable introduced. However, the greatest total improvement from the origin is achieved when x_2 is introduced. This can be found by multiplying the index row numbers by the maximum extent of introduction of the corresponding variable. Thus we could have seen, in advance, that point D would give $N = 644/9$ $(= 7 \times 92/9)$ and point A would give $N = 816/9 (= 6.8 \times 40/3)$. If x_2 had been introduced the optimum, B, would have followed after one further iteration. Sometimes these possibilities can be easily spotted and computational time saved.

3.5 Further Examples

Portfolio problems are frequently suitably structured for solution by programming methods. Some portfolio problems are quite difficult to solve and more substantial problems are discussed in the final chapter. However, the usefulness of a programming approach to this type of problem can be illustrated with relatively simple examples. The 'constrained choice of shares' and 'finance company' problems aim to demonstrate this point. The lengthier 'shift-pattern' example is based on a study undertaken by the author for a component supplier in the motor industry and is designed to illustrate how programming methods can be used to generate data for D C F calculations and hence the eventual investment decision.

Example One: Constrained Choice of Shares

In this problem the financial manager of a company with considerable cash resources has to decide on the percentages of a given sum to invest in various other companies. The yields per pound invested in each company are given below

	Unit trusts		Chemicals		Stores		Mines	
Company No.	1	2	3	4	5	6	7	8
Yield %	4.8	5.4	7.5	8.5	9	10	15	18

Company policy does not give the investment manager a completely free hand. At least 30% of any portfolio must be in unit trusts; no more than 25% may be invested in mining; at least 10% must be in chemicals and no more than 20% of the portfolio may be invested in any single company. The objective is to maximize the yield on the total sum invested. How should the portfolio be divided amongst the candidate companies?

Letting x_j represent the percentage of the portfolio invested in the jth company, and assuming that yield on the total sum is a weighted average of the individual yields, the problem can be expressed as:

$$\text{Maximize } F = 4.8x_1 + 5.4x_2 + 7.5x_3 + 8.5x_4 + 9x_5 + 10x_6 + 15x_7 + 18x_8$$

Subject to

$$
\begin{aligned}
x_1 + x_2 + x_3 + x_4 + x_5 + x_6 + x_7 + x_8 &= 100 \\
x_1 + x_2 &\geqslant 30 \\
x_7 + x_8 &\leqslant 25 \\
x_3 + x_4 &\geqslant 10 \\
x_1 &\leqslant 20 \\
x_2 &\leqslant 20 \\
x_3 &\leqslant 20 \\
x_4 &\leqslant 20 \\
x_5 &\leqslant 20 \\
x_6 &\leqslant 20 \\
x_7 &\leqslant 20 \\
x_8 &\leqslant 20
\end{aligned}
$$

This problem could be solved by use of the simplex method and larger problems with more involved constraints would be solved. The special structure of this problem (a 'sparse' matrix of coefficients and all non-zero coefficients being unity) enables a quick solution by inspection to be obtained.

Company eight is the most lucrative investment and x_8 is set at twenty. Company seven is the next most attractive, but x_7 may not exceed five because of constraint three. Clearly the best way of satisfying constraint two is to set x_2 equal to twenty and x_1 equal to ten. Constraint three is met by settling x_4 equal to ten. Constraint one then allows x_6 to be set at twenty and x_5 at fifteen. The full solution (but without slack variables) is then: $x_1 = 10$, $x_2 = 20$, $x_3 = 0$, $x_4 = 10$, $x_5 = 15$, $x_6 = 20$, $x_7 = 5$, $x_8 = 20$.

The index row of the final simplex tableau would enable a speedy evaluation of the elements of the companies investment policy which were predetermined. It would reveal the effects of relaxing some of the constraints. In the present example it is possible to do this without too much difficulty and without recourse to the simplex method. For example, if the policy was changed to the extent that 35% of the portfolio could be in mining, then the new optimal levels of x_5 and x_7 would be five and fifteen respectively and average yield would be up from 10.11% to 10.71%. This is a sensitivity analysis approach and is an illuminating way to present the consequences of policy at board level.

The constraints of this problem are one way of taking into account the riskiness of investments. Top management required at least a minimum investment in the relatively safe unit trust whilst a maximum was specified for the higher risk mining industry; furthermore, the eggs had to be divided amongst at least five baskets. In this instance risk itself was not quantified. The succeeding example includes a very simple measure of risk.

Example Two: Finance Company Problem

A finance company is considering lending up to a total of £100,000 to five prospective clients. The rates of interest that the potential customers are prepared to pay and the finance companies estimate of the default risk in each case is given below. In the event of default the entire loan will be written off.[5] The objective is to maximize the rate of interest earned on the £100,000, if there are no defaulters, subject to 'expected loss' not exceeding £1,000.

Company	1	2	3	4	5
Interest rate %	6.5	7	8.5	9.5	11.5
Default probability	0.006	0.008	0.013	0.015	0.024

Letting x_j represent the amount advanced to each company, the expected loss constraint is:

$$0.006\,x_1 + 0.008\,x_2 + 0.013\,x_3 + 0.015\,x_4 + 0.024\,x_5 \leqslant 1{,}000$$

Changing units of measure to £1,000 and multiplying both sides of the expected loss constraint by 1,000 the two constraints are

$$6\,x_1 + 8\,x_2 + 13\,x_3 + 15\,x_4 + 24\,x_5 \leqslant 1{,}000$$

$$x_1 + x_2 + x_3 + x_4 + x_5 \leqslant 100$$

and the objective function is

$$F = 6.5\,x_1 + 7\,x_2 + 8.5\,x_5 + 9.5\,x_4 + 11.5\,x_5$$

Figure 3.12 presents the solution of this problem by the simplex method.

To obtain the average interest rate in percentage terms the value of F should be

			6.5	7	8.5	9.5	11.5	0	0
			x_1	x_2	x_3	x_4	x_5	S_1	S_2
0	S_1	1,000	6	8	13	15	24	1	1
0	S_2	100	1	1	1	1	1	0	1
		0	−6.5	−7	−8.5	−9.5	−11.5	0	0
0	S_1	200	−2	0	5	7	16	1	−8
7	x_2	100	1	1	1	1	1	0	1
		700	0.5	0	−1.5	−2.5	−4.5	0	7
9.5	x_4	200/7	−2/7	0	5/7	1	16/7	1/7	−8/7
7	x_2	500/7	9/7	1	2/7	0	−9/7	−1/7	15/7
		5,400/7	−3/14	0	2/7	0	17/14	5/14	29/7
9.5	x_4	400/9	0	2/9	7/9	1	2	1/9	−6/9
6.5	x_1	500/9	1	7/9	2/9	0	−1	−1/9	15/9
		7,050/9	0	1.5/9	3/9	0	1	3/9	40.5/9

Figure 3.12 Solution of finance company problem

divided by 100. At the optimum an average rate of just over 7.83% is earned. Note that the selection of pivot columns was not determined by the most negative index row numbers. This was because it is fairly obvious that larger improvements in the objective function are possible by introduction of the variables indicated because of the extent to which they can be introduced. The number of iterations required can often be reduced in this way.

The optimal solution consists of $x_4 = 400/9$ and $x_1 = 500/9$. Only two of the five possible client companies should be lent money. This result was evident from the number of constraints in the problem. The final index row enables some evaluation of the risk policy of the finance company to be made. Each time the expected loss figure is raised by £100, x_4 increases by 100/9, x_1 decreases by 100/9 and F increases by 300/9. Alternatively, if risk had been ignored completely a sum of £68,116 [= 7,050 ÷ (9 x 11.5)] lent to company five alone would have given a return of 7.83% on the total of £100,000.

Realistic complicating considerations that this example ignores are the interdependence of risk from separate investments; the possibility that risk in an individual case may depend on the amount invested and the possibility that the rate of return required by the investor may affect the riskiness of the investment.

Significant interrelations of risk must be taken into account. How this can be accomplished by explained in the discussion of portfolio theory in the final chapter.

Example Three: Changing the Shift Pattern

This example is divided into two parts. Firstly comes a discussion in general terms of a way of 'formalizing' this type of problem. This is followed by a worked numerical example.

A firm can manufacture a range of n products. Only two resources are in limited supply, namely 'machine time' and 'labour time'. Other resources such as materials, can be obtained in any quantitites required. The firm's work is arranged into m shifts per time period. Let x_{ij} be the amount produced of the jth product on the ith shift and let π_j represent the profit per unit of product j. The objective is to maximize profit per time period, i.e. to maximize

$$\pi = \sum_j \pi_j \sum_i x_{ij} \tag{3.14}$$

Let a_j be labour time required to manufacture one unit of product j and let b_j be machine time required to manufacture one unit of product j. There are L_i man hours and K_i machine hours available on the ith shift. The two constraints can then be expressed as

$$\sum_j a_j x_{ij} \leqslant L_i \quad i = 1,2, \ldots, M \tag{3.15}$$

and

$$\sum_j b_j x_{ij} \leqslant K_i \quad i = 1,2, \ldots, M \tag{3.16}$$

Let the maximum of (3.14) subject to (3.15), (3.16) and sign requirements be $\bar{\pi}_m$. Under pressure from Trade Unions the firm is considering reducing the number of shifts that it operates. Consequently more labour time will be available per shift. Let the extra time available on the ith shift by ΔL_i. The problem would now be to maximize (3.14) to

$$\sum_j a_j x_{ij} \leqslant L_i + \Delta L_i \quad i = 1,2,\ldots,k \tag{3.17}$$

and

$$\sum_j b_j x_{ij} \leqslant K_i \quad i = 1,2,\ldots,k \tag{3.18}$$

where

$$k < m \quad \text{and} \quad \sum_{i=1}^{k} L_i + \Delta L_i = \sum_{i=1}^{M} L_i.$$

In the structure presented the new maximum of profit, $\bar{\pi}$ will be less than $\bar{\pi}_M$. In reality this would not necessarily be the case; unit profits may differ from shift to shift as a result of differing wage rates per shift [we should need to enter π_{ij} in (3.14)] or absenteeism may be lower with fewer shifts. These considerations have been omitted in this formulation but are included in the numerical example. Clearly if $\bar{\pi}_K > \bar{\pi}_M$ then (we shall ignore the costs associated with a changeover) the changed shift pattern should be implemented irrespective of union pressure.

However, suppose $\bar{\pi}_K < \pi_M$. What can be done about this? One way would be to see if productivity could be increased (reducing the a_j and or b_j). The tactic we shall examine here is that of increasing the machine time available. We have assumed in the writing of (3.18) that no more machine time is available in each shift than before. This situation can be changed by investing in more machines. If new machines were brought such that time available on the ith shift was $K_i + \Delta K_i$ then (3.14) would be maximized subject to (3.17) and

$$\sum_j b_j x_{ij} \leqslant K_i + \Delta K_i \tag{3.19}$$

For any given set of ΔK_i corresponding to a particular purchase of machines the problem can be solved by the simplex method and the new maximum profit calculated. Suppose the new level of profit is $\bar{\pi}_\Delta$. Then each period the new machines have added $\bar{\pi}_\Delta - \bar{\pi}_K$ to profits. If the discounted sum of these 'returns' exceeds the outlay required for the machines, then the investment is worthwhile. In general the optimal sector of ΔK_i (and the corresponding level of investment) cannot be obtained analytically. A series of L.P. problems has to be solved or the optimal ΔK_i obtained by some other numerical method.

Data for the numerical example is given below. The firm can manufacture three products and at present operates three shifts per day while 2,400 men and machine hours are available per shift.

			0.2	0.15	0.25	0	0
			x_1	x_2	x_3	S_1	S_2
0	S_1	2,400	0.2	0.4	0.8	1	0
0	S_2	2,400	0.5	0.3	0.3	0	1
			−0.2	−0.15	−0.25	0	0
0.15	x_2	6,000	0.5	1	2	2.5	0
0	S_2	600	0.35	0	−0.3	−0.75	1
		900	−0.125	0	0.05	0.375	0
0.15	x_2	36,000/7	0	1	17/7	25/7	−10/7
0.2	x_1	12,000/7	1	0	−6/7	−15/7	20/7
		7,800/7	0	0	−0.4/7	0.75/7	2.5/7
0.25	x_3	36,000/17	0	7/17	1	25/17	−10/17
0.2	x_1	60,000/17	1	6/17	0	−15/17	40/17
		21,000/17	0	0.4/17	0	3.25/17	5.5/17

Figure 3.13 Shift pattern example: three shift solution

Unit profits:	0.2	0.15	0.25	
	x_1	x_2	x_3	
Man hours:	0.2	0.4	0.8	$\leqslant$2,400
Machine hours:	0.5	0.3	0.3	$\leqslant$2,400

The solution of this problem is given in Figure 3.13.

The profit per shift is £21,000/17 which means £3,706 per day. Now, suppose that a two shift system is adopted, the third shift labour being equally divided between the first two shifts. Suppose also that the changeover means an increase in unit profits of 20% due to not having to pay high third shift wage rates, less intensive working of machinery, less absenteeism and lower service and supervisory charges. The right hand side of the labour time constraint is increased by 50%, machine time being unchanged as are the technical coefficients. All coefficients in the objective function are multiplied by 1.2. It will be seen in a later chapter that it is not necessary to start the problem again from scratch in order to accommodate such changes, but for the present we shall work the problem through with the new data.

Profit per shift is increased to £1,757.6 but since there are now only two shifts in operation daily profit comes down to £3,515. It is therefore preferable to stay with the existing three shift arrangement especially in view of the fact that changeover costs have not been included in these calculations.

Now, the firm can purchase machinery that would enable it to expand its machine hours available per shift by 25%. The cost of this machinery is £750,000; it would last 15 years and the firm's cost of capital is 12%. Should the machinery be bought if the two shift system has to be adopted? The reader may verify that

			0.24	0.18	0.30	0	0
			x_1	x_2	x_3	S_1	S_2
0	S_1	3,600	0.2	0.4	0.8	1	0
0	S_2	2,400	0.5	0.3	0.3	0	1
			−0.24	−0.18	−0.30	0	0
0	S_1	400	−1.4/3	0	0.4	1	−4/3
0.18	x_2	8,000	5/3	1	1	0	10/3
		1,400	0.06	0	−0.12	0	0.6
0.30	x_3	1,000	−3.5/3	0	1	1.5	−10/3
0.18	x_2	7,000	8.5/3	1	0	−2.5	20/3
		1,560	−0.08	0	0	0.3	0.2
0.30	x_3	66,000/17	0	7/17	1	25/17	−10/17
0.24	x_1	42,000/17	1	6/17	0	−15/17	40/17
		29,880/17	0	0.48/17	0	3.9/17	6.6/17

Figure 3.14 Shift pattern example: two shift solution

with machine hours at 3,000 per shift and man hours at 3,600 optimal outputs are $x_3 = 60{,}000/17$, $x_2 = 0$, $x_1 = 66{,}000/17$. Profit made would be £3,981 per day. Thus with the extra machinery daily profit rises by £466. Now assuming a 245 day working year, the annual increase in profits is £114,170. Therefore, treating the amounts £114,170 as if they occurred at the end of the year the 'project' to evaluate is

$$\text{NPV} = 114{,}170 \sum_{t=1}^{15} (1.12)^{-t} - 750{,}000$$

By reference to Appendix 3 it can be seen that NPV = £114,170 (6.8019) − 750,000 = £27,600. Thus the machinery should be bought if the two shift system is adopted. It may be noted that with the two shift system plus additional machinery the extra profit per year over the three shift system is £67,375 [=245(3,981 − 3,706)] which over 15 years gives a G.P.V. at 12% of £458,884. Therefore, if optimum decisions are made, the cost in present value terms of the changeover to a two shifts system is £291,116 (=£750,000 − £458,884). As an exercise the reader may calculate the opportunity cost of the changeover (where the original three shift system with extra machinery is presumed to be the foregone alternative).

3.6 The Lorie–Savage Problem Revisited

Investment problems of the form given by (2.8) to (2.11) can be solved by use of the simplex method. This is not always the most efficient way to tackle them, especially in respect of one constraint problems. The profitability index method has already been discussed and we shall be examining a special method of computation later in the book. However, something of the structure of these problems can be seen when constraints are arranged in tabular form and, as always, the simplex method generates useful interpretative data.

Let us solve the small and convenient problem of page 58 by the simplex method. Written out in full, the problem is to

$$\text{maximize } N = 9x_1 + 17x_2 + 12x_3 + S_0$$

$$\begin{aligned} \text{subject to} \quad & 5x_1 + 10x_2 + 6x_3 + S_0 = 11 \\ & x_1 + S_1 = 1 \\ & x_2 + S_2 = 1 \\ & x_3 + S_3 = 1 \\ & x_1, x_2, x_3, S_0, S_1, S_2, S_3 \quad 0 \end{aligned}$$

Slack variables have been included for all constraints including the $x_j \leqslant 1$ constraints. In formulating the objective function it has been assumed that the £11 is the inventor's own money and any unspent remainder is added to present value. Thus S_0 has a coefficient of unity in the objective function. An alternative formulation of the objective function in this case would have been $N = (9 - 5)$ $x_1 + (17 - 10)\,x_2 + (12 - 6)\,x_3 + 0S_1 + 11$. The coefficients of the *x*s are now how much is added to *N* by investment in the *x*s over the 'autonomous' amount £11. For instance if an extra £5 was available, if spent on x_1, this would increase *N* by £9, but *N* would have increased by £5 'autonomously' since it cannot be less than £16; so investment in x_1 adds a further £4 to the autonomous increase. With the original formulation of the objective function, Figure 3.15 shows the solution of the problem by the simplex method.

Fortunately, an integral solution has emerged without the recourse to explicit imposition of integer requirements. The optimal solution is, however, *degenerate* – although there are four constraints in the problem only three variables are positive at the optimum. This occurrence is noticed in the preceding solution when a tie occurred for the selection of the pivot row; both the x_2 and S_1 rows could have been chosen. Normally degeneracy is not much of a problem in hand computation, but it is possible that mechanistic adherance to the rule for selecting the pivotal column can cause the problem to 'cycle'. Charnes, Cooper and Henderson[6] have suggested a simple method of resolving a tied situation that eliminates the possibility of cycling. For the tied variables each rate of exchange in the row is divided by the pivot column number. These ratios are then compared column by column working from left to right starting with the slack variables and then proceeding, if necessary, with the structural variables. As soon as these ratios are unequal the tie is broken and that variable leaves the basis which has the algebraically smaller ratio. In the present case the tie is broken at once in the S_0 column. For S_1 the ratio is $0/1 = 0$ whilst for x_2 the ratio is $\frac{1}{2} \div \frac{1}{10} = 5$.

Interpretation of index row numbers in integer problems requires some care. This will be discussed in detail later, but note for the moment that an extra £1

			9	17	12	1	0	0	0
			x_1	x_2	x_3	S_0	S_1	S_2	S_3
1	S_0	11	5	10	6	1	0	0	0
0	S_1	1	1	0	0	0	1	0	0
0	S_2	1	0	1	0	0	0	1	0
0	S_3	1	0	0	1	0	0	0	1
		11	−4	−7	−6	0	0	0	0
1	S_0	1	5	0	6	1	0	−10	0
0	S_1	1	1	0	0	0	1	0	0
17	x_2	1	0	1	0	0	0	1	0
0	S_3	1	0	0	1	0	0	0	1
		18	−4	0	−6	0	0	7	0
12	x_3	1/6	5/6	0	1	1/6	0	−10/6	0
0	S_1	1	1	0	0	0	1	0	0
17	x_2	1	0	1	0	0	0	1	0
0	S_3	5/6	5/6	0	0	−1/6	0	10/6	1
		19	1	0	0	1	0	−3	0
12	x_3	1	0	0	1	0	0	0	1
0	S_1	1	1	0	0	0	1	0	0
17	x_2	1/2	1/2	1	0	1/10	0	0	−6/10
0	S_2	1/2	−1/2	0	0	−1/10	0	1	6/10
		41/2	−1/2	0	0	7/10	0	0	18/10
12	x_3	1	0	0	1	0	0	0	1
9	x_1	1	1	0	0	0	1	0	0
17	x_2	0	0	1	0	1/10	−1/2	0	−6/10
0	S_2	1	0	0	0	−1/10	1/2	1	6/10
		21	0	0	0	17/10	−1/2	0	18/10

Figure 3.15 Solution of Lorie–Savage problem via simplex method

available for investment will only increase NPV by 17/10{=(7/10) + 1} if x_2 can be set at the level 1/10. An increase in available funds of £10 would, of course, increase NPV by 17 since x_2 could then be set at unit level.

We were fortunate in the present problem in that the optimum was integral. Although this will not always be the case, Weingartner[7] has shown that the number of fractional projects at the optimum will not exceed the number of constraints (excluding the upper bounds and sign requirements). Hence in one constraint problems, however many variables there are, no more than one will be fractional, in two constraint problems no more than two will be fractional and so on. Thus the number of fractional projects that have to be dealt with may be quite small in relation to the total number of projects. If the cost of each project is not too large a

			x_1	x_2	x_3	S_0	S_1	S_2	S_3
			⋮	⋮	⋮	⋮	⋮	⋮	⋮
12	x_3	1	0	0	1	0	0	0	1
0	S_1	0	0	−2	0	−2/10	1	0	12/10
9	x_1	1	1	2	0	2/10	0	0	−12/10
0	S_2	1	0	1	0	0	0	1	0
		21	0	1	0	8/10	0	0	12/10

Figure 3.16 Degenerate problem: alternative form of solution

proportion of the total budget in each period then arbitrary rounding off of the L.P. solution should produce an all integer solution which has an objective function value within a few percent of the value of the objective function at the global integer optimum. This is often the most sensible way to proceed since the computational effort required to find the integer optimum is frequently very much greater than that required to produce the continuous L.P. optimum.

The optimal basic feasible solution $x_1 = 1, x_2 = 0, x_3 = 1, S_0 = 0, S_1 = 0, S_2 = 1, S_3 = 0$, could be described in tabular form in an alternative manner to that given in Figure 3.15. This would correspond to the selection of the x_2 row as pivot row in the preceding solution. The alternative presentation is given in Figure 3.16.

Although the value of the solution and the magnitudes of the variables are the same as in Figure 3.15, the index row numbers are different. In a degenerate solution the shadow prices are non-unique.[8] Which is the true set of shadow prices? The answer is that they are both valid *but only for movements in one direction.* The figure 7/10 for instance correctly states what would happen if one further unit of funds was available; x_2 would go up by 1/10, S_2 would decrease by 1/10 and N would rise by 7/10 over the autonomous increase of one. But 7/10 does not apply to decreases in available finance for, as can be seen from the rates of exchange, if S_0 was introduced to unit level (equivalent to a unit decrease of funds) the x_2 would have to decrease to −1/10, which is not feasible. However, Figure 3.16 does describe the situation for decreases in funds; x_1 would decrease by 2/10 and S_1 increase by that amount. N would diminish by 18/10 i.e. 8/10 more than the autonomous decrease of 1. Degeneracy is a knife edge situation and shadow prices are only appropriate for movements in particular directions.

3.7 Technical Difficulties and Simplifications

In this section some difficulties with different forms of constraint will be pointed out and resolved. Also, in some cases it is possible to reduce the apparent size of a problem by deletion of redundant constraints and dominated variables.

One of the most commonly encountered difficulties is the presence of 'greater than or equal to' constraints. For example, how might the constraint

$$3x_1 + 4x_2 \geqslant 12 \qquad (3.20)$$

be accommodated? Since the L.H.S. must not be less than the R.H.S. subtraction of a slack variable seems an obvious solution. The constraint could then be written as:

$$3x_1 + 4x_2 - S = 12 \tag{3.21}$$

where $S \geqslant 0$. This is quite correct but a problem arises when an initial basic feasible solution is being looked for. As we have seen, the simplest b.f.s. to find is most frequently the origin where the slack variables were set equal to the R.H.S. in the 'less than or equal to' constraints. Constraint (3.21) expressly rules out the origin since it would require $S = -12$. The difficulty is resolved by introduction of an additional variable known as an *artificial variable*, u, which is *added* to the L.H.S. of (3.21) to form

$$3x_1 + 4x_2 - S + u = 12 \tag{3.22}$$

u is introduced solely for the computational convenience of finding a starting b.f.s. in which x_1, x_2, $S = 0$ and $u = 12$. However, since $u > 0$ would permit the original constraint (3.20) to be violated no artificial variables must appear at positive levels in the final solution to the problem. To ensure this, a large penalty coefficient is attached to the variable u in the objective function. In hand computation this is (in a maximization problem) the unspecified number $-M$ where M is large enough to dominate any other number in the problem. Hence, no solution which has any positive artificial variables can be optimal. An example will illustrate the use of this device.

$$\begin{aligned} \text{Maximize } N = {} & 4x_1 + x_2 \\ \text{subject to} \quad & 5x_1 + 2x_2 \leqslant 16 \\ & 3x_1 + 4x_2 \geqslant 18 \\ & x_1, x_2 \geqslant 0 \end{aligned}$$

Firstly, introduce slack and artificial variables and modify the objective function.

$$\begin{aligned} \text{Maximize } N = {} & 4x_1 + x_2 + 0S_1 + 0S_2 - Mu_2 \\ \text{subject to} \quad & 5x_1 + 2x_2 + S_1 = 16 \\ & 3x_1 + 4x_2 - S_2 + u_2 = 18 \\ & x_1, x_2, S_1, S_2 u_2 \geqslant 0 \end{aligned}$$

Secondly, solve by the simplex method in the usual way.

In the final solution of Figure 3.17 the index row is all non-negative since the number $-(3/14) + M$ is positive. Any such number in which M appears with a positive coefficient, however small, is positive. Note that the 'most negative' number in the first index row is $-4M - 1$ since here M has its largest negative coefficient. As regards interpretation, the index row number 13/14 is interpretable in the usual way but the number 3/14 under S_2 relates to the increase in N as a result of a *reduction* in the R.H.S. of (3.20). Greater than or equal to constraints are relaxed when the R.H.S. is reduced and tightened when it is increased.

			4	1	0	0	$-M$
			x_1	x_2	S_2	S_1	u_2
0	S_1	16	5	2	0	1	0
$-M$	u_2	18	3	4	-1	0	1
		$-18M$	$-3M-4$	$-4M-1$	$+M$	0	0
0	S_1	28/4	14/4	0	2/4	1	$-2/4$
1	x_2	18/4	3/4	1	$-1/4$	0	1/4
		18/4	$-13/4$	0	$-1/4$	0	$1/4+M$
4	x_1	2	1	0	2/14	4/14	$-2/14$
1	x_2	3	0	1	$-5/14$	$-3/14$	5/14
		11	0	0	3/14	13/14	$-3/14+M$

Figure 3.17 Solution of problem with artificial variable

Sometimes the constraints are in the equality form to begin with before slack variables have been added. As with the greater than or equal to constraints the difficulty arises when a starting b.f.s. is being looked for. The problem is resolved in a similar manner by the addition of an artificial variable, but no slack variable is needed. For instance, the constraint

$$x_1 + x_2 = 20 \tag{3.23}$$

becomes

$$x_1 + x_2 + u = 20 \tag{3.24}$$

and in the objective function u appears with a coefficient of $-M$ as before. Note that alternatively (3.23) could have been replaced by the two constraints

$$x_1 + x_2 \leqslant 20 \tag{3.25a}$$

$$x_1 + x_2 \geqslant 20 \tag{3.25b}$$

an equally effective although more time-consuming device.

Sometimes, particularly in verbal statements of problems, the phrase 'about equal to' crops up. The symbol $\approx$ represents 'approximately equal to'. How can a constraint of the form

$$x_1 + x_2 \approx 20 \tag{3.26}$$

be accommodated? The best way is to oblige oneself to be a bit more specific about the limits to the acceptable range of variation of the L.H.S. of (3.26) and replace (3.26) with two constraints. For instance, if $x_1 + x_2$ less than say, 18, would be unacceptable and $x_1 + x_2$ greater than 23 would not be feasible, we could write

$$x_1 + x_2 \geqslant 18 \tag{3.27a}$$

$$x_1 + x_2 \leqslant 23 \tag{3.27b}$$

in place of (3.26). If, although 18 and 23 are the permitted extremes of variation of the L.H.S., it is 'more desirable' to have $x_1 + x_2$ rather nearer to 20 the slack variables of (3.27a) and (3.27b) can be given non-zero coefficients in the objective function which reflect the costs of being either side of 20.

Minimization Problems

The examples solved so far have all been ones in which the objective function was to be maximized. In many problems, minimization of a quantity (for instance cost or time) is the objective. Any minimization problem can be converted to a maximization problem by multiplying the objective function by -1. Minimizing $16y_1 + 12y_2$ is equivalent to maximizing $-16y_1 - 12y_2$. When the objective function has been expressed in maximizing terms the simplex method is applied but at the end it should be remembered that the negative objective function, value results (presumably) from the computational device of negation of the original function.

Redundant Constraints

In some problems, especially those in which there are more constraints than variables, the fact that certain of the constraints are satisfied may automatically mean that other constraints are also satisfied. Clearly, in this situation, some of the constraints can be dropped and time saved. For instance the constraint set:

$$
\begin{array}{lllll}
(1) & x_1 + 2x_2 & & & \leqslant 11 \\
(2) & x_1 + 2x_2 & & & \leqslant 10 \\
(3) & 3x_1 + x_2 & & & \leqslant 12 \\
(4) & 4x_1 + 3x_2 & & & \leqslant 23 \\
(5) & 2x_1 & + 3x_3 & & \geqslant 9 \\
(6) & x_1 & + x_3 & & \geqslant 3 \\
(7) & & x_3 & + 3x_4 & \leqslant 15 \\
(8) & 4x_1 + 3x_2 & & + 2x_4 & \leqslant 45
\end{array}
$$

Clearly (1) is redundant since (2) has the same L.H.S. and a smaller R.H.S. Adding (2) and (3) together gives $4x_1 + 3x_2 \leqslant 22$ which means that (4) can be dropped. Dividing (5) by 3 gives $\frac{2}{3}x_1 + x_3 \geqslant 3$ and if this is satisfied so must be (6). Now (3) sets a maximum of $x_1 = 4$, (2) gives a maximum of $x_2 = 5$ and (7) gives a maximum of $x_4 = 5$, thus $4x_1 + 3x_2 + 2x_4 \leqslant 41$ and (8) can be omitted. Therefore the original constraint set can be reduced to:

$$
\begin{array}{l}
x_1 + 2x_2 \leqslant 10 \\
3x_1 + x_2 \leqslant 12 \\
2x_1 + 3x_3 \geqslant 9 \\
x_3 + 2x_4 \leqslant 15
\end{array}
$$

which will effect a considerable time-saving.

Amongst equations it is sometimes possible to spot *linear dependence*, indeed this may be expected in some types of problem e.g. *distribution problems.*[9] For example the equations

$$(1) \quad 2x_1 + 3x_2 + x_3 = 20$$

$$(2) \quad 2x_1 + x_2 + x_3 = 15$$

$$(3) \quad 4x_1 + 8x_2 + 2x_3 = 45$$

are linearly dependent. (3) can be obtained by subracting (2) from (1) multiplied by 3. Any one of these three may be dropped – each one is implied by the other two.

Redundant Variables

Consider the problem:

$$\text{maximize } F = 12x_1 + 10x_2 + 11x_3$$

$$\begin{aligned} \text{subject to} \quad 3x_1 + 4x_2 + 2x_3 &\leqslant 20 \\ x_1 + 2x_2 + 4x_3 &\leqslant 25 \\ 2x_1 + 2x_2 + 6x_3 &\leqslant 40 \end{aligned}$$

In this problem x_2 is a redundant variable since it is dominated by x_1. Each unit of variable x_2 consumes more of the first and second resource than is required by unit level of x_1, and requires the same amount of the third resource. Also, its objective function coefficient is lower. In other words x_1 is no worse than x_2 in any respect and is better in some. Consequently x_2 could not be positive at a maximum of F and may be omitted. Sometimes a variable may be dominated by a group of two or more others and this may not be noticed at the outset. The only harm done by leaving in a redundant variable or constraint is that time will be wasted, but in searching for 'redundancy' the time consumed by the search must be taken into account.

Non-zero Lower Bounds

Frequently the lower bound (the lowest value that a variable is permitted to take) on a variable is greater than zero. It is possible to leave in the new lower bound conditions as additional constraints but this is computationally wasteful. Transforming the variables involved is a more efficient procedure. For example, consider the problem:

$$\text{maximize } F = 5x_1 + 4x_2$$

$$\begin{aligned} \text{subject to} \quad 2x_1 + 3x_2 &\leqslant 30 \\ 4x_1 + 2x_2 &\leqslant 40 \\ x_1 &\geqslant 2 \\ x_2 &\geqslant 3 \end{aligned}$$

Define $x_1^* = x_1 - 2$ and $x_2^* = x_2 - 3$ and substitute $x_1^* + 2$ for x_1 and $x_2^* + 3$ for x_2

in the constraints and objective function. The problem in the transformed variable is:

$$\text{maximize } F = 5x_1^* + 4x_2^* + 22$$

$$\text{subject to} \quad 2x_1^* + 3x_2^* \leqslant 17$$

$$4x_1^* + 2x_2^* \leqslant 26$$

$$x_1^*, x_2^* \geqslant 0$$

By the mechanism for choosing the pivot, the simplex procedure guarantees that no variable will be set at a negative level; thus explicit provision for non-negativity in the form of constraints is not required. Geometrically the substitution is simply a change of axes. Once the problem has been transformed it will be quicker to solve.

Non-unique Solutions

Consider the problem:

$$\text{maximize } F = 3x_1 + 1.5x_2$$

$$\text{subject to} \quad 2x_1 + 3x_2 \leqslant 18$$

$$4x_1 + 2x_2 \leqslant 20$$

Figure 3.18 presents the solution of this problem via the simplex method. The optimal solution is said to be *non-unique*; there is no other b.f.s. (in which x_2 replaces S_1) and a continuum of non-basic solutions (along the line BC in Figure 3.19) which also gives a value of 15 for F. In the simplex tableau this is evidenced by the zero index row number for x_2 in the solution at C. Basic variables always have zero index row numbers but if a non basic variable also does, then there are other solutions that are equally good. The alternative optimum at point B is also given in Figure 3.18.

No computational difficulties are caused by the phenomenon of non-uniqueness.

			3	1.5	0	0
			x_1	x_2	S_1	S_2
0	S_1	18	2	3	1	0
0	S_2	20	4	2	0	1
			−3	−1.5	0	0
0	S_1	8	0	2	1	−½
3	x_1	5	1	½	0	¼
		15	0	0	0	¾
1.5	x_2	4	0	1	½	−¼
3	x_1	3	1	0	−¼	3/8
		15	0	0	0	¾

Figure 3.18 A non-unique optimum

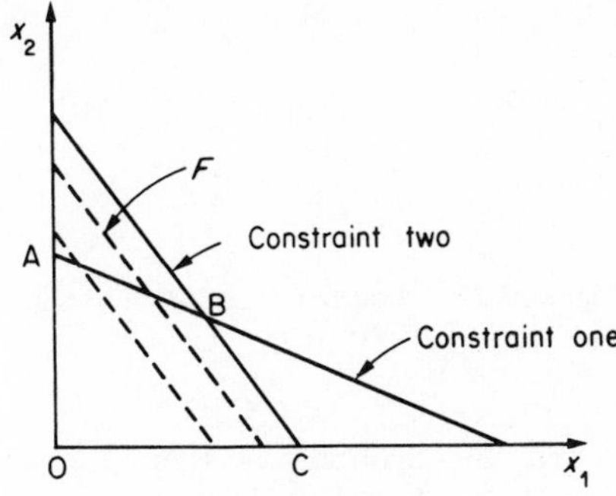

Figure 3.19 Graph of problem with non-unique optimum

Geometrically the non-uniqueness is recognized by the fact that slope of the objective function lines in Figure 3.19 are parallel to constraint two.

Optimality and Index Row Numbers

The obtaining of an all non-negative index row is a *sufficient* condition for optimality but it is not a *necessary* one. This is illustrated in the degenerate problem below.

$$\text{Maximize } F = 24x_1 + 30x_2$$

$$\begin{aligned} \text{subject to} \quad 4x_1 + x_2 &\leqslant 10 \\ 2x_1 + 2x_2 &\leqslant 20 \end{aligned}$$

A basic, feasible although degenerate solution to this problem is given in tableau form in Figure 3.20. The solution is, in fact, an optimal solution, even though the S_1 index row number is negative. Because x_1 is at zero level, S_1 can only be introduced to zero level thus leaving the value of F unchanged. This situation can only arise in degenerate problems and it must be possible to re-express the solution with an all non-negative index row. This is accomplished by introducing S_1 to zero level. The result is shown in Figure 3.21.

The shadow prices given in Figure 3.21 are appropriate for *increases* in resource one and *decreases* in resource two only. It is possible to re-express the solution in yet another way by bringing in S_2 at zero level. To accomplish this we must go via

			24	30	0	0
			x_1	x_2	S_1	S_2
24	x_1	0	1	0	$1/3$	$-1/6$
30	x_2	10	0	1	$-1/3$	$2/3$
		300	0	0	-2	16

Figure 3.20 Degenerate solution: first expression

			24	30	0	0
			x_1	x_2	S_1	S_2
0	S_1	0	3	0	1	−½
30	x_2	10	1	1	0	½
		300	6	0	0	15

Figure 3.21 Degenerate solution: second expression

the origin, first bringing in S_2 and dropping x_2, then reintroducing x_2 and dropping S_1. This will leave S_2 at zero level since there is a tie for choice of pivotal row. A non-human calculator would be unable to accomplish this exercise if programmed to prohibit reductions in objective function value. The restatement of the solution thus obtained is shown in Figure 3.22. This formulation of the solution gives shadow prices appropriate for *decreases* in resource one and *increases* in resource

			24	30	0	0
			x_1	x_2	S_1	S_2
30	x_2	10	4	1	1	0
0	S_2	0	−6	0	−2	1
		300	96	0	30	0

Figure 3.22 Degenerate solution: third expression

two. It is now apparent that the shadow prices of Figure 3.20 are not appropriate to any changes in resource levels. Only all non-negative index rows should be used for marginal resource valuations.

Some further interpretations of the problems in this chapter are given in Chapter 4 but before this can be accomplished some essential duality theory must be understood. It is to this task that we now address ourselves.

Notes

1. We are not at the moment considering the problem of changing an investment programme once it has been wholly or partly implemented. The discovery of new possibilities is either prior to implementation, or, if post implementation, the evidence produced will be only *prima facie* evidence for or against a more thorough enquiry into changeover possibilities.
2. It is not, strictly speaking, correct to say that a variable leaves a basis (which is a set of constants). However, the phrase has a clear 'commonsense' meaning and is employed in this text.
3. The new number/old number notation and the terms 'main row' and 'index row' are those used by R. W. Metzger in the well expounded text *Elementary Mathematical Programming*, Wiley, New York, 1958.
4. Redundant constraints are discussed in detail later in the chapter.
5. This is a naive default assumption and no account is taken of how many payments may be received or the timing of payments. For a more sophisticated model of default risk see Bierman, H., *Financial Policy Decisions*, Macmillan, New York, 1970, pp. 36–58.

6. Charnes, A., Cooper, W. W. and Henderson, A., *Introduction to Linear Programming*, Wiley, New York, 1953.
7. Weingartner, H. M., *Mathematical Programming and the Analysis of Capital Budgeting Problems*, Prentice-Hall, Englewood Cliffs, N.J., 1963.
8. In the simplex method as presented here. The fact that the dual problem (to be discussed in Chapter 4) is degenerate may cause minor difficulties if the dual simplex method of computation is being employed.
9. Such problems are discussed in Chapter 9.

Additional References

1. Beale, E. M. L., *Mathematical Programming in Practice*, Pitman, London, 1968.
2. Charnes, A. and Cooper, W. W., *Management Models and Industrial Applications of Linear Programming* (2 vols), Wiley, New York, 1961.
3. Dantzig, G. B., *Linear Programming and Extensions*, University Press, Princeton, N.J., 1963.
4. Dorfman, R., 'Mathematical or Linear Programming', *American Economic Review*, December, 1953.
5. Dano, S., *Linear Programming in Industry*, Springer-Verlag, Vienna, 1960.
6. Lusztig, P. and Schwab, B., 'A Note on the application of linear programming to capital budgeting'. *Journal of Financial and Quantitative Analysis*, December, 1968.
7. Masse, P. and Gibrat, R., 'Application of linear programming to investments in the electric power industry', *Management Science*, January, 1957.
8. Salkin, G. and Kornbluth, J., *Linear Programming and Financial Planning*, Haymarket Publishing Limited, London, 1973.
9. Sharpe, W. F., 'A linear programming algorithm for mutual fund portfolio selection', *Management Science*, 1967.
10. Weingartner, H. M., 'Criteria for programming investment project selection', *Journal of Industrial Economics*, November, 1966.
11. Whitmore, G. A. and Amey, L. R., 'Capital budgeting under rationing: comments on the Lusztig and Schwab procedure', *Journal of Financial and Quantitative Analysis*, September, 1972.
12. Vajda, S., *Readings in Linear Programming*, Wiley, New York, 1958.

CHAPTER 4

Dual Problems and Interpretation

The principal objectives of this chapter are to (a) explain and interpret the phenomon of duality in linear programming problems and (b) extend the sensitivity analysis begun in earlier chapters and to link this analysis with duality. The chapter is essentially preparation for application of the ideas developed to the more advanced capital rationing models in Chapter 5. The topic of non-zero objective function coefficients for slack variables is also discussed.

4.1 Duality

With every L.P. problem there is associated, in a remarkable symmetrical relationship, a *dual* problem. Consider the two constraint, two structural variable problem:

$$\begin{aligned} \text{maximize } F &= 10x_1 + 12x_2 \\ \text{subject to } \quad & 4x_1 + 2x_2 \leqslant 76 \\ & 3x_1 + 5x_2 \leqslant 85 \\ & x_1, x_2 \geqslant 0 \end{aligned}$$

The dual to this problem is:

$$\begin{aligned} \text{minimize } G &= 76y_1 + 85y_2 \\ \text{subject to } \quad & 4y_1 + 3y_2 \geqslant 10 \\ & 2y_1 + 5y_2 \geqslant 12 \\ & y_1, y_2 \geqslant 0 \end{aligned}$$

The maximization problem is usually referred to as the *primal* problem and the minimization problem as the dual, although strictly they are duals of each other. The dual problem employs all of the numbers (coefficients and constraint levels) of the primal problem but in a different arrangement. The coefficients of the objective function of the primal are the constraint levels of the dual; the constraint levels of the primal are the objective function coefficients of the dual; *columns* of constraint coefficients in the primal have become *rows* of constraint coefficients in the dual. Note that if 'primal' and 'dual' are interchanged in the previous sentence the statements are still valid; that is, there is *no asymmetry* between the problems. The primal and dual problems are graphed in Figure 4.1(a) and (b). The feasible area for the primal problem [4.1(a)] is OABC and the optimum is at joint B with the

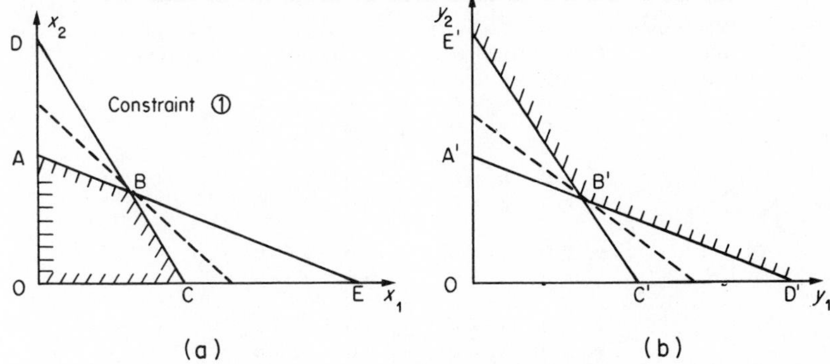

Figure 4.1 Graph of primal and dual problems

objective function shown as a dashed line. The feasible area for the dual [4.1(b)] is the open area with lower bound given by E′B′D′. The optimal solution is at point B′ since the objective is to minimize the dual objective function G. Each basic feasible solution of the primal problem has a corresponding basic (not necessarily feasible) solution in the dual. Indeed it turns out that there is only one b.f.s. in the primal problem that corresponds to a b.f.s. in the dual. These corresponding b.f.s. are also optimal! This is an important point which is true in general and will be returned to later. The dual constraints can be converted to equality form by *subtraction* of slack variables viz:

$$4y_1 + 3y_2 - t_1 = 10$$

$$2y_1 + 5y_2 - t_2 = 12$$

Figure 4.2. gives the corresponding basic solutions to the dual problems graphed in Figure 4.1 Primal slack variables are S_1 and S_2 In each basic solution to each problem there are of course, two non-zero variables and in basic *feasible* solutions, these are positive. Only at B and B′ is there a *corresponding* pair of feasible solutions. For every other feasible basic solution of one problem the corresponding solution of the other problem is infeasible. By study of Figure 4.2. the reader may detect a systematic correspondence between non-zero variables in one problem and zero variables in the corresponding solution to the dual problem. This point will be developed later on.

Further examples of primal–dual pairs are given below:

Example One

Primal: maximize $F = x_1 + x_2 + x_3$

subject to

$$2.5x_1 - x_2 + 4x_3 \leqslant 20$$

$$2x_1 + 6x_2 - 2x_3 \leqslant 10$$

$$x_1, x_2, x_3 \geqslant 0$$

Primal basic solution	Primal variables		Dual variables		Dual basic solution
0	$s_1 > 0$ $s_2 > 0$	$x_1 = 0$ $x_2 = 0$	$t_1 < 0$ $t_2 < 0$	$y_1 = 0$ $y_2 = 0$	0′
A	$s_1 > 0$ $x_2 > 0$	$x_1 = 0$ $s_2 = 0$	$y_2 > 0$ $t_1 < 0$	$t_2 = 0$ $y_1 = 0$	A′
D	$x_2 > 0$ $s_2 < 0$	$x_1 = 0$ $s_1 = 0$	$y_1 > 0$ $t_1 > 0$	$y_2 = 0$ $t_2 = 0$	D′
B	$x_1 > 0$ $x_2 > 0$	$s_1 = 0$ $s_2 = 0$	$y_1 > 0$ $y_2 > 0$	$t_1 = 0$ $t_2 = 0$	B′
C	$x_1 > 0$ $s_2 > 0$	$x_2 = 0$ $s_1 = 0$	$y_1 > 0$ $t_2 < 0$	$y_2 = 0$ $t_1 = 0$	C′
E	$x_1 > 0$ $s_1 < 0$	$s_2 = 0$ $x_2 = 0$	$y_2 > 0$ $t_2 > 0$	$t_1 = 0$ $y_1 = 0$	E′

Figure 4.2 Basic solutions to primal and dual problems

Dual:

$$\begin{aligned} \text{minimize } G = \;& 20y_1 + 10y_2 \\ \text{subject to } \;& 2.5y_1 + 2y_2 \geqslant 1 \\ & -y_1 + 6y_2 \geqslant 1 \\ & 4y_1 - 2y_2 \geqslant 1 \\ & y_1, y_2, y_3 \geqslant 0 \end{aligned}$$

The dual problem is graphed in Figure 4.3. No attempt is made to represent the primal problem in three dimensions. Note that the second and third dual constraint are upwards sloping. Dual constraint numbers are shown with rings and the feasible area is also indicated. The dashed line is the optimal contour of the objective function and the optimal solution is marked M.

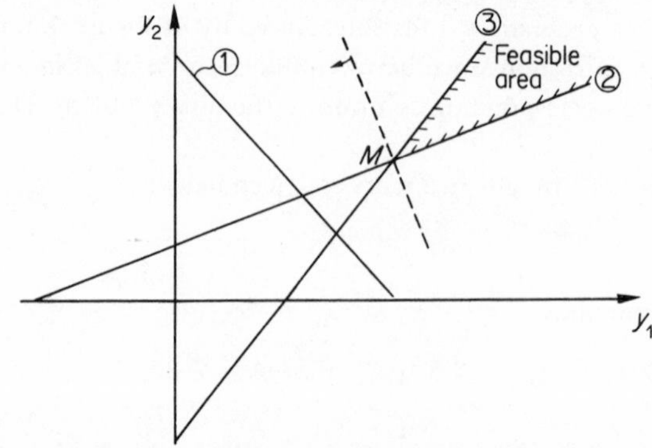

Figure 4.3 Graph of dual problem of Example one

Example Two

Primal: maximize $G = 3x_1 - x_2$

subject to

$$\begin{aligned} 2x_1 - 0.5x_2 &\leqslant 5 \\ x_1 \qquad &\leqslant 3.5 \\ 1.3x_1 - \quad 2x_2 &\leqslant 3 \\ x_1, x_2 &\geqslant 0 \end{aligned}$$

Dual: minimize $G = 5y_1 + 3.5y_2 + 3y_3$

subject to

$$\begin{aligned} 2y_1 + \quad y_2 + 1.3y_3 &\geqslant 3 \\ -0.5y_1 - \quad 2y_3 &\geqslant -1 \\ y_1, y_2, y_3 &\geqslant 0 \end{aligned}$$

The primal problem is graphed in Figure 4.4. The second constraint is an upper bound on x_1. The other constraints and the objective function slope up. Notice that in the dual of example two the second constraint could equally well be expressed by multiplying both sides of the inequality by -1, so the second dual constraint would be:

$$0.5y_1 + 2y_3 \leqslant 1$$

The conventional form of the primal problem is one of an objective function to be maximized subject to $\leqslant$ constraints and for the dual one of minimization subject to $\geqslant$ constraints. If a problem has mixed constraints, to find the dual first convert the problem to standard form. A couple of awkward looking examples follow.

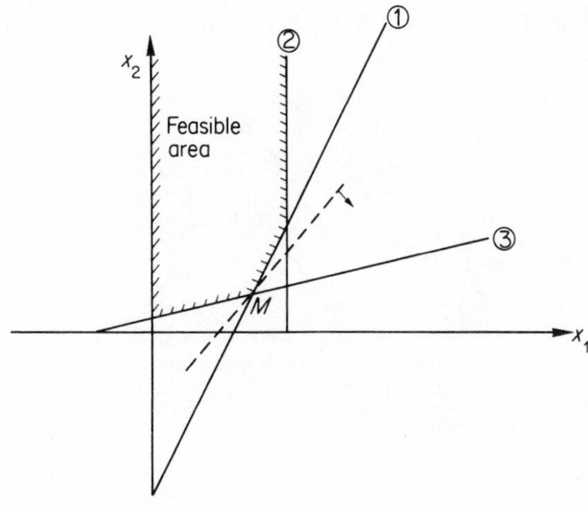

Figure 4.4 Graph of primal problem of Example two

Example Three

Primal: maximize $3x_1 + x_3$

subject to

$$2x_1 + x_2 + 2x_3 \leqslant 50$$
$$x_1 + 3x_2 + x_3 \geqslant 30$$
$$x_1, x_2, x_3 \geqslant 0$$

Dual: minimize $50y_1 - 30y_2$

subject to

$$2y_1 - y_2 \geqslant 3$$
$$y_1 - 3y_2 \geqslant 0$$
$$2y_1 - y_2 \geqslant 1$$
$$y_1, y_2 \geqslant 0$$

Equivalently, the dual form could be written as:

minimize $50y_1 + 30y_2$

subject to

$$2y_1 + y_2 \geqslant 3$$
$$y_1 + 3y_2 \geqslant 0$$
$$2y_1 + y_2 \geqslant 1$$
$$y_1 \geqslant 0 \; y_2 \leqslant 0$$

That is to say the presence of $\geqslant$signs in the maximization problem implies that corresponding dual variables are required to be non-*positive*, unless the maximization problem is first converted to a standard form. Note that the third of the dual constraints is redundant and could be omitted. This is reflected in the primal problem in *variable* x_3 being redundant, it is dominated by x_1. This is true in general as is the fact that if a primal constraint is redundant then a dual variable (the column of coefficients of which is the row of coefficients of the primal

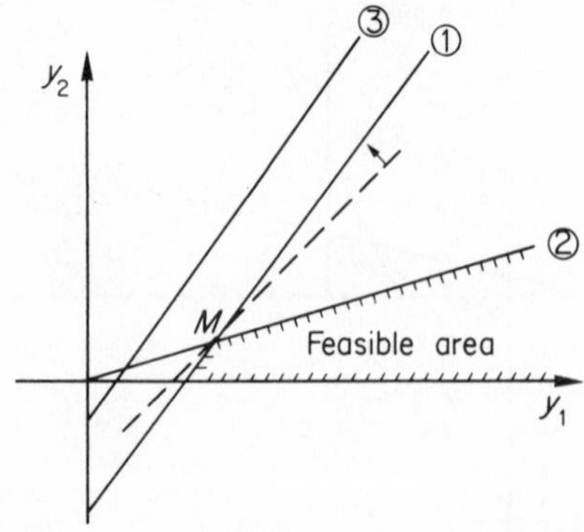

Figure 4.5 Graph of dual problem of Example three

constraint) is dominated. The redundant nature of the third dual constraint is evident from Figure 4.5. As an exercise it is suggested that the reader graph the primal problem minus x_3 and find corresponding basic solutions to the basic solution of the dual marked in Figure 4.5.

Example Four

Primal: maximize $x_1 + x_2$

subject to
$$3x_1 + 2x_2 \leqslant 20$$
$$x_1 + 4x_2 = 15$$
$$x_1, x_2 \geqslant 0$$

Dual: minimize $20y_1 + 15y_2 - 15y_3$

subject to
$$3y_1 + y_2 - y_3 \geqslant 1$$
$$2y_1 + 4y_2 - 4y_3 \geqslant 1$$
$$y_1, y_2, y_3 \geqslant 0$$

In this case, in order to obtain the dual the equality constraint of the primal is first replaced by the two inequality constraints $x_1 + 4x_2 \leqslant 15$ and $x_1 + 4x_2 \geqslant 15$ the second of which is then multiplied by -1. The dual problem could equally well be written as:

minimize $20y_1 + 15y_2^*$

subject to
$$3y_1 + y_2^* \geqslant 1$$
$$2y_1 + 4y_2^* \geqslant 1$$
$$y_1 \geqslant 0, y_2^* \text{ unrestricted}$$

An equality constraint in the primal problem means a dual variable of unrestricted sign. The two formulations of the dual are equivalent as $y_2^* \equiv y_2 - y_3$.

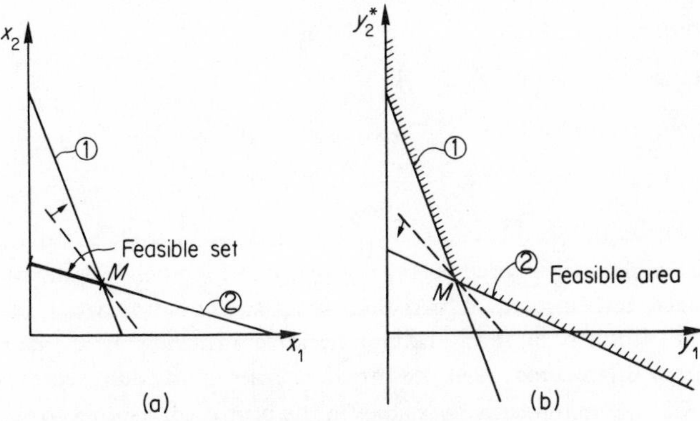

Figure 4.6 Graphs of primal and dual problems of Example four

The first formulation although more extensive, has the advantage of including only sign restricted variables. This raises the general point that whenever a problem arises in which a variable is unrestricted in sign it can always be replaced by the difference between two sign restricted varibles. As it happens in the above problem the optimal value of $y_2^* = +0.1$. Note that *absolute* values cannot uniquely be assigned to y_2 and y_3. The dual solution is *non-unique* in the 'extensive' formulation. Primal and dual are graphed in Figures 4.6(a) and 4.6(b). Note that the feasible area of the primal problem is a line segment and that this does not correspond to a similar restriction in the dual problem.

Example Five

'Primal': minimize $F = -4x_1 + x_2 + 2x_3$

$$x_1 - 0.5x_2 - 2x_3 \leqslant 0$$
$$3x_1 + x_2 + x_3 \leqslant 5$$
$$x_1, x_2 \geqslant 0.\ x_3 \leqslant 2$$

In this case the problem is one of minimization subject to $\leqslant$ constraints and variable x_3 has an upper bound but no lower bound i.e. x_3 is permitted to be negative. It is most convenient to transform the variable x_3. Let $x_3^* = 2 - x_3$ where $x_3^* \geqslant 0$. This will guarantee $x_3 \leqslant 2$. Then, all problem variables will have the usual sign requirements. Second substitute for x_3 in the constraints and objective function and third convert the objective function to one of maximization by multiplication by -1. The conventional form of the primal problem is then to

maximise $4x_1 - x_2 + 2x_3^* - 4$

subject to

$$x_1 - 0.5x_2 + 2x_3^* \leqslant 4$$
$$3x_1 + x_2 - x_3^* \leqslant 3$$
$$x_1, x_2, x_3^* \geqslant 0$$

and the dual is:

minimize $4y_1 + 3y_2$

subject to

$$y_1 + 3y_2 \geqslant 4$$
$$-0.5y_1 + y_2 \geqslant -1$$
$$2y_1 - y_2 \geqslant 2$$
$$y_1, y_2 \geqslant 0$$

The dual problem (in revised form) is graphed in Figure 4.7. If the upper bound on x_3 had been zero instead of two then the transformation would simply have redefined the problem in terms of non-negative variables. If x_3 had been left untransformed this would have resulted in the third dual constraint being $-2y_1 + y_2 \leqslant 2$, i.e. non-positive variables in the primal correspond to $\leqslant$ constraints in the dual.

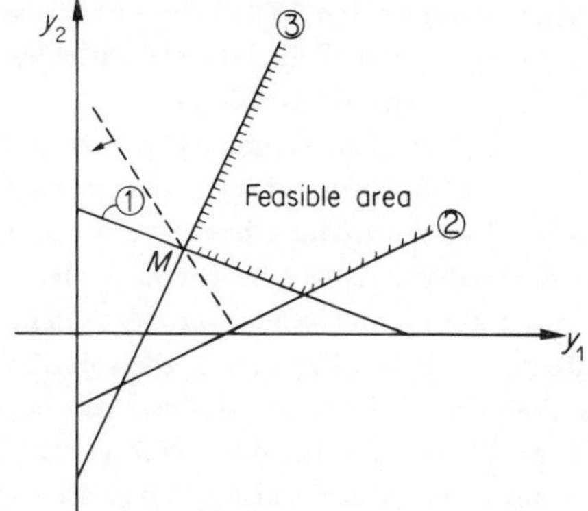

Figure 4.7 Graph of dual problem of Example five

Apart from the symmetrical relationship between primal and dual, why should the dual be of further interest? There are several reasons. Firstly, the dual structural variables, y, turn out to be none other than the shadow prices of the primal problem, i.e. the index row numbers under the slack variables. Thus the dual has great importance for economic interpretation and sensitivity analysis. Secondly, just as the optimal values of the dual variables can be found from the solution to the primal problem (being index row numbers) as also can the optimal values of primal variables be found from the solution to the dual problem. This is an important property since sometimes it is easier to solve the dual of a problem than the original problem. Thirdly, knowledge of duality facilitates a deeper understanding of what is involved in a number of computation procedures, for example the dual simplex method of Chapter 7. These later points will be developed presently. First let us examine the solutions, in tableau form, of the first problem of this chapter. These are given in Figure 4.8.

The maximum value of the primal objective function is achieved by setting $x_1 = 15, x_2 = 8, s_1 = 0, s_2 = 0$ for a value of F of 246. The shadow prices of the resources are 1 for resource one and 2 for resource two. In the dual problem the constraints are first converted to equalities by the subtraction of slack variables t_i, then artificial variables u_i are added in to provide a starting solution and are given weights of $+m$ in the dual objective function which is to be minimized. The objective function is then negated (in order that the maximization–geared simplex method may be used) and the simplex method then applied in the usual way. The optimal solution to the dual problem is to set $y_1 = 1, y_2 = 2, t_1 = 0, t_2 = 0$ for a value of G of 246.

The minus sign attached to 246 in Figure 4.8 results solely from the computational device of negation of the minimizing form of the objective function. It has no other significance. The equality of the optimal values of primal and dual objective functions is no coincidence. This is the case in general. All feasible solutions to the dual have values of G greater than or equal to all values of F for feasible solutions to the primal problem, with the equality holding only at the optimum. The dual 'shadow prices' are 15 for 'resource' one and 8 'for resource' two. The dual index row numbers under the artificial variables may be ignored; save for noting that they are both positive since $m > 15$.

The full extent of the primal–dual symmetry is now apparent. In the primal problem the optimal values of the structure variables, y, may be found in the final index row under the primal *slack* variables, hence $y_1 = 1$ and $y_2 = 2$. The optimal values of the dual slack variables, t, may be found in the final index row of the primal problem under the primal *structural* variables, hence $t_1 = 0$ and $t_2 = 0$. Precisely the same statements apply in respect of the solution to the dual problem. The optimal values of the primal structural variables may be found from the final index row of the dual problem under the dual slack variables, hence $x_1 = 15$ and $x_2 = 8$. The optimal values of the primal slack variables are found in the final index row of the dual problem under the structural variables. Consequently, once one problem is solved, so is its dual. Note that finding an optimal solution to the primal problem (finding a solution with a non-negative index row) is in fact the same as finding a feasible solution to the dual problem. If the dual was being solved the process would be equivalent to finding a feasible solution to the primal problem. Once corresponding feasible solutions to both problems have been found – so have the optimal solutions![1] It should be noted that if there is no feasible solution to either problem then the objective functions of the dual problem is unbounded. The converse statement also applies in that if an L.P. problem has no finite maximum solution then there exists no feasible solution to the dual problem.

Reference to the optimal solutions of Figure 4.8 illustrates a further aspect of the symmetrical relationship between primal–dual pairs. This is the *complementary slackness* condition. This may be stated succinctly as

$$\begin{aligned} &\text{(a) } s_1 y_1 = 0 \quad \text{and} \quad &&\text{(c) } x_1 t_1 = 0 \\ &\text{(b) } s_2 y_2 = 0 &&\text{(d) } x_2 t_2 = 0 \end{aligned} \tag{4.1}$$

That is, the products of corresponding pairs of primal structural variables and dual

			10	12	0	0
			x_1	x_2	s_1	s_2
0	s_1	76	4	2	1	0
0	s_2	85	3	5	0	1
		0	−10	−12	0	0
0	s_1	42	14/5	0	1	−2/5
12	x_2	17	3/5	1	0	1/5
		204	−14/5	0	0	12/5
10	x_1	15	1	0	5/14	−2/14
12	x_2	8	0	1	−3/14	4/14
		246	0	0	1	2

Figure 4.8a Solution to primal problem

			-76	-85	0	0	$-m$	$-m$
			y_1	y_2	t_1	t_2	u_1	u_2
$-m$	u_1	10	4	3	−1	0	1	0
$-m$	u_2	12	2	5	0	−1	0	1
		$-22m$	$-6m + 76$	$-8m + 85$	$+m$	$+m$	0	0
$-m$	u_1	14/5	14/5	0	−1	3/5	1	−3/5
-85	y_2	12/5	2/5	1	0	−1/5	0	1/5
		$-14/5m - 204$	$-14/5m + 42$	0	$+m$	$-3/5m + 17$	0	$8/5m - 17$
-76	y_1	1	1	0	−5/14	3/14	5/14	−3/14
-85	y_2	2	0	1	2/14	−4/14	−2/14	4/14
		−246	0	0	15	8	$-15 + m$	$-8 + m$

Figure 4.8b Solution to dual problem.

slack variables dual structural and primal slack variables must be zero at an optimum. Expression (4.1) (a) states that if $s_1 > 0$, $y_1 = 0$, i.e. if any of the first resource is left over the shadow price (marginal value) of that resource is zero. Also if $y_1 > 0$ then $s_1 = 0$, that is, any resource with positive value at the margin must be fully used. The condition (4.1) (c) states that if $x_1 > 0$ then $t_1 = 0$, i.e. if the first primal structural variable is positive then the first dual slack variable is zero. Dual slack variables can be interpreted as 'opportunity losses'. Consider the first dual constraint. It is

$$4y_1 + 3y_2 \geqslant 10 \tag{4.2}$$

Where t_1 is the difference between the L.H.S. and the R.H.S. of (4.2). The coefficients 4 and 3 are the amounts of resources one and two tied up in the production of one unit of x_1 whilst the magnitudes of y_1 and y_2 are the values per unit of each resource *if resources are used optimally*. In other words each unit of resource one can make a profit of y_1 and each unit of resource two can be used to make a profit of y_2. Consequently the L.H.S. of (4.2) is the *opportunity cost* of producing one unit of x_1 – it is therefore the profit foregone in using resources to produce x_1. Obviously, if the strict inequality holds in (4.2) this means that the profit foregone in producing x_1 is greater than the profit obtained on x_1. That is, if $t_1 > 0$ there is a positive opportunity loss involved in production of x_1. The optimal value of x_1 must then be zero. So, only when equality obtains in (4.2) will x_1 be positive. Note that in the nature of things there can never be an *opportunity* profit. y_1 and y_2 are determined by the *best* use of resources – these values allocate *all* profit to resources (the value of the dual objective function equals the value of the primal). In mathematical terms at best an equality can obtain in (4.2) in which case x_1 can be positive. All this is not to say that an *accounting profit* cannot be made but simply that there is no *better* use of resources than the best! When $t_1 > 0$ therefore, the optimal value of $x_1 = 0$ (although we should recall that x_1 may still make an accounting profit, production of x_1 would mean the presence of non-maximal profit level). The reader may interpret conditions (4.1) (b) and (d) in a similar manner.[2] The complementary slackness conditions are equivalent to the optimality conditions previously stated but stated in this way additional economic insight is obtained. This is of value in any decision making exercise – especially perhaps in the field of investment appraisal.

We can best illustrate the economic interpretation of dual problems by examination of the duals to the problems solved in Chapter 3. The first problem was:

$$\begin{aligned} &\text{maximize } N = 6x_1 + 4x_2 \\ &\text{subject to} \quad 4x_1 + 2x_2 \leqslant 16 \end{aligned}$$

where the coefficients of the objective function were present values and the constraint was on financial outlay. The dual problem is

$$\begin{aligned} &\text{minimize } M = 16y \\ &\text{subject to } 4y \geqslant 6 \\ &\qquad\qquad 2y \geqslant 4 \\ &\text{and} \qquad\quad y \geqslant 0 \end{aligned}$$

Evidently the first constraint is redundant. The second holds with equality at an optimum giving the minimum value of M as 32 for $y = 2$. An extra thousand pounds on the firm's capital expenditure budget would enable present value to be increased by £2,000. The opportunity loss on each machine of type one is given by the optimal value of dual slack variable one. Since $y = 2$, $t_1 = 2$. So although each machine of type one would make an accounting profit (in NPV terms) of £6,000 if one such machine is bought, then an opportunity is foregone to increase profits by another £2,000. The full solution to the dual is read from the index row in Figure 3.4 from which it is seen that $t_1 = 2$, $t_2 = 0$ and $y = 2$. The advent of additional investment opportunities as shown in Figure 3.5 alters the dual solution. The first three machines (including the previously optimal type two) all now show opportunity losses ($t_1 = 11/4$, $t_2 = 3/8$, $t_3 = 31/16$) and, since we have moved to a superior solution and there is only one scarce resource the marginal value of that resource *must* have risen ($y = 35/16$), and management will exert greater pressure to relax the financial constraint. Note that the change in optimal value of the objective function, 3, is equal to 3/8 multiplied by the value of x_2 in the previous solution and is also equal to the index row number of x_4 in the 'x_2 solution', 3/10 (ignoring sign) multiplied by the optimal value of x_4 in the final solution. The reader is asked to deduce the reasons for these equations.

In section 3.3 an additional constraint is introduced. If the constraint has any effect at all (i.e. is not redundant), the original optimum must now be infeasible. This means that the total value of resources ($16y_1 + 12y_2$) must be lower than previously and therefore the marginal *valuation of capital must fall.* It is now 5/4 – an extra £1,000 on the budget constraint would now increase NPV by only £1,250. This is because it cannot be used as effectively as before because of the new constraint. It is now optimal to purchase three machines of type one so, of course, the dual slack variable $t_1 = 0$ as can be seen from the final index row. The accounting profit of x_1 is unchanged and so is the accounting profit of x_2 but the reduced total imputed value of the resources ($(5/4)\ 16 + ½ \times 12$) has caused the opportunity loss on x_1 to fall to zero. As a last point on this problem it can be seen from Figure 3.9 that the dual infeasibility ($t_1 = -10/3$) does not imply primal infeasibility. If the original programme of buying only type two machines is adhered to a suboptimal solution is arrived at. Marginal valuation of funds is zero (only the floorspace constraint is binding), and total imputed value of resources is $0 \times 16 + (4/3)12 = 16$.

In respect of the three constraint problems of Figure 3.10 there is nothing to add at this stage to the discussion of the optimal solution given in Chapter three. However the preceding, suboptimal, solution is of interest. The value of y_1 (dual structural variable one) 33.2/7 is such as to attribute *more* than the total level of profit to resource one, finance; (33.2/7) 55 $\approx$ 261 and total profit = 90. So for an *average* valuation of resources suboptimal solutions cannot be relied upon. As a *marginal* valuation the figure is correct; an extra unit of finance would enable (ignoring whole number problems) an extra 33.2/7 to be added to NPV. It is therefore apparent that if a less than maximum profit is being made the marginal value of some of the resources can be greater than the value at the optimum. In other words, moving to a suboptimum position will not necessarily reduce the 'pressure' of all constraints. It should be noted that total valuation of resources: (33.2/7) 55 + 0 x 40 + (−13/7)92 = 90 is correct. Interpretation of the figure – 13/7 for y_3 requires care. It does not mean that one further unit of the third resource would reduce profit by 13/7. Relaxing a constraint cannot make things worse – the resource, machine time, could simply be left unused. This would mean a non-basic solution ($x_2 = 5, s_2 = 9, x_1 = 8, s_3 = 1$), but this is preferable to the neighbouring basic solution ($x_2 = 5 - 5/7$, $s_2 = 9 + 9/7$, $x_1 = 8 + 3/7$, $F = 90 - 13/7$). So the value of the objective function is only diminished if the investor is forced to use the additional 'resource' by marginal variation in the levels of basic variables – a situation nonsensical in practical terms.

The dual to the choice of shares problem is:

$$\text{Minimize:} \quad G = 100y_1 - 30y_2 + 25y_3 - 10y_4 + 20 \sum_{i=5}^{i=12} y_i$$

$$\begin{array}{llr}
\text{subject to} & y_1 - y_2 + y_5 & \geqslant 4.8 \\
& y_1 - y_2 + y_6 & \geqslant 5.4 \\
& y_1 - y_4 + y_7 & \geqslant 7.5 \\
& y_1 - y_4 + y_8 & \geqslant 8.5 \\
& y_1 + y_9 & \geqslant 9 \\
& y_1 + y_{10} & \geqslant 10 \\
& y_1 + y_3 + y_{11} & \geqslant 15 \\
& y_1 + y_3 + y_{12} & \geqslant 18 \\
& y_i \geqslant 0, \; i = 1,2, \ldots, 12. &
\end{array}$$

The solution is (positive variables only) $y_1 = 9$, $y_2 = 4.2$, $y_3 = 6$, $t_3 = 1$, $y_4 = 0.5$, $y_6 = 0.6$, $y_{10} = 1$, $y_{12} = 3$ and $G = 1{,}011$ (i.e. average yield = 10.11%). The value of $y_1 = 9$ means that for each 1% of the total budget left unspent average yield (over the *whole* budget including unspent balance) would be down by 0.09%. This corresponds to a reduction of x_5 to the level 14. The value 4.2 for y_2 means that if only 29% of the total budget had to be kept in unit trusts average yield would increase by 0.042% (x_5 increased to 16, x_1 decreased to 9). $y_3 = 6$ means that if 26% of the budget could be invested in mines then yield would be up by 0.06%. The reader is asked to interpret the remainder of the dual variables.

The dual to the finance company problem is:

$$\begin{aligned} \text{minimize} \quad & G = 1{,}000y_1 + 100y_2 \\ \text{subject to} \quad & 6y_1 + y_2 \geqslant 6.5 \\ & 8y_1 + y_2 \geqslant 7 \\ & 13y_1 + y_2 \geqslant 8.5 \\ & 15y_1 + y_2 \geqslant 9.5 \\ & 24y_1 + y_2 \geqslant 11.5 \\ & y_1, y_2 \geqslant 0 \end{aligned}$$

The optimal solution, obtainable directly from Figure 3.12 is $t_2 = 1.5/9$ $t_3 = 3/9$, $t_5 = 1$, $y_1 = 3/9$, $y_2 = 40.5/9$. The value of y_1 means that if the maximum expected loss figure was raised to £1,100 the average rate earned would increase by 1/3%. The value for y_2 means that if an extra £1,000 was available for loaning then total earnings would increase to 7090.5/9 but note that this would mean that *average* earnings would decline since

$$\frac{7090.5}{9(101)} < \frac{7{,}050}{9(100)}$$

This is due to the fact that the absolute level of expected loss remains unchanged. As an exercise the reader might care to work out the consequences if maximum expected loss was set at 1% of total investment.

In the 'shift pattern' problem the dual structural variables represent marginal valuations of machine time and man hours. The machine time valuations would be used to provide data for DCF calculations in respect of investment decisions about marginal variations in machine numbers. For instance if one further machine increased machine time to 2,820 hours, profit per shift would rise by £420 (5.5/17) = £136, which is almost £408 per day on the three-shift system. This increase in the profits stream (which does not include depreciation), would be set against the capital cost of the additional machine in the DCF calculation. As was seen in Chapter 3 substantial changes in constraint levels may require recalculation of the problem. This problem is discussed in the sensitivity analysis section to follow.

The dual to the Lorie–Savage problem is:

$$\begin{aligned} \text{minimize} \quad & M = 11y_0 + y_1 + y_2 + y_3 \\ \text{subject to} \quad & 5y_0 + y_1 \geqslant 9 \\ & 10y_0 + y_2 \geqslant 17 \\ & 6y_0 + y_3 \geqslant 12 \\ & y_0 \geqslant 1 \\ & y_0, y_1, y_2, y_3 \geqslant 0 \end{aligned}$$

where y_0 represents the marginal valuations of funds and y_1, y_2 and y_3 are the 'costs' of the upper bounds on the xs. The presence of integrality requirements (not explicitly incorporated in the formulation of the problem), and the degeneracy of the optimal solution mean that great care must be taken in use of the index row numbers, the dual solution, for decision-making purposes. A full discussion of use of dual values in integer problems follows in Chapter 7. However, a few remarks adding to the discussion of Chapter 3 are appropriate here. First if all variables must be integral then the marginal value of £1 more cash is not £1.7 but 1 since only S_0 can be increased. However, if a further *ten* pounds was available then N would increase by 17 since x_2 could be set at unit level. This is rather obvious, but the point is that inspection of the solution to a particular problem can give rise to more detailed statements about marginal values than can be made in general.

The ambiguity about shadow prices in the alternative forms of the solution shown in Figure 3.15 and 3.16 is illustrative of the general point that whenever a primal solution is degenerate the corresponding dual solution is non-unique, with one set of prices for movements in each direction. If the primal problem had been non-unique the dual solution would have been degenerate, i.e. the number of non-zero dual variables would have been less than the number of structural variables in the primal problem.

Even with the degeneracy removed because of integral requirements the dual solution is not all that it seems. We may anticipate the discussion of Chapter 7 by saying that a non-zero dual structral variable does not necessarily mean that more of the corresponding resource would increase profits and a zero shadow price, although correct (in non-degenerate cases) in implying that a marginal increase in the corresponding resource level would not increase profits, cannot be interpreted in general as meaning that there is no *sufficiently large* increment in that resource that would be profitable. All this is in sharp contrast with the continuous linear case. It is to the problem of substantial changes in problem parameters (in a continuous linear context) that we now turn.

4.2 Sensitivity Analysis

Sensitivity Analysis (sometimes, in the present context, referred to as post-optimality analysis) is concerned with the continuing optimality and/or feasibility of the original optimal b.f.s. to an L.P. problem when some of the parameters of that problem change. We shall examine the consequences of changes in objective function coefficients and changes in constraint levels. Changes in technical coefficients will be discussed briefly, but there is much less that can be said in general terms concerning the consequences of such changes. Many useful points concerning sensitivity analysis can be gleaned from geometrical consideration of 2 x 2 problems. The succeeding section examines changes in all types of parameter diagrammatically. This is followed by sensitivity analysis based on the Simplex tableau.

Graphical Analysis

In the context of investment decision-making this will usually mean changes in present values of projects or changes in the *estimates* of present values at the planning stage of an investment decision. First, however, let us examine the problem *in abstractio* and then apply the analysis to an investment problem.

In diagrammatic terms changes in objective function coefficients affect the slopes of the objective function. Consider the graph of the first problem in Section 4.1 as shown in Figure 4.1 (a). The slope of the objective function falls between the slopes of the constraints and consequently the optimal solution is at point B. Clearly, there is some variation possible in the slope of the objective function such that B remains optimal. As long as the objective function is no steeper than constraint one nor no flatter than constraint two point B will remain optimal. The slope of the objective function is given by the ratio of the coefficients of x_1 and x_2 in the function.

$$\text{i.e.} \quad \left(\frac{dx_2}{dx_1}\right)_{OF} = -\frac{10}{12}$$

For constraint one

$$\frac{dx_2}{dx_1} = -\frac{4}{2} = -2$$

and for constraint two

$$\frac{dx_2}{dx_1} = -\frac{3}{5} = -0.6$$

Now for unspecified objective function coefficients π_1 and π_2 point B will remain optimal provided that:

$$0.6 \leqslant \frac{\pi_1}{\pi_2} \leqslant 2 \tag{4.3}$$

For example if π_2 is set at the original value of 12 then B remains optimal provided (4.4) remains satisfied. This will be so if:

$$7.2 \leqslant \pi_1 \leqslant 24 \tag{4.4}$$

This is a considerable range of variation for the present value of a project. If the original value of π_1 had been 15, it could be argued that the optimal investment programme (B) is relatively insensitive to variations in NPV of investment one. If the original value of π_1 had been 8 then the programme is insensitive to improvements in NPV of x_1 but a cut of more than 10% would make point A (invest only in x_2) optimal.

For some specific value of π_1 the permitted range of variation of π_2 could be calculated using (4.3). For instance if $\pi_1 = 10$

$$5 \leqslant \pi_2 \leqslant 50/3 \tag{4.5}$$

for B to remain optimal.

In the context of 2 x 2 problems the effects of changes in technical coefficients can be illustrated diagrammatically. Such changes will affect the slopes of the

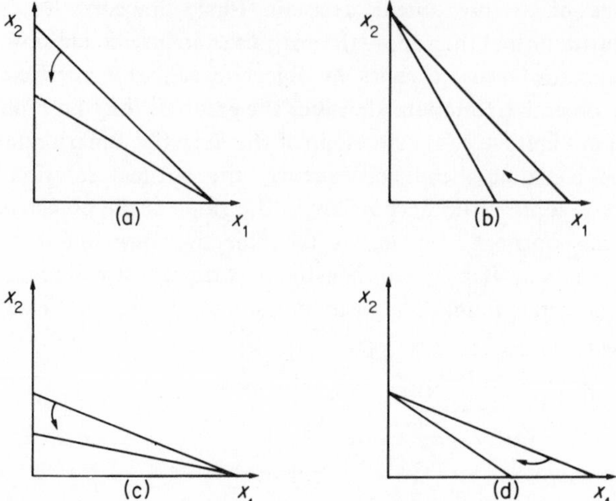

Figure 4.9 Effects of changed technical coefficients

constraints and leave unchanged the slope of the objective function, so long as the costs of the resources to which the technical coefficients relate are not included in objective function coefficients. Figure 4.9(a) shows the result on constraint one of an increase in the coefficient of x_2 in this constraint. (b) shows an increase in the coefficient of x_1; (c) and (d) show the consequences of increases in the coefficients of x_2 and x_1 in the second constraint. In general terms the constraints in a 2 x 2 problem can be written as:

$$a_{11}x_1 + a_{12}x_2 \leqslant b_1$$
$$a_{21}x_1 + a_{22}x_2 \leqslant b_2$$

where the 'a_{ij}' are the technical coefficients ($i = 1, 2, j = 1, 2$) the first subscription, the value of i, tells us the relevant constraint and the second subscript the relevant variable. The slope of constraint one is then a_{11}/a_{12}. This can readily be seen if the constraint is rewritten as:

$$x_2 = \frac{b_1 - s_1}{a_{12}} - \frac{a_{11}}{a_{12}} x_1$$

Similarly the slope of the second constraint is $-a_{21}/a_{22}$. The condition for optimality of point B can now be written. It is:

$$\frac{-a_{11}}{a_{12}} \leqslant \frac{-\pi_1}{\pi_2} \leqslant \frac{-a_{21}}{a_{22}}$$

Or, more conveniently, removing the minus signs as:

$$\frac{a_{21}}{a_{22}} \leqslant \frac{\pi_1}{\pi_2} \leqslant \frac{a_{11}}{a_{12}} \tag{4.6}$$

The original values of the π_js and the a_{ij}s satisified this condition. By the phrase 'point B remains optimal' it is meant that the optimal solution is at the intersection of the two constraints. If any of the a_{ij} change, the position of the point of intersection change relative to the origin. Consequently the *magnitudes* of x_1 and x_2 will change but both will remain the only non-zero variables in the solution.

With the π_js and the a_{ij}s except a_{11} fixed, the maximum range of variation can now be determined. We require that:

$$\frac{3}{5} \leqslant \frac{10}{12} \leqslant \frac{a_{11}}{2}$$

Consequently, point B remains optimal provided that $a_{11} \geqslant 5/3$. There is no upper limit on a_{11}. No matter how great the consumption of the first resource by x_1 some x_1 will still be desirable. This is a relatively rare 'counter-intuitive' result. As a_{11} increases point B slides upwards along constraint two. Only when $a_{11} = \infty$ and constraint one coincides with the vertical axis will no x_1 be desirable. At this point B has merged with A. Condition (4.6) does not tell the whole story however. As a_{11} is reduced point B slides *down* constraint two and indeed moves below the x_1 axis for $a_{11} < 228/85$, thus setting $x_2 < 0$ and rendering the intercept point B *infeasible*. Figure 4.10 graphs the problem for $a_{11} = 2$. The slope of the objective function still remains between those of the constraints and B would be optimal if *it could be achieved*. Of course point E is the optimal feasible solution and constraint one has become redundant. The lower bound on a_{11} is thus determined by considerations of feasibility and is 228/85.

This situation is in contrast to the objective function case when only optimality, not feasibility was the consideration. Thus even in graphical terms variations in technical coefficients can be troublesome. Add to this the possibility that the objective function coefficients may also depend on the a_{ij}, e.g. if the a_{ij} are cash outflows in a budgetary problem they will affect the NPVs of the xs and the magnitude of the problem technical coefficient changes emerges.

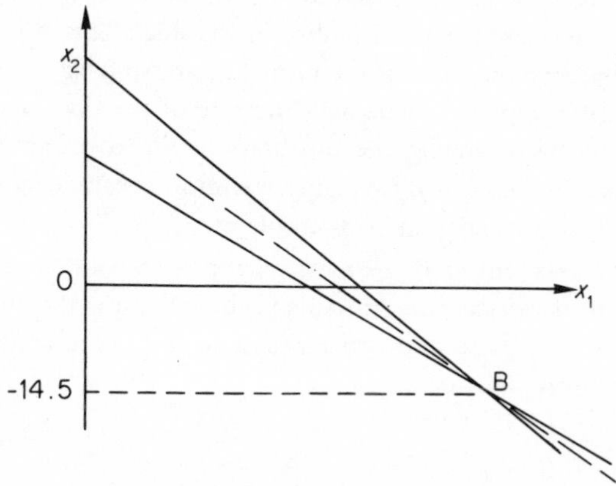

Figure 4.10 Large reduction in a_{11}

Changes in other of the a_{ij}s would be analysed in a similar fashion. Feasibility being borne in mind as well as optimality. For instance, the reader may verify that, in respect of point B, $a_{22} \geqslant 85/38$ for feasibility of the point, but $a_{22} \geqslant 3.6$ for optimality. Consequently, with the original values of the other parameters, point B will remain optimal provided $a_{22} \geqslant 3.6$.

We can now turn to discussion of changes in the b_i; the resource availabilities. Changes in the b_i mean that the positions of the constraints change, but not their slopes. In Figure 4.1(a), if more than 76 units of the first resource was available then constraint one would move away from the origin, moving point B downwards along constraint two. Since there are no changes in slope, point B will remain optimal. But clearly, if the increase in resource one is sufficiently large and there is no corresponding increase in resource two then the point of intersection of the constraints could be below the x_1 axis making the solution *infeasible*. This possibility is characteristic of situation involving changes in the b_i. The initial solution will remain optimal; only feasibility is in question.

Maximal changes in each resource level can be simply calculated. For constraint one this is when point B becomes coincident with E, i.e. the problem becomes degenerate. No further increases in resource one could be usable since they would imply negative x_2. At point E both constraints set the same limit on x_1. That is,

$$\frac{b_1}{4} = \frac{85}{3}; \quad \text{therefore} \quad b_1 = 113\tfrac{1}{3}$$

Similarly the maximum usable amount of the second resource (in conjunction with 76 units of resource one) is found when B becomes coincident with D. This is when $b_2 = 190$. In both cases if further increases occur the basis of the solution changes. At B, $x_1 > 0, x_2 > 0, S_1 = 0$, and $S_2 = 0$. If $b_1 > 113^1/_3$ then $x_1 > 0, S_1 \geqslant 0, x_2 = 0$. $S_2 = 0$ or if $b_2 > 190$ then $x_2 > 0$, $S_2 > 0$, $x_1 = 0$, and $S_1 = 0$. The group of positive variables remains the same (same basis) as long as point B remains in the non-negative quadrant.

All the discussion so far has been in terms of the primal problem. It could equally well have been put in terms of the dual. When we talk of optimality in the primal problem we are discussing feasibility in the dual. This is because changing the slope of the objective function of the primal means shifting the positions of the constraints in the dual. Equally, changing the slope of the dual objective function (dual optimality) means changing the positions of the constraints in the primal (feasibility therefore in question). Changing technical coefficients mean questions of both optimality and feasibility in both problems.

Although the (two-dimensional) geometrical approach could be extended to deal with three constraint, two structural variable problems (using the dual), diminishing returns soon set in. For these and larger problems it is more convenient to work with the Simplex tableau.

Tableau Analysis

First let us solve the initial problem of this chapter by thee Simplex method. Figure 4.11(a) gives the results. The optimum is obtained by setting $x_1 = 15, x_2 = 8$

for which $F = 246$ with $y_1 = 1$ and $y_2 = 2$. Now suppose the objective function coefficient of x_1 (π_1) goes down to 8, we know from the graphical discussion that only optimality, not feasibility is in doubt. All that needs to be done is to recalculate the index row of the 'optimal' solution. The result is shown in Figure 4.11(b). The new index row is all non-negative and so the original solution remains optimal (i.e. the *dual* remains feasible). When objective function coefficients change to check optimality all that needs to be done is to recalculate the index row. Now suppose that π_1 had dropped to 6, Figure 4.11(c) shows that the new index row has $y_1 = -6/14$ and the original optimum is no longer optimal. To obtain the new optimum the problem need not be started again from scratch. The x_1, x_2 solution is still *feasible* and the Simplex method can begin with any b.f.s.. So we simply iterate using B as the starting solution. Solution A is returned to as might be expected with x_1 dropping out. In larger problems this need not happen, but if the basis changes the new level of the less profitable variable will be lower. So, the procedure is relatively straightforward. Step one is to recalculate the index row. If this contains negative numbers reiterate to new optimum using the original optimum as initial b.f.s..

Maximum ranges of variations can be calculated for π_1 and π_2. For either coefficient all index row numbers must remain non-negative. So, for π_1 and $\pi_2 = 12$:

$$(5/14)\pi_1 - 3/14(12) \geqslant 0$$

and

$$(-1/7)\pi_1 + 2/7(12) \geqslant 0$$

which means that B remains optimal so long as:

$$7.2 \leqslant \pi_1 \leqslant 24$$

with $\pi_1 = 10$ the permitted range of π_2 is:

$$5 \leqslant \pi_2 \leqslant 50/3$$

As a final point it should be noted that if the objective function coefficient of a non-basic variable changes then the only index row number that is affected is its own. Thus if the coefficient of S_2 became +2 (unused units of resource two have salvage value), then its index row number becomes +2/7; no other index row numbers change. The subject of non-zero objective function coefficients for slack variables and the consequent changes in interpretion of dual variables is dealt with at the end of the chapter.

Changes in the b_i are a little more complicated to deal with than the changes in the π_j just considered. Figure 4.12 details the optimal solution of the dual problem (artificial variables omitted) and we recall that the index row numbers under the dual slack variables are the optimal values of the xs. If it is also recalled that constraint level variation in the primal is equivalent to objective function coefficient variation in the dual, it is clear that all that has to be done is to repeat the preceding analysis for the dual problem! If the coefficient of y_1 (level of

			10	12	0	0
			x_1	x_2	S_1	S_2
0	S_1	76	4	2	1	0
0	S_2	85	3	5	0	1
		0	−10	−12	0	0
0	S_1	42	14/5	0	1	−2/5
12	x_2	17	3/5	1	0	1/5
		204	−14/5	0	0	12/5
10	x_1	15	1	0	5/14	−1/7
12	x_2	8	0	1	−3/14	2/7
		246	0	0	1	2

(a)

			8	12	0	0
			x_1	x_2	S_1	S_2
8	x_1	15	1	0	5/14	−1/7
12	x_2	8	0	1	−3/14	2/7
		216	0	0	2/7	16/7

(b)

			6	12	0	0
			x_1	x_2	S_1	S_2
6	x_1	15	1	0	5/14	−1/7
12	x_2	8	0	1	−3/14	2/7
		196	0	0	−6/14	18/7
0	S_1	42	14/5	0	1	−2/5
12	x_2	17	3/5	1	0	1/5
		204	6/5	0	0	12/5

(c)

Figure 4.11 Original problem: changes in π_1

resource one) becomes 90 then x_1 (the t_1 index row number) becomes:

$$(-90)(-5/14) + (-85)(1/7) = 20$$

and the new level of x_2 is

$$(-90)(3/14) + (-85)(-2/7) = 5$$

Thus the dual solution is still optimal, i.e. the primal is still feasible with $x_1 = 20$, $x_2 = 5$ and $F = G = 260$. Maximum ranges of variation can now be worked out for

			−76	−85	0	0
			y_1	y_2	t_1	t_2
−76	y_1	1	1	0	−5/14	3/14
−85	y_2	2	0	1	1/7	−2/7
		−246	0	0	15	8

Figure 4.12 Dual to original problem: optimal solution

each resource individually. If b_1 represents the level of resource one then,

$$-b_1(-5/14) - 85(1/7) \geqslant 0 \quad \text{and} \quad -b_1(3/14) - 85(-2/7) \geqslant 0$$

Thus,

$$34 \leqslant b_1 \leqslant 113^1/_3$$

In a similar manner with $b_1 = 76$ the range of values for b_2 that keep both x_1 and x_2 non-negative (i.e. keep point B in the non-negative quadrant) is found to be:

$$57 \leqslant b_2 \leqslant 190$$

The above is all very well, but its value would be greatly reduced if the dual problem had to be solved separately before constraint level sensitivity analysis could begin. However, all the information relating to the dual solution is contained in the primal tableau. This includes rates of exchange as well as values for variables. The re-calculation of dual index row numbers above can be done with reference solely to the primal solution. Consider the rates of exchange under the slack variables S_1 and S_2. If we form the sum of products of elements in the first row of rates of exchange and respectively first and second resource levels we obtain:

$$5/14 \times 76 - 2/14 \times 85 = 15$$

i.e. the level of x_1. Now if the sum of products of elements in the second row of rates of exchange and first and second resource levels is formed we obtain

$$-3/14 \times 76 + 4/14 \times 85 = 8$$

i.e. the level of x_2. Now if resource one availability is 90 the new levels of x_1 and x_2 can be calculated in the above manner, viz.

$$x_1 = 5/14 \times 90 - 2/14 \times 85 = 20$$

$$x_2 = -3/14 \times 90 + 4/14 \times 85 = 5$$

In the primal, multiplying out rates of exchange and resource levels in this manner is equivalent to recalculating dual index row numbers. But the new non-zero dual index row numbers are precisely the new levels of primal variables that are being searched for!

To summarize so far: to find the new levels of solution variables in the primal sum the products of rates of exchange (under the Ss) and resource levels in the above manner. If the new levels are all non-negative the solution remains feasible and therefore, since optionality is not in question, no further work is needed. If one of the variables is now negative the solution is infeasible and at least one iteration is required. This will be dealt with momentarily.

What has been done in finding the sums of products above is *matrix multiplication*. A matrix is any rectangular array of members. For instance the array:

$$\begin{pmatrix} \frac{5}{14} & -\frac{2}{14} \\ -\frac{3}{14} & \frac{4}{14} \end{pmatrix} = \mathbf{A}$$

is a 2 x 2 matrix (two rows and two columns of numbers) and the array

$$\begin{pmatrix} 76 \\ 85 \end{pmatrix} = \mathbf{B}$$

is a 2 x 1 matrix (two rows and one column) or *vector*. The product of two matrices is also a matrix and elements (the numbers in the array) of the product matrix are formed by summing the products of elements in corresponding rows of the first matrix and columns of the second. The first element of the product of the above matrices is the sum of products of elements of the first row of **A** and the first (here the only) column of **B**. This will be the element in the first row of the first column of the product matrix **C**. The second element in the product matrix is found by summing products of the second row of **A** with the first column of **B**. This will be the element in the second row of the first column of **C**. Thus

$$\mathbf{A} \cdot \mathbf{B} = \begin{pmatrix} \frac{5}{14} & -\frac{2}{14} \\ -\frac{3}{14} & \frac{4}{14} \end{pmatrix} \cdot \begin{pmatrix} 76 \\ 85 \end{pmatrix} = \begin{pmatrix} 15 \\ 8 \end{pmatrix} = \mathbf{C}$$

completes the process since there are no further rows or columns to be dealt with. The product of a 2 X 2 matrix and a 2 X 1 matrix has been a 2 X 1 matrix. This result can be summarized as 2 X 2 X 2 X 1 = 2 X 1 from which it can be noted that the product of a 2 X 1 and a 2 X 2 matrix cannot be formed (this way round). In the above example **A** is said to premultiply **B**. A 2 X 1 matrix cannot premultiply a 2 X 2 matrix but it can postmultiply it, as has been seen. In general if the premultiplying matrix has m rows and n columns the postmultiplying matrix *must* have n rows (and any number of columns). For instance $m \times n \times n \times p = m \times p$. Two instances are given below:

$$\mathbf{A} \cdot \mathbf{B} = \begin{pmatrix} 4 & 8 \\ 3 & -2 \end{pmatrix} \begin{pmatrix} 7 & 1 \\ 5 & 6 \end{pmatrix} = \begin{pmatrix} 68 & 52 \\ 11 & -9 \end{pmatrix} = \mathbf{C}$$

Here, the element in the first row, second column of **C** is the first of **A** times the second column of **C**, and $-9 = 3.1 - 2.6$. Note that $\mathbf{A} \cdot \mathbf{B} \neq \mathbf{B} \cdot \mathbf{A}$.

$$\begin{pmatrix} 6 & 2 & -4 \\ -1 & 0 & 7 \end{pmatrix} \begin{pmatrix} 1 & 6 & \tfrac{1}{2} & 3 \\ 2 & -\tfrac{1}{4} & 7 & 4 \\ 8 & 2 & -4 & 0 \end{pmatrix} = \begin{pmatrix} -22 & 27\tfrac{1}{2} & 33 & 26 \\ 55 & 8 & -28\tfrac{1}{2} & -3 \end{pmatrix}$$

Note in this case that $\mathbf{B} \cdot \mathbf{A}$ does not exist.[3]

So, the level of solution variables is found by premultiplying the vector of resource levels by the matrix of exchange rates under the slack variables. This procedure can be used for determining maximum ranges of variation, viz.

$$\begin{pmatrix} \frac{5}{14} & -\frac{2}{14} \\ -\frac{3}{14} & \frac{4}{14} \end{pmatrix} \begin{pmatrix} b_1 \\ 85 \end{pmatrix} = \begin{pmatrix} \frac{5}{14} b_1 - \frac{170}{14} \\ -\frac{3}{14} b_1 + \frac{340}{14} \end{pmatrix} \geqslant \begin{pmatrix} 0 \\ 0 \end{pmatrix}$$

which, as we have seen leads to the result that $34 \leqslant b_1 \leqslant 113\tfrac{1}{3}$.

It was mentioned that all the rates of exchange of the dual solution are contained in the primal solution. This is so, but it is not always in precisely the rearrangement evident between the primal and dual solution tableau above. In this case multiplication by -1 and exchange or rows and columns under the slack variables of the primal gave rates of exchange under the slack variables of the dual. However, suppose that the objective function coefficient of x_2 was 20. Figure 4.13 gives optimal primal and dual solutions.

In this case given a change in resource level one to 90 the new values of S_1 and x_2 obtained by recalculating index row numbers for y_1 and t_2 in the dual are:

$$x_1 = (-14/5)0 + (2/5)(-85) + 90 = 56$$

$$y_2 = (-3/5)0 + (1/5)\,85 = 17$$

			−10	20	0	0
			x_1	x_2	S_1	S_2
0	S_1	42	14/5	0	1	−2/5
20	x_2	17	3/5	1	0	1/5
		340	2	0	0	4
			−76	−85	0	0
			y_1	y_2	t_1	t_2
0	t_1	2	−14/5	0	1	−3/5
−85	y_2	4	2/5	1	0	−1/5
		−340	42	0	0	17

Figure 4.13 Primal and dual optima: changed π_2

or, equivalently using the matrix of coefficients under the slack variables of the primal problem.[4]

$$\begin{pmatrix} S_1 \\ x_2 \end{pmatrix} = \begin{pmatrix} 1 & -2/5 \\ 0 & 1/5 \end{pmatrix} \begin{pmatrix} 90 \\ 85 \end{pmatrix} = \begin{pmatrix} 56 \\ 17 \end{pmatrix}$$

What happens, however, if the new optimal level of one of the variables in the solution is negative? The problem need not be started again from scratch. The *dual Simplex method* detailed in Chapter 7 can be applied with guaranteed success. However, at this stage an intuitively appealing rule of thumb will be suggested. Suppose that (with the original objective function coefficients) the level of resource one was raised to 120. The resulting values of x_1 and x_2 are

$$\begin{pmatrix} x_1 \\ x_2 \end{pmatrix} = \begin{pmatrix} \frac{5}{14} & -\frac{2}{14} \\ -\frac{3}{14} & \frac{4}{14} \end{pmatrix} \begin{pmatrix} 120 \\ 85 \end{pmatrix} = \begin{pmatrix} \frac{215}{7} \\ -\frac{10}{7} \end{pmatrix}$$

This infeasible solution and the return to feasibility is detailed in Figure 4.14. The negative x_2 has been *raised* to zero level by the introduction of S_1 which has a negative rate of exchange with x_2. The negative pivot element, −3/14, means that the variable replacing x_2 will be positive. The new optimum is arrived at in one iteration. Note that $850/3 < 1910/7$. This is because S_1 has a positive index row number. The original solution is optimal but infeasible. It is not always the case that only one iteration is required to get back to a feasible solution. x_2 might not have dropped out or some other variable may have become negative or the solution may become non-optimal depending upon choice of pivot column. There are two possible procedures that can be followed. Either x_1 is immediately raised to zero level and if this results in some other variable becoming negative this variable must be raised or, more systematically x_1 is raised to zero in as many stages as is necessary keeping all the other variables non-negative, the choice of pivotal row

		10	12	0	0
		x_1	x_2	S_1	S_2
10	x_1 215/7	1	0	5/14	−2/14
12	x_2 −10/7	0	1	−3/14	4/14
	1910/7	0	0	1	2
10	x_1 85/3	1	5/3	0	1/3
0	S_1 20/3	0	−14/3	1	−4/3
	850/3	0	14/3	0	10/3

Figure 4.14 Unfeasible solution: use of negative 'exchange rate'

being determined in the usual way – including the ratios of negative numbers. In Figure 4.14 the ratio $(-10/7)/(-3/14) < (215/7)/(5/14)$.

In problems of modest size there is little danger of 'cycling' between non-optimal, non-feasible solutions if common sense is applied in liberal proportions! The dual Simplex method in any case guarantees convergence and is explained later. So, if the new level of a variable is negative, introduce a variable into the basis which will raise the level of the errant variable, and, if necessary, season with wit.

Finally to bring together the discussion of resource level and objective function changes, from the optimal solution to the problem in its original form in Figure 4.11(a) it can be seen that the solution will remain optimal provided that:

$$(5/14)\Delta\pi_1 - (3/14)\Delta\pi_2 + 1 \geqslant 0 \quad \text{and} \quad (-1/7)\Delta\pi_1 + (2/7)\Delta\pi_2 + 2 \geqslant 0$$

where the $\Delta\pi_j$ are arbitrary changes in the π_j and it will remain feasible as long as:

$$(5/14)\Delta b_1 - (1/7)\Delta b_2 + 15 \geqslant 0 \quad \text{and} \quad (-3/14)\Delta b_1 + (2/7)\Delta b_2 + 8 \geqslant 0$$

where the Δb_i are arbitrary changes in the b_i. So, any given set of changes can be inserted into these four conditions for optimality and feasibility checks. The two sets of checks are independent of each other, containing only the $\Delta\pi_j$ or the Δb_i and not both, but have the common feature of using the same set of rates of exchange.

We now come to the knotty problem of changes in the technical coefficients. As has been seen these may affect both optimality and feasibility and, in addition it is more difficult to determine the size of the changes in primal and dual variables. Changing a technical coefficient also affects rates of exchange. If there are numerous changes in technical coefficients then it will normally be best to start the problem again.[5] However, if there are just one or two changes this will not be necessary. Consider the problem:

$$\begin{aligned}
&\text{maximize } F = 8x_1 + 10x_2 + 8x_3 \\
&\text{subject to} \quad 5x_1 + 4x_2 + 6x_3 \leqslant 134 \\
&\qquad\qquad\quad\; 3x_1 + 4x_2 + 3x_3 \leqslant 106 \\
&\qquad\qquad\quad\; 3x_1 + 6x_2 + 2x_3 \leqslant 150 \\
&\qquad\qquad\quad\; x_1, x_2, x_3 \geqslant 0
\end{aligned}$$

The solution to this problem is obtained in steps OAB of the Simplex tableau in Figure 4.15 to the left of the vertical line. In the light of knowledge of the optimal solution we can make some useful observations at once. Divide up the problem constraints as below

$$\begin{array}{l|l}
5x_1 + 4x_2 & + 6x_3 \leqslant 134 \\
3x_1 + 4x_2 & + 3x_3 \leqslant 106 \\
\hline
3x_1 + 6x_2 & + 2x_3 \leqslant 150
\end{array}$$

The solution has x_1 and x_2 and S_3 in the basis. Any changes in column 3 (the a_{i3})

				8	10	8	0	0	0	8	8
				x_1	x_2	x_3	S_1	S_2	S_3	x_1^*	x_3^*
	0	S_1	134	5	4	6	1	0	0	4	5
0	0	S_2	106	3	4	3	0	1	1	3	3
	0	S_3	150	3	6	2	0	0	0	3	2
			0	−8	−10	−8	0	0	0	−8	−8
	8	x_1	26.8	1	0.8	1.2	0.2	0	0		
A	0	S_2	25.6	0	1.6	−0.6	−0.6	1	0		
	0	S_3	69.6	0	3.6	−1.6	−0.6	0	1		
			214.4	0	−3.6	1.6	1.6	0	0		
	8	x_1	14	1	0	1.5	0.5	−0.5	0	0.5	1
B	10	x_2	16	0	1	−0.375	−0.375	0.625	0	0.375	0
	0	S_3	12	0	0	−0.25	0.75	−2.25	1	−0.75	−1
			279	0	0	0.25	0.25	2.25	0	−0.25	0
	8	x_1^*	28		0		1	−1	0	1	2
C	10	x_2	5.5		1		−0.75	1	0	0	−0.75
	0	S_3	33		0		1.5	−3	1	0	−1.5
			279		0		0.5	2	0	0	0.5

Figure 4.15 Changed technical coefficients: extended tableau

cannot affect the *feasibility* of the basis, only its optimality and that (as will be seen if not evident) only via the x_3 column of rates of exchange and index row number in solution B. Clearly, since increases in the a_{i3} will only make x_3 a less attractive proposition, it is only decreases or mixtures of decreases and increases that need concern us. Increases will increase the L.H.S. of the third dual constraint since $y_1, y_2, y_3 \geqslant 0$. Changes in row 3, corresponding to the resource constraint not binding at the optimum, cannot affect optimality,[6] only feasibility is in question if there are increases in the coefficients of x_1 and x_2. This feasibility question can most easily be checked by reference to the original inequality above. For example if a_{31} became 5 then the L.H.S. of constraint three becomes 145 for the current values of x_1 and x_2 so S_3 becomes 5 and the solution remains feasible. Changes in the remaining a_{ij}, increases or decreases can have widespread effects. We shall consider specifically a decrease of a_{11} to 4 along with a decrease in the coefficient of the non-basic variable x_3, a_{13}, to 5. We shall add to the tableau two further columns x_1^* with the new coefficients of x_1 and x_3^* with the new coefficients of x_3. Solutions prior to B may be worked through to get the rates of exchange of x_1^* and x_3^* but this is not necessary. Here the rates of exchange under the slack variables play an important role once more. It turns out that all the numbers in the whole tableau B are the original matrix of levels and coefficients in 0 premultiplied by the matrix or rates of exchange under the slack variables. This matrix is the *inverse of the basis.*[7] In other words:

$$\begin{pmatrix} 14 & 1 & 0 & 1.5 & 0.5 & -0.5 & 0 \\ 16 & 0 & 1 & -0.375 & -0.375 & 0.625 & 0 \\ 12 & 0 & 0 & -0.25 & 0.75 & -2.25 & 1 \end{pmatrix}$$

$$= \begin{pmatrix} 0.5 & -0.5 & 0 \\ -0.375 & 0.625 & 0 \\ 0.75 & -2.25 & 1 \end{pmatrix} \begin{pmatrix} 134 & 5 & 4 & 6 & 1 & 0 & 0 \\ 106 & 3 & 4 & 3 & 0 & 1 & 0 \\ 150 & 3 & 6 & 2 & 0 & 0 & 1 \end{pmatrix}$$

and so the rates of exchange between solution variables at B and 'new' variables x_1^* and x_3^* are given by the premultiplication of the new coefficients by the inverse of the basis. These numbers are appended to solution B to the right of the solid line. In detail:

$$\begin{pmatrix} 0.5 & 1 \\ 0.375 & 0 \\ -0.75 & -1 \end{pmatrix} = \begin{pmatrix} 0.5 & -0.5 & 0 \\ -0.375 & 0.625 & 0 \\ 0.75 & -2.25 & 1 \end{pmatrix} \begin{pmatrix} 4 & 5 \\ 3 & 3 \\ 3 & 2 \end{pmatrix}$$

Now, the change in a_{13} has made the optimum *non-unique*. The index row number of x_3^* is 0. The new x_3 could be introduced into the solution with no change in F. The old x_3 column is no longer relevant and may be deleted. The index row number of the new x_1, x_1^*, is as would be expected, negative. This is because x_1 now consumes less of a scarce resource than previously. In the dual the L.H.S. of constraint one is now less than the R.H.S. so the $\geqslant$ inequality is violated ($t_1 = -0.25$). Now x_1^* must be brought into the solution and x_1 eliminated from it. In the present case this can be accomplished in one step since x_1 happens to provide the pivot row. This will not always be the case, but since x_1^* dominates x_1 no solution containing both variables can be uniquely optimal, i.e. some of the index row numbers will be $\leqslant 0$ such that x_1 can eventually be 'pivoted out'. The new optimum for the current problem is shown in solution C where the x_1 and x_3 columns have been deleted. The original tableau size can be returned to simply by placing x_1^* in the former x_1 column and x_3^* in the former x_3 column. Note that x_3^* no longer provides an equally attractive alternative solution, its index row number being +0.5. Note also that in the previous solution x_3^* dominated x_1 but could not be used to improve things since its only superior quality was in consumption of a non-scarce resource.

Finally, in connection with technical coefficients it can be shown that:

$$\frac{\partial F_{\max}}{\partial a_{ij}} = -x_j y_i = \frac{\partial G_{\min}}{\partial a_{ij}}. \tag{4.7}$$

i.e. the rate of change of the objective functions at the optimum as coefficient a_{ij} is changed is minus the product of the optimum values of the corresponding x and y.[8] This result is not quite as useful as might first appear. The reason is that F_{max} is not a linear function of a_{ij}. Equation (4.7) gives only a slope at a point. If we were to use it to estimate the change in objective function in the case of a_{11} in Figure 4.15 we should have the formula:

$$\Delta F_{max.} = -x_j y_i \, \Delta a_{ij}$$

which in this case gives

$$\Delta F_{max.} \approx -14 \times 0.25 \times (-1) = 3.5$$

a considerable underestimate of the true change, seven. Note however that a better estimate of the change in F for finite Δa_{ij} can be obtained if either the *new* value of x and the *old* value of y is used or the old value of x and the new value of y. In these two cases respectively we should obtain

$$\Delta F_{max.} \approx -28 \times 0.25 \times (-1) = 7$$

and

$$\Delta F_{max.} \approx -14 \times 0.5 \times (-1) = 7$$

the correct value in each case! There is no guarantee of such pin-point accuracy in general, however, and the technique has the major disadvantage of requiring the new optimal value of either structural variable or shadow price. This is not so damning as it seems. In the present example all that is needed is the rate of exchange column for x_1^* with the old solution. Since x_1 is (in this case) the pivot row the new level of x_1 is 14/0.5. The new solution will be feasible since $16 - 0.375(14/0.5) = 5.5 > 0$ and $12 - (-0.75)(14/0.5) = 33 > 0$. But from this information we do not know the solution to be optimal; there may be further improvements to be gained. So what we estimate in this case is the lower bound on the change in F. The value of a reasonable estimate of the change in F for changed a_{ij} is in the evaluation of any proposals to make the change. Cuts in a_{ij} are increased efficiency and this will usually be obtained only at some cost. In assessing such proposals (which may involve purchase of new machinery) it is essential to have an estimate of benefits. The special characteristics of particular problems may enable estimates of benefit to be obtained with greater ease.

4.3 Non-zero objective function coefficients for slack variables

This discussion can usefully be appended here although it is only connected with sensitivity analysis insofar as *changes* in the objective function coefficients (ofcs) of slack variables are concerned. It has a more direct connection with the subject of duality since the economic interpretation of index row numbers is changed. An example will best illustrate these points. Take the data of the original problem of the chapter but now let unused units of resource two have a value of £1½ and unused units of resource one incur a cost of £¼ for their disposal. In the case of resource two the firm may be able to resell units at a price which is £1½ above that at which it buys. In the case of resource one we imagine that this resource is

			10	12	$-1/4$	$3/2$
			x_1	x_2	S_1	S_2
10	x_1	15	1	0	5/14	−2/14
12	x_2	8	0	1	−3/14	4/14
		246	0	0	$5/4$	$1/2$

Figure 4.16 Original problem: 'resaleable' resources

'prepaid' (the 76 units are already purchased) and that the £¼ is simply the disposal cost per unit. Figure 4.16 shows the optimal solution to the problem.

The optimum is therefore unchanged in that $x_1 = 15$, $x_2 = 8$ and $F = 246$. However, the dual solution is changed in the sense that the values of y_1 and y_2 though still both positive, are altered. In fact the value of the dual objective function appears to be $(5/4)76 + (1/2)85 = 275/2$, which is less than the primal value which duality theory tells us to be an impossible situation! The answer to this riddle is that the new index row numbers by themselves do not give the full marginal valuation of resources. They *are* correct in an opportunity loss sense in that if S_2 was brought into the solution to unit level then F would now only go down by ½; the changes in x_1 and x_2 would reduce F by 2 as before but the spare unit of resource two can now be sold for 3/2 producing a net loss of only ½ Similarly, if S_1 was brought in at unit level there would be a lost opportunity to make an additional profit of 5/4. F would go down by this amount. There would be a loss of one due to adjustments in the xs and an additional loss of ¼ incurred by the need to dispose of the unused unit of resource one. The net change in F is therefore $-5/4$.

However, the values 5/4 and 1/2 do *not* give the correct changes in F as a result of having one more unit of each resource. These values are *as before*. An additional unit of resource one would add £1 to F since x_1 would increase by 5/14 and x_2 decrease by 3/14 just as before. Likewise an additional unit of resource two would add £2 to F. These values can be obtained *by ignoring the ofcs of S_1 and S_2*. An element of asymmetry has been introduced. One set of values (5/4, 1/2) is appropriate to the setting of S_1 and S_2 at a positive level in the solution and another (1, 2) to the setting of S_1 and S_2 at negative level (equivalent to having more of the resource). This situation is *not* equivalent to the 'crossover' situation at a degenerate solution but results from true asymmetry in the profit function.

The dual problem can be written as:

$$\begin{aligned} \text{minimize } & 76y_1 + 85y_2 \\ \text{subject to } & 4y_1 + 3y_2 \geqslant 10 \\ & 2y_1 + 5y_2 \geqslant 12 \\ & 1y_1 + 0y_2 \geqslant -\frac{1}{4} \\ & 0y_1 + 1y_2 \geqslant \frac{3}{2} \end{aligned}$$

The non-zero, objective function coefficients of slack variables in the primal imply non-zero lower bounds on structural variables in the dual. The solution of Figure 4.16 now appears infeasible for the dual since $y_2 \geqslant 3/2$ and the index row number of $S_2 = 1/2$. However, it is not y_1 and y_2 that have been produced by the index row calculation. To see what has been produced the dual problem must be re-expressed.

The dual variables can be transformed to others with zero lower bounds. Let $\hat{y}_1 = y_1 + ¼$ and $\hat{y}_2 = y_2 - 3/2$. Insertion of these values into objective function and constraints gives:

$$\text{minimize } \hat{G} = 76\hat{y}_1 + 85\hat{y}_2 - ¼(76) + \frac{3}{2}(85)$$

$$\text{subject to } 4\hat{y}_1 + 3\hat{y}_2 \geqslant 13/2$$

$$2\hat{y}_1 + 5\hat{y}_2 \geqslant 5$$

$$\hat{y}_1, \hat{y}_2 \geqslant 0$$

The dual objective function has a constant term 217/2 which will be interpreted a little later. The dual constraint levels have changed and these are the new unit profits of the *x*s. These now bear in mind the alternative revenues and costs associated with non-use of the resources, but they do not tell the whole story.

In the primal problem the equivalent to removing the non-zero lower bounds in the dual is re-expressing the objective function to remove the non-zero ofcs of the slack variables. This can be done by expressing the slack variables as functions of the structural variables, viz.

$$S_1 = 76 - 4x_1 - 2x_2 \quad \text{and} \quad S_2 = 85 - 3x_1 - 5x_2$$

Accordingly the primal becomes;

$$\text{maximize } \hat{F} = 13/2x_1 + 5x_2 - ¼(76) + \frac{3}{2}(85)$$

$$\text{subject to } 4x_1 + 2x_2 \leqslant 76$$

$$3x_1 + 5x_2 \leqslant 85$$

$$x_1, x_2 \geqslant 0$$

The constant term, common to $\hat{F}$ and $\hat{G}$ can now be interpreted. It is the value of F that would have obtained had both *x*s been set at zero level. We might call this the *autonomous value* of F. This concept is important in capital rationing problems as will be seen in Chapter 5. Note that the autonomous value is only optimal (the dual is only feasible) if unit profits (as redefined) on the *x*s drop to zero or less. That is if the *original* unit profits are not more than 7/2 and 7 respectively.

Symmetry is thus re-established at the expense of an autonomous term in each objective function. In terms of marginal resource valuation, a further unit of resource two increases the autonomous term by 3/2 and since $\hat{y}_2 = ½$ the total change in the objective functions is 3/2 + ½ = 2. For resource one the net change in both functions is $5/4 - 1/4 = 1$. The $\hat{y}_1$ and $\hat{y}_2$ are appropriate therefore for computational purposes and the y_1 and y_2 for resource valuation purposes.

4.4 Resource Prices and ofcs

It was mentioned earlier that ofcs and resource prices may be interdependent. The relationship in its simplest form is seen in the context of a one-period profits maximization model.

A firm makes two products using three resources. x_1 and x_2 are the numbers of units of each product made. Constant per unit selling prices for each product are P_1 and P_2 respectively whilst the costs per unit of each resource are r_1, r_2 and r_3, respectively. The constraints are:

$$a_{11}x_1 + a_{12}x_2 \leqslant b_1$$

$$a_{21}x_1 + a_{22}x_2 \leqslant b_2$$

$$a_{31}x_1 + a_{32}x_2 \leqslant \text{unlimited}$$

Now unit profit equals unit revenue minus unit cost. Unit profit, $\pi_1 = P_1 - C_1$ and $\pi_2 = P_2 - C_2$ since unit revenue is price and C = unit cost. Now unit cost may be calculated quite simply in the current example. Each unit of x_1 requires a_{11} units of the first resource at a price of r_1 each, so the bill for resource one is $a_{11}.r_1$. Similarly the bills for resources two and three are $a_{21}r_2$ and $a_{31}r_3$ respectively. Total unit cost is therefore

$$\sum_{i=1}^{3} a_{i1}r_i = C_1$$

Similarly

$$C_2 = \sum_{i=1}^{3} a_{i2}r_i$$

The objective function can now be formed.

$$\text{Maximize } F = (P_1 - \sum_{i=1}^{3} a_{i1}r_i)x_1 + (P_2 - \sum_{i=1}^{3} {}_{i2}r_i)x_2$$

The third 'constraint' has played its entire role and can be eliminated. As a numerical example suppose $P_1 = 27$, $P_2 = 25$, $r_1 = 3$, $r_2 = 1$, $r_3 = 2$, and,

$$4x_1 + 2x_2 \leqslant 76$$

$$3x_1 + 5x_2 \leqslant 85$$

$$x_1 + x_2 \leqslant \text{unlimited}$$

then $C_1 = 4 \times 3 + 3 \times 1 + 1 \times 2 = 17$, $C_2 = 2 \times 3 + 5 \times 1 + 1 \times 2 = 13$. Therefore $\pi_1 = 27 - 17 = 10$ and $\pi_2 = 25 - 13 = 12$.

The cost calculation would also be necessary for cost minimization problems.

Where revenue is fixed profits are maximized by the minimization of costs. The characteristic problem of this type is to minimize $\Sigma C_j x_j$ subject to resource constraints and overall production requirements.

In both the profits maximization and cost minimization problems the ofcs are now functions of the a_{ij}. Sensitivity analysis of the a_{ij} is now even more complex than before. As well as introduction of 'starred variables' the ofc of x_j (for a change in a_{ij}) has to be re-calculated as will the whole index row if x_{ij} is a basic variable. The π_j are also functions of the P_j and all resource prices r_i. In sensitivity analysis if there is a change in P_j of ΔP_j then this is also the change in π_j. If r_i changes by Δr_i then the consequent change in π_j is $-a_{ij}\Delta r_i$. Sensitivity analysis of the selling prices and prices of resources proceeds first by recalculation of the objective function coefficients and then by redetermination of the index row. This procedure is worked through in the investment example of the succeeding chapter but as exercise the reader may determine arbitrary changes in the prices of the above problem and examine the solution sensitivity by reference to Figure 4.11(a).

4.5 Additional Variables and Constraints

Under this heading we shall also discuss the problem of the deletion of variables and the elimination of constraints.

First consider the case of additional variables. The discovery of additional opportunities for investment or production can be considered as part of the province of sensitivity analysis. The subject was introduced in Chapter 2 in a one-constraint problem, but the principle of approach to multi-constraint problems is identical. New columns are introduced to the tableau and the rates of exchange between the new variables and the existing basic variables are determined by pre-multiplication of the columns of constraint coefficients of the new variables by the inverse of the basis. The existing solution must remain feasible of course but it may not be optimal. If the index row numbers of any of the new variables are negative then further iterations are required; if not, the solution remains optimal. For instance, suppose there were two new opportunities to be added to the original problem of Figure 4.15, x_4 and x_5 with coefficients (objective function first) 7, 3 3 5 and 15, 7 6 9 respectively. Rates of exchange with the existing solution are

$$\begin{pmatrix} 0.5 & -0.5 & 0 \\ -0.375 & 0.625 & 0 \\ 0.75 & -2.25 & 1 \end{pmatrix} \begin{pmatrix} 3 & 7 \\ 3 & 6 \\ 5 & 9 \end{pmatrix} = \begin{pmatrix} 0 & 0.5 \\ 0.75 & 1.125 \\ 0.5 & 0.75 \end{pmatrix}$$

The optimal solution remains unchanged. The complete picture is given in Figure 4.17.

What if the investment opportunity set or possible product range is to be cut? If the cuts correspond to variables which are non-basic then the corresponding columns are deleted from the optimal tableau. For instance in Figure 4.15 if the opportunity to buy a type three machine (x_3 = number of these machines purchased) ceases to exist then the x_3 column of exchange rates is removed. The optimal solution is, of course, unchanged by this action. If on the other hand the

			8	10	8	7	15	0	0	0
			x_1	x_2	x_3	x_4	x_5	S_1	S_2	S_3
8	x_1	14	1	0	1.5	0	0.5	0.5	−0.5	0
10	x_2	16	0	1	−0.375	0.75	1.125	−0.375	0.625	0
0	S_3	12	0	0	−0.25	0.5	0.75	0.75	−2.25	1
		272	0	0	0.25	0.5	0.25	0.25	0.25	0

Figure 4.17 Simplex tableau: additional variables

variable concerned is a basic variable then it must be removed from the formerly optimal solution. This can be accomplished by the introduction of a non-basic variable with a positive rate of exchange with the outgoing basic variable. If the outgoing variable (say x_1) is not reduced to zero level in the next solution obtained then a further variable must be introduced. Once x_1 is out of the solution the column of rates of exchange is deleted. The objective function value of the solution thus obtained must be lower than that of the original optimum and indeed unless the correct selection of incoming variables is made the new solution may not be optimal. There will be several (in general) bases not containing x_1. However, a feasible solution will have been reached and optimality can then be acquired in the usual way. For instance consider the 'B' solution of the problem in Figure 4.15 (ignoring the technical coefficient changes) if x_1 is to be deleted then either x_3 or S_1 could be introduced and x_1 lowered. Now each unit of x_3 lowers x_1 by 1.5 and F by 0.25. S_2 also lowers F by 0.25 per unit but lowers x_1 by only 0.5, so it seems plausible to introduce x_3, This results in the new optimum, shown in Figure 4.18. The x_1 column, if not deleted, would have a negative index row number indicating that it would be profitable to introduce x_1 if this were possible. Note that the decrease in F, 7/3 between the two solutions is at once equal to (28/3) x 0.25 and (1/6) x 14.

Now consider the problem of deleted constraints. The limitation on use of a resource may be removed by factors external to the firm or as a result of the firm's activities. For example a firm may remove a bottleneck on machine time by investment in additional machines. Is the cost of purchasing the machines worth the gains by relaxation of the bottleneck? This is the kind of question we can answer here.

			8	10	8	0	0	0
			x_1	x_2	x_3	S_1	S_2	S_3
8	x_3	28/3	$2/3$	0	1	$1/3$	$-1/3$	0
10	x_2	39/2	$1/4$	1	0	$-1/4$	$1/2$	0
0	S_3	43/3	$1/6$	0	0	$5/6$	$-7/3$	1
		809/3	$-1/6$	0	0	$1/6$	$7/3$	0

Figure 4.18 Simplex tableau: elimination of x_1

If a constraint is deleted then basic solutions will contain one less variable. The old optimal b.f.s. is therefore no longer basic. If a constraint is deleted that corresponds with a slack variable that is positive in the old b.f.s. then the corresponding row is simply deleted from the tableau. In Figure 4.18, if constraint three was deleted the new optimal tableau would be as before with the S_3 row removed. Note that index row numbers and the value of F are unchanged since the ofc of S_3 is zero.[9] Note also that the rates of exchange between the basic variables x_2 and x_3 and the other variables are determined from the first two constraints only. So nothing else in the tableau is changed. The procedure is, for the dual, the deletion of a non-basic variable y_3 and the removal of the y_3 column from the dual tableau.

			10	12	0	0
			x_1	x_2	S_1	S_2
10	x_1	15	1	0	5/14	$-1/7$
12	x_2	8	0	1	$-3/14$	$2/7$
		246	0	0	1	2
10	x_1	85/3	1	$5/3$	0	$1/3$
0	S_1	$-112/3$	0	$-14/3$	1	$-4/3$
		850/3	0	14/3	0	10/3

Figure 4.19 Simplex tableau: deletion of binding constraint

If a binding constraint is relaxed then the procedure adopted in the primal must be equivalent to the removal of a basic variable from the solution to the dual. Some reworking will be necessary. As an example consider, for the first problem of this chapter, the deletion of constraint one, i.e. the company can now use as much of the first resource as it wishes and is limited only by consumption of resource two. Vis-a-vis the old solution it is as if S_1 is no longer required to have a minimum level of zero; it can be introduced into the solution at *negative level*. The situation is equivalent to that of the dual in Figure 4.18 when t_1 was introduced into the dual solution at level $-1/6$. The new optimum is shown in Figure 4.19. In the tableau the S_1 row is left in for completeness but it is of no relevance either in setting the level of x_1 or the rates of exchange and index row numbers. All that the value $S_1 = -112/3$ means is that the amount of resource one that the firm will require is $76 + 112/3$. It should be remembered that the index row number of S_1 in the original optimum, 1, meant that if S_1 could be brought into the solution at level -1 (i.e. if one more unit of the first resource was available) then F would increase by 1. The change in F between the two solutions is $(112/3) \times 1 = (14/3) \times 8$.

Now suppose that in order to remove constraint one a new machine had had to be obtained. Profit per period has been increased by $112/3$ ($= 850/3 - 246$) and the discounted sum of these returns would be compared with the outlay required to obtain the machine in order to arrive at the investment decision.

Notes

1. For a more extensive discussion and proof of this and other duality theorems see Baumol, W. J., *Economic Theory and Operations analysis*, 2nd Edn, Prentice-Hall, Englewood Cliffs, N. J., 1965, Chapter 6.
2. For an extensive economic and intuitive explanation of duality and opportunity losses see Baumol, W. J., *Economic Theory and Operation Analysis,* 2nd Edn., Prentice-Hall, Englewood Cliffs, N. J., 1965, Chapter 6.
3. For further discussion of matrix multiplication see Bellman, R., *Introduction to Matrix Analysis*, McGraw-Hill, New York, 1960.
4. For further details of the relationship between primal and dual optimal tableaux and a presentation of the 'concise' simplex tableau see Baumol, W. J., *Economic Theory and Operation Analysis*, 2nd Edn., Prentice-Hall, Englewood Cliffs, N. J., 1965, Chapter 6.
5. Unless there are special features of the problem which enable the consequences of changes to be deduced more easily than is usual.
6. Again we are assuming that objective function coefficients are not functions of the technical coefficients (the a_{ij}). An investment example where this is the case is examined at the end of the chapter.
7. The technicalities of matrix inversion will not be expounded here, see Bellman, R., *Introduction to Matrix Analysis*, McGraw-Hill, New York, 1960.
8. This is an intuitively sensible result but for a formal proof see Intriligator, M.D., *Mathematical Optimization and Economic Theory*, Prentice-Hall, Englewood Cliffs, N. J., 1971, Chapter 5.
9. The reader is asked to deduce the consequences of non-zero ofcs for such slack variables.

CHAPTER 5

Capital Rationing Models

The problem of project selection under constraints was introduced in Chapter 2 and constrained maximization problems and their interpretation have been the subject material of Chapters 3 and 4. Chapter 1 introduced the basic concepts of investment appraisal theory including present and terminal values. These threads can now be drawn together under the heading of *capital rationing*.

A capital rationing problem is one where not all projects with positive present values (determined at the prerationing discount rate) can be taken up because of limits on funds available for investment. It is also a situation in which some projects with negative present or terminal values may be accepted if they generate funds at crucial times. An interrelationship exists between projects because of the consumption of a common scarce resource: capital. Within the context of rationing models it is possible to include interrelationships due to the consumption of any scarce resource or resources. All this does not mean that the concepts of NPV, NTV and yield are not to be abandoned, although there can be considerable difficulties in defining NPV and NTV. What we shall frequently be concerned with is the NTV or yield of feasible groups of projects with the idea of maximizing terminal or present value *overall*.

We shall begin by examining problems with expenditure limit constraints only and later introduce other forms of financial constraints and physical constraints.

5.1 A One-constraint Problem Revisited

The simple one-constraint problem defined in section 2.14 provides a useful starting point and a vehicle for introducing some of the principles of problem formulation and interpretation useful in tackling larger problems. The problem was:

$$\begin{aligned} &\text{maximize } F = 9x_1 + 17x_2 + 12x_3 \\ &\text{subject to} \quad 5x_1 + 10x_2 + 6x_3 \leqslant 11 \\ &\qquad\qquad x_1, x_2, x_3 \geqslant 0 \end{aligned} \tag{5.1}$$

where the xs are amounts taken of each of three investments and the objective function coefficients are the NPVs per unit of each investment. Per unit capital outlays are given in the constraint and we shall assume that fractional values of the xs are meaningful and that there is no upper bound on any of the xs. Let us suppose that the NPVs of the objective function were due to incomes of 15.4, 29.7 and 19.8 after one year for each unit of each of the xs respectively and that the

			9	17	12	0
			x_1	x_2	x_3	S_0
0	S_0	11	5	10	6	1
		0	−9	−17	−12	0
12	x_3	11/6	5/6	10/6	1	1/6
		22	1	3	0	2

Figure 5.1 One-constraint problem: simplex solution

discount rate employed was 10%. In other words:

$$NPV_1 = (15.4/1.1) - 5 = 9$$

$$NPV_2 = (29.7/1.1) - 10 = 17$$

$$NPV_3 = (19.8/1.1) - 6 = 12$$

The form of the objective function in (5.1) would be appropriate in the case of a unit of a large organization constrained by head office to maximize present value, given a discount rate of 10% and where any unused funds return to a central source and are not relevant to the departments calculations. With S_0 as the slack variable in the equality form of the constraint, the solution of the problem by the simplex method is shown in Figure 5.1.

Maximum NPV is 22 with $x_3 = {}^{11}/_6$ and $x_1 = 0$ and $x_2 = 0$. The addition to NPV of having 12 units of capital available for investment would be 2. The opportunity costs (in present value terms) of units of x_1 and x_3 are 1 and 3 respectively. Suppose that the firm could relax the capital constraint by borrowing up to a limit of 5 extra units of capital at an interest rate of 20% (repayment of 1.2 per unit borrowed after one year). What is the new solution? To obtain this it is more convenient to express the objective function in *terminal value* terms and introduce a new variable, x_4, the amount borrowed, with objective function coefficient −1.2 and constraint coefficient −1. Terminal value is at $t = 1$, there being no unequal horizon problems in this example, and the coefficients of the existing xs are 9.9, 18.7 and 13.2. An additional constraint is also introduced and the solution is shown in Figure 5.2. The problem is started from the solution of Figure 5.1 with an extra

			9.9	18.7	13.2	−1.2	0	0
			x_1	x_2	x_3	x_4	S_0	S_1
13.2	x_3	11/6	5/6	10/6	1	−1/6	1/6	0
0	S_1	4	0	0	0	1	0	1
		24.2	1.1	3.3	0	−1	2.2	0
13.2	x_3	15/6	5/6	10/6	1	0	1/6	1/6
−1.2	x_4	4	0	0	0	1	0	1
		28.2	1.1	3.3	0	0	2.2	1

Figure 5.2 Simplex solution: expanded problem

column, the rate of exchange between x_3 and x_4 being the constraint coefficient, -1, multiplied by the inverse of the basis; an extra row is introduced with slack variable S_1 (since $x_4 + S_1 = 4$) at level 4.

There are several points of interest in Figure 5.2. Firstly the original multiplication of the objective function by the constant 1.1 changed nothing except the value of the solution and the index row numbers. This is true in general. Secondly if there had been no upper bound on x_4 then there would have been no limit to the value of F. This is so since x_4 has a negative rate of exchange between itself and x_3 and because the problem is linear. *Every* unit of x_4 introduced would increase F by one. An unbounded solution to the primal problem means that no feasible solution can be found to the dual. Thirdly it should be noted that 'project' x_4 has a *negative* NPV. In isolation, borrowing at 20% is loss making if discounting is at 10% but the important feature of x_4 is that it generates funds at the right time. From the tableau we can deduce the maximum borrowing interest rate that would be worthwhile for the company – up to 120%. Finally we observe that if central management allocated an extra unit of capital to the firm F would increase by 2.2, or if the borrowing ceiling could be relaxed by 25% F would increase by one.

In the original specification of the problem the circumstances were such that any unused funds of the allocation of eleven were returned to the central pool. What if the funds were provided by the firm itself? It would then be appropriate to include S_0 in the objective function with non-zero coefficient. The coefficient would be unity in the case of the present value form of F or 1.1 in the future value case. In terms of NPV it is as if there was an autonomous value of F of 11, and investment in the xs is thought of as an addition to this amount. The optimal solution is unaltered but dual variable y_0 drops to 1. If a further one unit of capital was possessed, investment of this in the xs increases present value only by one unit more than it would increase by if nothing was done. As was seen in chapter three, the objective function of such problems can be re-expressed so as to remove the non-zero coefficients of the slacks. In the present case since $S_1 = 11 - 5x_1 - 10x_2 - 6x_3$, F can be rewritten as:

$$F = 4x_1 + 7x_2 + 6x_3 + 11$$

where the coefficients of the xs show the increases over the autonomous value of F per unit of x_1, x_2 and x_3 respectively. The corresponding index row numbers are unchanged including that of S_0 which remains at unity. We turn now to a more involved example.

5.2 Multi-constraint Problems

Capital rationing problems vary greatly in complexity. The example of section 5.1 would provide a starting point for a simple two constraint model. A further constraint could be hypothesized in which R.H.S. and technical coefficients were predetermined as well as the coefficients of the objective function. If there was no transference of funds possible between periods then the formulation of the problem, its solution and its interpretation, would be uncomplicated and could proceed along the lines described so far. The question of slack variables in the objective function may arise depending on the circumstances of the problem. One of the principal objectives of this section is to describe how the objective function and constraints are arrived at, i.e. how problems can be described in mathematical terms and to provide interpretations of solutions in cases of varying difficulty. A basic model will be used throughout with restricting assumptions gradually relaxed, the consequences of alternative objectives deduced and statements of general results made.

Consider the problem facing an investor who has the choice of investing in either or both of two projects, or alternatively he may choose to invest in neither. In order to obtain one unit of project one, a sum of money K_{01} is required immediately, and subsequently a further sum K_{11} is required at the end of one year. The corresponding amounts for one unit of project two are K_{02} and K_{12}. Each unit of project one yields returns of R_{11} and R_{21} at the end of the first and second years respectively. Similarly project two yields R_{12} and R_{22} per unit. The investor has a sum of money of b_0 immediately available and a further sum b_1 available after one year. All or part of these funds may be inserted in short term securities at a rate of return j. The investor does not wish to raise further funds elsewhere, and seeks to maximize the terminal value of investments after two years. The data for the problem is presented in Figure 5.3 with the timing of outflows and inflows shown to the left.

$t = 2$	R_{21}	R_{22}	
$t = 1$	R_{11}	R_{12}	
	x_1	x_2	
$t = 0$	K_{01}	K_{02}	b_0
$t = 1$	K_{11}	K_{12}	b_1

Figure 5.3 Data layout for rationing problem

First the constraints must be formulated. For the initial period, zero, the constraint is:

$$K_{01}x_1 + K_{02}x_2 \leqslant b_0$$

or with the slack variable included:

$$K_{01}x_1 + K_{02}x_2 + S_0 = b_0$$

Now after one year the investor will have not only b_1 available but also any unused funds from $t = 0$ invested at $100j\%$ plus the first returns from the projects. So the total amount available is:

$$b_1 + R_{11}x_1 + R_{12}x_2 + S_0\ (1 + j)$$

and the period one constraint can be written as

$$K_{11}x_1 + K_{12}x_2 + S_1 = b_1 + R_{11}x_1 + R_{12}x_2 + S_0(1+j)$$

or, in order that only constant terms be on the R.H.S. of constraints:

$$(K_{11} - R_{11})x_1 + (K_{12} - R_{12})x_2 - S_0(1+j) + S_1 = b_1$$

The coefficients of the xs are then the *net* input required per unit of each project.

Now terminal value at $t = 2$ must be written down. There are the returns from the projects in year two, namely $R_{21}x_1 + R_{22}x_2$, plus any sum remaining unspent from year one invested at $100j\%$. The objective function could be written as:

$$F = R_{21}x_1 + R_{22}x_2 + S_1(1+j)$$

or, since

$$S_1 = b_1 + (R_{11} - K_{11})x_1 + (R_{12} - K_{12})x_2 + S_0(1+j)$$

and

$$S_0 = b_0 - K_{01}x_1 - K_{02}x_2$$

as

$$F = \pi_1 x_1 + \pi_2 x_2 + A$$

where:

$$\begin{aligned} \pi_1 &= R_{21} + (R_{11} - K_{11})(1+j) - K_{01}(1+j)^2 \\ \pi_2 &= R_{22} + (R_{12} - K_{12})(1+j) - K_{02}(1+j)^2 \\ A &= b_0(1+j)^2 + b_1(1+j) \end{aligned} \tag{5.2}$$

The coefficients π_1 and π_2 are the per unit NTVs of x_1 and x_2 and A is the autonomous terminal value arising from zero internal investments. As we have seen, division through of F by a positive constant will not alter the optimal levels of the xs. If F is divided by $(1+j)^2 > 0$ then the present value formulation is obtained since:

$$\pi_1(1+j)^{-2} = R_{21}(1+j)^{-2} + (R_{11} - K_{11})(1+j)^{-1} - K_{01} = N_1$$
$$\pi_2(1+j)^{-2} = R_{22}(1+j)^{-2} + (R_{12} - K_{12})(1+j)^{-1} - K_{02} = N_2$$

Using the terminal value formulations (which will be seen to be more convenient in less straightforward problems) the full problem is:

$$\begin{aligned} &\text{maximizing } F = \pi_1 x_1 + \pi_2 x_2 + A \\ &\text{subject to} \quad K_{01}x_1 + K_{02}x_2 + S_0 = b_0 \\ &\qquad (K_{11} - R_{11})x_1 + (K_{12} - R_{12})X_2 - S_0(1+j) + S_1 = b_1 \\ &\qquad x_1, x_2, S_0, S_1 \geqslant 0 \end{aligned} \tag{5.3}$$

Now consider a numerical example. Let $j = 0.1$ and the returns, costs and available fund data be:

	x_1	x_2	
$t = 2$	14	25	
$t = 1$	12	9	
$t = 0$	10	4	260
$t = 1$	7	17	120

Insertion of this data into expressions (5.2) and (5.3) results in the statement of the problem as:

$$\text{maximize } F = 7.4x_1 + 11.36x_2 + 446.6$$

$$\text{subject to} \quad 10x_1 + 4x_2 + S_o = 260$$

$$-5x_1 + 8x_2 - 1.1S_o + S_1 = 120$$

$$x_1, x_2, S_0, S_1 \geqslant 0$$

Now since S_0 is a somewhat unusual slack variable in that it appears with non-zero coefficient in another constraint it is necessary to introduce an artificial variable U_0 into the first constraint in order to obtain a starting solution. This done, the problem is solved via the simplex method. The iterations are laid out in Figure 5.4. Investment in 16 units of x_1 and 25 of x_2 would add 402.4 to the autonomous value of F of 446.6. Terminal value at $t = 2$ is then 849. The values of the dual structural variables are 1.16 and 0.84.

Diagrammatic representation of the problem reveals some interesting features. First consider the constraints. In Figure 5.5 the lines CE and AG show the two constraints with slack variables zero. The feasible region would appear to be the cross-hatched area OADE, but this is not the case. The variable S_0 appears with negative coefficient in constraint one. If S_0 is made positive funds are taken from the first period and transferred to the second. Constraint one, represented by line

			7.4	11.36	0	$-M$	0
			x_1	x_2	S_0	U_0	S_1
$-M$	U_0	260	10	4	1	1	0
0	S_1	120	-5	8	-1.1	0	1
		$-260M$	$-10M - 7.4$	$-4M - 11.36$	$-M$	0	0
7.4	x_1	26	1	0.4	0.1	0.1	0
0	S_1	250	0	10	-0.6	0.5	1
		192.4	0	-8.4	0.74	$0.74 + M$	0
7.4	x_1	16	1	0	0.124	0.08	-0.04
11.36	x_2	25	0	1	-0.06	0.05	0.1
		402.4	0	0	0.236	$1.16 + M$	0.84

Figure 5.4 Rationing example: simplex solution

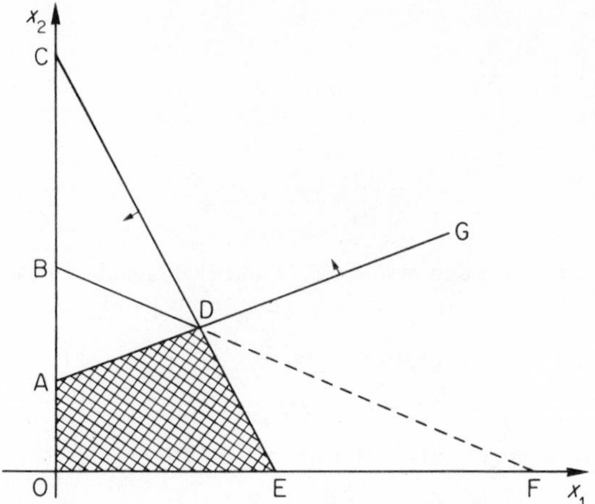

Figure 5.5 Diagram of rationing example

CE moves inwards as indicated by the arrow while AG moves upwards. The point of intersection moves along the line DB towards the x_2 axis. Thus points in ABD are also feasible and the total feasible region is OBDE. If borrowing from the supply in period two was possible at the same interest rate (i.e. if S_0 could be made negative) then the directions of movement of the constraints would be reversed and the intercept term D would move along the dashed line segment towards F. In the event of this possibility the total feasible region is OBF. The ability to transfer funds thus increases the feasible region. The two constraints are not independent and only determine the area OADE for the particular value of S_0 of zero. If S_0 does not have this lower bound there is in effect only one constraint; the two original constraints joining to form the line BF. The implication of this is quite striking. If there is no lower bound on S_0 and no upper bounds on the xs then only one project will be invested in. No more than one variable can be positive at an optimum.

This is not to say that our theoretical analyis predicts that in reality we shall find companies in capital rationing situations with all their eggs in one basket. Quite apart from considerations of risk there will be upper bounds on variables, borrowing limits, diminishing returns (an instance of non-linearity in the problem) and differential external borrowing and investment conditions. All of these factors will be examined in due course. First let us consider Figure 5.5 a little further. What is the equation of the line BF? The second constraint is:

$$-5x_1 + 8x_2 - 1.1S_0 + S_1 = 120$$

Now the first constraint is satisfied provided that:

$$S_0 = 260 - 10x_1 - 4x_2$$

substituting this into constraint two and setting $S_1 = 0$ gives:

$$-5x_1 + 8x_2 - 1.1(260 - 10x_1 - 4x_2) = 120$$

that is

$$6x_1 + 12.4x_2 = 406$$

This is the equation of the line BF. However, since at the moment S_0 is constrained to be non-negative the feasible area is generated by

$$6x_1 + 12.4x_2 \leqslant 406$$

and either:

$$10x_1 + 4x_2 \leqslant 260 \quad \text{(i.e. } S_0 \geqslant 0\text{)}$$

or:

$$x_1 \leqslant 16$$

Now the objective function lines have a slope of 7.4/11.36 (in absolute terms) which is steeper than the line BF which has a slope of 6/12.4. Thus point F would be optimal if only it was feasible. It is not feasible and since the $S_0 \geqslant 0$ constraint has a slope of 10/4 point D is optimal and in terms of the objective function it is as near to F as is possible.

We turn now to a detailed interpretation of the optimal solution to the problem in terms of the simplex tableau. The subject of borrowing (and borrowing proposals) is raised again shortly.

The index row number of artificial variable u_0 has a meaning once the M is removed. This is because in this problem u_0 is acting as the 'genuine' slack variable for constraint one. S_0 appears with a non-zero coefficient in the second constraint so that its column of rates of exchange cannot be elements of the inverse of the basis. This *is* however true of the u_0 column. The non-autonomous part of the dual objective function is:

$$(1.16)260 + (0.84)120 = 402.4$$

An extra £1 available at $t = 0$ would increase value at $t = 2$ by £1.16 over and above the autonomous increase of £1.21. The gross change in value at $t = 2$ is then £(1.16 + 1.21) = £2.37. Likewise, an extra £1 available at $t = 1$ would increase value at $t = 2$ by £0.84 over and above the autonomous increase of £1.1. The total change in this case is therefore £1.94.

It is these gross figures that enable maximum borrowing rates of interest to be calculated when the repayment date is $t = 2$. Clearly for £1 borrowed from an outside source at $t = 0$ the investor would be prepared to pay anything up to a maximum of £2.37 at $t = 2$. This means that the interest, annually compounded, charged on the loan could be up to 54%. If borrowing occurred at $t = 1$ with repayment at $t = 2$ the maximum borrowing rate would be 94%.

What if repayment of the loan had to be made prior to $t = 2$? The dual values enable us to rapidly evaluate such schemes in the following manner. If there is £1 borrowed at $t = 0$ and £D_2 repaid at $t = 2$ then the change in F, ΔF, is given by:

$$\Delta F = (1.16\ 0.84)\begin{pmatrix} +1 \\ 0 \end{pmatrix} + (1.21\ 1.1)\begin{pmatrix} +1 \\ 0 \end{pmatrix} - D_2$$

in which case, as we have seen D can be up to 2.37. If on the other hand a sum of money D_1 was repaid at $t = 1$ the change in F would be given by

$$\Delta F = (1.16\ 0.84)\begin{pmatrix} +1 \\ -D_1 \end{pmatrix} + (1.21\ 1.1)\begin{pmatrix} +1 \\ -D_1 \end{pmatrix} = 2.37 - 1.94D_1$$

So, in order that $\Delta F > 0$ it is required that $D_1 < 2.37/1.94$ implying a maximum borrowing rate of interest between $t = 0$ and $t = 1$ of 22.2%. The dual values enable any borrowing and repayment stream to be rapidly assessed. For arbitrary D_0 D_1 and D_2 we require

$$\Delta F = (2.37\ 1.94)\begin{pmatrix} D_0 \\ D_1 \end{pmatrix} - D_2 \geqslant 0$$

ΔF may be thought of as the negative of the opportunity loss on one unit of a new variable x_0 with coefficients in the constraints of $-D_0$ and $-D_1$ respectively and a coefficient of $-D_2$ in the objective function. If ΔF in (5.4) is positive it means that the borrowing scheme is worthwhile and x_0 should be brought into the solution.[1] In other words the borrowing is worthwhile and should be undertaken. A numerical example of the evaluation of a borrowing scheme is given later. The foregoing form of presentation of the problem, though usable is not the most convenient vehicle for such an analysis. The problem will now be represented in a format which does not include the NTVs of individual projects, does include non-zero objective function coefficients of at least one slack variable and has more general applicability in that it can be used in cases where there is no preassigned interest rate.

The formulation which we shall refer to as formulation two, has the constraints as before but the form of objective function is $F = R_{21}x_1 + R_{22}x_2 + S_1(1 + j)$. The solution to the problem in tableau form is shown in Figure 5.6.

In this formulation the 'full' shadow price for funds in period zero is given.

			14	25	0	$-M$	1.1
			x_1	x_2	S_0	u_0	S_1
$-M$	u_0	260	10	4	1	1	0
1.1	S_1	120	-5	8	-1.1	0	1
		$132 - 260M$	$-10M - 19.5$	$-4M - 16.2$	$-M - 1.21$	0	0
14	x_1	26	1	0.4	0.1	0.1	0
1.1	S_1	250	0	10	-0.6	0.5	1
		639	0	-8.4	0.74	$1.95 + M$	0
14	x_1	16	1	0	0.124	0.08	-0.04
25	x_2	25	0	1	-0.06	0.05	0.1
		849	0	0	0.236	$2.37 + M$	0.84

Figure 5.6 Simplex solution: formulation two

However since S_1 has an objective function coefficient of 1.1 this has to be added to the S_1 index row number, 0.84, to give the marginal value for funds at $t = 1$. In this formulation, if an artificial variable u_1 was added into constraint one its index row number would give the full marginal valuation at $t = 1$. This would not be the case with formulation one.

In formulation two the NTVs of the projects are not shown individually although it is terminal value that it is the objective to maximize. As will be seen in an example below there is no unambiguous value that can be put on terminal value or present value of a project in isolation when there are multiperiod constraints. The contribution of a given stream of costs and returns to terminal value depends upon the streams of return on other projects and the capital constraints. The contribution of an individual project to terminal value will change if it is adjoined to either a different set of other possible projects or a different set of constraints. This is an absolutely fundamental point in asset valuation. An asset *cannot* be valued in isolation from other assets to which it can be ajoined. An asset cannot be valued in isolation from the constraints which apply to its use.[2]

Let us now consider the borrowing possibility example mentioned earlier. Suppose the investor must repay £0.35 at $t = 2$ and £1 at $t = 1$ for each £1 borrowed at $t = 0$. No limit is set on the amount borrowed other than by the desire to borrow and the ability to repay. The borrowing scheme may be viewed as an additional investment project and adjoined to the constraint set and objective function of the problem. The problem becomes:

$$\text{maximize } F = 14x_1 + 25x_2 - 0.35x_3 + 1.15_1 - Mu_0$$

$$\text{subject to} \quad 10x_1 + 4x_2 - x_3 + S_0 = 260$$

$$-5x_1 + 8x_2 + x_3 - 1.1S_0 + S_1 = 120$$

$$x_1, x_2, S_0, S_1 \geqslant 0$$

For computation we start with the existing optimal tableau and add an extra column having determined the rates of exchange in the usual way. The new optimum is shown in Figure 5.7.

Extensive borrowing at $t = 0$ is indicated and only x_1 is invested in. If there had been an upper bound on borrowing of less than 500 then x_2 would have remained

			14	25	−0.35	0	−M	1.1
			x_1	x_2	x_3	S_0	u_0	S_1
14	x_1	16	1	0	−0.12	0.124	0.08	−0.04
25	x_2	25	0	1	0.05	−0.06	0.05	0.1
		849	0	0	−0.08	0.236	2.37 + M	0.84
14	x_1	76	1	2.4	0	−0.02	0.2	0.2
−0.35	x_3	500	0	20	1	−1.2	1	2
		889	0	1.6	0	0.14	2.45 + M	1

Figure 5.7 Borrowing possibility: simplex solution

in the solution at a reduced level.[3] The marginal valuations of funds are 2.45 at $t = 0$ and 2.1 (= 1 + 1.1) at $t = 1$. It should be noted that x_3 has been introduced into the solution despite having a negative NTV. (NTV = −0.24, NPV = −0.198.) Furthermore it has been introduced in preference to a project with NTV = 11.36. The reason is that x_3 provides funds at the right time. Its value in conjunction with x_1 is much greater than its value alone. NTV calculated with the discount rate of 10% does not measure the ability of the project to contribute to value at $t = 2$.

Whilst there is no *true* NTV for x_3, the index row number in the previous optimum shows the terminal value per unit of x_3 in conjunction with the asset set $A = (x_1, x_2)$ as 0.08. The solution also provides discount factors (or 'appreciation factors' in an NTV context) which allow this figure to be arrived at. These factors are of course the shadow prices. The opportunity loss on x_3 in the original optimum is t_3 where:

$$(2.37) \times 1 - (1.94) \times 1 - t_3 = -0.35$$

therefore $t_3 = -0.08$. This is the third constraint of the dual problem. Consequently the appropriate weights to attach to the stream of costs and income associated with x_3 are the marginal values of money given by the optimal solution. These marginal values can be broken down into implied interest rates from period to period. The equations to solve are:

$$(1 + i_0)(1 + i_1) = 2.37$$

$$(1 + i_1) = 1.94$$

where $100i_0\%$ is the implied interest rate prevailing from $t = 0$ to $t = 1$ and $100i_1\%$ prevails from $t = 1$ until $t = 2$. The rates are 22.16% and 94% respectively. NTV of x_3 with asset set A is then

$$[1(1 + i_0) - 1]\,(1 + i_1) - 0.35 = 0.08$$

In a similar fashion present value with asset set A is:

$$\frac{-0.35}{(1 + i_0)(1 + i_1)} \quad \frac{-1}{(1 + i_1)} + 1 = 0.0337$$

Once again is should be recalled that these figures for 'terminal value' and 'present value' are not NTV and NPV in the usual senses. The values for TV and PV for x_1 and x_2 obtained by using the dual discount factors illustrate this – they are both zero! This is a necessary and sufficient condition for a variable to be included in a basis. In other words only invest in those projects with zero present value! This is clearly *not* a view of present value that would be acceptable to the layman, but discounting by shadow prices will give optimal accept/reject decisions for additional projects since the shadow prices are the true opportunity costs of capital.

The point is a convenient juncture to dismiss a red herring that crops up in the capital budgeting literature from time to time. It is this. If the objective is to maximize present value and the correct discount factors to apply to determine present value come from the dual solution, then the primal objective function cannot be determined until the dual problem is solved. But of course the dual cannot be solved until both problems have been formulated![4] As we have seen this apparently unresolvable (in a linear framework) dilemma is a non-problem. Once the horizon has been set, and with the objective of maximizing value at the horizon given, the objective function consists of the horizon year returns from all projects (including 'slack projects'). The problem is solved with this function and optimal discount rates emerge. Further projects can then be assessed using these discount rates. Acceptable projects have zero or positive NPV at these rates. New maximum NPV will be zero using the new opportunity cost discount rates emerging from the optimal solution. Projects can only have positive NPVs when discounted with suboptimal opportunity cost discount factors. The propriety of present or terminal value formulations is discussed further in section 5.6.

Having considered the evaluation of a 'borrowing project', x_3, let us now consider the problem of borrowing from outside sources at predetermined interest rates. As has been seen, if a uniform interest rate applies to both borrowing and lending then only one project will be undertaken unless there are additional constraints. This will not necessarily be the case if borrowing and investment rates of interest differ. Let investment be possible at $100j\%$ and let $J = (1 + j)$. Borrowing is possible at $100i\%$ and $I = (1 + i)$. It is assumed that repayment is at will rather than at a specified date. Let S_t represent surplus cash at period t and $\bar{S}_t$ represent the level of borrowing at period t. New borrowing at t is $\bar{S}_t - \bar{S}_{t-1}$. In our current two constraint two investment context the constraints are:

$$(K_{01} - R_{01})x_1 + (K_{02} - R_{02})x_2 + \hat{S}_0 - \bar{S}_0 = b_0$$

$$(K_{11} - R_{11})x_1 + (K_{12} - R_{12})x_2 - J\hat{S}_0 + I\bar{S}_0 + \hat{S}_1 - \bar{S}_1 = b_1$$

where we are assuming that $R_{01} = R_{02} = 0$. In a larger problem with n investment opportunities the constraint for the tth period would be:

$$\sum_{h=1}^{n} (K_{th} - R_{th})x_h + J\hat{S}_{t-1} - I\bar{S}_{t-1} + \hat{S}_t - \bar{S}_t = b_t$$

In the two constraint example the objective function will be:

$$\text{maximize } F = R_{21}x_1 + R_{22}x_2 + J\hat{S}_1 - I\bar{S}_1$$

In a problem with horizon at $t = m$ the objective function would be

$$\text{maximize } F = \sum_{h=1}^{n} (R_{mh} - K_{mh})x_h + J\hat{S}_{m-1} - I\bar{S}_{m-1}$$

In such a problem, if there were constraints until only the $(M - p)$th period where $p \geqslant 2$ then 'part way' values of the objective function would have to be defined. For instance if $m = 6$ and $p = 2$ we should define

$$F_5 = \sum_{h=1}^{n} (R_{5h} - K_{5h})x_h + J\hat{S}_4 - I\bar{S}_4$$

and constrain

$$F_5 - \hat{S}_5 + \bar{S}_5 = 0$$

			14	25	0	0	1.1	−1.3	$-M$	$-M$	0	0
			x_1	x_2	$\hat{S}_0$	$\bar{S}_0$	$\hat{S}_1$	$\bar{S}_1$	u_0	u_1	S_0^*	S_1^*
$-M$	u_0	260	⑩	4	1	−1	0	0	1	0	0	0
$-M$	u_1	120	−5	8	−1.1	1.3	1	−1	0	1	0	0
0	S_0^*	100	0	0	0	1	0	0	0	0	1	0
0	S_1^*	100	0	0	0	0	0	1	0	0	C	1
		$(-380M)$	$(-5M-14)$	$(-12M-25)$	$(0.1M)$	$(-0.3M)$	$(-M-1.1)$	$(M+1.3)$	0	0	0	0
14	x_1	26	1	0.4	0.1	−0.1	0	0	0.1	0	0	0
$-M$	u_1	250	0	10	−0.6	0.8	1	−1	0.5	1	0	0
0	S_0^*	100	0	0	0	①	0	0	0	0	1	0
0	S_1^*	100	0	0	0	0	0	1	0	0	0	1
		$(364-250M)$	0	$(-19.4-10M)$	$(1.4+0.6M)$	$(-1.4-0.8M)$	$(-M-1.1)$	$(M+1.3)$	$(1.4+0.5M)$	0	0	0
14	x_1	36	1	0.4	0.1	0	0	0	0.1	0	0.1	0
$-M$	u_1	170	0	⑩	−0.6	0	1	−1	0.5	1	−0.8	0
0	$\bar{S}_0$	100	0	0	0	1	0	0	0	0	1	0
0	S_1^*	100	0	0	0	0	0	1	0	0	0	1
		$504-170M$	0	$(-19.4-10M)$	$(1.4+0.6M)$	0	$-1.1-M$	$M+13$	$(1.4+0.5M)$	0	$(1.4+0.8M)$	0

14	x_1	29.2	1	0	0.124	0	−0.04	0.04	0.08	−0.04	0.132	0
25	x_2	17	0	1	−0.06	0	0.1	−0.1	0.05	0.1	−0.08	0
0	$\bar{S}_0$	100	0	0	0	1	0	0	0	0	1	0
0	S_1^*	100	0	0	0	0	0	(1)	0	0	0	1
		833.8	0	0	0.236	0	0.84	−0.64	$2.37 + M$	$1.94 + M$	−0.152	0
14	x_1	25.2	1	0	0.124	0	−0.04	0	0.08	−0.04	0.132	−0.04
25	x_2	27	0	1	−0.06	0	0.1	0	0.05	0.1	−0.08	0.1
0	$\bar{S}_0$	100	0	0	0	1	0	0	0	0	(1)	0
−1.3	$\bar{S}_1$	100	0	0	0	0	0	1	0	0	0	1
		897.8	0	0	0.236	0	0.84	0	$2.37 + M$	$1.94 + M$	−0.152	0.64
14	x_1	12	1	0	0.124	−0.132	−0.04	0	0.08	−0.04	0	−0.04
25	x_2	35	0	1	−0.06	0.08	0.1	0	0.05	0.1	0	0.1
0	S_0^*	100	0	0	0	1	0	0	0	0	1	0
−1.3	S_1	100	0	0	0	0	0	1	0	0	0	1
		913	0	0	0.236	0.152	0.84	0	$2.37 + M$	$1.94 + M$	0	0.64

Figure 5.8 Different interest rates: example solution

which would be added to the list of constraints. This has to be done since *a priori* it is not known at what rate of interest to carry forward the sum F_5 into period six. If F_5 is positive, is should go forward at $100j\%$; if negative, the company is in debt and must pay interest at $100i\%$. $\hat{S}_5$ and $\bar{S}_5$ cannot both be positive *at an optimum* and optimality (and feasiblity) considerations will select the values of the variables in the course of solution of the problem. In the context of the numerical example let $i = 0.3$ and suppose that the maximum debt allowable at any time is 100. The problem is to:

$$\text{maximize } F = 14x_1 + 25x_2 + 1.1\hat{S}_1 - 1.3\bar{S}_1 - Mu_0 - Mu_1$$

$$\text{subject to} \quad 10x_1 + 4x_2 + \hat{S}_0 - \bar{S}_0 + u_0 = 260$$

$$-5x_1 + 8x_2 - 1.1\hat{S}_0 + 1.3\bar{S}_0 + \hat{S}_1 - \bar{S}_1 + u_1 = 120$$

$$\bar{S}_0 + S_0^* = 100$$

$$\bar{S}_1 + S_1^* = 100$$

$$x_1, x_2, \hat{S}_0, \bar{S}_0, \hat{S}_1, \bar{S}_1, u_0, u_1, S_0^*, S_1^* \geqslant 0$$

The slack variables in the upper bound restrictions have been distinguished by *. A second artificial variable, u_1, has been added in so that index row numbers can be used as they stand. All variables are to be non-negative. The solution to the problem is given in Figure 5.8. Pivotal elements are circled.

The borrowing opportunity raises F to 913; x_2 being raised to 35 and x_1 lowered to 12 in contrast to the 'x_3' borrowing scheme with compulsory part repayment at $t = 1$ in which x_1 (the $t = 1$ money generator) was raised to 76. Note that the marginal valuations of extra internal capital (2.37 and 1.94) are unchanged. Why then is it not worth setting $\bar{S}_0 = 1$ and having to repay only £1.69 at $t = 2$ when the extra £1 at $t = 0$ should increase TV by £2.37? The correct evaluation of $\bar{S}_0 = 1$ is shown to be -0.152, i.e. F would decrease by 0.152. This can be deduced from the marginal valuations of capital in the following way. An extra £1 at $t = 0$ would increase F by £2.37 but the L.H.S. of the constraint at $t = 1$ would have to be reduced by 1.3 because of the limit on $\bar{S}_1$ and on this account F would decline by $(1.3).(1.94) = 2.522$ making a net decrease of $2.522 - 2.37 = 0.152$. The figure 2.37 then shows how F would increase if £1 more of *internal* funds was available at $t = 0$.

A point of some computational interest emerges from Figure 5.8. The variable S_0^* that was in the original b.f.s. and dropped out in the second iteration returned in the fifth iteration which gave the optimal solution. A variable which drops out of a basis cannot be forgotten about – it may reappear at a later stage.

The problem is graphed in Figure 5.9. The original optimum with no borrowing or investment is D with optimal objective function line 00 indicated. The borrowing of 100 from outside sources moves constraint two upwards to A$'$G$'$ but leaves the original constraint unaltered at CE and the new optimum is at D$'$. The objective function through the point D$'$ can be thought of as having the same slope as through D but with 130 [= (100)1.3] deducted from its value or it can be envisaged as having different slope with no deduction but an addition. The latter formulation is

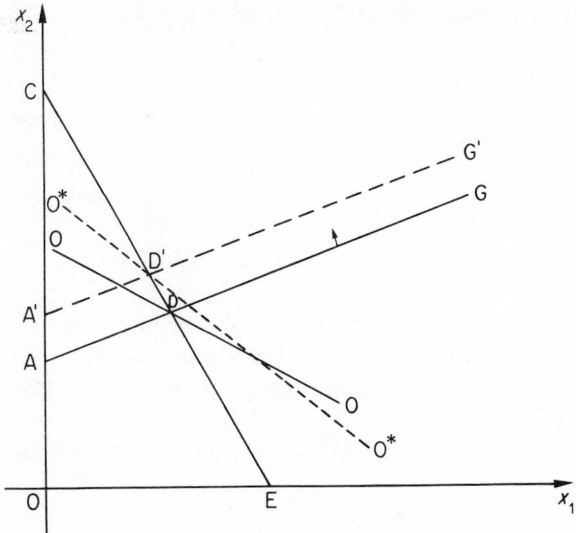

Figure 5.9 Diagram of borrowing/investment example

arrived at by writing F as

$$F' = 14x_1 + 25x_2 - 1.3(8x_2 - 5x_1 - 120) = 20.5x \;\; + 14.6x_2 + 156$$

since $8x_2 - 5x_1 - 120 = \bar{S}_1$ provided that all other Ss are zero. This is the form used for objective function line 0*0* and the constraints show that borrowing will always be up to the limit as this is raised. Point D′ remains optimal and moves up constraint CE towards C as the limit on $\bar{S}_1$ is raised. It should be recalled that, because of the non zero ofcs of slack variables and the autonomous components thus produced, the relative slope condition is no longer sufficient to prove optimality of D′. The autonomous components have to be considered too.

5.3 Further Numerical Examples

Return for the moment to a 'no-borrowing' situation. Let $b_0 = 100$, $b_1 = 80$, $K_{01} = 10$, $K_{11} = 20$, $K_{02} = 5$, $K_{12} = 5$, $R_{11} = 15$, $R_{21} = 25$, $R_{12} = 10$, $R_{22} = 10$ and $j = 0.2$. Substituting these figures into (5.3) gives the objective function for formulation one as:

$$\begin{aligned} F = {} & [25 + (15 - 20)(1.2) - 10(1.2)^2]x_1 \\ & + [10 + (10 - 5)(1.2) - 5(1.2)^2]x_2 \\ & + 100(1.2)^2 + 80(1.2) \end{aligned}$$

which gives

$$F = 4.6x_1 + 8.8x_2 + 240$$

The first of the constraints (the intitial constraint) is then $10x_1 + 5x_2 + S_0 = 100$

and the constraint after one year is $(20-15)x_1 + (5-10)x_2 - 1.2S_0 \leqslant 80$, so the problem can be written as:

$$\begin{aligned} \text{minimize} \quad & F = 4.6x_1 + 8.8x_2 + 240 \\ \text{subject to} \quad & 10x_1 + 5x_2 + S_0 = 100 \\ & 5x_1 - 5x_2 - 1.2S_0 \leqslant 80 \end{aligned}$$

and the sign requirements

$$x_1, x_2, S_0 \geqslant 0$$

The optimal solution to this problem is shown in the two formulations in Figures 5.10 (a) and 5.10 (b). The optimum is where $x_2 = 20$ and x_1 and $S_0 = 0$. That is, the investor should take twenty units of project two, ignore project one and fully use the initial budget of 100.

The maximal value of 176 for the objective function thus obtained in

			4.6	8.8	0	$-M$	0
			x_1	x_2	S_0	u_0	S_1
$-M$	u_0	100	(10)	5	1	1	0
0	S_1	80	5	-5	-1.2	0	1
4.6	x_1	10	1	(0.5)	0.1	0.1	0
0	S_1	30	0	-7.5	-1.7	-0.5	1
		46	0	-6.5	+0.46	-0.46	0
8.8	x_2	20	2	1	0.2	0.2	0
0	S_1	180	15	0	-0.2	1	1
		176	13	0	1.76	$1.76 + M$	0

(a)

			25x	10	0	1.2	$-M$	$-M$
			x_1	x_2	S_0	S_1	u_0	u_1
$-M$	u_0	100	(10)	5	1	0	1	0
$-M$	u_1	80	5	-5	-1.2	1	0	1
25	x_1	10	1	(½)	0.1	0	0.1	0
1.2	S_1	30	0	$-15/2$	-1.7	1	$-½$	1
		286	0	-6.5	+0.46	0	$1.9 + M$	$M + 1.2$
10	x_2	20	2	1	0.2	0	0.2	0
1.2	S_1	180	15	0	-0.2	1	1	1
		416	13	0	1.76	0	$3.2 + M$	$1.2 + M$

(b)

Figure 5.10 Simplex solutions to further example

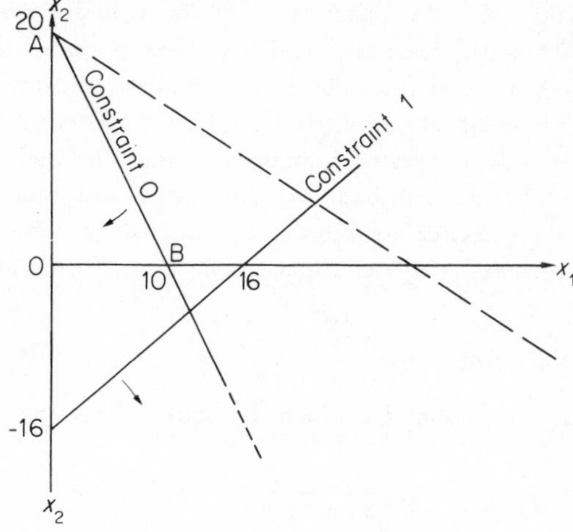

Figure 5.11 Graph of further example

formulation one is the gain in terminal value over and above that which would have been achieved if all the funds b_0 and b_1 had been invested in securities at 20%. Hence in total, TV after two years is

$$176 + 100(1.2)^2 + 80(1.2) = 416$$

The problem is graphed in Figure 5.11, with S_0 set at zero. The 'feasible area' is the triangle OAB, and the optimal position of the objective function is shown by the broken line. If S_0 was made positive – that is, if all the initial budget of 100 were not used – the constraints would move in the directions indicated by the arrows and clearly the optimal value of the objective function would be reduced.

The 'dual' to this problem in the form of formulation one can be written as:

$$\begin{aligned} \text{minimize} \quad & 100y_0 + 80y_1 \\ \text{subject to} \quad & 10y_0 + 5y_1 \geqslant 4.6 \\ & 5y_0 - 5y_1 \geqslant 8.8 \\ & y_0 - 1.2y_1 \geqslant 0 \end{aligned}$$

and

$$y_0, y_1 \geqslant 0$$

The dual objective function is minimized for

$$y_1 = 0, y_0 = 8.8/5 = 1.76$$

These values, 1.76 and 0, are the amounts by which TV would increase if one more unit of money were available in periods zero or one respectively over and above the sums 1.44 and 1.2 that TV would increase by anyway if the extra units were invested in securities at 20%. So, for instance, if the investor had had 101 at period zero instead of 100, the TV after two years would have been up by 3.2(= 1.76 + 1.44). Thus the investor would have been prepared to pay up to 3.2 after two years to obtain one extra unit for immmediate investment – an implied maximum borrowing interest rate of nearly 79%. Now consider some changes in the financial arrangements of the investor. Suppose that there are no internal funds and that the sums 100 and 30 represent bank overdraft limits with repayment of debt at will. For arithemtic convenience assume that the interest rate charged by the bank on loans is 30%. Surplus cash may be invested at 20% as before. The first constraint is:

$$10x_1 + 5x_2 + S_0 = 100$$

where S_0 represents the amount by which the bank is below its borrowing limit. The second constraint is:

$$5x_1 - 5x_2 + 1.3(100 - S_0) + \bar{S}_1 + \hat{S}_1 = 80$$

where $\bar{S}_1$ represents the amount by which the firm is below its overdraft limit. This variable is limited to 80. The other slack variable $\hat{S}_1$ is any positive surplus of cash that the firm has. After rearrangement the second constraint becomes:

$$-5x_1 + 5x_2 + 1.3S_0 - \bar{S}_1 - \hat{S}_1 = 50$$

and the upper bound on S_1 is written as:

$$\bar{S}_1 + S_1^* = 80$$

Now in the objective function, at $t = 2$ the firm will have $25x_1 + 10x_2$ in income from the investments minus its liabilities to the bank which amount to $1.3(80 - \bar{S}_1)$ plus any income from investment of surplus cash $1.2\ \hat{S}_1$. Clearly, $\hat{S}_1$ can only appear at positive level in the optimal solution provided that $\bar{S}_1 = 80$, that is $S_1^* \cdot \hat{S}_1 = 0$. The objective function is then:

$$F = 25x_1 + 10x_2 + 1.3\bar{S}_1 + 1.2\hat{S}_1 - 104$$

The problem, including artificial variables for the first two constraints is solved in Figure 5.12.

The overdraft ceiling is reached in period zero but not in period one. Again the only investment undertaken is x_2. Terminal value is 265 and the opportunity cost at $t = 2$ of taking one unit of investment one is 14.5. The value of *internal* capital at $t = 0$ is 3.3. The value of a one-unit extension in the overdraft limit is 1.61 (= 3.3 – 1.69). The component –1.3 in the index row number of U_1 results from the negative rate of exchange with $\bar{S}_1$. If U_1 was +1 then $\bar{S}_1$ would have to increase by one. Setting U_1 at unity is equivalent to raising the overdraft limit to 81. Consequently the investor would be 51 below the overdraft limit. There is no *net* saving of course for although $\bar{S}_1$ has an ofc of 1.3 the autonomous term in F increases to 105.3. Consequently there is no value in raising the overdraft limit in period one.

If instead of being overdraft limits the figures 80 and 100 represent borrowing limits for a firm from group funds with repayment at $t = 2$ (but not before) of what

			25	10	0	1.3	1.2	$-M$	$-M$	0
			x_1	x_2	S_0	$\bar{S}_1$	$\hat{S}_1$	u_0	u_1	S_1^*
$-M$	u_1	100	10	⑤	1	0	0	1	0	0
$-M$	u_1	50	-5	5	1.3	-1	-1	0	0	0
0	S_1^*	80	0	0	0	1	0	0	0	1
		$-150M$	$(-5M - 25)$	$(-10M - 10)$	$-2.3M$	$M - 1.3$	$M - 1.2$	0	0	0
$-M$	u_0	50	15	0	-0.3	①	1	1	-1	0
10	x_2	10	-1	1	0.26	-0.2	-0.2	0	0.2	0
0	S_1^*	80	0	0	0	1	0	0	0	1
		$(-50M + 100)$	$(-15M - 35)$	0	$0.3M + 2.6$	$-M - 3.3$	$-M - 3.2$	0	$2M + 2$	0
1.3	$\bar{S}_1$	50	15	0	-0.3	1	1	1	-1	0
10	x_2	20	2	1	0.2	0	0	0.2	0	0
0	S_1^*	30	-15	0	0.3	0	-1	-1	1	1
		265	14.5	0	1.61	0	0.1	$M + 3.3$	$M - 1.3$	0

Figure 5.12 Simplex solution: changed financial arrangements

is borrowed, and no addition is made to borrowing at $t = 1$ if less than 100 is borrowed at $t = 0$, the objective function would be

$$F = 25x_1 + 10x_2 - 1.69(100 - S_0) - 1.3(80 - \bar{S}_1) + 1.2\hat{S}_1$$
$$= 25x_1 + 10x_2 + 1.69S_0 + 1.3\bar{S}_1 + 1.2\hat{S}_1 - 273$$

and the constraints are:

$$10x_1 + 5x_2 + S_0 = 100$$
$$5x_1 - 5x_2 + \bar{S}_1 + \hat{S}_1 = 80$$
$$\bar{S}_1 + S_1^* = 80$$

The reader is invited to determine the solution to this problem.

5.4 The Time Horizon

In both of the basic problems used as examples in this section the time horizon of the investor had been set at two years. The approach to the solution of the problem would have been unchanged if some other predetermined horizon had been chosen. The problems of choice of horizon are manifold and are discussed shortly but as a preface to the discussion consider the consequences of an alternative horizon date being set for one of the problems already examined.

Suppose that in the second of the problems the horizon had been set at $t = 3$ and that it was the objective of the investor to maximize 'wealth' (defined as terminal value) at this point. Assume also that outside investment at 20% is possible but that borrowing is prohibited. Furthermore assume that it would have been possible to start further units of investment two at $t = 1$. The problem can be stated as

$$\begin{aligned} \text{maximize} \quad & F_3 = 10x_3 + 1.2S_2 \\ \text{subject to} \quad & 10x_1 + 5x_2 + S_0 = 100 \\ & 5x_1 - 5x_2 + 5x_3 - 1.2S_0 + S_1 = 80 \\ & -25x_1 - 10x_2 - 5x_3 - 1.2S_1 + S_2 = 0 \\ & x_1, x_2, x_3, S_0, S_1, S_2 \geqslant 0 \end{aligned}$$

The objective function appears rather sparse and has no terms in x_1 and x_2 directly in this form.[5] The contribution of x_1 and x_2 to value at $t = 3$ is reflected in the size of S_2, the surplus at $t = 2$. The variable x_3 represents further units of investment two undertaken from $t = 1$. The third 'constraint' simply defines S_2. The problem is solved by the simplex method in Figure 5.13. Artificial variables have been included but $-M$ ofcs have been omitted for convenience of presentation. From the solution it is seen that only investments of type two are undertaken, more being begun at $t = 1$ and a surplus of 380 is obtained at $t = 2$. Note that the marginal valuations of funds in $t = 0$ and $t = 1$ are greater by more than the factor 1.2 over their values in the $t = 2$ horizon case. This is because the rate of return that can be achieved on additional capital in these periods is in excess of the external rate of 20%.

So, once the horizon date has been set the problems are solvable by the usual

			0	0	0	0	10	1.2	0	0	0
			x_1	x_2	S_0	S_1	x_3	S_2	u_0	u_1	u_2
0	u_0	100	10	5	1	0	0	0	1	0	0
0	u_1	80	5	−5	−1.2	1	(5)	0	0	1	0
0	u_2	0	−25	−10	0	−1.2	−5	1	0	0	1
		0	0	0	0	0	−10	−1.2	0	0	0
0	u_0	100	10	5	(1)	1	0	0	1	0	0
10	x_3	16	1	−1	−0.24	+0.2	1	0	0	0.2	0
0	u_2	80	−20	−15	−1.2	−0.2	0	1	0	+1	1
		160	+10	−10	−2.4	+2	0	−1.2	0	+2	0
0	S_0	100	10	5	1	0	0	0	1	0	0
10	x_3	40	3.4	0.2	0	+0.2	1	0	0.24	0.2	0
0	u_2	200	−8	−7	0	−0.2	0	(1)	1.2	+1	1
		400	34	2	0	+2	0	−1.2	2.4	2	0
0	S_0	100	10	(5)	1	0	0	0	1	0	0
10	x_3	40	3.4	0.2	0	0.2	1	0	0.24	0.2	0
1.2	S_2	200	−8	−9	0	−0.2	0	1	1.2	+1	1
		640	24.4	−8.8	0	1.76	0	0	3.84	3.2	1.2
0	x_2	20	2	1	0.2	0	0	0	0.2	0	0
10	x_3	36	3	0	−0.04	0.2	1	0	0.2	0.2	0
1.2	S_2	380	10	0	1.8	−0.2	0	1	3	1	1
		816	42	0	1.76	1.76	0	0	5.6	3.2	1.2

Figure 5.13 Simplex solution: extended horizon

methods – but what criteria govern the choice of 'correct' date and how can post horizon phenomena be taken into account? The choice of horizon date (defined here as the last period for which the value of the objective function is explicitly considered and beyond which constraints are not explicitly formulated) is only problematical when investment projects are interdependent or the capital market is 'imperfect'. This means that we have a problem in all realistic cases. In neoclassical investment theory unlimited funds can be borrowed at a given interest rate and investment projects are not jointly constrained. Choice of horizon date is inconsequential in such cases.[6] If there are differential borrowing and investment rates or limits on borrowing then post-horizon returns cannot be considered independently of pre-horizon decisions. For instance, if the post-horizon returns are required to repay borrowing then the 'present' value of the returns at the horizon will differ from that when the returns are invested at some different interest rate.

We can distinguish between fixed horizons and rolling horizons. The latter refer to cases where new decisions are made (in the light of additional information) each period and the horizon rolls back to remain a pre-set distance from the current decision period. What is desirable here is that at $t = 0$ an optimal decision is made with respect to all possible futures. If there is complete probabilistic information about the future then ex-ante optimal decisions can be taken. Having decided upon this type of horizon then a decision is still to be made on the distance of the horizon from the present. A distinction can also be made between finite and infinite horizons. With infinite horizons it must be that after some value of t, say $\hat{t}$, all project returns are of the annuity form, otherwise an infinite quantity of information would be required. Having a finite horizon does not mean that no provision is made for the future beyond the horizon. Terminal value at the horizon is available for investment to generate future incomes and there may be post-horizon returns from some of the then ex-ante investments themselves.

The appropriate choice of horizon depends upon the 'utility function' of the investor – the formal representation of how the investor will benefit from the assets acquired. The choice will be subject to constraints imposed by data availability and computing capacity. In general we cannot say over what period an investor's utility function 'should' be defined. Some of us are myopic whilst others place great stock upon the future well-being of our grandchildren (or grand-brain-children). In general terms the investor has the objective of maximizing

$$U = U(E_0, E_1, \ldots, E_R, E_{R+1}, \ldots, E_\infty) \tag{5.5}$$

where (5.5) represents utility (sense of well-being) as a function of expenditure levels E_t. For a company these expenditure levels would be dividend payments. An ultra-myopic type would have the coefficients of E_t for $t > 0$ set at zero. At the other extreme Mr. Longsight, try as he might, cannot maximize a function of an infinite number of variables. Consequently he encapsulates the future beyond some period $t = n$ by the magnitude of a variable at n. We may think of this as wealth at $t = n, w_n$. The modified form of utility function is then

$$U' = U'(E_0, E_1 \ldots, E_n\ w_n). \tag{5.6}$$

There will be at least one constraint linking expenditures in the various periods. If there are such constraints they may be characterized by:

$$g_i(E_0, \ldots, E_n, w_n) \leqslant b_i \tag{5.7}$$

Where the functions of g_i are related to the revenues and costs that are associated with the investments which generate funds for expenditure. If there is a decision-making cost, C then this will certainly be an increasing function of n. That is $C = f(n)$ where $f'(n) > 0$. This cost would then have to be included in some of the constraints (5.7). Under certain conditions an *a priori* upper bound may be placed on the possible optimal value of n, say n^*. The investor would then have to solve at most $n^* + 1$ programming problems with U' and the g_i formulated for the horizon at n where $0 \leqslant n \leqslant n^*$. A sufficient condition for an upper bound on n at n^* is where the increase in decision-making cost (in present or terminal value terms) due to setting the horizon beyond n^* exceeded the increments in total net revenues from investments beyond n^*. That is $C_{t+1} - C_t > R_{t+1} - R_t + K_t - K_{t+1}$ for all $t > n^*$. It is being assumed there that any decrease in revenues automatically implies a decrease in the maximal value of U'. The cost of solving the $n^* + 1$ problems would be included in $f(n)$. The problem could be further complicated by decisions as to how many of the $n^* + 1$ problems it was worth solving. It is not the purpose here to detail a particular procedure for determining the optimal horizon; but simply to say that in principle an optimal value of the horizon can be found in some (we would suggest a representative selection of) problems. Any such procedure is likely to be overly sophisticated in practical terms even if it could be made operational. In practice if a 'natural' horizon does not suggest itself then the choice may be between two or three fairly widely spaced values ('short', 'medium' and 'long') with the final decision perhaps based on subjective reference to utility. Whilst on the subject it is noteworthy that a terminal value form of objective function is appropriate for a wide range of utility functions of the form (5.6) when unrestricted inter-period transfers of income are possible at a uniform rate for each period.[7] That is to say, maximization of terminal value will maximize U'.

The choice of horizon date may turn out to be a non-problem; for instance in situations where the optimal choice of investments is insensitive to selection of horizon date or where external circumstances dictate a particular time. An instance of the latter group of non-problem situations would be where terminal date was set by legal factors, e.g. expiration of lease of premises, expiration of patent rights or changes in overseas trade arrangements. An extreme instance of the former would be where the optimal investment programme remained precisely the same whatever the horizon date. A more common example would be where there was only a 'slight' penalty in the objective function (say present value) when the horizon date was changed from H_1 to H_2 if the H_1 optimal group of investments were retained in the H_2 situation even though the composition of the H_1 group was quite different from that of the H_2 optimal group. A further possibility is that some other group of investments might be undertaken which give near-optional values of the objective function for both H_1 and H_2. The investor may specify precisely, *a priori*, his requirements in terms of the two horizon dates by writing $F = \alpha_1 \mathrm{TV}_1 + \alpha_2 \mathrm{TV}_2$ as the objective function. The choice of values of α_1 and α_2 may reflect the investors' view of the probability of either horizon turning out to be the 'true' horizon (dictated by external factors) if this is not known *a priori*. In other cases α_1 and α_2 represent the relative importance to the investor of the value position at the two dates. For instance, a company has a liability that it may be called upon to meet in cash at either $t = 1$ or $t = 2$. Company policy dictates that as much as possible be repaid from internally generated funds in order that dependence on outside sources of capital be reduced. Management's view of possible and actual repayments is summarized in the expected *regret function*[8]

$$F = \alpha_1 (P_1^* - P_1) + \alpha_2 (P_2^* - P_2) \tag{5.8}$$

where P_1^* is maximum TV at $t = 1$ (representing the largest repayment that could be made at this time) and P_1 is actual TV at $t = 1$. Management feel that it is equally likely that the loan be recalled at $t = 1$ or $t = 2$. Accordingly it sets $\alpha_1 = \alpha_2 = 0.5$. Suppose that a one period capital constraint of £300,000 is faced and the net cash flows $(R_t - K_t)$ in each period for each of three projects are (in £000s)

A:	−60	162	30	
B:	−40	56	40	48
C:	−50	103	63	
Time	$t = 0$	$t = 1$	$t = 2$	$t = 3$

The constraint is: $60x_A + 40x_B + 50x_C \leqslant 300$. Now suppose that the £300,000 limit represents total retained earnings at $t = 0$ which could have earned 20% if invested elsewhere between $t = 0$ and $t = 1$ and 10% between $t = 1$ and $t = 2$. Earnings after $t = 1$ can be 'capitalized' at $t = 1$ (turned into a lump sum, say by sale to an outside factor) at 20% discount. The constraint was formulated easily enough but the objective function is a little more troublesome. The form of F in (5.8) is inconvenient in that it supposes knowledge of the maximal values at $t = 1$ and $t = 2$. Minimizing F is equivalent to maximizing $\hat{F} = -F$ where

$$\hat{F} = \alpha_1 P_1 + \alpha_2 P_2 - F^*$$

where F^* is the unknown constant $\alpha_1 P_1^* + \alpha_2 P_2^*$. Now

$$P_1 = 115x_A + 74.\overline{66}x_B + 95.5x_C$$

since, for example with respect to x_A

$$115 = [162 - 60(1.2)] + 30(1.2)^{-1}$$

with the coefficients of x_B and x_C determined in similar fashion. The term $\alpha_2 P_2$ is given by

$$0.5\,[129x_A + 88.8x_B + 110.3x_C]$$

where for instance

$$88.8 = (56 - 48)(1.1) + 40 + 48(1.2)^{-1}$$

Thus, weighting P_1 by 0.5 and summing gives the objective function as

$$\hat{F} = 122x_A + 81.7\overline{66}x_B + 102.9x_C - F^*$$

As was seen in Chapter 2, the solution to one constraint problems is found by selecting the variable with the greatest ratio of objective function coefficient to constraint coefficient. This is x_C with a ratio of 2.058 which gives the positive component of $\hat{F}$ as 617.4. The reader may verify that $F^* = 620.5$ so that expected regret is minimized at 3.1. Notice that x_C is selected despite the fact that x_A gives superior TV at $t = 1$ and x_B gives superior TV at $t = 2$.

This was an example where no single time horizon figure was set, but in the case of investment B returns continued to come in beyond the greater of the two values of t which formed the composite horizon. These returns (or return) were discounted, back to the $t = 2$ horizon to give a lump sum there. This is the 'normal' procedure for treatment of post-horizon returns insofar as these are known. The principal difficulty is in respect of the discount rate to be employed. Since this should reflect post-horizon conditions information relevant to this decision may be incomplete and as we have seen the rate of discount to apply to a stream of returns may depend upon other investment possibilities which are unknown. When it is impossible to determine precisely the post-horizon discount rate, an arbitrary choice will have to be made (or perhaps a weighted average of possible rates with the weights as subjective probabilities). The solution can then be found and analysed for its sensitivity to choice of post-horizon discount rate. The further is the horizon away then the lower will be the likelihood of the optimal choice of investments hinging upon post-horizon circumstances. As regards post-horizon constraints the approach adopted by Jaaskelainen[9] is recommended: 'We simply assume that the constraints relating to periods, 1, 2, . . . , n are stated explicitly and the constraints relating to the periods $n + 1$, $n + 2$, . . . are observed implicitly by the fact that a number of balance sheet items are required to obtain specified terminal values at n. In other words, the constraints for the periods $n + 1$, $n + 2$, are assumed to be built in in the form of target financial statements.

5.5 Investment Sequences

In this section we consider a rather special form of capital rationing problem. The case we have in mind is that of an investment which requires net inputs of capital in each of a number of years before positive returns start to come in. In a once only case the project would be assessed by NPV or NTV in the usual manner. Where repetition is possible, that is where several sequences of the same investment can be undertaken, commencing at different points in time and where initial capital is limited, the problem is somewhat more difficult. In the preceding section an illustration was given in which a second sequence of an investments costs and returns was possible starting from a later date. Whilst it is the case that such possibilities can be accommodated within the formulations given so far, in the case of only one investment possibility (available at varying levels) the special structure resulting can be exploited by a different computational approach.[10]

Consider in particular the case of a project that requires cash inputs in each of a number of years and gives a single postive return thereafter. Certain insurance policies are examples of this type of investment which can be thought of as the converse case of a one period outlay several return project. The problem will be to determine the points at which to start such investments and the scale of each so as to maximize terminal value at a specified date.

Consider the investment sequence -1, -2, 4, in other words, inputs required are £1 intially and £2 after one year yielding a return of £4 a further year thereafter. It is envisaged that several such sequences can be started; the number limited only by available funds of £4 initially. The objective is to maximize terminal value four years hence. Taking fractions of the project to be meaningful, it might be thought that the best policy would be as given by Figure 5.14 below.

Notationally it is convenient to refer to the intial year as one and the sequence started in that year as sequence one, so that 'year five' means 'at the beginning of the fifth year' – four years after sequence one was begun. The row labelled 'savings' shows funds available for investment in a year. The policy described by Figure 5.14 is to invest 4/3 in year one, 8/3 in year two, giving a return of 16/3 in year three,

Year	1	2	3	4	5
Savings	4	8/3	0	32/9	0
Sequence one	−4/3	−8/3	+16/3		
Sequence two			−16/9	−32/9	+64/9

Figure 5.14 Investment sequence example: naive solution

16/9 of which is used to start a second sequence which then results in savings of 32/9 in the fourth year, being just the amount required to complete the second sequence. The result is a terminal value of 64/9. This policy is not optimal. The optimum policy is that shown in Figure 5.15.

Three sequences should be completed (clearly there is no time for a fourth) as detailed and an improvement of 12½% in NTV over that of the naive pattern is achieved.

To ensure optimality it is only necessary that the sequences are such that there are no savings arising in any year after the first sequence has been completed. The problem is one of dynamic linear programming, but is uncharacteristic of such problems in that a relatively simple formula can be derived for its solution.

Let $\mathbf{Y}_t$ be the vector of the first inputs in the n sequences in the optimal programme beginning with the tth sequence. Then we can write

$$\mathbf{Y}_t = \frac{\mathbf{K}^{T-t}\,\mathbf{e}_r}{\mathbf{kK}^{T-1}\,\mathbf{e}_1}$$

where t is the subscript of the first element of the vector. For example if $t = 4$

$$\mathbf{Y}_4 = \begin{bmatrix} Y_4 \\ Y_5 \\ \vdots \\ Y_{4+n-1} \end{bmatrix}$$

and, for the example above, if $t = 1$

$$\mathbf{Y}_1 = \begin{pmatrix} Y_1 \\ Y_2 \end{pmatrix} = \begin{pmatrix} 1 \\ 1 \end{pmatrix}$$

Year	1	2	3	4	5
Savings	4	3	0	0	0
Sequence one	−1	−2	+4		
Sequence two		−1	−2	+4	
Sequence three			−2	−4	8

Figure 5.15 Investment sequence example: optimal solution

T is the number of periods to the horizon after the first sequence has been completed. There are n successive inputs in a sequence, $k_1\ k_2, \ldots, k_n$ leading to a return of R. Initial funds available are L. In the example above therefore, $T = 3$, $n = 2$, $k_1 = 1$, $k_2 = 2$, $R = 4$, $L = 4$. In general the matrix **K** has n rows and n columns. The only non-zero elements are the first row consisting of the k_h/R (in reverse order) and the diagonal below the principal diagonal, which consists of ones. It is written as

$$\mathbf{K} = \begin{bmatrix} \frac{k_n}{R} & \frac{k_{n-1}}{R} & \cdots & \frac{k_1}{R} \\ 1 & 0 & \cdots & 0 \\ 0 & 1 & \cdots & 0 \\ \vdots & \vdots & & \vdots \\ 0 & 0 & & 1 \end{bmatrix}$$

$\mathbf{e}_r$ is an n element column vector, only the first element being non-zero and equal to Lk_1/R. It is therefore written as

$$\mathbf{e}_r = \begin{bmatrix} \frac{Lk_1}{R} \\ 0 \\ \vdots \\ 0 \end{bmatrix}$$

$\mathbf{e}_1$ is an n element column vector. The first element is unity and the remainder are zero. We write:

$$\mathbf{e}_1 = \begin{bmatrix} 1 \\ 0 \\ 0 \\ \vdots \\ 0 \\ 0 \end{bmatrix}$$

k is a row vector with n elements. The first element is

$$\sum_{h=1}^{n} k_h/R$$

the second is

$$\sum_{h=1}^{n-1} k_h/R$$

and so on. The ith term therefore is

$$\sum_{h=1}^{n-i} k_h/r$$

and we write the vector k as a whole as:

$$\mathbf{k} = \left(\sum_{h=1}^{n} k_h/R, \ \sum_{h-1}^{n-1} k_h/R, \ldots, \sum_{h-1}^{n-(n-2)} k_h/R, \ k_1/R \right)$$

so, in order to obtain the vector of first inputs beginning with the tth, the $(T-t)$th and the $(T-1)$th power of the matrix **K** are required. This can be computationally tedious for large values of T and n, but for the data above the solution is quite simple. For example

$$\mathbf{Y}_2 = \begin{pmatrix} Y_2 \\ Y_3 \end{pmatrix} \quad \frac{\begin{pmatrix} ½ & ¼ \\ 1 & 0 \end{pmatrix}\begin{pmatrix} 1 \\ 0 \end{pmatrix}}{(¾ \quad ¼)\begin{pmatrix} ½ & ¼ \\ 1 & 0 \end{pmatrix}^2\begin{pmatrix} 1 \\ 0 \end{pmatrix}} = \begin{pmatrix} 1 \\ 2 \end{pmatrix}$$

That is, the second sequence should be started with an input of 1 (shown as −1 in Figure 5.15) and the third sequence should be begun with an input of 2 (shown as −2 in Figure 5.15) with these initial inputs and the resulting second inputs, savings are at zero level at the beginning of years three and four. Initial capital is exhausted at the start of the second year and subsequent inputs to existing and new sequences are provided out of returns from completed sequences. An ideal matching of the inflows from old sequences and the outflows due to new ones has been struck; such is the stuff of the dreams of financial managers!

The subject of the matching of cash flow patterns from projects is returned to in the financial planning models of chapter 6. In these models additional realistic financial constraints are introduced as, for instance, in paractice it will not normally be the case that zero reserves or zero payouts prior to the horizon date are acceptable.

5.6 Discounting Methods and Imperfect Capital Markets

'Imperfections' in the capital market can take many forms. The presence of a spectrum of interest rates rather than a uniform interest rate for financial transactions in a given time period does not necessarily imply imperfection when risks are taken into account. However many interest rates can prevail even in the absence of risk when monopoly forces act in the market or where information is imperfect or imperfectly disseminated. Another type of 'imperfection' occurs when there are effective constraints on borrowing and lending activities. Both of these circumstances have important implications concerning the appropriateness of discounting formulations of investor objectives. Discussion of these important matters has been left to this point in order that the material covered so far can be freely drawn upon.

First consider the case of unequal borrowing and lending rates of interest. As we all know there is no more a uniform rate for either of these categories than there is an overall uniform rate, but the use of just two interest rates brings out the important differences between the uniform interest rate case and the spectrum of interest rates case.

Assume that the investor's objective is to maximize 'satisfaction' or 'utility' from cash sums received over a given horizon of n years. This objective can be stated as:

$$\text{maximize} \quad U = U(w_t) \quad t = 0,1,2, \ldots, n$$

where the w_t are withdrawals from the income stream to be used for consumption (or if the investor is a company, the payment of dividends). The numbers w_t cannot all be chosen arbitrarily or no problem would exist. There must be at least one constraint linking the w_t. Such a constraint would relate to the total of expenditures possible given the income stream of the investor. The income stream will be determined by the returns from investments already in existence at $t = 0$ and the returns from projects yet to be decided upon. In the two interest rates case where a choice is to be made between the mutually exclusive projects R and S the single constraint could take the form

$$\sum_{t=0}^{n} (R_t + I_t - w_t)(1 + i)^{\alpha_t}(1 + j)^{n-t-\alpha_t} \geqslant T \tag{5.10)a}$$

or, if project S is selected:

$$\sum_{t=0}^{n} (S_t + I_t - w_t)(1 + i)^{\beta_t}(1 + j)^{n-t-\beta_t} \geqslant T \tag{5.10)b}$$

where the R_t and S_t are the returns from the two projects (in conventional investments $R_0 < 0$ and $S_0 < 0$), the I_t form the income stream from existing investments, $100i\%$ and $100j\%$ are respectively the borrowing and investment rates of interest and T is some minimum balance (perhaps zero) to obtain at the horizon. In the case of acceptance of project R, α_t is the number of years including and beyond t in which the investor is a net borrower and $n - t - \alpha_t$ is the number of periods including and beyond t in which the investor is a net creditor. β_t is defined similarly with respect to project S. No useful generality is lost by the assumption that the borrowing and investment rates are constant through time.

The crucial point is this: the values of α_t and β_t depend not only upon R_t and I_t or S_t and I_t but also upon the w_t selected, so that the terminal value of a project cannot be expressed independently of the values of w_t selected. In other words we cannot (at an exact, theoretical level) evaluate a project or choose between projects without reference to the utility function (5.9). This is not to say that the techniques based on present or terminal values should not be used in practice — other methods would run into the same or even greater difficulties. Where a utility function can be formulated so much the better. Where this is not practicable we have lost the *guarantee* of correctness of discounting methods. On the whole, we would argue, the consequences of this loss should be slight but since these consequences cannot be evaluated this statement is no more than an opinion. At any rate we have to manage some way without the reassurance of rigorous theoretical underpinning.

It is interesting to note how the difficulty disappears if $i = j$. The constraints given by the projects become:

$$\sum_{t=0}^{n} (R_t + I_t - w_t)(1 + i)^{n-t} \geqslant T \tag{5.11)a}$$

and

$$\sum_{t=0}^{n} (S_t + I_t - w_t)(1 + i)^{n-t} \geqslant T \tag{5.11)b}$$

respectively and, after rearrangement and division through by $(1 + i)^n$ they can be written as

$$\sum_{t=0}^{n} w_t(1 + i)^{-t} \leqslant \mathrm{PV}^* + \mathrm{PV}_R \tag{5.12)a}$$

and

$$\sum_{t=0}^{n} w_t(1 + i)^{-t} \leqslant \mathrm{PV}^* + \mathrm{PV}_S \tag{5.12)b}$$

where PV_R and PV_S are the net present values of the two projects and where:

$$\mathrm{PV}^* = \sum_{t=0}^{n} I_t(1 + i)^{-t} - T(1 + i)^{-n}$$

which is the present value of the existing income stream minus the present value of the required terminal balance. It is clear from (5.12)a and (5.12)b that the project with the greater NPV will be selected. It is not necessary to know the form of the utility function (5.9); all that is required is that utility be an increasing function of at least one of the w_t. It should be noted, however, that for some forms of (5.9) U may be unbounded unless there are lower bounds on the w_t.

If, with the uniform interest rate of $100i\%$ for all transactions there are limits placed on the amounts that can be transferred from one year to another, the project with the greater NPV at the rate i will not necessarily be preferred. Consider period zero. The net amount transferred from period zero with project R is given by the L.H.S. in (5.13). Suppose that

$$R_0 + I_0 - w_0 \geqslant A_0 \tag{5.13}$$

this amount is constrained to be no less than A_0. If $A_0 = 0$ then (5.13) represents a prohibition on borrowing, or if $A_0 < 0$ there is a limit to borrowings. In these circumstances it may no longer be possible for the returns from the project with greater NPV to be adjusted so that the choices available from the project with the

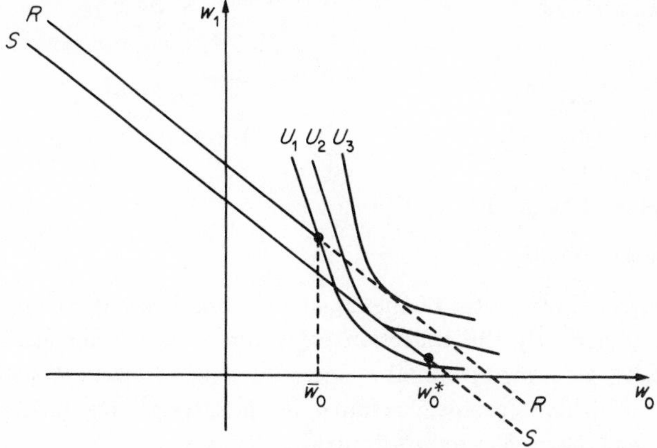

Figure 5.16 Utility maximization: restrictions on borrowing

lower NPV are dominated. The reason for this is that restrictions of the form (5.13) set different bounds on the w_t for different projects. For instance with the constraint on period zero activity the bounds on w_0 set by projects R and S are

$$w_0 \leqslant R_0 + I_0 - A_0$$

and

$$w_0 \leqslant S_0 + I_0 - A_0$$

A possible outcome is shown for the $n = 1$ case in Figure 5.16 in which the combinations of w_1 and w_0 achievable with project R with no limit on w_0 are shown by points along the entirety of the line RR including the dashed segment but with an effective bound on w_0 of $\bar{w}_0$ the permitted choices are bounded by the solid section of RR. For projects choices are similarly limited to the solid section of SS. With the indifference curves shown project S yielding utility level U_2 is preferred to project R which can give only $U_1 < U_2$. Without the limit A_0 project R would be preferred since $U_3 < U_2$ could be achieved. Of course project S need not have been preferred if the utility function and consequently the indifference curves had been different. The choice between R and S may also depend upon the existing income stream. With changed I_t the bound on the w_t are altered for given A_t.[11]

Problems with limits on transfers and non-uniform interest rates can, in principle, be solved exactly using programming models with the utility function explicitly stated and used as the objective function. The difficulty here lies not only in the formulation of the utility function but also in the fact that the constraints depend upon the projects chosen. If the utility function can be formulated and there are not 'too many' alternative groups of projects then the optimum group of projects can be determined by enumeration. For example if the choice lies between two mutually exclusive projects R and S two problems would be solved, which can be stated succinctly as

$$\begin{aligned}&\text{maximize} \quad U = U(w)\\&\text{subject to} \quad w \in W_R\end{aligned} \qquad (5.14)\text{a}$$

and

$$\begin{aligned}&\text{maximize} \quad U = U(w)\\&\text{subject to} \quad \mathrm{w} \in W_s\end{aligned} \qquad (5.14)\text{b}$$

where w represents the vector of the w_t, the symbol $\in$ means 'belongs to' and W_R and W_S are respectively the collection of vectors w which are feasible with the constraint sets resulting from the acceptance of project R and project S respectively. Whichever problem resulted in the greatest maximum value of U would determine the project to be selected.

We should expect such an approach to be rarely practicable however and in practice there will usually be no alternative but to use a simplifying assumption. Amongst the possibilities for such simplifications is the use of a terminal value formulation for the objective function along the lines suggested in previous models in this chapter. If such an approach is not considered to be satisfactory by the decision maker in a particular situation he may state an alternative objective within the context of a programming approach. In such an event it could nevertheless transpire that terminal value had a role to play – for instance a minimum level of terminal value may be included as a constraint – or terminal value may be one of several objectives.[12] In Chapter 6 the subject of alternative objectives is discussed within the context of the nature of company ownership and management. It is to such considerations that we now turn.

Notes

1. The reader is asked to deduce the equivalence of this procedure to the calculation of the index row number of a new variable given in Chapter 3.
2. For amplification of this point see Littlechild, S. C., and Samuels, J. M., 'On the valuation of assets', Management Centre Discussion Paper, University of Aston in Birmingham, July, 1970.
3. As an exercise the reader might consider the introduction of x_3 into formulation one. Its index row number is *positive* at the original optimum but its introduction is still indicated since something must be subtracted from this number. What?
4. For instance, see Baumol, W. J., *Economic Theory and Operations Analysis*, 2nd. Edn., Prentice-Hall, Englewood Cliffs, M.J., 1965, Chapter 19.
5. The reader is invited to express the problem in terms of formulation one.
6. See Weingartner, H. M., *Mathematical Programming and the Analysis of Capital Budgeting Problems*, Prentice-Hall, Englewood Cliffs, N.J., 1963, p. 154.
7. See section 5.6 below and also Wilkes, F. M., 'Inflation and capital budgeting decisions', *Journal of Business Finance,* 4, No. 3, Autumn 1974, pp. 52–53.
8. This is the simplest form of such a function. In general it may be a non-linear function of the $p_t^* - p_t$.
9. Wilkes, F. M., 'Inflation and capital budgeting decisions', *Journal of Business Finance,* 4, No. 3, Autumn 1972, p. 53.
10 The example that is to follow, with a minor alteration is taken from a paper by Gale, D., 'Optimal policy for sequential investments', The discussion as a whole constitutes a slightly modified précis of that paper.
11. Further discussion of the effects of existing income streams can be found in Wilkes, F. M.,

'Inflation and capital budgeting decisions', *Journal of Business Finance,* **4**, No. 3 Autumn 1972. The discussion therein is related to the context of differential borrowing and investment rates of interest.

12. For discussion of capital budgeting problems with multiple objectives see Chateau, J. P. D., 'The capital budgeting problem under conflicting financial policies', *Journal of Business Finance and Accounting,* **2**, No. 1, Spring, 1975. Many further references are contained in this article.

Additional References

1. Amey, L. R., 'Interdependencies in capital budgeting. A survey', *Journal of Business Finance,* **4**, No. 3, Autumn, 1972.
2. Baumol, W. J., and Quandt, R. E., 'Investment and discount rates under capital rationing: a programming approach', *Economic Journal,* **75**, 1965.
3. Bernhard, R. H., 'Mathematical programming models for capital budgeting. A survey, generalization and critique', *Journal of Financial and Quantitative Analysis,* **4**, No. 2, 1969.
4. Bhaskar, K. N., 'Borrowing and lending in a mathematical programming model of capital budgeting', *Journal of Business Finance and Accounting,* **1**, No. 2, Summer, 1974.
5. Carleton, W. T., 'Linear programming and capital budgeting models: a new interpretation', *Journal of Finance,* December, **1969**.
6. Elton, E. J., 'Capital rationing and external discount rates', *Journal of Finance,* June, **1970**.
7. Flavell, R. B., *Mathematical Programming and the Robustness of Solutions to Sequential Investment Problems*, Ph.D. Thesis, University of London, January, 1972.
8. Hughes, J. S., and Lewellen, W. G., 'Programming solutions to capital rationing problems', *Journal of Business Finance and Accounting,* **1**, No. 1, Spring 1974.
9. Lusztig, P., and Schwab, B., 'A note on the application of linear programming to capital budgeting', *Journal of Financial and Quantitative Analysis*, December, **1968**.
10. Ma, R., and Tydeman, J., 'Project selection criteria, wealth maximization and capital rationing', *Journal of Business Finance,* **4**, No. 4, Winter 1972.
11. Myers, S. C., 'A note on linear programming and capital budgeting', *Journal of Finance,* March, **1972**.
12. Pye, G., 'Present values for imperfect capital markets', *Journal of Business,* January, **1966**.
13. Roy, B., 'Problems and methods with multiple objective functions', *Mathematical Programming,* **1**, No. 2, 1971.
14. Weingartner, H. M., 'Criteria for programming investment project selection', *Journal of Industrial Economics,* **15**, No. 1, 1966.
15. Weingartner, H. M., 'Capital budgeting of interrelated projects: survey and synthesis', *Management Science,* **12**, No. 7, 1966.
16. Weingartner, H. M., *Mathemetical Programming and the Analysis of Capital Budgeting Problems*, Prentice-Hall, 1963.
17. Whitmore, G. A., and Amey, L. R., 'Capital budgeting under rationing: comments on the Lusztig and Schwab procedure', *Journal of Financial and Quantitative Analysis,* **8**, No. 1, 1973.
18. Wilkes, F. M., 'Dividend policy and investment appraisal in imperfect capital markets', *Journal of Business Finance and Accounting,* **4**, No. 2, Summer, 1977.

CHAPTER 6

Financial Planning Models

6.1 Introduction

A financial planning model is a capital rationing model broadly of the kind so far described but with the addition of constraints on the ranges of values that may be taken by some important financial variables and ratios. It is also possible that some financial statistics might appear in the objective function. Some of the more sophisticated models may be used not only to solve investment problems but also to project balance sheets for future years and so provide an overall picture of a company's financial position in the future. The presentation is centred around particular models. The first of these is a model developed by Charnes, Cooper and Miller which although very restricted in its objectives and range of possible application will serve both an introductory purpose and as a bridge between the models of Chapter 5 and the model of Samuels and Wilkes and the more sophisticated models of Chambers, Jaaskelainen and Deam, Bennett and Leather presented later. Before discussion of the Charnes, Cooper and Miller model however, some general observations would be in order.

Financial planning models are appropriate for and are used by larger companies and it is a characteristic of such enterprises that there is a separation of ownership from management. Although most managers are shareholders the majority of owners are not managers. Figure 6.1 illustrates this point with a Venn diagram.

Set A represents shareholders and B represents management (at the executive level). B is not wholly subsumed within A. This simple distinction between ownership and management, though an improvement on the classical economists' single concept of the entrepreneur, does not tell the whole story. Cyert and March consider that the activities of large companies are best described by separating out management, employees, ownership and customers. Management are viewed as the principal active participants and will pursue their own objectives (not always unambiguously defined or consistent amongst themselves), subject to the constraint that the other three groups are kept reasonably happy and therefore acquiescent. The three essentially passive groups are awarded 'side payments' by management in the forms of wages, dividends and 'service' respectively.

Nowadays this conception may need to be modified in the light of the increasingly active rôle that is being played by organized labour. More constraints are being imposed on management and a positive function in decision making is also being sought. The model might also be extended by adding in government or government agencies and by taking into account international and environmental

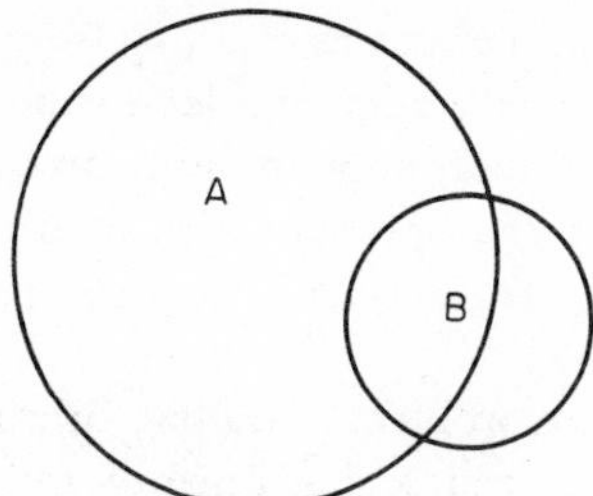

Figure 6.1 Owners and managers: overlap

considerations. Such models, however, would go much further than the scope of this chapter. The approach along such lines would perhaps be by simulation rather than by an optimization model. Further, we wish to concentrate upon financial considerations. To continue the discussion we shall therefore return to the division of Figure 6.1.

When questioned few owners would express a desire to make less profits rather than more. Apart from ethical reservations about *how* profits are made it is safe to assume that profits and security of profits are the principal concern of equity holders. Management, insofar as they are also equity holders, will have a vested interest in profits but this may not be their prime motivation. It is prestigious to be in control of a large organization and satisfying to be seen to have performed better than rivals with similar objectives.

Consequently, size (perhaps measured by trunover and aimed for by growth) and share of market may be the objectives of management, the achievement of which is constrained by satisfactory levels of attainment of shareholders' objectives. Baumol[1] produced a variant of the classical maximization model for the behaviour of firms in which sales revenue was maximized subject to a constraint on profits. This is a programming model and though hardly a financial planning model has the characteristic in common of maximization of a monetary objective function subject to a constraint imposed by the size of a financial statistic. Baumol's model is a static, one period model but could, no doubt, be extended to take account of several time periods but would continue to reflect the objectives of management rather than those of shareholders who, if they were fully aware and in charge, might be reasonably supposed to be more interested in the discounted value of cash flows or dividends with, possibly, constraints on revenues.

In either case, however, maximization of the chosen objective is subject to a financial constraint which is an alternative measure of performance. In addition to any constraints of this nature there will typically be both externally imposed and internally predetermined restrictions of a financial nature. The Charnes, Cooper and Miller model illustrates such a case.

6.2 The Charnes, Cooper and Miller Model

This model examines the following problem. Given the existing asset structure of a firm, what operating programme would yield the greatest prospective returns and what would be the change in the returns resulting from the various possible changes in the asset structure? Financial policy problems were introduced into the normal type of production-based linear-programming problem. The model therefore investigates the question of the optimal use of existing equipment resulting from prior investment decisions. The model is expressed within the framework of a warehousing problem.

In the classical warehouse problem, a trading firm has an opening inventory, it has estimates of the buying and selling price of the product over the next few periods, and there is a limit on the capacity of the warehouse. The problem is to decide when and in what quantities to buy the product and when and in what quantities to sell it so as to maximize a profit function over the planning horizon.

To this basic model, Charnes, Cooper and Miller (CCM) added financial constraints to include the possibility that purchases might be limited by the amount of cash available. The amount of cash available at any time is an opening balance plus value of sales minus value of purchases up to that time, less any minimum cash balance required. This definition of the cash position therefore assumes that cash surpluses earn zero interest. It would not be difficult to modify the model to relax this restriction. The model can be used to answer questions such as: If the company has the opportunity to borrow cash at any time what would be the maximum rate of interest that it would be prepared to pay? What would be the value of extra units of storage space?

Extensions of the basic model make it possible to examine the effects of trade credit if this is available and to evaluate any lending (as well as borrowing) possibilities that there may be.

Consider the basic warehouse model with one commodity (or several commodities with all transactions in fixed proportionate amounts). Adhering to the original CCM assumptions let:

P_j = estimated selling price (per ton) of the commodity in period j
C_j = estimated purchase price (per ton) of the commodity in period j
Y_j = the quantity to be sold in period j (tons)
X_j = the quantity to be purchased in period j (tons)

The X_j and Y_j are decision variables of the model whilst P_j and C_j are exogenously determined parameters. Now let

B = warehouse capacity (tons)
A = initial stock at warehouse (tons)
n = the number of periods within the planning horizon

The numbers B and A are fixed at the start of the problem but sensitivity analysis would show the effect of variations in B. The length of horizon is, strictly, a decision variable but we shall follow CCM in assuming that n is predetermined. CCM stated the objective as maximization of of total *undiscounted* profits over the horizon. On the basis of the work that we have done so far we may consider this to be a peculiar formulation but CCM are not unique in adopting such an objective. We shall see shortly that it is not difficult to modify the problem to use a weighted sum of profits but further discussions of the use of undiscounted sums as objectives is deferred until section 6.5. CCM's objective is then to:

$$\text{maximize } \Pi = \sum_{j=1}^{n} P_jY_j - C_jX_j \tag{6.1}$$

subject to n buying constraints of the form:

$$\sum_{j=1}^{n} X_j - \sum_{j=1}^{i=1} Y_j \leqslant B - A \quad (i = 1,2, \ldots n) \tag{6.2}$$

and n selling constraints expressed as:

$$\sum_{j=1}^{i} Y_j - \sum_{j=1}^{i=1} X_j \leqslant A \quad (i = 1,2, \ldots n) \tag{6.3}$$

and the sign requirements:

$$X_j \geqslant 0, \; Y_j \geqslant 0 \quad (j = 1,2, \ldots n) \tag{6.4}$$

Let us begin the verbal explanations of this model so far defined by (6.1), (6.2), (6.3) and (6.4), with the objective function (6.1). Profits, Π, as we have said are undiscounted in the CCM formulation but clearly we could write:

$$\Pi^* = \sum_{j=1}^{n} (P_jY_j - C_jX_j)(1 + r)^{n-j} \tag{6.5}$$

for a terminal value formulation. Alternatively, (6.1) can be thought of as terminal value if the nominal prices prevailing are $\hat{P}_j$ and $\hat{C}_j$ where $P_j = \hat{P}_j\,(1 + r)^{n-j}$ and $C_j = \hat{C}_j\,(1 + r)^{n-j}$.

The buying constraints relate to space available in the warehouse and state that in any period, i, purchases in that period, X_j, shall not exceed the warehouse capacity initially available $(B - A)$ plus sales up to $i(\Sigma_j^i = {}_1 Y_j)$ minus previous purchases $(\Sigma_{j=1}^{i-1} X_j)$. Thus, for example, the second-period $(i = 2)$ constraint requires that

$$X_2 \leqslant B - A + Y_1 + Y_2 - X_1.$$

The selling constraints require that no more is sold in a period than is available for sale then — that is, sales are made from inventory. The amount available for sale is the initial stock A plus total purchases up to and including the previous period $(\Sigma_{j=1}^{i-1} X_j)$ minus total sales up to and including the previous period $(\Sigma_{j=1}^{i-1} Y_j)$.

Therefore the third-period selling constraint requires that

$$Y_3 \leqslant A + X_1 + X_2 - Y_1 - Y_2$$

The buying and selling constraints above relate to physical capacity or availability. To introduce financial constraints let:

M_0 = the initial cash balance

M = the minimum cash balance permissible

Now, with C_j and P_j as the actual prices and with zero interest rate applying to cash transfer between periods it is required that:

$$\sum_{j=1}^{i} C_jX_j - \sum_{j=1}^{i-1} P_jY_j \leqslant M_0 - M \quad (i = 1,2, \ldots, n) \tag{6.6}$$

These financial requirements are now added to the constraints and the sign requirements above. Verbally the financial constraints require that the value of purchases in a period shall not exceed the excess of the initial cash balance over the requisite minimum cash balance ($M_0 - M$) plus the total value of sales up to and including the previous period ($\Sigma_{j=1}^{i-1} P_jY_j$) minus the total value of purchases up to and including the previous period ($\Sigma_{j=1}^{i-1} C_jX_j$). For example in the third period it is required that:

$$C_3X_3 \leqslant M_0 - M + P_1Y_1 + P_2Y_2 - C_1X_1 - C_2X_2$$

In the above it is being assumed that collection of debts takes one period but allowance can be made for lags in both collection of debts and the payment of creditors. If it is assumed that payments are made g periods after purchase, and cash is collected r periods after the sale, then the financial constraints would be:

$$\sum_{j=1}^{i} C_{j-g}X_{j-g} - \sum_{j=1}^{i} P_{j-r}Y_{j-r} \leqslant M_0 - M$$

For a numerical illustration let:

$A = 100$ tons, $n = 5$

$B = 125$ tons. $g = 0$

$M_0 = £1{,}000$, $r = 1$

$M = £500$

and assume that the costs and sales prices are

Period	c_j	p_j
1	25	20
2	25	35
3	25	30
4	35	25
5	45	50

The optimal solution of the direct problem involves purchases in the five time periods of 20, 0, 125, 0, 0, respectively. The initial purchase of 20 is the maximum permitted by the available funds ($M_0 - M$) of £500. The sales in the five periods are 0, 120, 0, 0, 125 respectively. The sales in period 2 are the opening stock plus purchases. The cash is realized in period 3 and the funds used for purchases up to the maximum permitted by the warehouse capacity. The resulting profit is £6,825 which is the difference between cash receipts and expenditure where the former are extended to include the collections at end of period 5. It includes the sale of the initial inventory, but not its cost, as this was incurred prior to this planning period.

The dual solution to the model is extremely useful. In this case the dual variables provide a means of determining the consequent increments in profits which can be secured if optimum use is made of asset increases. The dual will show, for example, the returns that would result from having one extra pound of cash initially. In the dual problem there will be a variable that is associated with each constraint in the primal or direct problem of maximizing profit. For instance, each of the n primal selling constraints has an associated dual variable u_k and each of the primal financial constraints has an associated dual variable v_k.

The dual objective function is the sum of the products of the primal constraint levels and their associated dual variables. The magnitudes of the dual variables (which must all be non-negative) show by how much profit (the value of the primal objective function) would increase if the corresponding constraint were relaxed by one unit. This is so because the optimum values of the primal and dual objective functions are the same. The dual objective function (to be minimized) can be written in either of two forms. It can be expressed as:

$$E = \sum_{k=1}^{n} (B - A)t_k + \sum_{k=1}^{n} Au_k + \sum_{k=1}^{n} (M_0 - M)v_k \tag{6.7}$$

or equivalently as

$$E = (B - A)T + AU + (M_0 - M)V \tag{6.8}$$

where the relationship between (6.7) and (6.8) is such that:

$$T = \sum_{k=1}^{n} t_k, \quad U = \sum_{k=1}^{n} u_k, \quad V = \sum_{k=1}^{n} v_k$$

Now since the optimum values of E and Π are equal, if $(B - A)$ was to go up by one because B increased by one – that is, there was one more ton of storage possible throughout the five periods – then E and therefore Π would increase by T^* (starred variables indicate optimum values). So clearly it would be worth paying anything up to T^* to obtain this extra storage capacity.

Solving the dual problem to the numerical illustration gives the following values:

Period	t^*	u^*	v^*
1	0	0	0
2	0	0	2/5
3	10	10	0
4	15	0	0
5	0	50	0

so that

$$T^* = \sum_{k=1}^{n} t_k = 25$$

$$U^* = \sum_{k=1}^{n} u_k = 60$$

$$V^* = \sum_{k=1}^{n} v_k = 2/5$$

So the financial constraint is seen to be binding only in period 1. An extra £25 available in period 1 would permit an additional unit to be purchased in that period, and hence an additional unit to be sold in period 2. The profit on this additional unit is £10 (=35 − 25), which on each extra pound above the existing constraint is 2/5 (=10/25), the value shown for $v_2{}^*$.

The value for T^* asserts that a one unit increment in warehouse capacity will, if used optimally, increase the total profit by £25. One extra unit could be purchased in period 3, held in inventory for that and the next period, and sold in period 5. An extra unit of opening inventory, 101 tons instead of 100, will lead to extra profits of £35, that is $U^* - T^*$.

All these values hold only within certain limits. When the constraints move outside these limits there will be different dual values. For instance, if the firm acquires more than 168 tons of warehouse capacity, the value for T^* will become zero, as the warehouse restriction will no longer be binding. A minimum capacity of 120 tons is necessary to validate the result T^* = £25, since reductions below this make the storage capacity constraint binding in period 1, not the cash constraint.

The figure V^* can be used to assess alternative applications of funds. For example, it can be used to evaluate proposed alterations in the parameters. Let us consider the desirability of altering B from 125 to 126, with M = £500. This would yield an increment in total profit of £25; the company being able to buy in period 3 at £25 and sell in period 5 at £50. The cost of securing this additional unit of capacity must be considered. Suppose the cost to be £20, and the additional facility is worth nothing at the end of the fifth period.

The return on the investment is 25% (=5/20); it is not sufficient to justify a diversion of funds from their original use, since the cost of the cash diversion as measured by V^* is 2/5 or 40%. Moreover, the investment in the added facility would not be warranted even if the extra £20 for the extra warehouse capacity could be secured at zero costs from external sources; for an increment ($\Delta M_0 <$ £125) in liquid funds can be more profitably employed in effecting purchases at period 1 prices and selling them in period 2.

On the other hand, under the liquidity constraints assumed for the firm, the extra warehouse space might be worth acquiring provided 'suitable' financing terms were offered by the builder. If, for example, the builder were willing to give terms of 50% down and 50% in period 3, then the cost of the diversion of funds would be only £4, which is less than the £5 net increment to profit from the extra space.

A simple extension to the model makes it possible to examine the effects of trade credit and the model can be generalized in other ways (for instance to deal with several products instead of one). However, the purpose here has been to illustrate the essential characteristics that would be common to all such generalizations.

6.3 The Samuels–Wilkes Model

In the CCM model just discussed a very simple objective was employed. As was mentioned in the introduction the question of an appropriate objective is a difficult one and varying choices will be made from case to case depending upon the nature of the separation of management from ownership and the particular aspirations of management. Where management act simply as the agents of the owners it is fair to assume (as is done throughout much of the received financial and economic theory), that the objective of a firm is to maximize the wealth of the shareholders. This involves maximizing in some sense the market value of the equity shares. This is usually taken to mean maximizing the market value of shares at a specific moment in time (usually the present). A present, or terminal value model would seem to be indicated here. However, operationally even this is a tall order. Not much is known other than generalities about the factors that explain share prices. Some models have expressed the objective function in terms of dividends, describing the present value of shares as the discounted stream of dividends.[2] Quite apart from the problem of the selection of discount rate there is the question of the correctness of equating discounted dividend streams with share price. The stock market may take a more short-sighted view of a company's future prospects than does the management of the company. The information available to the market may not be as comprehensive as information available to management and the information itself may bear more than one interpretation. For example dividend cuts are eschewed by managements because of the pessimistic interpretation of the cuts by the market. Notwithstanding bright long term prospects the market interprets a reduced dividend as a signal of declining fortunes and a case could be argued that the market typically considers only the *current* dividend. This may be greatly to be regretted by rational management but stock market myopia would be ignored at the company's peril.

Conventional capital budgeting theory suggests that a firm should seek to maximize the present value of its net cash flow. In the absence to tax distortions and in conditions of certainty with a perfect capital market this could lead to the maximization of the price of shares of the company.[3] But the stock market is not perfect, and factors additional to cash flow or even dividends need to be taken into account, when either the objective function or a constraint is expressed in terms of share price.

Investment decisions, where the share price is to be considered, must allow for the effect of reported accounting profits. Mao suggests that one reason why business has not been keen to adopt present value and yield criteria is because they fail to consider the effect of an investment on reported earnings.[4]

We shall not be concerned here with the question of whether in the objective function earnings or dividends provide the best surrogate for share price. Our interest in the Samuels–Wilkes (SW) model below is in showing the effects of alternative objectives to the maximization of present value (which is usually the form in which objective functions have been expressed notwithstanding the discounting problem), whether the present value is based on earnings or dividends. Two alternative objectives will be examined. The first will be the maximization of the minimum value of the company's share price within a given horizon. The second possibility is that of maximization of a measure of rate of growth of share price over the horizon.

Consider for the moment a case in which there are two investment opportunities, and the manager wishes to decide how many units of each investment to purchase. The returns from investment 1 are high in the early years of the planning period, but low in later years. Investment 2 on the contrary has low initial returns but high later returns. It is possible that, under a simple discounted cash flow approach, investment 2 appears the more profitable, and it would appear all the resources should be put in this type of investment. The result of such a decision could, however, be unfortunate as the low returns reported in the accounts in the early years of the planning period could give rise to a low market value if the market is sufficiently myopic. Such a company would be an ideal victim for the takeover bidder. A 'mixed strategy' would be more desirable – the firm's value would then not have to follow the undulating fortunes of a single investment.

As an illustration suppose that the two investment opportunities the company is considering run for four years each. The costs and return data can then be written as follows:

Period	0	1	2	3	4
Project 1	$-K_1$	R_{11}	R_{21}	R_{31}	R_{41}
Project 2	$-K_2$	R_{12}	R_{22}	R_{32}	R_{42}

where K_1 and K_2 are immediate costs incurred in the initiation of each project (at unit level) and the Rs are the net cash returns of each unit of each project invested in each of four periods with x_1 and x_2 representing the number of units of each investment taken; the year subscript being first. Total outlay and the total returns in each period are therefore as follows:

Period:	0	1	2
Returns:	$-K_1x_1 - K_2x_2$	$R_{11}x_1 + R_{12}x_2 (= F_1)$	$R_{21}x_1 + R_{22}x_2 (= F_2)$

Period:	3	4
Returns:	$R_{31}x_1 + R_{32}x_2 (= F_3)$	$R_{41}x_1 + R_{42}x_2 (= F_4)$

It is now assumed that the price of the shares of the company in period t will be some weighted average of the returns to accrue to each share in subsequent periods. Numerous alternative, more sophisticated assumptions regarding the mechanism of share-price determination, could have been made. It may even be argued that shareholders will be unlikely in many instances to be aware of the expected future returns to a company's investments. However, for the purposes of this example the precise workings of the share-price determination mechanism are immaterial as long as share price (and therefore total valuation, in which terms the numerical example is framed) in any period can be expressed, in the end, as a linear function of the investment levels we seek to determine. The coefficients of, and constants in, such functions can be themselves in whole or in part complicated functions of existing or past investment levels.

With the share price determination mechanism assumed, the total valuation of the company in period t, V_t, is given by:

$$V_t = W_1 F_{t+1} + W_2 F_{t+2} + W_3 F_{t+3} + \dots \tag{6.9}$$

and if for simplicity we assume that in equation (6.9) the coefficients $W_3, W_4, \dots$ are all zero and that only the initial valuations V_0 and V_1 are of concern, then we can write:

$$N_{11}x_1 + N_{12}x_2 = V_0 \quad \text{and} \quad N_{21}x_1 + N_{22}x_2 = V_1$$

where

$$\left.\begin{aligned} N_{11} &= W_1 R_{11} + W_2 R_{21} \\ N_{12} &= W_1 R_{12} + W_2 R_{22} \end{aligned}\right\}$$

Further, suppose that there is a budgetary constraint on the firm given by:

$$K_1 x_1 + K_2 x_2 \leqslant K \tag{6.10}$$

Here, the company's objective is to maximize the minimum of the two valuations V_0 and V_1 subject to (6.10) and the sign requirements, x_1 and $x_2 \geqslant 0$. Now as long as both V_0 and V_1 are positive for some values of the xs the budget must be fully used, so the problem can be written as:

$$\begin{aligned} &\text{maximize } V \\ &\text{subject to: } N_{11}x_1 + N_{12}x_2 \geqslant V \\ &\qquad N_{21}x_1 + N_{22}x_2 \geqslant V \\ &\qquad K_1 x_1 + K_2 x_2 = K \quad \text{and} \quad x_1, x_2 \geqslant 0 \end{aligned}$$

Define new variables $\tilde{x}_1$ and $\tilde{x}_2$ such that:

$$\tilde{x}_1 = \frac{K_1 x_1}{K}, \qquad \tilde{x}_2 = \frac{K_2 x_2}{K}$$

The problem can now be written as:

$$\begin{aligned} &\text{maximize } V \\ &\text{subject to: } \tilde{N}_{11}\tilde{x}_1 + \tilde{N}_{12}\tilde{x}_2 - V \geqslant 0 \\ &\qquad \tilde{N}_{21}x_1 + \tilde{N}_{22}\tilde{x}_2 - V \geqslant 0 \\ &\qquad \tilde{x}_1 + \tilde{x}_2 - 1 = 0 \\ &\qquad \tilde{x}_1, \tilde{x}_2 \geqslant 0 \end{aligned}$$

where

$$\tilde{N}_{11} = \frac{K}{K_1} N_{11},$$

and so on.

The problem now has the appearance of a two-player constant-sum 'game' in which the $\tilde{x}$s are analogous to the probabilities that a player A (the company) can attach to the selection of each of his possible courses of action, which are investment in x_1 and investment in x_2. However, we interpret the $\tilde{x}$s here as weights rather than probabilities. It is player A who wishes to maximize V the minimum valuation of the company, which the 'opponent', player B, is an imagined malevolent observer whose objective is to ensure that the only relevant valuation of the company is the lowest one.

Since the 'plays' of the game are sequential[5] B will always have at least one optimal pure strategy (investment in only one project) – a pure strategy will be chosen only if the matrix of $\tilde{N}$s contains a 'saddle point', which exists if an element is at once the minimum of its row and the maximum of its column. The data is now set out in the conventional game theory form.

$$\begin{array}{c} \text{Time} \\ \begin{array}{c} \tilde{x}_1 \\ \tilde{x}_2 \end{array} \begin{bmatrix} \tilde{N}_{11} & \tilde{N}_{21} \\ \tilde{N}_{12} & \tilde{N}_{22} \end{bmatrix} \end{array}$$

If a saddle point existed this would mean that at the time a project received its lowest valuation its $\tilde{N}$ number is the highest in that column. The $\tilde{N}$s can be interpreted as benefit/cost ratios. For example, if a saddle point existed in the first row, second column then by definition:

$$\tilde{N}_{21} \geqslant \tilde{N}_{22}$$

that is

$$\frac{K}{K_1} N_{21} \geqslant \frac{K}{K_2} N_{22}$$

where N_{21}/K_1 is the contribution of a unit of project one to valuation in year one and $\tilde{N}_{21}$ is the valuation in year one that would result if the entire budget was allocated to project one. Since only the minimum valuation of the two years is of concern to the investor, only x_1 would be taken. If $\tilde{N}_{12} \geqslant \tilde{N}_{11}$ the valuation in year zero would be improved by taking a positive amount of the second investment but only at the expense of a reduction in the year one valuation which is already the smallest. The absence of a saddle point implies the choice of a mixed strategy. A numerical example follows in which this is the case.

Consider a two-project example with the following cash-flow data:

Year	0	1	2	3	4
x_1 net returns (£)	−50	30	35	20	10
x_2 net returns (£)	−60	20	30	40	60

Let K = £300 (the sum available for investment in year zero). The firm's objective is to determine the levels of investment in the two projects so that it maximizes the minimum valuation that will be placed on its investments by the 'market' in the years zero, one and two (subsequent years being ignored for simplicity in the example). Assume that $W_1 = 0.8$, $W_2 = 0.5$, $W_3 = 0$, $W_4 = 0$, that is, the 'market' only considers returns accruing within a two-year horizon.

Before considering the optimal solution with maximum valuation objective let us examine the investments from a present value standpoint for comparative purposes. With a 20% discount rate it turns out that for project one:

$$\mathrm{GPV}_1 = 65.70 \qquad \mathrm{NPV} = 15.70$$

$$\frac{\mathrm{GPV}_1}{K_1} = 1.314 \qquad \frac{\mathrm{NPV}_1}{K_1} = 0.314$$

and for the second project:

$$\mathrm{GPV}_2 = 89.58 \qquad \mathrm{NPV}_2 = 29.58$$

$$\frac{\mathrm{GPV}_2}{K_2} = 1.493 \qquad \frac{\mathrm{NPV}_2}{K_2} = 0.493$$

So that in a non-rationing context the second project would be selected since it has the greater net present value. In the rationing situation the same choice would be made since project two has the greater ratio of present value (net or gross) to outlay. In this case x_1 would only be set at a positive level if a sufficiently low upper bound (less than five units) was placed on x_2.

The 20% discount rate case is equivalent to the setting of the weights $W_t = (1.2)^{-t}$ and taking into account only the situation at $t = 0$. In contrast with $W_1 = 0.8$ and $W_2 = 0.5$ as the only positive weights the N_{tj} ($j = 1,2$) turn out as:

$$N_{11} = 0.8(30) + 0.5(35) = 41.5$$

$$N_{12} = 0.8(20) + 0.5(30) = 31$$

$$N_{21} = 0.8(35) + 0.5(20) = 38$$

$$N_{22} = 0.8(30) + 0.5(40) = 44$$

$$N_{31} = 0.8(20) + 0.5(10) = 21$$

$$N_{32} = 0.8(40) + 0.5(60) = 62$$

The numbers $\tilde{N}_{t1}$ are obtained by multiplication of the N_{t1} by 6 (= 300 ÷ 50) and the $\tilde{N}_{t2}$ are the N_{t2} multiplied by 5 (= 300 ÷ 60). Consequently the data in the game formulation is:

$$\begin{array}{c} \\ \tilde{x}_1 \\ \tilde{x}_2 \end{array} \begin{array}{ccc} t = 0 & t = 1 & t = 2 \\ \left[\begin{array}{c} 249 \\ 155 \end{array}\right. & \begin{array}{c} 228 \\ 220 \end{array} & \left.\begin{array}{c} 126 \\ 310 \end{array}\right] \end{array}$$

in which it is evident that no saddle point exists since no element is simultaneously a row minimum and a column maximum. The problem can be stated as:

$$\text{maximize } V$$

$$\begin{aligned}\text{subject to: } 249\tilde{x}_1 + 155\tilde{x}_2 &\geqslant V \\ 228\tilde{x}_1 + 220\tilde{x}_2 &\geqslant V \\ 126\tilde{x}_1 + 310\tilde{x}_2 &\geqslant V \\ \tilde{x}_1 + \tilde{x}_2 &= 1\end{aligned}$$

and

$$\tilde{x}_1 \geqslant 0, \quad \tilde{x}_2 \geqslant 0$$

or, by substitution of $\tilde{x}_2 = 1 - \tilde{x}_1$ from the last constraint into the first three, the problem can be re-expressed as:

$$\text{maximize } V$$

$$\begin{aligned}\text{subject to: } V &\leqslant 94\tilde{x}_1 + 155 \quad (0) \\ V &\leqslant 8\tilde{x}_1 + 220 \quad (1) \\ V &\leqslant -184\tilde{x}_1 + 310 \quad (2) \\ \text{where } \quad 0 &\leqslant \tilde{x}_1 \leqslant 1\end{aligned}$$

Now, no more than two of the above constraints can simultaneously hold as strict equalities but it will be at one such point that the minimum value of V will be maximized. The situation is graphed in Figure 6.2. The lines marked 0, 1, and 2 show the values of V given by each constraint above as functions of $\tilde{x}_1$. For any value of $\tilde{x}_1$ whichever constraint gives the lowest valuation is the relevant one. The problem is to find the highest point of the lower boundary of all three lines. This is clearly at point A in the Figure at which constraints 0 and 2 are satisfied as equalities.

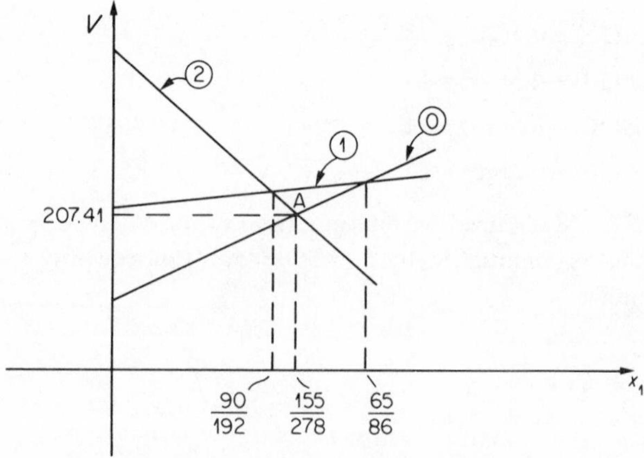

Figure 6.2 Diagram of S–W model example

The optimal solution in full is:

$$\tilde{x}_1 = \frac{155}{278}, \quad \tilde{x}_2 = \frac{123}{278}; \quad V_0 = 207.41, \quad V_1 = 224.46, \quad V_2 = 207.41$$

In terms of the original xs; $x_1 = 930/278$, $x_2 = 615/278$. In comparison to the maximum NPV solution at 20% in which $x_1 = 0$, $x_2 = 5$, and NPV = 147.90 the NPV from the maximin package is 117.96. The cost of the policy in present value terms is a drop in NPV of 20.24%. On the other hand with the NPV package the valuation that would have resulted are 155, 220 and 310 respectively. In this case although a doubling of valuation over the years is shown, the initial valuation would be down by 52.41 or 25.27%.

The maximin approach then results in substantial investment in x_1 and relatively smaller investment in x_2. Greater emphasis is placed on the project with the smaller fluctuations in returns/valuations. In general we should expect a maximin criterion to give a quite high initial valuation, and, from among projects with a similar scale of returns, to favour those with the most evenly spread returns and/or from within a group of projects select them in proportions which as far as possible cancel out the variations in returns to individual projects.

An alternative criterion with the objective of maximizing the average rate of growth of valuation over the considered horizon as a whole results in selecting just the one investment opportunity (x_2) which has the greater average rate of growth of valuation. Unless bounds are placed upon the size of individual xs the average growth rate criterion will select a single investment however many opportunities there are.

Another possible growth criterion is that of maximizing the minimum rate of growth of valuation between any two time periods. This objective might be described as maximization of the *sustainable* rate of growth of valuation and would, presumably, appeal to both managers and shareholders of a steady rather than speculative disposition. The problem in this case is to maximize the minimum value of V_{t+1}/V_t. With this criterion, in the numerical example once again x_2 alone would be selected.Unlike the average growth rate criterion however, this (selection of just one project) would not always result.

6.4 The Chambers Model

In the Samuels–Wilkes model bounds on variables and additional constraints relating to (say) liquidity or outlays in several periods could have been introduced. They were omitted here to emphasize the effects on project selection and value of the criteria given. Such further financial constraints were included in a financial planning model (with a 'classical' objective) developed by Chambers.[6] The model structure used is such as to allow any inclusion of such constraints.

Management of the company for which the model was designed wished to take account of the way that the allocation of investment funds affected other published financial results besides cash flows. Further, they considered that an important part of their skill in financial management lay in dovetailing projects so that funds were released by some investments as they were required by others. In the former respect

'. . . they (the managers) were unwilling altogether to neglect the changes which the project would bring about in other parts of the published accounts, derived on the basis not of cash flows but of accruals. They regarded the accounting convention of assigning costs and revenues to the periods judged to give rise to them as defining rules of a game in which they wanted a good score.'

The company prescribed that three financial measures should not fall below specified lower limits. They were earnings after tax; return (before tax) on gross assets; and the ratio of current assets to current liabilities. If these constraints were violated 'the price of the firm's shares and its ability to raise new funds might by impaired, and it might fall into the financial trap of not being able to finance projects essential to improving subsequent performance'. Of course it would be difficult to calculate precise values of the lower limits and ideally the functional relationship between these variables and the objective function would have been specified. This was not practicable however and would not be so in general. The performance of any model should be compared with the performance of alternative systems rather than with an unattainable global optimum. The description of the model to be given here is a slightly simplified and renotated version of the original.

The first financial constraint to be considered is the value taken by the 'current ratio', for which a predetermined minimum value was set. The constraint can be written as:

$$\frac{\text{current assets}}{\text{current liabilities}} \geqslant K \tag{6.11}$$

Now, current assets, V_t, are defined as:

$$V_t = V_t^0 + \sum_{j=1}^{n} \sum_{s=0}^{t} V_{js} x_j \tag{6.12}$$

where V_t^0 is the amount of current assets in period t attributable to investments undertaken before the commencement of the current planning period at $t = 0$. These investments will be referred to as 'old' investments which give rise to 'old' assets and 'old' liabilities. There are n new investments to choose from and x_j represents the level of the jth investment (in some cases x_j might only be allowed the values 0 or 1 but will be regarded as a continuous variable here) where $j = 1, 2, \ldots, n$. The coefficient V_{js} is the increase in current assets arising in the sth period per unit of investment j undertaken. The coefficients V_{js} are assumed constant, that is there are no economies or diseconomies of scale in this (or indeed any other) respect. The summation term in (6.12), then, is an unweighted sum of increase in current assets due to new investments in all periods from zero up to and including t. Current liabilities, b_t, are defined as:

$$B_t = B_t^0 + \sum_{j=1}^{n} \sum_{s=0}^{t} b_{js} x_j \tag{6.13}$$

where B_t^0 is the level of old current liabilities and b_{js} is the increase in current liabilities in the sth period per unit of project j. Substitution of (6.13) and (6.12) into (6.11) and rearrangement gives the form of the current ratio restriction most convenient for purposes of computation. It is:

$$\sum_{j=1}^{n} \sum_{s=0}^{t} (Kb_{js} - V_{js})x_j \leqslant V_t^0 - KB_t^0 \tag{6.14}$$

The next requirement for a financial statistic is the rate of return, pre-tax, on gross assets. Total gross assets in period t are defined as A_t where

$$A_t = A_t^0 + \sum_{j=1}^{n} \sum_{s=0}^{t} k_{js}x_j + \sum_{j=1}^{n} \sum_{s=0}^{t} (V_{js} - b_{js})x_j \tag{6.15}$$

where A_t^0 is the value in period t of gross assets acquired before $t = 0$ and not scrapped by period t. The coefficient k_{js} is the outlay in period s per unit of project j and the second summation term is new current assets minus new current liabilities in period t. Clearly (6.15) can be re-expressed concisely as:

$$A_t = A_t^0 + \sum_{j=1}^{n} \sum_{s=0}^{t} (k_{js} + V_{js} - b_{js})x_j \tag{6.16}$$

Now the rate of return on these assets in the tth period is defined as the ratio of earnings in this period to gross assets. Earnings (pre-tax and depreciation) in the tth period, R_t, are given by:

$$R_t = R_t^0 + \sum_{j=1}^{n} r_{jt}x_j \tag{6.17}$$

where R is the contribution to earnings (before tax and depreciation) in period t from old investments and the r_{jt} are the contributions to earnings (before tax and depreciation) expected to occur in period t per unit of project j. The r_{jt} are the 'net returns' of previous acquaintance in earlier models. The rate of return restriction is then given by

$$\frac{R_t}{A_t} \geqslant I \tag{6.18}$$

As a percentage the rate of return is $100i\%$ where: $I = (1 + i)$. Substitution of (6.17) and (6.16) into (6.18) and re-expression gives:

$$I \sum_{j=1}^{n} \sum_{s=0}^{t} (k_{js} + V_{js} - b_{js})x_j + \sum_{j=1}^{n} r_{jt}x_j \leqslant R_t^0 - IA_t^0 \tag{6.19}$$

Chambers' third financial requirement was a series of restrictions (one for each value of t as for (6.14) and (6.19) on earnings themselves. It was required that total earnings in each period net of tax and depreciation should not be less than a predetermined amount. This condition can be written as

$$E_t = E_t^0 + \sum_{j=1}^{n} e_{jt}x_j \geqslant E_t^* \tag{6.20}$$

where E_t is post-tax and depreciation earnings in period t, E_t^0 is that part of the total attributable to existing projects; the e_{jt} are the tax and depreciation netted r_{jt} and E_t^* is the assigned minimum value.

In addition to the three sets of restrictions above there are the familiar budget constraints in each period. These can be expressed as:

$$\sum_{j=1}^{n} k_{jt}x_j + D_t \leqslant F_t^0 + \sum_{j=1}^{n} f_{jt}x_j + N_t \tag{6.21}$$

where D_t are dividends to be paid in period t; the f_{jt} are the contributions to the flow of funds in period t per unit of project j; F_t^0 is the contribution to flow of funds in period t from old investments and N_t is the level of new long term finance becoming available during period t. The dividends D_t are set at a proportion of earnings post tax and depreciation in each period that is

$$D_t = d^{-1}E_t \tag{6.22}$$

Substitution of (6.20) into (6.22) and the result into (6.21) and rearrangement gives

$$\sum_{j=1}^{n} (k_{jt} - f_{jt} + d^{-1}\ e_{jt})x_j \leqslant F_t^0 + N_t - d^{-1}E_t^0 \tag{6.23}$$

The constraint set is completed by the usual sign requirements and upper limits on the scale of investment in each project, that is,

$$0 \leqslant x_j \leqslant x_j{}^* \qquad j = 1,2, \ldots, n$$

We now turn to consideration of the objective function. This is expressed in present value terms as the discounted sum of dividends to be paid over the planning period and the discounted value of 'wealth' at the horizon. The result, divided by the number of shares, would give share price according to a familiar model of share valuation. The objective function is written as:

$$\text{PV} = \sum_{t=0}^{H} D_t(1 + r)^{-t} + w_H(1 + r)^{-H} \tag{6.24}$$

where H is the predetermined horizon date. Now wealth at the horizon is defined as the discounted value at the horizon of post horizon cash flow from both old and new investments, that is,

$$W_H = \sum_{t=H+1}^{L} \sum_{j=1}^{n} f_{jt}x_j(1 + r)^{H-t} + W_H^0 \tag{6.25}$$

where L is the lifetime of the longest running new project and W_H^0 determined in a similar manner to the 'new' component of W_H but not spelled out here) in the discounted value of flow of funds from old investments. Now define

$$W_j = \sum_{t=H+1}^{L} f_{jt}(1 + r)^{H-t} \tag{6.26}$$

and substitute (6.20) into (6.23) and the result and (6.26) into (6.25) and rearranging, the objective function becomes

$$PV = \sum_{j=1}^{n} \left(\sum_{t=0}^{H} d^{-1} e_{jt}(1+r)^{-t} + w_j(1+r)^{-H} \right) x_j + C \tag{6.27}$$

where the constant term C is the present value due to old investments and is given by

$$C = d^{-1} \sum_{t=0}^{H} E_t^0 (1+r)^{-t} + W_H^0 (1+r)^{-H} \tag{6.28}$$

For convenience the complete problem is now reproduced in full. It is:

$$\begin{aligned}
&\text{maximize PV} = \sum_{j=1}^{n} \left(\sum_{t=0}^{H} d^{-1} e_{jt}(1+r)^{-t} + w_j(1+r)^{-H} \right) x_j + C \\
&\text{subject to} \quad \left.\begin{aligned}
&\sum_{j=1}^{n} \sum_{s=0}^{t} (Kb_{js} - V_{js}) x_j \leqslant V_t^0 - KB_t^0 \\
&\sum_{j=1}^{n} \left(r_{jt} + I \sum_{s=0}^{t} (k_{js} + V_{js} - b_{js}) \right) x_j \leqslant R_t^0 - IA_t^0 \\
&\sum_{j=1}^{n} (k_{jt} - f_{jt} + d^{-1} e_{jt}) x_j \leqslant F_t^0 + N_t - d^{-1} E_t^0
\end{aligned}\right\} t = 0,1,\ldots,H \\
&0 \leqslant x_j \leqslant x^*_j \quad j = 1,2,\ldots,n
\end{aligned} \tag{6.29}$$

The various coefficients of the x_j are not of course independently determined but arise from various manipulations of the costs for and returns from the individual projects. For instance, the after tax net cash flow figures f_{jt} are given by $f_{jt} = r_{jt} - \text{tax}(1) + \text{grant}(1) + V_{jt} + b_{jt} - k_{jt}$, and the after tax earnings (profit) $e_{jt} = r_{jt} - \text{tax}(2) + \text{grant}(2) - \text{depreciation}$. The terms tax (1) and grant (1) are respectively tax paid and grant received per unit of x_j and tax (2) and grant (2) are tax accrued and grant accrued. Depreciation is, as always an arbitrary figure being a proportion of previous capital outlays. The model could therefore be re-expressed in various ways eliminating many of the coefficients in (6.29) by substitution from the linear relationships defined above. The choice of formulation is a matter of convenience or aesthetics and makes no difference to the problem.

The reader will have noted the relative complexity of the model but will also have been aware of the considerable number of simplifying assumptions embodied in it. Noteworthy amongst these are

(i) the pre-set horizon date;

(ii) the predetermined discount rate for dividends, wealth and post-horizon returns;

(iii) the predetermined critical values of financial statistics;

(iv) the predetermined amounts of long term capital to be available in each year;
(v) the assumption that profits and taxes can be attributed to particular projects;
(vi) the absence of interactive affects between projects;
(vii) the absence of uncertainty;
(viii) the invariance of per unit project returns and costs with scale;
(ix) the exclusion of whole number requirements for the x_j.

This is not to be critical of the model. To be of use all models must bring a real world problem down to manageable proportions computationally. Simplifying and sometimes arbitrary assumptions must be made and it is worth repeating that the only relevant test of a model is whether or not it improves decision-making – not whether it produces a global optimum.

The appearance of arbitrary depreciation figures in a decision-making model (rather than in innocuous matters of report) may appear incongruous. Indeed if all the world, and in particular the financial world, behaved as the economists' 'rational man' then the inclusion of such items would lead to distortions in the problem and eventually to 'wrong' decisions being made. But the world is rarely as we would have it, and so long as important institutions and individuals set stock by figures including depreciation then we must include them in our models or suffer as a result. There are constraints that are defined by irrational attitudes, but these we must take as part of the environment within which economic decisions are to be made. As a final word on the subject of depreciation data they can be directly relevant to cash flows insofar as liability for taxation is partly dependent upon what is allowed by the tax authorities for depreciation purposes.

Suppose that in a practical instance an investment problem is structured as in (6.29) and solved. What should then occur? If time computational facilities permit, a sensitivity analysis of the solution should be undertaken. Whenever assumptions have to be made about particular values of the parameters of a problem it is as well to see what consequences would follow from changes in the values of some of the more important of these parameters. As was mentioned in the introduction the numbers N_t, representing increases in amounts of long term finance available at various times, would ideally be considered as decision variables themselves. Different values of at least some of the N_t could be assumed and the effects of these changes on the optimal investment programme derived by the sensitivity analysis methods discussed in chapter three. The dual solution of course has as structural variables the effect of marginal variations in the R.H.S. in (6.29) on the total present value. Those coefficients of the N_t which are positive indicate times at which it may be worth raising additional capital. The word 'may' is used because the marginal cost of funds may be in excess of the average cost of the existing amounts N_t. Those N_t which have zero shadow prices indicate times at which more funds than can be used are available. Consequently unless (a) the commitment to raise these funds is irrevocable or (b) substantial additional amounts are to be raised in periods in which finance is short, PV can be increased by reductions in the original levels of long term finance to be raised in such periods.

The sensitivity of the solution could also be examined in response to alternative values of the discount rate used in the objective function. There is as implicit assumption in the model that the investment programme decided upon does not alter the discount rate employed by the market to evaluate the company's future dividend stream. The rate may be expected to alter if the investments are of a diversifying nature and/or alter the risk class of the company. Changes in the value or r affect the objective function coefficients of the x_j and the final index row of the problem would be recalculated for different values of r.

The effect of a changed planning period can, in principle, also be determined. This will be a more involved process if (as is the case in the present model) the size of the constraint set is a function of H. In those cases in which only the objective function coefficients depend on H the matter is simpler. The higher the original value of H the less likely the solution is to be sensitive to marginal changes of horizon date but in any event the usual procedure for changes in objective function coefficients can be employed.

As we have already seen, changes in the profitability of projects, in that these affect the technical coefficients of the problem, are much more troublesome. If there are only one or two such changes anticipated then the problem need not be recomputed afresh but additional columns can be appended to the solution tableau. Another possibility is that all the r_{jt} are affected by changed external circumstances – say the overall state of the economy. In this event it might be useful to have (say) three runs of the programme for a 'most likely' outcome for a 'pessimistic' outcome and for an 'optimistic' outcome. It may then transpire that there is a 'core' of investments that would be desirable for all the economic scenarios. Plans could then be implemented to undertake these investments and a more detailed study (perhaps by way of a second stage, subsidiary problem) undertaken of the relative desirability of the remaining alternatives.

Apart from the property of being readily amenable to sensitivity analysis, financial planning models also enable predictions to be made of important financial statistics and balance sheet items or indeed comprehensive balance sheets. These forecasts derive from the optimal investment programme and will of necessity fall within the prescribed limits. In his article Chambers used his model to calculate reported after-tax earnings, return on gross assets (per annum) and the value of the current ratio over a period of five years. Furthermore, once this has been done the years in which these variables are at the minimum permitted levels ',. . . identify occasions on which the need to satisfy the corresponding financial restriction keeps the firm from exploiting investment possibilities which would increase the value of the whole programme. Valuable opportunities are excluded by the requirement that reported results should always meet the stated standards.'[7] In his post-optimality analysis Chambers points out that the results ' . . . suggest interesting motives for making these investments, and these are not motives which appear prominently in the orthodox canon of investment theory'.[8] Some projects proved attractive because they added to before tax earnings without adding to the asset base whilst another was undertaken because it would 'give a quick boost to after-tax earnings'. Chambers concluded that each of the projects undertaken offered '. . . a particular way of shifting profits, or return, or changes in current ratio, from one year to another. Financial managers can make use of these transformations to make published results more consistent from year to year. Such possibilities come as no news to the financial manager; what is novel in the current method is that it includes them in the formal analysis'.[9] And, consequently, it might be added, removes inevitable element of 'ad-hocery' from these manipulations. Finally Chambers showed how the question of the allocation of funds to projects could be related to other important management decisions; how 'a firm may so plan its borrowing as to escape from the trap of having to allocate funds to relatively unprofitable projects in order to meet short term restrictions on reported results' and detailed a method by which the effects of alternative dividend policies on the optimal investment programme may be deduced.

From the model developed by David Chambers we now turn to consideration of a larger financial planning model which although following the capital rationing and linear programming line of approach is more comprehensive in its consideration of the financing decision and taxation implications.

6.5 Jaaskelainen's Model[10]

The model developed by Veikko Jaaskelainen is sufficiently complex to require an entire book for its complete presentation. Therefore the description of the model given here must be greatly attenuated and many of the subtleties of application and interpretation omitted. However, it is hoped to convey most of the essentials of the model.

The model is specifically intended for the study of the interdependent nature of investment and financing decisions but despite the size of the model it contains a number of simplifying assumptions but of a different nature to those embodied in previous models that we have described. These assumptions are:

(i) the enterprise is a single product corporation;
(ii) only one type of fixed asset (a 'machine') is employed;
(iii) only one type of raw material is used.

These assumptions seem restrictive, but to quote: 'The purpose of the model is to serve as a basis for a whole class of models. Therefore only those aspects which seem to be essential are included to show the basic structure'. And further 'the inclusion of several plants, products, machines and raw materials would considerably complicate the model but would hardly bring in anything new that has not yet been treated in the literature'. The simplifications are made in the area in which L.P. theory is most developed – most of the applications of L.P. concern the area of production. 'Even with the simplifications the model will include several investment alternatives. The corporation may invest in fixed assets, inventories, cash and receivables, or any of their combinations.' The model therefore makes maximal simplifications on the production and physical investment alternative side in order that the financial aspects of the problem can be concentrated upon. It will be clear that the model could be expanded to relax (i), (ii) and (iii) above.

The tax environment in which the firm operates has the following main features.

(a) The basis of assessment is sales realized in the preceding period.
(b) Direct manufacturing cost of the product sold can be deducted from the sales revenue for the period.
(c) Depreciation charged to the books of the corporation as well as accrued interest and other overhead can be deducted from the sales revenue for the period.
(d) Depreciation of fixed assets can be computed on the declining balance method. The basis for the valuation of assets for depreciation is historic costs.
(e) If less than the full depreciation allowable is charged to the books in any given period the deficiency can be made good by prolongation of the period of depreciation.
(f) Losses may not be carried forward or backwards.
(g) Inventories may be valued at direct costs or at full costs. Reserves may be formed by writing down the value of inventories up to a given fraction of the costs at which they are originally valued.

These tax rules are roughly applicable to the present-day conditions in Finland. The principle differences between the above tax rules and those applicable to, say, a United States corporation appear to be the following two points.

1. A United States corporation can choose between the linear depreciation rule and the declining balance method but after a particular method is chosen it must be adhered to. The corporation under analysis can depreciate in a period any amount less than or equal to the maximum allowable amount under the declining balance method.
2. A United States corporation has carry-over rights. Hence, the loss of a period can be used to decrease the income tax of succeeding periods by applying it against the income of those periods. This possibility compensates for the strict depreciation rules. On the other hand, the corporation under analysis has no carry-over rights. Hence, it will try to avoid reporting losses. To this effect the corporation will depreciate less than the full allowable amount in the period of a loss and extend the depreciation interval further into the future than the minimum allowed by the tax law hoping that postponed depreciation charges can be applied against profit in future periods. Another possibility is to form a reserve in the carrying value of inventory in a profitable period and then reduce this reserve in the period in which a book loss would appear without this kind of special measure.

An interesting characteristic of these tax laws will be noted. It is that firms are allowed to form reserves against the carrying value of inventories. In other words, the value of inventories can be written down and the amount charged against the income for the period. The effect of the charge which creates this reserve is to reduce the accounting profit before tax and, hence, the income tax for the period during which the reserve is established, Of course, there will also be a corresponding decrease in the reported net profit for the period which is available for distribution in the next period, If this reserve is reversed in a later period it follows that the account profit before tax, and consequently, the corporate income tax for that period will be increased. It can therefore be said that the corporation can use the inventory reserve as a source of financing. The financing received is the deferral of the tax payment. This possible 'source' of finance will not be available to corporations in all countries. It is worth including however to illustrate (a) the complexity of the financing problem, and (b) its interdependence with investment and production decisions.

Apart from the usual cash flow estimates from the investment projects balance sheet data for the corporation at the time of analysis are required. Specifically:

Assets				*Liabilities*		
Cash in banks		E_1		Accounts payable	D_1	
Accounts receivable		E_2	E_3	Bank loans	D_2	D_3
Inventories						
Completed products	E_4			Share capital	D_4	
Raw materials	E_5	E_6		Accumulated		
				Undistributed profit	D_5	D_6
Less: reserve		E_7	E_8			
Fixed assets						
Machines			E_9			
Total			E_T	Total		D_T

Book value of inventories are included here for taxation purposes, otherwise as historic costs they are irrelevant for future planning unless they are included in some mystical views held by shareholders or financial institutions.

The coefficients and variables of the problem are now listed. The first subscript is used to distinguish separate entities and the second, i or j is a time subscript.

The constants used in the objective function and on the left-hand side of the restrictions:

a_{1i} = sales price of the product,
a_{2i} = direct variable costs of the product,
a_{3i} = direct wages per unit of the product,
a_{4i} = direct material cost per unit of the product, hence $a_{2i} = a_{3i} + a_{4i}$
a_{5i} = purchase price of a new machine,
a_{6i} = estimated depreciation of a new machine from the period it is purchased to the end of the horizon. This is a concept based on the estimated terminal

value of the machine at the end of the horizon and should not be confused with the depreciation allowed for tax purposes,

a_{7i} = the number of units of the product can be produced by a machine per period,

a_{8i} = the rate at which new shares are issued,

a_{9i} = an estimate made by the management of the rate at which the shareholders value the stock dividend,

a_{10i} = the maximum amount of bank loans that can be obtained in the ith period for each unit of equity,

a_{11i} = the coefficient that gives the relationship between the positive difference of the actual and target dividend in the ith period, $x_{di}-b_{6i}$, and the number of new shares that can be issued in the $\hat{n}$th period $x_{e\hat{n}}$,

a_{12i} = the minimum cash dividend per share that must be paid on the outstanding share capital according to the judgement of the managers in order to retain the present management in charge of the corporation,

a_{13i} = the corporate income tax rate,

a_{14i} = the maximum percentage reserve that can be built into carrying value of inventories according to the corporate income tax law,

a_{15i} = the maximum percentage depreciation that can be applied to the book value of fixed assets, net of previous depreciation (i.e. the depreciation rule is the so-called declining balance method),

a_{16i} = the rate of interest on bank loans,

At times the subscript i will be omitted from some of the as below. This implies that the respective constant is assumed to remain unaltered over all periods of the horizon.

The variables:

x_{si} = the number of units of sold products in the ith period,

x_{pi} = the units of products made in the ith period,

x_{ri} = the units of raw material purchased,

x_{mi} = the number of machines purchased,

x_{li} = the amount of bank loans taken,

x_{di} = the amount of cash dividends distributed,

x_{ei} = the amount (at par value) of new shares issued,

x_{wi} = the depreciation of machines charged to the books and allowed for tax purposes. This variable should not be confused with the constant a_{6i} which appears in the objective function and which is an opportunity cost concept,

x_{hi} = the accounting or book profit before taxes. The real or true profit is, of course, defined by the objective function,

x_{fi} = undistributed profit that is left unappropriated,

x_{gi} = undistributed profit that is formally incorporated in the share capital by means of an issue of stock dividend,

x_{qi} = the amount of reserve built into the carrying value of inventories.

The constants which appear on the right-hand side of the restrictions:

b_{1i} = the number of units of completed products per period which can be produced by the machines which the corporation has at the beginning of the analysis,

b_{2i} = the upper limit on sales during the ith period,

b_{3i} = the initial inventory of the completed products less the required closing inventory,

b_{4i} = cash in banks E_1 plus accounts receivable E_2 less accounts payable D_1 less bank loans D_2 of the opening balance less minimum safety cash balance less the cumulative fixed overhead costs from the beginning of the analysis to the end of the ith period,

b_{5i} = the maximum amount of bank loans that can be obtained on the basis of the equity which the corporation has at the beginning of the analysis,

b_{6i} = the minimum cash dividend that must be distributed on the share capital D_4 during the ith period in order to ensure a successful new issue,

b_7 = the maximum amount of new shares that can be placed on the market,

b_{8i} = the maximum depreciation coefficient multiplied by the net book value of the machines in the opening balance,

b_{9i} = the maximum inventory reserve coefficient multiplied by the initial value of the inventory of completed products and raw material,

b_{10i} = fixed overhead from the beginning of the analysis to the end of the ith period less the initial reserve against the carrying value of the inventories, E_7,

b_{11i} = the accumulated undistributed profit at the beginning of the analysis that could be distributed as cash dividends,

b_{12i} = the number of units of raw material in the initial inventory less the desired number of units in the closing inventory,

b_{13i} = the minimum cash dividend which according to the judgement of the managers must be distributed to the initial share capital during the ith period in order to keep the present management in power,

b_{14i} = the minimum overhead expenses that must be charged to the profit and loss account of the ith period according to the prevailing accounting standards (i.e. that part of the overhead which in no case can be interpreted as manufacturing overhead and carried over in the value of inventories),

b_{15} = the maximum stock dividend that can be distributed without a drop in the market value of the shares.

It is readily seen from this list that a number of the 'constants' will not usually be known with precision, for instance upper limits on sales and maximum stock dividends, whilst there are a number of judgemental items included. These may be varied in a subsequent sensitivity analysis.

The Constraints of the Problem

It will be recalled that the firm is a one product enterprise using one type of machine. Initial production capacity is for at most b_1 units of product per period but more machines may be purchased subsequently. If the corporation buys x_{mj} units on machines during the jth period, then the production capacity will be increased by $a_7 x_{mj}$ units of product per period. In the planning of the production we must take into account the fact that the planned amount of production for the ith period, x_{pi}, must be less than or equal to the initial production capacity, b_1, plus the new capacity acquired from the beginning to the end of the preceding period,

$$\sum_{j=1}^{i-1} a_{7j} x_{mj}$$

This means that we have to observe in the solution of the problem a separate restriction for each period limiting the production possibilities. These restrictions are called below capacity constraints, and can be stated as follows:

$$x_{pi} - \sum_{j=1}^{i-1} a_{7j} x_{mj} \quad (i = 1, 2, \ldots, n) \tag{6.30}$$

All machines purchased are assumed to be available for use throughout the n period horizon (the length of which we shall discuss later) but scrapping possibilities could be built into the model. The model does, however, allow for the purchase of machines principally for *tax reasons* so that the machines may not all be in use in every period so that in any case they would not necessarily be scrapped a set number of periods after acquisition. For reasons of simplicity sales of fixed assets are also not included as a possibility.

We now turn to consideration of sales of the product and the holding of unsold units as inventory. It has been assumed that there is an upper limit for the sales of the product in each period. This upper limit states that at price a_{1i} it is possible to sell at most b_{2i} units of product during the ith period. Hence, the demand side of the model is drastically simplified. Instead of assuming a whole range of possible sales prices and a quantity demanded at each price we are assuming that only one price, 'the prevailing market price' is considered by the firm and that the sales forecasts are made on the basis of this price. This condition adds a restriction for each period considered:

$$x_{si} \leqslant b_{2i} \qquad (i = 1,2,, \ldots ,n) \tag{6.31}$$

In a dynamic problem it is not necessary to assume that production equals sales for each period. On the contrary, if there are changes in the price level, or in the sales volume from period to period, it is quite possible that it pays to produce more than is sold in a period, store the excess products and sell them during a later period. Therefore the restrictions given in (6.32) are added.

$$\sum_{j=1}^{i} x_{sj} - \sum_{j=1}^{i} x_{pj} \leqslant b_{3i} \quad (i = 1,2, \ldots , n)$$

(6.32) states that the cumulative amount sold from the beginning of the analysis to the end of the ith period, Σx_{sj}, must be less than or equal to the amount produced from the beginning of the analysis to the end of the ith period, Σx_{pj}, plus the difference between the opening inventory and the desired closing inventory, b_{3i}. However, these restrictions do not prevent the production from being higher than the minimum needed to satisfy the sales requirements. The excess will be carried in inventory and will be available for sales in later periods.

We will later consider the possibility of investing in inventories not only for production capacity, price, or demand reasons, but also for tax reasons. It is also for this reason that we want to keep the restrictions (6.32) in the form in inequality rather than equality. Then it may happen in the optimal solution that the restrictions (6.32) remain as strict inequalities for some periods because of the need to obtain tax deferrals via inventory reserves which are formed by acquiring additional inventory and by forming a reserve against its carrying value in the closing balance for the period.

The next set of constraints that are considered are those imposed by liquidity requirements. The sources of cash inflow in the model are sales income, new loans, and the issue of new shares, All sales are assumed to be made on credit which matures in the period immediately following the sale. The cash outflow is again the result of payments for wages and raw material purchases, investment in new machines, repayment of bank loans, and payment of interest, taxes, and overheads as well as distribution of cash dividends.

Maintaining liquidity means that the cash inflow from different sources must at all times be large enough to cover the cash outflow. The constraints are therefore stated in cumulative form. The cash outflow from the beginning of the analysis to the end of the ith period must be less than or equal to the cash inflow from the beginning of the first period to the end of the ith period plus the difference between the initial cash balance and the desired minimum cash balance that the firm wants to hold at all times and carry to the $(n + 1)$th period to be used as a liquidity reserve for post-horizon operations. These restrictions can be stated in the form of inequalities (6.33).

$$-\sum_{j=1}^{i-1} a_{1j}x_{sj} + \sum_{j=1}^{i} a_{3j}x_{pj} + \sum_{j=1}^{i} a_{5j}x_{mj} + \sum_{j=1}^{i} a_{16j}x_{lj} - x_{li}$$

$$+ \sum_{j=1}^{i-1} a_{13j}x_{hj} + \sum_{j=1}^{i} x_{dj} + \sum_{j=1}^{i} a_{4j}x_{rj} \leqslant b_{4i} \qquad (i = 1,2, \ldots, \hat{n} - 1)$$

$$-\sum_{j=1}^{i-1} a_{1j}x_{sj} + \sum_{j=1}^{i} a_{3j}x_{pj} + \sum_{j=1}^{i} a_{5j}x_{mj} + \sum_{j=1}^{i} a_{16j}x_{lj} - x_{li} + \sum_{j=1}^{i-1} a_{13j}x_{hj}$$

$$+ \sum_{j=1}^{i} x_{dj} - a_8x_{e\hat{n}} + \sum_{j=1}^{i} a_{4j}x_{rj} \leqslant b_{4i} \qquad (i = \hat{n}, \hat{n} + 1, \ldots, n) \qquad (6.33)$$

The constant b_{4i} on the right-hand side of the restriction for the ith period stands for the initial cash balance E_1 plus the initial accounts receivable E_2 less the initial accounts payable D_1 less the intial bank loans D_2 less the minimum cash balance to be held at all times less the fixed overhead computed cumulatively from the beginning of the analysis to the end of the ith period.

As always happens, the financing problem is also in this model created by the fact that the total cash inflow may not equal the total cash outflow, and, secondly, by the fact that cash outlays usually precede the respective revenues. How much cash outflow leads the cash inflow depends partly on the policy of the management and partly on technical and other considerations.

In the present model it is assumed that there is a one period lag between sales and the respective cash inflow and, similarly, between reporting the profit before tax and the respective cash outflow in the form of income tax payment. All other cash in- and outflows are assumed to take place in the same period as the respective transaction. All bank loans are assumed to be one period loans with interest payable in advance. Hence, the cumulative amount of loans drawn down and paid back from the beginning of the analysis to the end of the ith period is simply the borrowing performed during the ith period, x_{1i} (excluding, of course the amount of bank loans outstanding at the beginning of the analysis).

On the basis of these observations we can give the following interpretation to the first $\hat{n} - 1$ restrictions : the constant b_{4i} plus the cumulative cash inflow from the sales to the end of the preceding period, $\Sigma_{j=1}^{1i-1} a_{1j}x_{sj}$, plus the cumulative net borrowing, x_{1i}, must be larger than or equal to the cumulative cash outflow for the payment of direct wages $\Sigma_{j=1}^{i} a_{3j}x_{pj}$, the purchase of new machines, $\Sigma_{j=1}^{i} a_{5j}x_{mj}$, the payment of interest, $\Sigma_{j=1}^{i} a_{16j}x_{1j}$, and the corporate income tax, $\Sigma_{j=1}^{i-1} a_{13j}x_{hj}$, as well as for the distribution of cash dividends, $\Sigma_{j=1}^{i} x_{dj}$, and the purchase of raw material, $\Sigma_{j=1}^{i} a_{4j}x_{rj}$.

The second set of restrictions for the periods, $\hat{n}$, $n + 1, \ldots, n$ is to be interpreted in exactly the same way, except for the fact that they also include the cash inflow from the issue of new shares during the $\hat{n}$th period, $a_8 x_{e\hat{n}}$. The cash inflow from this source is the effective net rate of issue, a_8, multiplied by the number of shares issued, $x_{e\hat{n}}$.

The next set of restrictions are on borrowing.

One of the basic assumptions of the model is that the firm is subject to capital rationing. During each period the corporation can obtain at most a given amount of bank loans. This upper limit is set by the suppliers of funds and reflects the uncertainty which the creditors feel about the prospects of the firm. In other words, we realize that the suppliers of funds may recognize the safety of their loans to be less than complete, even though the borrower may regard his prospects as certain.

It is assumed that the suppliers of funds set these limits in accordance with their own standards. The problem of whether these standards are objectively set from the point of view of the corporation need not concern us here. As far as the analysis is concerned, it is enough to recognize that such limits exist and that the corporation must observe them in the planning of future operations.

The model considers only short-term borrowing. All loans are assumed to be one-period bank loans, i.e. the loan drawn down in the ith period must be paid back in the $(i + 1)$th period. However, in the $(i + 1)$th period the corporation may obtain new loans up to a new limit. This simplifying assumption makes it unnecessary to set up restrictions which would interrelate the loans of different periods. We only need to add to the model a single restriction for each period stating that the amount of outstanding loans can at most be b_5 monetary units, i.e. the maximum amount that the suppliers are willing to extend on the basis of the share capital of the corporation at the beginning of the analysis, plus the coefficient a_{10} times the undistributed profit accumulated during the preceding periods plus a_{10} times the new issue of share capital. In other words, it is assumed that the suppliers of funds observe the total amount of equity of the corporation at the end of the preceding period and set a maximum debt-to-equity ration up to which limit the corporation may borrow in each period. The upper limits on borrowed funds are stated in the constraints:

$$x_{li} - a_{10,i-1}x_{f,i-1} \leqslant b_5 \quad (i = 1,2, \ldots, \hat{n}),$$
$$x_{li} - a_{10,i-1}x_{f,i-1} - a_{10\hat{n}}x_{e\hat{n}} \leqslant b_5, \quad (i = \hat{n}+1, \hat{n}+2, \ldots, \check{n})$$
$$x_{li} - a_{10,i-1}x_{f,i-1} - a_{10\hat{n}}x_{e\hat{n}} - a_{10\check{n}}x_{g\check{n}} \leqslant b_5 \quad (i = \check{n}+1, \check{n}+2, \ldots, n) \tag{6.34}$$

The first $\hat{n}$ restrictions state that the outstanding loans during the ith period, x_{li}, must be less than or equal to the maximum amount that can be borrowed against the equity the firm has at the beginning of the analysis, b_5, plus the amount that can be borrowed against the undistributed profit that has accumulated up to the $(i-1)$th period, $a_{10,i-1}x_{f,i-1}$

The following restrictions for the periods $\hat{n}+1$, $\hat{n}+2, \ldots, \check{n}$ are to be interpreted in the same way except that they also include the increase in the credit limits due to the issue of new share capital during the $\hat{n}$th period, $a_{10\hat{n}}x_{e\hat{n}}$.

Finally, the remaining restrictions for the periods $\check{n}+1, \check{n}+2, \ldots, n$ add to the previous credit limits the additional amount that can be borrowed due to the increase in the share capital resulting from an issue of a stock dividend during the $\check{n}$th period, $a_{10\check{n}}x_{g\check{n}}$.

The complex problem of the issue of new shares is now tackled. There has been much debate in the literature on dividend policy and share price but there is no generally accepted view of how investors actually consider the dividend policy of companies nor even a normative theory that is held to be definitive. Consequently any manner of incorporation of new share issues into a model is likely to prove controversial. However, one point would find consensus and that is that a firm cannot continue to issue new shares year after year with impunity. In the model it is assumed that management has chosen the $\hat{n}$th period for the new issue, if it is to be realized at all. Under these assumptions two types of restrictions are added to the problem.

$$x_{di} - a_{12}x_{e\hat{n}} \geqslant b_{6i} \quad (i = 1,2, \ldots, \hat{n}) \tag{6.35}$$

$$x_{e\hat{n}} \leqslant b_7 \tag{6.36}$$

Instead of the restrictions (6.35) and (6.36) it should actually be stated that if the cash dividends of the ith period, x_{di}, are larger than or equal to the target dividends for the period, b_{6i}, $i = 1, 2, \ldots, \hat{n}$, then the corporation may issue any amount of new shares which is less than or equal to the upper limit, b_7. This would require a multistage programming process, but this condition is approximated by the constraints (6.35) and (6.36).

The $\hat{n}$ restrictions (6.35) state that the more the actual dividends, x_{di}, exceed the target dividend on the original share capital b_{6i}, the larger can be the amount of new shares issued, $x_{e\hat{n}}$. (6.36) stipulates that the amount of new shares issued must be less than or equal to the upper limit, b_7. This upper limit represents the estimate, made by the management, of the maximum amount of new shares that can be offered at the planned rate of issue, a_8, without risking a saturation of the market.

As regards depreciation rules it is assumed that the corporation is operating in an economy where the tax law allows the use of the declining balance method of depreciation. The firm can choose to depreciate in period any amount which is less than or equal to the maximum allowed depreciation. This maximum is the coefficient a_{15} multiplied by the remaining book value of the assets at the end of the period, i.e. by the sum of the assets acquired during preceding periods, net of previous depreciation and the new acquisitions. If less than the full amount is depreciated in a period, this will only result in an extension of the interval in which the asset will be totally depreciated. The depreciation rules are expressed by the constraints (6.37)

$$-a_{15} \sum_{j=1}^{i} a_{5j}x_{mj} + a_{15} \sum_{j=1}^{i-1} x_{wj} + x_{wi} \leqslant b_8 \quad (i = 1, 2, \ldots, n) \tag{6.37}$$

These restrictions state the the depreciation for the ith period, x_{wi}, must be less than or equal to the maximum depreciation of the net book value of the fixed assets at the beginning of the analysis, b_8, plus the maximum allowed depreciation of the new acquisitions up to the end of the ith period, $a_{15} \sum_{j=1}^{i} a_{5j}x_{mj}$, less the actual depreciation charged to the books up to the end of the $(i-1)$th period, $a_{15} \sum_{j=1}^{i-1} x_{wj}$.

Items of depreciation therefore are included in the constraint set because of the way in which the tax liability of the corporation is arranged. These are based on the book value of assets which, unless owners, potential owners or financial sources regard such data as significant, are irrelevant to future decisions. As will be seen later Jaaskelainen includes depreciation of *new* fixed assets in his objective function. Jaaskelainen uses an opportunity cost argument in support of this.

Continuing with the formulation of the constraint set, it has been assumed that the corporation is operating in a tax regime which permits the establishment of reserves against the carrying value of inventories. The value of inventories in the closing balance for a period can be written down to at most a given fraction of the historic cost of acquisition and a corresponding charge made against the income of the period.

This reserve reduces the book profit before tax and, hence, also the income tax. But since the reported book profit before tax is reduced, it follows that the reported net profit, i.e. funds which could be distributed as dividends, are also reduced.

If this reserve is decreased during later periods, then the reported book profit before taxes for those periods and, consequently, the income tax as well as the net profit will increase. Therefore, the advantage that the firm gets from establishing the reserve is a deferral of the payment of the income tax. However, this advantage can be obtained only at the expense of a simultaneous reduction in the net profit which could be distributed to the shareholders.

By increasing its inventory at the date the balance sheet is drawn up, the firm can increase the basis for the reserve. It is therefore possible to increase the inventory reserve to a level which completely offsets the profit before tax that would appear without the reserve. But in order to increase the inventory, the firm must increase the purchases of raw material and these purchases must be paid for in due time. In other words, to reduce the cash outflow in the form of income tax the firm must increase the cash outflow in the form of payments for raw material purchases. Thus the firm's liquidity position is affected. Also, it may not be quite riskless, from the point of view of sales, to have large inventories. The problem is to find the optimum level of inventories and reserve. For this reason we must add to the problem n restrictions which indicate the upper limit to this reserve:

$$a_{14} \sum_{j=1}^{i} a_{2j}x_{sj} - a_{14} \sum_{j=1}^{i} a_{3j}x_{pj} - a_{14} \sum_{j=1}^{i} a_{4j}x_{rj} + x_{qi} \leqslant b_9 \qquad (i = 1,2, \ldots, n) \qquad (6.38)$$

The constant b_9 represents the maximum inventory reserve that can be formed against the carrying value of the initial inventory of completed products, E_4, and raw materials, E_5. The restrictions state that the reserve for the ith period, x_{qi}, must be less than or equal to b_9 plus the coefficient that indicates the maximum reserve per unit of acquisition costs, a_{14}, multiplied by the cumulative additions to inventory, i.e. the sum of direct wages, $\Sigma a_{3j}x_{pj}$, and the sum of raw material purchases, $\Sigma a_{4j}x_{rj}$, less the coefficient a_{14} times the cumulative decrease in inventory, i.e. the direct cost of sales, $\Sigma a_{2j}x_{sj}$. It may be noted that we are assuming here that during each period i the reserve made for the preceding period, $x_{q,i-1}$. is reversed and a new reserve, x_{qi}, is established.

This feature of tax law is, I believe, peculiar to the Finnish economy but there are good reasons for discussing it here quite apart from the fact that it forms part of the original model. These reasons are first that the interdependence of other management decisions (here the management of inventory) and investment decision making is illustrated. This interdependence will be present but in different ways in the particular circumstances prevailing in different countries. Secondly, as Jaaskelainen himself points out, a similar result may be obtained by appropriately timed sales promotion expenditure – at the end of the tax year. These expenses are charged against income in that year but the benefit in terms of sales occurs later.

We now turn to constraints of a more familiar nature namely lower bounds on profits before taxation.

It is assumed that the firm can and will influence the amount of income tax it pays. However, the firm can influence the amount of income tax to be paid only within certain limits. These limits are set by the tax laws. If the firm crosses these limits, it has to pay taxes, but if it stays within these limits it avoids the tax. Moreover, it is assumed that sometimes the corporation may even choose to pay income taxes voluntarily in some period if it finds this policy to be to its advantage. Therefore a set of cumulative restrictions (6.39) which represent the bounds set by the tax laws is appended to the constraint set.

$$\sum_{j=1}^{i} (a_{1j} - a_{2j})x_{sj} - \sum_{j=1}^{i} a_{16j}x_{1j} - \sum_{j=1}^{i} x_{hj} - \sum_{j=1}^{i} x_{wj} - x_{qi} \leqslant b_{10i}$$

$$(i = 1, 2, \ldots, n) \quad (6.39)$$

These restrictions state that if the gross profit on sales, $\Sigma(a_{1j} - a_{2j})x_{sj}$, less interest expenses, $\Sigma a_{16j}x_{lj}$, less depreciation charges, Σx_{wj}, less inventory reserve, x_{qi}, less overhead expenses, b_{10i}, is larger than zero, then the profit before taxes, Σx_{hj}, is also larger than zero. The restrictions allow, however, for the possibility that Σx_{hj}, is larger than zero although the corresponding restriction is not binding in the optimal solution.

The optimal value of the slack variable associated with the ith restriction shows how much the corporation could reduce the profit before taxes for the ith period within the limits set by the tax laws and without acquiring any additional deductible expenses.

However, it is evident from (6.39) that the firm may also reduce the profit before taxes by acquiring new deductible expenses. This can be done, for example, by investing in new machines and then increasing the corresponding depreciation, Σx_{wj}. In fact, if the terms of payment for the new machines are suitable, a growing firm may sometimes invest in new machines for income tax reasons earlier than it would do in a taxless economy.

The next set of restrictions concerns the maximal values of payment of dividends both in the forms of cash and stock. Of course optimal cash dividend policy is a book length subject in itself but there is universal agreement that cash dividends represent important policy decisions. Does anything really change when a stock dividend is issued? Some economists argue not on the grounds that a stock dividend is in reality a stock split and therefore has no economic significance. However in the case of a widely owned corporation the average shareholder can control neither the amount of the book profit that is reported nor the proportion of the reported net profit that is distributed. Moreover, the average shareholder's attitude is that his control of the corporation is not affected in any way whether he sells some of the shares he owns or not. In this case he is not indifferent to the number of shares which he receives from the corporation free of charge and can sell in the market at the prevailing market value.

If this view is accepted, then it follows that the management must pay careful attention to the questions of when to issue a stock divident and how large a dividend should be issued. For even if the corporation distributed cash dividends in the periods, $1, 2, \ldots, \check{n} - 1$, a stock dividend in the $\check{n}$th period, and then again distributed cash dividends in the periods $\check{n} + 1, \check{n} + 2, \ldots, n$, and if everyone concerned knew this beforehand, it might still happen that the market value of the shares would fall if many of those who received free shares went to the market to sell these shares because of a need for cash.

The management must therefore pay attention both to the timing and to the amount of stock dividends. As in the case of the issue of new shares, the problem of timing could be solved by a multi-stage programming process. To simplify the model, however, it is assumed that the management has decided to issue a stock dividend, if any, in the $\check{n}$th period and that this period comes after the $\check{n}$th period, which is the period for the prospective issue of new shares.

Under these assumptions we get n cumulative restrictions on the maximum amount that can be distributed as dividends in any period:

$$
\begin{aligned}
&-\sum_{j=1}^{i-1}(1-a_{13})x_{hj}+\sum_{j=1}^{i}x_{dj}+x_{fi}\leqslant b_{11}\,(i=1,2,\ldots,\check{n}-1)\\
&-\sum_{j=1}^{i}(1-a_{13})x_{hj}+\sum_{j=1}^{i}x_{dj}+x_{fi}+x_{g\check{n}}\leqslant b_{11}\,(i=\check{n},\check{n}+1,\ldots,n)
\end{aligned}
\qquad (6.40)
$$

The first $\check{n}-1$ restrictions of (6.40) state that the cumulative cash dividends, Σx_{dj}, plus the amount of accumulated undistributed profit at the end of the ith period, x_{fi}, must be less than or equal to the accumulated unappropriated profit at the beginning of the analysis, b_{11}, plus the cumulative net profit from the beginning of the analysis to the $(i-1)$th period, $\Sigma(1-a_{13})x_{hj}$.

The following restrictions for the periods, $\check{n}, \check{n}+1, \ldots, n$ are to be interpreted in the same way except that they also include the stock dividend during the $\check{n}$th period, $x_{g\check{n}}$.

Now unlike the Chambers model, in which cash dividend payments were a fixed (in any one run of the model) proportion of earnings, in Jaaskelainen's model there are upper bounds, as we have seen, and also lower bounds to which we now turn. In other words dividends are discretionary between lower and upper limits – a more common circumstance in reality. In Chambers' model, dividends and terminal wealth were the only components of the objective functions. We are delaying discussion of the objective function in the present model because of its unusual and controversial nature but it is not a function of dividend payments. However, the effects of dividends on the price of existing shares and the success of new shares issues must be, and is considered by Jaaskelainen. The restrictions are:

$$
\begin{aligned}
&x_{di} &&\geqslant b_{13i}(i=1,2,\ldots,\hat{n})\\
&x_{di}-a_{12}x_{e\hat{n}} &&\geqslant b_{13i}(i=\hat{n}+1,\hat{n}+2,\ldots,\check{n}-1)\\
&x_{di}-a_{12}x_{e\hat{n}}+a_9x_{gi} &&\geqslant b_{13i}(i=\check{n})\\
&x_{di}-a_{12}x_{e\hat{n}}-a_{12}x_{g\check{n}} &&\geqslant b_{13i}(i=\check{n}+1,\check{n}+2,\ldots,n)
\end{aligned}
\qquad (6.41)
$$

The first $\hat{n}$ restrictions state that the cash dividend, x_{di}, must for each period be larger than or equal to a given minimum dividend, b_{13i}. The following restrictions for the periods $\hat{n}+1, \hat{n}+2, \ldots, \check{n}-1$ required that the minimum dividend must include not only the payment on the original shares, b_{13i}, but also the target dividend on the new issue, $a_{12}x_{e\hat{n}}$. Since it is assumed that a stock dividend can be paid during the $\check{n}$th period, the corresponding restriction requires the sum of the cash dividend, x_{di} and the stock dividend, x_{gi}, weighed by the coefficient a_9, to be larger than or equal to the minimum dividend on the original shares, b_{13i}, plus the dividend on the new issue $a_{12}x_{e\hat{n}}$.

Finally, the restrictions for the periods $\check{n}+1, \check{n}+2, \ldots, n$ state that the cash dividend, x_{di} must be larger than or equal to the minimum dividend on the original shares, b_{13i}, plus the dividend on the new issue, $a_{12}x_{e\hat{n}}$, plus the dividend on the shares which were distributed in the form of stock dividend, $a_{12}x_{g\check{n}}$. It may happen that the firm does not make enough profit every period to satisfy the requirements (6.41). The constraints (6.40) are designed to take care of this possibility. The corporation can leave profit unappropriated during profitable periods to be able to satisfy the minimum cash dividend requirements during less profitable periods.

Finally on the matter of dividends we come to the stock dividend constraint. For the same reason as there is an upper limit to the amount of new shares issued, expressed by inequality (6.36) the management must estimate an upper limit to the issue of stock dividends. This upper limit can be expressed as the inequality:

$$x_{g\check{n}} \leqslant b_{15} \tag{6.42}$$

The restriction (6.42) states that if it is decided to issue a stock dividend during the $\check{n}$th period, then at most b_{15} shares can be issued without risking the saturation of the market, and, hence, a drop in the market value of the outstanding shares.

Next we turn to the question of raw materials purchases. In this model the value of raw material purchased can contribute to inventory reserve if more materials are purchased than are needed for production purposes in the immediate future. Consequently no upper bound is placed upon the value of raw material purchases in any period but there will of course be lower bounds defined by production requirements. These are stated as (6.43).

$$\sum_{j=1}^{i} x_{pj} - \sum_{j=1}^{i-1} \leqslant b_{12}, \quad (i = 1, 2, \ldots, n) \tag{6.43}$$

The restrictions stipulate that the number of units of raw material used to the end of the ith period, Σx_{pj}, must be less than or equal to the number of units of raw material ordered to the end of the preceding or $(i-1)$th period, Σx_{rj}, plus the amount of raw material available at the beginning of the analysis (from which the minimum safety inventory to be kept at all times has been deducted), b_{12}.

Next we turn to a restriction defined by accounting practices. The statistic profit before tax is regarded by most managements as an important measure of their performance and variations in this figure and more particularly variations in dividends payable as a result of this figure in any year are regarded as significant by the market.

Although the management tries to distribute a minimum dividend every period and although a part of the profit of good periods may be left unappropriated to ensure the possibility of distribution during the periods with insufficient profits, there is still a possibility that there may not be enough funds to be distributed during a given period.

In a situation like this the management might try to increase the amount of funds which can be distributed by manipulation of the profit before tax. One possibility is to depreciate fixed assets less than the usual amount or to leave out depreciation altogether. Another possibility is not to charge the overhead, or a part of it, against the income for the period, but carry it instead in the value of the closing inventory and charge it against the income for later periods. Obviously, these are not the only alternatives.

However, legislation and accounting conventions applicable to the corporation set given limits to this kind of manipulation. We must therefore add to the problem constraints which set an upper limit to the profit before tax for each period:

$$(a_{1i} - a_{2i})x_{si} - a_{16i}x_{1i} - x_{hi} \geqslant b_{14i} \quad (i = 1, 2, \ldots, n) \tag{6.44}$$

These restrictions require that the gross profit for the ith period, $(a_{1i} - a_{2i})x_{si}$, less interest expense, $a_{16}x_{li}$, less the part of the overhead expenses which in no case can be incorporated in the carrying value of the inventory, b_{14i}, must be larger than or equal to the reported profit before taxes for the same period, x_{hi}.

Last of all, the usual non-negativity constraints must be added to the problem. These constraints require that all variables of the model must be larger than or equal to zero:

$$x_{si}, x_{pi}, x_{ri}, x_{mi}, x_{li}, x_{di}, x_{ei}, x_{wi}, x_{hi}, x_{fi}, x_{gi}, \text{ and } x_{qi} \geqslant 0 \; (i = 1, 2, \ldots, n) \tag{6.45}$$

The sign requirements (6.45) then complete the constraint set of the model.

We now come to the question of the objective function. If the discounted (or terminal value) of dividends and wealth, acting as proxy for the value of the company, is not to be maximized what is? Jaaskelainen states: 'It is assumed in the present model that the object of the managers is the maximisation of the undiscounted cumulative profit over the horizon. The profit is undiscounted since it is not possible to know in advance the relevant discount rate'. The statement of the objective function is:

$$Z = \sum_{j=1}^{n} a_{1j}x_{sj} - \sum_{j=1}^{n} a_{2j}x_{pj} - \sum_{j=1}^{n} a_{6j}x_{mj} - \sum_{j=1}^{n} a_{16j}x_{lj} - \sum_{j=1}^{n} a_{13j}x_{hj} \tag{6.46}$$

The first term of the objective function $\Sigma a_{1j}x_{sj}$, represents the sales income over the horizon. Since it is assumed that all sales are made on credit that falls due in the next period, it follows that the term $a_{1n}x_{sn}$ represents the credit sales of the last period which mature only after the horizon and therefore must be discounted back to the horizon.

The following term, $\Sigma a_{2j},x_{pj}$, is the total of the direct costs of production over the horizon. The term $\Sigma a_{6j}x_{mj}$ represents the estimated depreciation of the machines which are purchased during the interval under analysis. The constant a_{6j}

stands for the purchase price of the machine in the jth period less the estimated residual value of the machine at the end of the horizon.

The next term,, $\Sigma a_{16j}x_{lj}$, gives the total interest payments over the horizon. In this model it is simply assumed that all bank loans are one period loans with interest payable in advance. Therefore, the cash outflow for interest payments and the reporting of interest as expense coincide. Interest is not treated as part of fixed overhead in the model. Since the methods and amounts of financing are to be determined by the model, the interest payments are not independent of the solution and cannot be treated as fixed overhead.

Finally, income tax is deducted from sales income. The term $\Sigma a_{13j}x_{hj}$ represents the total taxes. It is assumed that the corporation draws up a balance sheet at the end of each period. The respective profit and loss statement will then show a profit before tax of x_{hj} monetary units. The resulting income tax, $a_{13j}x_{hj}$, is paid in the following period. It follows that the payment of the income tax for the nth period, $a_{13n}x_{hn}$, will take place only after the horizon and must therefore be discounted back to the end of the horizon. The problem of the treatment of post-horizon reserves and costs has already been discussed in general terms. Jaaskalainen's model it is assumed 'that all sales are made on credit which is payable one period after the sale'. It follows that the total of accounts receivable at the end of the horizon equals the sales of the nth period. The terminal amount of accounts receivable becomes a cash inflow only after the horizon. It must somehow be observed in the objective. If we include in the objective only the cash inflow that obtains over the horizon, the accounts receivable at the end of the nth period would have no value. No sales would appear in the optimal programme for the last period because they would not contribute anything to the cumulative profit. This would be an inadmissible result equivalent to discounting the last period's sales income back to the end of the horizon with an infinite rate of interest.

On the other hand, if the objective function included in the sales income of the nth period at face value, it would imply that the relevant discount rate for the $(n + 1)$th period is zero. This is also inadmissible. We have to find a discount rate which is between these two extremes and somehow satisfactory. We simply select the rate of interest on bank loans as such a discount rate, recognizing at the same time that such a discount rate will necessarily be arbitrary and subject to criticism.

Similarly, we will assume in the model that taxes are paid in the period that follows the one used as the basis for the assessment. For the same reasons as in the case of accounts receivable we have to discount the income tax assessed on the basis of the results of the nth period and payable during the $(n + 1)$th period back to the end of the horizon. The same arbitrary rate is used as the discount rate. This is not controversial. In all capital rationing models known to the author this, or some equivalent, means of considering post-horizon phenomena is adopted.

What is not stated by Jaaskelainen in respect of the particular objective function employed is what the *underlying* objective of the company or management is. True, it is stated that a particular profit expression is to be maximized – but why? Most models assume the objective of maximization of 'value' or growth of value of a company defined in some way. It may result from Jaaskelainen's model that some definition of value *is* maximized but this is not clear. Value is usually expressed as some function of terminal wealth (or the present value of this), and dividend payments because these are important criteria in the determination of share prices. The major part of the work on the model is in the formulation of the constraint set and it is the comprehensive nature of this, including the tackling of the financing problem, that is the principal contribution made by Jaaskelainen. The objective function could be reformulated either completely or by the addition of important terms. In the latter case for example, consideration might be given to the inclusion of the slack variables from a modified form of the nth period liquidity constraint. In the model as presently formulated the firm is constrained not to have net investment 'in the bank' ($x_{li} \geqslant 0$). Depending on outside interest rates, the profitability of production, upper bounds on production (to be added to the model in practice) defined by possible sales or some capacity limit and the tax benefits from inventory reserve, the firm may wish to be a net investor in banks, the capital market or elsewhere (i.e. other companies). If the liquidity constraints, or at least the nth period liquidity constraint, were reformulated along the two slack variable lines ($\bar{s}$ and $\hat{s}$) of previous models we have described this would both add some flexibility to the model and bring the objective function somewhat nearer to a conventional form.

6.6 The 'FIRM' Model

The 'FIRM' model (or rather set of models) produced by Deam, Bennett and Leather was produced with reference to a large petroleum company with worldwide operations. At the time of writing further work is still being conducted on this comprehensive and ambitious corporate model. The description given here will be confined to a broad outline of the major model along with some discussion of the scope of application and some reference to corporate models in general. The reader may obtain further detail from reference 5. A corporate model is one which, as the name implies, can include all the principal activities of the corporation from long term financial planning to production planning and cash management. In the case of an enterprise that is a group of companies there may be a group model with submodels for individual firms or particular purposes. These submodels are not independent of the group model but are interlinked with it so that there are no inconsistencies either in objectives or constraints and parameters.

Before the FIRM model proper is introduced it would be constructive to consider a simpler model produced by Deam, Bennett and Leather (1975, p.35–37), which includes constraints relating to cash, labour and machine and new capital availability and output and dividend policy constraints. This particular formulation might prove useful to smaller scale enterprises (with adaptations to suit). The parameters of this model are:

Z = horizon data,
r = shareholders discount rate,
q_{ji} = value at the horizon of project i available at time j
v_j = horizon value of machine purchased at time j,

p_j = price of new machines at time j,
g_{ji} = net cash receipt per unit of product i at time j (selling price less unit variable cost),
f_j = fixed costs at time j,
a_{jik} = cash receipt (positive) or outlay (negative) at time k on project i available for acceptance at time j,
B_{ji} = net contribution to cash per unit of product i at time j,
h_{ji} = labour hours required per unit of product i at time j
L = lifetime of machines,
s_{ji} = machine hours required per unit of product i at time j,
t_j = hours of service available from a machine j years after purchase ($t_j = 0$ for > 1),
B = initial cash available (at $j = 0$),
H_j = labour hours available at time j,
Y_{ji} = maximum possible sales of product i at time j,
d_{-1} = dividend paid one year before time $j = 0$,
C_j = maximum cash that can be raised by the issue of ordinary shares at time j to existing shareholders,
m = number of investment projects available,
n = number of products in product range.

The reader will note the predetermined length of horizon and the known and constant market discount rate and the fact that C_j could be set at zero level if no new issue (restricted to existing shareholders in this model), of equity capital was being considered. In the g_{ji} it is assumed that there is no significant time lag between incurring costs and securing revenue from sales. The parameters q_{ji} and v_j (referred to by the authors as terminal value) are 'the value at the horizon date of cash flows associated with the item subsequently'. In other words post-horizon moneys are treated in the usual way by discounting back to the horizon; in this case at $100r\%$. The authors make the point that: 'This procedure involves an element of approximation: for example, projects available before the horizon are not exposed to competition with a project which might become available just after the horizon. Such approximation is inevitable, however. It is likely to be less serious, the further ahead the horizon is set.'

The decision variables of the model are:

b_j = cash balance carried forward on current account from time j,
c_j = cash raised from the issue of ordinary shares to existing shareholders at time j,
d_j = ordinary dividend at time j,
w_j = number of new machines purchased at time j,
x_{ji} = number of units taken of project i at time j,
y_{ji} = sales (and production) of product i at time j.

All decision variables are constrained to be non-negative. Sales are directly from production (no change in inventory). c_j can be thought of as a deduction from dividend at time j. Issue costs are ignored. 'Projects' and 'machines' are distinguished. The machines relate to the normal productive activity of the firm whilst projects (as will be seen from the constraints set out below), are separate entities which consume only financial resources and unscarce physical resources. The 'projects' may be no more than the $\hat{s}$ and $\bar{s}$ of previous acquaintance or they may be physical assets which do not compete with 'machines' for anything other than finance. Upper bounds may be required on some of the x_{ji} and some may be restricted to integral values (of which, more later).

The problem is to

$$\text{maximize } F = \sum_{j=0}^{z} (d_j - c_j)(1 - r)^{-j} + (1 + r)^{-z} \sum_{j=0}^{z-1} \sum_{i=1}^{m} q_{ji}x_{ji} + \sum_{j=z-L}^{z-1} V_j w_j \tag{6.47}$$

$$b_0 + d_0 + p_0 w_0 - \sum_{i=1}^{m} a_{0i0} x_{0i} \leqslant B \tag{6.48}$$

$$b_k + d_k + f_k + p_k w_k + c_k - b_{k-1} - \sum_{j=0}^{k} \sum_{i=1}^{m} a_{jik} x_{ji} - \sum_{i=1}^{n} g_{ki} y_{ki} \leqslant 0 \quad (k = 1,2, \ldots, z-1, z) \tag{6.49}$$

$$\sum_{i=1}^{n} h_{ji} y_{ji} \leqslant H_j \quad (j = 1,2, \ldots, z-1, z) \tag{6.50}$$

$$\sum_{i=1}^{n} S_{ji} Y_{ji} - \sum_{k=0}^{j-1} t_{j-k} w_k \leqslant 0 \quad (j = 1,2, \ldots, z-1, z) \tag{6.51}$$

$$y_{ji} - Y_{ji} \leqslant 0 \quad (j = 1,2, \ldots, z-1, z) \tag{6.52}$$

$$d_{j-1} - d_j \leqslant 0 \quad (j = 0,1,2, \ldots, z-1, z) \tag{6.53}$$

$$c_j - C_j \leqslant 0 \quad (j = 1,2, \ldots, z-z, z-1) \tag{6.54}$$

$$b_j, c_j, d_j, w_j, x_{ji}, y_{ji} \geqslant 0 \tag{6.55}$$

The objective function (6.47) is the present value of current and future dividends (net of new capital raised from the shareholders, plus the present value of the horizon value of projects and assets. Thus the objective function has a conventional underlying philosophy. The financial constraints are defined by (6.48) and (6.49), all of which, incidentally, will be satisfied as equalities in an optimal solution. This is because if the time j constraint was satisfied as a strict inequality then d_j or a future dividend could be increased thus increasing the value of F. It would not necessarily be the case that d_j could be increased because of the dividend constraints (6.53), but there is no explicit upper bound on d_z which could always be increased in these circumstances by inter-period transfers via the b_j. The dividend constraints (6.53) prevent dividend cuts which are normally eschewed for reasons discussed for minimal inter-period growth of dividend.

The physical constraints are defined by the remainder of the constraint set.

(6.50) relate to labour availability in each period the limit of which is predetermined for each period in any one run of the model. (6.51) relate to machine services availability and include the decision variables w_j thus there are no explicit upper bounds in this case. Production takes place from time one onwards. (6.52) are the upper bounds on sales. In the words of the authors: 'This would amount to a fairly crude representation of an assumed sales price–volume relationship i.e. the assumption that price is fixed as a policy decision and there is some maximum volume that can be sold at that price. Although crude, such a view of pricing policy is often adopted in practice'. The computational cost of allowing price to be a function of quantity sold can be considerable, but a linear price quantity relationship is used in a quadratic programming model in Chapter 10. (6.55) are the familiar sign requirements in addition to which (omitted here) the authors placed the requirement that some of the $x_{ij} \leqslant 1$, that is, no more than one unit of some investment projects may be taken. Although 'shares' in a project limited to 100% participation are often admissible (for instance where a contract is made jointly with another company and as a matter of course in insurance underwriting), frequently the requirements that $x_{ij} \geqslant 0$ and $x_{ij} \leqslant 1$ are in addition to the condition that x_{ij} be integral. This means that the only admissible values of such x_{ij} are 0 and 1; the projects must be accepted in full or rejected altogether. Discussion of such cases is postponed until the next chapter.

Naturally, since the model is a linear programming model sensitivity analysis procedures can be readily applied. Of particular interest in this respect would be an examination of the effects of changes in some of the financial variables and parameters. The effects of changed market discount rate in the objective function – perhaps allowing for changes in this rate over time, the effects of changing the upper limit on new capital c_j and the initial funds available, B and the effects of changed dividend policy requirements. In this latter respect it is quite possible that the $d_j \geqslant d_{j-1}$ requirement would mean that no feasible solution existed initially. The problem would then be to determine the 'best' dividend policy that could be adopted.

There is a further point in connection with sensitivity analysis that is worth making. This is that some of the parameters of the problem will be estimates and as we have seen in earlier work sensitivity analysis can be used to examine the consequence of errors in estimation. Also in connection with data requirements Deam, Bennett and Leather point out that: 'The estimation of the numerical data is likely to be a much more costly exercise than the formulation of the mathematical model the first time a linear programming exercise is undertaken. On subsequent occasions, much of the existing data can be reused subject to critical review and revision in the light of new information'. Further, the objection that is sometimes heard '.... that in practice the estimates of the data may seem so speculative that management may have little confidence in the exercise', is rather feeble. In the first place management is not bound to follow the decisions indicated by the computer output – it can simply be used as valuable additional information in the decision-making process. Secondly, the whole exercise can be repeated '... for a range of different estimates to discover which decisions are unaltered within the range of assumptions – and hence should be adopted with high confidence – and which are 'marginal' and require further investigation'. In addition, 'All the data required is relevant and some assumption about it is implied by any decision; the model building process requires the assumptions to be made explicit so that the consequences of the best estimates possible can be studied systematically'.

The FIRM model proper is on a substantially larger scale than the model just described but has structural similarities. It is an optimizing rather than a simulating type corporate model and seeks to maximize the NPV of after tax cash flows to shareholders. All operating (existing production) and investment activities are expressed in terms of cash flows and a series of financial matrices provides the linkage between successive time periods. To quote: 'within each period opportunities are represented by a static linear programming formulation. In any period net cash flow is equal to Revenue less Operating Costs (excluding Depreciation), Loan Interest and Company Tax, and may be invested, carried forward or paid out as dividend. It may be supplemented by New Share issues and net borrowing. Whilst the model is a cash flow model it does have the ability to report by years the projected conventional financial statement data (and tax information) associated with each solution. FIRM simultaneously determines optimal production, refining and marketing plans for each specific year together with their implicit investment decisions. Interrelationships between proposed investments and existing facilities, interrelationships between operations and equipment capacities, and interrelationships between investment, operations and finance are examined in an integrated manner which permits the interrelationships to be resolved automatically'. In addition: 'Financial policy is examined in a manner which recognizes the effect of debt on the required yield on equity capital and which also relates financial policy to the overall corporate plan. It does not associate the interest rate on incremental debt with the evaluation of any incremental investment opportunity'. This latter point, as we have already seen in the capital rationing discussion is an essential difference between rationing models and non-rationing discussion NPV maximization problems.

As was mentioned at the beginning of this section, Deam, Bennett and Leather produced a number of models including an overall Group FIRM model and associate models. The Group model is in reference to an international petroleum company with activities in many areas. To lead up to a description of this model we should start with what would be termed by the authors a 'static, long term planning, single area model' the structure of which is given in Figure 6.3. In the Figure, as usual, columns represent activities and rows constraints and the shaded areas denote the presence of non-zero coefficients. The R.H.S. of the constraints is separated off and the objective function is at the bottom. As can be seen, three types of activity are distinguished: refining marketing and investment with subdivisions within each category. In the objective function it will be seen that there are non-zero coefficients under all but the contractual marketing activities. The term produced by these activities is a constant and so does not affect the maximization exercise. The objective function is 'optimal revenues' less variable costs less annual capital charges relating to the investments. For a particular

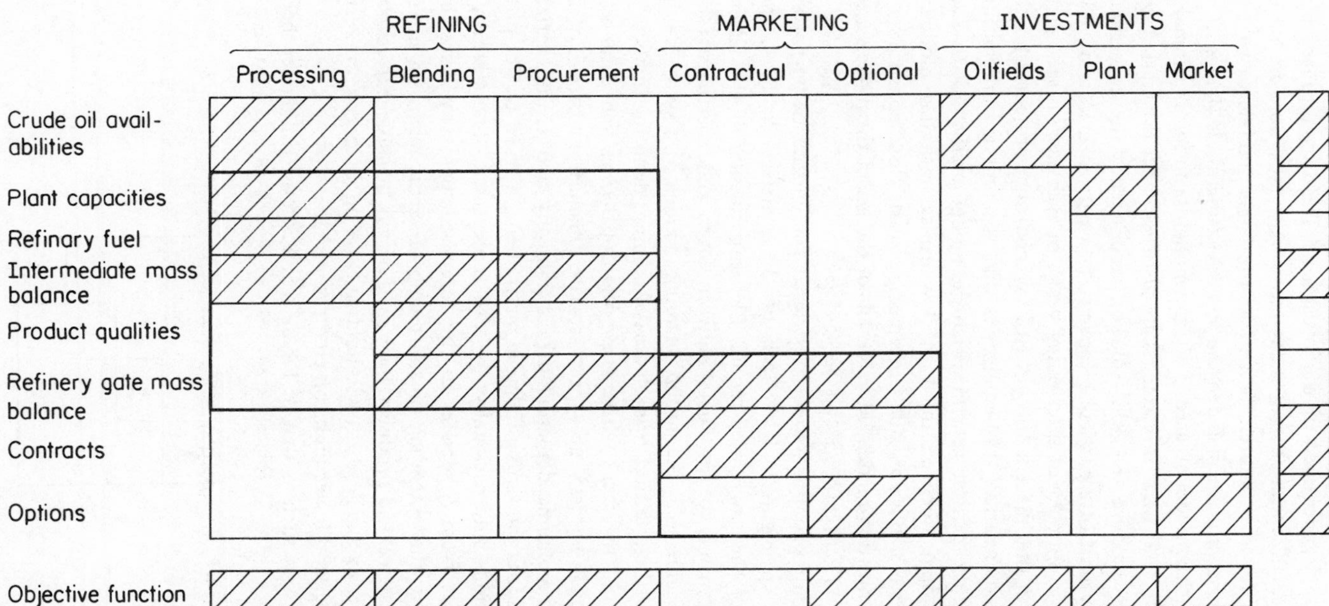

Figure 6.3 Structure of static, long term planning single area FIRM model

investment the 'annual capital charge' is that annuity figure running over the expected life of the investment, the present value of which is equal to the present value of capital outlays required on the investment. The discount rate employed to determine the annual capital charges is the cost of capital. There are no cash flow financial constraints incorporated as yet. In the larger models to follow, where these financial constraints are included the objective function is changed.

How would such a model be used? '. . . the model is run for a terminal year, say six years hence, to find what investments are justified under the market conditions projected. Let us suppose that this solution recommends the construction of a particular refinery unit of a particular capacity at a particular location. The model is then rerun for a number of intervening years, in each case to see whether that unit of that size in that place is still justified by conditions projected for the earlier years. The recommendation that emerges is that the unit is built in time to be commissioned by the earliest year in which the model justifies it'. In a sense this model is intermediate between the cash flow capital rationing models with an explicitly represented horizon and intermediate cash flow constraints and the earlier NPV maximization models. More details of the use of the models are given in Deam, Bennett and Leather (1975), pp. 53–54.

The larger group planning model (restricted for illustrative purposes to four areas), is shown in Figure 6.4.[12] Each of the matrices **A**, **B**, **C** and **D** are constructed as for the single area model. Elements outside of the lettered areas correspond to transfers of products between areas and coefficients in overall constraints. In Figure 6.5 the group planning model of Figure 6.4 has been '. . . expanded by the addition to each area of columns denoting financial balances and constraints, and the areas where these additional rows and columns overlap (marked with small letters), are the Associate financial matrices. In addition, further rows and columns depicting parent company and Group variables and constraints are added, the Group financial matrix being marked **G**. The possibilities of transferring funds internationally are also represented. These are by way of dividend payments from Associates to the parent company, by loans, by direct investment and by the extending or shortening of credit terms on international movements of crude oil and products. Each method will be subject to restraints and costs, for example, exchange costs, withholding taxes on dividends, interest charges on loans, and upper and lower limits on credit terms'.

Now, call a matrix such as that of Figure 6.5, **F**. In the full model there is an **F**

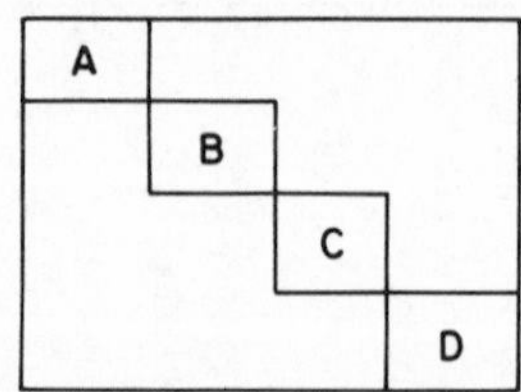

Figure 6.4 Structure of four area group planning model

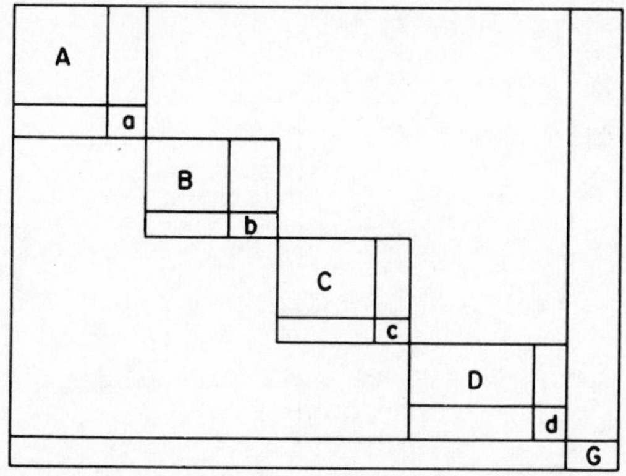

Figure 6.5 Group planning model with financial constraints

matrix for each time period that the model covers. The structure of the model in a four time period case would be as shown in Figure 6.6. in which $\mathbf{F}_t$ represents the **F** matrix for the *t*th time period so that as is usual, all time periods are handled simultaneously. There are non-zero coefficients below the $\mathbf{F}_t$ matrices in Figure 6.6. These represent the effects in future periods of activities undertaken in any given period. The objective function employed in this model represents current share price which is expressed as the sum of a function of historical share prices over the preceding average shareholding period and a discounted sum of all future dividends after 'allowance' for income and capital gains tax effects. A more detailed description of the objective functions will be given below.

The financial matrices (small letters in Figure 6.5), are of particular interest. A representation of such is given in Figure 6.7 for an Associate company in an initial year (one) and a subsequent year.[13] The authors describe this formulation as having only superficial representation of the parent company, it being assumed that the sole operating part of the group is the associated company. Further, costs and revenues are associated with cash flows (credit elements of transactions ignored). This is a simplification which will be removed in a later version of the model.

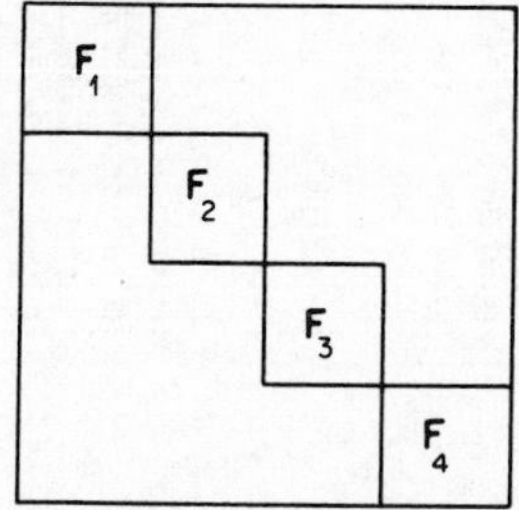

Figure 6.6 Structure of four period model

±	Row	1. Quantity Column	2. Costs	3. Revenues	4. Crude Profit	5. Investment	6. Operating Cash	7. Flow	8. Loan Taken	9. Loan Repaid	10. Interest Paid	11. Taxable Surplus	12. Tax Allowances Used	13. Tax Allowances C/F	14. Acc. Earnings + Before	15. Dividend	16. Dividend	17. Acc. Earnings After Dividend	18. Cash C/F	19. Cash Surplus To Investment	20. Borrowing Excess	21. New Issues	22. Dividend	23. Retained Cash
0	1. Investment Cash	-(7)				-1			+1	-1										-1		+1		
0	2. Tax Allowances	+(8)				-(1)							+1	+1										
0	3. Operating Cash	0	-1	+1			-1	+1			-1													
+	4. Loan Availability	+(9)							+1															
0	5. Loan Repayments	-(10)							+(2)	-1														
0	6. Interest	-(11)							+(3)		-1													
0	7. Taxable Surplus	0					+1					-1	-1											
0	8. Acc. Earnings	-(12)				-(4)	+1	-1				-(5)			-1	+1								
0	9. Div ⩽ Acc. Earnings	0													-1		+1	+1						
0	10. Div ⩽ Cash Flow	+(13)					+1	-1									-1		-1	+1				
+	11. Debt/Equity Ratio	+(14)							+1	-1											-1	-(6)		
0	12. Parent Co. Cash	0			+1												+1						-1	-1
+	13. Dividend Constraint	-(15)																					-1	
			←										Year 1											→
0	16. Investment Cash	0																	+1					+1
0	17. Tax Allowances	+(8)				-(1)		-1						-1										
0	18. Operating Cash	0																						
+	19. Loan Availability	+(9)																						
0	20. Loan Repayments	-(10)							+(2)															
0	21. Interest	-(11)							+(3)															
0	22. Taxable Surplus	0																						
0	23. Acc Earnings	-(12)				-(4)										-1		+1						
0	24. Div ⩽ Acc. Earnings	0																						
0	25. Div ⩽ Cash Flow	0										-(5)												
+	26. Debt/Equity Ratio	+(14)							+1	-1						+(6)		-(6)				-(6)		
0	27. Parent Co. Cash	0																						
+	28. Dividend Constraint	0																					+1	
Objective	S Type	(18)																				+(16)-(17)		
Functions	V-D Type	(18)							+(19)+(20)+(21)													+(22)-(23)		

Figure 6.7 Associate company financial matrix (part)

In the matrix of Figure 6.7 elements in the column labelled ± indicate the equation to zero (0) of the L.H.S. of the corresponding constraint or a weak inequality (+) in which the L.H.S. $\geqslant 0$. Elements in the matrix other than plus or minus unity are references to the explanatory notes below. A reference preceded by a minus sign indicates that the number entered is negative. To the right of the lower half of the array of coefficients in Figure 6.7 (opposite numbers 16–28), is an array identical to the upper half of the figure. These coefficients correspond to new activities undertaken in year two. The constraints 16–28 are spelled out in full after the explanatory notes.

Notes[14]

(1) The fraction of investment allowed as depreciation, investment allowances, etc. for corporation tax purposes. (2) The fraction of loan repayable (e.g. for 20-year loans repaid in equal instalments, the figures would all be 0.05). (3) The interest rate on loans. (By replicating the columns 8, 9, 10 with different figures it is of course possible to allow the model to choose between different terms of borrowing.) (4) The fraction of investment allowed as depreciation for accounting purposes. (5) The corporation tax rate. (6) The limiting debt/equity ratio. (7) Cash B/F from previous year. (8) Tax allowances available as a result of earlier operations. (9) Loan availability. (10) Sum of repayments, and (11) Interest payments, due on loans taken previously. (12) Initial value of accumulated earnings less current year's depreciation on existing assets (in year 1; In subsequent years only the depreciation on existing assets is given here, since the accumulated earnings figure is carried forward by the matrix itself). (13) Tax liability on previous year's operations. (14) (Limiting debt/equity ratio) x (Initial level of equity) – (Initial level of debt). (15) Minimum dividend (in year 1 only).

S TYPE Objective Function – (16) Cost of shareholder of one unit of cash raised by a new issue (including issue charges), discounted zero years in year 1, one year in 2, etc. (since issue is assumed to have been made during the previous year). (17)

$$\frac{\lambda^{j-1}(1-\beta)^{j-1}(1-b)}{(1+k_e^*)^j}$$

where b is the personal tax rate k_e^* is the shareholders' discount rate j is the year number and λ, β are correction factors for capital gains tax.[15]

(18) A constant,[16] the value of which will not affect the optimal strategy.

V-D TYPE Objective Function – (19) Loans taken are considered as involving cash flows from debt-holders in the previous period. Hence the coefficients for year j are:

$$\frac{1}{(1+k_w^*)^{j-1}} - \frac{1}{(1+k_i^*)^{j-1}}$$

where k_w^* is a weighted average cost of capital figure with the recognition of corporate and personal taxes, and k_i^* is the interest rate on debt capital, net of tax.

(20) As for (19) but shifted one year

$$\frac{1}{(1+k_w^*)^j} - \frac{1}{(1+k_i^*)^j}$$

(21) Debtholders' income is subject to personal tax, so coefficients become:

$$\frac{1-b}{(1+k_w^*)^j} - \frac{1-b}{(1+k_i^*)^j}$$

(22), (23) As for (16), (17) but with k_w^* replacing k_e^*.

The financial constraints can now be spelled out. The first states that investment in the first year does not exceed funds available then. In the identity form as presented in the matrix this reads:

– cash brought forward from previous year
– (−1 x year one investment +
+1 x loan taken +
−1 x loan repaid +
−1 x cash surplus to investment requirements +
+1 x cash raised by new share issues)
= 0

or alternatively it may be read as:

Year one investment = cash brought forward
plus loan taken
minus loan repaid
plus cash from new share issues
minus cash surplus

It is particularly instructive to examine constraints 16 to 28 i.e. those applying to the second year. It will be remembered that to the right of this lower half is another first half corresponding to activities started in year two. Thus row 16 can be expressed as:[17]

Year two investment = cash brought forward
plus retained cash
plus loan taken
minus loan repaid
plus new issues

Row 17 states that:

Tax allowance (to be used in year two or carried forward = tax allowances on investment (in year two year one and earlier)
plus operating loss in year one
plus tax allowances B/F from year one.

In row 18 operating cash flow may be either positive or negative and is represented by two variables in each year, one being positive cash flow the other the modulus of a negative cash flow.[18] This constraint states that:

Operating cash flow	=	operating revenues *minus* operating costs *minus* interest paid on loans

The remaining constraints state:

Row 19:	Loan taken	⩽	loan availability
Row 20:	Loan repayments	=	annual instalments due on earlier loans
Row 21:	Interest paid	=	interest rate *times* amounts of previous loans outstanding
Row 22:	Taxable surplus	=	operating surplus *minus* tax allowances used
Row 23:	Accumulated earnings (before year two dividend)	=	year one accumulated earnings *plus* current operating cash flow *minus* depreciation *minus* current tax liability
Row 24:	Accumulated earnings (after dividend)	=	accumulated earnings (before dividend) *minus* dividend
Row 25:	Dividend	=	operating cash flow *plus* cash surplus to investment requirements *minus* payment of previous years tax liability *minus* cash carried forward
Row 26:	'Borrowing Excess'[19]	⩾	book value of debt *minus* debt/equity limit *times* book value of equity
Row 27:	Retained cash	=	profit to parent company (from oil sales) *plus* dividend received from associate *minus* dividend to shareholders
Row 28:	Year two dividend to shareholders	⩾	year one dividend to shareholders

The 'borrowing excess' variable assumes a positive value when the debt/equity ratio is exceeded. This variable can be prevented from being positive in an optimum solution by attributing to it a suitably large, negative, objective function coefficient. On the other hand the model can allow for the possibility of the debt/equity limit being exceeded for individual years while holding on average. Many of the other variables in the model have no generally accepted unambiguous definitions. Whilst we shall not go into this matter here the interested reader is referred to Reference 5 pp. 66–67 for clarification.

The model was run with two versions of the objective function, most work being done with what the authors refer to as the 'S type' function. As we have already said, the function maximized is a definition of current share price which is the sum of:

(i) A function of historical share prices over the past N years where N is the average shareholding period;

(ii) A discounted sum of dividends over an infinite horizon after adjustment for income and gains tax effects.

The S type function is given in equation (6.56) where the first summation term is (i) above and the second summation term is (ii) and in which the P^* are historical share prices.

$$P_0 = \sum_{j=1}^{N} \left(\frac{\lambda(1-\beta)}{1+k_e^*}\right)^{j-1} \cdot \frac{\beta P^*_{-N+j}}{1+k_e^*} + \sum_{j=1}^{\infty} \left(\frac{\lambda(1-\beta)}{1+k_e^*}\right)^{j-1} \cdot \frac{d_j}{1+k_e^*} \qquad (6.56)$$

Clearly, since any model of share price determination can be disputed then P_0 as defined by (6.56) (referred to by the authors as the 'true value' of shares) could be criticized. Indeed the authors readily concede that capital gearing creates difficulties for functions (6.56) since the discount rate k_e^* was determined on the assumption that the limiting debt equity ratio held. In fact in use of the model this turned out to be perfectly reasonably (as we should expect since debt is cheaper as a source of finance than equity). The 'V–D' type objective function attempts to remedy this not-too-serious deficiency. In the V–D type function (with new issues allowed for), instead of the contribution to the objective function in year j being

$$\frac{S_j}{(1+k_e^*)^j}$$

where S_j is the total after tax cash flow to shareholders including dividends and new issues (negative) the contribution to the objective function is expressed as:

$$\frac{S_j + t_j}{(1+k_w^*)^j} - \frac{t_j}{(1+k_i^*)^j}$$

where t_j is the after tax cash flow to debtholders including interest payments, repayments and new loans (negative) and k_i^* is the after (personal) tax interest rate on debt and k_w^* is a weighted mean cost of capital figure independent of gearing. Extensive further discussion of the problems of determining the objective function is to be found in Deam, Bennett and Leather (1975, Chapter 3).

As regards computational feasibility the prototype FIRM model with one associate company and two refining and marketing areas and covering seven one-year periods contained about 2,800 rows and 5,500 columns. The initial run of this model (even after a fairly good starting point had been obtained piecemeal), took 15 hours on a large computer. However, after the problem has been solved once it is a much smaller task to solve a slightly different problem with the original solution as the starting point – 'This, together with improvements in the computer programme over recent years, means that it is now possible to run variant cases in an hour or two'. So that although computational effort is considerable the single associate model is currently a practical proposition. The full scale model described earlier is however an order of magnitude larger. Based on a Group planning model of 3,000 rows with 500 financial constraints and in excess of 6,000 columns over seven time periods there would be 24,500 rows. Whilst this is not currently feasible computationally ' . . . attempts to build and solve a representation of the group are now proceeding'. Further, the authors point out that (Deam, Bennett and Leather, 1975, p. 57) 'While the possibilities for optimization clearly increase as more and more of the Group's activities are included, nevertheless we feel that it is not premature to discuss openly the concept of such a model, which draws together much of the previously published work in the field of corporate financial planning'.

In conclusion it is useful to see the place within an overall planning context of models such as FIRM. A hierarchy of models can be constructed which can cover most, if not all, aspects of short, medium and long term planning. For instance, in the short term the problem of cash management could be approached with an appropriately designed model integrated into the overall planning system (see Figure 6.8). Deam, Bennett and Leather have constructed such a model to cover twelve one-month periods. The model ' . . . describes the periodic inflows and outflows of cash to and from the Group and the possible ways of investing or borrowing in the short term, the predictions of fluctuations in interest rates and exchange rates and the possible ways of transferring funds across natural boundaries, and attempts to maximize the value of the Group's current assets less current liabilities in one year's time'. In the short and medium term production and inventory control problems can be addressed with long term assets taken as fixed. Quarterly time periods might be convenient in such contexts. 'Such a model with, say, six time periods, three of one month and three of three months, could be used to break-down the medium term plan into short term operating patterns.'

Figure 6.8[20] illustrates the place of these models along with the long term Group and Associate models in the overall planning system. 'Data would be fed to each model consisting of quantities and prices of the Group's resources as determined by the next senior model(s) in the hierarchy. Thus, each aspect of the Group's activities would be optimized in a way that was subject to, and hence in

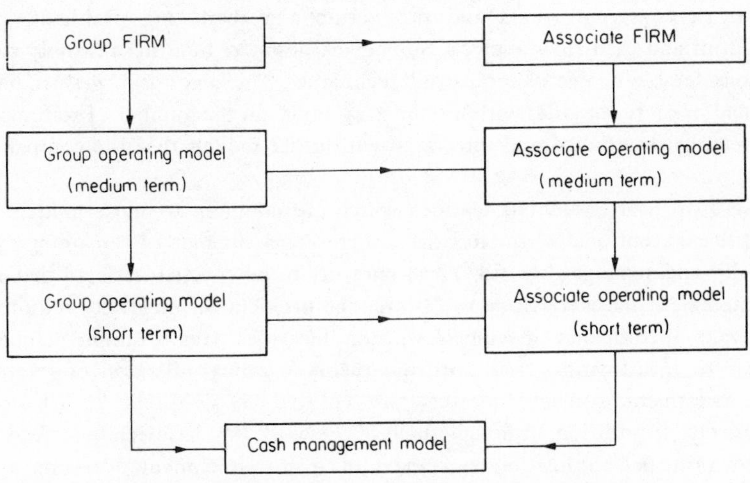

Figure 6.8 FIRM models within the overall planning system

accordance with, the objective of the whole. Suboptimization at the expense of the whole would thus be avoided.'

The implementation of such a comprehensive system of planning, quite apart from being a huge managerial task, would have wider ramifications in the area of organizational structure. Nevertheless it is along such lines that progress in scientific management will occur.

6.7 Concluding Remarks

Basic capital rationing models were introduced in Chapter 5 and in this chapter, five models of a financial planning nature at varying levels of complexity have been introduced. The size and sophistication of the models could be increased still further, but the objective of this chapter, as in other chapters, is to convey the *essence* of investment and financial decision making models along with a degree of technical knowledge sufficient to allow thorough understanding but stopping some way short of technical wizardry.

As has already been pointed out, in practice the detailed circumstances of particular cases usually require individual modelling. This does not imply an entirely unique model for each company: an existing model can often be modified to suit varying individual requirements. There are very many 'company' models in existence, both those that were designed by or for particular companies and those that are offered as adaptable packages by computing or consulting organizations. Those models in use in the U.K. are described in an excellent survey by Grinyer and Wooller (see references) in which the scope and limitations of each package are detailed.

The variation in sophistication is considerable, many being little more than a series of interconnected accounting identities that would find their principal use in the projection of profit and loss accounts, balance sheets, etc. under differing assumptions (i.e. sensitivity analysis). At the other extreme are corporate models of considerable complexity and adaptability with the ability to handle financial planning over several years and production and marketing problems, project evaluations and cash flow analysis. Some packages offer built-in sensitivity analyses and considerable choice of forecasting techniques. The larger packages can handle a thousand or more variables with 'no practical limit' on the number of statements.[21] Many can be interlinked and integrated with other models that the company may use.

Whilst we have presented features which are common to most models (along with some exceptional characteristics), there are a number of remaining areas of difficulty and some gaps to fill. The topics yet to be covered in detail that extend or complement the work done so far are: the problem of integrality requirements (fractional investments meaningless), non-linearities (for example diminishing returms to investments), and portfolio theory (optimal selection of interrelated risky investments). These matters are covered in Chapters 7, 10, and 11 respectively. In addition, although much of the work that has been described would find its principal application in respect of major investment decisions by large corporations, little has been said about the planning stage of projects and the application programming and capital budgeting techniques to the developmental phase of large investments. Chapters 8 and 9 introduce techniques that enable capital budgeting methods to be applied to such areas.

Notes

1. Baumol, W. J., *Economic Theory and Operations Analysis*, 2nd. edn., Chapter 13, Prentice-Hall, Englewood Cliffs, N. J., 1965.
2. See for example Gordon, M. J., *The Investment, Finance and Valuation of the Corporation*, Irwin, Homewood, Illinois, 1962.
3. For further discussion of this point see Section 6.6.
4. Mao, J. C. T., 'Survey of capital budgeting: theory and practice', *Journal of Finance*, May, **1970**.
5. A departure from the usual game situation in which 'plays' are simultaneous. There is also only one 'play' for each participant. Player A selects the levels of investment and player B selects the relevant (lowest) valuation of the investment.
6. Chambers, D. J., 'Programming the Allocation of funds subject to restrictions on reported results', *Operations Research Quarterly*, **18**, No. 4, 1967. The presentation given here is renotated but is otherwise precisely the model à la Chambers.
7. Chambers, D. J., 'Programming the allocation of funds subject to restrictions on reported results; *Operations Research Quarterly*, **18**, No. 4, 1967.
8. Chambers, D. J., 'Programming the allocation of funds subject to restrictions on reported results; *Operations Research Quarterly*, **18**, No. 4, 1967.
9. Chambers, D. J., 'Programming the allocation of funds subject to restrictions on reported results; *Operations Research Quarterly*, **18**, No. 4, 1967.
10. Jaaskelainen, V., 'Optimal financing and tax policy of the corporation', *Publications of the Helsinki Research Institute for Business Economics* No. 31, 1966. In the description of the model in this section many passages of text are taken verbatim from Jaaskelainen's book. In order to minimize clutter I have not cited such passages by use of footnotes, nor are all placed in quotation marks. Tables and notation are also identical. I am extremely grateful to Veikko Jaaskelainen for permission to do this. Needless to say, any misconstructions or misconceptions that may have crept in are my own.
11. Figure 4, p. 51, Reference 5. Reproduced by permission.
12. Figure 6.4 and 6.5 are Figures 5(a) and 5(b), p. 56, Reference 5. Reproduced by permission.
13. Figure 6.7 is part of Figure 8, pp. 62–63, Reference 5. Reproduced by permission.
14. These notes are those given by Deam, R. J., Bennett, J. W., and Leather, J. to Figure 8, pp. 62–63, Reterence 5. Reproduced by permission.
15. A detailed explanation of the objective function occupies a full chapter in Deam, Bennett and Leather and cannot be reproduced here. However, β is the ratio of capital gains tax rate to shareholding period and $\lambda = 1$ in the absence of gains tax. Otherwise λ satisfies $\lambda^N \nu - \lambda + 1 = 0$ where $\nu = \beta(1 - \beta)^{N-1} (1 + k_e^*)^{-N}$. The interested reader is referred to Reference 5, pp. 95–102. Some general remarks on the objective function are given below.
16. The second summation in equation 28, Reference 5, p.102.
17. From the text p. 63, Reference 5. It would appear that the 'retained cash' is held by the parent company whilst cash brought forward is held by the associate company.
18. This is a technique that we have seen in earlier work and is applied also to accumulated earnings.
19. For discussion of this variable see below.
20, Figure 9, p. 71, Reference 5.
21. In view of the computing difficulties encountered by the first full scale FIRM model it would appear that models with more than 20,000 constraints were not envisaged.

Additional References

1. Chambers, D., and Charnes, A., 'Inter-temporal analysis and optimization of bank portfolios', *Management Science*, **1961**.
2. Charnes, A., Cooper, W. W., and Miller, M. H., 'Application of linear programming to financial budgeting and the costing of funds', *Journal of Business*, January, **1959**.

3. Charnes, A., and Cooper, W. W., *Management Models and Industrial Applications of Linear Programming* (2 vols.), Wiley, London, 1961.
4. Cyert, R. M., and March, J. G., *A Behavioral Theory of the Firm*, Prentice-Hall, Englewood Cliffs, N. J., 1963.
5. Deam, R. J., Bennett, J. W., and Leather, J., 'Firm: a computer model for financial planning', *The Institute of Chartered Accountants Research Committee Occasional Paper No. 5*, 1975.
6. Demster, J., 'An accounting system structured on a linear programming model', *The Accounting Review*, October, **1967**.
7. Gordon, M. J., *The Investment, Financing and Valuation of the Corporation*, Irwin, Homewood, Illinois, 1962.
8. Gordon, M. J., 'Optimal investment and financing policy', *Journal of Finance*, **1963**.
9. Grinyer, J. R., 'Financial planning models incorporating dividend and growth elements', *Accounting and Business Research*, Spring **1973**
10. Grinyer, P. H., and Batt, C. D., 'Some tentative findings of corporate financial simulation models', *Operational Research Quarterly*, March, **1974**.
11. Grinyer, P. H., and Wooller, J., 'Corporate models today: a new tool for financial management', *The Institute of Chartered Accountants in England and Wales*, 1975.
12. Ijiri, Y., Levy, F. K., and Lyon, R. C., 'A linear programming model for budgeting and financial planning', *Journal of Accounting Research*, Autumn **1963**.
13. Lerner, E. M., and Carleton, W. T., 'The integration of capital budgeting and stock valuation', *American Economic Review*, September, **1964**.
14. Lerner, E. M., and Carleton, W. T., *A Theory of Financial Analysis*, Harcourt, Brace and World, New York, 1966.
15. Lutz, F., and Lutz, V., *The Theory of the Investment of the Firm*, University Press, Princeton, N. J., 1951.
16. Mansen, R. J., and Downs, A., 'A theory of large managerial firms', *Journal of Political Economy*, June, **1965**.
17. Salkin, G., and Kornbluth, J., 'Linear programming in financial planning', *Accountancy Age Books*, Haymarket Publishing, London, 1973.
18. Solomon, E., *The Management of Corporate Capital*, The Free Press of Glencoe, Glencoe, Illinois, 1959.
19. Solomon, E., *The Theory of Financial Management*, Columbia University Press, New York, 1963.
20. Warren, J. M., and Shelton, J. P., 'A simultaneous equation approach to financial planning', *Journal of Finance*, December, **1971** .
21. Williamson, O. E., *The Economics of Discretionary Behaviour: Managerial Objectives in a Theory of the Firm*, Prentice-Hall, Englewood Cliffs, N. J., 1964.
22. Wilkes, F. M., and Samuels, J. M., 'Stock market constraints and objectives in capital investment appraisal', *University of Aston in Birmingham Discussion Paper in Business and Organization No. 21*, July, 1970.

CHAPTER 7

Integer Linear Problems

Integer linear problems are those programming problems which would be linear were it not for the fact that some or all of the problem variables are not continuoulsy divisible. Such problems are sometimes referred to in the literature as discrete or diophantine programming problems. We may come across such problems in the capital budgeting area for two reasons. First there is the obvious case where only whole numbers of units of investments may be taken. Then there are those problems in which the formulation used requires the introduction of variables, not investment levels themselves, of a discrete nature. Such is the case in problems in which some of the constraints are of an 'either–or' nature and it can be convenient from a formulation point of view (if not from the computational standpoint) in such cases to introduce special additional variables that may take only integral values, usually just zero or one. Illustrations will be given below.

The chapter begins with some introductory observations, goes on to introduce two computational procedures for different types of integer problem, discusses other computational approaches and concludes with consideration of further applications in the capital budgeting area.

7.1 The Nature of the Problems

The class of discrete linear programming problems can be divided into a number of sub-types. A convenient classification is as follows:

(i) All integer problems.
(ii) Mixed integer-continuous variable problems.
(iii) Zero-one problems.

As the name suggests, the first category (also known as pure integer problems) consists of those problems in which all of the variables, including the slack variables, are required to take only whole number values in feasible solutions. Relatively few investment applications would be of such a nature but the pure problem provides a useful descriptive starting point and indeed the computational procedure that will be applied to such problems will be (with a minor modification) applied also to the more common mixed integer–continuous case. Consider the problem:

$$\text{maximize } F = 6x_1 + 7x_2$$

$$\text{subject to} \quad 2x_1 + x_2 \leqslant 13$$

$$x_1 + 2x_2 \leqslant 15$$

$$x_1, x_2, s_1, s_2 \geqslant 0$$

$$x_1, x_2, s_1, s_2 \text{ integral}$$

This problem is graphed in Figure 7.1. Were it not for the integrality requirements the feasible area would have been the familiar convex quadrilateral OABC of the continuous linear problem. With the integrality requirements, the feasible 'area' becomes the set of integer *lattice points* bounded by OABC.

It should be noted that in general, in an all-integer problem, some of the lattice points in $(x_2 x_1)$ space may not be feasible since they correspond to non-integral values of the slack variables. In the problem graphed it is evident that the basic feasible solutions, A, B, C, to the linear continuous problem are not feasible in the integral case, but this will not always be so since it may turn out that some of the b.f.s. correspond to lattice points.

On the face of it, the fact that a continuum of feasible solutions has been reduced to a finite number may seem a simplification; but it is not. Quite the reverse! It will be recalled that the fundamental theorem of linear programming allows the elimination of all feasible solutions save the basic solutions at the corner points of the feasible area. With the integrality requirements in force this is no longer possible. It will be seen that there are many more feasible lattice points in the integer problem than there are b.f.s. in the linear continuous case. This is the heart

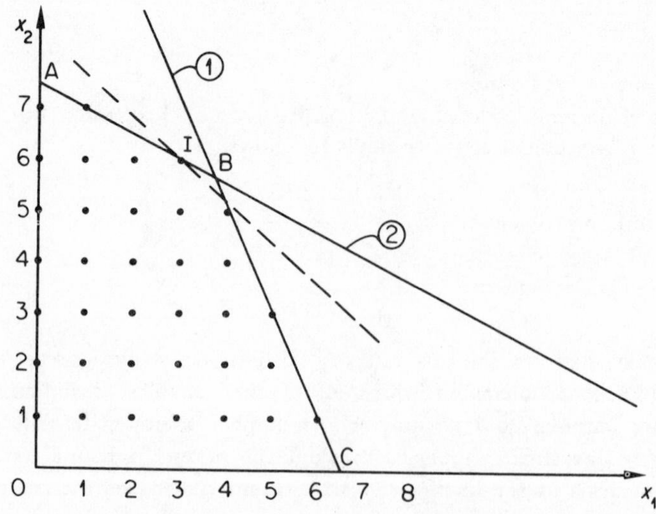

Figure 7.1 Graph of all integer problem

of the matter. It might be argued that only the five lattice points on the boundary of the feasible region need be considered, the remainder could not be optimal. Whilst this is correct it would be a prodigous computational task in problems of moderate size to identify and eliminate the 'dominated' lattice points. What is a simple task in a two-dimensional problem is quite out of the question in problems of realistic proportions and efficient (by integer programming standards) computational procedures do not approach the problem in this manner.

What alternative approaches suggest themselves? From Figure 7.1 it will be seen that the integral optimum, I, represents a rounding off of the continuous optimum at B. At point B the variables take the values $x_1 = 11/3$, $x_2 = 17/3$, $s_1 = 0$, $s_2 = 0$ and $F = 185/3$. At point I the values are $x_1 = 3$, $x_2 = 6$, $s_1 = 1$, $s_2 = 0$ and $F = 60$. It will be noted that at the integral optimum there are *three* strictly positive variables. Unless by chance the integral optimum coincides with a basic solution of the continuous problem there will be more positive variables than there are constraints (degeneracy aside) in the continuous problem. The integrality requirements themselves represent additional constraints which can be thought of as a set of mutually exclusive equality constraints, i.e. $x_1 = 0$, *or* $x_1 = 1$, *or* $x_1 = 2$ etc. Naturally, when constraints are added to a problem the value taken by the objective function cannot increase. Whilst rounding off is advisable in certain cases (see below) it is not a useful approach to finding the global integral optimum. This is so for two reasons.

Firstly, the integral optimum may not be a rounded-off version of the continuous optimum – it may have a very different composition.

Figure 7.2 illustrates a 2 x 2 problem in which rounding off the continuous optimum will not produce the integral optimum. Both structural variables must be integral and the fractional optimum is at point B with $3 < x_1 < 4$ and $3 < x_2 < 4$. B can be rounded off to either (3, 4) or (4, 3) but the solution I (5, 2) is superior to both as is evidenced by the objective function contours shown. It is worth noting, however, that there is not apparently a great difference between the values of the objective function at (3, 4), (4, 3) and I. The smaller are the fractional components of variables in a non-integral optimum relative to the 'whole' components the more likely this is to be the case. In such instances in larger problems (when the computational cost of obtaining I is considered) rounding off the fractional solution will be expected to optimize $F^* = F - C$, where F represents the objective function as previously considered and C is computational expense. This point is returned to later.

Secondly, the problem of rounding off is in itself an integer programming problem. As an instance of this point the problem of rounding off the continuous solution to the example above can be expressed as:

$$
\begin{aligned}
\text{maximize } F &= 6\Delta x_1^* + 7\Delta x_2^* + 13/3 \\
\text{subject to } \quad & 2\Delta x_1^* + \Delta x_2^* \leqslant -1 \\
& \Delta x_1^* + 2\Delta x_2^* \leqslant -1 \\
& \Delta x_1^* \ \Delta x_2^* \text{ integral} \\
& \Delta x_1^* \geqslant -4 \ \Delta x_2^* > -6
\end{aligned}
$$

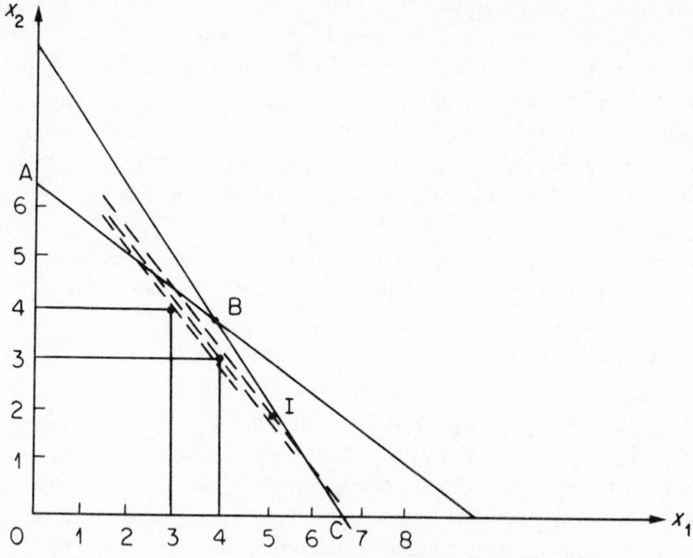

Figure 7.2 Failure of rounding off approach

where $\Delta x_1^* = \Delta x_1 - {}^1/_3$ and $\Delta x_2^* = \Delta x_2 - {}^1/_3$ and where Δx_1 and Δx_2 are the changes in x_1 and x_2 respectively from their values at the continuous optimum. Inspection of Figure 7.1 may suggest other lines of approach which would appear to be suitable for two-structural variable problems but the enthused reader should recall that in the diagram knowledge of the feasible set of lattice points has already been employed.

The second category consists of problems in which some, but not all of the variables must take only integral values. Typically in investment applications the slack variables relating to financial constraints are not required to be integral. Physical resources such as floor space, resource time (man hours, machine hours) and many physical quantities are continuously divisible. The set of integer-only variables is usually confined to certain of the investment possibilities and some variables introduced for formulational convenience (see Section 7.8). Figure 7.3 shows a two structural variable problem in which only x_2 is required to take an integral value, x_1 and the slacks being continuous variables. Feasible solutions are on the horizontal lines corresponding to integral values of x_2 bounded by the axes and the other constraints. As in the all-integer case there will typically be more positive variables at the optimum that there are constraints in the all-continuous problem.

It can sometimes turn out that an apparently mixed problem is in effect an all integer problem. For instance in the problem of Figure 7.1 if only the structural variables were required to be integral it would always turn out that the slack variables took on integral values at a feasible solution. Clearly, in problems in which all structural variables are required to be integral and in which technical coefficients

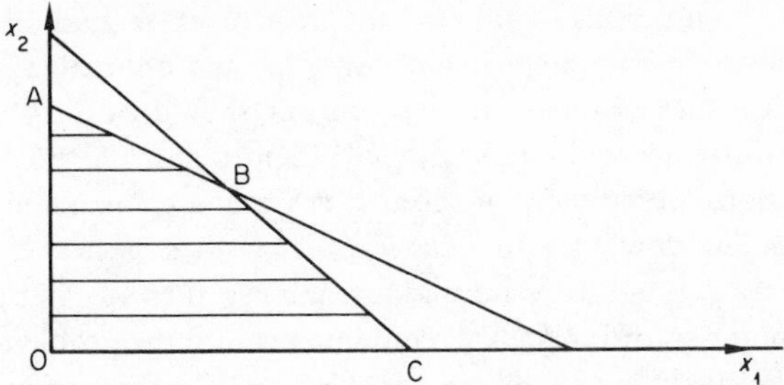

Figure 7.3 Graph of mixed integer–continuous problem

and right-hand sides are integral then slack variables will turn out to be integral too.

In zero-one problems the structural variables may assume only the values nought or one These variables are said to be 'two-state' and in an investment context would correspond to reject (zero) or accept (one). Investments which are of an all-or-nothing variety will have a two-state variable representing the investment level. The feasible set in an all two-state n structural variable problem comprises those 'corners' of the n dimensional hypercube which do not violate the financial and other constraints. Clearly such zero-one problems are special cases of the mixed integer-continuous variable problem and could employ the same solution procedure. However, as a rule, it is useful to exploit whatever special structure a problem has and a different solution method is presented later in the chapter. There will be problems of course in which not all of the investment levels are restricted to zero or one and in some problems only variables introduced for formulative convenience will be two-state. The choice of computational method in such cases would be from amongst those variables for mixed integer continuous problems in general.

We have mentioned that obtaining the global optimum (or in many instances just a 'good' solution) in integer problems will be much more time consuming and expensive than is the case in ordinary L.P. problems. So much so that Wagner[1] describes the problem of finding efficient algorithms as the 'quest for a philosopher's stone' whilst Woolsey[2] states 'This author has discovered the interesting fact from his experience that on many real world problems, people with experience can beat an elegant theoretical model all the time'. This suggests that there would be much to learn from a formal analysis of how 'experienced people' approach the problem. No doubt such studies will be undertaken in due course. Whilst in a heuristic context this writer's intuition suggests that an approach that utilizes the better qualities of both men and machines would have something to recommend it. Indeed it may transpire that some interactive procedure would get the best of both worlds – the machine possibly being helped along with one of the algorithms described below.[3]

It is hardly necessary to add that if integrality requirements can be sidestepped or otherwise not explicitly included in the problem at hand, they should be. What such cases arise? We have already discussed some difficulties associated with rounding off the continuous optimum. In practice there will be some readily identifiable cases where rounding down is simple[4] and optimal. If an automobile manufacturer finds that optimal monthly output should be 1, 413.2 units then rounding down this figure will be of negligible importance. The point is that in this instance the fractional component of the answer is minute compared to the integral component. Rounding down 1.4 to 1 however is another matter. If rounding off a fractional solution is straightforward and satisfactory then it will be preferable to the formal incorporation of integrality requirements into the problem.

Then it may be possible to redefine variables. In civilized society human beings are considered indivisible but man-hours are a continuous variable as are machine-hours. An indicated, production rate of 8.25 luxury cars per week means in reality 33 vehicles a month. Purchase of 1.3 computers by a department may suggest buying one and taking a 30% share in that of another department which (conveniently enough) requires 0.7 machines. And so on.

Finally there may be cases where the number of integral alternatives is so small that they can be completely enumerated. If for instance a company has just two large scale go/no go possibilities and twenty continuously divisible investment opportunities then four separate ordinary LP problems could be solved each corresponding to one pair of values of the two-state variables.

If the integrality requirements must remain, and we cannot avail ourselves of the very proper services of Woolsey's legendary 'little old ladies' then a formal integer alogorithm must be employed. One of the earliest approaches, that of integer forms, has yet to be significantly improved upon.[5]

7.2 A Cutting Plane Method

Figure 7.4 represents a two by two problem in which all x_1 x_2 lattice points in the non-negative orthant below ABC are feasible. It is clear that the set of feasible

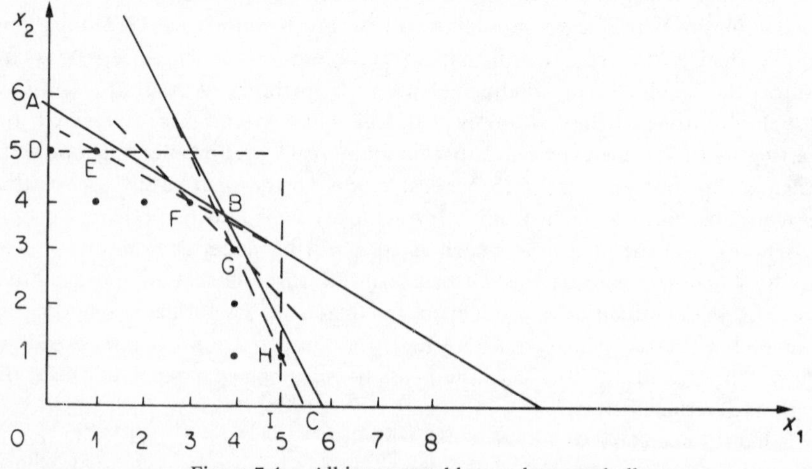

Figure 7.4 All-integer problem and convex hull

lattice points has a 'lower' upper bound than that defined by ABC. The polygon ODEFGHI shown in the figure is the smallest convex area that will contain all the feasible lattice points and is known as the *convex hull* of the constraint set. Clearly, the convex hull can be obtained by the addition of (in this case) five extra constraints which cut down the feasible area in the continuous case and so make the original constraints redundant. An important characteristic of the convex hull will be observed: the basic feasible solutions to the L.P. constraint set defined by the convex hull are feasible lattice points to the original integer problem. Since the objective function is linear one of the basic feasible solutions on the convex hull will be an optimal integral solution to the original problem. This would seem to indicate a solution procedure for the integer progamming problem: firstly find the convex hull and secondly, solve the problem with convex hull constraints as an ordinary L.P. problem by the simplex method. This procedure would indeed work but it is not operational in problems of any size because of the great computational effort required to determine the convex hull itself. Fortunately again it does not prove to be necessary to determine the entire convex hull. Additional constraints are introduced piecemeal to cut down the original area OABC towards the convex hull. This procedure is central to the approach now to be described.

The additional constraints that are added to the original constraint set define *cutting planes.* They are of such a nature as to exclude some of the non-integral region between the convex hull and the original constraints – consequently no feasible integral solution will be ruled out. We shall begin by examining an all integer problem and solve it using Gomory's cutting plane method for all integral problems.[6]

The procedure is as follows:

(i) Solve the problem by the simplex method ignoring integrality requirements. If the solution to this problem (call it P_0) is integral then the optimum has been reached. If the optimal solution to P_0 is not integral then:

(ii) introduce one extra constraint (cutting plane) to make the solution to P_0 infeasible but without excluding any feasible lattice points. Find the optimal feasible (in terms of the sign of variables) solution to this problem (P_1). If this solution is integral the optimum has been reached. If it is not integral then:

(iii) introduce a further constraint and find a sign – feasible optimum to this problem (P_2). If this solution is integral it is optimal. If not, introduce a further constraint – and so on.

Cuts can be defined in such a way that this procedure converges on the integral optimum in a finite (if possibly very large) number of steps. There are two details of the procedure that have yet to be explained. First how are the cuts generated and what computational procedure is applied to the problems P_1, P_2, etc? These questions are best answered in the context of a numerical example. Consider the following problem:

$$\text{maximize } F = 5x_1 + 3x_2$$

$$\text{subject to} \quad \begin{aligned} 2x_1 + x_2 &\leqslant 15 \\ x_1 + 3x_2 &\leqslant 12 \\ x_1, x_2 &\geqslant 0 \\ x_1, x_2 & \text{ integral} \end{aligned}$$

The problem is all integer since the slack variables will also be integral for integral x_1 and x_2. Figure 7.5 shows the solution to P_0 obtained in the usual way. The solution is non-integral, consequently stage 2 of the procedure must be entered and a cut generated. However, we must first explain the method by which non-integral numbers are divided into whole and fractional components. A number n_{ij} can be expressed as

$$n_{ij} = w_{ij} + f_{ij}$$

where w_{ij} is the 'whole' component, f_{ij} the fractional component and $f_{ij} \geqslant 0$. Thus for $n_{ij} = 2.4$, $w_{ij} = 2$ and $f_{ij} = 0.4$ and for $n_{ij} = -4.2$, $w_{ij} = -5$ and $f_{ij} = 0.8$. The reason for this procedure will become clear shortly. To produce a cut select one of the basic variables in the optimal solution to P_0 that should be integral but for which $f_{ij} > 0$, say x_2 in the current example. Next express all numbers in the x_2 row as $w_{ij} + f_{ij}$. Thus the x_2 row from Figure 7.5 can be written as:

$$1 + 0.8 \quad 0 + 0 \quad 1 + 0 \quad -1 + 0.8 \quad 0 + 0.4$$

Next take the fractional parts of these numbers and negate them producing

$$-0.8 \quad 0 \quad 0 \quad -0.8 \quad -0.4$$

The first -0.8 is the level of the slack variable in the new constraint (the first cut) when $x_1 = 6.6$ and $x_2 = 1.8$. The remaining numbers are the rates of exchange

			5	3	0	0
			x_1	x_2	S_1	S_2
0	S_1	15	(2)	1	1	0
0	S_2	12	1	3	0	1
		0	−5	−3	0	0
5	x_1	7.5	1	0.5	0.5	0
0	S_2	4.5	0	(2.5)	−0.5	1
		37.5	0	−0.5	2.5	0
5	x_1	6.6	1	0	0.6	−0.2
3	x_2	1.8	0	1	−0.2	0.4
		38.4	0	0	2.4	0.2

Figure 7.5 All-integer example: P_0 solution

between this variable (call it S_3) and x_1, x_2, S_1 and S_2 in the now non-feasible solution to the extended problem, P_1. The new S_3 row and an S_3 column are added to the tableau of Figure 7.5. The problem is now one in two structural variables and three constraints; consequently there will be three variables in any non-degenerate basic solution. The task now is to find a sign-feasible optimal solution to this problem.

We have already seen in sensitivity analysis how modest ingenuity can be employed to raise the level of a negative variable to zero or above by pivoting about a negative rate of exchange. It is now time to introduce a formal and foolproof procedure to move from the basic but infeasible solution to P_1 to a basic, sign-feasible and optimal solution to P_1. This procedure is the *dual simplex method.* The method consists in maintaining a positive index row (i.e. optimality of the primal and feasibility of the dual) and obtaining a sign-feasible solution to the primal problem. It will be recalled that in the (primal) simplex method dual feasibility was sought whilst maintaining feasiblity of the primal, where suboptimal solutions to the primal ($F < F$ max.) correspond to what might be termed 'superoptimal' and infeasible solutions to the dual ($G < G$ min.). The two methods are, therefore, symmetrical. In the dual simplex method the pivotal row is determined by a variable with negative value in the primal solution; S_3 being the only candidate in the current example. The pivotal column is determined by selection of the smallest ratio (ignoring sign) of index row number to rate of exchange in the pivotal row, the pivotal element being negative. This will ensure that the next solution obtained has an all non-negative index row for the same reasons that selection of the pivotal row in the primal simplex method guaranteed that the next solution obtained was primal-feasible. There is, however, no guarantee that only one iteration with the dual simplex method will produce a sign feasible primal. Several steps may be required before this is achieved and a particular subproblem P_t solved.

The first array of Figure 7.6 shows the additional row and column and the selection of pivotal row and column ($0.2/0.4 < 2.4/0.8$). Since S_3 is in the solution,

			5	3	0	0	0
			x_1	x_2	S_1	S_2	S_3
5	x_1	6.6	1	0	0.6	−0.2	0
3	x_2	1.8	0	1	−0.2	0.4	0
0	S_3	−0.8	0	0	−0.8	−0.4	1
		38.4	0	0	2.4	0.2	0
5	x_1	7	1	0	1	0	−0.5
3	x_2	1	0	1	−1	0	1
0	S_2	2	0	0	2	1	−2.5
		38	0	0	2	0	0.5

Figure 7.6 All-integer example: P_1 solution

albeit at an infeasible level, it has unity rate of exchange with itself and zeros elsewhere in the new column. The objective function coefficient of S_3 is, as with the other slack variables, zero. The lower array of Figure 7.6 shows the situation with one iteration complete. Dual feasibility has been maintained and, as it turns out, a sign and integer feasible solution to P_1 has been obtained. The original problem has therefore been solved with the addition of just one constraint (an extra constraint would have been required to generate the convex hull). The value of the objective function is reduced by 0.4, slack variable S_2 is integral and the solution to the dual to the original problem is also integral, a result which is true in general for all integer problems. In this case it has transpired that the optimal integral solution is a rounding off of the original continuous solution.

The reader will no doubt be curious as to the significance of the third constraint in terms of the original problem variables and why it is that a constraint so generated cannot exclude any feasible lattice points.

In respect of the first question the S_3 row of the first array of Figure 7.6 states that the value of S_3 is given by:

$$S_3 = -0.8 - 0x_1 - 0x_2 + 0.8S_1 + 0.4S_2$$

but from the original constraints

$$S_1 = 15 - 2x_1 - x_2 \quad \text{and} \quad S_2 = 12 - x_1 - 3x_2$$

Substituting for S_1 and S_2 in the expression for S_3 gives

$$S_3 = 16 - 2x_1 - 2x_2$$

which can be written as the inequality

$$2x_1 + 2x_2 \leqslant 16$$

which is the cut that was introduced. The problem is graphed in Figure 7.7. This displays an interesting feature of the problem in that constraint two is a convex hull constraint. The cut introduced, labelled 3 in the diagram, is another convex hull constraint, producing (7, 1) by intersection with constraint one and (6, 2) by intersection with the second restriction. The remaining convex hull constraint is $x_1 \leqslant 7$; this was not needed to produce the integral optimum.

What would have happened if a cut had been generated from the x_1 constraint in the solution of P_0? Figure 7.8 shows the calculations that would have resulted. The reader may verify that the constraint (corresponding to S_4) so introduced would have been

$$2x_1 + 3x_2 \leqslant 18$$

This is not a convex hull constraint, but does make the solution to P_0 infeasible without excluding any feasible lattice points. The problem is, in this case, not solved in one iteration. The sign feasible solution to P_1 is not integral, so that a further cut is required. This is shown in the second array of 7.8 and corresponds to

$$3x_1 + 4x_2 \leqslant 26$$

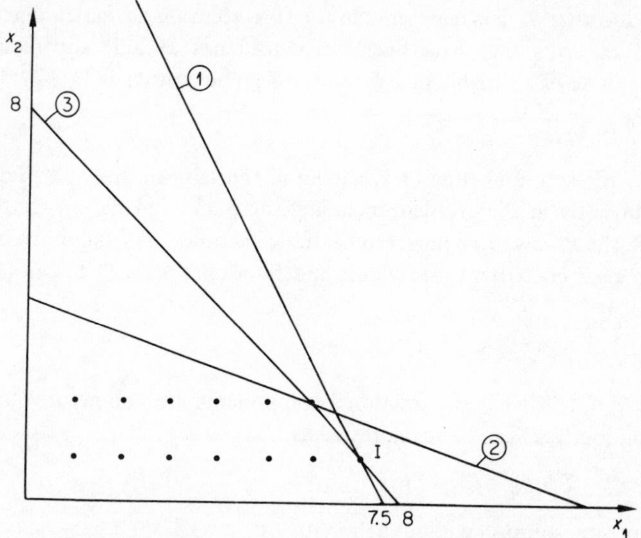

Figure 7.7 Graph of all-integer example

Again this is not a convex hull constraint but as will be seen from the third array of Figure 7.8 it does produce the integral optimum. Note that in the second array the S_5 constraint is generated either by the x_1 row or the S_2 row. In the final array the integral optimum is produced but contains an additional slack variable since there are now four constraints; dual values for the original constraints are unaffected

			5	3	0	0	0	0
			x_1	x_2	S_1	S_2	S_4	S_5
5	x_1	6.6	1	0	0.6	−0.2	0	
3	x_2	1.8	0	1	−0.2	0.4	0	
0	S_4	−0.6	0	0	−0.6	(−0.8)	1	
		38.4	0	0	2.4	0.2	0	
5	x_1	6.75	1	0	0.75	0	−0.25	0
3	x_2	1.5	0	1	−0.5	0	+0.5	0
0	S_2	0.75	0	0	0.75	1	−1.25	0
0	S_5	−0.75	0	0	−0.75	0	(−0.75)	1
		38.25	0	0	2.25	0	0.25	0
5	x_1	7	1	0	1	0	0	$-0.\overline{33}$
3	x_2	1	0	1	−1	0	0	$0.\overline{66}$
0	S_2	2	0	0	2	1	0	$-1.\overline{66}$
0	S_4	1	0	0	1	0	1	$-1.\overline{33}$
		38	0	0	2	0	0	$0.\overline{33}$

Figure 7.8 Solution with alternative cuts

however. Note that S_4 has re-entered in the final solution having disappeared in P_2.

Why do the cuts that have been introduced not exclude any feasible lattice points? The value of a variable in any solution can be written as

$$x_i = x_i^0 - \Sigma n_{ij} x_j \tag{7.1}$$

where x_i^0 is the solution value of x_i shown in the tableau, the x_j represent all the variables currently in the problem including the slacks and the n_{ij} are the rates of exchange in the x_i row, n_{ij} being zero for basic variables $i \neq j$ and unity if $i = j$. Now dividing up each coefficient into whole and fractional parts (7.1) can be rewritten as:

$$x_i = w_i^0 + f_i^0 - \Sigma(w_{ij} + f_{ij})x_j \tag{7.2}$$

where $0 \leqslant f_{ij} < 1$. That is the fractional components are non-negative as explained above. Equation (7.2) can be re-expressed as

$$x_i = w_i^0 - \Sigma w_{ij} x_j + f_i^0 - \Sigma f_{ij} x_j \tag{7.3}$$

Now any integral solution will be such that

$$x_i - w_i^0 + \Sigma w_{ij} x_j = \text{integer} \tag{7.4}$$

In other words all lattice points satisfy (7.4). Therefore if x_i is integral

$$f_i^0 - \Sigma f_{ij} x_j = \text{integer} \tag{7.5}$$

Now

$$\Sigma f_{ij} x_j \geqslant 0 \tag{7.6}$$

since $f_{ij} \geqslant 0$ and $x_j \geqslant 0$ and since by definition $f_i^0 < 1$ the integer in (7.5) cannot be positive. Therefore any integral solution (i.e. all the lattice points) must satisfy

$$f_i^0 - \Sigma f_{ij} x_j \leqslant 0 \tag{7.7}$$

that is

$$f_j^0 - \Sigma f_{ij} x_j + S_{m+1} = 0 \tag{7.8}$$

where S_{m+1} is an additional slack variable and is non-negative. Equation (7.8) can be re-expressed as

$$S_{m+1} = -f_i^0 + \Sigma f_{ij} x_j \tag{7.9}$$

which is the form of constraint proposed by Gomory and is that which we have used.

We come now to the question of which row in a solution should be used to determine the cut. Convergence on the integral optimum in a finite number of steps is only guaranteed if the row is selected in a particular way.[7] However this procedure is not very convenient in practice and simpler rules are used. Intuitively we want any cut to be as 'deep' as possible – to exclude as much of the original feasible area as possible (remember no feasible lattice point can be excluded). In fact ideally we should like all of the ratios f_i^0/f_{ij} to be as large as possible to ensure deepness since the larger is f_i^0/f_{ij} the larger will have to be the extent of the introduction of some previously not included variable and the further will be the movement away from the infeasible position. Typically however, for most rows some of the ratios are large and others small! As a rule of thumb (that has worked in practice) we simply select the largest of the f_i^0. This is the selection rule that was employed in the first instance in the numerical example above.

At first sight it would seem to be the case that the problem expands by one constraint and one variable (the new slack) every time that a cut is introduced and so rapidly may become daunting computationally. In fact there is an upper limit to the number of constraints that any problem P_t need have. This limit is the number of structural and slack variables, in the original problem, plus one. This is because the new Gomory constraints) need not always be satisfied (at a non-integral solution). Consequently, if say S_5 appears as a basic variable in P_3 it has done its job in making the solution to P_2 sign infeasible and may be removed from the problem. The S_5 row and column being deleted and the original variables used to generate further cuts. As the final worked example in all-integer problems,

$$\text{maximize } F = 5x_1 + 2x_2$$

$$\begin{aligned} \text{subject to} \quad 2x_1 + 3x_2 &\leqslant 22 \\ 3x_1 + x_2 &\leqslant 20 \\ x_1, x_2 &\geqslant 0 \\ x_1, x_2 &\text{ integral} \end{aligned}$$

The problem is all integer because of the integrality requirements for the structural variables conjoined with the integrality of all the parameters of the problem. Solution by Gomory's cutting plane method is shown in Figure 7.9. Note that there is a tie between the x_1 and S_1 rows in the penultimate array for the determination of the cut. The same cut, however, is generated by either row. The value of F at the integral optimum is 3.64% less than that at the continuous optimum. The two cuts introduced are:

$$3x_1 + 2x_2 \leqslant 23$$

and

$$4x_1 + 2x_2 \leqslant 28$$

respectively. Note that the dual solution *in terms of the original constraints* is integral. The reader will note that the value of the dual objective function, again in terms of the original constraints, is less than the optimal value of F. Why? Duality in integer problems is discussed in Section 7.5 below.

7.3 Mixed Problems

We now turn to consideration of problems in which some, but not all of the variables are required to be whole numbers. A common occurrence of such a

			5	2	0	0	0	0
			x_1	x_2	S_1	S_2	S_3	S_4
0	S_1	22	2	3	1	0		
0	S_2	20	3	1	0	1		
		0	−5	−2	0	0		
0	S_1	21/3	0	7/3	1	−2/3		
5	x_1	20/3	1	1/3	0	1/3		
		100/3	0	−1/3	0	5/3		
2	x_2	26/7	0	1	3/7	−2/7	0	
5	x_1	38/7	1	0	−1/7	3/7	0	
0	S_3	−5/7	0	0	−3/7	−5/7	1	
		247/7	0	0	1/7	11/7	0	
2	x_2	3	0	1	0	−1	1	0
5	x_1	17/3	1	0	0	2/3	−1/3	0
0	S_1	5/3	0	0	1	5/3	−7/3	0
0	S_4	−2/3	0	0	0	−2/3	−2/3	1
		103/3	0	0	0	4/3	1/3	0
2	x_2	2	0	1	0	−2	0	3/2
5	x_1	6	1	0	0	1	0	−1/2
0	S_1	4	0	0	1	4	0	−7/2
0	S_3	1	0	0	0	1	1	−3/2
		34	0	0	0	1	0	1/2

Figure 7.9 Further example: solution by cuts

problem is when the structural variables are required to be integral but the slack variables are not. There are also of course cases where not all of the xs are required to be integral.

The method of solution we shall employ is the same in principle to that already described for all-integer problems. The difference lies in the manner which cuts are determined. The method is unfortunately more complicated than in the all integer case but familiarity makes it more manageable than might appear at first sight. The slack variable in the new constraint appended to any problem is given by:

$$S = -f_i^0 + \Sigma d_{ij}x_j \tag{7.10}$$

where the terms d_{ij}, negated, will be the rates of exchange in the new row and where f_i^0 is given by a variable in the current solution which is required to be integral. Conventionally the non-integral variable with the highest fractional component (from amongst those variables required to be integral) is used to determine the cut. The d_{ij} are determined as follows:

$$d_{ij} = \begin{cases} n_{ij} & \text{if} \quad n_{ij} \geqslant 0 \\ \dfrac{-n_{ij}f_i^0}{1-f_i^0} & \text{if} \quad n_{ij} < 0 \end{cases} \quad \text{for variables not required to be integral}$$

$$\tag{7.11}$$

$$d_{ij} = \begin{cases} f_{ij} & \text{if} \quad f_{ij} \leqslant f_i^0 \\ \dfrac{f_i^0}{1-f_i^0}(1-f_{ij}) & \text{if} \quad f_{ij} > f_i^0 \end{cases} \quad \text{for variables required to be integral}$$

The n_{ij} of (7.11) are the rates of exchange in the selected row and the f_{ij} are the fractional components of the n_{ij} determined in the usual manner. Thus the d_{ij} for variables not required to be integral are determined without reference to the fractional components of the n_{ij}. The only fraction relevant here being f_i^0. For those variables that should become integral the d_{ij} are determined as for the all-integer situation provided that $f_{ij} \leqslant f_i^0$. If $f_i^0 < f_{ij}$ then the relevant d_{ij} is given by the last condition in (7.11). Note that

$$\frac{f_i^0}{1-f_i^0}(1-f_{ij}) < f_{ij}$$

when $f_{ij} > f_i^0$. Cuts generated in the manner (7.11) could also be employed in the all-integer case, the first half of (7.11) being irrelevant. The cuts so generated would be no shallower and often deeper than those generated in the $-f_{ij}$ manner. Let us now consider a numerical illustration of the use of the technique. The problem is:

$$\text{maximize } F = x_1 + 1.5x_2$$

$$\begin{aligned} \text{subject to} \quad 2x_1 + 2.5x_2 &\leqslant 12.25 \\ x_1 + 0.8x_2 &\leqslant 5.5 \\ x_1, x_2 &\geqslant 0 \\ x_2 &\text{ integral} \end{aligned}$$

The problem is graphed in Figure 7.10. The feasible set is the series of horizontal lines terminating on OABC and corresponding to integral values of x_2. The continuous optimum is at A where $x_2 = 4.9$. The 'integral' optimum is at A′ with $x_2 = 4$ and $x_1 = 1.125$. Note that the optimum must be on the boundary of the feasible set for the continuous case. Since the objective function coefficient of x_1, the continuous variable, is positive there can be no interior optimum. The solution of the problem by cuts is shown in Figure 7.11, where the single cut required is generated by (7.11). The x_2 row in the second array is used to generate the cut, since only x_2 is required to be integral. In this case the elements of the S_j row (the $-d_{ij}$) are easily determined, all being given by the first line of (7.11).

The optimal solution, with x_2 integral is obtained in one iteration, no further cuts

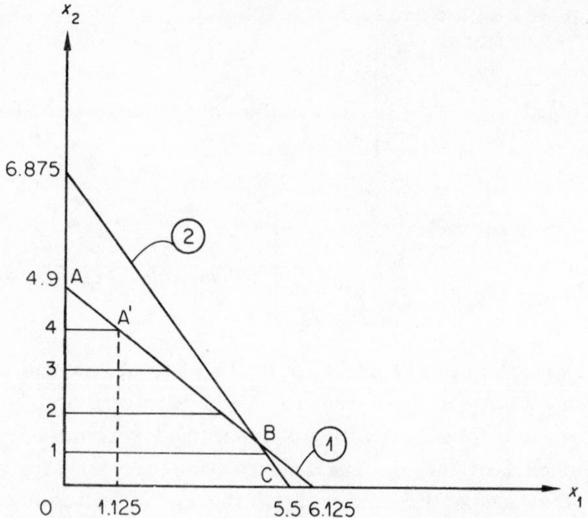

Figure 7.10 Graph of mixed integer–continuous example

being required. The cut is, in fact, an upper bound on x_2 being $x_2 \leqslant 4$. Note that the dual solution is not integral.

The problems solved in this and the preceding section have required few iterations to achieve the integral optimum. This will by no means always be the case in practice. Indeed the method of cut determination that we used in the all integer case does not guarantee convergence on the integral optimum in a finite number of iterations. The cuts (7.11) can be shown to lead to an optimum in a finite number of steps if the value of F is one of the variables required to be integral. This,

			1	1.5	0	0	0
			x_1	x_2	S_1	S_2	S_3
0	S_1	12.25	2	2.5	1	0	
0	S_2	5.5	1	0.8	0	1	
		0	−1	−1.5	0	0	
1.5	x_2	4.9	0.8	1	0.4	0	0
0	S_2	1.58	0.36	0	−0.32	1	0
0	S_3	−0.9	−0.8	0	−0.4	0	1
		7.35	0.2	0	0.6	0	0
1.5	x_2	4	0	1	0	0	1
0	S_2	1.175	0	0	−0.5	1	0.45
1	x_1	1.125	1	0	0.5	0	−1.25
		7.125	0	0	0.5	0	0.25

Figure 7.11 Mixed problem: solution by cuts

however, would represent an artificial restriction in many investment applications. It does turn out, nonetheless, that the solution procedures work quite well in actual use. We must bear in mind that the problems are much larger than those in continuous variables and too much must not be expected of the solution procedures. There can be difficulties if a completely automatic procedure is used to tackle integral problems. Quite aside from round-off difficulties in digital computers (only so many decimal places can be used) the 'finite-number' may be very large indeed. To quote Hadley[8] '... it seems that in many cases the number of iterations is so large that for practical purposes convergence is not obtained'. Continuous L.P. problems requiring less than twenty iterations to solve have been run for two thousand or more iterations without converging to an integer solution. Things are not always as depressing as this, however. The outcome depends very much on the type of problem that is tackled. The procedure does not work very well for sequencing problems – where the analytical formulation is large – but for ordinary problems as they arise in practice the cutting plane method can often be used to advantage. However it does begin to seem that a combination of man and machine in interaction is desirable for the solution to many integral problems.

There are numerous other approaches to the solution of integer linear problems that we cannot go into in this book. Branch and bound methods in particular have shown promise but have not on the whole been markedly more successful than Gomory-type methods. Apart from this fact the cutting plane approach can be grafted on to the simplex method and at least some of the flavour of convenience and simplicity of ordinary L.P. problems is retained.

7.4 Duality in Integer Problems

First consider all-integer problems. In the process of finding an integral solution to an otherwise linear problem, further constraints were added to the original set. Call the problem so arrived at (original constraints plus all requisite cuts) the *augmented* L.P. problem (it so happens that the solution is integral) and as such has a dual problem associated with it. The optimal value of the objective function in the augmented problem will be lower than in the original problem P_0, so from the point of view of resource valuation by shadow prices the total valuation of the original resources must drop (it being assumed that the optimal solution to P_0 was non-integral). The result can be stated as:

$$\Sigma b_0 y_0 > \Sigma b_0 y_0^a + \Sigma b^* y^* \geqslant \Sigma b_0 y_0^a \tag{7.12}$$

where the b_0 are the resource levels in the original L.P. problem (the R.H.S. of the constraints); the y_0 are the associated shadow prices in the optimal solution to P_0; the y_0^a are the shadow prices attached to the original resources in the optimal solution to the augmented problem; the b^* are the R.H.S. of the additional constraints defined by the appended cuts and the y^* are the dual variables associated with the R.H.S. of the new constraints. Except when the optimal solution to the augmented problem is degenerate, $\Sigma b^* y^* > 0$ so that strict

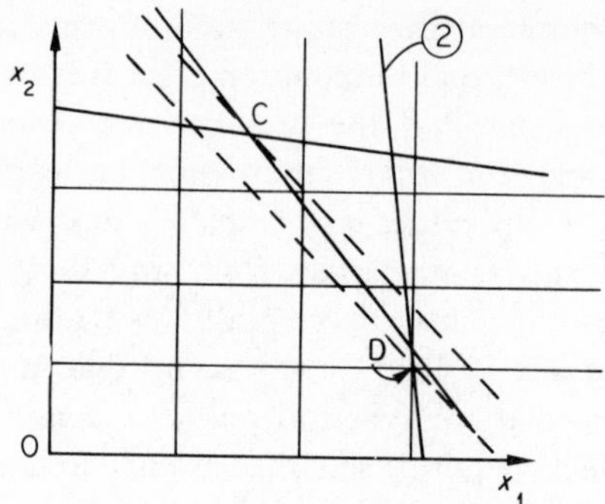

Figure 7.12 Integrality requirements and changes in dual values(i)

inequality would hold throughout (7.12). From (7.12) it can be seen that

$$\Sigma b_0(y_0 - y_0^a) > 0 \tag{7.13}$$

which allows the possibility that some of the original resources may receive increased valuation at the margin although some valuations must be reduced to such an extent that there is a net decrease. This situation is shown in Figure 7.12 where the shadow price of resource two is zero at the continuous optimum C but has become positive at the discrete optimum, D. The shadow prices themselves have to be carefully interpreted in an integer problem. A zero index row number corresponding to a constraint can no longer be taken to mean *necessarily* that further units of that resource are not worth having. Ruling out the case of degeneracy, a zero index row number means that the corresponding primal variable is at a positive level in the solution. If this primal variable is a slack variable then some of that particular resource is currently left unused. Consider the optimal solution to the first integer problem of this chapter. For convenience this is reproduced in Figure 7.13.

Resource two is not fully used here ($S_2 = 2$) and the index row number under S_2 is zero. A slight increase in the amount of resource two available would not allow a superior integral solution to the solution $x_1 = 7, x_2 = 1$ to be achieved. However, if there were an extra *three* units available ($b_2 = 15$ instead of 12) then the solution $x_1 = 6$, $x_2 = 3$ becomes feasible and optimal ($F = 39$). So three or more additional

			5	3	0	0	0
			x_1	x_2	S_1	S_2	S_3
5	x_1	7	1	0	1	0	−0.5
3	x_2	1	0	1	−1	0	1
0	S_2	2	0	0	2	1	−2.5
		38	0	0	2	0	0.5

Figure 7.13 Optimal solution of original problem

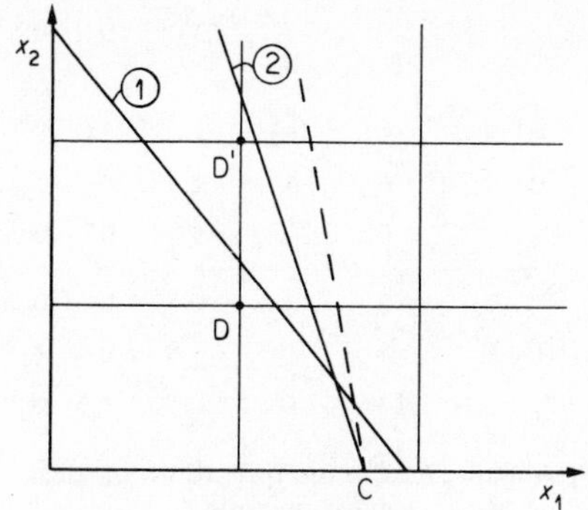

Figure 7.14 Integrality requirements and changes in dual values (ii)

units of the second resource are worth £1 (£39 – £38) to the problem solver. This possibility is not evident from the optimal tableau. In a small problem solved by hand the problem solver may be alive to this possibility and may look for it when conducting a sensitivity analysis. The fact that b_2 has a positive shadow price in P_0 does not necessarily mean that there may be some large worthwhile increase in b_2 in the integer case. Figure 7.14 illustrates such a case. The optimal continuous solution is at C in which $y_2 > 0$. The integral optimum is at D where $y_2 = 0$ but there is no worthwhile increase of any magnitude in resource two from the integral position.

Positive index row numbers in integer problems are also not all that they might seem. Although in the problem of Figure 7.13 a further unit of resource one *is* worth £2, enabling the solution $x_1 = 8$, $x_2 = 0$ to be achieved, the situation is not always so convenient. The rates of exchange under the slack variable corresponding to the increasing resource must be such that solution values for basic variables alter to new feasible levels. If this is not the case then the shadow price of the resource may give no useful information as to the value of marginal units. Consider the following problem.

$$\text{maximize } F = 7x_1 + 3x_2$$

$$\text{subject to} \quad 2x_1 + x_2 \leqslant 4$$

$$x_1 + 2x_2 \leqslant 6$$

$$x_1, x_2 \geqslant 0$$

$$x_1, x_2, S_1, S_2 \text{ integral}$$

The optimal solution is shown in Figure 7.15. It will be noted that the dual solution is not integral. The dual solution could be made integral by multiplication of the R.H.S. of the constraint set by a constant (in this case 0.5), but we shall not trouble to do this here.[9] If the problem was continuous a further unit of resource one would be worth £3.5 since x_1 would become 2.5 and $F = 17.5$ with $S_2 = 3.5$. The fractional solution is not permitted here but further units of resource one are of

			7	3	0	0
			x_1	x_2	S_1	S_2
0	S_1	4	(2)	1	1	0
0	S_2	6	1	2	0	1
		0	−7	−3	0	0
7	x_1	2	1	0.5	0.5	0
0	S_2	4	0	1.5	−0.5	1
		14	0	0.5	3.5	0

Figure 7.15 Interpretation of dual values: example

some value. Raising b_1 to 5 allows the solution $x_1 = 2$, $x_2 = 1$,to be achieved for $F = 17$. Consequently the extra unit of resource one is worth £3. In such a problem as this, in which the integral solution was arrived at without the addition of cuts, the index row numbers under the slacks provide *upper bounds* for changes in F following relaxation of the R.H.S. of the constraints. After cuts have been introduced however, the shadow prices may *underestimate* the value of extra resources. For example, suppose that constraint one was relaxed to 5 in the first instance. The tableau of the optimal integral solution is shown in Figure 7.16. If now the R.H.S. of constraint 1 is relaxed to 6 from 5, the integral solution $x_1 = 3$, $x_2 = 0$ becomes feasible. This gives $F = 21$ an increase of £4 over the $b_1 = 5$ case rather than the £3 increase that would be indicated by the shadow price in Figure 7.16. From the rates of exchange in the S_1 column it is evident that the solution $x_1 = 2$, $x_2 = 2$ is feasible for $b_1 = 6$, $b_2 = 6$ giving $F = 20$ and an increase over the previous solution of 3. The new solution $x_1 = 2$, $x_2 = 2$ is, as we know, suboptimal but it would appear to be optimal from the tableau since all variables are integral ($S_2 = 0$) and there is an all non-negative index row. What has gone wrong? The explanation lies in the fact that the cut constraints do not always have to be observed. The reader may verify the cut required to produce the Figure 7.16 solution from the continuous optimum for $b_1 = 5$, $b_2 = 6$ is $x_1 \leqslant 2$. As long as the resource levels remain at 5 and 6 then $x_1 \leqslant 2$ does not exclude any feasible lattice point, but when b_1 is relaxed to 6 the cut excludes $x_1 = 3$ which is now feasible.

			7	3	0	0	0
			x_1	x_2	S_1	S_2	S_3
7	x_1	2	1	0	0	0	1
0	S_2	2	0	0	−2	1	3
3	x_2	1	0	1	1	0	−2
		17	0	0	3	0	1

Figure 7.16 Example solution: increased b_1

What information then do shadow prices in such a solution as that in Figure 7.16 give us? The value of 3 for y_1 is in fact a *lower bound* on the change in F *provided* that the values of the variables in the solution and the S_1 column rates of exchange allow another feasible lattice point to be reached by alteration of the solution values using the rates of exchange. In our example $F = 20$ is reached for:

$$x_1 = 2 + (0) = 2$$

$$S_2 = 2 + (-2) = 0$$

$$x_2 = 1 + (1) = 2$$

Now let us conclude our discussion of zero shadow prices in integral solutions. Reference back to Figure 7.14 shows that it is possible for a resource to have zero shadow price in both the continuous optimum and the integral optimum and still it may be worth buying more of the resource if a sufficiently large increase is possible. Resource one in the diagram falls into this category. It is in surplus at both C and D but a 'large' increment would allow integral solution D′ (superior to D) to be reached. There is, of course, no increment sufficient to allow the objective function to exceed its value at the continuous optimum C.

The purpose of this discussion has been to illustrate some of the complexities of interpretation of shadow prices as resource valuations in integer problems. An exhaustive discussion would be of disproportionate length in the existing text. If so motivated the reader may show (most easily by diagrams) that all the combination of Figure 7.17 are possible. Column 1 gives the state (positive or zero) of a shadow price at a continuous optimum. Column 2 gives the state at the integral optimum. A tick in column 3 means that there are cases in which the integral solution can be improved by further units, in sufficient quantity, of the resource in question. A cross in column 3 indicates that there are cases where no increment in the resource will improve the integral position. The picture of Figure 7.17 may be further complicated by separation of cases where cuts have not been required to produce the integral optimum and further by separation of those cases where an upper bound or lower bound statement may be made.

A similar plethora of possibilities exists in the case of mixed integer-continuous

1	2	3
+	+	√
+	+	×
+	0	√
+	0	×
0	+	√
0	+	×
0	0	√
0	0	×

Figure 7.17 Shadow prices and improvement possibilities

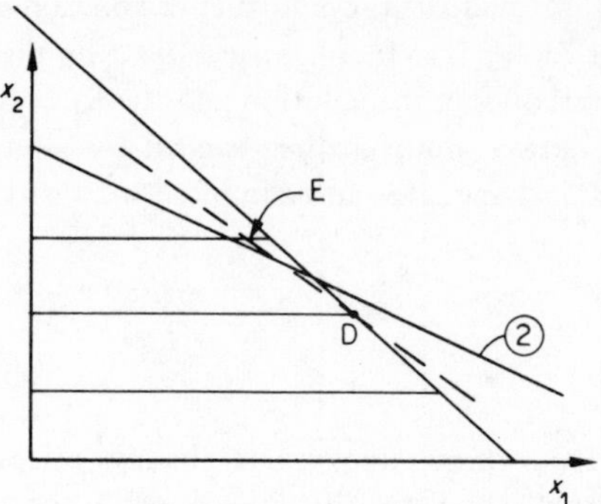

Figure 7.18 Mixed problem: difficulty with shadow prices

problems. It is possible that a shadow price be positive at an integral optimum but nevertheless no more of the resource can be used. Figure 7.14 can be used to illustrate such a case in a mixed problem in which the slack variables are not required to be integral. Figure 7.18 shows a problem in which one of the *x*s, x_1, is not required to be integral and in which resource two has zero shadow price at the integral optimum D but if the resource availability increases to permit points beyond E to be achieved then the objective function will be increased.

In general shadow prices may over- or understate the value of additional resources but frequently it is possible to say that the index row number represents a bound on the true value. For example consider the problem of Figure 7.11 and the index row number 0.5 in the final array – this suggests that an extra unit of the first resource would increase F to 7.625. This is not the case. If b_1 is increased by 0.25 to 12.5 the solution $x_2 = 5$, $x_1 = 0$ becomes feasible giving $F = 7.5$. Thus the ratio $\Delta F/\Delta b_1 = 1.5$ in this case. If $\Delta b_1 = 1$ however, x_2 cannot be increased beyond 5 but x_1 can be set at 0.375 giving $F = 7.875$ and $\Delta F = 0.75$ over the original value. Thus $\Delta F/b_1 = 0.75$ for $\Delta b_1 = 1$. Nevertheless the figure 0.5 in the tableau does convey some information, being a lower bound on the increase in F since the existing solution can be adjusted by the rates of exchange in the S_1 column. If in a solution to a problem in which cuts have been required the rates of exchange cannot be used to find a new feasible position it is not possible to say *a priori* whether the shadow price is an upper or lower bound to the true improvement. But when an integral optimum has been arrived at without cuts the shadow price will be an upper bound on the increase in F. For instance if in the first place $b_1 = 12.5$ then the optimum $x_1 = 5$, $x_2 = 0$, $S_2 = 1.5$ would have not required a cut and the index row number 0.6 under S_1, showing $\Delta F/\Delta b_1$ in the all-continuous case is an upper bound for the discrete problem. In this case if $\Delta b_1 = 1$ (from a base of 12.5) then the optimum has $x_2 = 5$, $x_1 = 0.375$ and $\Delta F = 0.375$ ($= 7.875 - 7.5$). If not cut has been required the shadow price cannot understate the true improvement.

7.5 Zero-one Problems

Whilst the relevance of non-zero-one discrete problems to capital rationing will have been apparent, the phenomenon of two-state variables is of especial importance. Frequently cases arise when an investment project has to be accepted or rejected in its entirety: that is either $x_j = 1$ or $x_j = 0$ any other values for x_j being meaningless. Also there are situations in which one or other of two projects, but not both must be undertaken. Such a condition defines a constraint for the problem. It can be stated as

$$x_i + x_k = 1 \tag{7.14}$$

which, in conjunction with the requirements that $x_j = 0$ or 1 and $x_k = 0$ or 1 produces the only two possibilities $x_j = 1$, $x_k = 0$ and $x_j = 0$, $x_k = 1$. Additional constraints of this type (also taken in conjunction with zero-one requirements) are:

$$x_j + x_k \leqslant 1 \tag{7.15}$$

which reads 'not both of x_j and x_k'

$$x_j - x_k \geqslant 0 \tag{7.16}$$

that is 'undertake project k only if project j is accepted' the solution $x_k = 1$, $x_j = 0$ being excluded.

$$x_j + x_k \geqslant 1 \tag{7.17}$$

which means accept 'either or both of' projects j and k. The restriction 'both or neither' can be accommodated by using constraint (7.16) plus

$$x_k - x_j \geqslant 0 \tag{7.18}$$

while

$$x_j + x_k + x_L = 2 \tag{7.19}$$

means any two of projects j, k and L. And so on. There are many other uses for two state variables in the area of problem formulation; some of which will be examined later in the chapter. For the moment however let us consider how the problems are to be solved.

A zero-one problem is a special case of integer programming, there being upper bounds of unity on the zero-one variables. Consequently the solution procedures with cuts that have been detailed in sections 7.4 and 7.5 will work also for zero-one problems. Indeed, in problems in which most of the problem variables are not two state, but a few are, then a cutting plane approach would prove to be amongst the more efficient procedures for solution. But in all-zero-one problems this special two-state characteristic can be exploited by specifically designed computational procedures.

There are very many algorithms to chose from. The relative efficiency of the algorithms in problem solution depends on the structure and size of the problem tackled. By 'structure' is meant considerations such as the signs of the a_{ij}, whether many of the a_{ij} are zero or not, whether or not those x_j with high a_{ij} in one constraint have high (relative to the other a_{ij}) a_{ij} in other constraints.

Algorithms especially designed for zero-one problems employ partial or implicit ennumeration. That is, not every feasible solution is actually evaluated, some may be eliminated without evaluation since it is known that there is at least one superior solution in such cases. There are very many all zero-one solution procedures. Approaches other than the one to be described here are briefly discussed in section 7.9.

The method that we have selected for discussion here is a 'pseudo-Boolean' method. Some simple ideas from Boolean Algebra (the algebra of systems of two-state variables) are employed. The technique is very simple to grasp and is well suited to solution of some small problems 'by hand' in that it allows human mental aptitudes some scope. It also provides a most suitable structure for useful sensitivity analysis as will be seen later. There are disadvantages however. In comparison to some other procedures relatively few solutions are not explicitly evaluated. This disadvantage will be of less importance the fewer in number are the feasible solutions to the problem. The technique is therefore better suited to those problems in which the principal computational difficulty is in determining a relatively small feasible solution set. Such problems are those in which most of the technical coefficients are 'large' relative to the R.H.S. of the constraints. The technique then, will be more efficient in larger scale investment applications than to 'shop floor' scheduling problems for which there are superior methods.

Consider the following problem.

$$\text{maximize } F = 10x_1 + 6x_2 + 7x_3 - x_4 + 5x_5$$

$$\text{subject to (1)} \quad 5x_1 + 6x_2 - x_3 + 2x_4 + 2.5x_5 \leqslant 9$$

$$(2) \quad -2x_1 + 4.5x_2 + 6x_3 - 0.5x_4 + 7x_5 \geqslant 10$$

$$(3) \quad 4.5x_1 + 4x_2 + 1.5x_3 + 4x_4 + 3x_5 \leqslant 8.5$$

$$x_1, x_2, x_3, x_4, x_5 \text{ 0 or 1}$$

It turns out that the form of constraints (1), (2) and (3) is not the most convenient way that the restrictions can be expressed. The first step in the computational procedure is to convert the constraints to 'canonical' form. The canonical form of constraints is one in which all coefficients are positive and the constraints are of $\geqslant$ variety. It will also prove convenient to re-arrange and relabel variables so that their coefficients are in descending order of magnitude from left to right. Starting with the first constraint begin by converting it to $\geqslant$ form by multiplication through by -1. It becomes

$$-5x_1 - 6x_1 + x_3 - 2x_4 - 2.5x_5 \geqslant -9 \qquad (1)'$$

which does not appear to be more manageable than the original form. However, define new variables y as follows:

$$y_1 = 1 - x_2 \quad y_3 = 1 - x_5 \quad y_5 = x_3$$

$$y_2 = 1 - x_1 \quad y_4 = 1 - x_4$$

It is a useful simplification to write $\bar{x}_2$ for $1 - x_2$, etc. This will be done from now on. It will be noted in the above that where an x variable appears with negative coefficient in $(1)'$ it is replaced by a y variable that will be of opposite state, i.e. if $x_2 = 0$, $y_1 = 1$ and if $x_2 = 1$, $y_1 = 0$. The ys have been subscripted so that y_1 has the highest coefficient down to y_5 with the lowest. Substitution of ys for xs in $(1)'$ gives

$$6y_1 + 5y_2 + 2.5y_3 + 2y_4 + y_5 \geqslant 6.5 \qquad (1)''$$

The task now is to find so called 'basic solutions' of $(1)''$. A basic solution in this context is one in which if any variable set at unit level in the solution is changed to zero level then the constraint is violated. For example one basic solution to $(1)''$ is $y_1 = 1$, $y_3 = 1$, $y_2, y_4, y_5 = 0$ whereas $y_1 = 1$, $y_2 = 1$, $y_3 = 1$, $y_4 = 0, y_5 = 0$ is non-basic. The basic solutions to $(1)''$ are tabulated below.

y_1	y_2	y_3	y_4	y_5
1	1	0	0	0
1	0	1	0	0
1	0	0	1	0
1	0	0	0	1
0	1	1	0	0
0	1	0	1	0

As will be seen from the layout of the table the basic solutions can be systematically found by first finding those which contain y_1 at unit level; next find those in which y_1 is at zero level but y_2 is at unit level and so on. In the present example there are no basic solutions in which both y_1 and y_2 are at zero level.

The next stage in the procedure is to convert the basic solutions to the first constraint into 'families' of solutions. A family of solutions comprises *fixed variables*: those which are set at zero or one and may not be altered) and *free variables* which are allowed to be zero or one. The families of solutions are:

y_1	y_2	y_3	y_4	y_5
1	1	–	–	–
1	0	1	–	–
1	0	0	1	–
1	0	0	0	1
0	1	1	–	–
0	1	0	1	–

The dashes represent the free variables. It will be seen that a family is obtained from the corresponding basic solution by replacing the zero after the last unit entry in the row with dashes. It will thus follow that in each family the group of fixed variables is such that if any one of the variables at unit level is reduced to zero the constraint is violated. The constraint is satisfied whatever the values of the free variables are. Normally it is possible to obtain the families of solutions directly from the constraint without writing the basic solutions down separately. Lastly the families of solutions are reconverted to expression in the xs and each labelled.

	x_1	x_2	x_3	x_4	x_5
a_1	0	0	–	–	–
b_1	1	0	–	–	0
c_1	1	0	–	0	1
d_1	1	0	1	1	1
e_1	0	1	–	–	0
f_1	0	1	–	0	1

The same process is now applied to the other constraints. Constraint (2) is written as

$$7y_1 + 6y_2 + 4.5y_3 + 2y_4 + 0.5y_5 \geqslant 12.5 \tag{2''}$$

where $y_1 = x_5$, $y_2 = x_3$, $y_3 = x_2$, $y_4 = \bar{x}_1$, $y_5 = \bar{x}_4$. The transformation of x variables will differ from one constraint to the next. The y variables are used only as 'intermediaries'. The solution families to the second constraint, in terms of the ys are:

y_1	y_2	y_3	y_4	y_5
1	1	–	–	–
1	0	1	1	–
0	1	1	1	–

which on reconversion to xs become

	x_1	x_2	x_3	x_4	x_5
a_2	–	–	1	–	1
b_2	0	1	0	–	1
c_2	0	1	1	–	0

Now, before the process is applied to the third constraint families of solutions which are feasible for both of the first two constraints are found. Starting with the family a_1, appropriate setting of the free variables produces

	x_1	x_2	x_3	x_4	x_5
a_1a_2	0	0	1	–	1

a family of solutions which satisfies both a_1 and a_2. Again by appropriate choice of free variables it will be seen that all the solutions below are members of a family of solutions to each of the constraints

	x_1	x_2	x_3	x_4	x_5
a_1a_2	0	0	1	–	1
c_1a_2	1	0	1	0	1
d_1a_2	1	0	1	1	1
e_1c_2	0	1	1	–	0
f_1a_2	0	1	1	0	1
f_1b_2	0	1	0	0	1

So the above are families of solutions to each of the first two constraints. We can now tackle the third constraint. It can be written as:

$$4.5y_1 + 4y_2 + 4y_3 + 3y_4 + 1.5y_5 \geqslant 8.5 \qquad (3)''$$

where $y_1 = \bar{x}_1$, $y_2 = \bar{x}_2$, $y_3 = \bar{x}_4$, $y_4 = \bar{x}_5$, $y_5 = \bar{x}_3$. In terms of the ys the families of solutions are

y_1	y_2	y_3	y_4	y_5
1	1	—	—	—
1	0	1	—	—
1	0	0	1	1
0	1	1	1	—
0	1	1	0	1
0	1	0	1	1
0	0	1	1	1

which are in terms of the xs

	x_1	x_2	x_3	x_4	x_5
a_3	0	0	—	—	—
b_3	0	1	—	0	—
c_3	0	1	0	1	0
d_3	1	0	—	0	0
e_3	1	0	0	0	1
f_3	1	0	0	1	0
g_3	1	1	0	0	0

Common solutions to all three constraints are then:

	x_1	x_2	x_3	x_4	x_5
$a_1a_2a_3$	0	0	1	—	1
$e_1c_2b_3$	0	1	1	0	0
$f_1a_2b_3$	0	1	1	0	1
$f_1b_2b_3$	0	1	0	0	1

It is from amongst these solutions that the optimal feasible solution will be found. There is only one free variable left in one family and since this variable, x_4, has a negative coefficient in the objective function it will be set at zero level. At this stage of the solution procedure free variables in each family are set at zero or one depending on the coefficient in the objective function. The optimal solution is now obtained by evaluating each solution. In matrix form the results can be written as:

$$\begin{pmatrix} 0 & 0 & 1 & 0 & 1 \\ 0 & 1 & 1 & 0 & 0 \\ 0 & 1 & 1 & 0 & 1 \\ 0 & 1 & 0 & 0 & 1 \end{pmatrix} \begin{pmatrix} 10 \\ 6 \\ 7 \\ -1 \\ 5 \end{pmatrix} = \begin{pmatrix} 12 \\ 13 \\ 18 \\ 11 \end{pmatrix}$$

The optimal solution therefore is $x_1 = 0$, $x_2 = 1$, $x_3 = 1$, $x_4 = 0$, $x_5 = 1$ giving $F = 18$. This completes the solution procedure. A fair amount of work has been involved in obtaining the optimum, but this will be true of any exact solution procedure. The major problem lay in finding feasible solutions to the entire constraint set. Once the feasible solutions have been found some are eliminated without evaluation when the remaining free variables in each family are set at the appropriate state determined by the signs of objective function coefficients. All solutions that then remain have to be evaluated. Note that there is no feasible solution with $x_1 = 1$. It is instructive to see by reference back to the original constraints how difficult this fact would be to establish by an inspection procedure.

The method that has been described is particularly amenable to sensitivity analysis of the objective function coefficients. If present values of projects are changed the new values are inserted into the column vector in the evaluation stage. If the R.H.S. of a constraint alters then the families of solutions appropriate to the new resource level must be found and the 'intersection' of these families with the (unchanged) families of solutions to the other constraints determined. The new optimal solution would then be determined. If a technical coefficient changes, the effect on the optimum is calculated in a similar manner. Additional constraints can be incorporated by finding the families of solutions to the new constraints and forming the intersection of these with the existing solutions to the problem (prior to selection of values for the free variables in these solutions). Finally, if a new variable is added to the original problem then the number of basic solutions to each constraint may increase. Each existing basic solution will still be basic with the new variable at zero level, but there may be more solutions with the new variable at unit level which are basic. These new basic solutions are found and the intersection of families of solutions redetermined.

7.6 Special Cases

A number of special case problems involving two-state variables are of interest in an investment context and also as exercises in problem formulation. We shall briefly examine five such problems.

Fixed Charges Problem

Suppose that an investor is to select from amongst n possible investments so as to maximize total net present value. Suppose also, for the time being, that the constraint set does not include an initial capital expenditure constraint.[10] The net present value resulting from x_j units of investment j is given by:

$$\left.\begin{matrix} N_j x_j - F_j & \text{if } x_j > 0 \\ 0 & \text{if } x_j = 0 \end{matrix}\right\} \tag{7.20}$$

The capital outlay required for $x_j > 0$ has two components, an amount which depends upon the level of the investment and which is included in the N_j of (7.20) in the usual manner and a *fixed charge* F_j which is incurred only if the investment is undertaken at *any* positive level. The F_j may be thought of as certain of the administrative expenses connected with a project. In a production planning exercise the F_j are often described as 'set up' costs.

What difficulties are caused by (7.20)? We observe that it is incorrect to express the objective function as:

$$N = \sum_{j=1}^{n} N_j x_j - \sum_{j=1}^{n} F_j \tag{7.21}$$

since the effect of the formulation (7.21) is that the F_j are ignored by the L.P. optimization process. In (7.21) the F_j are included in N even if the x_j are zero, whereas we know from (7.20) that this is not the case. The difficulty is resolved in the following manner. Introduce n new variables w_j where $w_j = 0$ or 1. Redefine the objective function as:

$$N = \sum_{j=1}^{n} N_j x_j - \sum_{j=1}^{n} F_j w_j \tag{7.22}$$

Now if we can ensure that $w_j = 1$ if and only if $x_j > 0$ the correct level of N will be obtained. To accomplish this introduce n new constraints of the form

$$x_j - M_j w_j \leqslant 0 \quad j = 1, 2, \ldots, n \tag{7.23}$$

where M_j are constants of such magnitude that $x_j \leqslant M_j$ is certainly satisfied in any optimal solution. Now observe that if $w_j = 0$ (7.23) along with the sign requirements on x_j means that $x_j = 0$ and the contribution to N is zero. If $w_j = 1$ then (7.23) means that $x_j \leqslant M_j$ which will, from the definition of M_j be an ineffective restriction and the contribution to N will be $N_j x_j - F_j$.

With the other joint constraints on x_j represented in the usual manner the full formulation of the problem is

$$\left.\begin{aligned}
&\text{maximize } N = \sum_{j=1}^{n} N_j x_j - \sum_{j=1}^{n} F_j w_j\\
&\text{subject to}\\
&\quad \Sigma a_{ij} x_j \leqslant b_i \qquad i = 1, 2, \ldots m\\
&\quad x_j - M_j w_j \leqslant 0 \; j = 1, 2, \ldots n\\
&\quad w_j \leqslant 1\\
&\quad x_j, w_j \geqslant 0\\
&\quad w_j \text{ integral}
\end{aligned}\right\} \tag{7.24}$$

The upper (1) and lower (0) bounds on w_j conjoined with the integrality requirement that the only permissible values of the w_j are 0 and 1. It only remains to determine suitable values of the M_j. An obvious possibility would be to set $M_j = \text{Max}_i\ (b_i)/a_{ij}$ so that (7.23) are redundant if $w_j = 1$.

For computation a mixed integer continuous programming algorithm would be employed. The computational burden depends upon how many of the investments have a fixed charge associated with them, since for each such case a new variable, a new constraint and an integrality requirement are introduced.

Earlier on we stated that the validity of the formulation (7.24) was contingent upon there being no constraint on initial outlay. The reason for this can now be seen. If there was such a constraint a fixed charge element would be introduced into the constraint set since the outlay required for x_j units of the jth investment would be:

$$\begin{array}{ll} k_j x_j + F_j & \text{if} \quad x_j > 0 \\ 0 & \text{if} \quad x_j = 0 \end{array}$$

where K_j represents that part of outlay variable directly with x_j.[11] Fixed charges in a constraint may be handled by the same device employed on the objective function. Call the initial capital constraint constraint zero and express it thus:

$$\sum_{j=1}^{n} K_j x_j + \Sigma F_j w_j \leqslant b_0 \tag{7.25}$$

Now simply append (7.25) to the problem given by (7.24). Any further constraints with fixed charges could be included in a similar fashion.

The Minimum Size Problem

Suppose that an investment can be varied in scale but there is a smallest possible size if the investment is to be undertaken. That is:

$$\begin{array}{ll} \text{either } & x_j = 0 \\ \text{or} & x_j \geqslant X_j \end{array}$$

This dichotomy can be accommodated by a means similar to that in the fixed charges problem. For each investment with minimum feasible level include two additional constraints of the form

$$\left.\begin{array}{l} x_j - M_j w_j \leqslant 0 \\ \text{and} \quad x_j - X_j w_j \geqslant 0 \end{array}\right\} \tag{7.26}$$

where the w_j are two-state, M_j are defined as above and X_j are the minimum positive levels. If $w_j = 0$ then (7.26) restricts x_j to zero. If $w_j = 1$ the first constraint in (7.26) is redundant and the second states that $x_j \geqslant X_j$ as required.

Specific Alternatives

In some problems an investment level may be restricted to zero or certain specified alternative possible values which may not be neighbouring integers. For instance suppose that there are only three permissible positive values of investment one. Label these values:

$$0, x_{11}, x_{12}, x_{13}$$

In the objective function (in place of $N_1 x_1$) write:

$$N_{11}x_{11} + N_{12}x_{12} + N_{13}x_{13}$$

and in the constraints (in place of $a_{i1}x_1$) write:

$$a_{i11}x_{11} + a_{i12}x_{12} + a_{i13}x_{13}$$

and add the condition that

$$x_{11} + x_{12} + x_{13} \leqslant 1$$

where the coefficients in the objective function are the net present values corresponding to the alternative levels of investment and the constraint coefficient shows resource consumptions corresponding to each level. Finally add the requirement (in whatever form the particular algorithm requires) that x_{11}, x_{12} and x_{13} are either zero or one.[12]

Alternative Constraints

There may arise cases in which although there are m individually defined constraints only k of these need necessarily hold. Management efforts or 'mobile resources' may be employed to relax $m - k$ of the constraints as required. How can such a possibility be allowed for? The m constraints in familiar form are given by:

$$\Sigma a_{ij}x_j \leqslant b_i \quad i = 1, 2, \ldots m$$

Now introduce m zero-one variables w_i and the constraint

$$\Sigma w_i \geqslant k$$

Define numbers M_i such that

$$\Sigma a_{ij}x_j \leqslant M_i \quad i = 1, 2, \ldots m \tag{7.27}$$

is satisfied in any optimal solution and rewrite the original constraints as:

$$\Sigma a_{ij}x_j \leqslant b_i w_i + M_i(1 - w_i) \quad i = 1, 2, \ldots m \tag{7.28}$$

From (7.28) it is evident that if a particular $w_i = 1$ then the constraint in original form must be observed (it is not relaxed) but if $w_i = 0$ then (7.28) reduces to (7.27) which is ineffective. Note that the constraints (7.28) could be re-expressed in conventional form (with variables on the L.H.S.) as:

$$\Sigma a_{ij}x_j + (M_i - b_i)w_i \leqslant M_i$$

The Single Project Problem

A special case of mixed integer continuous programming that is of interest in an investment context is the situation where there is only one 'project' to be accepted or rejected in its entirety but more than one source of finance and more than one potential outlet for surplus funds. In practice there will be limits to the amounts of cash that can be raised from given sources and there may be external or self-imposed limits on the amounts placed in individual institutions or bonds. The rate of return required for acceptability of the project will, in these circumstances, depend not only on the rates of interest in the problem but also upon the upper bounds. This will be the case more generally too, but the relatively simple cases considered below allow functional relationships between required yield from the project and upper bounds and rates of interest to be determined. Consider the problem:

$$\text{maximize } F = 1.13x_1 + 1.11x_2 - 1.05z_1 - 1.14z_2 + R_3x_3$$

$$\text{subject to} \qquad x_1 + x_2 + 1{,}000x_3 - z_1 - z_2 \leqslant 0$$

$$z_1 \leqslant 800$$

$$x_1, x_2, z_1, z_2 \geqslant 0 \; x_3 = 0 \text{ or } 1$$

The single project is represented by variable x_3 which would cost £1,000 to initiate and give a single return of R_3 after one year. The variables z represent amounts raised from the two possible sources of finance at costs of 5% and 14% and x_1 and x_2 represent deposits in financial institutions giving interest at 13% and 11%. If the project is not taken ($x_3 = 0$) F is maximized for $x_1 = 800$ and $z_1 = 800$. Therefore $\overline{F} = 800\ (1.13 - 1.05) = 64$. Now for the project to be acceptable the value of F with $x_1 = 1$ must be at least 64. With $x_3 = 1$, F is maximized for $z_1 = 800$, $z_2 = 200$ and the constraint on F is given by:

$$\overline{F} = R_3 - 800(1.05) - 200(1.14) \geqslant 64$$

which means that $R_3 \geqslant 1{,}132$ for acceptability so that the requisite yield on the project is 13.2%. This yield figure, it will be noted, is different from any of the interest rates in the problem even though the horizon is only one period. This is because of the upper bound on the cheap source of finance. The required minimum return R_3 is, in fact,

$$\hat{R}_3 = 800(1.13) + 200(1.14)$$

or, with an upper bound $z_1^* \leqslant 1{,}000$ on z_1

$$\hat{R}_3 = z_1^*(1.13) + (1{,}000 - z_1^*)(1.14)$$

in which it will be noted that $\hat{R}_3$ does not depend at all on the cost of the 'cheap' finance provided that this does not exceed 13%. The term z^* (1.13) is an opportunity cost due to the fact that the return on x_1 is not earned if $x_3 = 1$. If the cheap finance cost 13.5% then x_1 would never have been worthwhile and $\hat{R}_3$ would have been given by

$$\hat{R}_3 = z_1^*(1.135) + (1{,}000 - z_1^*)(1.14)$$

which is £1,136 for $z_1^* = 800$. To further illustrate the importance of bounds for requisite yield append one further constraint to the original problem namely

$x_1 \leqslant 500$. The best alternative values of R are now

$$x_3 = 0 \quad \left.\begin{array}{l} x_1 = 500 \\ x_2 = 300 \\ z_1 = 800 \end{array}\right\} F = 500(1.13) + 300(1.11) - 800(1.05) = 58$$

$$x_3 = 1 \quad \left.\begin{array}{l} x_3 = 1 \\ z_1 = 800 \\ z_2 = 200 \end{array}\right\} F = R_3 - 800(1.05) - 200(1.14)$$

therefore $\hat{R}_3 = 500(1.13) + 300(1.11) + 200(1.14) = 1{,}126$ so that the minimum yield required on the project is 12.6%. That is, the required yield is less than the return on the best alternative investment forsaken (x_1).

7.7 Alternatives and Conclusions

Various alternative computational procedures have been alluded to in the course of this chapter. There is no single procedure that is best for all types of integer problem. Different procedures exploit, to better advantage, different problem structures. None are anywhere near being entirely satisfactory.

The most important class of computational methods not discussed so far are *branch and bound* methods. Variations on the basic theme can be applied to pure, mixed and zero one problems. In broad terms the branch and bound approach is as follows.[13]

For each variable required to be integral determine a lower bound and an upper bound on the value of that variable, viz. for x_j integral

$$L_j \leqslant x_j \leqslant H_j \tag{7.29}$$

where L_j and H_j are such that the optimal value of x_j will be included. Usually $L_j = 0$ and H_j need be no greater than the integer at or below $\text{Max}_i\ (b_i/a_{ij})$. As will be seen if the circumstances of a particular problem allow tighter bounds to be inserted in (7.29) this will diminish computational effort.

Having initially determined the optimal solution to the continuous L.P. problem suppose that it turns out that in this solution $x_j = 2.5$. Now clearly in the integral optimum either

$$L_j \leqslant x_j \leqslant 2 \tag{7.30}$$

or

$$3 \leqslant x_j \leqslant H_j \tag{7.31}$$

since (7.30) and (7.31) cover all permissible integral values of x_j. Now solve separately two L.P. problems with the original constraints to which is added (7.30) in one case and (7.31) in the other.[14] If both of these problems have an optimal solution integral in the required variables then the integral optimum corresponds to the greater of the two values of the objective function. Usually one or other problem does not have an optimum solution which satisfies all of the integrality requirements. Further iterations are then required. At any stage of these iterations there is a 'master list' of problems which differ in the bounds that are placed on individual variables required to be integral. Problems are selected from and added to the master list as the bounds (7.30) and (7.31) on each variable are revised. When any problem that is solved has an integral optimum the value of the objective function for this solution is recorded. It determines a *lower bound* for the integral optimum objective function. If at some iteration a problem has an optimum solution with objective function value less than or equal to the current lower bound or there is no feasible solution then that branch need not be investigated further.[15] If on the other hand a problem has an integral optimum and the value of the objective function is greater than the current lower bound, the lower bound is replaced by the new value. Computations cease when the master list is empty. The optimal solution corresponds to the last bound thus obtained.

This approach seems to work well for problems in which there are few integer valued variables. But, if the number of such variables is large or if the solution to the original L.P. problem is a long way (in terms of the values of the variables in the solutions) from the integral optimum then the number of iterations required may be impractically large. A rather obvious difficulty here is that whilst the former situation can be spotted in advance the latter cannot be. The procedure can be efficiently coded for machine computation without intervention being required.[16] A variation of the procedure can be used to solve all zero-one problems.

In summary, we have examined the various types of integer linear programming problems. They are relevant to consideration of capital rationing problems whenever all or some of the investment alternatives may take only certain discrete values. We have seen that interpretations of solutions to integer problems is less straightforward than in the linear continuous case – indeed the solutions are much less informative. Of the very many computational approaches possible we selected two: a 'pseudo Boolean' method for zero-one problems and cutting plane methods for nonzero-one mixed and all integer problems. Of these techniques not detailed the most important are 'branch and bound' methods. On the whole, these are about as successful as the cutting plane approach but it was not our objective to review all the algorithms in use.

Notes

1. Wagner, H. M., *Principles of Operations Research with Applications to Managerial Decisions*, Prentice-Hall, Englewood Cliffs, N.J., 1969. Chapter 13.
2. Woolsey, R. E. D., 'A candle to Saint Jude, or four real world applications of integer programming', *Management Science Interfaces,* 2, No. 2, 1972.
3. On rereading this pious hope, I decided, perhaps unwisely, not to delete it. As Woolsey suggests we should certainly 'tell it as it is' but at the same time we can see it as it might be.
4. As in the case where all technical coefficients are non-negative and constraints are all $\leqslant$ inequalities.
5. Except for some problems of special structure.
6. Gomory, R. E., *All-Integer Programming Algorithm*, IBM Research Centre, Research Report RC–189, 1960.
7. For an explanation of this selection procedure see Hadley, G., *Non-linear and Dynamic Programming*, Addison-Wesley, Reading, Massachusetts, 1964, p. 278.
8. Hadley, G., *Non-linear and Dynamic Programming*, Addison-Wesley, Reading, Massachusetts, 1964, p. 281.

9. Making the dual solution integral in this way is possible provided that the dual variables are rational numbers – which will always be the case so long as there are no irrational parameters in the problem.
10. This assumption will later be dropped. It is made, for a reason that will become apparent, to simplify the intial presentation.
11. In the objective function $N_j = G_j - K_j$ where G_j is the gross present value per unit of x_j.
12. There is an application of this procedure in certain problems involving non-linearities.
13. I have based the following short discussion on the very clear presentation of Wagner, H. M., *Principles of Operations Research with Applications to Managerial Decisions*, Prentice-Hall, Englewood Cliffs, N.J., 1969, Chapter 13. The reader is referred to this source for further analysis and detailed descriptions of the methods in use.
14. The reader will recall from previous work that it will not be necessary to solve the two 'new' L.P. problems completely from scratch. We have seen how to add in additional constraints as they rise.
15. Wagner suggests that the technique might well be retitled Branch and Prune!
16. As may the cutting plane method. An operator may well be required to truncate the proceedings however!

Additional References

1. Abadie, J. (Ed)., *Integer and Non-Linear Programming*, North Holland, Amsterdam, 1970.
2. Alcaly, R. E., and Klevorick, A. K., 'A note on the dual prices of integer programs', *Econometrica,* 34, 1966.
3. Balas, E., 'An additive algorithm for solving linear problems with zero-one variables', *Operations Research,* **13**, 1965.
4. Balas, E., *'Duality in Discrete Programming: IV Applications*, Management Sciences Research Report No. 195. Pittsburg: Carnegie-Mellon University, October, 1968.
5. Balinski, M. L., 'Integer programming: methods, uses, computation', *Management Science,* **12**, 1965.
6. Beale, E. M. L., 'Survey of integer programming', *Operational Research Quarterly,* **16**, 1965.
7. Charnes, A., and Cooper, W. W., *Management Models and Industrial Applications of Linear Programming Vol. 11*, Wiley, New York, 1961.
8. Cooper, L., and Drebes, C., 'An approximate solution method for the fixed charge problem', *Naval Research Logistics Quarterly,* **14** 1967.
9. Dantzig, G. B., 'On the significance of solving linear programming problems with some integer variables', *Econometrica,* **28**, 1960.
10. Faaland, R., 'An integer programming algorithm for portfolio selection', *Management Science,* **20** Series B, 1973–74.
11. Geoffrion, A. M., and Marsten, R. E., 'Integer programming algorithms; a framework and state of the art survey', *Management Science,* **18** Series A, 1972.
12. Gomory, R. E., 'An algorithm for integer solutions to linear programs' in *Recent Advances in Mathematical Programming,* Graves, R. L., and Wolfe, P., (Eds), McGraw-Hill, New York, 1963.
13. Gomory, R. E., 'On the relation between integer and noninteger solutions to linear programs', *National Academy of Sciences,* **53**, 1965.
14. Hammer, P. L., and Rudeanu, S., 'Pseudo Boolean programming', *Operations Research,* **17**, 1969.
15. Hirsch, W. M., and Dantzig, G. B., 'The fixed charge problem', *Naval Research Logistics Quarterly,* **15**, 1968.
16. Hu, T. C., *Integer Programming and Network Flows,* Addison-Wesley, Reading Massachusetts, 1969.
17. Jensen, R. E., 'Sensitivity analysis and integer programming', *The Accounting Review,* **1968.**
18. Kaplan, S., 'Solution of the Lorie–Savage and similar integer programming problems by the generalised Lagrange multiplier method', *Operations Research,* **XIV**, 1966.
19. Lawler, E. L., and Bell, M. D., 'A method for solving discrete optimization problems', *Operations Research,* **XIV**, 1966.
20. Lawler, E. L., and Wood, D. E., 'Branch and bound methods: a survey', *Operations Research,* **XIV**, 1966.

21. Mao, J. C. T., and Wallingford, B. A., 'An extension of Lawler and Bell's method of discrete optimization with examples from capital budgeting', *Management Science,* **XV**, No. 2, October, 1968.
22. Salkin, H. M., *Integer Programming*, Addison-Wesley, 1975.
23. Senzu, S., and Toyoda, Y., 'An approach to linear programming with 0–1 variables', *Management Science*, **XV**, Series B, 1968–9.
24. Trouth, C. A., and Woolsey, R. E., 'Integer linear programming: a study in computational efficiency', *Management Science,* **XV**, Series A., 1968–9.
25. Weingartner, H. M., *Mathematical Programming and the Analysis of Capital Budgeting Problems*, Prentice-Hall, Englewood Cliffs, N.J., 1963.
26. Weingartner, H. M., 'Captial budgeting of interrelated projects: survey and synthesis', *Management Science,* **XII**, 1966.
27. Ziemba, W. T., 'A myopic captial budgeting model', *Journal of Financial and Quantitative Analysis,* **1970**.

CHAPTER 8

DCF and Project Networks

8.1 Introduction

Large scale investment projects may involve a preproduction period of several years. Such is the case particularly in respect of public utilities. Discounted cash flow methods will, of course, still be appropriate for and applicable to such investments. One of the most important tools of scientific management that has been developed in the past two decades, Critical Path Method (CPM) is now applied to the planning and control of all such projects. The objective of this chapter is to develop the linkages between critical path based methods and the DCF approach to capital budgeting.

As we shall see, the pattern of cash flows associated with a project can be obtained from certain CPM diagrams and the present value consequences of alterations to the initial network can be deduced. Indeed to the extent that such alterations are discretionary in nature the consequences for present value *must* be deduced if an optimization rather than a satisficing approach is employed by management.

Consequently it is rather surprising that the development of CPM methods has been essentially divorced from the methods of investment appraisal. In Chapter 1 we saw something of the background to and development of DCF methods of project appraisal. So before commencing the study of CPM and related methods proper it would be appropriate to discuss briefly the history of the techniques. At the end of the chapter the CPM and DCF methods will be drawn together in the context of large scale investments.

Critical Path Method is one of the modern techniques of network analysis and is used for the planning, scheduling and analysis of projects which consist of a large number of sequentially interrelated operations. The construction of highways, buildings, ships and aircraft provide examples of projects to which CPM methods have been applied with much success.

Until the mid fifties Gantt charts, and various other forms of bar charts, were one of the most important tools of project planning.[1] Although they continue to be useful in various guises today the place in project analysis has been largely taken by Critical Path and similar methods. The concept of a critical sequence of tasks which determine the minimum completion time of a project was known in England by 1955 and shortly afterwards was developed, publicized and somewhat oversold in the United States.

There are numerous techniques more or less similar to CPM, most being conceived at around the same time (1957–58), differences between the methods arising primarily as consequences of the particular characteristics of the problems which the methods were originally developed to address. PERT (Programme Evaluation and Review Technique) is the best known of these but some others are PEP PRISM IMPACT, SCANS and RAMPS.

In the earliest applications of CPM, time was the only relevant consideration, lateness penalties were very great. In most commercial applications nowadays cost is an equally important factor. Some of the typical objectives are: to arrange jobs and allocate resources to jobs to secure a required completion time subject to a cost or resource constraint or to minimize project cost subject to a time constraint. We shall examine CPM/time, PERT/time and PERT/cost. Problems arising from resource limitations will be analysed and linear programming formulations of some of the problems developed. The capital budgeting aspects are emphasized as the basic groundwork is accomplished.

8.2 CPM/Time

The most efficacious way to explain CPM is to consider a problem at once. Consider the hypothetical manufacturing and assembly line process presented in tabular form (the *project table*) in Figure 8.1. Column 1 describes each task of which the project is comprised and the jobs are identified by alphabetical label in column 2. The sequence in which the jobs are to be performed is given in the immediate predecessor column and the initial estimates of job times are given in column 4.

Although we shall take the project table as a starting point we should note that it presupposes that a good deal of work has already been done in respect of data gathering and determining sequences. This point will be returned to later on. Our task is now to represent the information of Figure 8.1 in diagrammatic form.

To accomplish this, each job is represented by a circle which includes the job label and time estimate. Ordering is represented by linear connections between jobs

Job	Job label	Immediate predecessor	Original job time estimate (minutes)
Set up machinery	a		10
Assemble materials	b	a	20
Select and prepare materials for component I	c	b	20
Select and prepare materials for component II	d	b	15
Select and prepare materials for component III	e	b	20
Mould I	f	c	40
Turn I	g	f	10
Paint I	h	g	10
Turn II	i	d	15
Turn III	j	e	15
Assemble II, III	k	i, j	10
Polish II, III	l	k	20
Assemble I, II, III	m	h, l	25
Inspect and pack	n	m	15

Figure 8.1 Example problem: project table

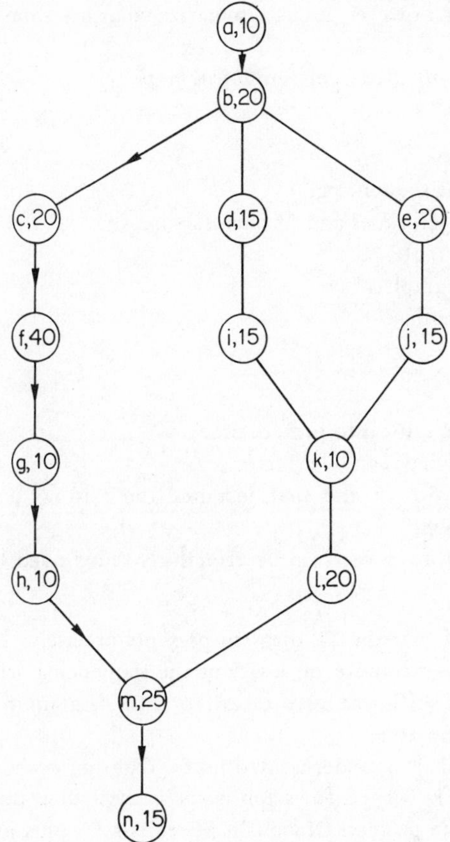

Figure 8.2 Example problem: CP diagram

in sequence. The whole is presented in Figure 8.2. It should be noted that only jobs in sequence are connected by lines, i.e. where there is no connecting line the jobs may be performed simultaneously.

The *critical path*, indicated by arrows, is the longest path (in time) through the network of Figure 8.2. (The *CP diagram*); this is the 'bottleneck route' and it comprises jobs abcfghmn. The critical path is the sequence of jobs which determines the minimum completion time for the project as a whole. If any time savings are to be made attention must first be focused on jobs on the critical path – there is no point in trying to speed up or rearrange other jobs, project completion time cannot be reduced this way. This latter pointer, telling us where *not* to expand effort is most important for in large networks there are many more non-critical jobs than critical ones. More of this later. At this stage the critical path can be found by enumeration – taking each path through the system and summing job times thereon. We shall shortly develop an alternative method of finding the critical path which yields valuable additional information.

Before proceeding, however, let us summarize what has gone so far.

Initial order of work for CPM/time (graphical method)

(i) Obtain data.
  (a) Define jobs.
  (b) Determine sequencing.
  (c) Estimate job times and (if necessary) costs..
(ii) Form project table.
(iii) Form project graph.
(iv) Find critical path.

CPM/time shows

(i) which jobs are critical to project time;
(ii) where time savings can be affected;
(iii) what not to do: in the first instance there is no point in speeding up non-critical jobs;
(iv) ways in which resources can be effectively redeployed within the project as a whole.

It should be noted that the CP diagram presents precisely the same information as the project table – no more no less, but the sequencing arrangements are now clearly visible. This is sufficient justification for a CP diagram in itself – but there is much more that can be done.

For each job we shall now derive two useful data: an *early start* time (ES) and *early finish* time (EF). The ES for a job is the earliest time that it can begin after commencement of the project. Obviously EF equals ES plus job time, since EF is the earliest time by which a job can be completed. Alongside each job we shall now write ES and EF in the following manner.

First of all, the start time for the initial job is fixed at $t = 0$; this is the ES of job a. The EF will then be at $t = 10$. Now job b can commence as soon as job a is completed so the ES of job b is the EF of job a. Job c can be started as soon as b is finished; f can be started when c is finished and so on down the left hand branch of the CP diagram as far as job h.

However, we cannot proceed directly from h to m as the early start of m is determined by the later of the EFs of h and l since both must be completed before m can begin. This gives the rule for determining early start time, manely: ES of a job is the latest of the EFs of the immediate predecessors of the job. Thus where a job has only one predecessor there is no possible ambiguity, but when there are several we take the largest of the preceding EF times.

Consequently in order to eventually determine the early start time for job m we must now return to job d in the centre branch. Its ES is 30, being equal to the EF

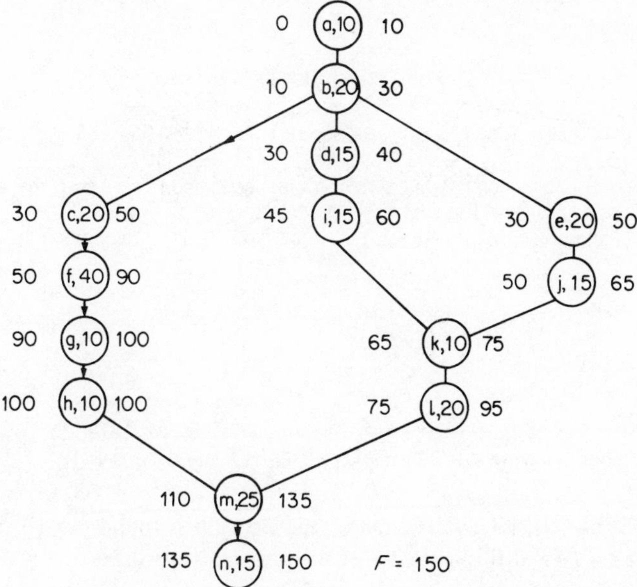

Figure 8.3 Example problem: ES and EF times

of b. We can proceed to find the EF of job i, 60. But because k succeeds both i and j we must now return to job l. In so doing it turns out that the ES of k is the EF of j (65) rather than i (60). Consequently the EF of l is 95 and therefore the ES of m is set by the EF of h rather than l. The EF of job n follows readily at 150 and this time of course is the EF time for the project as a whole. Call this time $F = 150$, i.e. the project takes a minimum of 150 minutes to complete, this time being determined by the left-hand branch – the critical path. ES and EF information is presented in Figure 8.3.

For any project there will normally be some idea of a time by which it *should* be completed – call this time T ('target time' – perhaps a contractual deadline or some *a priori* notional time). For initial feasibility of course $T \geqslant F$ but in many practical cases T is less than F even to begin with. We shall come to this situation later on. Firstly suppose the project is time-feasible – say $T = 160$. We shall now determine further data; the *late start* (LS) and *late finish* (LF) times for each job.

The LF of a job is the time a job must be completed by in order that the whole project is finished by T. Of course, LS = LF – job time. To determine LF and LS times we begin with the last job n, and work backwards. Clearly n must be completed by $t = 160$ so it has LF = 160 and therefore LS = 145. Job m is thus found to have LS = 120 which will be the LF of both h and l. It is a simple matter now to find the LS of jobs c, d and e. Now the LF of job b is the *earliest* of the LS times for c, d and e since if b is not completed by this time at least one path will push completion time beyond 160. This leads us to the operating definition of LF: the late finish time for a job is the earliest of the late start times for the immediate

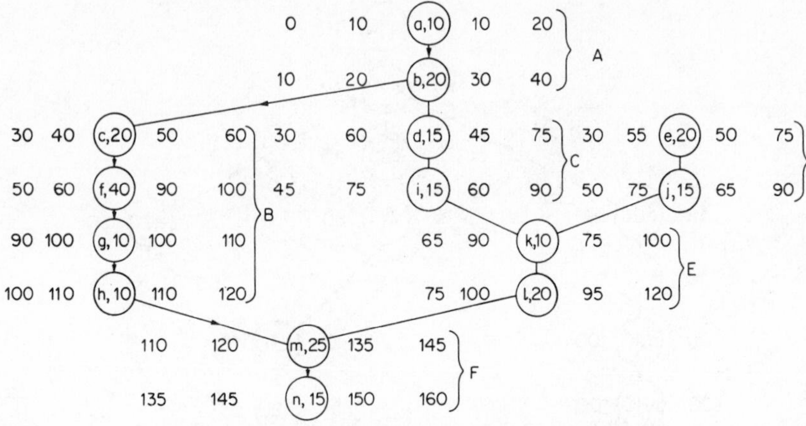

Figure 8.4 Example problem: LS and LF times

successors of the job. Late start time of the first job is found (as we should have suspected) as $t = 10$ and this is the LS of the project as a whole.

LS and LF information presented: LS (job) LF, is shown in Figure 8.4. Finding LS of the entire project is not the point of the exercise however. It is valuable to know the amount of 'sparetime' in a job — things may not go precisely according to plan, delays may occur or jobs take longer than scheduled, but this may not be important if there is sufficient flexibility in the timing of the start of future jobs. Such flexibility is called 'slack' or 'float'.

There are in fact three concepts of slack. The most frequently used is *total slack* (TS) which is, for each job, the length of time a job may be delayed its ES without causing the project as a whole to be delayed beyond T, the deadline time. Therefore TS in each job will be LS − ES or equivalently LF − EF. Total slack is defined for each job individually. In saying that TS = LS − ES it is being assumed that there are no delays in previous jobs (so that ES is unaffected) or subsequent jobs (so that the LS time is still relevant). Reference to Figure 8.4 shows that all critical jobs have ten minutes TS. That is, TS for critical jobs is $T - F$. It will also be seen from the figure that all non-critical jobs have TS $\geqslant$ 10. This is true generally and enables a further definition of 'criticalness' to be made:

> A critical job is one having minimum total slack, (i.e. TS = $T - F$).

So having found ES, LS, EF and LF times for each job, the critical path (or paths — there may be several) is found by joining up jobs with minimum TS. Two results should be pointed out here. Firstly, there will always be at least one path through the network that consists only of critical jobs. Secondly, all critical jobs are on a critical path.[2]

The second type of slack is *free slack* (FS). Again defined independently for each job FS is the delay possible in a job such that subsequent jobs can still begin at their ES time. In other words for job x and the succeeding job x + 1, free slack for job x,

$FS_x = ES_{x+1} - EF_x$. The only jobs in the example system with FS $\geqslant 0$ are jobs i and l. FS in job i is five minutes and FS in job l is fifteen minutes. Roughly speaking, FS is the delay possible without affecting F and TS is the delay possible without affecting T. However, this definition, though useful conceptually, is not precisely accurate. Some jobs with FS = 0 can be delayed without affecting F. This point will be dealt with shortly when an alternative view of slack is presented. Obviously, all critical jobs will have zero FS and for any job FS $\leqslant$ TS provided that there is initial feasibility ($T \geqslant F$). If however $T < F$ then FS may exceed the (negative) TS for some jobs.

The statement that FS $\leqslant$ TS is readily shown. For any job x, $TS_x = LF_x - EF_x = LS_{x+1} - EF_x$ since $LS_{x+1} = LF_x$. Now if there is initial feasibility ($T \geqslant F$) then for all jobs LS $\geqslant$ ES so for job x + 1 we can write $LS_{x+1} = ES_{x+1} + \Delta$ where $\Delta \geqslant 0$. Thus $TS_x = ES_{x+1} + \Delta - EF_x$. Now $FS_x = ES_{x+1} - EF_x$ by definition. Consequently, $TS_x - FS_x = \Delta \geqslant 0$, i.e. $TS_x \geqslant FS_x$ provided $T \geqslant F$.

The third type of slack, *independent slack* (IS), is the time remaining between the late finish of a job and the earliest of the early starts of subsequent jobs. So $IS_x = ES_{x+1} - EF_x$. Not surprisingly there are few occasions in practice where jobs are found to have positive IS. Any job with positive IS is a very long way from being critical. Clearly for all projects with $T \geqslant F$ then for any job TS $\geqslant$ FS $\geqslant$ IS. The reader may care to formulate a proof or the latter part of this relationship along the lines of the proof given above.

The concept of slack really comes into its own when the problem of time reductions is considered. Total slack as we have seen helps in identification of the critical path and hence those jobs on which attention should first be directed when speeding up is being considered. Now there are two distinct ways in which F can be reduced. The first is by speeding up jobs and the second is by rearrangement of job ordering (when there is flexibility in this).

To begin with, consider the problem of speeding up jobs. It can be convenient to divide up a network into branches as has been done in Figure 8.4 and discuss time savings within branches. The CP is, initially, ABF but branches A and F are on *any* path through the system. A consequence of this is that any time savings (through the speeding up of jobs), in branches A and F *cannot alter the position of the CP* and are fully reflected in early finish time for the project as a whole.

Speeding up of jobs in A means that the ES time of *all* succeeding jobs is reduced. For example if the duration of job b is cut from 20 min to 17 then the ES of all subsequent jobs is reduced by 3 min thereby increasing TS by 3 min in all succeeding jobs. Minimum TS is now 13 min. Note that the total slack in job a is also increased to 13 since its LS and LF times are increased by 3 min and for job b itself EF is reduced by 3 min and LS is increased to 23.

In Section F too, time savings cannot alter the position of the CP. Late finish times of all preceding jobs are increased by the amount of time saved in F. So to make things awkward let us rule out any time savings in sections A and F. We must therefore concentrate on section B.

Suppose time on job F can be reduced to 30 min. This will reduce EF of f to 60 and the ES and EF of g and h by 10 min so that EF of h becomes 100. Now the ES of job m is the later of the EFs of h and l so that the start time for m is still governed by EF of h, 100. Consequently, EF of job n becomes 140, 10 min is saved overall, minimum TS is 20 min, TS in branches E and D remains at 25 min and in branch C TS is still 30 min.

Now suppose it would be possible to save a further 10 min in job f, reducing job time to 20 min. The EF of job h is now 90 min but the ES of job m is 95 since EF of l remains unchanged. Early finish for the entire project *F*, is 135. The further 10 min saved in job f have resulted in only 5 min saving for the project as a whole. This is because the CP has switched from ABF to ADEF. Minimum TS is now 25 min. Slack in D and E was not increased as time on job F was reduced because F is not in sequence with jobs in D and E. Section A *is* in sequence with B so why did not slack here continue to increase as time on job F was reduced? The answer is that A is *also* in sequence with D and E and the LF time of job b is fixed by the earliest of the LS times of its successors c, d and e, and LS times of c and d do not change as time on job f is altered. The LF time of job b eventually becomes 55 but cannot go to the 60 which is the LS of c when f is reduced to 20.

A valuable role for TS in time savings problems is emerging. In the present context it is useful to think of TS in *branches* of the system rather than individual jobs. The preceeding analysis showed that every minute saved in job f increased TS in c, g and h by one minute also and it is of no importance *where* in branch B time is saved as far as TS in jobs in C, D and E is concerned. The maximum amount of time it is worth saving in B is the difference between TS in this branch and the next lowest level of TS in a branch not in sequence with B. So having found TS we then have valuable information for time savings by comparing TS in 'unsequenced' branches.

In fact it can be useful to aggregate the jobs within branches in the format shown in Figure 8.5. Here, ES and EF, LS and LF times are calculated for branches as a whole. Time saved (or indeed added), anywhere in a branch affects LS and EF of the branch. This done, suppose that it was required to save more than the 15 min originally saved in project time. Having ruled out time savings in A and F time must now be saved in D or E *as well as* A. Another CP has been picked up and ideally (so that no time saving is wasted) each path should be kept *jointly critical.*

Now time saved in E will not alter the CP between D and C so, to be awkward

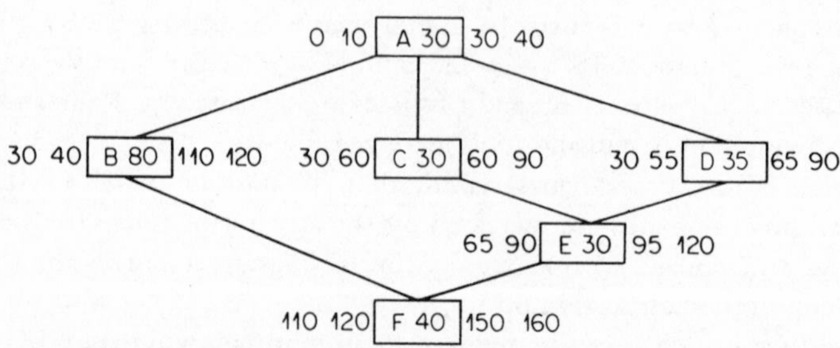

Figure 8.5 Example problem: aggregation

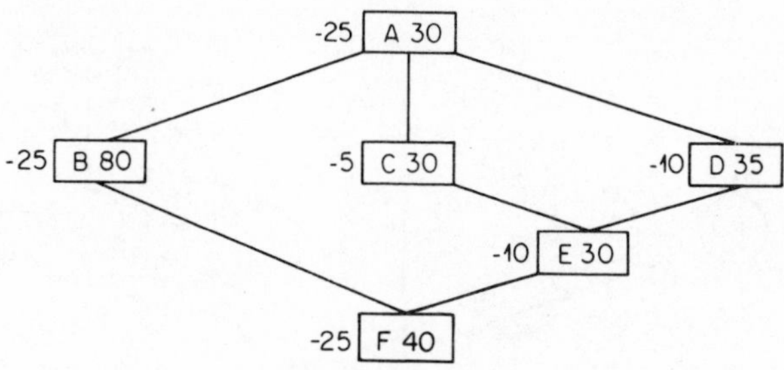

Figure 8.6 Infeasible situation: negative TS

again, rule out time savings in E. If EF of B is now 90, up to 5 min can usefully be saved in D but no more otherwise ACEF would become uniquely critical. If greater time savings are required then at least three jobs must be simultaneously speeded up: one job in B, one in C and one in D. This is a characteristic of time savings achieved by speeding up jobs; gradually more critical paths are picked up and an increasing number of jobs are to be worked on.

Suppose now that to begin with there was the infeasible situation in which $T < F$. In particular say $T = 125$, i.e. 25 min must be saved. We can readily see the saving necessary in each branch if TS is calculated as before but now of course minimum TS is negative. Figure 8.6 presents the informantion with TS indicated alongside each branch box instead of ES, EF, LS, LF data. Minimum TS is -25 and maximum TS is -5 and to achieve feasibility TS everywhere in the system must be non-negative. It can readily be seen therefore that if time savings in A and F in total are α and time savings in E are β then the requisite saving in B is $25 - \alpha$ (for $\alpha \leqslant 25$), in D $10 - (\alpha + \beta)$ must be saved (for $\alpha + \beta \leqslant 10$) and in c, $5 - (\alpha + \beta)$ is to be saved (for $\alpha + \beta \leqslant 5$). Thus the objective is to get minimum TS up to zero and to accomplish this, aggregation of jobs into branches can be convenient.

By what means are the time savings in the jobs being effected? It is being assumed that time savings in certain of the jobs are technically feasible or that delays between jobs (see below) can be cut. The problem is complicated somewhat if job time variations are not continuous, e.g. time on job f is 50 min, 40 min, 33 min, 29 min or 20 min, in which case it will not always be possible to keep several paths jointly critical. But here the objective will be to get as near as possible to the joint-critical situation.

What about the costs of time savings and any resources needed to effect them? If cost is to be considered explicitly as well as time, and resources needed for speeding up one job have to be taken from another then the problem is very much more complicated and 'trades-off' have to be considered. Discussions of these questions is postponed until section 8.4.

Time savings may also be achieved by rearranging job orderings where this is feasible. To the extent that there is discretion in 'network logic' a combinatorial element is introduced. This can rapidly assume formidable proportions. For instance if a project consists of one hundred jobs (small by practical standards),

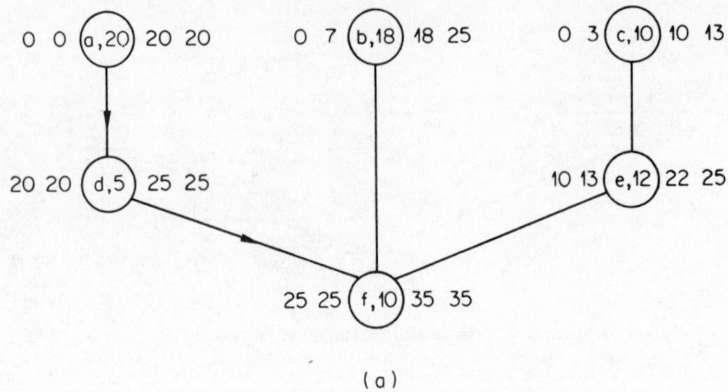

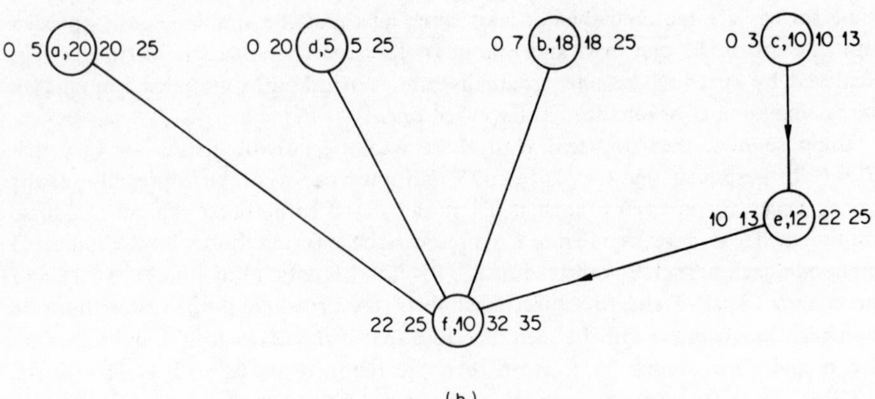

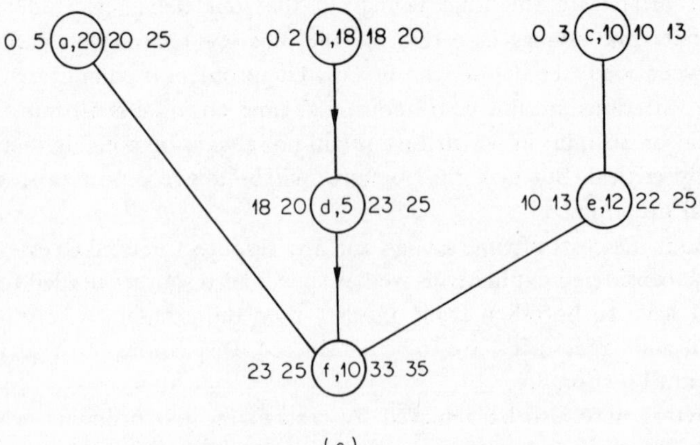

Figure 8.7 Job relocation example

ninety-five of which have a predetermined sequential relationship whilst the remaining five can be fitted in anywhere, then in fact there are over eight thousand million possible arrangements of jobs! The rescheduling problem is thus formidable and some approximation approaches are discussed in the context of resource problems below. However, a few points relevant to small degrees of discretion in small networks are appropriate here.

Firstly, and rather obviously, to be effective on project time any rearrangement of jobs must affect the critical path. No time can be saved by rescheduling amongst only non-critical jobs. Secondly, some jobs must be taken *out* of the present CP. Now if any job is introduced into the CP then F is increased by the duration of that job. But if a job is removed from the CP then F will be reduced by the job time only if the original path (minus the one job) remains critical. Without study of a particular network all that can definitely be said (if in the first instance, the path is uniquely critical) is that ES time of all succeeding jobs is lowered and LF time of all preceding jobs is raised. In other words slack in the CP is increased. The concept of TS in fact can be of value in a rescheduling context. If the position of a job is changed then the saving in project time will be the difference between the old value of minimum TS and the new value. More specifically, if the job is relocated in an independent position – one that does not decrease TS on any other branch – then total time saved is the difference between minimum TS and the next lowest level of TS or job time whichever is smaller.

Consider the system of Figure 8.7 (a) where F is 35 and since it is the only relevant project time $T = F$. The CP is adf with TS = 0. Relocation of job d as in 8.7 (b) could be seen, before the event to bring a saving of $\Delta t = 3$, the difference between critical TS, 0, and the next lowest TS, that in branch ce of 3. In 8.7 (b) it is readily seen that new minimum TS = 3 job a has TS = 5 and is no longer on the critical path. If further manipulations were carried out the total time savings would give minimum TS at any stage. If, alternatively it was possible only to sequence d after b then we know that TS in job a must go up by 5 and TS in B must decrease by 5 so that time saved will be $TS_b - 5 - TS_a$ or 5 whichever is the smaller.

8.3 PERT/Time

The original PERT/time system was developed by the United States Navy at around the same time that CPM was developed by the Du Pont Company. PERT/time has as its central feature the notion of a critical path, but differs from CPM in respect of job-time estimates. PERT is concerned with situations in which job times are random variables. It may be that job time is simply unknown in the case of an entirely new project or that job times are influenced by uncontrollable variables (e.g. the weather).

Ideally we should like the *probability distribution* of job times. When there are discrete alternatives this is a list of possible job times and the associated chance of occurrence of each time. Figure 8.8 details an instance where there are four possible durations for a job. These times are listed in column 1. Probability of occurrence is given in column 2 and column 3 elements are summed to give the expected duration of the job. Things are rarely as convenient as this of course. The

Time (t)	Probability (p)	$t \cdot p$
22	0.2	4.4
32	0.2	6.4
46	0.3	13.8
56	0.3	16.8
	Expected time =	41.4

Figure 8.8 A discrete distribution of job times

underlying probability distribution of job times will be more complicated in many instances and the duration of different jobs may be interdependent (joint probability distributions). All is not lost, however, if we know the *type* of probability distributions (e.g. discrete (as above), Normal, Gamma or Beta), and some of its parameters – in particular the mean and variance. It is most unlikely that these parameters will be known *a priori* and the PERT/time method gives a simple and practicable means of obtaining 'reasonable' estimates of mean and variance.

The person in charge of each job is asked to provide three estimates of job time: a 'pessimistic' estimate, an 'optimistic' estimate and a 'most likely' estimate. The investigator may quantify 'optimistic' and 'pessimistic' for example by defining the pessimistic time as one for which there are 95 chances out of a 100 of getting the job done within this time. This statistic may be based on past experience with the job or may be an *a priori* subjective estimate (i.e. a guess) if the job has never been done before 'optimistic' would then be that time for which there were only 5 chances out of 100 of completing the job by this time. Alternatively in qualitative terms the pessimistic estimate defined as: 'the time taken to complete the job if everything goes wrong short of total disaster' and the optimistic estimate as: 'everything goes well short of a miracle'. Figure 8.9 places these estimates and the most likely figure (m) on the graph of a possible underlying distribution. Numerically, arithmetic mean time (expected time), e, can be approximated as a function of a, b and m once the underlying distribution is fixed. For example if the underlying distribution is a Beta distribution then the value of e can be

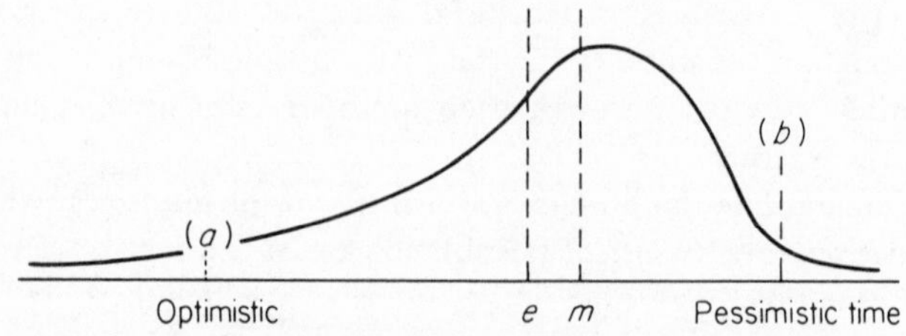

Figure 8.9 PERT job time estimates

approximated as:

$$e \simeq \frac{1}{6}(a + b) + \frac{2}{3}m \tag{8.1}$$

In (8.1) the coefficients 1/6 and 2/3 are weights appropriate for the Beta distribution.[3] How do we know what the underlying distribution is like? In general we have to specify this *a priori*. 'Experience' on the one hand and operations research theory on the other may have to be called on. This point will be mentioned again in the comments of review of the procedure.

Once the mean time has been determined this is used as in the CPM diagrams and analysis proceeds à la CPM. Occasionally, the CPM may be derived using the pessimistic estimates if at all events a project *must* be completed in such and such a time. Unscrupulous or naive contractors may employ optimistic estimates in tender preparation. However, these are (one trusts) uncommon situations.

The job time variance can also be estimated from a, b and m in fact variance, σ^2, is approximated as:

$$\sigma^2 \simeq \frac{1}{36}(b - a)^2 \tag{8.2}$$

Where (8,2) is appropriate for a Beta distribution.

Having obtained estimates of mean times and variances for individual jobs the mean times and variances of strictly ordered sequences of jobs may be found. For instance if a series of n jobs are in strict sequence and the distributions of individual job times are independent of each other, then mean time for completion of the sequence is the sum of the individual mean job times, i.e.

$$E(T) = \sum_{i=1}^{n} E(t_i)$$

and the variance of time for completion of the n jobs is the sum of the individual job time variances, i.e.

$$\sigma_T^2 = \sum_{i=1}^{n} \sigma_i^2$$

Having found the expected completion time for a branch of a system and total variance for that branch a *confidence interval* can be found for completion time for the branch.[4]

For instance if individual job times in the branch are normally distributed then it is known that for the ith job there is a 95% chance that the job time will actually lie in the interval: $E(t_i) \pm 1.96\sigma_i$. This is because 95% of the area under a Normal curve lies within 1.96 standard deviations of the mean. Each extreme tail contains only 2½% of the area under the curve; that is only a 2½% chance that job time will take more than $E(t_i) - 1.96\sigma_i$. The 95% confidence interval for the branch as a whole is

$E(t_i)$	σ_i^2
8.4	0.9
12.5	1.7
15.0	2.6
9.3	0.6
14.8	2.2
$\Sigma E(t_i) = 60.0$	$\Sigma \sigma_i^2 = 8.0$

Figure 8.10 Data for confidence interval calculation

given by equation (8.3).

$$C_{95} = E(T) \pm 1.96\sigma_T = \Sigma E(t_i) \pm 1.96(\Sigma\sigma_i^2)^{1/2} \tag{8.3}$$

If a branch consists of five jobs with expected times and variances as given in Figure 8.10 with each job time independently normally distributed then the 95% confidence interval for completion time for the branch is given by equation (8.4)

$$C_{95} = 60 \pm 1.96\sqrt{8} = 54.45\overline{6} \text{ to } 65.5\overline{43}$$

If some of the job times are not independent of each other but are *jointly distributed* (i.e. the probability distribution of times for job i depends on the time taken for other jobs) the estimated mean time and variance of a sequence can still be found analytically although the situation is more complicated. Real difficulties arise when all jobs are not in strict sequence – as in the typical networks that have been considered so far – and a confidence interval for completion time for the whole project is desired.

To illustrate: when two or more branches join up, as do branches C and D in branch E in Figure 8.4 then the early start time for E depends upon which of C and D is finished first but times for C and D are now random variables. The expected early start for E is the expected value of the maximum of TC and TD i.e. $E(\max T_C, T_D)$ where T_C is completion time for branches A and C and T_D is completion time for branches A and D. Mathematical analysis of such cases is, however, beyond the scope of this text and would only be warranted on very small networks in practice. A *simulation* exercise would be more rewarding.

In such a simulation exercise the procedure would be to insert probability distributions of job times along with the network logic into a computer and the distribution of F would then be determined empirically after many runs through of the system. Mean and confidence intervals could then be estimated for the project as a whole (or for particular non strictly sequenced parts of the system).

Multiple time estimates in network analysis are not quite as fashionable nowadays as they were in the early and mid sixties. This may be because the approach is overly sophisticated in respect of many applications and because in many PERT/time analyses a single figure estimate is worked with eventually and unless the complications of PERT produce a significantly better mean figure they will not be worth the cost and time involved. Whether a single figure estimate or the PERT procedure is superior cannot be determined in abstraction. The choice of method in any case should be determined by the particular circumstances obtaining in that case.

We conclude with a few points in support of a CPM rather than PERT approach when job times are uncertain. First, is what might be called the 'levels of criticalness approach'. In this, critical jobs now become 'first level critical' and near-critical jobs become 'second level critical'. For instance in a building operation jobs with three days TS may be first level critical and jobs with four to six days TS second level critical. If all goes well the second level critical jobs would not determine the minimum completion time for the project. But if, for instance, some of these job times depend on extraneous factors (e.g. the performance of a subcontractor) they may be 'unreliable' and become critical. If likely cases can be identified in advance it would be useful to have some contingency plans worked out for speeding up of some of the subsequent newly critical jobs.

Finally if one wished to err on the side of caution a fixed percentage could be added on to the initial time estimate for each job so that although single figure estimates are then used there is a built-in 'safety margin' for delays. This approach along with the previous two, is one of approximation. The degrees of approximation are not specified, but the methods should not be dismissed as 'ad-hocery'. It is modifications such as these that make theoretical models tractable in practical usage. There is scarcely an area of quantitative decision making in management that does not require some unspecified degree of compromise with exactness. We turn now to another area of critical path analysis that usually requires approximation approaches.

8.4 PERT/Cost

To employ CPM methods in problems where cost as well as time, is a relevant consideration, it is necessary to relate cost to time in a systematic manner. New time/cost systems are being developed continually – a fact which illustrates the point that there is, as yet, no all purpose solution procedure available. Many of the new systems are in relation to specific projects and will therefore have only a limited range of applicability.

The complexity of the problem hinges a good deal upon how cost varies with time. If for a particular job the rate of change of cost with time is positive, i.e.. $dc/dt > 0$ then minimization of job time will result in minimization of cost. For a project as a whole, in these circumstances, all time saved implies reduction of cost and the minimization of completion time overall is a necessary condition for the minimization of cost.

Things are rarely so convenient. We shall begin by illustrating a system in which job cost and job time are inversely related, i.e. with $dc/dt < 0$ for every job. Subsequently a case will be encountered in which some types of job have $dc/dt < 0$ whilst others have $dc/dt > 0$.

A simple approach, which we shall PERT/cost, is as follows. For each job in the system two figures for time and two figures for cost are determined. The figures are a minimum cost estimate and the associated time and a minimum time estimate and the associated cost. Sometimes the least cost estimate is linked with the 'normal'

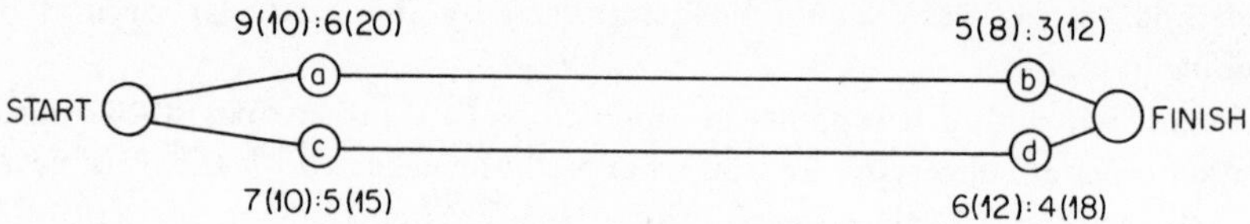

Figure 8.11 PERT/cost example

job time whilst the high cost method involves 'crashing' the job. Whatever, the objective will be to secure a minimum figure for the cost of completing a project subject to the condition that it is finished within a specified deadline. The problem will be the more difficult if in order to speed up one job resources have to be taken from others (the problem of *resource trade-offs*). Thus jobs are interrelated by common use of scarce resources as well as by logical sequence.

Of course, what has been defined is a programming problem and where the structure and size of the task permits, the established computational procedures can be employed. Such is the case in the example to follow, in which it will be assumed that when a job is to be speeded up the resources needed to accomplish this are brought in from outside the system. The very simple network of Figure 8.11 shows jobs as circles and the relevant time and cost figures associated with them – the cost figures being bracketed. Thus the minimum cost estimate for job a is £10, and the completion time associated with this is 9 hours, and the minimum time estimate is 6 hours and its associated cost is £20. The jobs are to be performed in the orders indicated and all four jobs must be completed in 11 hours. There are two notional jobs 'start' and 'finish'. The network corresponds to a partial ordering of the jobs such that it can be separated into upper and lower routes, i.e. there is no ordering between (a) and (c) and both can be worked on simultaneously.

The problem is to minimize the cost of completing the whole system in 11 hours. This means the completion of each branch in 11 hours. Now, we shall assume that the two pairs of values for time and cost represent extremes and that cost is a linear function of time over the time range for each job. Thus dc/dt for job a is the constant term $- 10/3$ $[\{(10-20)/(9-6)\}]$ and for job b it is 4/2. In the lower branch $dc/dt_c = -2.5$ and $dc/dt_d = -3$. Figure 8.12(a) shows the situation graphically for jobs in the upper branch. Incidentally it should be noted that packages offered by computing companies allow alternative assumptions about dc/dt as a function of time. Some of these are graphed in Figure 8.12(b). The convex to the origin or piecewise linear assumptions would seem the more plausible of the three.

With the highly tractable linearity assumption shown in Figure 8.12(a) the solution procedure suggests itself. This is to begin by doing each job the slow, cheap way. If the time constraint is violated speed up the job with the lowest (in absolute terms) value of dc/dt and save as much as is necessary or as much as is possible on this job. If more time savings are required than can be affected on the 'cheapest' (in time-savings terms) job then the job with the next lowest value of dc/dt is selected – and so on. In the current example on the upper branch if each job is

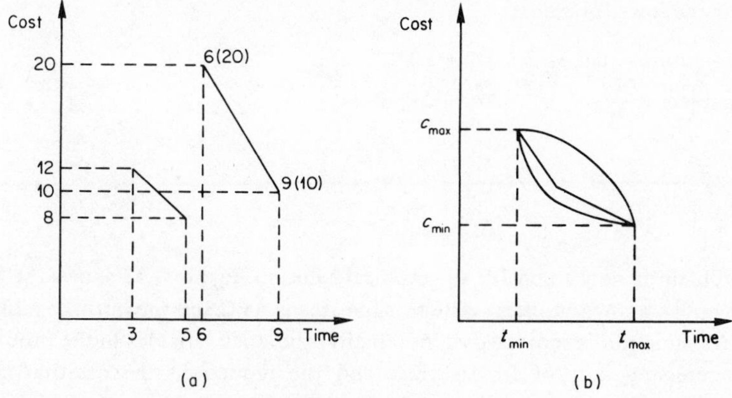

Figure 8.12 Time–cost trade offs

done at the normal time the branch is completed in 14 hours, so that three need to be saved. Job b is the cheapest for savings here and two hours can be saved at an addition to cost of £4. The remaining hour necessary is then saved in job a at a cost of £3.33. On the lower branch the two hours needed to be saved can be found in job c at a total cost of £5. Letting Δt_j represent the time saved on job j the problem can be expressed in L.P. form as:

$$\text{minimize } \Delta C = 3.\overline{33}\Delta t_a + 2\Delta t_b + 2.5\Delta t_c + 3\Delta t_d$$

$$\begin{aligned}\text{subject to} \quad & \Delta t_a + \Delta t_b \geqslant 3\\ & \Delta t_c + \Delta t_d \geqslant 2\\ & \Delta t_a \leqslant 3\\ & \Delta t_b \leqslant 2\\ & \Delta t_c \leqslant 2\\ & \Delta t_d \leqslant 2\\ & \Delta t_j \geqslant 0 \text{ for } j = \text{a, b, c, d}\end{aligned}$$

The problem can be divided into two halves, which is a desirable feature computationally. They are:

$$\text{minimize } \Delta C_u = 3.33\Delta t_a + 2\Delta t_b$$

$$\begin{aligned}\text{subject to:} \quad & \Delta t_a + \Delta t_b \geqslant 3\\ & \Delta t_a \leqslant 3\\ & \Delta t_b \leqslant 2\\ & \Delta t_a \quad \Delta t_b \geqslant 0\end{aligned}$$

and, for the lower branch:

$$\text{minimize} \quad \Delta C_l = 2.5\Delta t_c + 3\Delta t_d$$

$$\begin{aligned} \text{subject to:} \quad & \Delta t_c + \Delta t_d \geqslant 2 \\ & \Delta t_c \leqslant 2 \\ & \Delta t_d \leqslant 2 \\ & \Delta t_c \,;\; \Delta t_d \geqslant 0 \end{aligned}$$

The problem is now amenable to graphical solution. Figure 8.13 shows the solution to the upper branch problem. The feasible area is ABC and the optimal value of the objective function is indicated at A. Finally, the dual variables in the problem give the incremental cost of time savings and the reductions in cost that could be obtained by relaxation of the upper bounds. If such relaxation is achieved by purchase or hire of additional resources then the dual variables allow such investments to be evaluated.

In more complex networks not so conveniently subdivided into strictly sequenced branches, the programming formulation is not so straightforward. For instance consider the system of Figure 8.6. Essentially there will be a constraint corresponding to each path through the network. Time on each path must be within the limit allowed. Assume for simplicity that each rectangle represents a job and that costs for the ith job are given by

$$C_i = \alpha_i - \beta_i t_i$$

where $\alpha_i, \beta_i > 0$ and where $t_i^L \leqslant t_i \leqslant t_i^u$ and i = A, B, C, D, E, F. If time on each job is a continuous variable between the given limits the cost minimization problem subject to a time constraint can be written as:

$$\text{maximize} \quad F = \sum_i \beta_i t_i$$

$$\begin{aligned} \text{subject to} \quad & t_A + t_B + t_F = T \\ & t_A + t_C + t_E + t_F = T \\ & t_A + t_D + t_E + t_F = T \\ \text{and} \quad & t_i^L \leqslant t_i \leqslant t_i^u \text{ for all } i \end{aligned}$$

The deadline time is T and the constraints can be written as equalities given the linearity of costs. If some of the β_i were negative then the $\leqslant$ inequality would replace the equality sign in the constraints.

Suppose now that the time taken on each job is a function (assumed linear here) of the resources used on the job and that resources are limited in total. By assumption we can write:

$$t_i = L_i(x_{ij}) \quad \text{for} \quad j = 1, 2, \ldots, n$$

that is, time on the ith job is a linear function of the n resource inputs; x_{ij} being the quantity of the jth resource used on the ith job. Substitution of the $L_i(x_{ij})$ for the

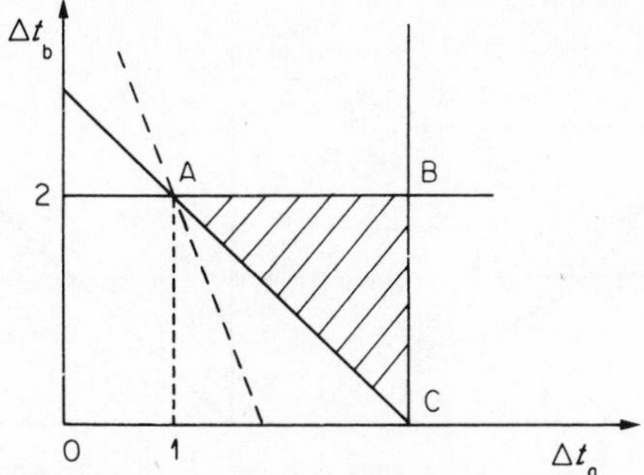

Figure 8.13 Solution to upper branch problem

t_i in the constraint set and objective function leaves both as linear expressions in the x_{ij} and in addition the resource usage constraints:

$$\sum_i x_{ij} \leqslant x_j \quad \text{for} \quad j = 1, 2, \ldots, n$$

would be appended to the constraint set. In principle the technique applies to problems of any size but in practice the usage would be conditioned by consideration of computational feasibility (and cost) and the plausibility of the linearity assumptions.

8.5 Optimum Project Duration

So far we have been considering problems in which a particular time constraint had been set. We turn now to consider the problem of optimum project duration. In concrete terms how many months or years and months should be spent on a large construction task when there is some discretion as to duration? To begin to answer the question it is useful to divide costs into those which increase with time and those for which $\mathrm{d}c/\mathrm{d}t < 0$. Into the former category would fall 'indirect' costs; costs of administration, financing, hire of plant and equipment, rent, etc. The 'direct' costs, attributable unambiguously to particular tasks would generally fall into the latter category. How can these different characteristics be optimally reconciled?

First consider the direct costs (we shall include all costs with $\mathrm{d}c/\mathrm{d}t < 0$ under this heading) for the project as a whole. Beginning by doing each job the long, cheap way and finding the critical path we obtain one pair of values for project time and total direct costs. The objective here is to obtain the graph of total direct costs against time and in principle we should like to find the cheapest way of saving each unit of time. As mentioned above, this problem can be computationally formidable. Where this is the case the following approximate procedure is suggested. Consider just two possible times for each job – normal (cheap) time and crash (costly) time. Begin with each job assumed to be done the normal way and find what would be total cost and the critical path. Now crash the cheapest (in

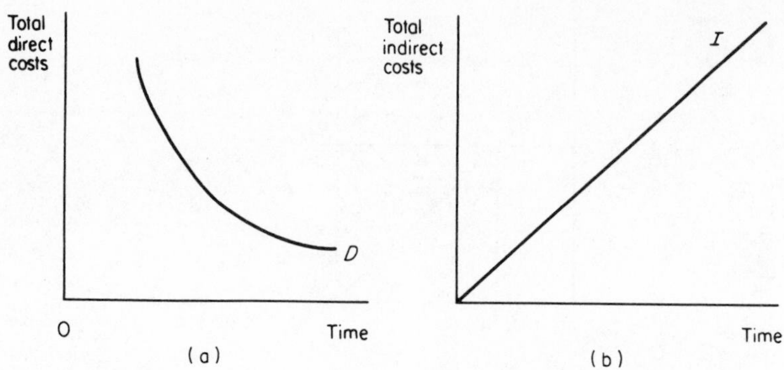

Figure 8.14 Project duration and present values of costs

terms of 'crashing') job on the CP. Find the new level of total direct cost and time and the new CP. Now crash the cheapest job on this path and so on. By this means (or by an L.P. approach in smaller problems) time/direct cost data is obtained and a possible graph of direct costs against time can be produced. If an investment decision is being taken (whether or not to undertake the project) the cost data may be put in present value form. This will be assumed to be done in the context of the present discussion. A procedure for obtaining the present value of costs associated with a network is given in the following sections. A plausible shape for a graph of the present value of direct costs against time is shown in Figure 8.14(b) shows a possible graph of the present value of total indirect costs against time. Whilst we should not conclude that discounted indirect costs are necessarily a linear function of time, a monotonic increasing relationship is to be expected. In Figure 8.15 the line $D + I$ gives the present value of total costs, direct plus indirect and the line shows the present value of the return on the project (assumed here to be a lump sum payment occurring when the project is complete). The line π shows net present value against time $[= R - (D + I)]$. This is maximized at $t = \bar{t}$, the optimal duration. Breakeven durations are t_1 and t_2 whilst the minimum cost duration is t_3. Note that if R is a declining function of time (as in the case of a fixed payment on completion) then the minimum cost duration for the project will not be chosen if the objective is maximization of present value of profits. The cost minimizing time would only be chosen if there was provision (say by an inflation clause in the contract) to increase the terminal payment at a compound rate equal to the rate of discount, i.e. to keep the present value constant.

The diagram of Figure 8.15 allows of further analysis. Suppose the company that is involved with the project is in a bidding situation and in order to secure the contract has to promise completion by $t_4 < \bar{t}$. Presumably penalty payments will be due in the event of delay. The optimum project duration in this instance would be found by subtracting the curve showing lateness penalties as a function of time from the previous profit function as given by π. The high point of this new curve would determine optimum (from the point of view of the constructor) project duration. If as seems reasonable the lateness penalties are an increasing function of

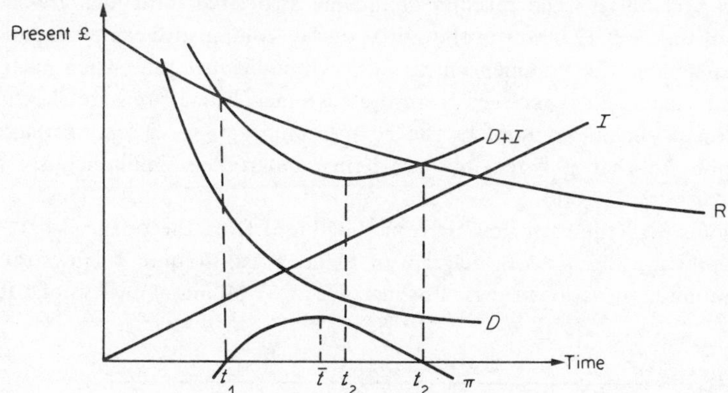

Figure 8.15 Optimal project duration

time the new optimum duration will be less than $\bar{t}$. Though the argument here seems rather unscrupulous, if the lateness penalties reflect something in excess of the true costs of lateness to the customer, the solution would prove mutually beneficial!

8.6 Critical Path Method and Discounted Cash Flow

We shall now consider in greater detail the relationship between CPM and DCF analysis. In lengthy investment projects (for which CPM is a must) involving several outflows of capital the timing of the outflows will be important from both the liquidity and present value standpoints. Most probably there will also be cash inflows at various stages of the operation representing payments for part completion (say of a ship or a building) or income resulting from partial operation (of plant and equipment). The timing of these inflows is also important from both standpoints.

Firstly, an alternative graphical form of CPM is essential. In Figure 8.16 the network of Figure 8.2 is reproduced but with an alternative presentation in which line segments represent the jobs and circles are 'nodes' or 'events' representing the completion of one task and the commencement of another. The length of the lines is proportional to the job durations. Horizontal lines do not represent jobs but are simply to separate several jobs with a common predecessor. Dashed lines show amounts of free slack (what does this suggest about the presence of free slack and increases in total slack?).

In contrast to the data in the project table, Figure 8.1, let the units of time be weeks rather than minutes and envisage a manufacture and assemble operation with six basic stages (representing the branches of the network) which are divided into a total of 14 jobs. Suppose that jobs a and b represent materials collection and erection of plant whilst jobs c, f, g, and h, d, and i, e and j, represent fabrication of components. Jobs k and l are sub-assembly operation and job m represents final assembly and inspection whilst jobs n corresponds to testing and delivery.

The capital outlays and receipts of income associated with jobs are shown in £1,000s in Figure 8.17. Data in the initial outlay column give capital expenditures consequent upon the commencement of each individual job. When each job is completed a payment is received from the customer. These sums are shown in the completion payments column. In the next column data for weekly variable costs are per job, so that if three jobs are being undertaken simultaneously weekly variable costs are £30,000.

In Figure 8.18 the cash flow pattern is deduced from the financial data of the project table and the network diagram of Figure 8.16. Column 1 shows the initial outlays required at various times. For instance at t = 30 initial outlays of £100,000

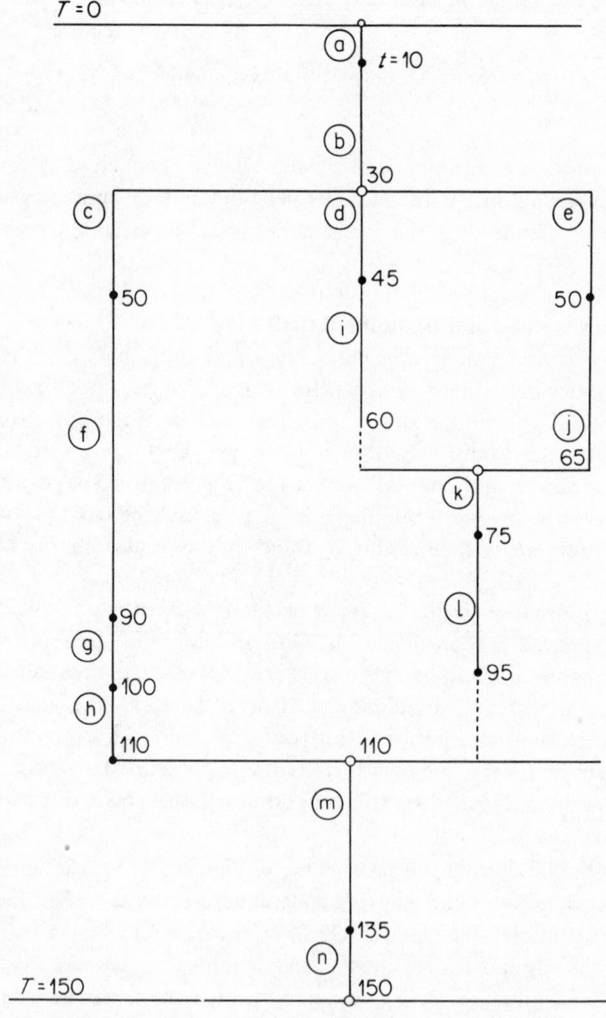

Figure 8.16 Alternative form of network diagram

Job classification	Job	Duration (weeks)	Initial outlay	Completion payment	Weekly variable costs	Job preceding
Assemble materials	a	10	150		10	
Erect plant	b	20	150	250	10	a
Fab 1	c	20	100	300	10	b
Fab 2	d	15	100	75	10	b
Fab 3	e	20	100	225	10	b
Fab 1	f	40	200	100	10	c
Fab 1	g	10	50	175	10	f
Fab 1	h	10	100	650	10	g
Fab 2	i	15	100	250	10	d
Fab 3	j	15	150	450	10	e
Sub-assembly 1	k	10	250	125	10	i, j
Sub-assembly 2	l	20	75	150	10	k
Final assembly	m	25	250	500	10	h, l
Delivery	n	15		2,000	10	m

Figure 8.17 Network cost and revenue data

are required on each of jobs c, d, and e, so that the total outflow at this point is £300,000. Column 2 shows the timing of completion payments. For example at $t = 50$ completion payments of £525,000 are due in: £225,000 for job e and £300,000 for completion of job c. Column 3 shows weekly variable costs aggregated over five week periods (for simplicity in this example). For example at $t = 35$ the bill for variable costs is £150,000 relating to expenses on three jobs (c, d and e) over a five week period. Column 4 [=2 – (1 + 3)] shows net cash flow for each value of t. For example at $t = 45$ there is a net outflow of £175,000, being £75,000 – (£100,000 + £150,000).

As regards discounting assume that interest is compounded quarterly at the rate of 3% per quarter and that the first compounding is at $t = 13$. Column 5 in 8.18 brings the cash flow items forward to the next compounding point. The procedure here is one which could be adopted in any capital budgeting problem in which cash flows arise in between compounding points. It proves to be convenient to alter the cash flows to an equivalent stream of flows occurring at the compounding points. Then discount factors can be applied to this adjusted pattern of cash flows in the familiar fashion.

To see how the process works consider the first entry in column 5. What is implied here is that, in present value terms, a single outflow of 458.3 at the end of the first quarter is equivalent to the individual flows of 200 out at once plus 50 out after 5 weeks plus 200 out after 10 weeks. The initial –200 is carried forward at the full 3% and so would become $-200(1 + 0.03)$ at $t = 13$. The next outflow, of 50 at $t = 5$ occurs with 8/13 of the first quarter still to go. Thus the interest on this sum will be 8/13 of 3%, so that the –50 is brought forward to $t = 13$ as $-50\{1 + (8/13).0.03\}$. Finally the –200 flow at $t = 10$ occurs with 3/13 of the initial quarter remaining and so is equivalent to $-200\{1 + (3/13) \cdot 0.03\}$ at $t = 13$.

All this is summarized as:

$$-458.3=-200(1+0.03)-50\left(1+\frac{8}{13}\cdot 0.03\right)-200\left(1+\frac{3}{13}\cdot 0.03\right) \tag{8.5}$$

Further applying this procedure the equivalent cash flow at the second compounding point is given by equation (8.6)

$$-102.0=-50\left(1+\frac{11}{13}\cdot 0.03\right)-50\left(1+\frac{6}{13}\cdot 0.03\right) \tag{8.6}$$

and so on for the remaining entries in column 5

t	1	2	3	4	5	6	7
0	150		50	−200			
5			50	−50			
10	150		50	−200			
13					(1) − 458.3	0.9709	−445.0
15			50	−50			
20			50	−50			
26					(2) − 102.0	0.9426	−96.1
30	300	250	50	0			
35			150	−150			
39					(3) − 151.4	0.9151	−138.6
40			150	−150			
45	100	75	150	−175			
50	350	525	150	+25			
52					(4) − 302.4	0.8885	−268.7
55			150	−150			
60		250	150	+100			
65	250	450	100	+100	(5) + 47.7	0.8626	+41.1
70			100	−100			
75	75	125	100	−50			
78					(6) − 152.2	0.8375	−127.5
80			100	−100			
85			100	−100			
90	50	100	100	−50			
91					(7) − 254.0	0.8131	−206.5
95		150	100	+50			
100	100	175	50	+25			
104					(8) + 76.3	0.7894	+60.2
105			50	−50			
110	250	650	50	+350			
115			50	−50			
117					(9) + 254.0	0.7664	+194.7
120			50	−50			
125			50	−50			
130			50	−50	(10) − 151.7	0.7441	−112.9
135	5	500	50	+450			
140			50	−50			
143					(11) + 408.0	0.7224	+294.7
145			50	−50			
150		2,000	50	+1,950			
156					(12) + 1,925.7	0.7014	1,350.7
							Σ = +546.1

Figure 8.18 Network cash flow and present values

Column 6 shows the present value factor associated with each compounding point. Column 7 ((=5 x 6) then gives the present value of each item in the modified cash flow. Net present value is the sum of entries in column 7 and is £546,100. Consequently, from the standpoint of net present value the project is seen to be worthwhile and would be undertaken if any other constraints on for instance time, resources of liquidity are met and if there are no superior alternative projects.

We now turn to the matter of changes in job times and the resultant effects on NPV. First consider increases or decreases in the durations of non-critical jobs. These will not affect the overall completion time and will also leave unchanged the cash flow items associated with critical jobs. To the extent that such time changes are discretionary their desirability will be determined by the effects on NPV. If jobs i and l, for instance, are speeded up then the completion payments associated with them are brought forward. NPV must increase on this account. If the increase in NPV as a result of the earlier payments for completion exceeds the present value of the increases (if any) in variable costs for the jobs speeded up then (assuming that there are no deleterious effects on other jobs) the speeding up is worthwhile.

For example suppose that job l is speeded up so that it is completed in 15 weeks instead of 20. The effect of this change is two-fold. Firstly, the completion payment for l would be received at $t = 90$ instead of $t = 95$. Secondly, the weekly variable costs during the 15 weeks now required for the completion of job l may be changed. Let us suppose that variable costs for l are the same overall, viz. 200. This would mean $13\frac{1}{3}$ per week for each of the 15 weeks. Throughout this period from $t = 75$ to $t = 90$ one other job is being worked on which incurs weekly variable costs of 10. Thus, weekly variable costs now total $23\frac{1}{3}$ that is $116\frac{2}{3}$ per five week period.

Thus the entries in column 3 of Figure 8.18 for $t = 80$, 85 and 90 will now be $116\frac{2}{3}$ instead of 100. From $t = 90$ to $t = 95$ only one job will now be worked on so that variable costs for this period will be 50. This is the new $t = 95$ entry in column 3. In column 2 the $t = 95$ entry of 150 is deleted and the $t = 90$ entry is increased to 250. The change in net present value will therefore be:

$$\left[-16\tfrac{2}{3}\left(1+\frac{11}{13}.03\right)-16\tfrac{2}{3}\left(1+\frac{6}{13}.03\right)-16\tfrac{2}{3}\left(1+\frac{1}{13}.03\right)\right.$$

$$\left.+150\left(1+\frac{1}{13}.03\right)\right]0.8131+\left[+50\left(1+\frac{9}{13}.03\right)\right.$$

$$\left.-150\left(1+\frac{9}{13}.03\right)\right]0.7894=0.449$$

Suppose now that a critical job is speeded up. There are two possibilities here. Either the start times of subsequent jobs can be brought forward or some free slack (equal to the time saving) is introduced for that particular job. Subsequent jobs are not *automatically* started earlier (unless a time constraint is to be met – the original completion time being infeasible) since in general the effect on NPV is not known *a priori*. Ideally, alternative possibilities in the earlier starting of subsequent groups of jobs would be evaluated in terms of their effects on NPV. That rearrangement of start times which gave the maximal increase in NPV would then be adopted. But this is a combinatorial problem and in large systems there may be very many possibilities and complete enumeration may be expensive or infeasible computationally.

Fortunately, in many practical problems by far the largest cash inflow will occur at the completion of the last job, as is the case in the current illustrative example and the bringing forward of this item may be expected to dominate any adverse effects on NPV resulting from earlier capital expenditures at the commencement of preceding jobs. Alternatively, there may be only a small number of rearrangements of start times which are possible for resource availability reasons (rather than for logical reasons). In this case evaluation of each case might prove to be feasible.

In the current example suppose that a technicai innovation allowed the completion of job f in 20 weeks instead of 40. The extreme alternatives are (a) to bring the start and completion of g and h forward by 20 weeks and the start of m and n forward by 15 weeks and (b) to allow 20 weeks of slack in f itself and start subsequent jobs on the critical path at the existing times. Between these extrema are compromise possibilities of allowing some slack in the critical path from f and completing n sooner by an amount of $\Delta_t < 15$ weeks. Clearly, the earlier payment of the substantial cash inflows presently scheduled for $t = 100$, $t = 135$ and $t = 150$ will dominate other considerations and alternative (a) brings the greatest improvement in NPV.

Now consider the possibility of rescheduling jobs so as to improve NPV. Present-value favourable reschedulings do not necessarily imply time reductions overall although in practice this will often be the case. Also there may arise the questions of delay penalties for late completion and bonuses for early delivery, but these we shall ignore here. Again, the problem is one of choosing from a potentially large number of possible combinations without the possibility of expressing the objective *a priori* as a function of the possible courses of action. If the number of alternatives is small then enumeration is feasible but otherwise fairly cavalier assumptions and simplifications may be called for.

8.7 A Programming Formulation

Essentially the problem confronting the investor is one of choosing between a number of mutually exclusive 'projects' corresponding to different timings or alternative schedulings of the original project. So far we have discussed the relationship between project networks and present value and shown how the network layout can be used to assess charges in present value in very restricted cases: Two questions remain to be considered. Firstly, can an optimizing algorithm be developed, and secondly, is such an algorithm likely to be useful on problems of practical size where the number of alternatives is large?[5]

To answer the second question first. There does not exist at present, nor is there likely to exist in the near future, an exact optimizing algorithm for present value maximization in large networks with many alternative timings and schedulings. At the end of this chapter we shall mention some practical possibilities for such cases.

To answer the first query, let us consider the problem as a programming problem

Job	Predecessor	Duration
0	–	d_0
1	0	d_1
2	0	d_2
3	1	d_3
4	2, 3	d_4

Figure 8.19 Project table for programming example

for a very small network. It will prove to be convenient to consider a variation of the approach so far with a network representation of the 'arc-node' type. Suppose that there are just three real jobs labelled 1, 2, 3 with additional jobs 0 (representing the imaginary job 'start' which precedes all other jobs) and 4 (the imaginary 'finish' job, succeeding all other jobs). The system is described in the project table of Figure 8.19 and reproduced in arc-node diagrammatic form in Figure 8.20. in the diagram, circles represent 'events' or nodes and correspond to the completion of all of the immediately preceding jobs. The nodes also mark the starting point of subsequent jobs which are identified by subscript. The length of the job lines has no significance in this type of diagram.

Suppose now that cash flows are associated with the occurrence of the events. For example, event 2 represents the completion of job 1 and the start of job 3. The cash flows at event 2 would, in the context of earlier illustrations correspond to the completion payment for job 1 and the initial outlay on job 3. With the arc-node network we can replicate any of the networks so far considered by suitable use of 'dummy' jobs.[6] By suitable definition jobs cash flows items that are essentially of a variable cost nature could be made to correspond to nodes. Otherwise regular or minor cash flows may be aggregated.[7]

Now let R_i be the cash flow (positive or negative) that is associated with node i. In general the objective function would be given by (8.7)

$$V = \sum_{i=1}^{n} R_i W_i \tag{8.7}$$

where V represents net present value to be maximized. In (8.7) the W_i are

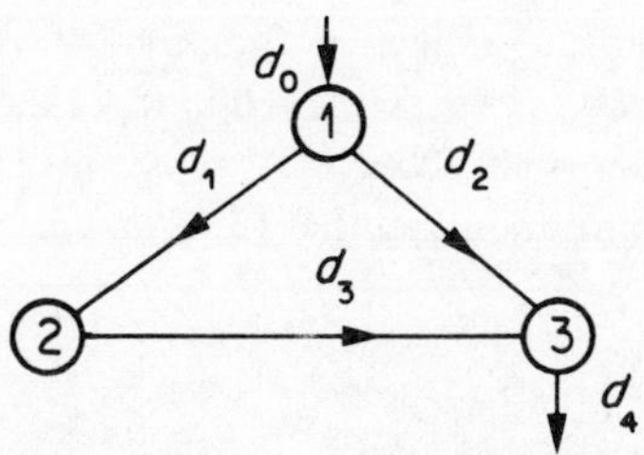

Figure 8.20 Arc-node representation of network

discount factors determined by the rate of interest, the time of occurence of the nodes and the nature of the compounding process. This point will be returned to shortly. We should note for the moment simply that V is a non-linear function of the event times (which we shall represent by t_i). In the example network the t_i observe the following restrictions (in which d_4 is assumed to take the value zero).

$$\left.\begin{aligned} t_0 &= d_0 \\ t_2 &= t_1 + d_1 \\ t_3 &\geqslant t_1 + d_2 \\ t_3 &\geqslant t_2 + d_3 \end{aligned}\right\} \tag{8.8}$$

Now suppose that individual job times may be varied continuously between lower and upper limits. That is:

$$d_j^L \leqslant d_j \leqslant d_j^u \quad \text{for} \quad j = 0, 1, 2, 3 \tag{8.9}$$

Clearly for different values of the d_j the critical path may change, but (8.8) must always be observed. Now on the basis of (8.9) let d_j^* be the difference between actual job time and minimum job time for each job. Thus

$$\begin{aligned} d_j^* &\geqslant 0 \\ d_j^* &\leqslant d_j^u - d_j^L \end{aligned} \tag{8.10}$$

and the constraint set can be written as:

$$\left.\begin{aligned} t_1 + d_0^* &= d_0^L \\ t_2 - t_1 - d_1^* &= d_1^L \\ t_1 - t_3 + d_2^* &\leqslant - d_2^L \\ t_2 - t_3 + d_3^* &\leqslant - d_3^L \\ d_0^* &\leqslant d_0^u - d_0^L \\ d_1^* &\leqslant d_1^u - d_1^L \\ d_2^* &\leqslant d_2^u - d_2^L \\ d_3^* &\leqslant d_3^u - d_3^L \\ d_j^* &\geqslant 0 \quad \text{for} \quad j = 0, 1, 2, 3 \end{aligned}\right\} \tag{8.11}$$

Now let us reconsider the objective function. If the discrete compounding process used throughout this text is employed in (8.7) then an integer programming formulation of the problem is necessary.[8] To avoid this eventuality assume that the compounding process is continuous, so that (8.7) may be written as:

$$V = \sum_{i=1}^{n} R_i e^{-rt_i} \tag{8.12}$$

If the compounding process is in fact discrete then in (8.12) we shall have made the

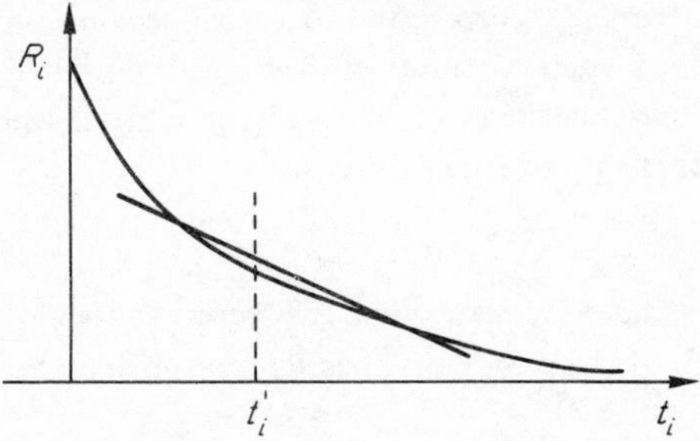

Figure 8.21 Linear approximation to PV graph

first of two approximations. In comparison with the next approximation to be made, that in (8.12) is very minor. As an aside, it is worth noting that (8.12) could equally well have been written as:

$$V = \sum_{i=1}^{n} R_i(1 + s)^{-t_i} \tag{8.13}$$

where for any value of the interest rate s in (8.13) we can choose r in (8.12) such that $r = \log_e(1 + s)$ so that (8.12) and (8.13) are equivalent.

The next stage is to develop a linear approximation to (8.12). In Figure 8.21 the declining curve graphs $V_i = R_i e^{-rt_i}$, t_i' is a 'current' value for t_i (to be further discussed shortly) and the straight line represents a linear approximation to R_i. In fact, as the linear approximation to be used here, we shall take the tangent of the V_i function at t_i. Now the value given by the tangent, $\hat{V}_i$, will, except at t_i' itself always understate V_i. At first glance this does not seem good and it might appear preferable to use a line, such as that in Figure 8.21 which at $t_i = t_i'$ is above V_i. However, only the slope of the linear approximation is important, the position of the line relative to the origin provides a constant term in the approximated objective function and so does not affect the outcome of the maximization exercise. Use of the tangent was suggested by Russell in an article in 1970.[9]

Russell pointed out that provided the optimal event times were sufficiently close to the current times t_i' then the approximation is valid. The computational approach involved here and as suggested by Russell would normally be one of successive approximations in which a series of linear programming problems are solved. This will be discussed below. If for the moment we envisage a one-stage procedure (which may be indicated for very large networks) in respect of the accuracy of the approximation we shall simply have to hope for the best. Remember that a procedure is justified provided it improves on what otherwise would have been done. Once an optimum has been attained with the approximated objective function the true value of V can be obtained by substitution of the event times into (8.12). This will determine (and, hopefully, verify) that an improvement has been effected.

The current event times t_i' correspond to a feasible solution to the constraint set (8.11). Assuming that such a solution has been obtained, the approximated objective function can be worked out. The present value of the cash flow associated with an individual event i is approximated as:[10]

$$\hat{V}_i = R_i e^{-rt_i'} + rt_i' R_i e^{-rt'_i} - rt_i R_i e^{-rt_i'} \tag{8.14}$$

Given t_i' and the interest rate, r, the first two terms in (8.14) are constants and we shall call their sum R_i^*. Labelling $R_i e^{-rt_i}$ as R_i' the approximation to (8.12) is

$$\hat{V} = \sum_{i=1}^{n} \hat{V}_i = \sum_{i=1}^{n} R_i^* - r \sum_{i=1}^{n} t_i R_i' \tag{8.15}$$

The problem is now expressed as a continuous linear programming problem in which a maximum of (8.15) is sought subject to (8.11)[11].

Now, where computational facilities permit, it would be possible to extract a more accurate answer by the following procedure. Beginning with a feasible set of values for the t_i', form the objective function (8.14) and optimize. The resulting values of the t_i become the t_i' in the objective function of the next problem – and so on until the solution converges.[12] However the simplex method would not represent a very effecient means of solution since it does not exploit the special structure of the problem at all. Russell suggests a method using a fluid flow interpretation of the dual problem.[13]

An important conclusion of the study of network cash flow problems is that the time-critical path may not be particularly important in financial terms. To quote Russell: 'It has been shown that the critical path may not be very cost significant but that there exists a cost-critical tree of activities to each of which a marginal cost of lengthening the duration may be ascribed'.[14] Interpreted in the context of the constraint set (8.11) there will emerge shadow prices associated with the R.H.S. of the constraints. The shadow prices will be the present value implications of marginal alterations to the bounds on job durations. The cost of altering an optimal job duration that falls strictly within the given bounds can also be determined. In terms of an L.P. formulation, this latter value will be given by the sum of products of rates of exchange (in the row of the duration being altered) and corresponding index row numbers.

There is considerable scope for further research in the network cash flow area and as Russell points out the possible applications are almost as numerous as are the applications of CPM/time. In particular Russell cites six types of problem:

(i) The pricing of delays in contractual situations.
(ii) The optimum timing of logically dependent investments.
(iii) The avoidance of payment structures which positively discourage the early completion of a project.
(iv) The identification of 'cost-critical' jobs during progress of a contract.
(v) The optimum timing of major projects in a developing national economy.
(vi) The use of the 'duration price' as the criterion for resource allocation decisions of for decisions in time-cost trade-off problems.

Notes

1. For discussion of these charts see Starr, M. K., *Production Management : Systems and Synthesis*, Prentice-Hall, Englewood Cliffs, N. J., 1964.
2. Many of the results from Critical Path analysis will be simply stated here without proof. The interested reader is referred to Muth, J. F., and Thompson, G L., (eds.) *Industrial Scheduling*, Prentice-Hall, Englewood Cliffs, N. J., 1964, Chapter 22.
3. See Starr, M. K., *Production Management : Systems and Synthesis*, Prentice-Hall, Englewood Cliffs, N. J., 1964. p.123. Technical discussions of the properties of Beta distributions can be found in Weatherburn, C. E., *A First Course in Mathematical Statistics*, Cambridge University Press, London, 1961.
4, For the essential statistics see Yamane, T., *Statistics, An Introductory Analysis*, Harper and Row, New York, 1964.
5. Large scale projects may involve thousands of jobs broken down into several subnetworks which are interlinked into a master network. Some experienced practitioners that I have met prefer to tackle ordinary CP problems of less than five hundred jobs by hand – so tractable is the basic CPM/time procedure.
6. We shall not need this device in this chapter so discussion of zero and real time dummies is omitted. See Barnetson, P., *Critical Path Planning*, Newnes–Butterworth, London, 1969.
7. Or possibly treated separately in an approximation approach if regular day to day cash flows were more or less independent of the important capital items.
8. The interested reader might care to attempt this as an exercise in the use of two-state variables.
9. Russell, A. H., 'Cash flows in networks', *Management Science (A)*, **16**, No. 5, January, 1970. Incidentally, the 'discrete compounding' process suggested as an alternative by Russell (p. 360) is not quite the one that we have been using in this text. In this book we assume (as is normally the case) that compounding takes place at set dates, rather than at given intervals beginning for each receipt at exactly the time of that receipt.
10. Readers familiar with the calculus may verify that (8.14) is the equation of the tangent to V_i at t_i' being the linear terms in the Taylor expansion of V_i about t_i'.
11. In some problems it may be necessary to add an upper bound on the last event time to the constraint set (8.11). Apart from time Feasibility requirements if R_n is sufficiently large and negative PV may be maximized by setting t_n at $+\infty$
12. Although convergence will occur in a finite number of steps in this procedure it is not clear how rapid this convergence process is in practice. We have seen the magnitude of problems that can arise in this connection in integer programming. Further, only convergence on a local optimum is guaranteed (this is usually as much as can be expected of approximation procedures). However, Russell suggests a special computational procedure which appears promising. 'There should be no difficulty in solving maximum present value network problems involving several hundred nodes and arcs in a matter of a few minutes judging by Ford and Fulkerson's results' (Russell, A. H., 'Cash flows in networks', *Management Science (A)*, **16**, No. 5, January, 1970, p. 367.)
13. For the details of this special technique the reader is referred to Russell, A. H., 'Cash flows in networks', *Management Science (A)*, **16**, No. 5, January, 1970, pp. 368–372.
14. Russell, A. H., 'Cash flows in networks', *Management Science (A)*, **16**, No. 5, January, 1970, p. 368.

Additional References

1. Adelson, R. M., 'Criteria for capital investment: An approach through decision theory', *Operations Research Quarterly*, **16**, 1965.
2. Archibald, R. D., and Villoria, R. L., *Network Based Management Systems*, Wiley, New York, 1967.
3. Arisawa, S., and Elmaghraby, S. E., 'Optimal time – cost trade-offs in Gert networks', *Management Science*, **18(A)**, 1972.
4. Barnetson, P., *Critical Path Planning*, Newnes – Butterworth, London, 1969.
5. Battersby, A., *Network Analysis*, Macmillan, London, 1964.
6. Berman, E. C., 'Resource allocation in PERT networks under continuous time – cost functions', *Management Science*, **10**, 1964.
7. British Productivity Council, *Eighteen Case Studies in the Use of Critical Path Method*, 1964.

8. Carruthers, J. A., and Battersby, A., 'Advances in critical path methods', *Operations Research Quarterly*, **17**, 1966.
9. Chapman, C. B., *Project Planning: A General Programming Model for Practical Problems* University of Southampton Discussion Paper No. 6804.
10. Charnes, A., and Cooper, W. W., 'A network interpretation and a directed sub-dual algorithm for critical path scheduling', *Journal of Industrial Engineering*, **12**, 1961.
11. Clark, C. E., 'The optimum allocation of resources among the activities of a network', *Journal of Industrial Engineering*, **12**, 1961.
12. Croft, F. M., 'Putting a price tag on PERT activities', *Journal of Industrial Engineering*, **21**, 1970.
13. Elmaghraby, S. E., 'On the expected duration of PERT type networks', *Management Science*, **13**, 1967.
14. Ford, L. R. J., and Fulkerson, D. R., *Flows in Networks*, University Press, Princeton, N. J., 1962.
15. Fulkerson, D. R., 'A network flow computation for project cost curve', *Management Science*, **7**, 1961.
16. Hill, L., 'Some cost accounting problems in PERT/cost", *Journal of Industrial Engineering*, **17**, 1966.
17. Jewell, W. S., 'Optimal flow through network with gains', *Operations Research*, **10**, 1962.
18. Kelly, J. E., 'Critical path planning and scheduling: mathematical basis', *Operations Research*, **9**, 1961.
19. Muth, J. F., and Thompson, G. L., (eds.) *Industrial Scheduling*, Prentice-Hall, Englewood Cliffs, N. J., 1963.
20. Wagner, H. M., *Principles of Operations Research*, Prentice-Hall, Englewood Cliffs, N.J., 1969.

CHAPTER 9
Distribution Problems

9.1 Introduction

The large corporation nowadays has typically a number of geographically separate production plants and trades with customers located in various regions of a country and/or with clients overseas. Problems arise as to how warehouses should best draw their supplies from factories and in respect of how customer demands should be met from warehouses. These are essentially continuing short-term problems, once the production and distribution facilities have been established. Prior to commencement of operations there is the major investment problem of determining the scale and location of plant and buildings.

As demand or production conditions change then further investment decisions arise. Over time, decisions will be required as to which plants to invest capital in and to build up and which production facilities to run down (Government policies permitting). If a company is moving into a new region there will be problems of where to locate production and storage facilities or in which cities to purchase plant and equipment. Such investment problems have a distributional character. As we shall see, distribution problems are particular cases of linear programming problems (representing the more general allocation problem) but although distribution problems can be formulated as linear programming problems, the special structure of distribution problems allows a more efficient computational procedure to be devised. Also it will be shown, later in the chapter, that certain financial problems can be expressed as distribution problems.

9.2 Linear Programming Formulation

In this chapter we shall concentrate our attentions on two-dimensional distribution problems (no intermediate destinations). Let us consider an example of such a problem.

A company has, at present, three factories that produce a single product. The product is supplied to four (potential) customers. Factory A has unit costs of £2 for the product whilst in the newer factories B and C each unit of the product costs only £1 to produce. The entries in Figure 9.1 are cost data shown as negative numbers and represent the production plus transportation cost per unit from each factory to each customer. Thus for one unit of the product made in factory A and shipped to customer one the cost is £6. This is made up of £2 in production costs and £4 in transportation costs. The remaining entries in this row under columns 2, 3, and 4 are the production costs of £2 plus respectively £3, £1 and £3 transportation costs. The final column gives production capacity figures (for arithmetic convenience these are kept unrealistically small). Rows B and C again show production plus transportation costs from the remaining factories to the four customers. It seems odd to express this data with negative values and indeed this is not strictly necessary, but it is the conventional format (to convert the problem to a maximizing problem rather than minimize costs) and will be used here. The final row shows the requirements of each customer.

We shall assume that the price of the product p is the same to each customer and in particular that $p \geqslant 8$. The objective of the firm is assumed to be the maximization of profits. Shipments from factories to customers will be determined accordingly. The profit per unit shipped from factory to a customer is selling price, p, minus unit production and transportation cost as given in Figure 9.1. Total profit is the sum of unit profits times shipments from each source to each destination. It should be noted that the assumption of a common price charged to all customers is not, in fact, restrictive. If the price to customer one was $p + 1$ then the same unit profit position is achieved by considering the price to be p and deducting 1 from the shipment costs.

To / From	Cust. 1	Cust. 2	Cust. 3	Cust. 4	Supply capacity
Factory A	−6	−5	−3	−5	10
Factory B	−2	−7	−6	−4	8
Factory C	−4	−8	−5	−3	14
Demand	6	12	8	8	

Figure 9.1 Data for transportation problem

There are, however, implicit in the problem two linearity assumptions that will not always hold up in practice. Firstly there are the constant per unit productive and shipment costs. There are assumed to be no economies or diseconomies of scale in either production or transportation and no divisibility problems (as there would be if one truckload was 1.5 units). There are also assumed to be no 'externalities', e.g. more shipped from factory A does not mean less shipment capability from factories B and C. On the demand side it is being assumed that each customer will take any size of shipment (up to the amount entered in the demand row) at the going price. That is to say there is no 'all or nothing' situation as regards the orders for goods. It is also assumed that price is invariant with respect to quantity taken. The objective is to arrange shipments so as to maximize profits.

The problem is clearly a linear programming problem and could be written as follows.

$$
\left.
\begin{array}{lll}
\text{Maximize} & F = \sum_i \sum_j (p - c_{ij})X_{ij} & \\
\text{subject to} & \sum_j x_{1j} \leqslant 10 & \sum_i x_{i1} \leqslant 6 \\
 & \sum_j x_{2j} \leqslant 8 & \sum_i x_{i2} \leqslant 12 \\
 & \sum_j x_{3j} \leqslant 14 & \sum_i x_{i3} \leqslant 8 \\
 & & \sum_i x_{i4} \leqslant 8 \\
 & x_{ij} \geqslant 0 &
\end{array}
\right\} \quad (9.1)
$$

Where x_{ij} represents the amount produced at factory i and sent to customer j (factory A is represented by the subscript $i = 1$ for convenience, B = 2 and C = 3). The supply capacity limits clearly require $\leqslant$ signs in the constraints, but what of the demand requirements? Sometimes these are expressed as $\geqslant$ conditions. This would mean that, for example, customer 1 was to receive *at least* eight units. Clearly, the relevant specification depends on the particular problem faced. Note, however, that there would be no feasible solution to the problem (9.1) if $\geqslant$ inequalities were specified on the demand side. As we shall see the matter is really a non-issue as the problem will be modified by addition of a constraint so that strict equalities must obtain in all of the constraints of (9.1).

It would be possible to solve the problem defined by (9.1) using the simplex method. This would be very extravagant computationally however. It will be noted that the set of technical coefficients in the problem consists only of zeros and ones; with the vast majority being zeros. Consequently it is not surprising that the simplex method can be bettered for problems of this type.

9.3 The Modified Distribution Method

The special method of solution begins by making supply equal demand. If, as in the present example, it is demand that exceeds supply an additional row is introduced to make up the deficit. This can be thought of as an imaginary source of supply – any customer 'receiving' goods from the imaginary supplier (known usually as the dummy) will be just that many units short on his order. There are no costs associated with the dummy factory (prohibitions on supply to certain customers can be introduced).[1] When supply equals demand the problem is said to be one in *balanced rim conditions*.

Since the problem is an L.P. problem the optimal solution will be a basic solution and the first requirement is to find a starting basic solution. Such a solution is shown in Figure 9.2. Circled numbers in the squares represent *assignments* – values of the x_{ij}.

Thus, for example $x_{32} = 6$, $x_{13} = 8$ and so on. Since $x_{42} = 2$ customer 2 will receive in total only ten of the twelve units that he would be prepared to take. The

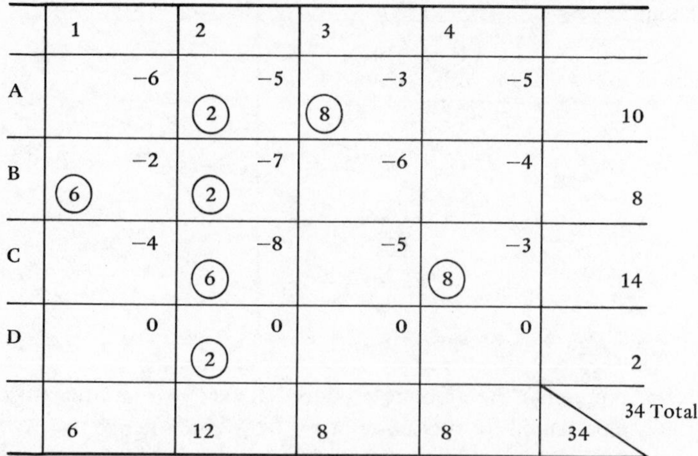

	1	2	3	4	
A	−6	(2) −5	(8) −3	−5	10
B	(6) −2	(2) −7	−6	−4	8
C	−4	(6) −8	−5	(8) −3	14
D	0	(2) 0	0	0	2
	6	12	8	8	34 / 34 Total

Figure 9.2 Transportation problem: initial solution

sum total of costs associated with this solution,

$$\sum_i \sum_j x_{ij} C_{ij}$$

is

$$2.5 + 8.3 + 6.2 + 2.7 + 6.8 + 8.3 + 2.0 = 132.$$

If we now suppose that $p = 10$ the value of F for the solution will be

$$10 \sum_{i=1}^{3} \sum_{j=1}^{4} x_{ij} - 132 = 10.32 - 132 = 188$$

Note that the x_{ij} are summed only over the first three rows – corresponding to real assignments. The dummy assignment is not in reality made and yields no revenue. It will be observed that only seven of the x_{ij} are not zero although there are eight constraints including the constraint for the fourth row $\Sigma_j x_{4j} \leqslant 2$. This does not mean that the solution is degenerate. Since each constraint is in fact satisfied as a strict equality and since total supply equals total demand any one of the constraints can be dropped from the problem. If seven of the constraints are satisfied the eighth will automatically be fulfilled. The constraints are said to be *linearly dependent*. There are only seven independent constraints; consequently, a basic solution will have no more than seven assignments. In general, if there are m rows and n columns a basic solution will have no more than $m + n - 1$ positive assignments. Note that in the problem defined by (9.1) plus the fourth row constraint, since by definition $p \geqslant c_{ij}$ for all i,j, an optimum cannot have a strict inequality obtaining in any pair of constraints. In such a solution at least one of the x_{ij} could be increased thus increasing F.

The solution shown in Figure 9.2 was obtained by inspection. To begin with an assignment was made to the square with the lowest cost figure – somewhere in the fourth row. It was placed in the second column in view of the fact that costs within that column are large (in absolute terms), relative to costs elsewhere. Next x_{21} was set equal to six – the maximum value for x_{21} since $\Sigma_i x_{i1} \leqslant 6$. No further assignments can now be made (in this solution), in the first column. x_{13} was then set at eight and also x_{34} was set at eight. x_{12} was then put equal to two and consequently the assignments $x_{22} = 2$ and $x_{32} = 6$ followed of necessity. Fortuitously this made seven assignments in all and so the solution is basic.[2] It is no great problem if it turns out that an inspection solution contains more than $m + n - 1$ assignments. We shall discuss this matter in the sensitivity analysis section and for the moment we shall assume that a basic feasible solution has been found.

Thus the first difference between the solution procedure here and the simplex method emerges. The starting solution is not the origin. However, the rationale of the methods are the same. A basic solution is determined, then an optimality check (as outlined below) is made. If the solution is not optimal a new variable is introduced at positive level and a move is made to a neighbouring basic feasible solution. This process is repeated until the optimum is reached.

The next task is therefore to check the starting solution for optimality. This is done by seeing if there are any neighbouring basic solutions that would improve the objective function. A neighbouring solution is one in which only one of the variables presently at zero level is made positive and one or more of the existing basic variables set at zero. In what follows we shall be calculating what would be the index row numbers of the x_{ij}. Consider x_{11}. If this is made positive (some of factory A's output is assigned to customer one) then corresponding reductions must be made elsewhere in the first row and column, which will in turn necessitate changes in existing assignments elsewhere in the matrix in order to satisfy the rim conditions. This process is equivalent to adjusting the level of the variables currently in the solution when the simplex method is employed. If x_{11} is set at unit level the consequent adjustments in the existing assignments are shown in Figure 9.3. It is as if one unit had been shifted round the arrowed path; x_{11} and x_{22} increasing and x_{12} and x_{21} decreasing as indicated by the signs.

Such a path is called a 'closed path' since it begins and ends at the same square. Has the readjustment of assignments via the closed path improved F? Revenue is unchanged of course but costs are altered. One unit is now shipped to customer 1 from factory A at a cost of £6, one more unit shipped from B to 2 thus adding £7 to costs here but since x_{12} and x_{21} are both decreased by one there are savings of £5 and £2 respectively. The net change is therefore $+ 6 + 7 - 5 - 2 = 6$ so that the rearrangement adds to costs and is not worthwhile. The index row number of x_{11} in the present solution is +6. The solution with $x_{11} = 1$ is non-basic having eight $x_{ij} > 0$. The neighbouring basic solution is found by 'routing' one more unit round the closed path to produce the pattern shown in Figure 9.4, the remaining x_{ij} being unchanged. This solution will cost £12 more than the original. But is the rearrangement shown the only way of accommodating $x_{11} > 0$? The answer is no. What has been found is a neighbouring basis which shows a decrease in F. It is the

	1	2	3	4	
A	−6 (1) + →	−5 − (1)	−3 (8)	−5	10
B	↑ −2 (5) − ←	↓ −7 + (3)	−6	−4	8
C	−4	−8 (6)	−5	−3 (8)	14
D	0	0 (2)	0	0	2

Figure 9.3 Evaluating vacant square 11

only way that x_{11} can be made positive without making some other variable, presently zero, positive too. As in the simplex method the optimum can be reached in a myopic fashion by movement between neighbouring bases. The closed path adjustments lead to the only neighbouring basis with $x_{11} > 0$, so if there is no improvement represented by this change we can safely investigate other neighbouring bases in which x_{11} remains at zero level.

For each vacant square (corresponding $x_{ij} = 0$) in the problem a closed path is formed. Since the closed path relates to the introduction of one new variable only and the adjustment of existing variables the 'turning points' on a closed path (at which changes in assignments are made), will occur only at assignment squares (corresponding $x_{ij} > 0$). For each vacant square in a non-degenerate solution there will be exactly one closed path. For example (with the original basis), turning points in the closed path for square x_{23} are x_{13}, x_{11} and x_{21}. The closed paths for squares (3, 3) and (4, 4) are illustrated in Figures 9.5(a) and (b).

Starting with the square under investigation alternate plus and minus signs are put at turning points in the path to indicate the occurrence of respectively, increases and decreases in assignments. It should be noted that it is of no account in which direction the attachment of signs proceeds since including the intial plus there are an even number of changes to be made. Having attached the appropriate

	1	2
A	−6 (2)	−5
B	−2 (4)	−7 (4)

Figure 9.4 Closed path reassignments for positive x_{11}

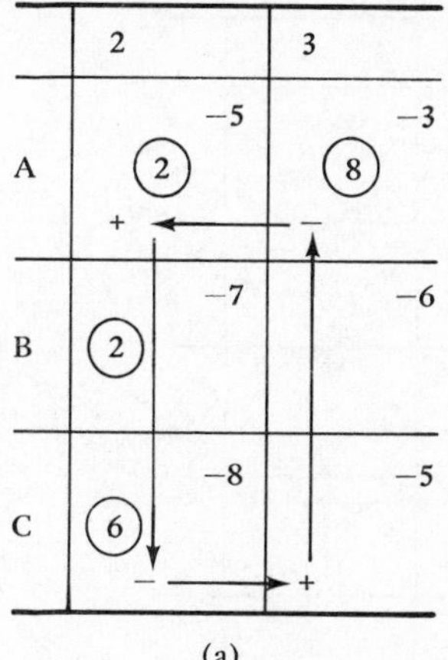

(a)

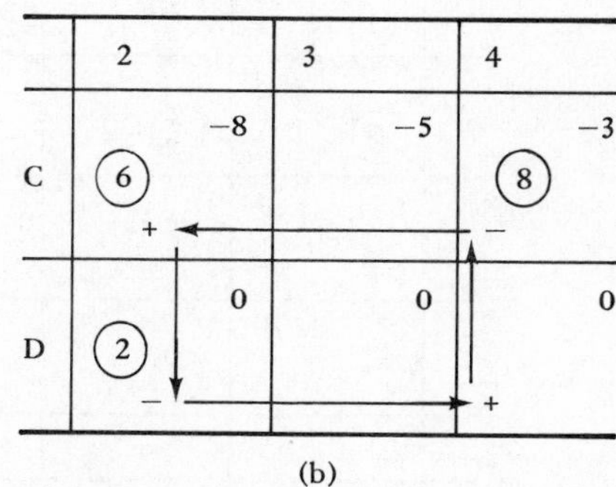

(b)

Figure 9.5 Other closed paths

signs, costs are then summed for the 'positive' squares and the 'negative' squares. If decreases in cost exceed increases then the re-routing is worthwhile. This is not the case for square x_{23}; the evaluation for which (the index row number of x_{23}) is $+5+6-3-7=+1$. The closed paths for the remaining vacant squares are all rectangular in form; which will not always be the case. As we have seen, in forming a closed path it is sometimes necessary to 'jump over' an assignment square. For example x_{22} is unaltered in the adjustments for $x_{14} > 0$. The x_{14} closed path turns at x_{12}, x_{32} and x_{34}.

Only square x_{33} has a negative evaluation $(5+5-(8+3)=-1)$. In general the variable corresponding to the square with 'most negative' evaluation will be introduced into the basis. There is no choice in the present situation. Each unit x_{33} improves the objective function by one so that x_{33} will be introduced to its maximum possible extent. The limit is, as in the simplex method, set by the first variable that becomes zero as x_{33} is increased. This will be the smallest assignment at a 'negative' place in the closed path. This will be six in the present case. Consequently x_{33} is introduced at level 6 and the improved solution is shown in Figure 9.6. Costs in total for this solution will $132 - 6.1 = 126$, so $F = 194$.

Is further improvement possible? We now have a viable if not particularly efficient solution procedure. Closed paths can be formed for each vacant square in Figure 9.6 and the corresponding possibility of an assignment evaluated. The vacant squares in this solution do not all have rectangular closed paths. Figure 9.7 shows the closed path for square (2, 4). The reader may verify that the other non-rectangular closed paths are for x_{31} (path is: x_{31}, x_{21}, x_{22}, x_{12}, x_{13}, x_{33}, x_{31}) and x_{44} (path is: x_{44}, x_{34}, x_{33}, x_{13}, x_{12}, x_{42}, x_{44}). Every vacant square in the solution has a positive evaluation, i.e. there is no neighbouring basis that is not inferior to the present basis. Consequently the solution $x_{12}=8$, $x_{13}=2$, $x_{21}=6$, $x_{22}=2$, $x_{33}=6$, $x_{34}=8$, $x_{42}=2$ is optimal and unique. The value of F is thus maximized at 204.

	1	2	3	4	
A	−6	−5 (8)	−3 (2)	−5	10
B	−2 (6)	−7 (2)	−6	−4	8
C	−4	−8	−5 (6)	−3 (8)	14
D	0	0 (2)	0	0	2
	6	12	8	8	

Figure 9.6 Improved solution

It will be noted that the solution is also integral. The structure of distribution problems is such that provided the R.H.S. of the constraints are integers all basic solutions will be integral. We shall return to this point subsequently, but will note here that, unfortunately, this integrality property of the solutions to distribution problems cannot be exploited to provide a useful algorithm for integer problems generally.

We shall now consider refinements to the computational procedure so far outlined. The first improvement relates to the way in which vacant squares are evaluated. The new procedure will be detailed and then an explanation of 'why' will be given. The procedure is known as the modified distribution method (MODI) and is as follows. To each row and column a number, u_i for a row v_j for a column, is determined such that at each *assignment square* i, j $u_i + v_j = -c_{ij}$. Thus in the

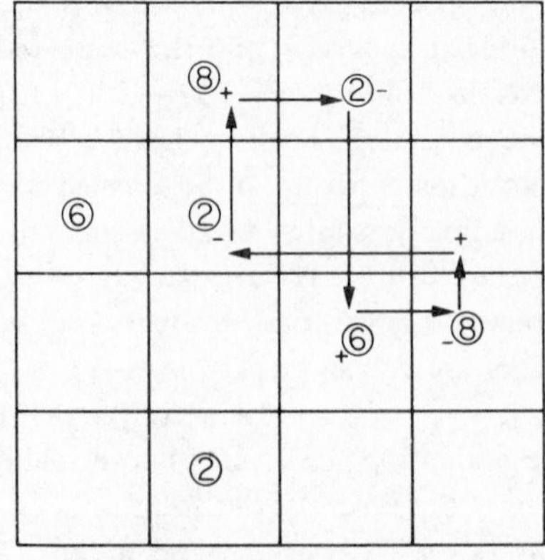

Figure 9.7 Non-rectangular closed path

original inspection solution the numbers should be such that:

$$
\begin{aligned}
u_1 + v_2 &= -5 \\
u_1 + v_3 &= -3 \\
u_2 + v_1 &= -2 \\
u_2 + v_2 &= -7 \\
u_3 + v_2 &= -8 \\
u_3 + v_4 &= -3 \\
u_4 + v_2 &= 0
\end{aligned}
$$

It will be seen that we have seven linear equations in eight unknowns. This means that we can solve for any seven of the u_i and v_j in terms of the eighth. That is, we can determine relative values of the u_i and v_j but not unique absolute values. Relative values are all that is required, since we shall be using the u_i and v_j to evaluate neighbouring bases relative to a current solution. In order that actual numbers can be worked with, an arbitrary value is assigned to one of the unknowns. It is conventional to set $u_1 = 0$ and this is done here. From the equations, the remaining values are then: $u_2 = -2$, $u_3 = -3$, $u_4 = +5$, $v_1 = 0$, $v_2 = -5$, $v_3 = -3$, $v_4 = 0$.

In the process of calculation it is convenient to write in the u_i and v_j numbers to the left of each row and at the head of each column respectively. Once that has been done, as shown in Figure 9.8, these row and column numbers can be used to speedily determine the improvement potential of each vacant square in the solution.

The process of evaluation of the vacant squares is as follows. For each vacant square determine the number e_{ij} given by:

$$e_{ij} = u_i + v_j + c_{ij}$$

The sign of e_{ij} indicates whether improvement is possible or not. The magnitude (if

		0 1	−5 2	−3 3	0 4	
0	A	−6	−5 (2)	−3 (8)	−5	10
−2	B	−2 (6)	−7 (2)	−6	−4	8
−3	C	−4	−8 (6)	−5	−3 (8)	14
+5	D	0	0 (2)	0	0	2
		6	12	8	8	34

Figure 9.8 MODI method: row and column numbers

negative) gives the size of the per unit improvement in the objective function as a result of the introduction of x_{ij} into the solution. The e_{ij} are in fact the index row numbers for the x_{ij} if the simplex method of computation had been employed. Thus the e_{ij} are the evaluations previously arrived at by use of individual closed paths for each square.

So, for the vacant squares in the original solution of Figure 9.8 the e_{ij} are:

square: 1,1 = 0 + 0 + 6 = +6
1,5 = 0 + 0 + 5 = +5
2,3 = −2 − 3 + 6 = +1
2,4 = −2 + 0 + 4 = +2
3,1 = −3 + 0 + 5 = +1
3,3 = −3 − 3 + 5 = −1
4,1 = +5 + 0 + 0 = +5
4,3 = +5 − 3 + 0 = +2
4,4 = +5 + 0 + 0 = +5

Thus only x_{33} has a negative index row number and will be made positive in the next solution to improve F. As an exercise the reader may verify that the evaluations remain the same, if, say, u_3 had been set equal to an arbitrary constant M. It will be seen that the 'M components' of the u_i and v_j cancel out in each evaluation. Note also that the evaluation of each assignment square must be zero.

Once the direction of improvement has been found in the above manner the MODI method proceeds to 'route round' the closed path in the manner already detailed. This completes the procedure. As soon as a solution has been found in which $u_i + v_j + c_{ij} \geqslant 0$ for all i,j an optimum has been reached. As further practice the reader may verify that for the solution of Figure 9.6 and with $u_1 = 0$ the remining row and column numbers are $u_2 = -2$, $u_3 = -2$, $u_4 = +5$, $u_1 = 0$, $u_2 = -5$, $u_3 = -3$, $u_4 = -1$ and that each vacant square evaluation is accordingly positive.

Why does the procedure above produce the index row numbers? Omitting the revenue side of the objective function the distribution problem can be stated as:

maximize $F = -\Sigma\, c_{ij}x_{ij}$

subject to: $\sum_{j} x_{ij} = s_i \forall i$

$\sum_{i} x_{ij} = D_j \forall j$

$x_{ij} \geqslant 0 \forall i,j$

where the symbol ∀ means 'for all' and it will be recalled that the formulation of the problem we are using here is for balanced rim conditions.

Now, using notation that rather betrays the answer to the question the dual problem is to:

minimize $G = \sum_{i} u_i s_i + \sum_{j} v_j d_j$

subject to $u_i + v_j \geqslant -c_{ij} \forall_{ij}$

u_i, v_j unrestricted

It will be recalled from Chapter 4 that equality constraints in a primal problem imply corresponding dual structural variables of unrestricted sign. For a variable that is basic (i.e. positive in a non-degenerate solution), the corresponding dual constraint is satisfied as a strict equality. Thus for all $x_{ij} > 0$, $u_i + v_j = -c_{ij}$. That is, $u_i + v_j + c_{ij} = 0$ which are precisely the conditions used to determine the row and column numbers above. Consequently the u_i and v_j are the shadow prices of the problem. In any L.P. problem the index row numbers of the primal beneath the x_{ij} are the values of the dual slack variables t_{ij}. The dual slacks are defined by

$$t_{ij} = u_i + v_j + c_{ij}$$

and are therefore the evaluations of squares. In a non-optimal solution to the primal problem the corresponding dual solution is infeasible ($t_{ij} \geqslant 0$ is a requirement for feasibility; dual slacks are not unrestricted), and some of the $t_{ij} < 0$.

A further improvement of the solution procedure would be effected if a starting solution could be found in 'reasonable' time that was on average superior to casual inspection. Vogel's approximation method provides such a solution.[3] It amounts to intelligent inspection and quite frequently produces the optimum straight off. However the MODI method must be used as an optimality check and to improve if necessary. Vogel's method (VAM) proceeds as follows. For each row and column determine the difference between the two smallest c_{ij} figures and attach these numbers to the row and columns. Select that row or column with the greatest such number and assign as much as possible to the square with lowest c_{ij} in that row/column. For our example problem the result is shown in Figure 9.9.

Column 2 has the largest VAM number and the smallest c_{ij} element is zero in the dummy row (remember that the data in the tableau are $-c_{ij}$). The maximum assignment that can be made to this square is two. No further assignments can be placed in row 4. At each stage of the VAM procedure maximal assignments will be made being the smallest of the two figures – remaining supply and remaining demand in the row and column of the square selected. The row or column thus

VAM Nos.	2	5	3	3	
2	−6	−5	−3	−5	10
2	−2	−7	−6	−4	8
1	−4	−8	−5	−3	14
0	0 X	0 (2)	0 X	0 X	2
	6	12	8	8	

Figure 9.9 VAM: first assignment

	~~2~~ 2	~~5~~ 2	~~3~~ 2	~~3~~ 1	
2	−6 X	−5	−3	−5	10
2	−2 (6)	−7	−6	−4	8
1	−4 X	−8	−5	−3	14
~~0~~	0 X	0 (2)	0 X	0 X	2
	6	12	8	8	

Figure 9.10 VAM: second assignment

'satisfied' is temporarily deleted and the process repeated ignoring the deleted row/column. In the example row 4 is deleted and new VAM numbers calculated. These, and the next assignment are shown in Figure 9.10.

Old VAM numbers are crossed out and it is seen that there is a five-way tie for the row or column to be chosen next. In such an event the assignment is made to the square with the lowest c_{ij} in all of the tied rows/columns. This is square (2, 1) and the greastest assignment possible here is six. This causes column 1 to be deleted and leaves two units of supply remaining in row 2. Figure 9.11 shows the solution eventually arrived at by VAM.

In the next application there is again a five-way tie and the assignment of eight was accordingly made to square (1, 3) and column three deleted. The next assignment is eight to square (3, 4) deleting column 4 and the remaining assignments follow of necessity. The solution obtained turns out to be the original

−6 X	−5 (2)	−3 (8)	−5 X	10
−2 (6)	−7 (2)	−6 X	−4 X	8
−4 X	−8 (6)	−5 X	−3 (8)	14
0 X	0 (2)	0 X	0 X	2
6	12	8	8	

Figure 9.11 Completed VAM solution

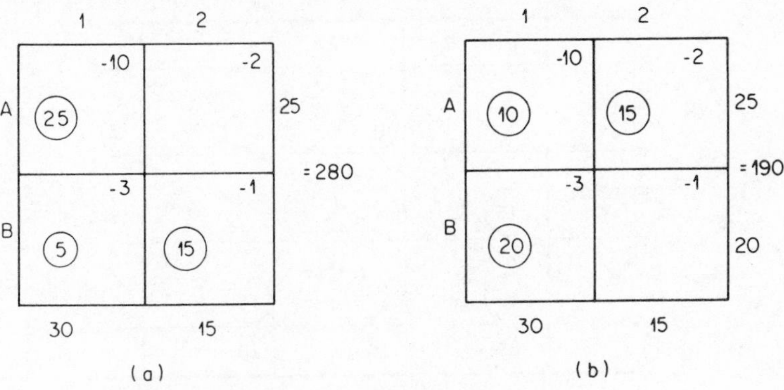

Figure 9.12 Naive inspection and VAM solution

inspection solution. The smaller the problem the more likely this is to be the case expecially if inspection is relatively subtle.

Intuitively VAM produces good starting solutions because of its emphasis on the differences between low cost squares. If a row/column with large differences is not 'attended to' until several assignments have already been made then it may prove necessary to make large assignments to high cost squares in that row/column. In the case of a column this would mean supplying a customer much of his order from an expensive source when a *much* cheaper source has supplied another customer that could have been supplied from elsewhere at only *slightly* greater cost. For instance, consider the two by two problem in Figure 9.12(a) and (b). Figure 9.12(a) shows a naive inspection solution in which the first assignment is to the overall least cost square (2, 2). This assignment of 15 units means that customer 1 has, in the main, to be supplied from the expensive source A when B would have been better employed supplying customer one and A customer two. Solution (b) is the VAM initial solution which is optimal.

9.4 Non-uniqueness and Degeneracy

As in ordinary L.P. problems it is quite possible that a given value of the objective function is generated by more than one basic solution to the problem. Each of the solutions which give this particular value of F is said to be non-unique and is evidenced in the simplex tableau by a zero index row number under non-basic variable. In distribution problems a solution is non-unique if a vacant square has zero evaluation. Such a situation is shown in the optimal solution to the problem in Figure 9.13. Here, square 1, 1 has zero evaluation and the basic solution $x_{11} = 5$, $x_{12} = 10$, $x_{21} = 15$, $x_{31} = 15$, $x_{33} = 20$ gives the same value of F as the solution shown in the figure. There are therefore just two optimal basic solutions. There is, of course, a continuum of fractional solutions representing rerouting of Δ round the closed path for square 1, 1 where $0 < \Delta < 5$. Of more interest is the fact that there are six optimal integral solutions corresponding to integral values of Δ between and including 0 and 5. Non-uniqueness of the primal causes no

	$u_1 = -13$	$u_2 = -8$	$u_3 = -12$	
$u_1 = 0$	−13	−8 (10)	−12 (5)	15
$u_2 = +7$	−6 (15)	−7	−6	15
$u_3 = +3$	−10 (10)	−11	−9 (15)	25
	25	10	20	

Figure 9.13 Non-unique solution

computational problems. The dual solution to a non-unique primal solution will be degenerate.

This brings us to the problem of degeneracy in the primal itself. A degenerate basic solution has less than $m + n - 1$ assignments. This will cause some problems. Figure 9.14 shows a degenerate basic solution to the problem of Figure 9.13. There are only four positive assignments. The difficulty that this causes can be expressed in two equivalent ways. Since there are only four assignments there will be only four equations to solve for six unknown u_i and v_j, so that numbers cannot be established for some rows and columns. The numbers u_3 and u_1 cannot be determined with the solution of Figure 9.14. It will also not be possible to find a closed path for at least one vacant square. The lack of assignments means that there are not enough 'turning points' to go round. In the current example a closed path can be found for only one square, (1, 2).

The degeneracy is resolved by first adding in a small assignment at an appropriate place and adjusting the rim conditions of the problem accordingly. In Figure 9.15 a small assignment ϵ is placed in square (1, 1) and to keep rim conditions unviolated the supply at A and the demand from 1 are both increased by

		$u_2 = -13$	$u_3 = -12$	
$u_1 = 0$	−13	−8	−12 (15)	15
$u_2 = +6$	−6	−7 (10)	−6 (5)	15
	−10 (25)	−11	−9	25
	25	10	20	

Figure 9.14 Degenerate solution

	$u_1 = -13$	$u_2 = -13$	$u_3 = -12$	
$u_1 = 0$	−13 (ε)	−8	−12 (15)	15 + ε
$u_2 = +6$	−6	−7 (10)	−6 (5)	15
$u_3 = +3$	−10 (25)	−11	−9	25
	25 + ε	10	20	

Figure 9.15 'Resolution' of degeneracy

ε. We now have the correct number of assignments and the problems will be worked out with the new rim conditions and at the end ε will be set at zero. No precise value is given to ε before the end of the problem but throughout it is understood that ε is smaller than any other assignment in the problem. If ε appears at a negative place in a closed path then all that can be routed round that path is ε. Thus the problem will not be distorted. With ε placed in square (1, 1) values for all of the u_i and v_j can now be determined and closed paths established for each vacant square.

Could the ε assignment have been placed elsewhere and what would have been the result? When degeneracy arises the ε assignment (or assignments in cases of multiple degeneracy) can be placed in any *independent* square. An independent square is any square for which a closed path consisting entirely of assignment squares at turning points cannot be established. Thus all vacant squares except (1, 2) are independent. The problem will be solved here for ε placed in (1, 1) but the reader may verify that although the u_i and v_j will be different if ε is placed elsewhere the optimal solution will be arrived at just the same. If the primal is degenerate the corresponding dual solution is non-unique. Different positioning of the ε assignment will correspond to different (but equal in terms of the objective function), dual solutions and consequently different shadow prices and index row numbers. However, since ε will eventually be put equal to zero, nothing in reality will be changed.

Now with ε in square (1, 1) and the u_i and v_j that this produces, the evaluations of the vacant squares are $e_{12} = -5$, $e_{21} = -1$, $e_{32} = +1$, $e_{33} = 0$. Thus an improvement of 50 in the objective function can be effected by routing ten units round the closed path for square (1, 2). The result of this is shown in Figure 9.16. The u_i and v_j values for this solution give evaluations of $e_{21} = -1$, $e_{22} = +5$, $e_{32} = +6$, $e_{33} = 0$. Thus square (1, 2) is the only one that shows improvement potential. But how much improvement in the objective function can be achieved by routing round the closed path for square (1, 2)? The smallest assignment at a negative place in the path is ε itself. Thus by routing round this closed path no real improvement is effected. All that happens is that the ε assignment is repositioned. This, however, is important. The new location of ε will allow a real improvement in

	$v_1 = 13$	$v_2 = -8$	$v_3 = -12$
$u_1 = 0$	-13; ϵ	-8; (10)	-12; (5)
$u_2 = +6$	-6	-7	-6; (15)
$u_3 = +3$	-10; (25)	-11	-9

Figure 9.16 Improved degenerate solution

the objective function to be effected at the next iteration. Figure 9.17 shows the situation with ϵ repositioned.

What has occurred between the solutions of Figure 9.17 and Figure 9.16 would have been evidenced in the simplex tableau by there being just one negative index row number (under x_{21}) and the pivotal row for x_{21} being x_{11} row in which x_{11} is at zero level. Thus the same degenerate solution is being re-expressed, but in such a way as to allow the introduction of a variable with a (now) negative index row number at a strictly positive level. If it had turned out that there was no relocation of the ϵ assignments such that a positive amount could be rerouted to improve F then the optimum would have been reached. In this event there must be some positioning of ϵ such that all vacant squares have positive (assuming uniqueness) evaluations. Recall that the absence of negative index row numbers is a *sufficient* condition for optimality but is not *necessary.*

Returning to the solution of Figure 9.17, the vacant square evaluations are: $e_{11} = +1$, $e_{22} = +5$, $e_{32} = +5$, $e_{33} = -1$. The closed path for square (3, 3) is: (3, 3),

	$v_1 = -12$	$v_2 = -8$	$v_3 = -12$
$u_1 = 0$	-13	-8; (10)	-12; (5) $+ \epsilon$
$u_2 = +6$	-6; ϵ	-7	-6; (15) $- \epsilon$
$u_3 = +2$	-10; (25)	-11	-9

Figure 9.17 Repositioned ϵ assignment

	$v_1 = -13$	$v_2 = -8$	$v_3 = -12$	
$u_1 = 0$	−13	−8 (10)	−12 (5) + ϵ	15 + ϵ
$u_2 = +7$	−6 (15)	−7	−6	15
$u_3 = +3$	−10 (10) + ϵ	−11	−9 (15) − ϵ	25
	25 + ϵ	10	20	

Figure 9.18 Degenerate problem: optimal solution

(2, 3), (2, 1), (3, 1), (3, 3) in which the ϵ assignment occurs at a positive place. A total of $15 - \epsilon$ may be routed round the path to give the solution shown in Figure 9.18, in which it is evident that setting $\epsilon = 0$ gives the solution of Figure 9.13 which is an optimal one.

Situations of multiple degeneracy, in which there are $m + n - 3$ or fewer assignments, are handled in a similar fashion. If there were $m + n - 3$ assignments then two small assignments ϵ and v are placed in independent locations and the rim conditions adjusted accordingly.

Degeneracy is more likely to occur when there are individual supply and demand figures that are the same. Maximum degeneracy [number of assignments = max (m, n)], occurs when all supply and demand figures are the same. Such a problem is called an *assignment problem* and although the ϵ technique can be used to solve such a problem there is a different and more efficient solution procedure available.[4]

9.5 Sensitivity Analysis

The principal subjects we shall consider in this section are; changes in costs, changes in supply and demand figures and changes in the numbers of suppliers and demanders. To begin with however, we shall examine a problem that may already have occurred to the reader.

In the original problem of this chapter demand exceeded supply so that a fictitious source of supply was intoroduced to balance the rim conditions. When demand exceeds supply in reality it may be desirable to ensure that some particular customers at least receive their full requirement. This can be accomplished by attaching a distribution cost of £M to the appropriate square in the dummy row. For instance if management decreed that customer two must not be short on his order then the figure $-M$ would appear in square (4, 2) with zeros elsewhere in the fourth row. The number M is sufficiently large to dominate any other number in the problem so that the variable x_{42}, with coefficient $-M$ in the objective function, cannot be positive at an optimum. However, extra information can be obtained if zeros are entered intially in the dummy row and the optimum obtained for this problem. If it has turned out that customer two was not supplied from D the

	$v_1 = 0$ 1	$v_2 = -5$ 2	$v_3 = -3$ 3	$v_4 = -1$ 4	
$u_1 = 0$ A	−6	−5 (8)	−3 (ϵ)	−5	10
$u_2 = -2$ B	−2 (6)	−7 (2)	−6	−4	8
$u_3 = -2$ C	−4	−8	−5 (6)	−3 (8)	14
$u_4 = +3$ D	0	$-M$	0 (2)	0	2
	6	12	8	8	

Figure 9.19 Optimal solution: prohibition on dummy supply

optimum would have been obtained. Since this is not the case the $-M$ figure is now entered in square (4, 2); the u_i and v_j are then recalculated. The only number to change is u_4 which becomes $+ 5 - M$ so that each vacant square in the fourth row has negative evaluation. The 'most negative' square is (4, 3) with evaluation $+ 2 - \mathrm{M}$, which means in fact that each unit routed round the corresponding closed path will add 2 to costs. The new optimum is shown in Figure 9.19. The solution is degenerate and an ϵ assignment was placed in square (1, 3). The corresponding u_i and v_j are shown. All vacant squares have squares have positive evaluation.

The difference between the value of F in the original optimum and the new optimum will be the cost of keeping customer two happy. This is 4. Management, with this information, can now determine whether this is worthwhile. Incidentally, the location of the ϵ assignment in square (1, 3) was not crucial. The ϵ assignment can be located in any independent square. If the square chosen produces u_i and v_j which give all non-negative evaluations for vacant squares then the optimum has been reached. There is no need to worry that some other location of ϵ might have produced a negative evaluation since we know that an all non-negative index row is a sufficient condition for optimality.

Let us now consider the consequences of cost changes in general. The rationale of the procedure is identical to that for the simplex tableau. When costs changed the index row was recalculated and in distribution problems the evaluations of vacant squares are redetermined. If a cost figure in a vacant square alters then this will not affect the u_i and v_j since these are determined only by the assignment squares. All that is affected is the evaluation of the vacant square itself. If the cost changes by Δ_{ij} then the evaluation also changes by Δ_{ij}, no other squares are affected. When the cost at an assignment square alters this is equivalent to a change in the objective function coefficient of a basic variable. The

		$v_1 = 0$ 1	$v_2 = -7.5$ 2	$v_3 = -3.3$ 3	$v_4 = -1.1$ 4	
$u_1 = 0$	A	−6.6	−7.5 (8)	−3.3 (2)	−5.5	10
$u_2 = 2.2$	B	−2.2 (6)	−9.7 (2)	−6.6	−4.4	8
$u_3 = 2.2$	C	−4.4	−10.8	−5.5 (6)	−3.3 (8)	14
$u_4 = 5.5$	D	0	−2 (2)	0	0	2
		6	12	8	8	

Figure 9.20 Differential selling prices: example

u_i and v_j are affected and the evaluation of many vacant squares may change. All that is required is to recalculate the u_i and v_j for the new cost data. If it emerges that some vacant squares now show improvement, one is selected and the solution procedure reapplied.

As an example, suppose that in the context of the original problem price to customers one, three and four was raised by one pound and price to customer two was reduced by one pound whilst all costs increased by 10%. The resultant changes in coefficients and the u_i v_j are shown in Figure 9.20. It is assumed that rim conditions are unchanged. Clearly the original solution remains optimal. It should be noted that the financial entries in the squares are no longer the $-c_{ij}$ throughout since not all customers are now charged the same price. The entries are $-(c_{ij} - \Delta p_j)$ where Δp_j is the deviation for the jth customer, from the maximum price charged to any customer.

The original problem was to maximize $\Sigma_i\Sigma_j(p - c_{ij})x_{ij}$. The term $\Sigma_i\Sigma_j p x_{ij} = p\Sigma_i\Sigma_j x_{ij} = p\Sigma_j d_j$ being a constant would not influence the optimality calculation. Consequently in the tableau only the c_{ij} appeared and $\Sigma_i\Sigma_j - c_{ij}x_{ij}$ was maximized. When prices are different between customers the objective function of the problem can be expressed as:

$$\text{maximize } F = \sum_i \sum_j (p_h - c_{ij} - \Delta p_j)x_{ij}$$

where p_h is the highest price obtained from any customer and the Δp_j are the amounts below this price charged to individual customers. Except for the dummy row the data in Figure 9.20 are the terms $-(c_{ij} + \Delta p_j)$ where $\Delta p_j = 2$ for $j = 2$ and $\Delta p_j = 0$ otherwise. The term $p_h\Sigma_i\Sigma_j x_{ij} = dp_h$ being constant. In the original problem coefficients of zero were used in the dummy row. We could equally well have used coefficients of $-p$. There are no costs or revenues associated with dummy assignments. For $i = 4$ the objective function coefficients should, strictly, be zero. Since $c_{4j} = 0 \; \forall \; i$ we should write $\Sigma_i(p - c_{4j} - p)x_{4j}$ for the fourth row. However adding a constant to the objective function coefficients in any row or column will not change the optimal solution and p was added throughout the dummy row.

In general if k_j is added to the ofcs in the jth column and r_i added to the ofcs in the ith row the objective function becomes

$$F^* = \sum_i \sum_j (p + k_j + r_i - c_{ij})x_{ij}$$

so that

$$F^* = \sum_i \sum_j (p - c_{ij})x_{ij} + \sum_i \sum_j k_j x_{ij} + \sum_i \sum_j r_i x_{ij}$$

but

$$\sum_i k_j x_{ij} = k_j d_j \quad \text{therefore} \quad \sum_j \sum_i k_j x_{ij} = \sum_j k_j d_j = \text{constant}$$

similarly since

$$\sum_j r_i x_{ij} = r_i s_i, \quad \sum_i \sum_j r_i x_{ij} = \sum_i r_i s_i = \text{constant}$$

so that

$$F^* = \sum_i \sum_j (p - c_{ij})x_{ij} + \text{constant}$$

and the optional x_{ij} are unchanged. Consequently in Figure 9.20 in the second column the coefficients -5.5, -7.7, -8.8, 0 could have been used and the optimal solution would have been unaffected. Note that if the constant +2 is added to the coefficients in the second column only v_2 changes, becoming -5.5. All the u_i and the remaining v_j are unaltered as are all all of the vacant square evaluations.

We now turn to consider changes in the rim conditions – changes in supplies and emands. To take a simple case to begin with suppose that there is a 'balanced' change in supplies and demands. By 'balanced' it is meant that the change in demand is equal to the change in supply. For instance let demand from customer 3 increase to 12 units and supply at plant B increase to 12 units. How can these changes be accommodated without starting the problem again?

For convenience of reference let us work with the financial data of Figure 9.20. The procedure is first to assign the amount of the increase in supply to the customer whose demand has also increased. Thus an assignment of four would be made in square (2, 3). There are now more assignments than necessary but the (2, 3) assignment can readily be eliminated by routing it round a closed path which initially consists entirely of assignment squares. The steps are shown in Figure 9.21(a) and (b). Only the relevant part of the array is reproduced here, the other assignments being unchanged.

The 'new' solution must be optimal since the u_i and v_j will be unchanged. The cost of handling such extra unit in a balanced increase for row i and column j is

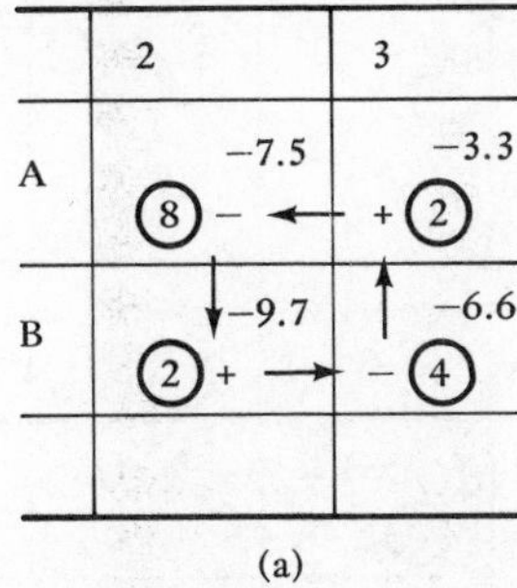

2
3
A
−7.5
−3.3
8
2
B
−9.7
−6.6
2
4
(a)

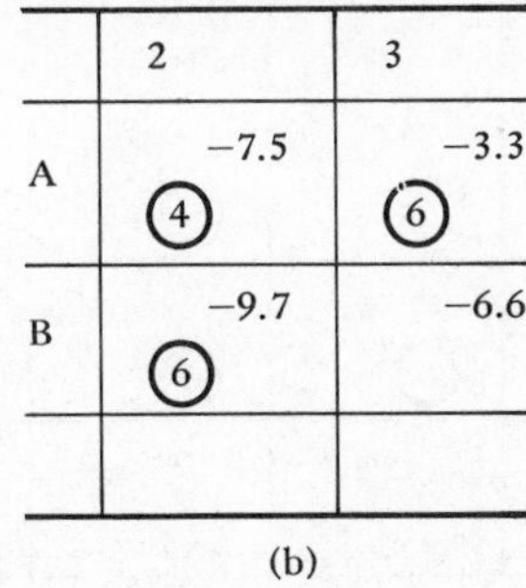

2
3
A
−7.5
−3.3
4
6
B
−9.7
−6.6
6
(b)

Figure 9.21 Balanced change in rim conditions: example

$u_i + v_j$ provided that the original basis does not become infeasible. An even simpler case would be where the square at the intersection of the row and column concerned was already an assignment square. All that would be required here is an increase in the assignment so conveniently located.

Suppose now that the increase in demand and supply from 3 and at B was 10. Routing this amount round the closed path gives the solution in Figure 9.22(a). The solution is optimal but infeasible. The problem need not be started again, but a procedure analogous to the dual simplex method can be applied. A new variable is introduced into the solution such that square (1, 2) appears at a positive place in its closed path. Possibilities are x_{23}, x_{24}, x_{43} and x_{44}. Of these variables that with the lowest $u_i + v_j +$ 'c_{ij}' evaluation is chosen. This will preserve optimality though not necessarily, in general, achieve feasiblity in one iteration. Both x_{23} and x_{24} have evaluations of +1.1 and the decision between them is arbitrary. x_{23} is introduced in Figure 9.22(b) producing a feasible optimum but, of course, one which is non-unique since x_{24} has zero evaluation for this solution.

Balanced changes involving more than one supplier and demander can be dealt with in a similar fashion. Firstly the extra allocations are made, secondly the number of assignments is reduced to $m + n - 1$ and thirdly feasibility is restored. Not all of these steps will be necessary in each case.

(a)

	2	3
A	−7.5 (−2)	−3.3 (12)
B	−9.7 (12)	−6.6

(b)

	2	3
A	−7.5	−3.3 (10)
B	−9.7 (10)	−6.6 (2)

Figure 9.22 Balanced changes: further example

	1	2	3	4	5	
A	−6.6	−5.5 (6)	−3.3 (4)	−5.5	$-P_h$	10
B	−2.2 (6)	−7.7 (4)	−6.6	−4.4	$-P_h$ (5)	15
C	−4.4	−8.8	−5.5 (6)	−3.3 (8)	$-P_h$	14
D	$-P_h$	$-P_h$ (2)	$-P_h$	$-P_h$	$-P_h$	2
	6	12	10	8	5	

Figure 9.23 Unbalanced changes: sub optimal solution

Balance can frequently be achieved by adjusting dummy supply when the demand charge from real customers is different from the supply change from real suppliers. This will not always be possible however. Suppose that supply from factory B increases to a possible fifteen units but the only increase in demand is 2 units from customer 3. Supply now exceeds demand by three units, and if the problem was being solved from scratch all that would be required would be an imaginary customer with a demand of three units and no dummy producer. Rather than start again, however, first introduce a dummy customer with a demand of 5 units and leave in the imaginary producer for the time being. This will enable use to be made of the work done so far. Assign 2 units to square (2, 3), route this round the one assignment closed path consisting of squares (2, 3), (1, 3), (1, 2) and (2, 2). The remaining 5 units at factory 2 are assigned to the dummy customer. The result is shown in Figure 9.23. It will be noted that the financial entries in both dummies have been set at $-p_h$ and two has been added throughout the second column. As we have seen this is quite proper. It would be possible also to add p_h to each square in row D and column 5 giving 'cost' figures of zero throughout the row and column except for the intersection square where the figure would be $+p_h$. This could be done at once on future occasions to avoid changing to the $-p_h$ format but was not done here because of the lack of intuitive clarity. The dummy to dummy cost of $+p_h$ will make this square 'attractive'. No real transaction takes place if an assignment is placed here but a 'dummy-to-real' or 'real-to-dummy' assignment means a lost opportunity to earn revenue of $+p_h$. This essential difference would be encapsulated in the distinctive figure of $+p_h$ for square (4, 5) if zeros were employed elsewhere. The question now is whether the distribution of Figure 9.23 is optimal or not. Calculation and use of the u_i and v_j reveal that square (4, 5) has an evaluation of $7.7 - p_h$ which is negative. Thus the solution is not optimal and two units are routed round the closed path for square (4, 5). Figure 9.24 gives the result in which the dummy row has now been deleted. The

	1	2	3	4	5	
A	−6.6	−5.5 (6)	−3.3 (4)	−5.5	$-P_h$	10
B	−2.2 (6)	−7.7 (6)	−6.6	−4.4	$-P_h$ (3)	15
C	−4.4	−8.8	−5.5 (6)	−3.3 (8)	$-P_h$	14
	6	12	10	8	3	

Figure 9.24 Unbalanced changes: optimal solution

only assignment in the dummy row is two units to the dummy customer – a phantom transaction which can be ignored. All that needs to be done is to adjust the demand from the dummy customer to 3 units. Note finally that the optimum is non-unique; square (3, 5) having zero evaluation.

9.6 Investment Applications (i) Size and Location of Plant

In this section we shall begin to examine the application of the techniques developed so far in this chapter to problems in which a capital element is explicitly identified. Firstly the problem of adjusting the sizes of existing plant is considered. This is a case of running down or increasing capacity at plants to meet changing demand (and more generally cost) conditions. Then the problem of altogether new plant at new locations is considered.

To start with, consider the problem of expansion or contraction of production capability of existing factories. The problem is one of optimal investment in new equipment or disinvestment in existing facilities. Consider a simple example. In the problem as originally formulated in this chapter and solved in Figure 9.6 two units less than the demand limit were supplied to customer two. Suppose that management wished to rectify this situation by expanding capacity at A, B or C by two units. Assume for the moment that the capital costs of the expansion at all factories would be zero. The objective is to supply 2 more units to customer 2 from a real source at lowest variable cost.

If we recall the formulation of the dual problem the u_i and v_j were seen to be shadow prices and for arbitrary Δd_j (changes in demand) and Δs_i (changes in supply) the minimum change in the dual (and hence the primal) objective function is $\Sigma_i u_i \Delta s_i + \Sigma_j u_j \Delta d_j$. Thus for a given set of Δd_j the least cost changes in supply to meet this changed demand are found by minimizing $\Sigma u_i \Delta s_i$ such that $\Sigma_i \Delta s_i = \Sigma_j \Delta d_j$. Where possible this would mean selecting that row corresponding to the 'appropriate' u_i and changing supply there by $\Sigma_j \Delta d_j$. For a net demand increase the appropriate u_i is the greatest value. In our example we are setting $\Delta d_j = 0 \ \forall j$. Also, we wish to eliminate supply from the dummy source and so set $\Delta s_4 = -2$ consequently since $\Sigma_i \Delta s_i = 0$ then $\Sigma_{i \neq 4} \Delta s_i = 2$. The values of the u_i in the solution of Figure 9.8 were $u_1 = 0$, $u_2 = -2$, $u_3 = -2$ and $u_4 = +5$. Therefore it is clearly optimal to increase supply at factory one. The increase in total cost will be $\Sigma_i - u_i \Delta s_i = 10$ and the increase in profits will be $2p - 10$. Consequently production capacity should remain unchanged at factories B and C. There would be an *opportunity loss* of $2(u_2 - u_1)$ if capacity at factory B had been expanded instead.

The question of capital costs can now be considered. Suppose that the capital costs of expansion of capacity at each plant had been, K_A, K_B, K_C respectively and that the supply and demand figures represent weekly flows. If these flows are aggregated over an interest compounding period of n weeks and the relevant interest rate is $100i\%$ the choice is between three projects that can be compared on a NPV basis. The return in each compounding period (consisting of n of the time units for which supply and demand figures are given) in the case of factory A would be $n(2p - 10)$ and in the case of factories B and C the return is $n(2p - 14)$. Clearly the choice between B and C would be trivial (depending only on the outlays) if the expanded capacity at both plants had the same life expectancy.

However, suppose now that the new capacities at each location have different lifetimes. Investments at the three locations represent mutually exclusive alternatives and the one with the greatest NPV will be selected. The respective net present values can be calculated from a simple formula. If an investment gives a constant return R at the end of each of T years, with an interest rate of $100i\%$ then the gross present value is given by:

$$\text{GPV} = R\left[\frac{1-(1+i)^{-T}}{i}\right] \tag{9.2}$$

so that in the present context the choice is between the NPVs as given in (9.3), where the respective lifetimes are T_A, T_B and T_C years.

$$\left.\begin{aligned} &n(2p-10).\ \frac{1-(1+i)^{-T_A}}{i} - K_A \\ &n(2p-14).\ \frac{1-(1+i)^{T_B}}{i} - K_B \\ &n(2p-14).\ \frac{1-(1+i)^{-T_C}}{i} - K_C \end{aligned}\right\} \tag{9.3}$$

The next illustration concerns the choice of factory location at the planning stage of operations. Suppose a company wishes to get established in a region or country and has a range of alternative sites for production facilities. Assume that the locations of the demand points (the customers) are predetermined but that the company has a number of possible sites at which to locate factories. How can the company arrive at the set of optimal factory locations? As we shall see the problem is combinatorial in character and several subproblems may have to be solved. The first step however would be to eliminate the 'dominated' locations. Logically, this is a trivial exercise once the relevant information has been assembled.[5] Location X

Factory \ Customer		$v_1 = -9$ 1	$v_2 = -5$ 2	$v_3 = -5$ 3	$v_4 = -11$ 4	$v_5 = 0$ 5	
$u_1 = 0$	A	−10	−5 (80)	−7	−15	0 (20)	100
$u_2 = +1$	B	−8 (30)	−12	−4 (70)	−14	0	100
$u_3 = 0$	C	−9 (20)	−6	−14	−12	0 (80)	100
$u_4 = +1$	D	−11	−4 (40)	−9	−10 (60)	0	100
$u_5 = 0$	E	−10	−6	−6	−12	0 (100)	100
		50	120	70	60	200	

Figure 9.25 Location of plant example

dominates location Y if costs per unit (production and shipment) at Y are greater for every destination than at X.

Having eliminated such alternatives several questions remain, including those of how many factories to build and where to locate them amongst the non-dominated alternative sites. To simplify the illustration assume that technological considerations dictate that the maximum production capacity at a factory in any location is 100 and that there are five possible locations. Demand from each of four customers are, respectively, 50, 120, 70 and 60 units. Figure 9.25 below gives the production plus transportation costs and the optimal solution to the naive problem where 'fixed' capital costs (the total of initial outlays) are assumed to be independent of the number of factories established. Selling price is assumed to be the same from each factory and the fifth column is the dummy customer taking up the 200 units of slack capacity.

Several results are clearly apparent. Although only three plants are needed to supply existing customer demand, four are called for in the transportation solution. Location E is apparently undesired and location A would produce only at 80% whilst C has 80% unutilized capacity in the current solution. Now unless rapid expansion of demand is envisaged if capital costs are anything near to realistic levels only three plants will be desired initially. The static decision problem where a demand of 300 is to be satisfied is how to accomplish this optimally with three plants. If capital costs differ between plant locations the problem is considerably more complicated computationally than if capital costs are the same everywhere.

First consider the differing capital costs case. From Figure 9.25 it would appear that location E can be eliminated; but this is not the case as the 9.25 solution has not considered capital costs. It may well turn out that plant at E is not optimal but we cannot say so yet. As was mentioned earlier the problem is combinatorial and unless a rather involved integer programming formulation is employed the 5C3 = 10 possible combinations of three plants from 5 will have to be solved as separate subproblems and NPVs calculated from expression similar to those in (9.3). Although such an exercise would be rather tedious by hand it would of course take little time by computer and would certainly be a worthwhile exercise to eliminate possibilities.

One useful piece of information can readily be obtained from Figure 9.25 however, and that is an upper bound (not necessarily the least upper bound in general) on the increase in variable costs of the three plant optimum over the four plant solution. Notice that the evaluation of vacant square A1 is only +1 and that routing 20 units round the corresponding closed path would produce a three plant (A, B and D) feasible solution (albeit degenerate) with total production plus distribution costs only 20(= 20 x 1) per 'supply and demand' period greater than in the four plant solution.

If capital costs and lifetimes are the same in all locations, then the ABD three plant solution is in fact optimal. This can be seen without solving the ten subproblems in the following way. Notice that no vacant square evaluation is less that +1. This means that *any* reassignment of one unit from the solution of Figure 9.25 will cost at least 1 unit of money per supply and demand period. Further, at least 20 units must be reassigned from the solution of Figure 9.25 to effect a three plant solution (in which there must be precisely two positive entries in the dummy column). Therefore 20 is the least possible increase in variable costs and the ABD solution must be an optimum. In fact ABD is the unique optimum since every other three plant departure from the solution of Figure 9.25 must involve reassignment of more than 20 units.

9.7 Investment Applications (ii) A Financing Problem

There are many possible 'physical' investment situations involving geographically separate plant and differing production and/or distribution and capital costs that can profitably be approached from the standpoint of distribution problems. It is also possible to formulate certain financing problems in the form of a distribution problem. Consider the following example.

A holding company owns three firms A, B and C. Each firm is at the point of requiring capital inputs of amounts 140, 70 and 90 capital units respectively. The holding company can obtain funds from three sources. It can issue shares in each of the companies held which will represent differing costs to existing shareholders in the holding company depending on the risk class of the individual firm. Let us suppose that there is an overall limit (imposed by the holding company) of 100 units of finance raised by equity issue. In addition debt may be increased by up to 80 units and the holding company has 120 units of retained earnings available. Figure 9.26 shows this financing problem and its solution in a distributional format.

In the figure the cost entries are the costs to the holding company of finance for the three firms from the different sources and 'assignments' represent the amounts to be raised from each source for each firm. This example is one of a rather simple

	Firm A	Firm B	Firm C	Sums available
Equity	−15 (90)	−20	−14 (10)	100
Debt	−12	−15	−10 (80)	80
R.E.	−8 (50)	−8 (70)	−8	120
Requirements	140	70	90	300 / 300

Figure 9.26 Financing example

financing problem. Typically, financing problems will have the structure of more complicated programming problems and indeed, ideally, the problems of optimal sources and uses of funds should be examined simultaneously. This will not always be possible, but occasionally computational techniques originally designed for quite different management applications can suit the structure of simplified financing problems.

However, in section 9.9 a recently developed application of distribution methods to a short term investment problem is given. The problem is considerably more involved than the example that has just been studied and some knowledge of a special class of distribution problems is called for. The following section develops this material prior to presentation of the model itself.

9.8 Transshipment Problems[6]

Transshipment problems are distribution problems in which 'goods' may be moved through intermediate locations (i.e. transshipped). The 'goods' may be physical commodities or, as we shall see, money. The transshipment problem is best illustrated in the context of the movement of goods between locations. The financial application will come in the subsequent section.

Consider the case of a retailing chain that has stores at six different locations. At present although the total amount of stocks of a certain commodity that the company has is satisfactory the distribution between stores is not as desired and a redistribution is planned. In Figure 9.27 each numbered circle represents a store and the figures alongside each store represent the excess (if positive) or deficiency (if negative) in stocks of the item that are held by the store. Thus for instance store No. 1 has a surplus of 6 units, store No. 5 requires 7 units whilst the stock position at store N. 4 is as desired. Movements of stock may proceed in the directions indicated by the arrows and the c_{ij} figures show the cost of moving one item of stock between adjacent stores. Note that stocks can move either way between stores 4 and 3 but we are not assuming that the costs of movement are the same in

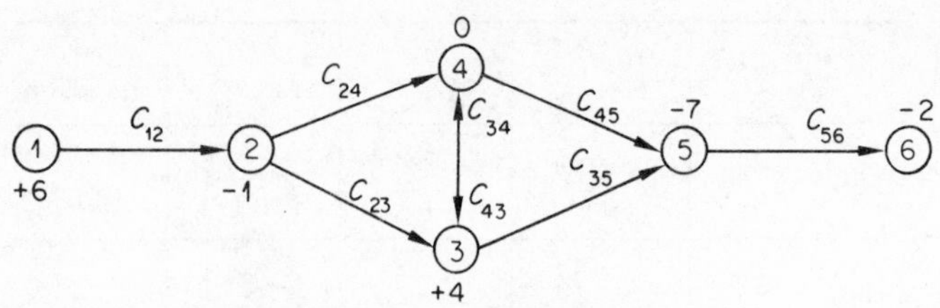

Figure 9.27 A transshipment problem

each direction. In general $c_{ij} \neq c_{ji}$. Usually of course stocks can be moved either way between any pair of stores directly or through intermediate points. In this example the possibilities have been restricted to keep the problem size small. Observe that there are still four different ways in which goods may be moved from store 1 to store 5, viz. 1, 2, 4, 5 or 1, 2, 3, 5 or 1, 2, 4, 3, 5 or 1, 2, 3, 4, 5. In each of these cases store 2 acts as a transshipment point along with 3 and/or 4 as the case may be. How may the desired redistribution be effected at least cost?

Demand point / Supply point	2	5	6	
1	$-c^*_{12}$	$-c^*_{15}$	$-c^*_{16}$	6
3	$-M$	$-c^*_{35}$	$-c^*_{36}$	4
	1	7	2	10 / 10

Figure 9.28 Transshipment problem: 'compact' distributional formulation

The problem can be expressed in distributional form in either of two ways. In the first method designate a row in the distribution tableau for each store with surplus stock and a column for a store with stock deficiency. Thus in Figure 9.28 there are two rows corresponding to stores 2, 5 and 6. Rim conditions represent surpluses and deficiencies in the usual manner. Now, as regards the cost data there is no way that store 3 can supply store 2 so a cost figure of M is entered in this square. The remaining entries are starred to indicate that they represent the *least cost* means of moving stocks between stores. Let us introduce some numerical cost data to illustrate this point. This is done in Figure 9.29 where, for instance, $c_{34} = 4$, $c_{43} = 6$, and $c_{56} = 11$. Since there is only one way of moving stock from store 1 to

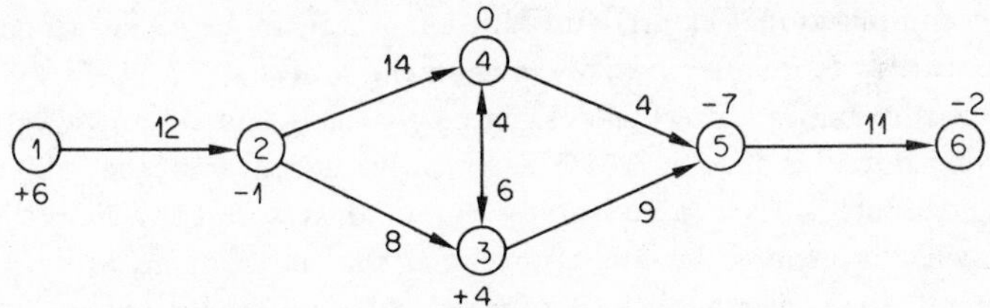

Figure 9.29 Transshipment problem: cost date

store 2, $c_{12}^* = c_{12} = 12$. But consider the cost of shipments between stores 3 and 5. A direct shipment would cost 9 per unit, but if transshipment via store 4 occurred the cost would be $c_{34} + c_{45} = 8$ per unit. Thus $c_{35}^* = 8$. The reader may verify that the remaining cost entries are as shown in Figure 9.30, where for instance the cheapest way of moving one unit from store 1 to store 5 is via stores 2, 3 and 4 as intermediaries, giving $c_{15}^* = 28$. The optimal solution is also shown in the figure, and is interpreted as follows:

Supply point \ Demand point	2	5	6	
1	−12 (1)	−28 (3)	−39 (2)	6
3	−M	−8 (4)	−19	4
	1	7	2	10 \ 10

Figure 9.30 Transshipment problem: optimal solution

Six units leave store 1, of which 1 unit stays at store 2 the remaining 5 units going via stores 3 and 4 to store 5. Two of the 5 units arriving at store 5 go on to store 6. The remaining deficiency of 4 units at store 5 are made up by a shipment from store 3 via store 4. It will have been noted that it is quite arbitrary which two of the 9 units arriving at store 5 are then shipped to store 6. These 2 units may have originated from either of the supply points. This fact is evident in the solution of Figure 9.30 in that the solution is non-unique.

The procedure that has just been described leads to a compact distribution tableau but requires prior determination of the least cost routes between supply and demand points. The alternative distributional formulation has a more extensive layout but does not require the least cost route calculations (which can entail considerable computational effort). In addition it can more easily accommodate such additional restrictions as capacity limits on the routes.

In the extensive tableau a row is designated for each 'source' and a column for each 'sink'. A 'source' is a point which has positive supply and cannot be used as a transshipment point – it is a 'pure' supply point. Thus store 1 is a source but store 3 is not. A 'sink' is a 'pure' demand point; being the end of a line. Store 6 is thus a sink. In general there may be several sources and sinks in a problem. In the rim conditions the s_i figure for a source is its supply and the d_j figure for a sink is its demand. For each transshipment point both a row and column is assigned. Now let p_k represent the initial net stock level of transshipment point k. If point k is a supply point then $p_k > 0$, if it is a demand point then $p_k < 0$. In the rim conditions we set the s_k figure at $p_k + T$ and the d_j figure at level T where T is the total amount of stock to be redistributed. In the present problem the value of T is therefore ten units. Note that the net figure for point k is p_k. The reason that T is added to both supply and demand figures (one of which would otherwise be zero) is that the store may have to handle up to $p_k + T$ units due to a possible transshipment function. As we shall see in computational terms the device prevents negative entries in the extensive tableau. Finally, positive x_{ij} (for $i \neq j$) are permitted only as allowed by the arrows in the original network. Thus x_{24} may be positive but x_{42} must be zero; prohibitive cost figures being entered accordingly.

The tableau layout and optimal solution are shown in Figure 9.31. Zero cost entries will be noted at the junction of the kth row and kth column. Prohibited movements between adjacent points are ensured with M cost figures which are also attached to the intersection of rows and columns corresponding to non-adjacent points. The remaining c_{ij} entries are the original data. The solution of Figure 9.31 can be seen to give exactly the optimal arrangement that had been determined in

	2	3	4	5	(Sink) 6	
(Source) 1	−12 (6)	−M	−M	−M		6
2	0 (4)	−8 (5)	−14	−M	−M	9
3	−M	0 (5)	−4 (9)	−9	−M	14
4	−M	−6	0 (1)	−4 (9)	−M	10
5	−M	−M	−M	0 (1)	−11 (2)	3
	10	10	10	10	2	

Figure 9.31 Transshipment problem: 'extensive' format

the tableau of Figure 9.30. Establishment of u_i and v_j values for the extensive tableau will reveal that the optimum is unique; no distinction being made in this tableau regarding the alternative origins for the the supply to store 6. The interested reader may find it instructive to compare the u_i and v_j values in the two tableau and to verify that the optimal solution in the extensive layout does not depend upon the precise value of 10(= T) units being added to supplies and demands at transshipment points. As will be seen, to prevent negative entries in the tableau of 9.31 any number of nine or above will suffice.

9.9 Investment Applications, (iii) A Short Term Investment Model

In an article in 1974, V. Srinivasan produced an intriguing application of distributional methods in the area of cash management.[7] The problem of cash management '. . . is concerned with optimally financing net cash outflows and investing net inflows of a firm while simultaneously determining payment schedules for incurred liabilities'.[8] The operational research approach to this problem has been two-pronged; inventory based models have been suggested and linear programming formulations have been produced.[9] Srinivasan's model uses the approach of Orgler but with a distributional formulation and solution procedure. In the model four major types of decision variable are distinguished: payment schedules, short term financing, securities transactions and the cash balance. The objective in the model is to minimize net cost (taking into account timings of receipts and payments) from the cash budget over the planning horizon.[10] The optimization is, of course, subject to constraints (of an interperiod nature) on the decision variables.

The unusual feature of Orgler's model is that the period lengths are unequal ranging from one day to three months in the illustration to follow. This device enables the day-to-day aspects of cash management to be taken into account without producing a model of impracticable size. In use, at the end of the first (day length) period the model is recomputed so that only the period one decisions are actually implemented but the longer run implications of these decisions have been taken into account. Srinivasan employed the same numerical example as Orgler (for comparative purposes) but with a distributional formulation that provides greatly increased computational efficiency. This point will be discussed further below, but for the moment let us examine the example itself.[11]

Six time periods are considered. The lengths are:

Period No.	*Length (days)*
1	1
2	1
3	10
4	20
5	60
6	90

Within this time structure decisions are to be made regarding the following.

(i) The payment schedules for predicted purchases in all periods.

(ii) The transactions to be made on the portfolio of securities that is held by the firm at the start of the planning period.
(iii) The extent of any new investments in marketable securities.
(iv) The use (or non-use) of credit facilities available to the firm.

In order to set up the 'transportation' tableau it is necessary to specify the following.

(a) The total number of sources of funds (in total P).
(b) The total number of uses of funds (in total Q).
(c) The amounts available at each of the sources (represented by a_i where $i = 1, 2, \ldots P$).
(d) The amounts required at each of the uses (i.e. the 'demands' represented by r_j where $j = 1, 2 \ldots Q$).
(e) The cost of putting one dollar from source i to use j (represented by c_{ij}).

These are the data requirements. With x_{ij} representing the amount of the ith source that is allocated to use j, the problem can be expressed as:

$$\begin{aligned}
&\text{minimize} && \sum_{i=1}^{P} \sum_{j=1}^{Q} c_{ij} x_{ij} \\
&\text{subject to:} && \sum_{j=1}^{Q} x_{ij} = a_i \quad (i = 1, 2, \ldots P) \\
& && \sum_{i=1}^{P} x_{ij} = r_j \quad (j = 1, 2, \ldots Q) \\
& && x_{ij} \geqslant 0 \quad \text{for all} \quad i, j
\end{aligned} \tag{9.4}$$

The problem is clearly a transportation problem and the MODI method may be applied to its solution. In addition to the constraints of (9.4) prohibitions may be incorporated in the usual manner, viz. if source i may not be employed for use j then $c_{ij} = M$. Now cash may be a source; for instance in the making of payments and a 'destination' as when securities are sold to generate cash. Consequently cash will appear in both rows and columns. In Figure 9.32 the first six rows correspond to sources of cash and the first six columns represent uses of cash in each of the periods. Figure 9.32 is Srinivasan's figure one.[12] It will be noted that Srinivasan's presentation is a little different from that developed in this chapter. As in our style assignment squares are identified by circles but it is the cost figure that is circled rather than the assignment level. Also as evidenced in the key at the bottom of the tableau the c_{ij} are entered in (rather than $-c_{ij}$ in our style).[13]

Now, as regards the rim conditions and particular cost data in the example rows 7 to 12 correspond to securities held by the firm at the start of the planning period each having a different maturity date. For instance the unit entry in the availabilities column, seventh row corresponds to a security of \$10,000 which matures at the end of the first period and so provides a sum of \$10,000 available for use during the second period. It will be noted that row 12 corresponds to a security of $500,000 face value which matures after the end of the sixth period (i.e. beyond the horizon). All but the first security can be sold prior to the maturity date. Row 13 corresponds to an 'open line of credit' of $2,500,000 that may be drawn on, if desired. Row 14 is a dummy and denotes uses not satisfied during the time horizon. The figure of $1,000,000 entered in this availability column is arbitrary and can be shown not to affect the optimal solution. It is inserted so that optimum cash balance can be easily determined, otherwise it could be deleted since the model does not allow accounts payable to be postponed beyond the horizon.

The accounts payable (again in units of $10,000) are shown in the requirements row, columns 7 to 12. Column 13 is a dummy representing unused sources and corresponds to securities that are allowed to mature beyond the horizon and line of credit not being fully utilized. The requirement level r_{13}, shown as $6,470,000 is determined so as to balance the rim conditions, i.e.

$$\sum_{i=1}^{14} a_i = \sum_{j=1}^{13} r_j$$

The determination of this value for r_{13} comes after all the other rim conditions have been entered in.

Now before the rim conditions can be completed we shall need to examine the cost data.[14] 'Shipments' from sources $i = 1, 2, \ldots 6$ to uses $j = 2, 3, \ldots 6$ and 13 with $i < j$ represent investments in marketable securities. For example if the firm invests $1 of first period cash in a security which matures at the beginning of the sixth period it receives 1.2 cents interest, which figure is entered as a negative cost. All 'cost' figures are given in cents. Similarly investing $1 in the second period in a security which matures beyond the horizon earns 2.4 cents interest; hence the entry of −2.4 dummy column 13 row 2.

Squares with $j < i$ and $i = 2, 3, \ldots 6$ correspond to the taking of short term loans. An assignment in square (4, 2) would correspond to the taking of a loan at the beginning of period two and paying back at the start of period four. Provision is not made in the model for such loans and a cost figure of M is entered in squares with $j < i$ and $i = 2, 3, \ldots 6$. Where $i = j$ an assignment would represent a shipment from a cash source to a cash use hence $c_{ij} = 0$ for $i = 1, 2, \ldots 6$.

The c_{ij} for $i = 7, 8, \ldots 12$ relate to sales of securities in the initial portfolio prior to maturity. These costs are interpreted by Srinivasan as losses in yield – which will in general be uncertain so that expected values would have to be used. The actual nature of these c_{ij} in any situation depend upon the particular circumstances. For instance if no interest payments are due on the securities (as might be the case if interest is paid at six monthly intervals) the c_{ij} would represent discounts. It would seem desirable to keep data on an actual cash flow basis wherever possible. Since securities cannot be sold after they have matured cost figures of M are entered for all post maturity periods for each security. Accounts are paid only from cash hence $c_{ij} = M$ for $i = 7, 8, \ldots 12$ and $j = 7, 8, \ldots 12$.

The remaining c_{ij} relate to cash-to-accounts payable assignments and credit. A 2% discount is assumed to apply if accounts are settled within 10 days. If payment is made within 10–30 days there is no discount. It is assumed accounts may not be

Sources \ Uses	1	2	3	4	5	6	7	8	9
	Cash						A		
Cash 1	2,945 0	25 −.01	30 −.025	−.16	−.40	−1.20	−2.0	M	M
2	M	3,000 0	−.01	−.15	−.40	−1.20	−2.0	−2.0	M
3	M	M	2,992 0	−.13	−.40	−1.20	5 −2.0	3 −2.0	−
4	M	M	M	2,900 0	−.26	−1.06	0	0	4 −
5	M	M	M	M	3,000 0	−.80	M	M	0
6	M	M	M	M	M	3,000 0	M	M	M
Securities 7	.02	1 0	M	M	M	M	M	M	M
8	.04	.02	12 0	M	M	M	M	M	M
9	.21	.19	5 .17	0	M	M	M	M	M
10	10 .50	.50	.50	.33	0	M	M	M	M
11	25 1.5	1.5	1.5	1.33	1.0	0	M	M	M
12	50 3.0	3.0	3.0	2.83	2.5	1.5	M	M	M
13	3.6	3.58	23 3.56	205 3.38	3.0	1.8	M	M	M
14	M	M	M	M	M	M	M	M	M
Requirements r_j (in 10,000$)	3030	3026	3062	3105	3000	3000	5	3	40

e → 11	12	Slack 13	Availabilities (in 10,000$)	
M	M	−2.4	3,000	Cash 1st pd.
M	M	−2.4	3,000	Cash 2nd pd.
M	M	−2.4	3,000	Cash 3rd pd.
M	M	−2.26	3,000	Cash 4th pd
150 (−2.0)	M	440 (−2.1)	3,590	Cash 5th pd.
0	570 (−2.0)	85 (−1.2)	3,655	Cash 6th pd.
M	M	M	1	Sec. 2nd pd.
M	M	M	12	Sec. 3rd. pd.
M	M	M	5	Sec. 4th pd.
M	M	M	10	Sec. 5th pd.
M	M	M	25	Sec. 6th pd
M	M	0	50	Sec.Beyond horizon
M	M	22 (0)	250	Line of credit
M	M	100 (0)	100	Slack
150	570	647		

x_{ij} / c_{ij}	c_{ij}: costs in cents/\$, M = 99,999 x_{ij}: optimum amounts in 10,000\$ (x_{ij} = 0 for uncircled cells)

Fig. 9.32 Srinivasan/Orgler example

settled beyond 30 days (the maximum period of trade credit here). Accordingly, cost entries of −2, 0 and M are made in squares ij for $i = 1, 2, \ldots 6$ and $j = 7, 8, \ldots 12$.

Row 13 corresponds to the line of credit on which loans can be obtained at the beginning of any period repayable after one year. Monthly simple interest is charged at 0.6%. Early repayments are prohibited. The c_{ij} for $i = 13, j = 1, 2, \ldots 6$ show the interest charges until the horizon. Accounts are settled only in cash hence $c_{13j} = M$ for $j = 7, 8, \ldots 12$. Since all credit need not be used $c_{13\ 13} = 0$. In this problem all accounts payable must be settled within the horizon so that the dummy source 14 may ship only to the dummy use, 13. Thus $c_{14j} = 0$ for $j = 1, 2, \ldots 12$ and $c_{14\ 13} = 0$.

We can now return to complete the rim conditions. We need data for availabilities at sources $1, 2, \ldots 6$ and requirements at use $1, 2, \ldots 6$. In this example the net exogenously determined cash flows are expected to be −300,000, −260,000, −620,000, −1,050,000 +5,900,000 and +6,550,000 in each of the periods respectively. Initial cash balance is 90,000 so that with maturing securities of 10,000 in the first period the initial cash balance may be regarded as 100,000. Now, the minimum cash balance that is to be held at any time is 100,000 and this is treated by subtracting it from the initial balance to get a zero figure. As Srinivasan points out, it is as if the initial cash balance is set aside to meet the minimum cash balance requirement.

Now it will have become evident to the reader that the tableau of Figure 9.32 is the extensive layout of a transshipment problem. 'Cash' in all the periods represent transshipment points. Cash may be moved around from one period to another (in this case not backwards in time) as goods may be moved from one store to another (with certain prohibitions). In obtaining the a_i and r_j figures for rows 1–6 and columns 1–6, Srinivasan has simply added a large number (30,000,000) to the exogenously determined cash supply or demand. This is a minor variation on the device that we suggested in the previous section ($a_k = p_k + T$, $r_k = T$). Note that if this technique had been used with $T = 30{,}000{,}000$ the s_i figures would have been 2,970, 2,974, 2,938, 2,895, 3,590 and 3,655 respectively whilst all d_j figures (for columns 1 to 6, that is) would have been 3,000. In this case all that would have changed are the 'i to i' notional transshipment figures on the diagonal up to $i = 6$; no real cash transfers would have been affected. To complete the rim conditions r_{13} is determined so that

$$\sum_{i=1}^{14} a_i = \sum_{j=1}^{13} r_j$$

thus $r_{13} = 647$.

The solution of Figure 9.32 may be arrived at by the MODI method and is interpreted as follows. The accounts payable billed in periods $1, 2, \ldots 6$ are paid in full in periods 3, 3, 4, 4, 5 and 6 respectively. For example $x_{37} = 50{,}000$ and $x_{6,12} = 5{,}700{,}000$. Credit is drawn upon to the tune of 230,000 at the start of period three ($x_{13,3} = 230{,}000$) and 2,050,000 at the start of period four

($x_{13,4}$ = 2,050,000). The securities maturing in periods five and six and beyond the horizon are sold in the first period; those maturing in period four are sold in period three whilst the remainder are allowed to mature. In the first period amounts of 250,000 and 300,000 are invested in securities maturing in the second and third periods respectively (x_{12} = 250,000 and x_{13} = 300,000). In the fifth and sixth periods 4,400,000 and 850,000 are invested in securities that mature beyond the horizon.

Since the problem is in distributional format sensitivity analysis may readily be undertaken. The dual solution is shown in Figure 9.33[15] in which the entry in each square is the sum of row and column numbers (the u_i and v_j of previous acquaintance) associated with each square. Entries in Figure 9.33 have been rounded off to two places of decimals and it should be borne in mind that Srinivasan's cost entries are the c_{ij} themselves rather than the $-c_{ij}$ that we have used in the remainder of the chapter. Let us follow Srinivasan and call the entries of 9.33 d_{ij}. Thus d_{ij} shows the rate at which the optimal level of cost would increase (decrease) if the availability at the ith source and the requirement of the jth use were simultaneously increased (decreased).

As an illustration of the use of the d_{ij} consider the effect of having one more unit of cash in period 1. The result would be to decrease the optimum value of the objective function (i.e. reduce cost) by 3.58 cents. The appropriate d_{ij} is $d_{1,13} = -3.58$ since one more unit of cash would increase the requirement of the slack use. The extra cash helps by reducing the amount borrowed from the line of credit in period three (saving 3.56 cents) and yields 0.02 cents from investment in securities from period 1 to 3.

In respect of accounts receivable by the firm some initial assumption regarding the use of credit facilities by the firm's customers must be made. Suppose payment of accounts receivable was one month beyond the due date, then $d_{45} = -1.28$ shows the effect of tightening credit policy so that bills due in period 4 (which would normally have been paid in period five) are paid in period 4. This will increase the cash source in period 4 at the expense of period 5, it is as if the *use* in period 5 had increased. The net effect is an improvement of 1.28 in the objective function.

The d_{ij} for $j = 1, 2, \ldots 6$ with $i < j$ bring out the effects of short term loans if these were available. For instance $d_{35} = -1.46$ shows that if a loan could be obtained at the start of period 3 and repayed at the start of period 5 total cost would be reduced by 1.46 cents. This would be an alternative to the line of credit facility and determines the maximum acceptable monthly interest rate (1.46%) that would be attractive over this period.

The d_{ij} in the fourteenth row for $j = 7, 8, \ldots 12$ show the effects on the minimal level of costs resulting from increasing the accounts payable (note that slack supply will be increase to balance the increase of the requirement r_j). Total cost would increase if these accounts payable were to increase since 'to pay the accounts payable due in period 1, for instance, a loan is obtained from the line of credit costing 3.56 cents/\$ so that even after subtracting the discount of 2.0 cents/\$ there is a net cost of $d_{14,7}$ = 1.56 cents/\$. However, $d_{14,12}$ = –0.8 cents since the

Sources \ Uses		Cash 1	Cash 2	Cash 3	Cash 4	Cash 5	Cash 6	Cash 7	Accounts payable 8	Accounts payable 9	Accounts payable 10	Accounts payable 11	Accounts payable 12	Slack 13	
Cash	1	0	−0.01	−0.02	−0.20	−1.48	−2.38	−2.02	−2.02	−2.20	−2.20	−3.48	−4.38	−3.58	Cash 1st pd.
Cash	2	0.01	0	−0.01	−0.19	−1.47	−2.37	−2.01	−2.01	−2.19	−2.19	−3.47	−4.37	−3.57	Cash 2nd pd.
Cash	3	0.02	0.01	0	−0.18	−1.46	−2.36	−2.00	−2.00	−2.18	−2.18	−3.46	−4.36	−3.56	Cash 3rd pd.
Cash	4	0.20	0.19	0.18	0	−1.28	−2.18	−1.82	−1.82	−2.00	−2.00	−3.28	−4.18	−3.38	Cash 4th pd.
Cash	5	1.48	1.47	1.46	1.28	0	−0.90	−0.54	−0.54	−0.72	−0.72	−2.00	−2.90	−2.10	Cash 5th pd.
Cash	6	2.38	2.37	2.36	2.18	0.90	0	0.36	0.36	0.18	0.18	−1.10	−2.00	−1.20	Cash 6th pd.
Securities	7	0.01	0	−0.01	−0.19	−1.47	−2.37	−2.01	−2.01	−2.19	−2.19	−3.47	−4.37	−3.57	Sec. 2nd pd.
Securities	8	0.02	0.01	0	−0.18	−1.46	−2.36	−2.00	−2.00	−2.18	−2.18	−3.46	−4.36	−3.56	Sec. 3rd pd.
Securities	9	0.19	0.18	0.17	−0.01	−1.29	−2.19	−1.83	−1.83	−2.01	−2.01	−3.29	−4.19	−3.39	Sec. 4th pd.
Securities	10	0.50	0.49	0.48	0.30	−1.98	−1.88	−1.52	−1.52	−1.70	−1.70	−2.98	−3.88	−3.08	Sec. 5th pd.
Securities	11	1.50	1.49	1.48	1.30	0.02	−0.88	−0.52	−0.52	−0.70	−0.70	−1.98	−2.88	−2.08	Sec. 6th pd.
Securities	12	3.00	2.99	2.98	2.80	1.52	0.62	0.98	0.98	0.80	0.80	0.48	−0.38	−0.58	Sec. Beyond horizon
	13	3.58	3.57	3.56	3.38	2.10	1.20	1.56	1.56	1.38	1.38	0.10	−0.80	0	Line of credit
	14	3.58	3.57	3.56	3.88	2.10	1.20	1.56	1.56	1.38	1.38	0.10	−0.80	0	Slack

Figure 9.33 Srinivasan/Orgler example: dual solution

2.0 cents/$ discount on accounts payable is more attractive than the yield of 1.2 cents/$ obtainable by investing in securities maturing beyond the horizon. The effect of postponing purchases so that accounts payable currently due in, say, the third period would be due only in, say, the sixth period is given by $-d_{14,9} + d_{14,12} = -2.18$ cents/$ (since a simultaneous decrease of r_9 and increase of r_{12} is equivalent to simultaneous decrease of (a_{14}, r_9) and an increase of (a_{14}, r_{12})).'[16] Finally, note that since $d_{13,13} = 0$ increasing the line of credit limit would not reduce optimal cost.

As usual we should add that all of the values above apply only so long as changes do not alter the optimal b.f.s. Further interpretations would also be possible.[17] All of the sensitivity analysis could, of course, have been conducted with an L.P. formulation but not with such facility as in the transportation layout of Srinivasan.

The other advantages of the distributional layout are that it may be more attractive to management (and therefore find wider use) than the L.P. formulation due to its 'inherent simplicity and intuitive appeal'. The approach is also attractive computationally being 'more efficient by a factor of about 30 to 1 than the linear programming formulation of the problem. Since the model is to be recomputed daily the savings involved would be substantial.' The sole disadvantage of the transshipment formulation is that it is considerably less flexible (than the L.P. version) in incorporating institutional constraints on average cash balances, financial ratios etc. If more than one such constraint was to be included 'one would have to resort to decomposition techniques with such constraints constituting the master problem and the transshipment formulation defining the subproblem'.

Finally, along with the L.P. approach the transshipment model requires systematic setting down of data, constraints and objectives: '. . . the financial manager needs to state in tabular form the various sources and uses of funds and their timing and provide the amounts and the unit costs involved. Thus, the transshipment formulation serves as a very useful tool in organizing data in management information systems for financial control'.[18]

9.10 Concluding Remarks

Distribution problems are particular cases of linear programming problems for which efficient special computational procedures have been developed. Consequently those investment problems which have a distributional character are usually best solved by the modified distribution method (at least in terms of hand computation). We have discussed the solution of profits maximizing and cost minimizing distribution problems in general, and have considered some particular investment applications.

In addition to the cases that we have examined in some detail, certain network problems can be formulated as distributional problems and therefore solved by distributional methods. Of particular interest in this respect is the network cash flow problem of Chapter 8. The dual of this problem has the form of a transportation problem and distribution methods could be applied to its solution. Although useful insights may be gleaned by such an exercise the 'network flow' approach is more efficient as a solution procedure.[19]

In this chapter, as in Chapter 8, one of the objectives has been to apply techniques from the area of operational research to aspects of certain large-scale investment problems that are at best only superficially covered in the established literature on capital budgeting. These deficiencies remedied (at least in part) we now turn our attention to the subjects of non-linearities and risky interrelated investments.

Notes

1. Coefficients of $-p$ could equally have been used in the dummy row. This matter is discussed later in the chapter.
2. As will be seen later, the fact that a solution has $m + n - 1$ assignments does not necessarily mean that the solution is not degenerate. It will however be basic.
3. See Reinfeld, N. V., and Vogel, W. R., *Mathematical Programming*, Prentice-Hall, Englewood Cliffs, N.J., 1958.
4. See for example Sasieni, M., Yaspan, A., and Friedman, L., *Operations Research*, Wiley, New York, 1959.
5. It will be assumed that the costs of obtaining information are negligible in comparison with other costs in the problem.
6. The presentation given here is based on that of Wagner, *op. cit.*, Chapter 6, to which the reader is referred.
7. Srinivasan, V., 'A transshipment model for cash management decisions', *Management Science*, **20**, (Series B), 1973–4.
8. Srinivasan, V., 'A trasshipment model for cash management decisions, *Management Science,* **20**, (Series B), 1350, (1973–4).
9. We have already discussed the Charnes, Cooper and Miller model in Chapter 6. For discussion of the cash management problem in general see Samuels, J. M., and Wilkes, F. M., *op. cit.*, Chapter 12 in which some discussion of the inventory theoretic approach may be found. See also (i) Miller, M. H., and Orr, D., 'An application of control limit models to corporate cash balances', In Robichek, A. A., *Financial Research and Management Decisions*, Wiley, New York, 1967; (ii) Baumol, W. J., 'The transactions demand for cash: an inventory theoretic approach', *Quarterly Journal of Economics,* **66**, 1952; (iii) White, D. J., and Norman, J. M., 'Control of cash reserves', *Operational Research Quarterly,* **16**, 1965. On the Linear Programming front see (i) Robichek, A. A., Teichroew, D., and Jones, J. M., 'Optimal short term financing decisions', *Management Science,* **12**, 1965; (ii) Archer, S. H., 'A model for the determination of firm cash balances', *The Journal of Financial and Quantitative Analysis,* **1**, 1966; (iii) Orgler, Y., 'An unequal-period model for cash management decisions', *Management Science,* **16** (Series B), 1969.
10. This will be spelled out in more detail below.
11. In the example we shall employ Srinivasan's notation.
12. Srinivasan, V., 'A transshipment model for cash management decisions, *Management Science,* **20**, (Series B), 1354. The use of the word 'source' is Srinivasan's and does not in this context correspond to a 'pure supply' point in the transshipment sense.
13. Consequently.
14. The solution is akin to that of determining the R.H.S. of the constraints in the capital rationing models of Chapter 5. The figures that we ended up with there depended on the rate of interest at which funds may be transferred from one period to another.
15. This is Srinivasan, V., 'A transshipment model for cash management decisions', *Management Science,* **20**, (Series B), Figure 2, (1973–4).
16. Srinivasan, V., 'A transshipment model for cash management decisions', *Management Science*, **20**, (Series B), 1359 (1943–4).
17. In the article Srinivasan goes on to determine the optimal level of the cash balance – previously arbitrarily set at 100,000. This is a further advantage of the distributional layout.
18. Srinivasan, V., 'A transshipment model for cash management decisions', *Management Science*, **20**, (Series B), 1352 (1973–4).
19. See Russell, A. H., 'Cash flows in networks', *Management Science (A),* **16**, No. 5, 360, January, 1970. For discussion of networks in a transportation context see Wagner, H. M.,

Principles of Operations Research with Applications to Managerial Decisions, Prentice-Hall, Englewood Cliffs, N.J., 1969, Chapter 7.

Additional References

1. Balinski, M. L., and Gomory, R. E., 'A primal method for the assignment and transportation problems', *Management Science,* **10**, 1964.
2. Charnes, A., and Cooper, W. W., *Management Models and Industrial Applications of Linear Programming,* Vols. 1 and 2, Wiley, London, 1961.
3. Charnes, A., and Cooper, W. W., 'The stepping-stone method of explaining linear programming calculations in transportation problems', *Management Science,* **1**, 1954.
4. Hadley, G., *Linear Programming*, Addison-Wesley, Reading, Massachusetts, 1962.
5. Klein, M., 'A primal method for minimal cost flows with applications to the assignment and transportation problems', *Management Science,* **14**, 1967.
6. Metzger, R. W., *Elementary Mathematical Programming*, Science Editions, 450, 1963.
7. Orden, A., 'The transshipment problem', *Management Science,* **2**, 1956.
8. Orgler, Y., *Cash Budgeting, the Payment Schedule, and Short Term Financing by Business Firms*, Ph.D. Dissertation Graduate School of Business, Carnegie-Mellon University, 1967.
9. Orgler, Y., *Cash Management: Methods and Models,* Wadsworth, Belmont, California, 1970.
10. Srinivasan, V., *A Transshipment Model for Cash Management Decisions*, Management Sciences Research Report No. 243, Graduate School of Industrial Administration, Carnegie-Mellon University, Pittsburgh, 1971.
11. Szwarc, W., 'The initial solution of the transportation problem', *Operations Research,* **8**, 1960.
12. Szwarc, W., 'The transportation problem with stochastic demand', *Management Science*, **11**, 1964.
13. Wagner, H. M., 'On a class of capacitated transportation problems', *Management Science,* **5**, 1959.
14. Wagner, H. M., *Principles of Operations Research with Applications to Managerial Decisions*, Prentice-Hall, Englewood Cliffs, N.J., 1969.
15. Williams, A. C., 'A treatment of transportation problems by decomposition', *SIAM J. on Applied Mathematics*, **10**, 1962.

CHAPTER 10

Non-Linear and Stochastic Problems

10.1 Introduction and Overview

In this chapter we examine, in general terms, problems of non-linear maximization both with and without constraints. In section 10.2 a brief overview of constrained and unconstrained maximization problems is presented; the principal objective being to determine those conditions which characterize optima. The section is intended to provide only the minimum coverage necessary to gain some insight into the nature of the problems and to understand and employ the optimality conditions to solve some particular cases of non-linear programming problems in subsequent work.

Whilst the principal emphasis is on non-linear programming problems the special case of linear programming is reconsidered in this more general context with the objective of deepening the understanding of such problems. The problem of 'classical programming' – the maximization of a non-linear function subject to equality constraints and with unrestricted variables – is not explicitly considered for two reasons. Firstly, most investment problems are not of this nature and secondly classical programming problems are special cases of non-linear programming problems (see sections following) and so are included implicitly in this discussion. However in section 10.3 we examine an unconstrained maximization problem in an investment context and in section 10.4 the relationship of pricing decisions to terminal values is examined. As will be noted in the discussion of this latter problem one equality constraint might be included in certain contexts.

In section 10.5 we develop a quadratic programming investment problem and show how the solution may be found by use of the simplex method.

Whilst non-linearities in general are the subject of the introductory discussion a detailed solution procedure (for an exact solution) is given only for a special subclass of non-linear programming problems. These are problems in which only the objective function is non-linear (in particular being quadratic and concave). This work will subsequently be built upon in respect of the portfolio analysis of Chapter 11. So far as investment applications are concerned the case of non-linear objective function is likely to be the most important subclass. The additional references at the end of the chapter contain sources for further reading in this area.

10.2 Review of Maximization Problems

Consider the problem of finding the maximum value that a function of a single variable takes when the only constraint is that the variable is a real number. The

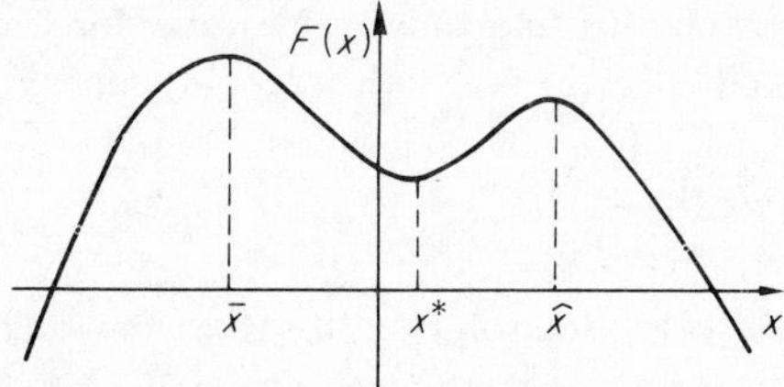

Figure 10.1 Maximization: illustrative function

problem can be stated as:

$$\underset{x}{\text{Max}}\, F(x) \quad \text{s.t.} \quad x \in R \tag{10.1}$$

In words the statement of the problem in (10.1) reads 'maximize over x the function $F(x)$ such that the value of x belongs to the set of real numbers' (i.e. is anywhere between minus infinity and plus infinity). Now consider the particular case where $F(x)$ takes the form shown in Figure 10.1. The maximizing value of x is $\bar{x}$ and in this case $\bar{x} \leqslant 0$. The maximum is characterized by the slope of the function $F(x)$ being zero. Symbolically:

$$\frac{\mathrm{d}F(x)}{\mathrm{d}x} = 0 \tag{10.2}$$

at a maximum. The condition of zero slope given by (10.2) is the equation to zero of the *first derivative* of $F(x)$ with respect to x. The first derivative is the rate of change of $F(x)$ as x changes. In the work that follows we shall be concerned only with polynomial functions. A polynomial function of a single variable x may in general be written as:

$$F(x) = a_0 x^n + a_1 x^{n-1} + a_2 x^{n-2} + \ldots + a_{n-1} x + a_n \tag{10.3}$$

where (10.3) represents an nth order polynomial provided that $a_0 \neq 0$. Now the slope of $F(x)$ at any point is the value of the derivative of the function at that point and the derivative of a function such as (10.3) is obtained by finding the derivative (differentiating) each term individually and summing. Now:

$$\frac{\mathrm{d}(ax^m)}{\mathrm{d}x} = max^{m-1} \tag{10.4}$$

that is the derivative with respect to x of ax^m where the coefficient, a, and the exponent, m, are constants is obtained by multiplying by the 'old' exponent and reducing the exponent by one. So the derivative of (10.3) with respect to x is

$$\frac{\mathrm{d}F(x)}{\mathrm{d}x} = na_0 x^{n-1} + (n-1)a_1 x^{n-2} + (n-2)a_2 x^{n-3} + \ldots + a_{n-1} \tag{10.5}$$

and the slope of $F(x)$ for any value of x is obtained by substituting that value of x

in (10.5). Thus if we wanted to find those values of x for which the slope of $F(x)$ was zero we should have to solve the $(n-1)$th order polynomial equation:

$$\frac{dF(x)}{dx} = na_0x^{n-1} + (n-1)a_1x^{n-2} + (n-2)a_2x^{n-3} + \ldots + a_{n-1} = 0 \quad (10.6)$$

Except for some special cases, the solution of (10.6) for values of n in excess of 4 would be obtained by numerical methods. There will be $n-1$ values of x which satisfy (10.6); these are termed *roots*. Some of the roots may be identical (so that we do not have $n-1$ different numbers) and some roots may not be real numbers (they may involve the square root of -1) but this possibility need not concern us here.

Now, to return to our consideration of conditions for a maximum of $F(x)$ in general. Each point which satisfies (10.2) is termed a *stationary value* of the function. A stationary value, in the case of a function of a single variable, may be a maximum, a minimum or a point of inflexion.[1] The condition of zero slope is necessary but is not sufficient to ensure the overall, *global maximum* of $F(x)$.

At the point $x = \hat{x}$ the function takes on a *local maximum* value. That is, small variations, increases or decreases, in x around the value $\hat{x}$ produce a reduced value of $F(x)$. A sufficiently large reduction in the value of x to bring it near to $\bar{x}$, would produce a higher value of $F(x)$. Of course, a global maximum is also a local maximum. The function takes on a local minimum at $x = x^*$. This turning point is also characterized by (10.2). The distinction between local maxima and local minima is that the rate of change of the slope of $F(x)$ is negative for a maximum (slope decreasing) and positive for a minimum (slope increasing).[2]

The rate of change of the slope of a function is given by the derivative of the expression for the slope; remember that the slope is itself a function of x. Thus the rate of change of the slope of $F(x)$ in (10.3) is given by the derivative of (10.5). This is called the second derivative of the original function and is given by (10.7).

$$\frac{d^2F(x)}{dx^2} = (n-1)na_0x^{n-2} + (n-2)(n-1)a_1x^{n-3},$$
$$+ (n-3)(n-2)a_2x^{n-4} + \ldots + 2a_{n-2} \quad (10.7)$$

In (10.7) it is assumed that n is at least 5. For example if $n = 5$ then (10.7) in full would be:

$$\frac{d^2F(x)}{dx^2} = 20a_0x^3 + 12a_1x^2 + 6a_2x + 2a_3 \quad (10.8)$$

Now for a local maximum we have stated that the rate of change of the slope of $F(x)$ should be negative. Thus (10.9) should hold for a maximum. For a local minimum (10.10) applies.

$$\frac{d^2F(x)}{dx^2} < 0 \quad (10.9)$$

$$\frac{d^2 F(x)}{dx^2} > 0 \tag{10.10}$$

The conditions (10.2) and (10.9) apply to all local maxima and do not enable us to distinguish between local and global maxima. Unless it is known *a priori* that a local maximum is also the global maximum, the global maximum can be found by reference to the value of $F(x)$ itself, i.e. by evaluating $F(x)$ at each point satisfying (10.2) and (10.9).

Now suppose that not all real values of x are permissible. In particular consider the case where only non-negative values of x are allowed. The problem now becomes:

$$\underset{x}{\text{Max}}\ F(x) \quad \text{s.t.} \quad x \geqslant 0 \tag{10.11}$$

(10.11) defines a non-linear programming problem (provided of course that $F(x)$ is not a linear function) the choice of real values of x is restricted. What conditions now characterize maxima? Reference to Figure 10.1 suggests that there are two types of point at which maxima can occur – a turning point of $F(x)$ such as $\hat{x}$, or a *boundary point*. The only boundary point in the current problem is $x = 0$. At $x = 0$ the only permitted direction of change in x is an increase in the value of x and it is evident from the graph that $F(x)$ diminishes for increasing x at $x = 0$. Consequently $x = 0$ is a candidate for the global maximum of $F(x)$ because of the sign requirement.[3] If $F(x)$ had been as in Figure 10.2(a) the boundary point $x = 0$ would have provided the global maximum even though it is not a turning point of $F(x)$. In Figure 10.2(b) $x = 0$ is a local maximum since decreases in x are not allowed but $\hat{x}$, an *interior* turning point, is the global maximum. In Figure 10.2(c) the boundary point is not a local maximum since $F(x)$ is increasing for increasing x.

Now the local maxima in the diagrams of Figure 10.2 satisfy one or other of two sets of conditions. Namely either

$$x = 0 \quad \text{and} \quad \frac{dF(x)}{dx} < 0 \tag{10.12a}$$

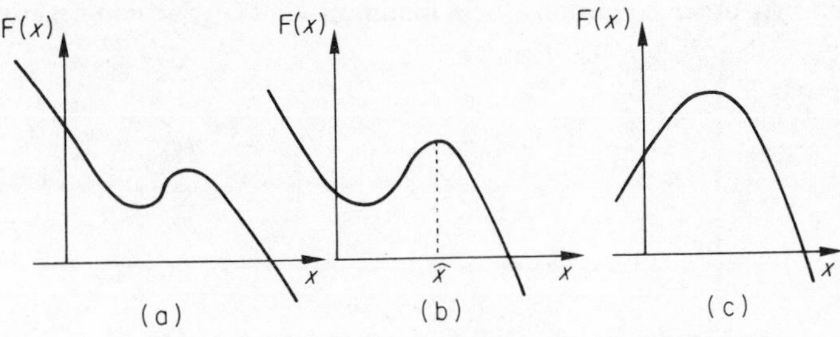

Figure 10.2 Boundary and interior maxima

or

$$x > 0 \quad \text{and} \quad \frac{dF(x)}{dx} = 0 \tag{10.12b}$$

The local minima in the diagrams satisfy one or other of:

$$x = 0 \quad \text{and} \quad \frac{dF(x)}{dx} > 0 \tag{10.13a}$$

or

$$x > 0 \quad \text{and} \quad \frac{dF(x)}{dx} = 0 \tag{10.13b}$$

It should be noted that (10.12a) and (10.13a) unambiguously identify a local maximum and a local minimum respectively, whilst (10.12b) and (10.13b) are identical. One further possibility that is not represented in Figure 10.2 is that of a stationary value occuring at $x = 0$ that is:

$$x = 0 \quad \text{and} \quad \frac{dF(x)}{dx} = 0 \tag{10.14}$$

Note that condition (10.14) will be satisfied if, and only if, there is no constant term in the derivative of $F(x)$.

The characteristics of a local maximum of $F(x)$ subject to $x \geqslant 0$ can be summarized as:

$$\left.\begin{array}{l} x \geqslant 0 \\ \dfrac{dF(x)}{dx} \leqslant 0 \\ \dfrac{dF(x)}{dx} \cdot x = 0 \end{array}\right\} \tag{10.15}$$

Note that (10.15) includes (10.12a) and (10.12b) but since (10.15) also includes (10.13a) and (10.14) then (10.15) must be described as necessary conditions only.

Necessary first order conditions for a minimum of $F(x)$ for non-negative x are:

$$\left.\begin{array}{l} \dfrac{dF(x)}{dx} \geqslant 0 \\ \dfrac{dF(x)}{dx} \cdot x = 0 \\ x \geqslant 0 \end{array}\right\} \tag{10.16}$$

In the case of a minimum, for a boundary point to be optimal the function must be downward sloping at the boundary (i.e. decreasing with increasing x).

So far we have examined cases in which x was restricted to non-negative values.

Conceivably, situations may arise in which it would be convenient to formulate a problem such that x was restricted to non-positive values. In this case necessary conditions for a maximum of $F(x)$ in the permitted range of values of x are:

$$\left.\begin{aligned} &\frac{\mathrm{d}F(x)}{\mathrm{d}x} \geqslant 0 \\ &x \cdot \frac{\mathrm{d}F(x)}{\mathrm{d}x} = 0 \\ &x \leqslant 0 \end{aligned}\right\} \tag{10.17}$$

Conditions (10.18) are necessary for a minimum of $F(x)$ for non-positive values of x.

$$\left.\begin{aligned} &\frac{\mathrm{d}F(x)}{\mathrm{d}x} \leqslant 0 \\ &x \cdot \frac{\mathrm{d}F(x)}{\mathrm{d}x} = 0 \\ &x \leqslant 0 \end{aligned}\right\} \tag{10.18}$$

The reader may find it instructive to check conditions (10.17) and (10.18) by constructing diagrams of the type shown in Figures 10.1 and 10.2.

The conditions set out above can be readily extended to cases where the lower or upper bound on x is not zero. For instance, suppose that it is required that x be not less than some specified value x min. The conditions for a maximum subject to this requirement are

$$\left.\begin{aligned} &\frac{\mathrm{d}F(x)}{\mathrm{d}x} \leqslant 0 \\ &(x - x\ \mathrm{min}) \cdot \frac{\mathrm{d}F(x)}{\mathrm{d}x} = 0 \\ &x - x\ \mathrm{min} \geqslant 0 \end{aligned}\right\} \tag{10.19}$$

Now consider the extension of the results to the case of a function of two variables.

Suppose first that we wish to find an unconstrained maximum of the function:

$$F = F(x_1, x_2) \tag{10.20}$$

Consider the function of Figure 10.3. The function takes on its maximum value at the point $(\bar{x}_1, \bar{x}_2)$. In the case illustrated in the figure the problem is akin to finding the coordinates of the highest point of a hill. Interpret the value of x_2 as the distance moved in a northerly direction (from an arbitrary origin or starting point) and the value of x_1 as the distance travelled eastwards from the origin. The value of F corresponds to the height of the hill. Obviously at the highest point the hill must have zero slope in both the northerly and eastwards directions otherwise it would be possible to gain height by moving north (or south) or/and east (or west).

Let the slope in the northerly (x_2) direction be represented by $\partial F/\partial x_2$ and the

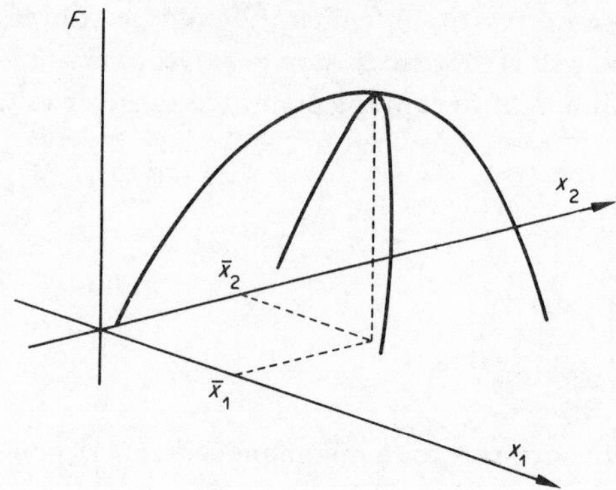

Figure 10.3 Maximization: a function of two variables

slope in the x_1 direction be represented by $\partial F/\partial x_1$. These slopes are called the *partial derivatives* of the function and are the rate of change of the function in the *fundamental directions*. Thus $\partial F/\partial x_2$ is the slope in the x_2 direction, there being no change in the value of x_1 and in the case of $\partial F/\partial x_1$ we consider the slope in the x_1 direction allowing no change in x_2. Now, for a small change in x_1, of amount Δx, and with no change in the value of x_2 the change in $F, \Delta F$, is approximately slope (at the point from which movement starts) times distance moved. That is:

$$\Delta F \simeq \frac{\partial F}{\partial x_1} \Delta x_1 \tag{10.21}$$

Similarly for a small movement x_2 in the x_2 direction alone we can write:

$$\Delta F \simeq \frac{\partial F}{\partial x_2} \Delta x_2 \tag{10.22}$$

and for small movements in both directions at once:[4]

$$\Delta F \simeq \frac{\partial F}{\partial x_1} \Delta x_1 + \frac{\partial F}{\partial x_2} \Delta x_2 \tag{10.23}$$

Now the expression:

$$\mathrm{d}F = \frac{\partial F}{\partial x_1} \mathrm{d}x_1 + \frac{\partial F}{\partial x_2} \mathrm{d}x_2 \tag{10.24}$$

is called the total differential of F. Revealingly, $\mathrm{d}F$ is sometimes called the *principal part* of ΔF. In (10.24) $\mathrm{d}x_1$ and $\mathrm{d}x_2$ are called the differentials of x_1 and x_2 respectively and may be of arbitrary size (i.e. they need not be small). In general $\mathrm{d}F \neq \Delta F$. however if $\Delta x = \mathrm{d}x$ and $\Delta y = \mathrm{d}y$ are small then $\mathrm{d}F$ will be a 'close' approximation to ΔF. The partial derivatives give both the slopes of the surface in the fundamental directions and the slopes of the *tangent plane* in these directions. Thus $\mathrm{d}F$ is the increment in height of the tangent plane for arbitrary $\mathrm{d}x_1$ and $\mathrm{d}x_2$. For a function to have a stationary value at a point $\mathrm{d}F$ must be zero for arbitrary $\mathrm{d}x_1$ and $\mathrm{d}x_2$. In other words the principal part of ΔF must be zero at such a point.

As regards the 'mechanics' of partial differentiation, when differentiating partially with respect to one variable, all terms and parts of terms in other variables are treated as constants – they 'come down into' the derivative just as a constant would. Consider an example. Suppose that

$$F = 128x_1 + 84x_2 + 5x_1x_2 - 7x_1^2 - 9x_2^2$$

then

$$\frac{\partial F}{\partial x_1} = 128 + 5x_2 - 14x_1$$

and

$$\frac{\partial F}{\partial x_2} = 84 + 5x_1 - 18x_2$$

The function F takes a stationary value when these two partial derivatives are equal to zero. The reader may verify that this is the case for $x_1 = 12$ and $x_2 = 8$. The character of the stationary value may be determined by reference to higher order derivatives (which we shall not go into here). However, if we happened to know by some other means that the function F was *concave* in the neighbourhood of a point satisfying first order conditions we should know that a local maximum had been obtained at that point. Intuitively a surface (or in general a hypersurface) is concave in a region if a straight line joining any two points (on the surface above the region) lies on or below the surface.[5] Obviously, if a function happens to be everywhere concave then first order conditions will be sufficient. The functions that we deal with in this chapter will everywhere be concave functions.

Thus to summarize, if an unconstrained maximum of $F(x_1, x_2)$ is sought then first order conditions are:

$$\frac{\partial F}{\partial x_1} = 0 \quad \text{and} \quad \frac{\partial F}{\partial x_2} = 0 \tag{10.25}$$

which are necessary conditions in general, but are both necessary and sufficient if $F(x_1, x_2)$ is generally concave.[6]

Now consider the problem of maximizing $F(x_1, x_2)$ subject to the sign requirements $x_1 \geqslant 0$ and $x_2 \geqslant 0$. It turns out that first order conditions are what would seem the obvious generalization of the conditions (10.16) in the case of a function of a single variable. They may be stated as:

$$\left.\begin{array}{ll} \text{(i)} & \dfrac{\partial F}{\partial x_1} \leqslant 0 \\[2ex] \text{(ii)} & \dfrac{\partial F}{\partial x_2} \leqslant 0 \\[2ex] \text{(iii)} & x_1 \cdot \dfrac{\partial F}{\partial x_1} + x_2 \dfrac{\partial F}{\partial x_2} = 0 \\[2ex] \text{(iv)} & x_1 \geqslant 0 \\ & x_2 \geqslant 0 \end{array}\right\} \tag{10.26}$$

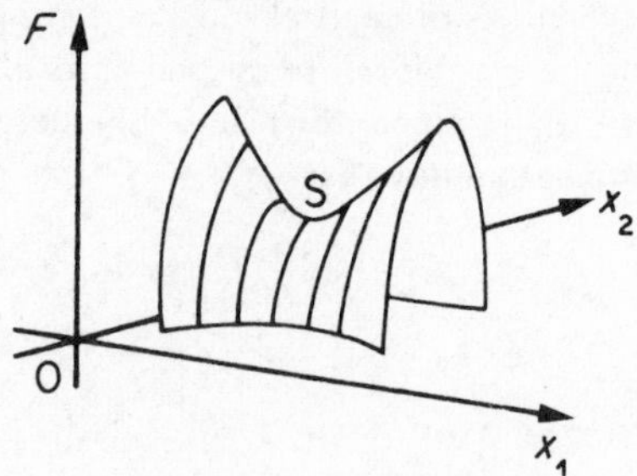

Figure 10.4 Saddle point

(i) and (ii) state that both first order *partial derivatives* have to be non-positive. Condition (iii), taken in conjunction with (i), (ii) and (iv) means that both $x_1 . (\partial F/\partial x_1)$ and $x_2 (\partial F/\partial x_2) = 0$; since neither of these terms can be positive, in order for the sum to be zero each individual term must be zero. For a minimum of F subject to the same sign requirements the directions of the weak inequalities in (i) and (ii) are reversed.

On occasion it may be desired to find a *saddle point* of a function such as F. This is a maximum with respect to one variable and a minimum with respect to the other. The descriptive term 'saddle-point' is apropos since the graph of the function near such a point has the appearance of a saddle. This is illustrated in Figure 10.4 in which the Function $F(x_1, x_2)$ has, at the saddle point S, a maximum in the x_2 direction and a minimum in the x_1 direction.

For a maximum in the x_2 direction and a minimum in the x_1 direction subject to the sign requirements necessary conditions are:

$$\left.\begin{aligned} \frac{\partial F}{\partial x_1} &\geqslant 0 \\ x_1 \frac{\partial F}{\partial x_1} &= 0 \\ x_1 &\geqslant 0 \\ \frac{\partial F}{\partial x_2} &= 0 \\ x_2 \frac{\partial F}{\partial x_2} &= 0 \\ x_2 &\geqslant 0 \end{aligned}\right\} \qquad (10.27)$$

Note that in this case there is no convenient summarizing as was possible with (10.26) (ii) of the requirement that the product of the level of each variable and the corresponding partial derivative be zero. The reader may find it instructive to write down necessary conditions for maxima, minima and saddle points when one or both of the variables is required to be non-positive or has a non-zero lower bound.

Now consider the case where there are constraints in addition to sign requirements. Suppose that the values of x_1 and x_2 chosen must satisfy the requirements that $g(x_1, x_2) \leqslant b$, where $g(x_1, x_2)$ has continuous first order partial derivatives and b is a constant. The full problem with sign requirements is:

$$\left.\begin{array}{ll} \text{maximize } F = F(x_1, x_2) & \\ \text{subject to } g(x_1, x_2) \leqslant b & \\ \text{and} \qquad x_1 \geqslant 0, x_2 \geqslant 0 & \end{array}\right\} \tag{10.28}$$

necessary conditions are obtained by formulating the *Lagrangian function, L*, where L is given by

$$L = F(x_1, x_2) + y(b - g(x_1, x_2)) \tag{10.29}$$

and y is the *Lagrange multiplier*. It turns out that a maximum of F subject to the constraint and the sign requirements occurs when a saddle point of L is found such that the value of L is a maximum in both the x_1 and x_2 directions and a *minimum* in the y direction.[7] Treating y in the same way as the xs we wish to find a saddle point of $L = L(x_1, x_2, y)$ for $x_1 \geqslant 0$, $x_2 \geqslant 0$ and $y \geqslant 0$. The problem of maximizing F subject to a constraint and sign requirements has been transformed into one of finding a saddle point of L, a function of three variables subject only to sign requirements. An intuitive notion of why this procedure works can be developed once optimality conditions have been set out. The first order conditions are:

$$\left.\begin{array}{l} \dfrac{\partial L}{\partial x_1} = \dfrac{\partial F}{\partial x_1} - y\dfrac{\partial g}{\partial x_1} \leqslant 0 \\[2ex] \dfrac{\partial L}{\partial x_2} = \dfrac{\partial F}{\partial x_2} - y\dfrac{\partial g}{\partial x_2} \leqslant 0 \\[2ex] x_1 \dfrac{\partial L}{\partial x_1} + x_2 \dfrac{\partial L}{\partial x_2} = 0 \\[2ex] x_1 \geqslant 0 \\[1ex] x_2 \geqslant 0 \\[1ex] \dfrac{\partial L}{\partial y} = b - g(x_1, x_2) \quad 0 \\[2ex] y \dfrac{\partial L}{\partial y} = 0 \\[2ex] y \geqslant 0 \end{array}\right\} \tag{10.30}$$

The derivative with respect to the Lagrange multiplier is the statement of the constraint itself so that provided the constraint is incorporated in the Lagrangian as in (10.29) and a minimum of the function with respect to the multiplier is sought, the conditions (10.30) known as the *Kuhn–Tucker conditions*, guarantee that the values of x_1 and x_2 chosen will satisfy the constraint. The Kuhn – Tucker conditions characterize local maxima of F subject to the constraint and the sign requirements. If the objective function satisfies a condition (is concave) and the constraint is convex and provided that a *constraint qualification* condition is met the Kuhn – Tucker conditions are both necessary and sufficient for local maximum of F.[8]

The conditions are easily extended to the case of a function of n variables subject to m constraints. Each constraint is included in the Lagrangian as in (10.19) so that there will be m multipliers required. We shall conclude this section with consideration of a more involved example but for the moment let us consider the special case of the application of the Kuhn – Tucker conditions in the linear programming case.

The 2 x 2 L.P. problem can be stated as:

$$\begin{aligned} &\text{maximize } \pi = \pi_1 x_1 + \pi_2 x_2 \\ &\text{subject to} \quad a_{11}x_1 + a_{12}x_2 \leqslant b_1 \\ &\qquad\qquad\quad a_{21}x_1 + a_{22}x_2 \leqslant b_2 \\ &\qquad\qquad\qquad x_1 \geqslant 0, x_2 \geqslant 0 \end{aligned}$$

The Lagrangian is:

$$L = \pi_1 x_1 + \pi_2 x_2 + y_1(b_1 - a_{11}x_1 - a_{12}x_2) + y_2(b_2 - a_{21}x_1 - a_{22}x_2)$$

and the Kuhn–Tucker conditions are:

$$\left.\begin{aligned} &\frac{\partial L}{\partial x_1} = \pi_1 - a_{11}y_1 - a_{21}y_2 \leqslant 0 \\ &\frac{\partial L}{\partial x_2} = \pi_2 - a_{12}y_1 - a_{22}y_2 \leqslant 0 \\ &x_1 \frac{\partial L}{\partial x_1} + x_2 \frac{\partial L}{\partial x_2} = 0 \\ &x_1 \geqslant 0 \\ &x_2 \geqslant 0 \\ &\frac{\partial L}{\partial y_1} = b_1 - a_{11}x_1 - a_{12}x_2 \geqslant 0 \\ &\frac{\partial L}{\partial y_2} = b_2 - a_{21}x_1 - a_{22}x_2 \geqslant 0 \\ &y_1 \frac{\partial L}{\partial y_1} + y_2 \frac{\partial L}{\partial y_2} = 0 \\ &y_1 \geqslant 0 \\ &y_2 \geqslant 0 \end{aligned}\right\} \qquad (10.31)$$

Several points will be apparent from the conditions (10.31). Firstly, the derivatives of the Lagrangian with respect to the multipliers are the statements of the primal constraints. Secondly, the derivatives with respect to the primal variables are the statements of the dual constraints; from which it is evident that the multipliers are the dual structural variables – the shadow prices! Thirdly, let us interpret the conditions:

$$x_1 \frac{\partial L}{\partial x_1} + x_2 \frac{\partial L}{\partial x_2} = 0$$

and

$$y_1 \frac{\partial L}{\partial y_1} + y_2 \frac{\partial L}{\partial y_2} = 0$$

As we have seen it is implied that each component of these conditions is zero. Consider

$$y_1 \cdot \frac{\partial L}{\partial y_1} = 0$$

Now it is clear that y_1 can be positive only if $\partial L/\partial y_1 = 0$ that is to say: $a_{11}x_1 + a_{12}x_2 = b_1$ and the first constraint is binding, i.e. $s_1 = 0$, i.e. a resource can only have positive shadow price if there are no unused units of that resource. We could equally well write this condition as:

$$y_1 s_1 = 0$$

By the same process of argument, it follows that

$$y_2 s_2 = 0$$

$$x_1 t_1 = 0$$

$$x_2 t_2 = 0$$

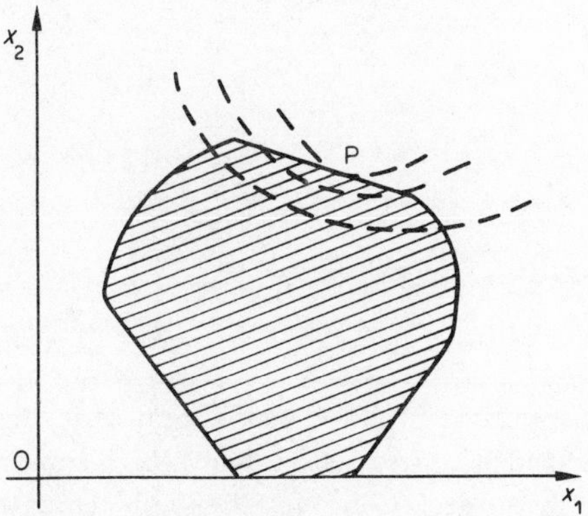

Figure 10.5 A non-linear programming problem

where t_1 and t_2 are the slack variables in the dual constraints. From the last but one condition it emerges that x_1 can only be positive if there is no opportunity loss involved in its 'production'. Similarly for x_2 from the last condition. These conditions, $y_i x_j = 0$ for $i = j$ and $x_j t_i = 0$ for $i = j$ are the *complementary slackness* conditions and the Kuhn – Tucker conditions could be written as:

$$\left.\begin{aligned}
&\frac{\partial L}{\partial x_1} = \pi_1 - a_{11}y_1 - a_{21}y_2 + t_1 = 0 \\
&\frac{\partial L}{\partial x_2} = \pi_2 - a_{12}y_1 - a_{22}y_2 + t_2 = 0 \\
&\frac{\partial L}{\partial y_1} = b_1 - a_{11}x_1 - a_{12}x_2 - s_1 = 0 \\
&\frac{\partial L}{\partial y_2} = b_2 - a_{21}x_1 - a_{22}x_2 - s_2 = 0 \\
&x_1 \geqslant 0 \quad s_1 \geqslant 0 \\
&x_2 \geqslant 0 \quad s_2 \geqslant 0 \\
&y_1 \geqslant 0 \quad t_1 \geqslant 0 \\
&y_2 \geqslant 0 \quad t_2 \geqslant 0 \\
&y_1 s_1 + y_2 s_2 + x_1 t_1 + x_2 t_2 = 0
\end{aligned}\right\} \tag{10.32}$$

Finally note that the Kuhn – Tucker conditions stated as (10.31) or (10.32) mean that a corresponding pair of feasible solutions to the primal and dual problems implies optimality of the primal. If the dual problem is formulated as a Lagrangian and the Kuhn – Tucker conditions are derived it will be seen that these are identical to (10.31) meaning that a pair of feasible solutions to both problems means optimality for both problems. Consider now the non-linear case. The general non-linear programming problem can be stated as:

$$\text{maximize } F(x_1, \ldots x_n)$$

$$\text{subject to: } \left.\begin{aligned}
&g_1(x, \ldots x_n) \leqslant b_1 \\
&\quad \vdots \\
&g_m(x_1, \ldots x_n) \leqslant b_m \\
&x_1 \geqslant 0, \ldots, x_n \geqslant 0
\end{aligned}\right\} \tag{10.33}$$

In the case where $n = 2$ the problem may appear as in Figure 10.5 in which the feasible region is the shaded convex set (all points on a straight line joining any two points in the set are in the set). Contours of the objective function are shown by dashed curves and the optimum solution is (in this case) the boundary point P.

Unlike linear programming an interior optimum is possible in which case all the constraints (including the sign requirements) are satisfied as strict inequalities. In the case of $n = 2$ it may be helpful to think of the problem as one of finding the highest (or lowest in a minimization problem) point in an area of ground corresponding to the feasible area. No generality is lost in formulating the problem as in (10.33) which is one of maximization subject to $\leqslant$ inequalities with all x_j required to be non-negative. If minimization of a function is required the function is simply multiplied by -1 and maximized. Similarly, $\geqslant$ inequalities can be converted to $\leqslant$ inequalities by negation. Variables constrained to be other than non-negative can be transformed to non-negative variables, e.g. if $x_6 \leqslant 10$ define $x_6^* = 10 - x_6$ (so that $x_6^* \geqslant 0$ implies $x_6 \leqslant 10$) and substitute for x_6 in the constraints and objective function. If x_j is unrestricted it can be expressed as the difference between two non-negative variables $x_j^* - \hat{x}_j$. Thus in the constraints and the objective function the unrestricted variable x_j would be replaced by $x_j^* - \hat{x}_j$ where $x_j^* \geqslant 0$ and $\hat{x}_j \geqslant 0$. If $x_j^* > \hat{x}_j$ than this corresponds to $x_j > 0$. Conversely if $x_j^* < \hat{x}_j$ then $x_j < 0$. Finally an equality constraint

$$g_i(x_1, \ldots, x_n) = b_i \tag{10.34}$$

can be replaced by the two constraints

$$g_i(x_i, \ldots, x_n) \leqslant b_i \text{ and } -g_i(x_1, \ldots, x_n) \leqslant -b_i$$

which can only be satisfied simultaneously if (10.34) holds.

Thus in the general non-linear case the Lagrangian function is:

$$L = F(x_1, \ldots, x_n) + \sum_{i=1}^{m} y_i(b_i - g_i(x_1, \ldots x_n))$$

and the Kuhn–Tucker conditions are:[9] (10.35)

$$\left.\begin{aligned}
&\frac{\partial L}{\partial x_j} = \frac{\partial F}{\partial x_j} - \sum_{i=1}^{m} y_i \frac{\partial g}{\partial x_j} \leqslant 0 && (j = 1, 2, \ldots n)\\
&\sum_{j=1}^{n} x_j \frac{\partial L}{\partial x_j} = 0 &&\\
&x_j \geqslant 0 && (j = 1, 2, \ldots n)\\
&\frac{\partial L}{\partial y_i} = b_i - g_i(x_i, \ldots x_n) \geqslant 0 && (i = 1, 2, \ldots m)\\
&\sum_{i=1}^{m} y_i \frac{\partial L}{\partial y_i} = 0 &&\\
&y_i \geqslant 0 && (i = 1, 2, \ldots m)
\end{aligned}\right\} \tag{10.36}$$

In the non-linear programming case the 'economic' interpretation of the Lagrange multipliers is awkward and not so useful as in the linear programming case. In an article in 1967 Balinski and Baumol expressed the position well.[10] 'The specification, interpretation and uses of the dual problem corresponding to any linear programme are well known and well documented in the literature. Among economists it is, however, not widely known that duals can be paired with *non-linear* programming problems and that many of the duality relationships which hold in linear programming continue to hold for certain classes of non-linear programmes. Specifically, if the entire primal problem is characterized by diminishing returns then many of the standard duality properties retain their validity, though certain symmetries of the linear case are lost.'

Later in the chapter we shall examine a non-linear programming problem in which a quadratic objective function is minimized subject to linear constraints. The objective function employed will be concave (thus exhibiting 'diminishing returns' and we shall see that useful sensitivity analysis may be carried out.

An important point remains to be made in connection with the primal problem. It was not a difficult matter to obtain the conditions (10.36) that correspond to a saddle point of (10.35) and thus a local maximum of $F(x_1, \ldots, x_n)$ subject to the constraints $g_i(x_1 \ldots x_n)$ but whilst the Kuhn–Tucker conditions characterize optimal solutions it does not follow that once these conditions have been set out the solution is almost at hand.

This fact can be seen even in the linear case where the Kuhn–Tucker conditions are the primal and dual constraints plus complementary slackness conditions and sign requirements. A solution to these conditions has still to be found by the simplex method or otherwise. This state of affairs is the case *a fortiori* in non-linear problems for which there are a great many computational approaches, both exact and approximate. In this chapter we shall detail only one of the several quadratic programming algorithms that are available, otherwise confining the discussion to descriptive form or to generalities. Before turning to some particular classes of non-linear problems we shall consider some simpler cases in which non-linearities arise in investment problems outside of a programming context.

10.3 Size of Investment

Even when there is only one investment opportunity there can be problems of non-linearity. In chapter one when NPV and NTV methods were discussed, the scale of each project was considered fixed. There will, however, be occasions when it may be possible to invest in several units of the same project. The problem of choosing the optimum number of units to invest in is not trivial if the initial outlay and receipts in each period are not linear functions of the number of units obtained, even if there is no constraint on total expenditure.

Consider a continuously divisible project X which yields returns at the end of each of two years. Let x represent the number of units of X and let $R_1(x)$, $R_2(x)$, $K(x)$ represent the receipts and the initial outlay as functions of x. Thus, with a uniform discount of $100i\%$, NTV for any value of x is given by

$$\text{NTV} = (1+i)R_1(x) + R_2(x) - (1+i)^2 K(x) \tag{10.37}$$

which is to be maximized. Assuming $R_1(x)$, $R_2(x)$, and $K(x)$ to be differentiable functions, we require the first derivative of NTV with respect to x to be zero. That is:

$$(1 + i)R_1'(x) + R_2'(x) = (1 + i)^2 K'(x) \tag{10.38}$$

where $R_1'(x)$, $R_2'(x)$, and $K'(x)$ are the derivatives of $R_1(x)$, $R(x)$, and $K(x)$ with respect to x. Verbally, (10.38) represents the equation of *marginal terminal revenue* (MTR) with *marginal terminal cost* (MTC). MTR is the left-hand-side of (10.38) and is (approximately) the addition to revenue at the end of the project caused by the purchase of an extra unit of X now. MTC, the right-hand side of (10.38) is (approximately) what would be the terminal value of the cost (incurred at the present) or an extra unit of X. Of course the derivative of (10.37) gives the rate of change of net terminal value at a point – that is for a particular value of x. The approximate statements above, corresponding to finite increments in x are 'good' approximations in general, only when the increment in x is 'small'.

Now the first order condition expressed as (10.38) applies to any stationary value of (10.37). To ensure a maximum it is further required that MTC be increasing faster (or decreasing less rapidly) than MTR. This is a sufficient second-order condition, and can be stated formally as:

$$(1 + i)^2 K''(x) > (1 + i)R_1''(x) + R_2''(x) \tag{10.39}$$

where $K''(x)$, $R_1''(x)$ and $R_2''(x)$ are the second derivatives of $K(x)$, $R_1(x)$, and $R_2(x)$ with respect to x.

In general, several values of x may satisfy both the first and the second-order conditions and from among these the best value giving the global optimum may usually be determined by evaluating (10.37) for each value of x satisfying both (10.38) and (10.39). If only whole-number values of x are meaningful then (10.37) should be evaluated for the whole numbers immediately above and below each fractional value of x that satisfies (10.38) and (10.39). In the absence of constraints on the values that x may take, the integral optimum must be 'next to' one of the 'fractional' maxima (assuming that the local optima are not themselves integral). However, it should be pointed out that the global integral optimum is not necessarily a rounding off of the global fractional optimum.

10.4 Product Pricing and Terminal Values

In some circumstances terminal value methods can give useful information to help solve the problem of product pricing. This fact is perhaps best illustrated by way of an example. Consider the case of a firm interested in the possible introduction of new capital equipment. Suppose for simplicity that the project has no external effects – for example, reduction in profitability of other investments – and that it would be financed entirely from the firm's own funds which otherwise would have been invested in the capital market (say) at $100i\%$. If the available funds are L and the cost of the equipment which lasts for n years is K, then the NTV of the investment is given by

$$\text{NTV} = \sum_{h=0}^{n} R_h(1 + i)^{n-h} - L(1 + i)^n \tag{10.40}$$

where $R_0 = L - K$. The remaining returns

$$R_1, \ldots, R_n$$

are after-tax profits. Suppose that tax is at a flat rate of $100t$% then expressing revenue each year as pq_h (price times quantity sold in the hth year) and costs each year as c_h, then the post-tax return in the hth year is given by:

$$R_h = (1 - t)(p_h q_h - c_h) \tag{10.41}$$

Now the quantity that can be sold in any year, let us suppose, is a function of price alone and costs of production are a function of quantity produced in that year (equals quantity sold, here) which is in turn a function or price. Consequently if the relation between price and quantity (the product demand curve) is known, the only unknown in (10.40) is price, so that NTV can be maximized with respect to price, or set to some particular value and solved for price. This latter approach could be useful in respect of the problem of the pricing of certain public utilities – with 'profit' margins predetermined and demand estimates already made.

For a numerical example, consider a machine with a two-year life-time to be used to produce a single product in quantities q_1 and q_2 (as yet undetermined) in each of the two years and sold at prices of p_1 and p_2 respectively. The demand conditions in each year are given by

$$q_1 = 100 - p_1 \quad \text{and} \quad q_2 = 300 - 4p_2 \tag{10.42}$$

Cost of production in each year are given by

$$c_1 = 20 + 2q_1 \quad \text{and} \quad c_2 = 10 + 3q_2 \tag{10.43}$$

Profits are taxed at the flat rate of 40% each year, and the purchase price of the machine is £2,800. An interest rate of 10% is appropriate for the calculations throughout, and the investor wishes to determine the prices to charge in each period so as to maximise the NTV of the investment. Substitution of (10.41) into (10.40) for $t = 0.4$ and $i = 0.1$ gives:

$$\text{NTV} = -2{,}800(1.1)^2 + (1 - 0.4)(p_1 q_1 - c_1)(1.1) + (1 - 0.4)(p_2 q_2 - c_2) \tag{10.44}$$

in which the terms in L have cancelled out due to the uniform interest rate. Now (10.44) can be written in terms of the prices alone as

$$\text{NTV} = -2{,}800(1.1)^2 + 0.6(1.1)(102p_1 - p_1^2 - 220) + 0.6(312p_2 - 4p_2^2 - 910) \tag{10.45}$$

since (10.42) gives the relationships between prices and quantities and substitution of these expressions into (10.34) gives $c_1 = 220 - 2p_1$ and $c_2 = 910 - 12p_2$.

Necessary conditions for a maximum of NTV with respect to the prices p_1 and p_2 are by differentiation of (10.45).

$$\left.\begin{aligned} 0.66(102 - 2p_1) &= \frac{\partial \text{NTV}}{\partial p_1} = 0 \\ \text{and} \\ 0.6(312 - 8p_2) &= \frac{\partial \text{NTV}}{\partial p_2} = 0 \end{aligned}\right\} \tag{10.46}$$

Therefore, the only turning point (which can be shown to be a maximum) is at

$$p_1 = 51, \quad p_2 = 39$$

thus:

$$q_1 = 49, \quad q_2 = 144 \text{ and NTV} = 1{,}287.86$$

Thus the project is worthwhile, and appropriate prices and corresponding quantities are determined.

In a more general context, for example, where the demand conditions in any one period depend on prices charged and quantities sold in other periods, if forecasts are revised and interest rates and cost structures change over time, then at any moment of time corrections are possible to the calculated optimum prices and quantities for future periods. That is, calculations of optimal prices and quantities from time t onwards can be 'updated' in the light of the changed interest rates and cost conditions that might apply beyond t.

The model developed in this section, with the objective function being a quadratic function of the decision variables, can be used as the lead-in to a quadratic programming investment problem. This will now be developed.

10.5 A Quadratic Programming Investment Model

Suppose that a firm faces the following investment problem.

$$\left.\begin{aligned} &\text{maximize } N = N_1(x_1) + N_2(x_2) \\ &\text{subject to} \quad a_{11}x_1 + a_{12}x_2 \leqslant b_1 \\ &\qquad\qquad\quad a_{21}x_1 + a_{22}x_2 \leqslant b_2 \quad x_1 \geqslant 0, x_2 \geqslant 0 \end{aligned}\right\} \tag{10.47}$$

In (10.47) x_1 and x_2 represent the amounts taken of two investments. The constraints are linear and may be thought of as corresponding to the consumption of physical resources. The objective function is however, non-linear. The term $N_1(x_1)$ represents the net present value resulting from accepting x_1 units of the first investment and similarly $N_2(x_2)$ implies that present value from the second investment is a function of the amount taken of that investment alone. Thus there is assumed to be no interdependence between the investments so far as the objective function is concerned. The function N is said to be separable and additive. The xs are related only by the consumption of scarce resources.

Let us now see how the functions $N_1(x_1)$ and $N_2(x_2)$ are obtained in this case.

The net present values from the two investments can be written in familiar form as:

$$N_1 = R_{1t}(1+i)^{-t} - K_1 \quad \text{and} \quad N_2 = R_{2t}(1+i)^{-t} - K_2 \tag{10.48}$$

Consider the case of the x_1 project in particular. The project returns are given by:

$$R_{1t} = I_{1t} - c_{1t} \tag{10.49}$$

where I_{1t} is income in period t and c_{1t} is variable costs in period t. Now suppose that x_1 represents machinery and b_1 and b_2 in the constraints represent manpower and materials all being combined to produce an output q_1. Now $I_{1t} = p_{1t}q_{1t}$ and $c_{1t} = c_1(q_{1t})$. If, as in the previous case, selling price of q_1 is linearly related to volume this can be written as:

$$p_{1t} = a_{1t} - b_{1t}q_{1t} \tag{10.50}$$

where the parameters of the relationship may differ from year to year. Suppose variable costs are given by

$$c_{1t} = g_{1t}q_{1t} + h_{1t}q_{1t}^2 \tag{10.51}$$

where g_{1t} and h_{1t} are positive constants. Substitution of (10.51) into (10.49) and since $I_{1t} = p_{1t}q_{1t}$ where p_{1t} is defined by (10.50) the expression for R_{1t} becomes:

$$(a_{1t} - g_{1t})q_{1t} - (b_{1t} + h_{1t})q_{1t}^2 \tag{10.52}$$

Now let output in each year, q_{1t}, be proportional to the number of units of investment taken, where the factor of proportionality, m_{1t} may vary from year to year thus:

$$q_{1t} = m_{1t}x_1 \tag{10.53}$$

If the initial outlay is given by

$$K_1 = e_1x_1 + f_1x_2 \tag{10.54}$$

where e_1 and f_1 are constants we can now write $N_1(x_1)$ as:

$$N_1(x_1) = A_1x_1 - B_1x_1^2 \tag{10.55}$$

where

$$A_1 = \sum_t (a_{1t} - g_{1t})m_{1t}(1+i)^{-t} - e_1$$

and

$$B_1 = \sum_t (b_{1t} + h_{1t})m_{1t}^2(1+i)^{-t} + f_1$$

It will now be assumed that both A_1 and B_1 are positive numbers.

If production, demand, cost and outlay conditions are similar for investment x_2 the objective function becomes

$$N = A_1x_1 - B_1x_1^2 + A_2x_2 - B_2x_2^2 \tag{10.56}$$

Equation (10.56) is to be maximized subject to the constraints and sign requirements. Now set the problem up in Lagrangian form and establish the Kuhn–Tucker conditions. The Lagrangian is:

$$\begin{aligned} L = A_1x_1 - B_1x_1^2 + A_2x_2 - B_2x_2^2 + y_1(b_1 - a_{11}x_1 - a_{12}x_2) \\ + y_2(b_2 - a_{21}x_1 - a_{22}x_2) \end{aligned} \tag{10.57}$$

and the Kuhn–Tucker conditions are:

$$\left.\begin{aligned} &\frac{\partial L}{\partial x_1} = A_1 - 2B_1x_1 - a_{11}y_1 - a_{21}y_2 + t_1 = 0 \\ &\frac{\partial L}{\partial x_2} = A_2 - 2B_2x_2 - a_{12}y_1 - a_{22}y_2 + t_2 = 0 \\ &x_1t_1 = 0 \\ &x_2t_2 = 0 \\ &\quad x_1 \geqslant 0 \quad t_1 \geqslant 0 \\ &\quad x_2 \geqslant 0 \quad t_2 \geqslant 0 \\ &\frac{\partial L}{\partial y_1} = b_1 - a_{11}x_1 - a_{12}x_2 - s_1 = 0 \\ &\frac{\partial L}{\partial y_2} = b_2 - a_{21}x_1 - a_{22}x_2 - s_2 = 0 \\ &y_1s_1 = 0 \\ &y_2s_2 = 0 \\ &\quad y_1 \geqslant 0 \quad s_1 \geqslant 0 \\ &\quad y_2 \geqslant 0 \quad s_2 \geqslant 0 \end{aligned}\right\} \tag{10.58}$$

The Kuhn – Tucker conditions have been expressed in complementary slackness form since this will prove to be more convenient from the computational viewpoint. The crucial point about conditions (10.58) is that, apart from the complementary slackness requirements, they are *linear*. The constraint set is convex and the objective function is strictly concave so that a feasible solution to (10.58) will produce the global maximum value of N; indeed there will be only one set of values of the xs, ss and ys that satisfy (10.58) and this will be optimal.

The question now is: how is a feasible solution to (10.58) to be found? The answer is that a variation of the simplex method in linear programming can be employed. The original objective function (10.56) is not employed. Instead a substitute objective function (or, as we shall see two substitute objective functions) is employed such that the optimal solution to the new problem gives a feasible solution to (10.58) and hence an optimal solution to the original problem. The algorithm that will be described here is a modified version of Wolfe's simplex method for quadratic programming.[11] The procedure is best explained in the context of an example.

Let the problem be to:

$$\left.\begin{aligned} \text{maximize} \quad & N = 40x_1 + 60x_2 - x_1^2 - 2x_2^2 \\ \text{subject to} \quad & 5x_1 + 4x_2 \leqslant 120 \\ & 10x_1 + x_2 \leqslant 140 \\ & x_1 \geqslant 0, \quad x_2 \geqslant 0 \end{aligned}\right\} \tag{10.59}$$

The problem is of the form discussed above with $A_1 = 40$, $A_2 = 60$, $B_1 = 1$ and $B_2 = 2$. The objective function is strictly concave and the constraints form a convex set. The Kuhn – Tucker conditions are necessary and sufficient for an optimal solution. The Lagrangian function [the equivalent of (10.57)] and the Khun–Tucker conditions [corresponding to (10.58)] are

$$L = 40x_1 + 60x_2 - x_1^2 - 2x_2^2 + y_1(120 - 5x_1 - 4x_2) + y_2(140 - 10x_1 - x_2)$$

$$\left.\begin{aligned} \frac{\partial L}{\partial x_1} &= 40 - 2x_1 - 5y_1 - 10y_2 + t_1 = 0 \\ \frac{\partial L}{\partial x_2} &= 60 - 4x_2 - 4y_1 - y_2 + t_2 = 0 \\ & x_1 t_1 + x_2 t_2 = 0 \\ & x_1 \geqslant 0 \quad x_2 \geqslant 0 \\ \frac{\partial L}{\partial y_1} &= 120 - 5x_1 - 4x_2 - s_1 = 0 \\ \frac{\partial L}{\partial y_2} &= 140 - 10x_1 - x_2 - s_2 = 0 \\ & y_1 s_1 + y_2 s_2 = 0 \\ & y \geqslant 0 \quad y_2 \geqslant 0 \end{aligned}\right\} \tag{10.60}$$

The procedure begins by re-expressing the constraints corresponding to the partial derivatives in (10.60) so that the constant terms are on the R.H.S. and adding in artificial variables (since we are dealing with equality constraints). We then have:

$$\left.\begin{aligned} 2x_1 + 5y_1 + 10y_2 - t_1 + u_1 &= 40 \\ 4x_2 + 4y_1 + y_2 - t_2 + u_2 &= 60 \\ 5x_1 + 4x_2 + s_1 + u_3 &= 120 \\ 10x_1 + x_2 + s_2 + u_4 &= 140 \end{aligned}\right\} \tag{10.61}$$

For the objective function, coefficients of -1 are attached to the artificial variables and zero for all other variables. The objective function is then maximized. The maximum value of this objective function will be zero and this will be taken when the artificial variables have been removed from the basis – in other words when a feasible solution has been found to (10.60) provided that the complementary slackness conditions are observed. This solution will, as we have seen, be the optimal solution to the original problem. The non-linear complementary slackness conditions are observed during the calculations by making sure that the xs and ts and also the ys and ss do not enter a solution simultaneously. Thus if x_2 was in the solution at some stage t_2 would not be introduced even if it had the 'most negative' index row number; some other variable with a negative index row number would be brought in.

Now it turns out to be convenient to tackle the calculation in two stages. In stage one only u_3 and u_4 are given -1 coefficients and only the xs are permitted to replace us in the basis. In stage two, in which u_3 and u_4 have been driven out of the basis -1 coefficients are attached to u_1 and u_2 and the ys and the ss may now enter subject to the complementary slackness provisions. It should be noted that if it was not possible for the xs alone to replace u_3 and u_4 there would be no feasible solution to the original constraints in which both xs were positive. Such a circumstance would violate the 'constraint qualification' condition that was referred to earlier on.

The calculations of stage one are shown in Figure 10.6. For clarity no index row numbers are shown under the variables that are not permitted to enter the basis in this phase. Otherwise the usual simplex procedure is applied and pivotal elements are circled. The calculation is not quite as tedious as might seem from the size of the tableau since whole rows or columns of rates of exchange (corresponding to zero pivotal column or main row numbers) remain unchanged from one basis to the next.

The stage two calculations are shown in Figure 10.7 in which it will be seen that the u_3 and u_4 columns are deleted. It turns out that in this problem there is never a 'clash' between corresponding pairs in the complementary slackness conditions, but as we have seen this would not have caused difficulty. The optimal solution to the quadratic programming problem (10.59) is to set $x_1 = 88/7, x_2 = 100/7$ and $s_1 = 0$ and $s_2 = 0$ giving a value of $N = 38{,}896/49$.

What interpretations may be made of the optimal solution – in particular what is the significance of the optimal values of the Lagrange multipliers and what sensitivity analysis can be accomplished at reasonable computational expense?

Firstly, consider sensitivity analysis. In the last array of Figure 10.7 the inverse of the basis can be obtained from the last four columns of ıates of exchange. In the original tableau (Figure 10.6) the four columns under the artificial variables in the first array form an identity matrix. Now u_3 and u_4 were deleted in phase two of the calculation but it will be noted that the columns of coefficients under s_1 and s_2 are identical to those under u_3 and u_4. Therefore the columns of rates of exchange under u_1, u_2, s_1, s_2 respectively, form the inverse of the basis. That is to say, the optimal values of the solution variables can be expressed as:

$$\begin{pmatrix} y_2 \\ y_1 \\ x_2 \\ x_1 \end{pmatrix} = \frac{1}{49}\begin{pmatrix} 5.6 & -7 & 8.32 & -5.28 \\ -1.4 & 14 & -16.08 & 8.32 \\ 0 & 0 & 14 & -7 \\ 0 & 0 & -1.4 & 5.6 \end{pmatrix}\begin{pmatrix} 40 \\ 60 \\ 120 \\ 140 \end{pmatrix} = \frac{1}{49}\begin{pmatrix} 63.2 \\ 19.2 \\ 700 \\ 616 \end{pmatrix} \tag{10.62}$$

			0	0	0	0	0	0	0	0	0	0	−1	−1
			x_1	x_2	y_1	y_2	t_1	t_2	S_1	S_2	u_1	u_2	u_3	u_4
0	u_1	40	2	0	5	10	−1	0	0	0	1	0	0	0
0	u_2	60	0	4	4	1	0	−1	0	0	0	1	0	0
−1	u_3	120	5	4	0	0	0	0	1	0	0	0	1	0
−1	u_4	140	(10)	1	0	0	0	0	0	1	0	0	0	1
		−260	−15	−5										
0	u_1	12	0	−0.2	5	10	−1	0	0	−0.2	1	0	0	−0.2
0	u_2	60	0	4	4	1	0	−1	0	0	0	1	0	0
−1	u_3	50	0	(3.5)	0	0	0	0	1	−0.5	0	0	1	−0.5
0	x_1	14	1	0.1	0	0	0	0	0	0.1	0	0	0	0.1
		−50	0	−3.5										
0	u_1	104/7	0	0	5	10	−1	0	0.4/7	1.6/7	1	0	0.4/7	−1.6/7
0	u_2	20/7	0	0	4	1	0	−1	−8/7	4/7	0	1	−8/7	4/7
0	x_2	100/7	0	1	0	0	0	0	2/7	−1/7	0	0	2/7	−1/7
0	x_1	88/7	1	0	0	0	0	0	−0.2/7	0.8/7	0	0	−0.2/7	0.8/7
		0	0	0							0	0	1	1

Figure 10.6 Quadratic programming: stage one

			0	0	0	0	0	0	0	0	−1	−1
			x_1	x_2	y_1	y_2	t_1	t_2	s_1	s_2	u_1	u_2
−1	u_1	104/7	0	0	5	(10)	−1	0	0.4/7	−1.6/7	1	0
−1	u_2	20/7	0	0	4	1	0	−1	−8/7	4/7	0	1
0	x_2	100/7	0	1	0	0	0	0	2/7	−1/7	0	0
0	x_1	88/7	1	0	0	0	0	0	−0.2/7	−0.8/7	0	0
		−124/7	0	0	−9	−11	1	1	7.6/7	−2.4/7	0	0
0	y_2	10.4/7	0	0	0.5	1	−0.1	0	0.04/7	−0.16/7	0.1	0
−1	u_2	9.6/7	0	0	(3.5)	0	0.1	−1	−8.04/7	4.16/7	−0.1	1
0	x_2	100/7	0	1	0	0	0	0	2/7	−1/7	0	0
0	x_1	88/7	1	0	0	0	0	0	−0.2/7	0.8/7	0	0
		−9.6/7	0	0	−3.5	0	−0.1	1	8.04/7	−4.16/7	0.9	0
0	y_2	63.2/49	0	0	0	1	−0.8/7	1/7	8.32/49	−5.28/49	0.8/7	−1/7
0	y_1	19.2/49	0	0	1	0	0.2/7	−2/7	−16.08/49	8.32/49	−0.2/7	2/7
0	x_2	100/7	0	1	0	0	0	0	2/7	−1/7	0	0
0	x_1	88/7	1	0	0	0	0	0	−0.2/7	0.8/7	0	0
		0	0	0	0	0	0	0	0	0	1	1

Figure 10.7 Quadratic programming: stage two

Consequently the effects of variations in A_1, A_2, b_1 and b_2 (currently at levels 40, 60, 120 and 140 respectively) can be readily determined. The analysis is conducted as for variations in resource levels in linear programming. Note that the optimal values of the xs are functions only of b_1 and b_2. So long as A_1 and A_2 change in such a manner as to leave y_1 and y_2 non-negative the levels of the xs will be unaffected.

What of changes in the resource levels b_1 and b_2? If the objective function had been linear, y_1 and y_2 would have been the shadow prices of the resources and would have shown how much the objective function would change, per unit of change in the resource levels. Our objective function is strictly concave however. The result of this is that y_1 and y_2 represent *upper bounds* on the change in N. The value of y_2 is the rate of change of the constrained maximum of N as b_2 is changed, but this rate of change is itself variable (unlike the linear case 'within' a basis) and is in fact diminishing. This can be seen from the coefficients of b_1 and b_2 for y_1 and y_2 in (10.62). The coefficients are -16.08 and -5.28 respectively. Consequently for any finite increase Δb_2 in b_2 the increase in N, $\Delta N \leqslant \Delta b_2 \cdot y_2$. For instance if 141 units of the second resource were available from (10.62) it will be seen that the new optimal values of the xs are 621.6/49 and 99/7 for x_1 and x_2 respectively; consequently the new optimal value of N is 38,956.56/49 an increase of 60.56/49 which is less than the value of y_2 of 63.2/49. The new value of y_2 corresponding to 141 units of the second resource is seen to be (63.2/49) $-$ (5.28/49) = 57.92/49 which is less than the increase in N, as we should expect.

The reader may verify that a unit increase in the first resource causes N to increase by $11.16/49 < 19.2/49$. In this case the actual change in N is further away from the value of y_1 than was the case for ΔN and y_2 when b_2 increased. Intuitively, this can be seen to be due to the fact that it is x_2 that increases with increasing b_1, and x_2 has a bigger negative coefficient of the quadratic term ($B_2 = -2$) in N and the quadratic term becomes more important as x_2 is increased.

Note that y_2 is an increasing function of b_1, and y_1 is also an increasing function of b_2, i.e. the marginal value of each resource increases as the amount of the other resource increases, the rate of change being the same (8.32/49) in each case. This results from the fact that for 'well-behaved' functions second order cross-partial derivatives (which is what the number 8.32/49 is) are equal. A second order cross-partial derivative of a function is obtained by differentiating the function partially first with respect to one variable then with respect to another. In our case we have:

$$y_1 = \frac{\partial L}{\partial b_1} \quad \text{and} \quad y_2 = \frac{\partial L}{\partial b_2}$$

If now we differentiate y_1 partially with respect to b_2 we obtain:

$$\frac{\partial y_1}{\partial b_2} \equiv \frac{\partial^2 L}{\partial b_2 \partial b_1} \tag{10.63}$$

and differentiating y_2 partially with respect to b_1:

$$\frac{\partial y_2}{\partial b_1} \equiv \frac{\partial^2 L}{\partial b_1 \partial b_2} \tag{10.64}$$

The second order cross-partial derivatives (10.63) and (10.64) will be equal if they are continuous. They are continuous here and are both equal to 8.32/49 at the optimum.

Returning to consideration of the values of y_1 and y_2 themselves, how may these values be used? Given any finite increase in the amount of an individual resource available the product of the increase in resource level and the corresponding Lagrange multiplier gives an upper bound on the change in N, which if exceeded by the additional cost of the resource increment, would be sufficient to reject the resource increase possibility. It is a necessary but clearly not sufficient condition for the acceptance of a resource increment for the cost of the increment to be strictly less than the upper bound on the increase in N.

The effects of variations in the parameters B_1 and B_2 in the objective function are less readily evaluated. A change in B_j affects the 'technical coefficient' in the Kuhn–Tucker constraint corresponding to the partial derivative with respect to x_j. As was seen in Chapter 4, sensitivity analysis for changes in technical coefficients in linear problems can be a long-winded business involving the introduction of an extra column into the tableau and the determination of new rates of exchange for this column. The process is the same in the present case and the description will not be repeated. Thus working with the Kuhn–Tucker conditions changes in the Bs are dealt with as were changes in technical coefficients.

Changes in the Bs are, of course, changes in objective function coefficients of the problem as originally formulated in (10.59). Diagrammatically, what happens is that the slopes of the objective function contours change, and in the case of an optimum at a point of tangency between a contour of the objective function and a constraint, the point of tangency will change. Thus the situation is unlike that in the linear case for changed objective function coefficients. In the linear case such changes meant either remaining at the original basis (with unchanged xs) or moving to a new corner point solution.

Of course, the coefficients A_1, A_2, B_1 and B_2 are arrived at after present value calculations have been made. Changes in the discount rate, length of horizon, future prices and so on will normally cause simultaneous changes in both the A and B coefficients. Consequently sensitivity analysis on (say) the discount rate would be cumbersome. In most cases it would be preferable to solve separate problems for alternative values of the discount rate rather than attempt post-optimality analysis in the usual manner.

The problem structure that we have set out above is useful for economic decision making problems that are not usually thought of as investment problems. The case of the 'multi-product monopolist' would be an example where x_1 and x_2 represent output levels and N represents a profit function for a single time period; in fact our original problem formulation was a generalization of this problem.

10.6 A Quadratic Constraint

In this section we consider the problem of maximizing a linear objective function subject to a set of linear constraints and one quadratic constraint. In general the problem can be expressed as:

$$\left.\begin{array}{lll} \text{maximize} & F = \sum_{j=1}^{n} R_j x_j & \\ \text{subject to:} & \sum_{j=1}^{n} a_{ij} x_j \leqslant b_i & (i = 1, 2, \ldots, m) \\ \text{and} & \sum_{j=1}^{n} d_j x_j + \sum_{h=1}^{n} \sum_{j=1}^{n} d_{hj} x_h x_j \leqslant b_0 & \\ & x_j \geqslant 0 & \end{array}\right\} \tag{10.65}$$

In (1065) the R_j, a_{ij}, d_j, d_{hj}, b_i and b_0 are constants and where at least one of the d_{hj} is non-zero. If $d_{jj} \neq 0$ then the requirements for the zeroth resource by the jth activity is a non-linear function of activity level and if $d_{hj} \neq 0$ there exists interdependency between the zeroth resource consumption by the hth and jth activities. Consider a small-scale example.

A company wishes to choose the amounts to take of two investments subject to a linear initial outlay constraint and a quadratic constraint on consumption of some fixed resource. Suppose that the coefficients of the problem are as in (10.66).

$$\left.\begin{array}{ll} \text{maximize} & F = 7x_1 + 8x_2 \\ \text{subject to} & x_1 + 3x_2 \leqslant 15 \\ \text{and} & 10x_1 + 12x_2 + 0.2x_1^2 + 0.5x_2^2 + 0.6x_1x_2 \leqslant 100 \\ & x_1 \geqslant 0 \quad x_2 \geqslant 0 \end{array}\right\} \tag{10.66}$$

The Lagrangian function and the Kuhn–Tucker conditions would then be:

$$\left.\begin{array}{l} L = 7x_1 + 8x_2 + y_1(15 - x_1 - 3x_2) + y_2(100 - 10x_1 \\ \quad - 12x_2 - 0.2x_1^2 - 0.5x_2^2 - 0.6x_1x_2) \\ \dfrac{\partial L}{\partial x_1} = 7 - y_1 - y_2(10 + 0.4x_1 + 0.6x_2) \leqslant 0 \\ \dfrac{\partial L}{\partial x_2} = 8 - 3y_1 - y_2(12 + x_2 + 0.6x_1) \leqslant 0 \\ x_1 \dfrac{\partial L}{\partial x_1} + x_2 \dfrac{\partial L}{\partial x_2} = 0 \\ x_1 \geqslant 0, \quad x_2 \geqslant 0 \\ \dfrac{\partial L}{\partial y_1} = 15 - x_1 - 3x_2 \geqslant 0 \\ \dfrac{\partial L}{\partial y_2} = 100 - 10x_1 - 12x_2 - 0.2x_1^2 - 0.5x_2^2 - 0.6x_1x_2 \geqslant 0 \\ y_1 \dfrac{\partial L}{\partial y_1} + y_2 \dfrac{\partial L}{\partial y_2} = 0 \\ y_1 \geqslant 0, \quad y_2 \geqslant 0. \end{array}\right\} \tag{10.67}$$

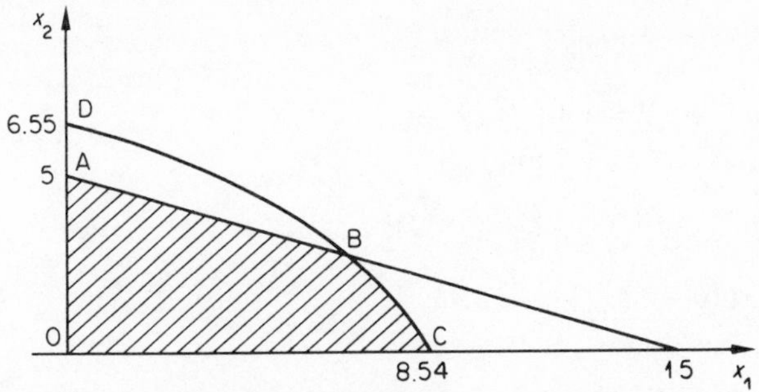

Figure 10.8 Quadratic constraint example

As in all programming problems the Kuhn–Tucker conditions characterize an optimum but as in many cases they are not particularly helpful in finding it. Finding solutions to the conditions of (10.67) is by no means easy even though the problem itself is one in two variables and two constraints only. Where the dimensions of the problem permit, diagrams can be of considerable help. The constraint set in the current problem is graphed in Figure 10.8 where the feasible region is shaded. It will be noted that the feasible region is convex[12] and that since the objective function is linear the optimal solution will be *either* at one of the points OABC *or* a point of tangency between points B and C. The values of x_2 and x_1 at points B and C are obtained by setting x_1 and x_2 (respectively) equal to zero in the quadratic constraint. Now the objective function contours have a slope of −0.875 and are thus steeper (in absolute terms) than the linear constraint. Thus point A will not be optimal. As x_1 increases, the slope (in absolute terms) of the quadratic constraint also increases, so that if the slope of the quadratic constraint at point C is less than the slope of the objective function contours then point C will be optimal. If the slope of the quadratic constraint at point C is greater (again in absolute terms) than the objective function contours, then the optimum will be either at point B or at a point of tangency between B and C.

Now the slope of the objective function contours being linear is easily found to be given by the ratio of the coefficients of x_1 and x_2 in the objective function. It will be noted that these coefficients are the partial derivatives of F with respect to x_1 and x_2. In other words the slope of the objective function contours is minus the ratio of the partial derivatives of the function. The same applies in the case of the quadratic constraint. If the R.H.S. is at the level b_0, then recalling our earlier discussion of differentials:

$$\mathrm{d}b_0 = \frac{\partial b_0}{\partial x_1}\,\mathrm{d}x_1 + \frac{\partial b_0}{\partial x_2}\,\mathrm{d}b_2$$

but along the constraint there must be no change in b_0 therefore $\mathrm{d}b_0 = 0$ and so:

$$\frac{\mathrm{d}x_2}{\mathrm{d}x_1} = -\frac{\dfrac{\partial b_0}{\partial x_1}}{\dfrac{\partial b_0}{\partial x_2}}$$

thus in the present example:

$$\frac{dx_2}{dx_1} = -\frac{(10 + 0.4x_1 + 0.6x_2)}{(12 + x_2 + 0.6x_1)}$$

and at point C, where $x_1 = 0$ and $x_2 = 8.54$

$$\frac{dx_2}{dx_1} = -\frac{(10 + 0.4x_1)}{(12 + 0.6x_1)} = -\frac{13.42}{17.12} = -0.78$$

Thus the objective function is steeper than the quadratic constraint at point C and so point C is optimal giving a value of F of 59.78.

In theory the optimality of a point obtained by means other than solution of the Kuhn–Tucker conditions can be verified by substitution into the conditions (and solving for the Lagrange multipliers). However, the problem of rounding errors arises here. The value of x_1 at C is only *approximately* 8.54. The Kuhn–Tucker conditions can be usefully employed to find (in this case approximately) the values of the Lagrange multipliers. Here we have found $x_1 = 8.54$, $x_2 = 0$ and since the first constraint is not binding $y_1 = 0$. Also since $x_1 \geqslant 0$ then $\partial L/\partial x_1 = 0$ thus

$$7 - y_2(10 + 0.4(8.54)) = 0,$$

therefore

$$y_2 \simeq 0.52$$

The value of y_2 is the rate of change of the optimal value of F as the R.H.S. of the quadratic constraint is altered but since the constraint is non-linear the value of y_2 is not constant for a finite change in b. Thus it can be used only to place a bound (upper) on the change in F. For example, if 110 units of the second resource were available the upper bound on the increase in F given by use of the Lagrange multiplier y_2 is 5.2. As the reader may verify the new value of x_1 is approximately 9.28 and the corresponding value of F is 64.96, an increase of 5.18. Thus the use of y_2 in this instance for a 10% increase in resource 2 availability is accurate to one decimal place.

Whilst we are able to tackle two variable problems with a quadratic constraint by hand (using such ingenuity as we can muster) this approach is not practicable for larger problems. Van de Panne[13] developed a solution procedure for these problems. The method will not be detailed here, but is in fact 'an application of the simplex and dual methods for quadratic programming to parametric quadratic programming problems'. Although the algorithm will terminate in a finite number of iterations the calculations involved may be lengthy although the method lends itself well to computer application. Unfortunately the method cannot cope with more than one quadratic constraint. If the feasible area for the quadratic constraint is non-convex, considerable computational difficulty arises and Van de Panne's method cannot be employed and an approximation method (these are discussed briefly below) is indicated.

A special case of problems with one quadratic constraint is of some

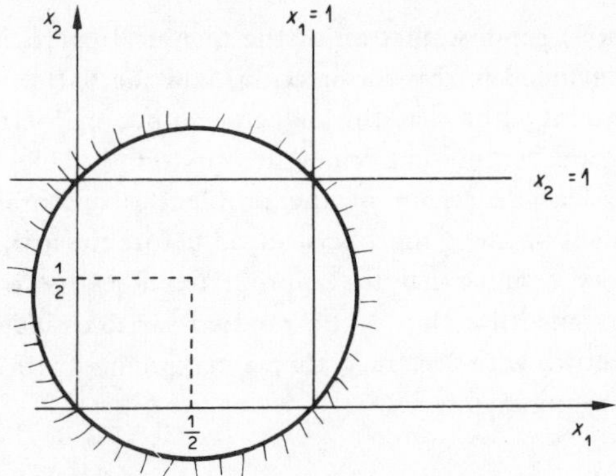

Figure 10.9 Formulation of zero-one integer problem

formulational interest. Consider the problem:

$$\left.\begin{array}{ll} \text{maximize} & R_1x_1 + R_2x_2 \\ \text{subject to:} & a_{11}x_1 + a_{12}x_2 \leqslant b_1 \\ & a_{21}x_1 + a_{22}x_2 \leqslant b_2 \\ & (x_1 - \frac{1}{2})^2 + (x_2 - \frac{1}{2})^2 \geqslant \frac{1}{2} \\ & x_1 \leqslant 1, \quad x_2 \leqslant 1, \quad x_1 \geqslant 0, \quad x_2 \geqslant 0 \end{array}\right\} \tag{10.68}$$

The quadratic constraint defines a non-convex feasible region – not inside a circle radius $0.5\sqrt{2}$ centred at the point ½, ½. The reader may recognize the problem as a zero-one integer programming problem. The quadratic constraint and upperbounds are graphed in Figure 10.9 in which the feasible region for the quadratic constraint is indicated. In conjunction with the unity upper bounds and the sign requirements, the only feasible points are the zero-one lattice points (some of which may, of course, not satisfy the linear constraints of (10.68). Now (10.68) would not appear to be a computationally efficient way to formulate the zero-one problem, but, if a problem appeared to have the form of (10.68) (perhaps after transformation of variables) the zero-one algorithms could be applied to its solution. As further formulational practice we shall see in the next section how certain chance constrained problems can be expressed as problems with a quadratic constraint.

10.7 Stochastic Problems

In this section we shall briefly examine some stochastic linear programming problems and see how their solutions may be approached.[14] Consider a simple problem to begin with.

$$\left.\begin{array}{ll} \text{Maximize} & N = \sum_{j=1}^{n} N_j x_j \\ \text{subject to:} & \sum_{j=1}^{n} a_{ij}x_j = b_i \quad (i = 1, 2, \ldots, m) \\ & x_j \geqslant 0 \quad (j = 1, 2, \ldots, n) \end{array}\right\} \tag{10.69}$$

In the problem (10.69) suppose that all of the technical coefficients (those of the slack variables are included in this formulation) and the R.H.S. of the constraints are known with certainty but that the objective function coefficients (which we shall interpret as per unit net present values) are random variables.

Now clearly the feasible region of the problem is determined but we shall suppose that the values of the x_j must be selected before the actual values of the N_j become known. If we assume that the appropriate objective is to maximize the expected value of N and that the N_j are random variables independent of all x_j, with the a_{ij} and b_i known with certainty, then a maximum of (10.70)a subject to the constraints and sign requirements

$$E(\Sigma N_j x_j) \tag{10.70)a$$

is obtained for the levels of x_j which maximize (10.70)b subject

$$\Sigma E(N_j) x_j \tag{10.70)b$$

to the constraints and sign requirements. This result is known as the linear certainty equivalence theorem and where if applies the problem is reduced to an ordinary linear programming problem in which the coefficients of the x_j are the expectations of the unit net present values. The problem is much more complex if some of the x_j may be set *after* some of the N_j have become known or if there are other random elements.

Consider now a more involved problem. Suppose that in (10.69) the N_j are random variables as before but that in addition some of the a_{ij} are also random. We shall make a number of simplifying assumptions namely:

(i) The value of each random element is independent of the levels of all of the x_j.
(ii) The values of x_j for $j = 1, 2, \ldots, k \leqslant n$ must be determined before any exact values of the random elements are known (this will be called the *first stage* of the problem and x_j for $j \leqslant k$ are first-stage variables).
(iii) The constraints $i = 1, 2, \ldots, g \leqslant m$ contain only the first-stage variables and the technical coefficients and R.H.S. in these constraints are known with certainty.
(iv) There always exist feasible levels for the *second-stage* variables (there are the x_j for $j = k + 1, \ldots, n$) and these levels are to be set after all of the values of the random elements have become known.
(v) There is only a finite number, Q, of possible sets of values for the random elements and each possible set of values has a known probability of occurrence.
(vi) It is appropriate to maximize the expected value of N.

These assumptions underlie the two-stage linear model in which the levels of the first-stage variables are decided upon initially as are *decision rules* for the selection of the second-stage variables. Once the first-stage variables are set at particular values the decision rules tell us what levels to choose for the second-stage variables in each and every possible outcome (Q possibilities in total) for the random coefficients. Following Wagner's notation let the sets of possible values of the random N_j, a_{ij}, and b_i be denoted by:

$N_{qj}, a_{qij}, b_{qi})$

with probability of occurrence p_q for the qth set where $q = 1, 2, \ldots, Q$. An optimal decision rule is now found by solving the linear programme:

$$\left.\begin{array}{lll} \text{maximize:} & \sum_{j=1}^{n} E(N_j)x_j + \sum_{q=1}^{Q} p_q \left(\sum_{j=k+1}^{n} N_{qj}x_{qj} \right) & \\ \text{subject to:} & \sum_{j=1}^{k} a_{ij}x_j = b_i \quad (i = 1,2, \ldots, g) & \\ \text{and:} & \sum_{j=1}^{k} a_{qij}x_j + \sum_{j=k+1}^{n} a_{qij}x_{qj} = b_{qi} & (i = g+1 \ldots m) \\ & & q = (1, 2, \ldots Q) \\ & x_j \geqslant 0, \quad x_{qj} \geqslant 0 & \end{array}\right\} \quad (10.71)$$

Where, in (10.71) the first g constraints relate to the first stage of the problem and the remaining $m - g$ are the second-stage decision rules. Note that the x_j for $j = 1, \ldots k$ appear in the second stage of the problem and once the random coefficients are known all terms in x_j assume constant values. The number of possible values of the N_j for $j = 1, 2, \ldots k$ is not restricted to Q. A numerical example will help to understand the use and validity of the model (10.71).

A firm has three investment projects that it may undertake. Let the levels of these investments be represented by x_1, x_3 and x_4. Investment 1 can produce three alternative values for per unit Gross Present Value of 8, 13 and 14 with probabilities 0.1, 0.7 and 0.2 respectively. Gross Present Values per unit from the other investments and initial outlays per unit on all investments are random variables as is the amount of finance to be made available. Two possible sets of values of these random elements are possible (i.e. $Q = 2$). They are:

with probability 0.4: (12, 23, 5, 7, 11, 50) $(q = 1)$

with probability 0.6: (17, 23, 6, 8, 12, 60) $(q = 2)$

where the elements within the parentheses are from left to right: GPV per unit of investment 3, GPV per unit of investment 4, outlay per unit of investment 1, outlay per unit of investment 3, outlay per unit of investment 4 and available funds. In addition, investment 1 has an upper bound of 3 and its level must be decided upon before any of the random elements take known values. The values of x_3 and x_4 are to be set when the actual values of the random elements are known.

In the first summation term of the objective function in (10.71) there is just one element in this example since we shall take it that the objective function coefficient of the slack variable (x_2) in the upper bound on x_1 is zero. The upper bound is written as:

$$x_1 + x_2 = 3$$

Thus $g = 1$ and $k = 2$ and in the objective function $E(N_1)$ is

$$E(N_1) = 0.1(8) + 0.7(13) + 0.2(14) - 0.4(5) - 0.6(6) = 7.1$$

The second summation term in the objective function is:

$$0.4[(12 - 7)x_{13} + (23 - 11)x_{14} + x_{15}]$$
$$+ 0.6[(17 - 8)x_{23} + (23 - 12)x_{24} + x_{25})]$$

where x_{15} and x_{25} are the slack variables in the 'two' constraints relating to outlay and unused funds are included in the objective function here. These are:

$$5x_1 + 7x_{13} + 11x_{14} + x_{15} = 50$$

and

$$6x_1 + 8x_{23} + 12x_{24} + x_{25} = 60$$

Note that x_{14} represents the level of x_4 if the first set of values of the random elements materializes, otherwise x_4 will assume the level x_{24}. The full problem in the form of (10.71) is:

$$\left.\begin{aligned}
&\text{maximize:} && F = 7.1x_1 + 2x_{13} + 4.8x_{14} + 0.4x_{15} \\
& && \quad + 5.4x_{23} + 6.6x_{24} + 0.6x_{25} \\
&\text{subject to:} && x_1 + x_2 = 3 \\
& && 5x_1 + 7x_{13} + 11x_{14} + x_{15} = 50 \\
& && 6x_1 + 8x_{23} + 12x_{24} + x_{25} = 60 \\
& && x_1 \geqslant 0 \quad x_2 \geqslant 0 \quad x_{13} \geqslant 0 \quad x_{23} \geqslant 0 \\
& && x_{14} \geqslant 0 \quad x_{24} \geqslant 0 \quad x_{15} \geqslant 0 \quad x_{25} \geqslant 0
\end{aligned}\right\} \qquad (10.72)$$

Now the procedure is that x_1 must be determined first and the full L.P. problem (10.72) is solved to give values for x_1 and x_2. Then, once these values have been obtained and the actual values of the random elements have become known the remainder of the *x*s are determined (which will be a trivial exercise here). The calculations for the first-stage variables are shown in Figure 10.10 from which it is evident that x_1 is set at its maximal level of three units. Now if the first possible set of values of the random elements arises then x_4 should be set equal to 35/11. If the second set of values of the random element arises then x_3 should be set at the level 21/4. These values for x_4 and x_3 can be checked by looking at the second-stage problem in either event. If $q = 1$ then having set $x_1 = 3$ the problem is to:

$$\begin{aligned}
&\text{maximize} && 5x_{13} + 12x_{14} + x_{15} \\
&\text{subject to:} && 7x_{13} + 11x_{14} + x_{15} = 35 \\
& && x_{13} \geqslant 0, \quad x_{14} \geqslant 0, \quad x_{15} \geqslant 0
\end{aligned}$$

which is achieved for $x_{14} = 35/11$, $x_{13} = 0$, $x_{15} = 0$. The net present value obtained will thus be 420/11 plus that resulting from three units of x_1 (which will depend on the actual figure for GPV, that occurred).

			7.1	0	2	4.8	0.4	5.4	6.6	0.6
			x_1	x_2	x_{13}	x_{14}	x_{15}	x_{23}	x_{24}	x_{25}
0	x_2	3	1	1	0	0	0	0	0	0
0.4	x_{15}	50	5	0	7	11	1	0	0	0
0.6	x_{25}	60	6	0	0	0	0	8	12	1
		56	−1.5	0	0.8	−0.4	0	−0.6	0.6	0
7.1	x_1	3	1	1	0	0	0	0	0	0
0.4	x_{15}	35	0	−5	7	11	1	0	0	0
0.6	x_{25}	42	0	−6	0	0	0	8	12	1
		60.5	0	1.5	0.8	−0.4	0	−0.6	0.6	0
7.1	x_1	3	1	1	0	0	0	0	0	0
0.4	x_{15}	35	0	−5	7	11	1	0	0	0
5.4	x_{23}	21/4	0	−3/4	0	0	0	1	3/2	1/8
		63.65	0	3.05	0.8	−0.4	0	0	1.5	0.075
7.1	x_1	3	1	1	0	0	0	0	0	0
4.8	x_{14}	35/11	0	−5/11	7/11	1	1/11	0	0	0
5.4	x_{23}	21/4	0	−3/4	0	0	0	1	3/2	1/8
		64.923	0	0.868	1.055	0	0.036	0	1.5	0.075

Figure 10.10 Stochastic example: calculations

If, on the other hand, the $q = 2$ values arose the second-stage problem would be:

$$\begin{aligned} \text{maximize} \quad & 9x_{23} + 11x_{24} + x_{25} \\ \text{subject to} \quad & 8x_{23} + 12x_{24} + x_{25} = 42 \\ & x_{23} \geqslant 0, \quad x_{24} \geqslant 0, \quad x_{25} \geqslant 0 \end{aligned}$$

which is solved for $x_{23} = 42/8$ (i.e. 21/4), $x_{24} = 0$, $x_{25} = 0$. The reader will recall from earlier work that in these one-constraint problems the one positive variable will be that having the greatest ratio of GPV to outlay.

The solution to (10.71) given in tableau like that of Figure 10.10 will give the optimal values of the second-stage variables since the second-stage constraint set divides into Q separate sections once the levels of the first-stage variables have been set and in the original objective function of (10.71) the objective function of each possible second-stage problem is simply multiplied through by a constant (the probability of occurrence).

Now the two-stage procedure that has been outlined here can be generalized to multi-stage problems which can be written as very large ordinary linear programming problems. This factor of size can render the approach impracticable. In a two-stage problem, for example, there will be $Q(m-g)$ second-stage constraints and if $m - g = 100$ (not at all large by 1975 standards) and $Q = 20$ there will be two thousand second-stage constraints. However, in such cases it is possible to obtain bounds on the optimal value of the objective function without too much difficulty.[15]

There is an alternative approach which (at the cost of a few more simplifying assumptions) retains the same number of constraints as in the original stochastic programming in which, as the name would suggest, the constraints of the original problem need be satisfied only with a particular minimum level of probability. This is chance constrained programming. That is (with slack variables not explicitly included)

$$P(\sum_j a_{ij}x_j \geqslant b_i) \geqslant p_i \quad \text{for} \quad i = 1, 2, \ldots, m \tag{10.73}$$

In (10.73) it is assumed that the a_{ij} are known with certainty but the b_i are random variables independent of the x_j. The chance constraints (10.73) can be shown to imply an equivalent set of m deterministic constraints

$$\sum_j a_{ij}x_j \leqslant B_i \quad i = 1, 2, \ldots, m \tag{10.74}$$

where each B_i in (10.74) is the largest number such that $P[b_i \geqslant B_i] \geqslant p_i$. The objective function $\Sigma E(N_j)x_j$ is then maximized subject to (10.74).

To see how the numbers B_i are determined suppose that b_1 has the discrete marginal probability distribution:

$$P(b_1 = 5) = 0.3$$

$$P(b_1 = 9) = 0.4$$

$$P(b_1 = 12) = 0.2$$

$$P(b_1 = 14) = 0.1$$

This data is shown in Figure 10.11(a) and from this is obtained Figure 10.11(b) the probabilities that b_1 is at least specified amounts (the B_1). Thus for instance if p_1 in (10.73) is 0.6 then the appropriate B_1 figure is 5. For $0.1 \leqslant p_1 \leqslant 0.3$ then $B_1 = 9$.

The chance constrained approach is not without limitations, however. As Wagner points out there is no differential penalty attached to the various amounts by which $\Sigma a_{ij}a_j$ may exceed b_i for different x_j. In fact specifying the appropriate values for

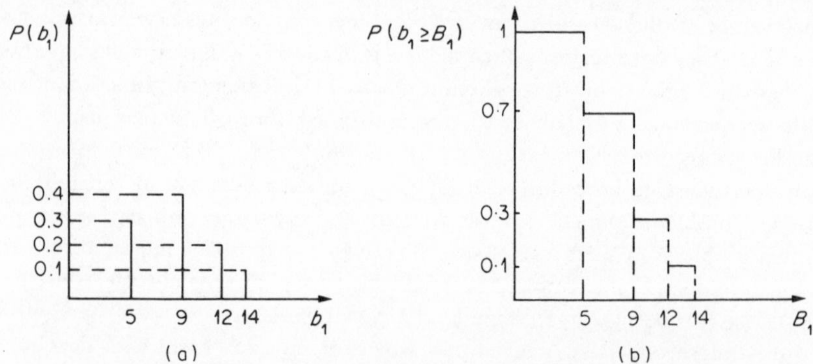

Figure 10.11 Chance constrained example: probabilities

the p_i should be part of the optimization problem. Furthermore in a multi-stage situation the conceptual difficulties in a chance constrained approach increase enormously, but the method can be applied to cases where there are several joint chance constraints. In this case the probability that a group of constraints are jointly satisfied at the original values of the b_i must not be less than a particular figure. In addition the chance constrained approach can be used (at the price of non-linearity) in cases where the a_{ij} are stochastic and the problem becomes one of programming with a quadratic constraint or constraints (if there is more than one chance constraint with stochastic coefficients).[16] Thus the quadratic constraint problem discussed in section 10.6 represents a possible means of formulating a class of stochastic problems and Van de Panne's method would find application in this area.

10.8 Advanced Topics

In this chapter we have looked at the generalities of non-linear programming problems but have considered in detail only one solution procedure for one (very important) special case. Some observations on computation in non-linear programming problems in general are worth adding here.

There is a class of procedures known as *gradient methods* in which the principle used is that of changing the x vector in such a way as to move in the 'direction' in which the objective function is increasing most rapidly. There are various manners in which this principle is employed in the presence of constraints depending upon the way in which it is modified to take account of the constraints. Even though gradient methods are not of the same ilk as the simplex method (they are not 'adjacent extreme point' methods) the simplex algorithm is frequently of use in determining the direction in which to move if moving in the direction of the gradient vector (the direction of steepest ascent) is ruled out by constraints or sign requirements. However, gradient methods, as Hadley points out '. . . will normally converge at best to a local optimum, and perhaps not even a local optimum. It is only when the problem possesses the appropriate convexity or concavity properties that we can be sure that the process will converge to the global optimum. Generally, an infinite number of iterations may be required for convergence, although for certain special cases such as linear programming problems, convergence can always be made to take place in a finite number of steps.[17] This is not to condemn the methods. It is frequently out of the question to determine the global optimum (or to know that it has been found). Gradient methods are among the best available and it should be recalled that a technique is justified if it improves on what otherwise would have been done.

In those problems in which the objective function and constraints are separable and can therefore be written as:

$$\left.\begin{aligned} &\text{maximize } F = \sum_{j=1}^{n} f_j(x_j) \\ &\text{subject to:} \quad \sum_{j=1}^{n} g_{ij}(x_j) \leqslant b \quad (i = 1, 2, \ldots, m) \\ &\text{and} \quad x_j \geqslant 0 \quad (j = 1, 2, \ldots, n) \end{aligned}\right\} \tag{10.75}$$

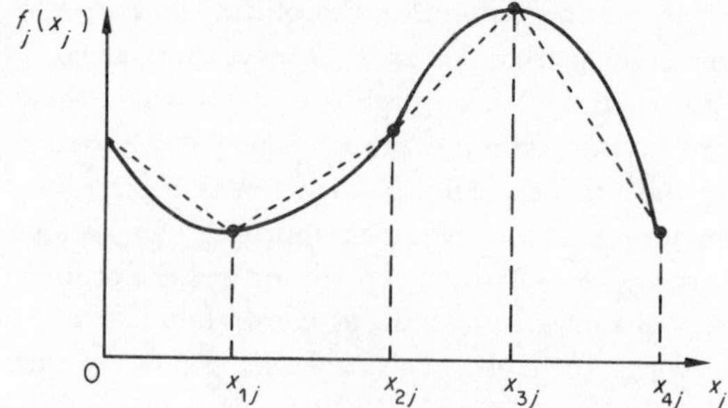

Figure 10.12 Polygonal approximation to curvilinear function

the functions $g_{ij}(x_j)$ and $f_j(x_j)$ in (10.75) can be replaced by polygonal approximations. Such an approximation is shown in Figure (10.12) where $f_j(x_j)$ is rather crudely approximated by the series of dashed lines. The approximation can be made as good as is desired (at the price of computational effort) by appropriate selection of the x_{kj} (above, $k = 1, \ldots 4$) and fine enough division of the interval over which x_j is permitted to vary. Having made such approximations a local maximum for the approximating problem is found. Only when the appropriate convexity/concavity conditions are satisfied will there be an assurance of finding the global optimum to the approximating problem. One word of caution however. Apparently innocuous approximations can have surprisingly dramatic effects in terms of the original problem.

In those problems in which only the objective function is non-linear extensions of the simplex method can be applied. The problem becomes difficult, however, when the partial derivatives of the objective function with respect to the x_j are not linear. A quadratic programming approach to such problems has been developed by Fletcher and extended by Murray and Biggs to problems with non-linear constraints.[18] When the objective function is linear but the constraint set is not, Kelley suggested that a cutting plane approach may be employed.[19] In this approach a set of linear constraints is generated that contain the original feasible region (which must be convex). This L.P. problem is then solved by the simplex method. The solution produced will not in general be feasible in terms of the original constraints and a cutting plane is introduced rendering the L.P. solution infeasible but not cutting off any of the original feasible region. The new L.P. problem is then solved and a new cut generated. Convergence, however, may require an infinite number of steps so that in practical terms there appears to be little advantage over other approximating techniques.

In stochastic problems with a present value criterion, the problem in general is to determine that feasible set of investments for which the probability distribution of present value maximizes the expected utility of the investor. A formidable problem. Indeed it is only when the investor's utility function satisfies particular axioms that there will exist a utility function with the property that the investor may proceed by maximizing expected utility. As Hadley points out: 'Procedures for cases where it cannot be assumed that the decision maker has a utility function of the type needed and/or where the probability distributions for the random variables are not known are much less clear cut and also more controversial'.[20] In addition, when the problem is of a sequential nature (as would seem to be the case in many practical situations) difficulties are vastly magnified in comparison with non-sequential problems. Our objective in this chapter has been a very limited one, namely to discuss approaches to solution in some simplified cases. The word 'simplified' should be interpreted in a relative sense.

We asserted at the beginning of the chapter that in an investment context problems with non-linear objective functions and linear constraints were 'more important' than those in which the objective was linear but the constraints were not. We would argue a similar point in a stochastic context. That is, problems in which the objective function alone is stochastic are of most importance (more frequently occurring). Let us briefly consider some more advanced material in this area.[21]

If projects are interrelated then the return in any year from one of them depends upon the choice of other investments that are made and the actual returns that these investments give. Let $N(I)$ be the net present value of a set, I, of investments giving aggregate cash flows $X_t(I)$ in the years $t = 1, 2, \ldots n$. Aggregate initial outlay K is assumed known with certainty. $N(I)$ is normally distributed whenever the joint distribution of $X_1(I), X_2(I), \ldots, X_n(I)$ is multivariate normal. I is a set of values I_k where $I_k = 1$ if the kth investment is accepted or zero if the kth investment is rejected. In this case (multivariate normal distribution of returns) the expected net present value is given by:

$$E[N(I)] = -K + \sum_{t=1}^{n} E[X_t(I)] \left[\prod_{s=1}^{t} (1 + i_s(I)) \right]^{-1} \tag{10.76}$$

where the discount factor for each year [the second square bracketed term in (10.76)] allows for different interest rates between each adjacent pair of years and the rates themselves may depend upon the set of investments I. Thus the interest rate applying in the sth year for set of investments I is $i_s(I)$. If a uniform rate of discount (over time and sets of investments) prevailed then the discount factor for year t would be the familiar $(1 + i)^{-t}$. So the assumptions made enable us to write in (10.76), the expected net present value of the set of investments, as the sum of the discounted returns in each year minus aggregate outlay.

However, expressions for the individual $E[X_t(I)]$ and the variance of net present value, var$[N(I)]$ are complicated. $X_t(I)\{\Pi_{s=1}^{t} [1 + i_s(I)]\}^{-1}$ is a random variable which is itself a sum of random variables and $N(I)$ is the sum of these (less K). Under certain conditions the distribution of a sum of a large, finite number of these random variables is asymptotically normal, so that $N(I)$ should be approximately normal if these conditions hold for the random variables whose sum is $N(I) + K$. The 'Central Limit Problem' is the problem of determining these conditions.

Knowledge of the probability distribution of $N(I)$ for all feasible I provides a substantial basis for a subjective selection of I.[22] For computational purposes it is very convenient if we can write:

$$N(I) = \sum_{k=1}^{m} N_k I_k + \sum_{j=1}^{m} \sum_{\substack{k=1 \\ k \neq j}}^{m} u_{jk} I_j I_k \tag{10.77}$$

where in (10.77) the u_{jk} are specified constants and $u_{jk} = u_{kj}$. For this to be so we need to assume a particular model of cash flows; the same cost of capital i_t in the tth year irrespective of I and that interactive effects are pairwise additive or the cumulation of pairwise effects. The problem would then be to maximize the quadratic function:

$$E[N(I)] = \sum_{k=1}^{m} u_k I_k + \sum_{j=1}^{m} \sum_{\substack{k=1 \\ j \neq 1}}^{m} u_{jk} I_j I_k \tag{10.78}$$

subject to constraints. It will be recalled that the I_k are two-state variables so that we are confronted with something more than an ordinary quadratic programming problem. Possible exact solution procedures (in differing constraint circumstances) are as follows:

(i) If all zero-one investment combinations are feasible then an algorithm by Reiter[23] can be applied. Reiter's procedure can be used to find optimal or 'near optimal' solutions. The method is a stochastic algorithm (using random starting programs) and can be shown to converge on an optimal program in a finite number of steps although the probability that an optimum (global) will be found in a 'relatively small' number of steps is 'large'. In addition, the probability of finding a 'nearly optimal' solution in a small number of steps (two or three trials with randomly selected starting programs) is 'substantial'.

(ii) If in addition to the zero-one requirements there are L.P. type constraints and provided rounding off is possible then a non-concave quadratic programming method due to Candler and Townsley[24] may be employed.

(iii) If the situation is as in (ii) but the objective function is concave[25] then there is a choice among several methods of quadratic programming. The problem is a 'conventional' Q.P. problem and the simplex method outlined in section 10.5 could be employed.

(iv) If the matrix of the u_{jk} is negative definite then (in principle) an integer solution can be obtained by integer Q.P. algorithms.[26]

In more general terms Hillier[27] discusses the problem of maximizing the expected utility (maximize $E\{u[N(I)]\}$) from investments and gives an approximate L.P. approach in which a sequence of L.P. problems is solved. Firstly, an approximate solution to: maximize $E[N(I)]$ subject to L.P. type requirements with $0 \leqslant I_k \leqslant 1$; is found which enables a good linear approximation of $E\{U[N(I)]\}$ to be obtained and a solution found in a similar (approximate) manner.

Notes

1. We shall shamelessly eliminate all but the barest essentials from this discussion. For discussion of inflexion points (and other subtleties) see Allen, R.G.D., *Mathematical Analysis for Economists*, Macmillan, London, 1960.
2. Strictly speaking the rate of change of the slope of $F(x)$ should be non-increasing for a maximum and non-decreasing for a minimum. If the rate of change of the slope of $F(x)$ is zero at a point which satisfies (10.2) to determine the character of the stationary value we should have to investigate higher-order derivatives. See Allen, R.G.D., *Mathematical Analysis for Economists*, Macmillan, London, 1960 for discussion of this point. We shall adopt the sufficient [along with the first order condition (10.2)] second order condition.
3. We refer of course to the global maximum within the feasible region (given by $x \geqslant 0$).
4. (10.23) is a most important relationship although by no means all people find it intuitively appealing. The fact of the matter is that a movement (say) in a northeasterly direction can be broken down into two parts – a movement north and a movement east. A function with continuous first order partial derivatives in the neighbourhood of a point cannot have zero slopes in the fundamental directions and non-zero slopes in other directions at that point. For formal discussion of this material see Allen, R.G.D., *Mathematical Analysis for Economists*, Macmillan, London, 1960 Chapter XIII. If F has continuous first order partial derivatives in a region where ϵ_1 and ϵ_2 approach zero as Δx_1 and Δx_2 approach zero, we could write as an equation

$$\Delta F = \frac{\partial F}{\partial x_1} \Delta x_1 + \frac{\partial F}{\partial x_2} \Delta x_2 + \epsilon_1 \Delta x_1 + \epsilon_2 \Delta x_2$$

5. For a proper discussion of concavity of a function over a convex region see Hadley, G., *Nonlinear and Dynamic Programming*, Addison-Wesley, Reading, Massachusetts, 1964, Chapter 3.
6. We shall assume throughout that F has continuous first partial derivatives.
7. For further description and a diagrammatic illustration of the saddle point property see Henderson, J. M., and Quandt,, R. E., *Microeconomic Theory*, McGraw-Hill, New York, 1958.
8. For a discussion of the constraint qualification condition see Intriligator, M. D., *Mathematical Optimization and Economic Theory*, Prentice-Hall., Englewood Cliffs, N. J., 1971, Chapter 4, pp. 57–60. For discussion of concavity and convexity properties of functions see Hadley, G., *Nonlinear and Dynamic Programming*, Addison-Wesley, Reading, Massachusetts, 1964, pp. 83–87.
9. For full discussion of these conditions see Hadley, G., *Nonlinear and Dynamic Programming*, Addison-Wesley, Reading, Massachusetts, 1964, and Intriligator, M. D., *Mathematical Optimization and Economic Theory*, Prentice-Hall, Englewood Cliffs, N. J., 1971.
10. Balinski, M. L., and Baumol, W. J., 'The dual in non-linear programming and its economic interpretation', *Review of Economic Studies,* **1967**. Quote from Page 237.
11. See Wolfe, P., 'The simplex method for quadratic programming', *Econometrica,* **27**, 1959, and Carr, C. R., and Howe, C. W., *Quantitative Decision Procedures in Management and Economics*, MGraw-Hill, New York, 1964.
12. A sufficient condition for this is that the d_{hj} in the constraints (10.65) form a positive semi-definite matrix.
13. Van de Panne, C., 'Programming with a quadratic constraint', *Management Science,* **12**, 1966.
14. Much of the treatment in this section is based upon Wagner's discussion (*Principles of Operations Research with Applications to Managerial Decisions*, Prentice-Hall, Englewood Cliffs, N.J., 1969, pp. 658–671) to which the reader is referred for further development.
15. See Wagner, H. M., *Principles of Operations Research with Applications to Managerial Decisions*, Prentice-Hall, Englewood Cliffs, N. J., 1969, pp.664–667.
16. See Van de Panne, C., *Programming with a Quadratic Constraint*, University of Birmingham Discussion Paper Series A, No. 45, January, 1964.
17. Hadley, G., *Nonlinear and Dynamic Programming*, Addison-Wesley, Reading, Massachusetts, 1964, p. 296.
18. See: Fletcher, R., *An Efficient, Globally Convergent, Algorithm for Unconstrained and Linearly Constrained Optimization Problems*, Paper presented at Seventh International

Mathematical Programming Symposium, The Hague, 1970; Murray, W., 'An algorithm for constrained minimization', in *Optimization*, Fletcher, R., (Ed.), Academic Press, London, 1969; Biggs, M. C., *A New Method of Constrained Minimization using Recursive Equality Quadratic Programming*, Technical Report No. 24, The Numerical Optimization Centre, The Hatfield Polytechnic, 1971.

19. Kelley, J. E., 'The cutting plane method for solving convex programs' *Journal of the Society for Industrial and Applied Mathematics,* **8**, 1960.
20. Hadley, G., *Nonlinear and Dynamic Programming*, Addison-Wesley, Reading Massachusetts, 1974, p. 159.
21. This presentation is drawn from Hillier, F. S., *The Evaluation of Risky, Interrelated Investments*, North Holland Publishing Company, Amsterdam, 1969. We attempt to simplify the material a little.
22. See Hillier, F. S., Derivation of probabilistic information for the evaluation of risky investments, *Management Science,* **9**, 1963.
23. Reiter, S., 'Choosing an investment program among interdependent projects', *The Review of Economic Studies,* **30**, No. 2, February, 1963.
24. Candler, W., and Townsley, R. J., 'The maximization of a quadratic function of variables subject to linear inequalities', *Management Science,* **10**, 1964.
25. The objective function will be concave if the matrix of the U_{jk} is negative semi-definite.
26. See Boot, J. C. G., and Theil, H., *A Procedure for Integer Maximization of a Definite Quadratic Function*, Econometrics Institute of the Netherlands School of Economics, Reprint Series No. 93. See also Kunzi, H. P., and Oettli, W., 'Integer quadratic programming', in *Recent Advances in Mathematical Programming*, Groves, R. L., and Wolfe, P., (Eds.), McGraw-Hill, New York, 1963.
27. Hillier, F. S., *The Evaluation of Risky, Interelated Investments*, North Holland Publishing Company, Amsterdam, 1969.

Additional References

1. Abadie, J. (Ed.), *Non-linear Programming*, North Holland, Amsterdam, 1967.
2. Beale, E. M. L., *Mathematical Programming in Practice*, Pitman Publishing, London, 1968.
3. Braitsch, R. J., 'A Computer comparison of four quadratic programming algorithms', *Management Science*, (Series A), 1972.
4. Dixon, L. C. W., *Non-Linear Optimization*, The English Universities Press, London, 1972.
5. Dorn, W. S., 'Duality in quadratic programming', *Quarterly of Applied Mathematics,* **18**, 1960.
6. Dorn, W. S., 'On Lagrangian multipliers', *Operations Research,* **9**, 1963.
7. Dorn, W. S., 'Non-linear programming – a survey', *Management Science,* **9**, 1963.
8. Hartley, H. O., 'Non-linear programming by the simplex method', *Econometrica,* **29**, 1961.
9. Intriligator, M. D., *Mathematical Optimization and Economic Theory*, Prentice-Hall, Englewood Cliffs, N. J., 1971.
10. Kuhn, H. W., and Tucker, A., 'Non-linear programming', in Neyman, J. (Ed.), *Proceedings of the Second Berkeley Symposium on Mathematical Statistics and Probability*, University of California Press, Berkeley, 1951.
11. Naylor, T. H., and Vernon, J. M., *Microeconomics and Decision Models of the Firm*, Harcourt, Brace and World, New York, 1969.
12. Reiter, S., and Sherman, G. R., 'Allocating indivisible resources affording external economies or diseconomies', *International Economic Review*, January, **1962**.
13. Rockafeller, R. T., 'Duality in nonlinear programming', in Dantzig, G. B., and Veinott, A. F., (Eds.), *Mathematics of the Decision Sciences Part I, Providence R. I.*, American Mathematical Society, 1968.
14. Van de Panne, C., and Whinston, A., 'Simplicial methods for quadratic programming', *Naval Research Logistics Quarterly,* **11**, 1964.
15. Van de Panne, C., and Whinston, A., 'A comparison of two methods of quadratic programming', *Operations Research,* **14**, 1966.
16. Wagner, H. M., *Principles of Operations Research with Applications to Managerial Decisions*, Prentice-Hall, Englewood Cliffs, N. J., 1969.
17. Wolfe, P., 'A duality theorem for non-linear programming', *Quarterly of Applied Mathematics,* **14**, 1961.
18. Wolfe, P., 'Methods of non-linear programming', in Abadie J. (Ed.), *Non-linear Programming*, North Holland, Amsterdam, 1967.

CHAPTER 11
Portfolio Theory

Portfolio theory is concerned with the problem of selecting (and in general building and revising) an optimal set of investments (the portfolio) bearing in mind the anticipated returns to these investments, the risk associated with them and the utility of the investor. As will be seen there is considerable overlap between the material of this chapter and the quadratic programming and stochastic problems of Chapter 10. Whilst this work will be drawn upon frequently, portfolio theory is presented separately since it is so important a special case. Portfolio theory is a vast subject in its own right. We shall principally be concerned here with the problem of the selection of one optimal portfolio in relatively convenient circumstances. These will be such that the Lagrange multiplier methods and the quadratic programming algorithm that has been expounded, can be employed. More advanced material, simplified models and problem areas are contained in the later sections.

11.1 Background

Modern approaches to the problem of portfolio selection began with Markowitz and nowadays most theorists take his work as a starting point.[1] The principal advance that Markowitz made over preceding theories of portfolio selection was the manner in which the risks associated with investments were taken into account. The variance (or standard deviation) of the return on an investment was used as a measure of risk, in place of the old idea of a risk premium. Variance is not always a suitable measure of risk (this point will be returned to later) but on the whole the idea of using statistical measures of dispersion as measures of risk was a significant advance. Investors were assumed to be rational insofar as they would prefer greater returns to lesser ones given equal or smaller risk, and 'risk aversion'. As was seen in Chapter 1, risk aversion means that as between two investments with equal expected returns, the investment with the smaller risk would be preferred. 'Return' could be any suitable measure of monetary inflows but, on the whole, yield is the most convenient measure of return to adopt in this context, so that when the standard deviation of returns is referred to we shall mean the standard deviation of yield about its expected value.

The objective of the investor is assumed to be the maximization of expected utility. It is worth recalling that it is only when the investor's utility function satisfies certain axioms that the maximization of expected utility will be the appropriate objective. The variables in the problem are the investments of which the portfolio is comprised and it will be assumed that expected utility can be written as a function of expected portfolio return and the variance or standard deviation of return as surrogate for risk. There is a further assumption implicit here. Neo-classical economics expresses utility as a function of *goods consumed* in the current period and to be consumed in future time periods. In the neo-classical analysis income is considered 'utile' in that it allows consumption of goods. If we are thinking of a utility function in this traditional sense we are one step removed from the real arguments of the function. Whilst these considerations are important when 'the investor' is an individual person (income would appear in a constraint), are they relevant when the investor is a bank or insurance company? For what purposes and by whom are the returns eventually used? Do all persons concerned with the investments (managers and shareholders) have the same utility functions? Can an aggregate measure of utility be arrived at?

We shall sidestep these questions by regarding the utility functions used as measures of performance that have been decided upon in advance of the exercise. It would be utterly impracticable to do anything else. Thus we shall write:

$$E(U) = f(\bar{R}, \sigma) \tag{11.1}$$

where $E(U)$, expected utility, is a single index of performance, $\bar{R}$ is the expected return on the portfolio as a whole and σ is the associated standard deviation of return. The function (11.1) 'maps' a two-dimensional measure into one dimension. Although the function (11.1) relates to a single time period this is the entire planning horizon. More involved models may include several time periods. Note that in maximizing $E(U)$ in (11.1) we shall be maximizing what we expect 'utility' to be and not what it will actually turn out to be since this is unknown at the time the decision has to be taken. Henceforward for convenience, we shall write simply U for 'expected utility'.

In passing it is worth noting what the function (11.1) would imply in the absence of risk (where $\sigma = 0$ for all portolios and $\bar{R}$ is the actual return). In this situation of perfect certainty this would mean choosing a portfolio of investments to maximize net present value or yield (subject to scale considerations). If the world is linear and continuously divisible as well as certain, this would mean selecting one investment alone, that is, no diversification whatever. Since, however, diminishing returns and an insistence on being integral are quite natural, a limited amount of diversification would be suggested even by traditional theory. This degree of diversification, however, falls far short of that which is commonly observed – a compelling explanation of which is that risk is undesirable and that diversification can reduce risk. As we shall see, however, not all rules that give rise to diversification of investment do reduce risk. In fact some naive diversification rules can actually cause the level of risk to increase.

Returning now to cases where risk is strictly positive, the assumption of 'rationality' and 'risk aversion' mean that U will change in the same direction as a change in $\bar{R}$ alone (written $\partial U/\partial \bar{R} > 0$) and that U will change in the opposite direction to a change in σ alone (writtin $\partial U/\partial \sigma < 0$). The objective then is to choose a portfolio of investments that maximizes (11.1) subject to whatever financial and other contraints may apply.[2] It is clear that a portfolio which

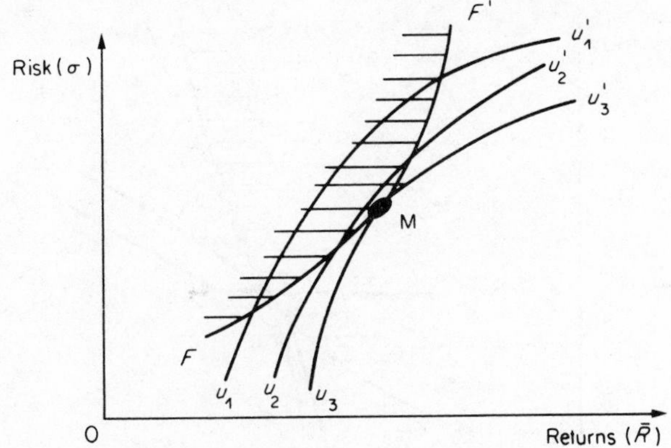

Figure 11.1 Optimal risk–return combination

maximizes (11.1) must satisfy the following condition: the portfolio of investments must have maximum expected return for all risk levels (measured by standard deviation here) not exceeding its own, and it must have minimum standard deviation of return for all levels of return not lower than its own.

There will in general be many portfolios which satisfy the above condition. These are known as the *mean-variance efficient portfolios* (variance will be employed in place of standard deviation later on). All that has been done is the weeding out of the inefficient portfolios. The investor must now make a choice between the mean-variance efficient portfolios.

Graphically the mean-variance efficient portfolios lie on a line such as FF' – the efficiency frontier – in Figure 11.1. All portfolios in the shaded area to the left of FF' are mean-variance inefficient – that is to say there are other portfolios (nearer to FF') which have greater expected returns for the same or smaller risk or smaller risk for the same or greater returns.

The lines uu' in the figure are indifference curves. All points on any one such curve are combinations of risk and return which are equally satisfactory for the investor. Curves further to the right correspond to greater levels of utility, that is, $u_3 > u_2 > u_1$. They possess the curvature (convex to the risk axis) as drawn, if investors have a diminishing marginal rate of substitution between expected return and risk. This would mean that invesotrs were decreasingly willing to accept higher returns to compensate for greater risk. If all assets are risky, the optimal portfolio is portfolio M, at a point of tangency between an indifference curve and the efficiency frontier.

If there is a 'riskless' investment, however, the investor may be able to improve on M. For instance, Government securities are usually taken to be risk free. Once the security has been purchased the return is known and assured. Such a riskless rate of return is called the pure interest rate. Figure 11.2 graphs the situation. The pure interest rate is R_p, and, by investing partly in the riskless asset and partly in portfolio N the investor could obtain risk/return combinations along the line R_pN.

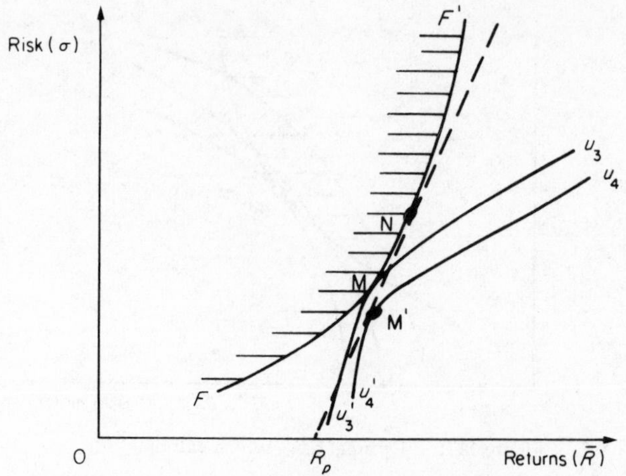

Figure 11.2 Utility maximization with riskless asset

If $\bar{R}_N$ is the expected rate of return on portfolio N and σ_N the standard deviation of this return, then for $0 \leqslant \alpha \leqslant 1$ by investing in the proportions α in the riskless asset and $1-\alpha$ in portfolio N the investor can achieve an expected return of $\bar{R}_{p,N}$ where

$$\bar{R}_{p,N} = \alpha R_p + (1-\alpha)\bar{R}_N \tag{11.2}$$

with an associated level of risk given by

$$\sigma_{p,N} = (1-\alpha)\,\sigma_N \tag{11.3}$$

The optimum position is now M′. If borrowing was possible at the pure interest rate then risk/return combinations above N on the extension of the line R_pN would be attainable. If borrowing was possible at a rate of interest greater than R_p then the line through R_p and N would kink at N and slope more steeply above N. Borrowing could be thought of as the *issue* of a security by the investor. Although this is not always possible in practice, where stocks of the riskless asset are already held, disinvestment in this asset could be interpreted as borrowing at the rate of interest R_p. The investor with the indifference curves above, however, would not choose to borrow; clearly M′ could not be improved upon by borrowing.

Let us now begin to examine the portfolio problem in algebraic terms. As we have seen it so far the problem can be broken down into two parts: firstly, find the efficient portfolios; secondly, choose one of the efficient portfolios so as to maximize investor utility. As will be seen later on, the two parts can be brought together so that a utility maximizing efficient portfolio is selected in one go. However, it will be convenient first to examine the problem of determining the efficient set of portfolios.

11.2 Two Securities

Consider a problem in just two securities. The investor has L pounds at his disposal. If the prices of the two securities are, respectively, S_1 and S_2 per unit and n_1 and n_2 units respectively of each security are purchased, then the budget constraint can be written as:

$$n_1 s_1 + n_2 s_2 \leqslant L \tag{11.4}$$

or alternatively as:

$$\frac{n_1 S_1}{L} + \frac{n_2 S_2}{L} \leqslant 1 \tag{11.5}$$

Now define $x_1 = n_1 S_1/L$ and $x_2 = n_2 S_2/L$ and impose the restrictions that the entire budget be spent.[3] The constraint can now be written as:

$$x_1 + x_2 = 1 \tag{11.6}$$

Now let $\bar{R}_1$ and $\bar{R}_2$ be the expected values of the yields from each security. The expected value of yield on the portfolio, written as $\bar{R}$, will then be given by:

$$\bar{R} = x_1 \bar{R}_1 + x_2 \bar{R}_2 \tag{11.7}$$

clearly (11.7) could be rewritten in terms of x_1 or x_2 alone because of (11.6), but for expository reasons we shall leave (11.7) as it stands.

R_{1h}	R_{2h}	p_h
R_{11}	R_{21}	p_1
R_{12}	R_{22}	p_2
R_{13}	R_{23}	p_3

Figure 11.3 Yield possibilities: example

Now, what about the variability of the yield figures? Suppose that there are just three pairs of values of yield figures which may emerge. Write these as (R_{1h}, R_{2h}) where $h = 1, 2, 3$ with probabilities of occurrence p_h where $\Sigma_{h=1}^{3} p_h = 1$ Figure 11.3 presents this information in tabular form. From this we can readily calculate the expected returns on the portfolio for proportions x_1 and x_2 of the budget spent on the two securities respectively. We obtain:

$$\begin{aligned}\bar{R} &= p_1(x_1 R_{11} + x_2 R_{21}) + p_2(x_1 R_{12} + x_2 R_{22}) + p_3(x_1 R_{13} + x_2 R_{23})\\ &= x_1(R_{11}p_1 + R_{12}p_2 + R_{13}p_3) + x_2(R_{21}p_1 + R_{22}p_2 + R_{23}p_3)\\ &= x_1 \bar{R}_1 + x_2 \bar{R}_2\end{aligned}$$

Now consider variance of return on the portfolio as a whole. Recall that variance is the sum of the products of the squared deviations of individual portfolio return figures from the mean return and the probability of occurrence of each figure. Thus portfolio variance, V, is given by:

$$V = \sum_{h=1}^{3} p_h d_h^2 \tag{11.8}$$

$$\text{where } d_h = x_1 R_{1h} + x_2 R_{2h} - x_1 \bar{R}_1 - x_2 \bar{R}_2$$
$$= x_1 (R_{1h} - \bar{R}_1) + x_2 (R_{2h} - \bar{R}_2)$$

Now the first term in the summation (11.8), $p_1 d_1^2$ is given by

$$p_1 d_1^2 = p_1 [x_1 (R_{11} - \bar{R}_1) + x_2 (R_{21} - \bar{R}_2)]^2$$
$$= p_1 [x_1^2 (R_{11} - \bar{R}_1)^2 + 2x_1 x_2 (R_{11} - \bar{R}_1)(R_{21} - \bar{R}_2)$$
$$+ x_2^2 (R_{21} - \bar{R}_2)^2]$$

thus

$$\sum_{h=1}^{3} p_h d_h^2 = x_1^2 \sum_{h=1}^{3} p_h (R_{1h} - \bar{R}_1)^2 + 2x_1 x_2 \sum_{h=1}^{3} p_h$$

$$(R_{1h} - \bar{R}_1)(R_{2h} - \bar{R}_2) + x_2^2 \sum_{h=1}^{3} p_h (R_{2h} - \bar{R}_2)^2 \tag{11.9}$$

from which we observe that the first summation on the R.H.S. of (11.9) is the variance of return on the first security which we shall write as σ_1^2. The third summation on the R.H.S. is the variance of return on the second security, σ_2^2. The second summation is the *covariance* of returns on the two securities. This may be written as either σ_{12} or σ_{21}. Covariance measures the extent to which the possible returns on the securities vary together. The lower is the value of σ_{12} the less 'in step' are the possible returns to the two investments. We can now rewrite (11.9) more conveniently as:

$$V = x_1^2 \sigma_1^2 + 2x_1 x_2 \sigma_{12} + x_2^2 \sigma_2^2 \tag{11.10}$$

Now standard deviation of portfolio return (which we were referring to earlier on as σ_p) would be the square root of V in (11.10). From here onwards however, we shall employ the variance rather than the standard deviation of returns as the measure of risk. This is conventional since variance is a much more convenient measure of risk in the context of solution by Lagrange multiplier or programming methods.

Now having obtained $\bar{R}$ as a function of x_1 and x_2 in (11.7) and V as a function of x_1 and x_2 in (11.10) the next step is to obtain V as a function of $\bar{R}$. This will give the equation of the efficiency frontier (with variance, on the vertical axis, as the risk measure). Using the relationship of (11.6) we can write variance as

$$V = x_1^2 \sigma_1^2 + 2x_1 (1 - x_1) \sigma_{12} + (1 - x_1)^2 \sigma_2^2$$

so that

$$V = x_1^2 (\sigma_1^2 - 2\sigma_{12} + \sigma_2^2) + 2x_1 (\sigma_{12} - \sigma_2^2) + \sigma_2^2 \tag{11.11}$$

from which it will be noted that if $x_1 = 0$, $V = \sigma_2^2$, the only factor producing variability in this case being x_2. If $x_1 = 1$ then from (11.11) $V = \sigma_1^2$.

Returning to (11.7) and again employing (11.6) we can write

$$\bar{R} = x_1 \bar{R}_1 + (1 - x_1)\bar{R}_2 = \bar{R}_2 + x_1(\bar{R}_1 - \bar{R}_2)$$

thus

$$x_1 = \frac{\bar{R} - \bar{R}_2}{\bar{R}_1 - \bar{R}_2} \tag{11.12}$$

Now substituting the R.H.S. of (11.12) for x_1 in (11.11) gives

$$V = [\bar{R}^2(\sigma_1^2 - 2\sigma_{12} + \sigma_2^2) - 2\bar{R}(\sigma_1^2\bar{R}_2 - \sigma_{12}(\bar{R}_1 + \bar{R}_2) + \sigma_2^2\bar{R}_1) + \bar{R}_2^2\sigma_1^2 - 2\bar{R}_1\bar{R}_2\sigma_{12} + \bar{R}_1^2\sigma_2^2](\bar{R}_1 - \bar{R}_2)^{-2} \tag{11.13}$$

From which it is evident that the efficiency frontier is a quadratic in $\bar{R}$, if rather a cumbersome one. It is important to note that no optimization has been involved in the obtaining of (11.13). For this reason the problem in two securities (with all the buget to be spent) is sometimes described as trivial but it will be noted that the investor has yet to select a point on the frontier.

Some further study of (11.13) is rewarding. The constant term is typically non-zero which implies that the portfolio with zero expected return will not in general have zero variance. Figure 11.4 gives a diagrammatic representation of equation (11.13) from which it is evident that the portfolio with least return will not usually be the least risky. Having obtained the efficiency frontier it is easy enough to obtain the composition of the variance minimizing portfolio. From (11.11) we obtain:

$$\frac{dV}{dx_1} = 2x_1(\sigma_1^2 - 2\sigma_{12} + \sigma_2^2) + 2(\sigma_{12} - \sigma_2^2) \tag{11.14}$$

and

$$\frac{d^2V}{dx_1^2} = 2(\sigma_1^2 - 2\sigma_{12} + \sigma_2^2) \tag{11.15}$$

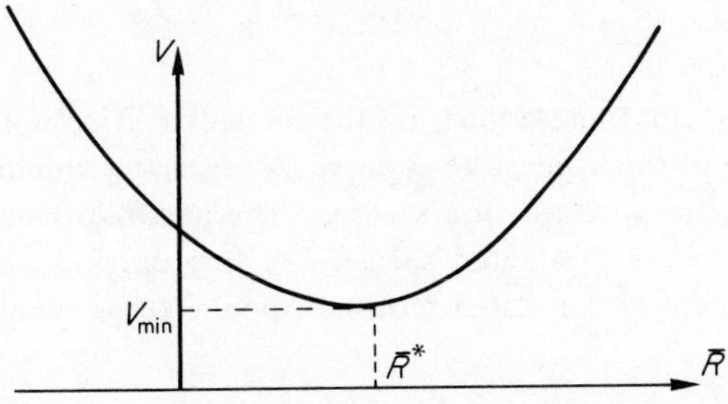

Figure 11.4 Graph of V against $\bar{R}$

Let us first examine the second derivative. This is twice the coefficient of $\bar{R}^2$ in (11.13). If this coefficient is positive then the turning point of V is a minimum.[4] Now the *coefficient of linear correlation*, r, between two variables measures the degree of linear relationships between them and is written as:

$$r = \frac{\sigma_{12}}{\sigma_1 \sigma_2} \tag{11.16}$$

where it can be shown that $-1 \leqslant r \leqslant +1$. A value of $r = +1$ implies a perfect positive linear relationship between the variables and $r = -1$ implies a perfect negative linear relationship. Now *in the extreme* $\sigma_{12} = \sigma_1 \sigma_2$ and substituting this into (11.15) gives:

$$\sigma_1^2 - 2\sigma_1 \sigma_2 + \sigma_2^2 = (\sigma_1 - \sigma_2)^2 \geqslant 0 \tag{11.17}$$

Thus (11.15) must be non-negative so that the equation of the R.H.S. of (11.14) to zero will produce the variance minimizing condition for x_1. The variance minimizing portfolio therefore has:

$$x_1 = \frac{\sigma_2^2 - \sigma_{12}}{\sigma_1^2 - 2\sigma_{12} + \sigma_2^2} \quad \text{and} \quad x_2 = \frac{\sigma_1^2 - \sigma_{12}}{\sigma_1^2 - 2\sigma_{12} + \sigma_2^2} \tag{11.18}$$

in which it is quite possible that either x_1 or x_2 is less than zero. We shall take up this point again shortly.

The value of variance at a minimum is obtained by substituting for x_1 from (11.18) which gives

$$V\text{min} = \frac{\sigma_1^2 \sigma_2^2 - \sigma_{12}^2}{\sigma_1^2 - 2\sigma_{12} + \sigma_2^2} = \frac{1 - r^2}{C} \tag{11.19}$$

where

$$C = \frac{\sigma_1^2 - 2\sigma_{12} + \sigma_2^2}{\sigma_1^2 \sigma_2^2}$$

From (11.19) it is clear that only if returns are perfectly correlated can a risk-free portfolio be obtained. This is intuitively plausible in the case of perfect negative correlation but is not so clear if $r = +1$. In this case $\sigma_{12} = \sigma_1 \sigma_2$ and from (11.18) it emerges that the values of the xs are:

$$x_1 = \frac{\sigma_2}{\sigma_2 - \sigma_1} \quad \text{and} \quad x_2 = \frac{\sigma_1}{\sigma_1 - \sigma_2} \tag{11.20}$$

Clearly if $\sigma_1 = \sigma_2$ no finite values of the xs will suffice unless $\sigma_1 = \sigma_2 = 0$. If $\sigma_1 \neq \sigma_2$ then one of the xs must be negative. A negative x would correspond to the *issue* rather than the purchase of a security. The portfolio would be *leveraged.* If leveraged portfolios are prohibited then a risk free portfolio cannot be obtained with perfectly positively correlated returns. Where returns are perfectly negatively correlated then:

$$x_1 = \frac{\sigma_2}{\sigma_2 + \sigma_1} \quad \text{and} \quad x_2 = \frac{\sigma_1}{\sigma_2 + \sigma_1} \tag{11.21}$$

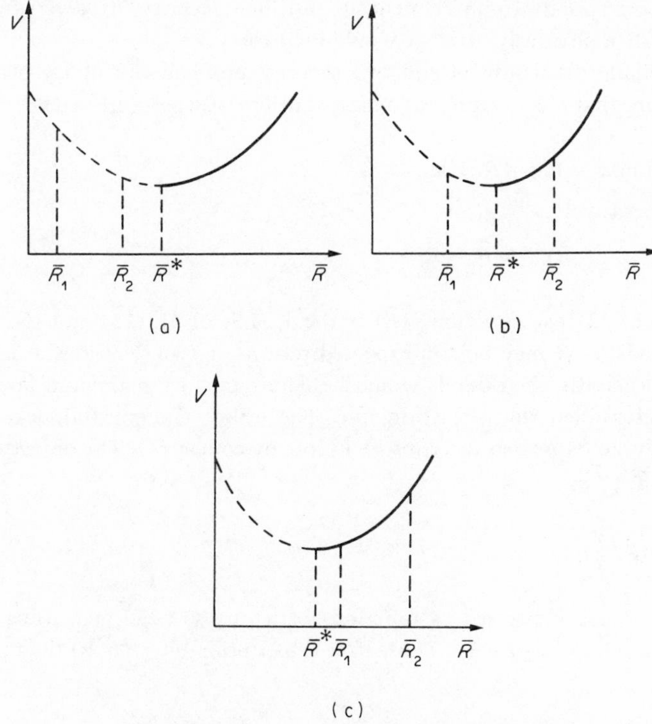

Figure 11.5 Relevant and obtainable sections of frontier

so that if $\sigma_1 = 5$ and $\sigma_2 = 7$ then investment of 7/12 of the sum available in security 1 and 5/12 of the sum available in security 2 would eliminate variation in return and give an assured return figure of $(7\bar{R}_1 + 5\bar{R}_2)/12$.

Such cases are unlikely extremes and something resembling the diagram of Figure 11.4 would be typical, but not all of the curve will normally be relevant or obtainable. Firstly, only that section of the frontier that is positively sloped will be relevant for the 'rational' investor. Secondly, if leveraged portfolios are excluded the obtainable section of the frontier is that point over the interval bounded by the individual expected return figures $\bar{R}_1$ and $\bar{R}_2$. Possiblities are illustrated in Figure 11.5(a), 11.5(b) and 11.5(c). In the case of 11.5(a) the minimum variance portfolio is leveraged (negative x_1) and unattainable. The risk-averse investor would set $x_1 = 0$ and $x_2 = 1$ for an expected return of $\bar{R}_2$ and corresponding minimal (given the leverage prohibition) variance. In the case of Figure 11.5(b) the relevant section of the frontier is over the interval $\bar{R}^*$ to $\bar{R}_2$. In Figure 11.5(c) the minimum variance portfolio is leveraged (negative x_2) and the relevant section of the frontier is over the interval $\bar{R}_1$ to $\bar{R}_2$.

Non-zero limits on leverage could be incorporated and would extend the attainable section of the efficiency frontier. One further point can be illustrated in terms of Figure 11.5. In cases (a) and (c) the minimum variance that can be achieved corresponds to investment in just one security. If diversification was compelled then obviously variance would increase.

To conclude discussion of the two security problem the utility maximization part (recalling that U is to represent expected utility) can be expressed as:

$$\begin{aligned} &\text{maximize} \quad U = f(\bar{R}, V) \\ &\text{subject to:} \quad V = g(\bar{R}) \\ &\text{and} \quad \bar{R}_L \leqslant \bar{R} \leqslant \bar{R}_U \end{aligned} \tag{11.22}$$

where in (11.22) the function $g(\bar{R})$ is the R.H.S. of (11.13) and the lower and upper bounds on $\bar{R}$ may be the expected returns on two securities if no leverage is allowed. Otherwise the bounds would be determined by maximum leverage limits or a predetermined diversification rule. The utility maximization exercise could alternatively be expressed in terms of x_1 (or of course x_2). The objective function is, as before

$$U = f(\bar{R}, V)) \tag{11.23}$$

but V and $\bar{R}$ are expressed as functions of x_1 by (11.11) and, using (11.7) and (11.6) $\bar{R} = x_1(\bar{R}_1 - \bar{R}_2) + \bar{R}_2$. Thus, after substitution into $f(\bar{R}, V)$ the problem can be written as:

$$\begin{aligned} &\text{maximize} \quad U = h(x_1) \\ &\text{subject to} \quad L_1 \leqslant x_1 \leqslant U_1 \end{aligned} \tag{11.24}$$

where, in (11.24) the lower and upper bounds on x_1, would be zero and one if no leverage was permitted and no diversification compelled.

11.3 Three Securities: A Diagrammatic Approach

Now consider a three security problem. As before let x_i represent the proportion of the total budget that is invested in the ith security, and other notation as before we have:

$$\begin{aligned} 1 &= x_1 + x_2 + x_3 \\ \bar{R} &= x_1 \bar{R}_1 + x_2 \bar{R}_2 + x_3 \bar{R}_3 \\ V &= x_1^2 \sigma_1^2 + x_2^2 \sigma_2^2 + x_3^2 \sigma_3^2 + 2x_1 x_2 \sigma_{12} + 2x_1 x_3 \sigma_{13} + 2x_2 x_3 \sigma_{23} \end{aligned} \tag{11.25}$$

In the variance expression of (11.25) we see that variance of return on the portfolio as a whole depends on variances in the returns of individual securities and the covariance of returns between each pair of securities. The end objective of the exercise would be to secure a maximum of (11.23).

In general, for n securities we have:

$$\left.\begin{aligned} 1 &= \sum_{i=1}^{n} x_i \\ \bar{R} &= \sum_{i=1}^{n} x_i \bar{R}_i \\ V &= \sum_{i=1}^{n} x_i^2 \sigma_i^2 + \sum_{i=1}^{n} \sum_{\substack{j=1 \\ j \neq i}}^{n} x_i x_j \sigma_{ij} \end{aligned}\right\} \tag{11.26}$$

where in the variance expression in (11.26) σ_{ij} represents the covariance of returns between securities i and j. The more important of the two summation terms in V is the second, the covariance summation. In fact for a portfolio consisting of a large number of securities typically the variances of returns on individual securities are relatively unimportant contributors to the variance of return on the portfolio as a whole. The important factor is how the returns on securities vary together. There are just n terms in the variance summation but $n(n-1)$ in the covariance summation.[5] Note that if one more possible security was to be considered this would add one term to the variance summation but $2n$ further terms would have to be included in the covariance summation.[6]

Problems in three or more securities can be approached in a two-part manner. Firstly, the efficiency frontier is determined and secondly, a portfolio somewhere on the frontier is selected. Later we shall describe a procedure by which the problem may be solved in one stage but it will be instructive to begin discussion of solution procedures with a two-part approach seen in diagrammatic terms.

Consider the problem in three securities. For graphical analysis the problem can be reduced to one in two variables by substitution. Since $x_3 = 1 - x_1 - x_2$ the expected portfolio return is:

$$\begin{aligned} \bar{R} = x_1 \bar{R}_1 + x_2 \bar{R}_2 + (1 - x_1 - x_2)\bar{R}_3 &= x_1(\bar{R}_1 - \bar{R}_3) \\ &+ x_2(\bar{R}_2 - \bar{R}_3) + \bar{R}_3 \end{aligned} \tag{11.27}$$

and the variance will be:

$$\begin{aligned} V &= x_1^2 \sigma_1^2 + 2x_1 x_2 \sigma_{12} + 2x_1(1 - x_1 - x_2)\sigma_{13} + \\ &\quad x_2^2 \sigma_2^2 + 2x_2(1 - x_1 - x_2)\sigma_{23} + (1 - x_1 - x_2)^2 \sigma_3^2 \\ &= x_1^2(\sigma_1^2 + \sigma_3^2 - 2\sigma_{13}) + x_2^2(\sigma_2^2 + \sigma_3^2 - 2\sigma_{23}) \\ &\quad + 2x_1 x_2(\sigma_3^2 + \sigma_{12} - \sigma_{13} - \sigma_{23}) + 2x_1(\sigma_{13} - \sigma_3^2) \\ &\quad + 2x_2(\sigma_{23} - \sigma_3^2) + \sigma_3^2 \end{aligned} \tag{11.28}$$

In Figure 11.6 the ellipses are *isovariance contours* showing combinations of x_2 and x_1 (and by implication x_3) which along any one contour give portfolios of equal

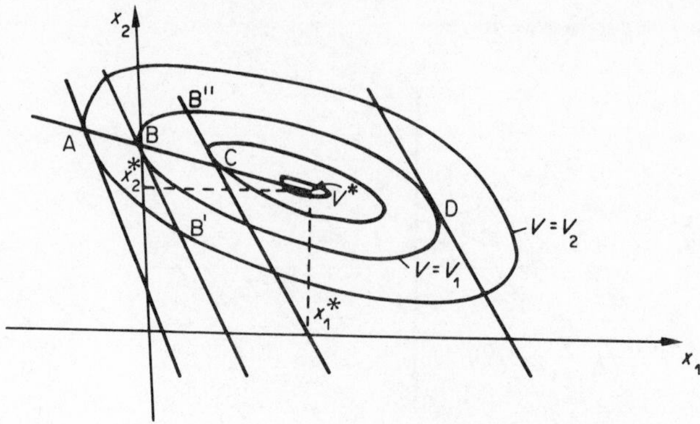

Figure 11.6 The critical line

variance. Contours nearer to the centre point correspond to lower values of V. The point V^* (given by $x_1 = x_1^*$ and $x_2 = x_2^*$) is the minimum variance portfolio. The parallel straight lines in the figure are iso-return contours. Along any one such line the values of x_1 and x_2 give portfolios with equal expected return. With security three representing the highest expected return investment, iso-return contours further to the left correspond to greater values of $\bar{R}$.

The mean-variance efficient portfolios correspond to values of the xs on the locus of points of tangency between isovariance curves and iso-return lines to the left of V^*. This locus is a straight line through points such as A, B and C and is called the *critical line.* A point such as B$'$, off the critical line, is not mean variance efficient. B$'$, on the same iso-return line as B, is on a higher isovariance curve ($V_2 > V_1$). The point B$''$ corresponds to xs that give the same variance as at B but B$''$ is on a lower iso-return line. It is important to note that points of tangency to the right of V^*, such as point D, correspond to portfolios giving minimum return for given variance lying on the irrelevant negatively shaped section of the graph of V against $\bar{R}$.

Once the critical line has been found the efficiency frontier can be plotted. Each point on the critical line corresponds to a value of V (given by the isovariance line through the critical line) and a value of $\bar{R}$ (given by the iso-return line through the critical line) and these pairs of values are the coordinates of points on the efficiency frontier. If the investor's risk-return preferences are represented in the same diagram the optimal combination of return and variance can be obtained. The analyst then refers back to Figure 11.6 to find the corresponding values of x_1 and x_2 and, by implication x_3.

Finally with reference to Figure 11.6 it should be noted that the minimum variance portfolio, V^* may not be one of maximum diversification in that it may consist largely of two securities or perhaps one security. If an investor is obliged to 'diversify' (say be putting $^1/_3$ of the budget in each security) risk will actually increase.

11.4 Lagrange Multiplier Treatment

With sufficiently skilled draftsmanship a portfolio problem in four securities (and hence three dimensions with one x treated implicitly) could be solved graphically. Problems in more than four securities require a non-graphical approach. The problem of finding the set of mean-variance efficient portfolios is one to which the Lagrange Multiplier approach seems suited since it is one in constrained minimization (or maximization). For each given value of portfolio return we require minimum variance. The problem is to:

$$\left.\begin{array}{ll} \text{minimize} & V = \sum_{i=1}^{n} x_i^2 \sigma_i^2 + \sum_{i=1}^{n} \sum_{\substack{i=j \\ j\neq i}}^{n} x_i x_j \sigma_{ij} \\ \\ \text{subject to} & \sum_{i=1}^{n} x_i \bar{R}_i = \bar{R} \\ \text{and} & \sum_{i=1}^{n} x_i = 1 \end{array}\right\} \qquad (11.29)$$

for each possible value of $\bar{R}$. In this formulation negative values of the xs are not excluded as possibilities. A negative x would represent a 'leveraged' portfolio, the investor would be issuing a security. This will not always be possible, but for the time being we shall allow this. Of course, in principle there will be no finite bound on the portfolio return (if the $\bar{R}$s differ) if there are no lower bounds on the xs since we are considering a case of constant returns to scale. In this approach bounds can be introduced at a later stage of the calculations.

It will be recalled that the two security case of (11.29) is trivial since for any given value of $\bar{R}$ there will be a unique solution to the two constraints, both being linear. For each value of portfolio return there is a unique portfolio and therefore just one corresponding value of V. The risk-return efficiency frontier is then easily graphed.

In the three security case the Lagrangian function is written as:

$$L = x_1^2\sigma_1^2 + x_2^2\sigma_2^2 + x_3^2\sigma_3^2 + 2x_1x_2\sigma_{12} + 2x_1x_3\sigma_{13} + 2x_2x_3\sigma_{23} + y_1(\bar{R} - x_1\bar{R}_1 - x_2\bar{R}_2 - x_3\bar{R}_3) + y_2(1 - x_1 - x_2 - x_3) \qquad (11.30)$$

Investment	Mean return ($\bar{R}_i$)	Variance (σ_i^2)	Covariance (σ_{ij})
x_1 (Safebet consolidated)	0.06	0.0004	$\sigma_{12} = 0.0005$
x_2 (Bothworlds Ltd)	0.12	0.0036	$\sigma_{23} = 0.0015$
x_3 (Sleeveace prospecting)	0.30	0.0625	$\sigma_{13} = 0.0002$

Figure 11.7 Data for Lagrange multiplier example

where y_1 and y_2 are the multipliers. Since the constraints are equalities and there are, as yet, no sign requirements the first order conditions are:

$$\left.\begin{aligned}
\frac{\partial L}{\partial x_1} &= 2\sigma_1^2 x_1 + 2\sigma_{12}x_2 + 2\sigma_{13}x_3 - y_1\bar{R}_1 - y_2 = 0\\
\frac{\partial L}{\partial x_2} &= 2\sigma_2^2 x_2 + 2\sigma_{12}x_1 + 2\sigma_{23}x_3 - y_1\bar{R}_2 - y_2 = 0\\
\frac{\partial L}{\partial x_3} &= 2\sigma_3^2 x_3 + 2\sigma_{13}x_1 + 2\sigma_{23}x_2 - y_1\bar{R}_3 - y_2 = 0\\
\frac{\partial L}{\partial y_1} &= \bar{R} - x_1\bar{R}_1 - x_2\bar{R}_2 - x_3\bar{R}_3 = 0\\
\frac{\partial L}{\partial y_2} &= 1 - x_1 - x_2 - x_3 = 0
\end{aligned}\right\} \tag{11.31}$$

Since conditions (11.31) are five linear equations in five unknowns; the three *xs* and two Langrange multipliers, there will be a unique solution which because of the convexity of the function V, will give the variance minimizing values of the *xs*. It can be shown that the Langrange multiplier $y_1 = \mathrm{d}V\min/\mathrm{d}\bar{R}$; the rate of change of the minimum value of variance as required return changes. y_1 is therefore the slope of the efficiency frontier if variance is represented on the vertical axis.

Before passing on to a numerical exercise, consider briefly the case of *riskless assets*. Although theoretically no investment is entirely free of risk for most practical purposes government securities (and perhaps the issues of some government backed agencies and large non-government financial institutions) may be considered to be free of risk. 'Risk-free' is taken to mean zero variance in the security return (and therefore of course zero covariance with the returns from other securities). The basic model structure used so far can accommodate such assets. The matrix of the first derivatives of the Lagrangian will contain zero entries corresponding to the risk free investment. For example in a three security problem with x_3 risk free we should have to solve:

$$\begin{pmatrix}
2\sigma_1^2 & 2\sigma_{12} & 0 & -\bar{R}_1 & -1\\
2\sigma_{21} & 2\sigma_2^2 & 0 & -\bar{R}_2 & -1\\
0 & 0 & 0 & -\bar{R}_3 & -1\\
1 & 1 & 1 & 0 & 0\\
\bar{R}_1 & \bar{R}_2 & \bar{R}_3 & 0 & 0
\end{pmatrix}
\begin{pmatrix} x_1\\ x_2\\ x_3\\ y_2\\ y_1 \end{pmatrix}
=
\begin{pmatrix} 0\\ 0\\ 0\\ 1\\ \bar{R} \end{pmatrix}$$

If many securities are risk free the matrix above would be rather 'sparse' (containing many zeros) and reformulations of the problem might be investigated.

Consider the following numerical example. Mean return, variance and covariance data are given in Figure 11.7. The returns are yield figures expressed as decimals.

Portfolio return will then be given by:

$$\bar{R} - 0.06x_1 + 0.12x_2 + 0.30x_3$$

Portfolio variance is:

$$V = 0.0004x_1^2 + 0.0036x_2^2 + 0.0625x_3^2$$
$$+ 0.001x_1x_2 + 0.0004x_1x_3 + 0.003x_2x_3$$

The equations (11.31) for the above data are solved for the xs and the Lagrange multipliers as functions of $\bar{R}$; the required portfolio return. With $\bar{R}$ expressed as a percentage figure instead of a decimal (e.g. 10 instead of 0.1) the solution is:

$$x_1 = \frac{10{,}272 - 685\bar{R}}{6{,}054} \qquad x_2 = \frac{577\bar{R} - 3{,}606}{6{,}054}$$

$$x_3 = \frac{108\bar{R} - 612}{6{,}054} \qquad y_1 = \frac{62.02\bar{R} - 364.9}{6{,}054}$$

$$y_2 = \frac{26.2608 - 3.649\bar{R}}{6{,}054}$$

The solution has several points worthy of note. First, not all of the xs are non-negative for all values of $\bar{R}$. It will be seen that x_1 is positive only if $\bar{R}$ is less than 10,272/685, x_2 is positive only if $\bar{R}$ exceeds 3,606/577 and x_3 will only be positive if $\bar{R}$ exceeds 612/108. Consequently variance minimizing portfolios are unleveraged only for values of $\bar{R}$ between (approximately) 6.25% and 15%. If values of $\bar{R}$ outside of this interval are required and the investor may not issue securities (negative xs prohibited) then the calculations have to be modified to include the sign requirements. The means by which this provision can be included are described later on.

The second point is that the variance minimizing portfolios for 6%, 12% and 30% do not consist of single investments in x_1, x_2 and x_3 respectively. For instance the variance minimizing portfolio for $R = 30$ is:

$$x_1 = \frac{-10{,}278}{6{,}054}, \quad x_2 = \frac{13{,}704}{6{,}054}, \quad x_3 = \frac{2{,}628}{6{,}054}$$

Clearly if negative xs are unfeasible, then a return of 30% can only be secured by $x_1 = 0$, $x_2 = 0$, $x_3 = 1$; only x_3 is taken as intuition would suggest. However the variance minimizing portfolio for 12% contains all positive xs with:

$$x_1 = \frac{2{,}052}{6{,}054}, \quad x_2 = \frac{3{,}318}{6{,}054}, \quad x_3 = \frac{684}{6{,}054}$$

The corresponding value of V for this portfolio is 0.002312 (to be related to the return in decimal form, $R = 0.12$) whereas with $x_2 = 1$ the corresponding variance figure is 0.0036. Incidentally the variance figure 0.002312 is quite large relative to a mean return of only 12%. In percentage terms the standard deviation is about 4.8% so that there is only a (just over) 95% chance of the actual return falling between 2.4% and 21.6%.

The third point concerns the optimal value of the Lagrange multiplier y_1. As we have said, y_1 represents the rate of change of the minimum value of variance as required expected return changes. The value of y_1 becomes zero for $R = (364.9/62.02) \simeq 5.88$ (corresponding to $x_1 \simeq 1.031$, $x_2 \simeq -0.035$, $x_3 \simeq 0.004$). As required return falls towards 5.88% so variance falls, but as return decreases below 5.88% so the corresponding minimum variance figure rises. That is to say an attempt to secure lower overall variance by reducing required return below 5.88% would fail; 5.88% is the return on the overall variance minimizing portfolio. The point is somewhat 'academic' however as portfolios with return below 6.25% are leveraged.

Fourth, it should be noted that there is no limit to the expected return on the portfolio if leveraging is permitted. High values of $\bar{R}$ produce positive values of x_3 and x_2 and negative x_1. The investor is adding to his original funds by issuing securities at 6% and investing the monies thus raised at 12% (to keep down variance) and 30%.

Fifthly, the optimal value of y_2 is interesting. The Lagrange multiplier y_2, at an optimum, can be shown to be $dV\text{min}/db$, where b, expressed as a decimal is the proportion of the total budget that the investor spends. We have set $b = 1$ in writing $x_1 + x_2 + x_3 = 1$ and the investor is constrained to spend his entire budget on the 'real' investments; there is no cash in this model (though it could be included by introducing x_4 with return and variance zero). In fact for some low values of portfolio expected return the investor could reduce variance by not spending his entire budget. We see that y_2 is positive for $\bar{R} < 26.2608/3.649 \simeq 7.2$ meaning that changes in b bring changes of Vmin in the same direction; a reduction in the proportion of the budget spent brings a reduction in minimum value of variance that can be achieved. However, in order to restrict the problem to one in three variables we shall largely ignore the matter of proportion of budget expended.

The equations of the isovariance contours in x_2x_1 space (for a diagram similar to Figure 11.6) can be found by substitution of $x_3 = 1 - x_1 - x_2$ into the formula for variance. The result is:

$$V = 0.0625x_1^2 + 0.0631x_2^2 + 0.1226x_1x_2 - 0.1246x_1 - 0.122x_2 + 0.0625 \tag{11.32}$$

Setting V equal to a particular value in the above equation generates one isovariance contour. In comparison with Figure 11.6 the contours are rotated clockwise and V^* is positioned just beneath the horizontal axis.

The equations of the iso-return lines are obtained by substitution of $x_3 = 1 - x_1 - x_2$ into $\bar{R} = 6x_1 + 12x_2 + 30x_3$ so that:

$$x_2 = \frac{30 - \bar{R}}{18} - \frac{4x_1}{3}$$

Changing $\bar{R}$ simply alters the position of the return line relative to the origin. All iso-return lines have a slope of $-4/3$.

The equation of the critical line can be found by expressing x_2 as a function of x_1 and $\bar{R}$ (from the solutions for x_1 and x_2 given above) and making the substitution $\bar{R} = 6x_1 + 12x_2 + 30(1 - x_1 - x_2)$. The result is (approximate coefficients):

$$x_2 = 0.834 - 0.842x_1$$

The critical line, the locus of points of tangency of iso-return lines and isovariance contours is a straight line of slope -0.842 the relevant section being above and to the left of V^*.

To obtain the risk-return efficiency frontier first substitute for x_1 and x_2 their solutions as functions of $\bar{R}$ into (11.32). This gives minimum variance as a function of expected return. The result is (approximate coefficients and with $\bar{R}$ as a percentage figure)

$$V = 21.69 - 6.03\bar{R} + 0.512\bar{R}^2 \tag{11.33}$$

We must now tackle the problem of preventing leverage. Clearly one way of doing this would be to set the problem up in the first instance as a quadratic programming problem and work with the Kuhn–Tucker conditions which contain explicit provisions that the xs be non-negative. But there is another procedure which does not require a Q.P. approach. We have expressed the optimal x_j as functions of $\bar{R}$ and so long as $\bar{R}$ (in the numerical illustration) is not outside of the range 3,606/577 to 10,272/685 there are no negative xs. Consider the upper bound first of all. When $\bar{R}$ reaches this value x_1 becomes zero. At this point x_1 is removed from the analysis and the problem is reduced to one in two securities, x_2 and x_3. In general when x_j becomes zero in an n security problem it is dropped from the analysis and the remaining $n-1$ xs are solved for afresh as linear functions of the portfolio return. Continuing with the variation in $\bar{R}$, when the next x reaches zero level it, in turn, is deleted and for values of $\bar{R}$ further in the direction of change the problem becomes one in n–2 securities – and so on. Although the logic of the procedure is straightforward the computational effort is considerable – a new problem is only one less variable having to be solved at each stage.

However, as we have seen, when a problem is reduced to one in two securities the determination of the efficiency frontier is a trivial problem (provided that all the budget has to be spent) and in our example when R exceeds 10,272/685 the values of x_2 and x_3 in the portfolio can be obtained by reference to the portfolio return equation alone. That is

$$R = 12x_2 + 30x_3$$

but since we obstinately persist in the requirement that the budget be spent; $x_3 = 1 - x_2$ so that

$$x_2 = \frac{30 - \bar{R}}{18} \quad \text{and} \quad x_3 = \frac{\bar{R} - 12}{18}$$

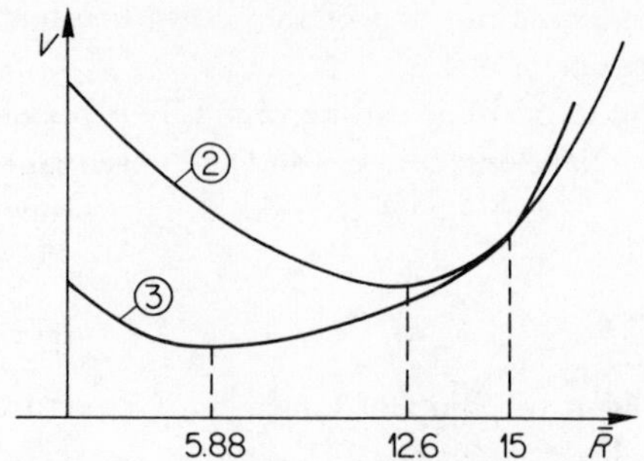

Figure 11.8 Relationship of 2 and 3 security frontiers

Variance as a function of $\bar{R}$ is obtained as before. That is

$$V = 0.0036x_2^2 - 0.0625x_3^2 + 0.003x_2x_3$$

substituting $1 - x_2$ for x_3 gives

$$V = 0.0631x_2^2 - 0.122x_2 + 0.0625$$

substituting $(30 - R)/18$ for x_2 gives (approximate coefficients and with $\bar{R}$ as a percentage figure)

$$V = 344.44 - 49.074\bar{R} + 1.9475\bar{R}^2 \tag{11.34}$$

The two expressions for variance, (11.33) and (11.34) give the same figure for V at $\bar{R} \simeq 15$ (any difference due to errors in rounding). The situation is illustrated in Figure 11.8 (not to scale). The lower curve marked (3) is the three security efficiency frontier and the upper curve is the efficiency frontier in securities 2 and 3 only. The two curves touch at $\bar{R} \simeq 15$ but the two security curve is steeper as $\bar{R}$ increases above 15. It is this upper curve that is the relevant one for these values of $\bar{R}$ if the leverage is prohibited. Of course the maximum values of $\bar{R}$ that can be achieved in the absence of leverage is 30. The reader may verify the tangency at $R \simeq 15$ and the fact that the two security frontier is steeper above this value of $\bar{R}$ by reference to the equations for the slopes of the frontiers. These are:

$$\text{(a)} \quad \frac{dV}{d\bar{R}} = -6.03 + 1.024\bar{R} \quad \text{(three securities)}$$

$$\text{(b)} \quad \frac{dV}{dR} = -49.074 + 3.895\bar{R} \quad \text{(two securities)} \tag{11.35}$$

Setting the R.H.S. of (11.35) (b) to be not less than the R.H.S. of (11.35) (a) gives the result that $\bar{R} \geqslant 15$.

A similar procedure can be applied for low values of $\bar{R}$. When $\bar{R} = 3{,}606/577 > x_2 = 0$ and for further reductions in $\bar{R}$, x_2 is omitted. It follows that since:

$$\bar{R} = 6x_1 + 30x_3 \quad \text{and} \quad x_1 + x_3 = 1 \tag{11.36}$$

$$x_1 = \frac{30 - \bar{R}}{24} \quad \text{and} \quad x_3 = \frac{\bar{R} - 6}{24}$$

and since V is now given by

$$V = 0.0004x_1^2 + 0.0625x_3^2 + 0.0004x_1x_3$$

we can write

$$V = 0.0625 - 0.1246x_1 + 0.0625x_1^2$$

and substitution for x_1 with $\bar{R}$ as a percentage figure (approximate coefficient of $\bar{R}^2$)

$$V = 44.0625 - 13.1875\bar{R} + 1.0851\bar{R}^2 \tag{11.37}$$

Again the corresponding efficiency frontier given by (11.37) is within the old frontier; variance/return combinations implying negative x_2 being excluded. The range of application of (11.37) and (11.36) is small however, being for $6 \leqslant \bar{R} \leqslant 6.25$ (approx.). It will be seen from (11.36) that x_3 would become negative for $\bar{R} < 6$. Unleveraged portfolios with expected return less than 6% cannot be achieved and portfolios with expected return in excess of 6¼% are more efficient with x_2 included.

The reader may wish to verify that (11.37) gives lower values of V in the range $6 \leqslant \bar{R} \leqslant 6.25$ than does the two security frontier consisting of x_1 and x_2. This frontier is given by

$$V = 32 - 9.6667\bar{R} + 0.8333\bar{R}^2 \tag{11.38}$$

We have seen therefore that the unleveraged efficiency frontier, at least in the three security problem, is comprised of sections of three and two security frontiers each of which is a quadratic in $\bar{R}$. Thus, aside from the leverage prohibition we are concerned with quadratic expressions. This will always be the case irrespective of the number of securities involved since the solution of the n security equivalent of conditions (11.31) will give each x_i as a linear function of $\bar{R}$. Consequently substitution for the x_i in the expression for V will give a quadratic function of $\bar{R}$.

Despite this fact that, in the end, we are dealing with only quadratic expressions in $\bar{R}$ it is evident that the obtaining of the unleveraged efficiency frontier is a considerable computational task. Also, the investor has yet to decide upon the particular combination of variance and return on the efficiency frontier that he wishes to have.

11.5 Representation of Investor Preferences

As we have already seen, this problem can be represented as that of finding the point on the efficiency frontier which is on the highest variance/return indifference curve. But although this approach is theoretically elegant and would round off the analysis nicely it would not usually be employed in practice. The investor would normally select the efficient portfolio that is 'most appealing' to him (by furtive reference to his utility function no doubt!) or else would incorporate some unsophisticated representation of preferences in an alternative objective function to that of (11.29).

There is a formulation of the efficiency frontier determination problem which allows the incorporation of the investor's risk return preferences so that the overall optimum portfolio can be identified along with production of the efficiency frontier itself. The objective is to maximize a weighted average of expected return and variance: that is; maximize

$$F = w\bar{R} - V \tag{11.39}$$

subject to the expenditure constraint $\Sigma x_j = 1$. The function F can be interpreted as a utility function. In general the investor's ex-ante satisfaction with a portfolio depends on both expected return and variance and can in principle at least be written as a function of these variables. That is

$$U = f(\bar{R}, V) \tag{11.40}$$

where U represents expected utility. Any such function would on the basis of the assumptions discussed at the beginning of the chapter, have the property that utility is an increasing function of portfolio variance. Mathematically the first-order partial derivatives of U are of opposite sign.

$$\frac{\partial U}{\partial \bar{R}} > 0 \quad \text{and} \quad \frac{\partial U}{\partial V} < 0$$

These conditions are satisfied by (11.39) provided $w > 0$ since

$$\frac{\partial F}{\partial \bar{R}} = w \quad \text{and} \quad \frac{\partial F}{\partial V} = -1$$

The slope of the indifference curves (the rate at which the investor is prepared to trade security for return, at a point, so as to maintain an unchanged level of satisfaction) is called the marginal rate of substitution, In general this can be found in the following manner by

$$\mathrm{d}U = \frac{\partial U}{\partial \bar{R}}\,\mathrm{d}\bar{R} + \frac{\partial U}{\partial V}\,\mathrm{d}V$$

Now along an indifference curve, by definition, $\mathrm{d}U = 0$ (there must be no change in utility). Thus

$$\frac{\partial U}{\partial \bar{R}}\,\mathrm{d}\bar{R} + \frac{\partial U}{\partial V}\,\mathrm{d}V = 0$$

so that the slope of the indifference curves, $\mathrm{d}V/\mathrm{d}\bar{R}$, is given by

$$\frac{\mathrm{d}V}{\mathrm{d}\bar{R}} = -\frac{\partial U/\partial \bar{R}}{\partial U/\partial V} \tag{11.41}$$

which in the case of (11.39) is:

$$\frac{dV}{d\bar{R}} = \frac{-w}{-1} = w$$

so that the weight w expresses the rate at which variance must increase to offset an increase in expected return. Alternatively $d\bar{R}/dV = 1/w$ expresses the rate at which expected return must increase to compensate for increased variance. The lower the value of w the more averse to risk the investor is. For a given value of w the indifference curves are straight lines in V, $\bar{R}$ space as shown in Figure 11.9.

Utility increases as return for given variance increases so that lines further to the right in Figure 11.9 correspond to increased utility ($U_3 > U_2 > U_1$). In Figure 11.10 the effects of varying w are seen. The effect is to rotate an indifference line about an imaginary (variance cannot be negative) point on the V axis. For given U, with line D the investor requires increased 'compensation' in terms of return for a given increase in variance in comparison to lines A B and C.

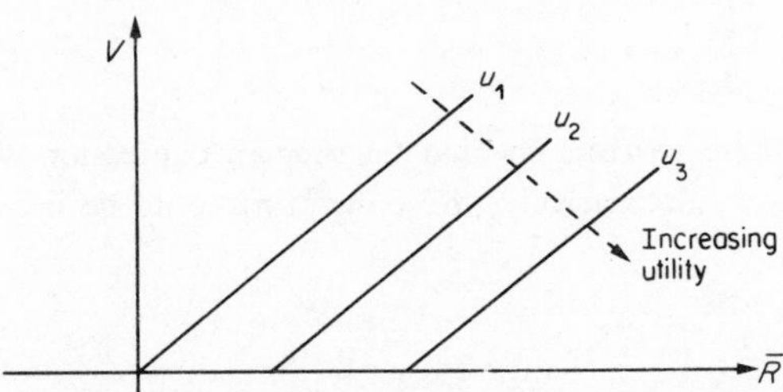

Figure 11.9 Constant m.r.s. indifference curves

Now consider the maximization of (11.39). Suppose we fix $\bar{R}$ at some arbitrary value $\bar{R}^0$. In this event for any value of w the difference $w\bar{R}^0 - V$ can be maximal only if V is minimized; that is, if a point on the efficiency frontier is selected. If we now fix V at V^0 for any w the difference can be maximal only if R is maximized – again a point on the efficiency frontier is selected. So, no matter what the value of w is the investor will always choose a point on the efficiency frontier. This means that the optimum will be a point of tangency between an indifference line and the efficiency frontier so that continuous variation of w will produce the efficiency frontier itself. This fact is illustrated in Figure 11.11 in which point A is selected when the value of w used is greater than that which produces A$'$. It should be noted that points below A$'$ correspond to negative utility; the intercept point of the indifference lines being above the origin. Such points would be of mathematical significance only. Points to the left of A$''$ on the efficiency frontier are obtained only if w is allowed to become negative.

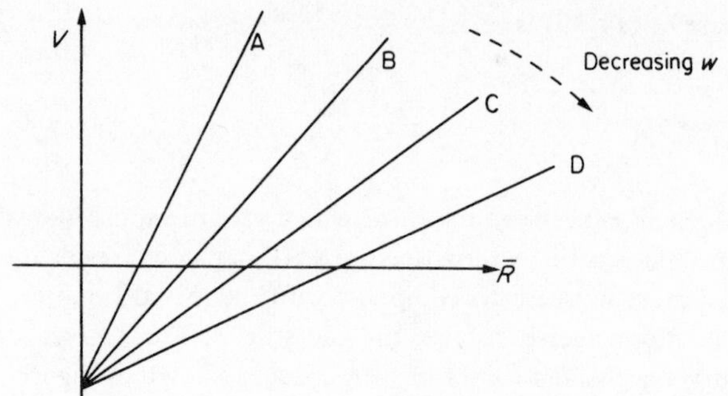

Figure 11.10 Effect of different values of w

Formally, the problem of maximization of (11.39) can be written in terms of the xs as:

$$\left.\begin{aligned} &\text{maximize: } w \sum_{i=1}^{n} x_i \bar{R}_i - \sum_{i=1}^{n} x_i^2 \sigma_i^2 - \sum_{i=1}^{n} \sum_{\substack{j=1 \\ j \neq i}}^{n} x_i x_j \sigma_{ij} \\ &\qquad \text{subject to} \qquad \sum_{i=1}^{n} x_i = 1 \end{aligned}\right\} \tag{11.42}$$

The problem could be written up as a Lagrangian expression with the constraint explicitly included or, alternatively, the constraint could be included implicitly by substituting

$$x_n = 1 - \sum_{i=1}^{n-1} x_i$$

for x_n in the objective function itself. Either way the optimal values of the xs would emerge as linear functions of w producing return/variance combinations on the efficiency frontier. This will be left as an exercise for the interested reader to perform on the numerical data of Figure 11.7.

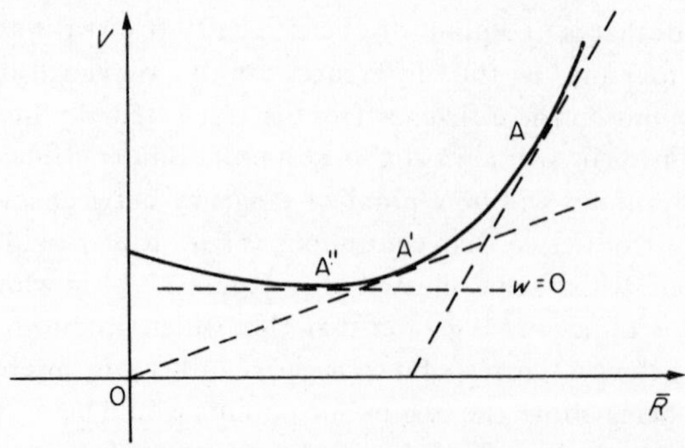

Figure 11.11 The efficiency frontier and variation in w

Since we have already obtained the efficiency frontier by the minimization approach we have the expression for variance as a function of expected return given by (11.33). Upon substitution, (11.39) for the numerical example becomes:

$$F = (w + 6.03)R - 0.512\bar{R}^2 - 21.69 \qquad (11.43)$$

which can now be maximized with respect to $\bar{R}$. The conditions are:

$$\frac{dF}{d\bar{R}} = (w + 6.03) - 1.024\bar{R} = 0$$

and

$$\frac{d^2F}{d\bar{R}^2} = -1.024 \qquad < 0$$

Thus the optimal value of $\bar{R}$ is given by:

$$\bar{R}(\text{opt}) = \frac{w + 6.03}{1.024} \qquad (11.44)$$

and the corresponding value of F is, unsurprisingly, a quadratic in w given by:

$$F_{\text{max}} = 0.488w^2 + 5.888w - 3.936 \qquad (11.45)$$

In the special case where $w = 0$ (the investor is concerned only with variance) equation (11.44) gives the return associated with the variance minimizing portfolio, and (11.45) gives (negated) the minimum value of variance itself.

The optical level of variance as a function of w is found by substituting (11.44) into (11.37). The result is:

$$v(\text{opt}) = 0.488w^2 + 3.936$$

If a linear utility function such as (11.39) provides an adequate representation of the investor's preferences then a one-stage procedure of maximization of this function will be indicated. If a more sophisticated utility function is to be employed then a two-stage solution procedure is preferable. First the efficiency frontier is determined and then the utility function is introduced and maximized with the efficiency frontier as a constraint.

As an example of the latter procedure suppose that the investor's utility function was of the Cobb–Douglas type.[7] That is:

$$U = A\bar{R}^{\alpha}(k + V)^{-\beta} \qquad (11.46)$$

where $A > 0$, $\alpha > 0$, $\beta > 0$, $k > 0$ and $\alpha < \beta$. The constant k is included so that utility is finite for zero variance. If $\alpha < \beta$ as supposed then the indifference curves are as shown in Figure 11.12 being concave to the $\bar{R}$ axis. It would be reasonable to suppose that $\alpha < 1$ so that the marginal ultility of return ($\partial U/\partial \bar{R}$) is diminishing. The slope of the indifference curves as given by (11.46) is:

$$\frac{dV}{d\bar{R}} = \frac{\alpha(k + V)}{\beta R}$$

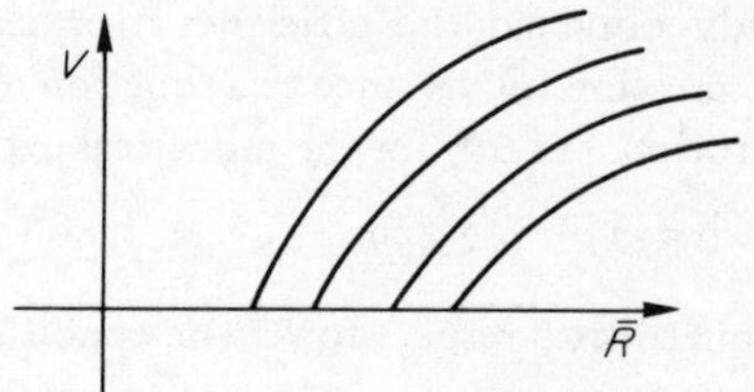

Figure 11.12 Indifference curves: Cobb–Douglas case ($\alpha < \beta$)

which can be shown to diminish as $\bar{R}$ increases for given utility so long as $\alpha < \beta$. That is, as variance increases for given utility the investor requires increasing increments in return to compensate. Intuitively this is more appealing than the linear indifference curve case in which the increments in $\bar{R}$ are constant.

In passing it would be rather neat if utility could be expressed as a function of arguments which contribute positively to satisfaction. We might think of utility as a function of return and 'security'. For example:

$$U = A\bar{R}^{\alpha} S^{\beta}$$

where S is an index of security and $\beta > 0$. Obviously there would need to be some upper bound on S (although we have not yet introduced the notion of risk free investments). The index of security $S = 1/(k + V)$ has an upper bound of $1/k$ and produces the form (11.46).

Now consider a numerical illustration. Let

$$U = \bar{R}^{0.8}(1 + V)^{-1.5}$$

and with V given by (11.33) the Lagrangian is:

$$L = \bar{R}^{0.8}(1 + V)^{-1.5} + \lambda(V - 21.69 + 6.03\bar{R} - 0.512\bar{R}^2)$$

and first order conditions are:

$$\frac{\partial L}{\partial \bar{R}} = 0.8\bar{R}^{-0.2}(1 + V)^{-1.5} + 6.03\lambda - 1.024\bar{R}\lambda = 0$$

$$\frac{\partial L}{\partial V} = -1.5\bar{R}^{0.8}(1 + V)^{-2.5} + \lambda = 0$$

$$\frac{\partial L}{\partial \lambda} = V - 21.69 + 6.03\bar{R} - 0.512\bar{R}^2 = 0$$

Substituting for λ from the second condition into the first gives:

$$0.8\bar{R}^{-0.2}(1 + V)^{-1.5} + 9.045\bar{R}^{0.8}(1 + V)^{-2.5} - 1.536\bar{R}^{1.8}(1 + V)^{-2.5} = 0$$

multiplying through by $\bar{R}^{0.2}(1 + V)^{2.5} \neq 0$ and solving for V gives:

$$V = \frac{1.536\bar{R}^2 - 9.045\bar{R} - 0.8}{0.8}$$

Substitution into the third condition produces:

$$1.1264\bar{R}^2 - 4.221\bar{R} - 18.152 = 0$$

of which the positive root is $\bar{R} = 6.304$. This is the utility maximizing value of portfolio return.

A more general form of utility function is worth mentioning at this point not only because it may be useful in itself but also because it produces the functions we have used so far and indeed other expressions of interest as special cases. Let utility be given by[8]

$$U = a_0(a_1\bar{R}^{-b} + a_2(k + V)^{-b})^{-c/b} \tag{11.47}$$

where $a_0 > 0$, $a_1 \geqslant 0$ and $a_2 \leqslant 0$. In interpretation of (11.47) we begin by noting that in a portfolio context the value of a_0 is unimportant and would normally be set at unity but if U was attatched to a *single investment* and the utility of different, mutually exclusive projects was being considered, then a_0 could be interpreted as a 'project-specific' coefficient being different between projects. The coefficients a_1 and a_2 are distribution parameters and the relative magnitudes of these reflect the relative importance attached by the investor to return and risk. The value of b determines the curvature of the indifference curves; b is known as the substitution parameter and $b \geqslant -1$. The parameter c, the degree of homogeneity of the function, is difficult to interpret in the present context but might be thought of as measuring the overall 'sensitivity' of the investor.

In an application, the investor would select values of the parameters of (11.47) and solve the portfolio problem by the two-stage procedure. Selection of certain values of the parameters produces (perhaps as a limiting case) simpler and more familiar forms of function. For example as the value of b approaches zero then U approaches the Cobb–Douglas form:

$$U \rightarrow a_0\bar{R}^{a_1c}(k + V)^{a_2c} \quad \text{as} \quad b \rightarrow 0$$

If $b = -1$ and $c = 1$ the linear case is produced. That is:

$$U = a_0(a_1\bar{R} + a_2(k + V))$$

so that if $a_2 = -a_0^{-1}$ then the linear form (11.39) is produced (set $k = 0$ here and where $w = a_0a_1$). When $b = -1$ and $c = 2$ (11.47) is a quadratic expression.

The use of CES functions in investment appraisal generally is discussed in the Appendix to this chapter and there are cases other than those mentioned above which are generalized by expressions like (11.47). The purpose of utility functions is to derive a one-dimensional measure of the desirability of a project or portfolio with may have several important characteristics. The form of function used is at the discretion of the investor.

11.6 Quadratic Programming Solution

Suppose that the investor's preferences regarding return-variance combinations can be described by (11.39). For the problem data of Figure 11.7 we shall now use the quadratic programming procedure of Chapter 10 to solve the portfolio problem for $w = 5$. With return and variance data in percentage terms the objective will be to maximize:

$$F = 30x_1 + 60x_2 + 150x_3 - 4x_1^2 - 36x_2^2 - 625x_3^2 - 10x_1x_2 - 4x_1x_3 - 30x_2x_3 \tag{11.48}$$

Let us suppose, for a change, that not all the budget need be spent, but continue to assume that leveraged portfolios are prohibited. Thus the constraint set is given by:

$$\left.\begin{array}{l} x_1 + x_2 + x_3 \leqslant 1 \\ x_1 \geqslant 0, \quad x_2 \geqslant 0, \quad x_3 \geqslant 0 \end{array}\right\} \tag{11.49}$$

If it should turn out that, at an optimum, not all of the budget is spent, then the variance of portfolio return that is arrived at, and the return figure itself are still related to the total budget, not just that part which is actually spent. It is as if there were a fourth security (proportion invested being s below) cash, giving zero actual and expected return and zero variance and covariance with other securities. The Lagrangean function will be:

$$L = F + y(1 - x_1 - x_2 - x_3) \tag{11.50}$$

and the Kuhn–Tucker conditions corresponding to (10.58) will be:

$$\left.\begin{array}{l}
\dfrac{\partial L}{\partial x_1} = 30 - 8x_1 - 10x_2 - 4x_3 - y + t_1 = 0 \\
\dfrac{\partial L}{\partial x_2} = 60 - 72x_2 - 10x_1 - 30x_3 - y + t_2 = 0 \\
\dfrac{\partial L}{\partial x_3} = 150 - 1250x_3 - 4x_1 - 30x_2 - y + t_3 = 0 \\
x_1t_1 = 0 \\
x_2t_2 = 0 \\
x_3t_3 = 0 \\
x_1 \geqslant 0 \quad t_1 \geqslant 0 \\
x_2 \geqslant 0 \quad t_2 \geqslant 0 \\
x_3 \geqslant 0 \quad t_3 \geqslant 0 \\
\dfrac{\partial L}{\partial y} = 1 - x_1 - x_2 - x_3 - s = 0 \\
ys = 0 \\
y \geqslant 0 \quad s \geqslant 0
\end{array}\right\} \tag{11.51}$$

Now since F is concave and the constraints (11.49) form a convex set, the Kuhn–Tucker conditions are both necessary and sufficient for a global optimum. Following the procedure of chapter ten we now re-express the Kuhn–Tucker

			0	0	0	0	0	0	0	0	0	0	0	−1
			x_1	x_2	x_3	y	t_1	t_2	t_3	s	u_1	u_2	u_3	u_4
0	u_1	30	8	10	4	1	−1	0	0	0	1	0	0	0
0	u_2	60	10	72	30	1	0	−1	0	0	0	1	0	0
0	u_3	150	4	30	1,250	1	0	0	−1	0	0	0	1	0
−1	u_4	1	(1)	1	1	0	0	0	0	1	0	0	0	1
0	u_1	22	0	2	−4	1	−1	0	0	−8	1	0	0	−8
0	u_2	50	0	62	20	1	0	−1	0	−10	0	1	0	−10
0	u_3	146	0	26	1,246	1	0	0	−1	−4	0	0	1	−4
0	x_1	1	1	1	1	0	0	0	0	1	0	0	0	1

Figure 11.13 Q.P. example: phase one calculations

conditions corresponding to the partial derivatives in (11.51) so that constant terms only are on the R.H.S. Adding in artificial variables gives:

$$\left.\begin{aligned} 8x_1 + 10x_2 + 4x_3 + y - t_1 + u_1 &= 30 \\ 10x_1 + 72x_2 + 30x_3 + y - t_2 + u_2 &= 60 \\ 4x_1 + 30x_2 + 1{,}250x_3 + y - t_3 + u_3 &= 150 \\ x_1 + x_2 + x_3 + s + u_4 &= 1 \end{aligned}\right\} \qquad (11.52)$$

The phase 1 calculations are shown in Figure 11.13 and the phase 2 calculations in Figure 11.14. In phase 2 pivotal elements have been chosen with an eye to arithmetic convenience rather than automatic selection of the most negative index row number. Starred zero are zero to three decimal places. The optimal solution is seen to consist of $x_1 = 0.479$, $x_2 = 0.430$, $x_3 = 0.091$ giving an expected portfolio yield of 10.764%. Reference to equation (11.44) gives, for $w = 5$, a value of $R = 10.771\%$. The difference is attributable to rounding errors.

11.7 Index Models

For operational purposes the amount of information required for the Markowitz model can be a severe disadvantage. If n securities are being considered then n expected returns, n variances and $n(n-1)/2$ covariances would be needed. In total then $(n/2)(n + 3)$ bits of data are necessary. Ball and Brown[9] cite the example that if all of the 1,300 or so stocks traded on the New York Stock Exchange were being considered, then the number of estimates required as data inputs would be approximately 850,000. This would be quite impracticable.

Markowitz was aware of this limitation of his original model (now referred to as the Markowitz full covariance model, MFC) and suggested a simplification drastically reducing the volume of data that would be required. Subsequently Sharpe produced his 'diagonal' or 'single-index' model.[10]

The single index model assumes that the returns to individual securities are related only through their own particular relationships with a market index. In

			0	0	0	0	0	0	0	0	−1	−1	−1
			x_1	x_2	x_3	y	t_1	t_2	t_3	s	u_1	u_2	u_3
−1	u_1	22	0	2	−4	(1)	−1	0	0	−8	1	0	0
−1	u_2	50	0	62	20	1	0	−1	0	−10	0	1	0
−1	u_3	146	0	26	1,246	1	0	0	−1	−4	0	0	1
0	x_1	1	1	1	1	0	0	0	0	1	0	0	0
		−218	0	−90	−1,262	−3	1	1	1	22	0	0	0
0	y	22	0	2	−4	1	−1	0	0	−8	1	0	0
−1	u_2	28	0	(60)	24	0	1	−1	0	−2	−1	1	0
−1	u_3	124	0	24	1,250	0	1	0	−1	4	−1	0	1
0	x_1	1	1	1	1	0	0	0	0	1	0	0	0
		−152	0	−84	−1,274	0	−2	1	1	−2	3	0	0
0	y	126.4/6	0	0	−28.8/6	1	−1.2/6	0.2/6	0	−47.6/6	1.2/6	−0.2/6	0
0	x_2	2.8/6	0	1	2.4/6	0	0.1/6	−0.1/6	0	−0.2/6	−0.1/6	0.1/6	0
−1	u_3	676.8/6	0	0	(7,442.4/6)	0	3.6/6	2.4/6	−1	28.8/6	−3.6/6	−2.4/6	1
0	x_1	3.2/6	1	0	3.6/6	0	−0.1/6	0.1/6	0	6.2/6	0.1/6	−0.1/6	0
		−676.8/6	0	0	−7,442.2/6	0	−3.6/6	−2.4/6	1	−28.8/6	9.6/6	8.4/6	0
0	y	21.503	0	0	0	1	−0.177	0.035	−0.005	−7.914	0.177	−0.035	0.005
0	x_2	0.430	0	1	0	0	0.017	−0.017	0*	−0.035	−0.017	0.017	0*
0	x_3	0.091	0	0	1	0	0*	0*	−0.001	0.004	0*	0*	0.001
0	x_1	0.479	1	0	0	0	−0.017	0.016	0.001	1.019	0.017	−0.016	−0.001
		0	0	0	0	0	0	0	0	0	1	1	1

Figure 11.14 Q.P. example: phase two

particular:

$$R_i = A_i + B_i I + C_i \quad (i = 1, 2, \ldots, n) \tag{11.53}$$

where R_i is the return (actual) on the ith security, I is the level of a market or economic index, A_i and B_i are parameters and C_i is a random variable with expected value zero and variance Q_i. The error terms for different securities are uncorrelated with each other, i.e. the covariance between C_i and C_j is zero $i \neq j$. The future level of the index is given by:

$$I = A_{n+1} + C_{n+1} \tag{11.54}$$

where A_{n+1} is a parameter and C_{n+1} is a random variable with expected value zero and variance $Qn + 1$. The model is pictured in Figure 11.15. The horizontal axis is the level of the index and the value of R_i is measured on the vertical axis above the origin. A_i is the intercept term and the slope of the straight line is B_i. The variance of the C_i is assumed independent of the level of the index. Beneath the horizontal axis the probability distribution of the value of the index is illustrated.[11]

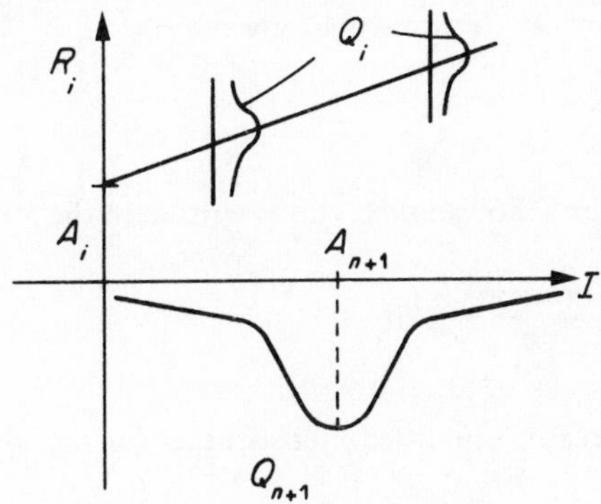

Figure 11.15 Sharpe's single index model diagram

The following relationships may be obtained:

$$\left.\begin{aligned} \bar{R}_i &= A_i + B_i A_{n+1} \\ \sigma_i^2 &= B_i^2 Q_{n+1} + Q_i \\ \sigma_{ij} &= B_i B_j Q_{n+1} \end{aligned}\right\} \tag{11.55}$$

Where, in (11.55) the two components of σ_i^2 have been described as systematic risk and unsystematic risk respectively.

If it was desired to use the MFC model the covariance data can be obtained from (11.55) having estimated only $2n$ values of the B_i. This alone would go a long way towards making the MFC model practicable for large scale applications. However, the portfolio problem can be reformulated altogether.

Consider portfolio return. The actual value of this, R is given by:

$$R = \sum_{i=1}^{n} x_i R_i$$

$$= \sum_{i=1}^{n} x_i(A_i + B_i I + C_i)$$

$$= \sum_{i=1}^{n} x_i(A_i + C_i) + I \sum_{i=1}^{n} x_i B_i$$

$$= \sum_{i=1}^{n+1} x_i(A_i + C_i) \qquad (11.56)$$

where, in (11.56),

$$x_{n+1} \equiv \sum_{i=1}^{n} x_i B_i$$

Sharpe viewed the portfolio as an investment in n 'basic securities' and an investment in the index [the $n + 1$th term in the summation (11.56)]. The expected value of portfolio return will be given by:

$$\bar{R} = \sum_{i=1}^{n+1} x_i A_i \qquad (11.57)$$

Now. as regards portfolio variance, this is written in the MFC model as:

$$V = \sum_{i=1}^{n} x_i^2 \sigma_i^2 + \sum_{i=1}^{n} \sum_{\substack{j=1 \\ j \neq 1}}^{n} x_i x_j \sigma_{ij} \qquad (11.58)$$

which can now be greatly simplified. Substituting for the σ_i^2 and σ_{ij} from (11.55) gives:

$$V = \sum_{i=1}^{n} x_i^2 (B_i^2 Q_{n+1} + Q_i) + \sum_{i=1}^{n} \sum_{\substack{j=1 \\ j \neq 1}}^{n} x_i x_j B_i B_j Q_{n+1} \qquad (11.59)$$

(11.59) is obviously rewritable as:

$$V = \sum_{i=1}^{n} x_i^2 Q_i + \sum_{i=1}^{n} x_i^2 B_i^2 Q_{n+1} + \sum_{i=1}^{n} \sum_{\substack{j=1 \\ j \neq i}}^{n} x_i x_j B_i B_j Q_{n+1}$$

$$= \sum_{i=1}^{n} x_i^2 Q_i + Q_{n+1} \left(\sum_{i=1}^{n} x_i B_i \right)^2 \qquad (11.60)$$

$$= \sum_{i=1}^{n+1} x_i^2 Q_i$$

so that the variance equation contains only $n + 1$ terms! The name 'diagonal model' arises from the fact that if (11.60) is expressed in matrix form only elements in the principal diagonal of the resulting matrix are non-zero. (11.60) would appear as

$$(x_1, x_2, \ldots, x_{n+1}) \begin{pmatrix} Q_1 & & & \\ & Q_2 & & \text{O} \\ & & \ddots & \\ \text{O} & & & Q_{n+1} \end{pmatrix} \begin{pmatrix} x_1 \\ x_2 \\ \vdots \\ x_{n+1} \end{pmatrix}$$

Viewed as a two-phase procedure the investor's problem is to determine the efficiency frontier from (11.57) and (11.60) and then to choose a point on it. The efficiency frontier thus provided will differ somewhat from the MFC frontier. Theoretically the MFC frontier has maximal efficiency and the single index frontier will be within or, in the extreme, not to the right of the MFC frontier. Further comparisons, resulting from empirical work are discussed below.

Now let us consider briefly a two index model. Suppose we order the securities so that the first m are correlated higher with index 1 (I_1) than index 2 (I_2) whilst the remaining $n-m$ are correlated more highly with the second index. The actual returns on the securities will be given by:

$$\left.\begin{aligned} R_i &= A_i + B_i I_1 + C_{1i} \quad (i = 1, 2, \ldots, m) \\ R_i &= A_i + B_i I_2 + C_{2i} \quad (i = m+1, \ldots, n) \end{aligned}\right\} \qquad (11.61)$$

where

$$E(C_{1i}) = 0, \quad E(C_{2i}) = 0, \quad E(C_{1i}^2) = Q_{1i}, \quad E(C_{2i}^2) = Q_{2i}$$

and where all pairs of securities have uncorrelated error terms. The levels of the indices are given by:

$$\begin{aligned} I_1 &= A_{n+1} + C_{n+1} \\ I_2 &= A_{n+2} + C_{n+2} \end{aligned} \qquad (11.62)$$

and where, in (11.62) $E(C_{n+1}) = 0$, $E(C_{n+2}) = 0$, $E(C_{n+1}^2) = Q_{n+1}$, $E(C_{n+2}^2) = Q_{n+2}$. Actual portfolio return is given by:

$$\begin{aligned} R &= \sum_{i=1}^{n} x_i R_i \\ &= \sum_{i=1}^{m} x_i(A_i + C_{1i}) + \sum_{i=m+1}^{n} x_i(A_i + C_{2i}) + I_1 \sum_{i=1}^{m} x_i B_i \\ &\quad + I_2 \sum_{i=m+1}^{n} x_i B_i \\ &= \sum_{i=1}^{n+2} x_i(A_i + C_i) \end{aligned} \qquad (11.63)$$

where, in (11.63), $C_i = C_{1i}$ for $i \leqslant m$; $C_i = C_{2i}$ for $m < i \leqslant n$; $C_i = C_{n+1}$ for

$i = n + 1$ and $C_i = C_{n+2}$ for $i = n + 2$. Also

$$x_{n+1} \equiv \sum_{i=1}^{m} x_i B_i \quad \text{and} \quad x_{n+2} \equiv \sum_{i=m+1}^{n} x_i B_i$$

The expected value of portfolio return will be:

$$\bar{R} = \sum_{i=1}^{n+2} x_i A_i \tag{11.64}$$

Now, as regards variances and covariances we have:

$$\left.\begin{array}{ll} \sigma_i^2 = B_i^2 Q_{n+1} + Q_{1i} & (i = 1, 2, \ldots, m) \\ \sigma_i^2 = B_i^2 Q_{n+2} + Q_{2i} & (i = m+1, \ldots, n) \\ \sigma_{ij} = B_i B_j Q_{n+1} & (i, j \leqslant m) \\ \sigma_{ij} = B_i B_j Q_{n+2} & (i, j > m) \\ \sigma_{ij} = B_i B_j Q_{12} & (i \leqslant m, j > m \quad \text{or} \quad i > m, j \leqslant m) \end{array}\right\} \tag{11.65}$$

where, in (11.65) the term Q_{12} is the covariance between C_{n+1} and C_{n+2}. Substitution into (11.58) yields:

$$\begin{aligned} V = {} & \sum_{i=1}^{m} x_i^2 Q_{1i} + \sum_{i=m+1}^{n} x_i^2 Q_{2i} + Q_{n+1} \sum_{i=1}^{m} x_i^2 B_i^2 + Q_{n+2} \sum_{i=m+1}^{n} x_i^2 B_i^2 \\ & + Q_{n+1} \sum_{\substack{i=1 \\ i \neq j}}^{m} \sum_{j=1}^{m} x_i x_j B_i B_j + Q_{n+2} \sum_{\substack{i=m+1 \\ i \neq j}}^{n} \sum_{j=m+1}^{n} x_i x_j B_i B_j \\ & + 2Q_{12} \sum_{i=1}^{m} \sum_{j=m+1}^{n} x_i x_j B_i B_j \end{aligned} \tag{11.66}$$

which can be rewritten as:

$$\begin{aligned} V = {} & \sum_{i=1}^{m} x_i^2 Q_{1i} + x_{n+1}^2 Q_{n+1} + \sum_{i=m+1}^{n} x_i^2 Q_{2i} + x_{n+2}^2 Q_{n+2} \\ & + 2Q_{12} \sum_{i=1}^{m} \sum_{j=m+1}^{n} x_i x_j B_i B_j \end{aligned} \tag{11.67}$$

which can be seen to contain no less than $n + 2 + m(n-m)$ terms. Note that if $m = 0$ or $m = n$ the model wouod be single index and would contain only $n + 1$ terms. Whilst (11.67) contains fewer terms than the MFC equivalent (about 423,000 for a 1,300 security problem if $m = 650$) it too is impracticable unless the two indices are uncorrelated. If this was the case then $Q_{12} = 0$ and there are only $n + 2$ terms. Clearly it is highly desirable to select uncorrelated indices. Finally, note that the approach could be used with three, four or more indices and that the MFC model could be viewed as an n index model with each security as its own index.

The comparative performances of the MFC, single index and two index models are most interesting. Clearly the index models have the enormous advantage of requiring much lower information requirements than MFC. However, as Sharpe himself pointed out in connection with his own single index model:

> 'The assumptions of the diagonal model lie near one end of the spectrum of possible assumptions about the relationships among securities. The model's extreme simplicity enables the investigator to perform a portfolio analysis at a very small cost, as we have shown. However, it is entirely possible that this simplicity so restricts the security analyst in making his predictions that the value of the resulting portfolio analysis is also very small.'[12]

Investigating this possibility Sharpe conducted a small scale experiment with twenty securities randomly selected from those traded on the New York stock exchange. The performances of these securities over the period 1940–51 was used to obtain two sets of data. Firstly, the mean returns and variances and covariances of returns over the period were obtained directly. Secondly, parameters of the diagonal model were estimated by regression techniques from the performance of the securities over the period. A portfolio analysis was then performed on each set of data. The results indicated that '. . . the 62 parameters of the diagonal model were able to capture a great deal of the information contained in the complete set of 230 historical relationships. An additional test, using a second set of 20 securities gave similar results'. Sharpe concluded that:

> 'These results are, of course, too fragmentary to be considered conclusive but they do suggest that the diagonal model may be able to represent the relationships among securities rather well and thus that the value of the portfolio analyses based on the model will exceed their rather nominal cost. For these reasons it appears to be an excellent choice for the initial practical applications of the Markowitz procedure.'[13]

Subsequently, a considerable amount of further resting has been undertaken. Wallingford, like Sharpe, employed samples containing just twenty securities but he conducted experiments using actual historical data and as an alternative, simulated data.[14] He found that, within this context, two index models produced more efficient portfolios than single index models. This is not altogether surprising and indeed must be the case if the increased computational effort and cost resulting from the use of two indices is to be justified.

However, a study conducted shortly before Wallingford's work (the results of which in fact surprised and motivated Wallingford) by Cohen and Pogue found that the single index model outperformed a two index model.[15] Cohen and Pogue used one hundred and fifty randomly selected common stocks and found that the MFC model, naturally, generated the dominant efficiency frontier but, in the context of their study, found that Sharpe's single index model matched or outperformed a two index model based upon that outlined above. What explanations can be offered for this result? First, as Cohen and Pogue themselves pointed out, their sample, being entirely of common stocks, was fairly homogeneous and thus particularly suitable for single index treatment. This fact alone however is not sufficient to explain away their results. There is, of course, the outside possibility that some peculiarities of the sample or of the indices used could have influenced the results.[16] This seems unlikely, however. A much more likely explanation was provided by Wallingford. Whilst Cohen and Pogue drew from 'a fairly large universe' of common stocks they added institutional constraints limiting the amount invested in any one security. Wallingford's work did not do this. In Wallingford's words: 'This reduction in the size of the universe and the elimination of the investment constraints is a major deviation from the Cohen and Pogue analysis and may help to explain any differences in the results of the studies'.[17] Thus the two studies are not directly comparable. Bearing in mind the possible undesirable consequences of arbitrary diversification rules and notwithstanding the smaller scale of Wallingford's study, it is suggested here that Wallingford's results are more likely to be representative of the comparative performances of the models in actual use.

11.8 Data Problems

Whilst we have discussed the quantities of information required for the various models we have said very little in respect of the means of obtaining the data. Clearly the quality of the information used is of great importance. As Francis and Archer point out: 'The efficient portfolios generated by portfolio analysis are no better than the statistical inputs on which they are based'.[18] Francis and Archer suggest three different approaches for generating the data inputs required: '(a) ex-post data may be tabulated and projected into the future with or without being adjusted; (b) ex-ante probability distributions can be compiled; or (c) a simple econometric relationship may be used to forecast returns'. They further suggest that: 'Ideally, all three approaches should be pursued independently for each of the n assets. These independent forecasts could then be compared and contrasted by a committee of security analysts and a concensus of opinion reached as a final step in security analysis. This final consensus of opinion would represent the best attainable statistics and could be given to the portfolio analyst'.[19] Whilst the words 'independent' and 'best' may be contestible, there seems much to commend the testing of such a combined approach rather than relying exclusively on either historical data or subjective prior probability distributions.

Briefly, approach (a) involves calculating historical values for the security returns, variances and covariances, possibly adjusted on a subjective basis as a result of changed company or economic circumstances. Approach (b) ideally develops subjective probability distributions of returns to each security over all possible business conditions that may obtain. Rather a tall order, one might feel, but sufficiently experienced and daring analysts may be persuaded to attempt this exercise. Approach (c) generates the required inputs using regression analysis. Blume carried out an investigation of some simple-econometric forecasting models.[20] Whilst concluding that security returns conformed more closely to a non-normal stable Paretian distribution than to a normal distribution, he found that the assumptions underlying the least-squares regression model (regarding the error terms) were not significantly violated in the post war period. In common with the approach (a) this third method encounters difficulty in respect of new issues.

The consequences of Blume's stable-Paretian result, and Fama's subsequent work[21] seem, on the face of it, rather ominous. The particular form of the Paretian distribution that describes the ex-post returns of many assets has infinite variance. If this was also the case for ex-ante returns, the Markowitz model would appear to be unusable. In fact there are two possible ways out of the difficulty. Firstly, variance need not be used as the measure of risk. Secondly, if variance was chosen approximations could be made to restrict variances to finite values. Fried[22] has suggested a method of obtaining *a priori* distributions of asset returns for Markowitz-type models using standard forecasting methods and has provided a rationale for the continued use of these models despite the presence of infinite variance in the *ex-post* distribution of asset returns.

11.9 Use of the Models

The formal portfolio models that we have been describing have been little used in practice so far. This is disappointing. There is a number of good reasons for this. In addition, however, a number of dubious excuses have been proferred from time to time.

Whilst computational costs for the simplified models need not be excessive in respect of the obtaining of an original portfolio, there is the problem of updating. As time goes on fresh data on prices, returns and variances come in. The updating means further work for the analysts and more computing expenses. Significant changes in parameters can render the original efficient portfolio very inefficient. There are also various legal and administrative constraints that will need to be incorporated. Taxation can give rise to complex problems and ideally we should include all variable costs that are identified with the portfolio. These problems have been considered by various authors.

Mao,[23] Evans and Archer,[24] and Latane and Young[25] have examined some of the problems caused by non-zero transactions and information costs. Whilst further work by Pogue[26] has extended the basic Markowitz model to include the possibility of selling short as well as transactions costs, leverage policies, and the effects of taxation. Under these circumstances by no means all available securities will be included in a portfolio and the problems arise of how many and which securities to include in a portfolio. A marginal analysis of the costs and benefits of increased diversification is undoubtedly required to answer the former question but selection criteria are still a source of some debate.

As regards the dynamics of portfolio management, clearly over time the information available changes a portfolio that is on the efficiency frontier at time t may not be on the frontier at time $t + 1$. Smith[27] developed a model for portfolio revision which takes account of both transaction costs and capital gains taxation, and Evans[28] presented an evaluation of the so-called buy-and-hold strategy and a version of the fixed-proportions strategy. The buy-and-hold strategy is that the investor should sell securities a predetermined number of periods after their purchase, reinvesting dividends in the securities on which they were paid. The fixed-proportions strategy differs in that reinvestment is such as to maintain the original holdings of the various assets proportionately in monetary terms. Evans assumed equal proportionate holdings and discovered that the choice between the two rules depended upon the amounts of the initial investments and the marginal capital gains tax rate of the investor.

Despite these constructive efforts to make the models both realistic and workable many problems remain. Not all practitioners, apparently, take a positive standpoint. Firth[29] reports that '. . . it is worth noting that many managers say that until analysts forecasting abilities improve, further development of portfolio theory or its application is not warranted. The contention is that the resources spent on portfolio theory would be better expended on improving forecasting techniques and on the formation of probability distributions'. One is tempted to conclude that, until then, these particular managers will rely on the 'proven' merits of ad-hocery, 'hunch', 'experience', 'skill', 'Fundamentalism' and the hocus-pocus of Chartism; but one will not.

To conclude with, let us briefly consider the investment performance of large companies and the question of whether or not any significant improvement can be made on random portfolios. There has been a good deal of work done, of an essentially discriptive nature, on the performance of mutual funds and other large public portfolios in the United States.[30] Francis and Archer[31] cite evidence that the performance of mutual funds is poor and results from poor management practices, principally naive diversification. A study by Farrar[32] however, comparing mutual fund portfolios to efficient portfolios produced by the Markowitz model, found that the characteristics of the mutual funds portfolios were similar to those of corresponding efficient portfolios. This study shows the mutual funds in the best light. In contrast Cohen and Pogue found that even when using as naive an estimate of expected return as the average of past returns the performance of portfolios that were selected by the Markowitz model was as good as, or better than, the actual performance of the mutual funds.

There have been numerous tests where the performance of a randomly generated portfolio of shares has been compared with the performance of a selected portfolio, such as a unit trust or mutual fund. In his extremely detailed study of 115 United States mutual funds over the ten-year period from 1955 to 1964, Jensen found that the risk-return combination for 58 of the funds was below the 'market line', they performed less well than the index of general market performance. As would be expected, a number of funds *did* perform better than the index, but Jensen found no evidence that certain funds consistently perform better than the norm. Above-average performance in one period was not associated with above-average performance in other periods. This confirms the findings of other studies.[33] It has been shown with U.K. unit trusts that during 1964–66 the average unit trust performed no better than random portfolios selected from the same industries in which the trusts themselves invested.[34]

The findings, in general, offer strong support for more widespread use of MFC or simplified models. Whilst there undoubtedly are difficulties with the scientific method of analysis, there can be no doubt that they will eventually prevail.

Appendix

CES Functions in Project Appraisal and Risk Measurement

In this appendix some of the utility discussion and other principles of approach in the portfolio analysis chapter are drawn upon and employed within a project selection context. The objective is to show how a functional form, widely used in economic theory is also useful in an investment context. The function will be used in two ways, (a) to allow the investor to use several risk factors in producing a one-dimensional measure of risk and (b) to use the approach to produce a one-dimensional evaluation of a project where, in general, several risk factors and measures of return may be incorporated.

There are two characteristic extremes of types of approach to the problem of risk. The first type of approach (which we shall call the portfolio analysis approach) is to attempt to estimate the probability distribution of the measure of return employed and to use one of the parameters of the probability distribution (usually the variance, but the use of higher moments has been suggested) as a surrogate measure of risk. The investor subsequently assesses each project or each portfolio with direct or implicit reference to a utility function of the measure of return and the measure of risk. The second type of approach is to use a simple criterion (or a simple modification of a deterministic criterion) which presumably subsumes information about risks associated with projects and the investor's attitude towards risk. We have in mind such techniques as payback period and the risk discount method. The second type of approach is less intellectually satisfying but in practice is highly tractable, cheap, quick and easily understood. The portfolio analysis approach whilst being theoretically optimal has so far gained only limited acceptance.

Sensitivity analysis (SA) and multi criterion (MC) (sometimes known as filtering or hurdle procedures) methods may be thought to lie somewhere between the above extrema. In principle they allow the investor to decide on the degree of complexity of his approach and can combine some of the better features of each. Both SA and MC methods, however, present the investor with a set of information rather than a single measure (either of risk or acceptability). Here we are aiming for the 'middle ground' now occupied by SA and MC methods. The approach proposed will allow the investor to decide which risk criteria should be emphasized and to choose a parameter value to represent his overall attitude to risk. The methods described can be used to produce a single composite measure of risk or acceptability.

(1) A CES Composite Measure of Risk

The measure of risk proposed is:

$$r = a_0(a_1 F_1^{-b} + a_2 F_2^{-b})^{-c/b} \qquad \text{(A1)}$$

The measure takes the form of a CES function each element of which has a plausible interpretation in the context of risk.

The variables F_1 and F_2 are measures of project characteristics that are (in any one investor's mind) associated with riskiness. For example F_1 or F_2 might be project length, a function of length, outlay required for the project, payback period, variance of return, etc. The constants a_1 and a_2 are 'distribution parameters' where $a_1, a_2 \geqslant 0$. The relative magnitude of a_1 and a_2 indicates the relative importance attached by the investor to each risk factor. The degree of homogeneity of the function, c, measures the overall 'risk sensitivity' of the investor. The greater is the value of c the greater will be the value of r for given F_1 and F_2, i.e. the greater is the investor's view of the riskiness of the project. a_0 is a project-specific coefficient and is an arbitrary constant that might, for example, take different values for investments in different industries; for instance, a low value for an investment in foodstuffs processing and a high value for Australian mines. The substitution parameter, $b(\geqslant -1)$, determines the elasticity of substitution (s) between the risk factors. This is less easy to interpret. The elasticity of substitution, $(1 + b)^{-1}$, is inversely related to the curvature of the iso-risk lines generated by (A1). Therefore, the greater the value of b, the greater the curvature of the iso-risk lines. The greater the curvature of the lines the more sensitive is the investor to changes in the relative levels of F_1 and F_2. For example if b was large, a relatively small increase in F_1 (F_2) would mean that the risk level rose much more rapidly for a given increase in F_2 (F_1) than previously.

The investor employs the measure by choosing the risk factors, determining their levels and setting the values of the parameters.

The function A(1) (in a production context) was devised to provide generalizations of a number of well-known functions. Those of interest in the present context are:

(*a*) *The Cobb–Douglas (Wicksell) Case*. As $b \to 0$ then

$$r \to a_0 F_1^{a_1 c} F_2^{a_2 c} \tag{A2}$$

and the elasticity of substitution between F_1 and F_2 $\to$ unity. The Cobb–Douglas form is more convenient analytically and would be used if $s = 1$ accurately reflected the sensitivity of the investor to changes in the relative levels of F_1 and F_2. Scale distribution and investment specific factors may still be chosen at will.

(*b*) *The Linear Case*. If $b = 1$ and $c = 1$ then (A1) reduces to

$$r = a_0(a_1 F_1 + a_2 F_2) \tag{A3}$$

Risk level is linearly homogeneous in the two factors and the factors are perfect substitutes. The marginal rate of substitution (MRS) between the risk factors is a_1/a_2 and $s = \infty$. The constant MRS implies that whatever the relative magnitudes of F_1 and F_2 the investor is indifferent between a change in F_1 of Δ and a change in F_2 of $a_1\Delta/a_2$. This is of course less plausible than the Cobb–Douglas case but (A3) is still more convenient than (A2). It is worth noting that if F_1 is an estimate of the variance of the measure of return to the investment and $a_2 = 0$, $a_1 = a_2^{-1}$

then variance is the measure of risk – no other project characteristics being taken into account.

(c) The Quadratic Case. When $b = -1$ and $c = 2$ then (A1) is a quadratic expression in the risk factors. A somewhat more general form of (A1) might be appropriate here namely

$$r = a_0(a_1 F_1^{-b} + a_2 F_2^{-b} + a_3)^{-c/b} \tag{A4}$$

which in the quadratic case reduces to

$$r = a_0 \sum_{i=1}^{3} \sum_{j=1}^{3} a_i a_j F_i F_j \tag{A5}$$

where $F_3 = 1$ and $a_0 = 0$ for the homogeneous case. If $a_3 > 0$ and if r_h is the measure of risk in the homogeneous case than the non-homogeneous risk measure is given by

$$r_n = r_h + a_0 a_3 (a_1 F_1 + a_2 F_2 + a_3) \tag{A6}$$

which is greater than r_h and biased towards one of the factors if $a_1 \neq a_2$. The marginal rate of substitution between the factors in (A5) is constant and as in the linear case is equal to a_1/a_2. The elasticity of substitution is infinite – since the factors are perfect risk substitutes (the iso-risk lines are straight).

(d) The input–output case. As $b \to \infty$ and $c = 1$ then (A1) approaches the input–output case. In the input–output case the iso-risk lines are rectangular, for if the risk factors are in the 'right' proportions an increase in either factor (however large) makes no difference to the level of risk.

(2) A CES Unidimensional Measure of Project Desirability

The function (A1), or a generalization of (A1) to include more factors, provides a measure of project desirability if some of the factors relate to the return from the project. The CES measure generalizes three existing measures as well as in genral terms being a utility function the parameters of which reflect an investor's attitudes to return and risk. The factors included in the function are also at the investor's discretion.

The first generalization is that of the coefficient of variation decision rule. If F_1 = NPV, F_2 = standard deviation of NPV and the values of the parameters are $a_0 = 1$, $a_1 = c^{-1}$, $b \to 0$ and $a_2 = -c^{-1}$, then r = coefficient of variation.

If F_1 = expected return and F_2 = standard deviation of return and the parameter values chosen are $a_0 = 1$, $a_1 = 1$, $b = -1$, $c = 1$ and $a_2 < 0$ then Baumol's intuitively appealing L criterion is generated.

If $a_0 = 1$ (or an interest rate i), $b \to 0$, $a_1 = c^{-1}$, $a_2 = -c^{-1}$ and if F_1 = NPV and $F_2 = K[1 - \{1/(1+i)\}n[$ where K represents project outlay then (1) is equivalent to a rate of return concept proposed by Ramsey (1970).

Ramsey's rate of return is given by:

$$i_r = i\left\{\frac{\text{NPV}}{K[1-(1+i)^{-n}]}+1\right\} \tag{A7}$$

In general terms if F_1 is 'return' and F_2 is 'risk' ($a_2 < 0$) then parameter variation in (1) will allow utility functions of CES, Cobb–Douglas linear or polynomial forms to be derived. In this connection it may prove to be more convenient (so that $a_2 > 0$) to interpret F_2 as a measure of security ($0 \leqslant F_2 \leqslant 1$) rather than risk. If $F_2 = 1$ the deterministic case is generated.

In the context of (A1) we can also describe a mechanism by which 'certainty equivalents' (see Shackle, 1952) are formed. For any project with $0 < F_2 < 1$ and for given F_1 say F_1^u a value of r is generated; call this r_u. Now set $r_u = a_0(a_1 F_1^{-b} + a_2 1^{-b})^{-c/b}$ and solve for F_1. The value of F_1 is the certainty equivalent of F_1^u.

The CES approach can be made multi-factor of course with

$$r = a_0 [\Sigma a_i F_i^{-b}]^{-c/b} \tag{A8}$$

in which if some F_i are risk factors the corresponding $a_i < 0$. Or, if the investor prefers to consider risk and return separately, but where many factors go into the determination of both we can write for 'return'.

$$\text{return} = a_{0r} [\Sigma a_{ir} F_{ir}^{-b_r}]^{-c_r/b_r} = V \tag{A9}$$

and for 'risk'

$$\text{risk} = a_{0u} [\Sigma a_{iu} F_{iu}^{-b_u}]^{-c_u/b_u} = R \tag{A10}$$

and return and risk brought together in the second phase of a two-stage procedure as:

$$r = \alpha_0 [\alpha_1 V^{-\beta} + \alpha_2 R^{-\beta}]^{-v/\beta}$$

References

A1. Brems, H., *Quantitative Economic Theory: A Synthetic Approach*, Wiley, New York, 1968.

A2. Ramsey, J. B., 'The marginal efficiency of capital, the internal rate of return, and net present value: an analysis of investment criteria', *Journal of Political Economy*, **78**, No. 5, October, 1970 (and subsequent reply).

A3. Shackle, G., *Expectations in Economics*, Cambridge University Press, New York, 1952.

A4. McFadden, D., 'Further results on CES production functions', *The Review of Economic Studies*, **30**, No. 2, June, 1963.

Notes

1. Markowitz, H. M., *Portfolio Selection: Efficient Diversification of Investments*, Wiley, New York, 1959.
2. The next few paragraphs essentially reproduce the discussion of risk in Chapter 1. The ground is briefly covered again for completeness in the present context.
3. No generality is lost by this convenient assumption. One of the 'securities' is an n security problem can be cash, the stock variable with a price of unity and a yield of zero percent.
4. We should be in dire straits indeed if the coefficient of $\bar{R}^2$ was positive. Since a quadratic can have only one turning point a negative coefficient of the squared term would eventually imply negative variance!

5. The reader will note that this is a substantial information requirement. We shall return to this matter later on.
6. $2n$ terms are added since as the covariance summation is written σ_{ij} and σ_{ji} are included separately.
7. For discussion of Cobb–Douglas utility functions see for example Brems, H., *Quantitative Economic Theory: A Synthetic Approach*, Wiley, New York, 1968.
8. This form of utility function goes under the same CES (Constant Elasticity of Substitution). For further discussion, see Brems, H., *Quantitative Economic Theory: A Synthetic Approach*, Wiley, New York, 1968.
9. Ball, R., and Brown, P., 'Portfolio theory and accounting', *Journal of Accounting Research*, Autumn **1968.**
10. Sharpe, W. F., 'A simplified model for portfolio analysis', *Management Science*, **9**, 1963.
11. Note that this distribution will not be exactly normal (for most indices at least) negative values being unobtainable. Figure 11.15 is Sharpe's Figure 2.
12. Sharpe, W. F., 'A simplified model for portfolio analysis', *Management Science*, **9**, 291 (1963).
13. Sharpe, W. F., 'A simplified model for portfolio analysis', *Management Science*, **9**, 292 (1963).
14. Wallingford, B. A., 'A survey and comparison of portfolio selection models', *Journal of Financial and Quantitative Analysis*, June **1967**.
15. Cohen, K. J., and Pogue, J. A., 'An empirical evaluation of alternative portfolio selection models', *Journal of Business*, April **1967**.
16. Wallingford's indices were computed from the sample itself whereas Cohen and Pogue computed their indices from a larger population. Strictly speaking, the index on to which the ith securities returns are regressed should not have the ith security as a component or the model will be 'overspecified'. However the effects are infinitesimal. See Fama, E., 'Risk, return and equilibrium: some clarifying comments', *Journal of Finance*, March, **1968.**
17. Wallingford, B. A., 'A survey and comparison of portfolio selection models, *Journal of Financial and Quantitative Analysis*, p. 99, June, **1967**.
18. Francis, J. C., and Archer, S. H., *Portfolio Analysis*, Prentice-Hall Foundations of Finance Series, Englewood Cliffs, N.J., 1971, chapter 3.
19. Francis, J. C., and Archer, S. H., *Portfolio Analysis*, Prentice-Hall Foundations of Finance Series, Englewood Cliffs, N.J., 1971, p. 47.
20. Blume, M., 'Portfolio theory: a step towards its practical application', *Journal of Business*, April, **1970**.
21. Fama, E., 'The behaviour of stock market prices', *Journal of Business*, January, **1965**. Also 'Portfolio analysis in a stable paretian market', *Management Science*, January, **1965**, and Mandelbrot, B., 'The variation of certain speculative prices', *Journal of Business*, October, **1963**.
22. Fried, J., 'Forecasting and probability distributions for models of portfolio selection', *Journal of Finance*, June, **1970**.
23. Mao, J. C. T., 'Essentials of portfolio diversification strategy', *Journal of Finance*, December, **1970**.
24. Evans, J. L., and Archer, S. H., 'Diversification and the reduction of dispersion: an empirical analysis', *Journal of Finance*, December, **1968**.
25. Latane, H. A., and Young, W. E., 'Test of portfolio building rules', *Journal of Finance*, September, **1969**.
26. Pogue, J. A., 'An extension of the Markowitz portfolio selection model to include variable transaction costs, short sales, leverage policies and taxes', *Journal of Finance*, December, **1970**.
27. Smith, K. V., 'A transition model for portfolio revision', *Journal of Finance*, September, **1967**.
28. Evans, J. L., 'An analysis of portfolio maintenance strategies', *Journal of Finance*, June, **1970**.
29. Firth, M., *Investment Analysis: Techniques of Appraising the British Stock Market*, Harper and Row, New York, 1975, pp. 236–237.
30. See for instance (a) Jensen, M. C., 'The performance of mutual funds in the period 1945–1964', *Journal of Finance*, May, **1968**; (b) Sharpe, W. F., 'Mutual fund performance', *Journal of Business*, January, **1966**; (c) Treynor, J. L., 'How to rate management of

investment funds', *Harvard Business Review*, Jan.–Feb., **1965**; (d) Jensen, M. C., 'Risk, the pricing of capital assets, and the evaluation of investment portfolios', *Journal of Business*, April, **1969**.

31. Francis, J. C., and Archer, S. H., *Portfolio Analysis*, Prentice-Hall Foundations of Finance Series, Englewood Cliffs, N.J., 1971, Chapter 8.
32. Farrar, D. E., *The Investment Decision Under Uncertainty*, Prentice-Hall, Englewood Cliffs, N.J., 1965.
33. Such as those by Sharpe, W. F., 'A simplified model for portfolio analysis, *Management Science,* **9**, 1963 and 'Risk aversion in the stock market', *Journal of Finance*, September, **1965**.
34. See Samuels, J. M., 'The performance of unit trusts', *The Bankers' Magazine*, August, **1968**.

Additional References

1. Baumol, W. J., 'An expected gain-confidence limit criterion for portfolio selection', *Management Science*, October, **1963**.
2. Chen, A. H. Y., Jen, F. C., and Zionts, S., 'The optimal portfolio revision policy', *Journal of Business*, January, **1971**.
3. Cohen, J. B., and Zinbarg, E. D., *Investment Analysis and Portfolio Management*, Irwin, Homewood, Illinois, 1967.
4. Hastie, K. L., 'The determination of optimal investment policy', *Management Science*, August, **1967**.
5. Hester, D., and Tobin, J. (Eds.), *Risk Aversion and Portfolio Choice*, Wiley, New York, 1967.
6. Hodges, S. D., and Brealey, R. A., 'Using the Sharpe model', *Investment Analysis*, September, **1970**.
7. Horowitz, I., 'The varying quality of investment trust management', *Journal of the American Statistical Association*, December, **1963**.
8. Jacob, N. L., 'A limited diversification portfolio selection strategy for the small investor', *Journal of Finance*, June, **1974**.
9. Jones-Lee, M., 'Portfolio adjustments and capital budgeting criteria', *Journal of Business Finance*, No. 2, Autumn, **1969**.
10. Lee, S. M., and Lerro, A. J., 'Optimizing the portfolio selection for mutual funds', *The Journal of Finance*, December, **1973**.
11. Lintner, J., 'The evaluation of risk assets and the selection of risky investments in stock portfolios and capital budgets', *Review of Economics and Statistics*, Feburary, **1965**.
12. Lintner, J., 'Security prices, risk and maximal gains from diversification', *Journal of Finance*, December, **1965**.
13. Martin, A. D., 'Mathematical programming of portfolio selections', *Management Science*, **1** , 1955.
14. Markowitz, H., 'The optimization of a quadratic function subject to linear constraints, *Naval Research Logistics Quarterly,* **3**, 1956.
15. Markowitz, H., 'Portfolio analysis', *Journal of Finance*, March, **1952**.
16. Mossin, J., 'Optimal multiperiod portfolio policies', *Journal of Business*, April, **1968**.
17. Paine, N. R., 'A case study in mathematical programming of portfolio selections', *Applied Statistics,* **1**, 1966.
18. Renshaw, E. F., 'Portfolio balance models in perspective: some generalizations that can be derived from the two asset case', *Journal of Financial and Quantitative Analysis*, June, **1967**.
19. Sarnat, M., 'A note on the prediction of portfolio performance from ex-post data', *The Journal of Finance*, September, **1972**.
20. Sharpe, W. F., 'A linear programming algorithm for mutual fund portfolio selection', *Management Science*, **March**, 1967.
21. Sharpe, W. F., *Portfolio Theory and Capital Markets*, McGraw-Hill, New York, 1970.
22. Smith, K. V., 'A portfolio analysis of conglomerate diversification', *The Journal of Finance*, June, **1969**.
23. Smith, K. V., 'Stock price and economic indices for generating efficient portfolios', *Journal of Business*, July, **1969**.
24. Szego, G. P., and Shell, K., *Mathematical Methods in Investment and Finance*, North Holland, Amsterdam, 1972.
25. Tobin, J., 'Liquidity preference as behaviour towards risk', *Review of economic Studies*, February, **1958**.

Appendix 1

Present value of £1 at compound interest: $(1 + r)^{-n}$

Years (n)	Interest rates (r) 1	2	3	4	5	6	7	8	9	10	11	12	13	14	15	
1	0.9901	0.9804	0.9709	0.9615	0.9524	0.9434	0.9346	0.9259	0.9174	0.9091	0.9009	0.8929	0.8850	0.8772	0.8696	1
2	0.9803	0.9612	0.9426	0.9246	0.9070	0.8900	0.8734	0.8573	0.8417	0.8264	0.8116	0.7972	0.7831	0.7695	0.7561	2
3	0.9706	0.9423	0.9151	0.8890	0.8638	0.8396	0.8163	0.7938	0.7722	0.7513	0.7312	0.7118	0.6931	0.6750	0.6575	3
4	0.9610	0.9238	0.8885	0.8548	0.8227	0.7921	0.7629	0.7350	0.7084	0.6830	0.6587	0.6355	0.6133	0.5921	0.5718	4
5	0.9515	0.9057	0.8626	0.8219	0.7835	0.7473	0.7130	0.6806	0.6499	0.6209	0.5935	0.5674	0.5428	0.5194	0.4972	5
6	0.9420	0.8880	0.8375	0.7903	0.7462	0.7050	0.6663	0.6302	0.5963	0.5645	0.5346	0.5066	0.4803	0.4556	0.4323	6
7	0.9327	0.8706	0.8131	0.7599	0.7107	0.6651	0.6227	0.5835	0.5470	0.5132	0.4817	0.4523	0.4251	0.3996	0.3759	7
8	0.9235	0.8535	0.7894	0.7307	0.6768	0.6274	0.5820	0.5403	0.5019	0.4665	0.4339	0.4039	0.3762	0.3506	0.3269	8
9	0.9143	0.8368	0.7664	0.7026	0.6446	0.5919	0.5439	0.5002	0.4604	0.4241	0.3909	0.3606	0.3329	0.3075	0.2843	9
10	0.9053	0.8203	0.7441	0.6756	0.6139	0.5584	0.5083	0.4632	0.4224	0.3855	0.3522	0.3220	0.2946	0.2697	0.2472	10
11	0.8963	0.8043	0.7224	0.6496	0.5847	0.5268	0.4751	0.4289	0.3875	0.3505	0.3173	0.2875	0.2607	0.2366	0.2149	11
12	0.8874	0.7885	0.7014	0.6246	0.5568	0.4970	0.4440	0.3971	0.3555	0.3186	0.2858	0.2567	0.2307	0.2076	0.1869	12
13	0.8787	0.7730	0.6810	0.6006	0.5303	0.4688	0.4150	0.3677	0.3262	0.2897	0.2575	0.2292	0.2042	0.1821	0.1625	13
14	0.8700	0.7579	0.6611	0.5775	0.5051	0.4423	0.3878	0.3405	0.2992	0.2633	0.2320	0.2046	0.1807	0.1597	0.1413	14
15	0.8613	0.7430	0.6419	0.5553	0.4810	0.4173	0.3624	0.3152	0.2745	0.2394	0.2090	0.1827	0.1599	0.1401	0.1229	15
16	0.8528	0.7284	0.6232	0.5339	0.4581	0.3936	0.3387	0.2919	0.2519	0.2176	0.1883	0.1631	0.1415	0.1229	0.1069	16
17	0.8444	0.7142	0.6050	0.5134	0.4363	0.3714	0.3166	0.2703	0.2311	0.1978	0.1696	0.1456	0.1252	0.1078	0.0929	17
18	0.8360	0.7002	0.5874	0.4936	0.4155	0.3503	0.2959	0.2502	0.2120	0.1799	0.1528	0.1300	0.1108	0.0946	0.0808	18
19	0.8277	0.6864	0.5703	0.4746	0.3957	0.3305	0.2765	0.2317	0.1945	0.1635	0.1377	0.1161	0.0981	0.0829	0.0703	19
20	0.8195	0.6730	0.5537	0.4564	0.3769	0.3118	0.2584	0.2145	0.1784	0.1486	0.1240	0.1037	0.0868	0.0728	0.0611	20
25	0.7795	0.6095	0.4776	0.3751	0.2953	0.2330	0.1842	0.1460	0.1160	0.0923	0.0736	0.0588	0.0471	0.0378	0.0304	25
30	0.7419	0.5521	0.4120	0.3083	0.2314	0.1741	0.1314	0.0994	0.0754	0.0573	0.0437	0.0334	0.0256	0.0196	0.0151	30
35	0.7059	0.5000	0.3554	0.2534	0.1813	0.1301	0.0937	0.0676	0.0490	0.0356	0.0259	0.0189	0.0139	0.0102	0.0075	35
40	0.6717	0.4529	0.3066	0.2083	0.1420	0.0972	0.0668	0.0460	0.0318	0.0221	0.0154	0.0107	0.0075	0.0053	0.0037	40
45	0.6391	0.4102	0.2644	0.1712	0.1113	0.0727	0.0476	0.0313	0.0207	0.0137	0.0091	0.0061	0.0041	0.0027	0.0019	45
50	0.6080	0.3715	0.2281	0.1407	0.0872	0.0543	0.0339	0.0213	0.0134	0.0085	0.0054	0.0035	0.0022	0.0014	0.0009	50

Years (n)	Interest rates (r)															
	16	17	18	19	20	21	22	23	24	25	26	27	28	29	30	
1	0.8621	0.8547	0.8475	0.8403	0.8333	0.8264	0.8197	0.8130	0.8065	0.8000	0.7937	0.7874	0.7812	0.7752	0.7692	1
2	0.7432	0.7305	0.7182	0.7062	0.6944	0.6830	0.6719	0.6610	0.6504	0.6400	0.6299	0.6200	0.6104	0.6009	0.5917	2
3	0.6407	0.6244	0.6086	0.5934	0.5787	0.5645	0.5507	0.5374	0.5245	0.5120	0.4999	0.4882	0.4768	0.4658	0.4552	3
4	0.5523	0.5337	0.5158	0.4987	0.4823	0.4665	0.4514	0.4369	0.4230	0.4096	0.3968	0.3844	0.3725	0.3611	0.3501	4
5	0.4761	0.4561	0.4371	0.4190	0.4019	0.3855	0.3700	0.3552	0.3411	0.3277	0.3149	0.3027	0.2910	0.2799	0.2693	5
6	0.4104	0.3898	0.3704	0.3521	0.3349	0.3186	0.3033	0.2888	0.2751	0.2621	0.2499	0.2383	0.2274	0.2170	0.2072	6
7	0.3538	0.3332	0.3139	0.2959	0.2791	0.2633	0.2486	0.2348	0.2218	0.2097	0.1983	0.1877	0.1776	0.1682	0.1594	7
8	0.3050	0.2848	0.2660	0.2487	0.2326	0.2176	0.2038	0.1909	0.1789	0.1678	0.1574	0.1478	0.1388	0.1304	0.1226	8
9	0.2630	0.2434	0.2255	0.2090	0.1938	0.1799	0.1670	0.1552	0.1443	0.1342	0.1249	0.1164	0.1084	0.1011	0.0943	9
10	0.2267	0.2080	0.1911	0.1756	0.1615	0.1486	0.1369	0.1262	0.1164	0.1074	0.0992	0.0916	0.0847	0.0784	0.0725	10
11	0.1954	0.1778	0.1619	0.1476	0.1346	0.1228	0.1122	0.1026	0.0938	0.0859	0.0787	0.0721	0.0662	0.0607	0.0558	11
12	0.1685	0.1520	0.1372	0.1240	0.1122	0.1015	0.0920	0.0834	0.0757	0.0687	0.0625	0.0568	0.0517	0.0471	0.0429	12
13	0.1452	0.1299	0.1163	0.1042	0.0935	0.0839	0.0754	0.0678	0.0610	0.0550	0.0496	0.0447	0.0404	0.0365	0.0330	13
14	0.1252	0.1110	0.0985	0.0876	0.0779	0.0693	0.0618	0.0551	0.0492	0.0440	0.0393	0.0352	0.0316	0.0283	0.0254	14
15	0.1079	0.0949	0.0835	0.0736	0.0649	0.0573	0.0507	0.0448	0.0397	0.0352	0.0312	0.0277	0.0247	0.0219	0.0195	15
16	0.0930	0.0811	0.0708	0.0618	0.0541	0.0474	0.0415	0.0364	0.0320	0.0281	0.0248	0.0218	0.0193	0.0170	0.0150	16
17	0.0802	0.0693	0.0600	0.0520	0.0451	0.0391	0.0340	0.0296	0.0258	0.0225	0.0197	0.0172	0.0150	0.0132	0.0116	17
18	0.0691	0.0592	0.0508	0.0437	0.0376	0.0323	0.0279	0.0241	0.0208	0.0180	0.0156	0.0135	0.0118	0.0102	0.0089	18
19	0.0596	0.0506	0.0431	0.0367	0.0313	0.0267	0.0229	0.0196	0.0168	0.0144	0.0124	0.0107	0.0092	0.0079	0.0068	19
20	0.0514	0.0433	0.0365	0.0308	0.0261	0.0221	0.0187	0.0159	0.0135	0.0115	0.0098	0.0084	0.0072	0.0061	0.0053	20
25	0.0245	0.0197	0.0160	0.0129	0.0105	0.0085	0.0069	0.0057	0.0046	0.0038	0.0031	0.0025	0.0021	0.0017	0.0014	25
30	0.0116	0.0090	0.0070	0.0054	0.0042	0.0033	0.0026	0.0020	0.0016	0.0012	0.0010	0.0008	0.0006	0.0005	0.0004	30
35	0.0055	0.0041	0.0030	0.0023	0.0017	0.0013	0.0009	0.0007	0.0005	0.0004	0.0003	0.0002	0.0002	0.0001	0.0001	35
40	0.0026	0.0019	0.0013	0.0010	0.0007	0.0005	0.0004	0.0003	0.0002	0.0001	0.0001	0.0001	0.0001	0.0000	0.0000	40
45	0.0013	0.0009	0.0006	0.0004	0.0003	0.0002	0.0001	0.0001	0.0001	0.0000	0.0000	0.0000	0.0000	0.0000	0.0000	45
50	0.0006	0.0004	0.0003	0.0002	0.0001	0.0001	0.0000	0.0000	0.0000	0.0000	0.0000	0.0000	0.0000	0.0000	0.0000	50

Appendix 2

Amount of £1 at compound interest: $(1 + r)^n$

Years (n)	Interest rates (r) 1	2	3	4	5	6	7	8	9	10	11	12	13	14	15	
1	1.0100	1.0200	1.0300	1.0400	1.0500	1.0600	1.0700	1.0800	1.0900	1.1000	1.1100	1.1200	1.1300	1.1400	1.1500	1
2	1.0201	1.0404	1.0609	1.0816	1.1025	1.1236	1.1449	1.1664	1.1881	1.2100	1.2321	1.2544	1.2769	1.2996	1.3225	2
3	1.0303	1.0612	1.0927	1.1249	1.1576	1.1910	1.2250	1.2597	1.2950	1.3310	1.3676	1.4049	1.4429	1.4815	1.5209	3
4	1.0406	1.0824	1.1255	1.1699	1.2155	1.2625	1.3108	1.3605	1.4116	1.4641	1.5181	1.5735	1.6305	1.6890	1.7490	4
5	1.0510	1.1041	1.1593	1.2167	1.2763	1.3382	1.4026	1.4693	1.5386	1.6105	1.6851	1.7623	1.8424	1.9254	2.0114	5
6	1.0615	1.1262	1.1941	1.2653	1.3401	1.4185	1.5007	1.5869	1.6771	1.7716	1.8704	1.9738	2.0820	2.1950	2.3131	6
7	1.0721	1.1487	1.2299	1.3159	1.4071	1.5036	1.6058	1.7138	1.8280	1.9487	2.0762	2.2107	2.3526	2.5023	2.6600	7
8	1.0829	1.1717	1.2668	1.3686	1.4775	1.5938	1.7182	1.8509	1.9926	2.1436	2.3045	2.4760	2.6584	2.8526	3.0590	8
9	1.0937	1.1951	1.3048	1.4233	1.5513	1.6895	1.8385	1.9990	2.1719	2.3579	2.5580	2.7731	3.0040	3.2519	3.5179	9
10	1.1046	1.2190	1.3439	1.4802	1.6289	1.7908	1.9672	2.1589	2.3674	2.5937	2.8394	3.1058	3.3946	3.7072	4.0456	10
11	1.1157	1.2434	1.3842	1.5395	1.7103	1.8983	2.1049	2.3316	2.5804	2.8531	3.1518	3.4785	3.8359	4.2262	4.6524	11
12	1.1268	1.2682	1.4258	1.6010	1.7959	2.0122	2.2522	2.5182	2.8127	3.1384	3.4985	3.8960	4.3345	4.8179	5.3503	12
13	1.1381	1.2936	1.4685	1.6651	1.8856	2.1329	2.4098	2.7196	3.0658	3.4523	3.8833	4.3635	4.8980	5.4924	6.1528	13
14	1.1495	1.3195	1.5126	1.7317	1.9799	2.2609	2.5785	2.9372	3.3417	3.7975	4.3104	4.8871	5.5348	6.2613	7.0757	14
15	1.1610	1.3459	1.5580	1.8009	2.0789	2.3966	2.7590	3.1722	3.6425	4.1772	4.7846	5.4736	6.2543	7.1379	8.1371	15
16	1.1726	1.3728	1.6047	1.8730	2.1829	2.5404	2.9522	3.4259	3.9703	4.5950	5.3109	6.1304	7.0673	8.1372	9.3576	16
17	1.1843	1.4002	1.6528	1.9479	2.2920	2.6928	3.1588	3.7000	4.3276	5.0545	5.8951	6.8660	7.9861	9.2765	10.7613	17
18	1.1961	1.4282	1.7024	2.0258	2,4066	2.8543	3.3799	3.9960	4.7171	5.5599	6.5436	7.6900	9.0243	10.5752	12.3755	18
19	1.2081	1.4568	1.7535	2.1068	2.5270	3.0256	3.6165	4.3157	5.1417	6.1159	7.2633	8.6128	10.1974	12.0557	14.2318	19
20	1.2202	1.4859	1.8061	2.1911	2.6533	3.2071	3.8697	4.6610	5.6044	6.7275	8.0623	9.6463	11.5231	13.7435	16.3665	20
25	1.2824	1.6406	2.0938	2.6658	3.3864	4.2919	5.4274	6.8485	8.6231	10.8347	13.5855	17.0001	21.2305	26.4619	32.9190	25

Years (n)	Interest rates (r)														
	16	17	18	19	20	21	22	23	24	25	26	27	28	29	30
1	1.1600	1.1700	1.1800	1.1900	1.2000	1.2100	1.2200	1.2300	1.2400	1.2500	1.2600	1.2700	1.2800	1.2900	1.3000
2	1.3456	1.3689	1.3924	1.4161	1.4400	1.4641	1.4884	1.5129	1.5376	1.5625	1.5876	1.6129	1.6384	1.6641	1.6900
3	1.5609	1.6016	1.6430	1.6852	1.7280	1.7716	1.8158	1.8609	1.9066	1.9531	2.0004	2.0484	2.0972	2.1467	2.1970
4	1.8106	1.8739	1.9388	2.0053	2.0736	2.1436	2.2153	2.2889	2.3642	2.4414	2.5205	2.6014	2.6844	2.7692	2.8561
5	2.1003	2.1924	2.2878	2.3864	2.4883	2.5937	2.7027	2.8153	2.9316	3.0518	3.1758	3.3038	3.4360	3.5723	3.7129
6	2.4364	2.5652	2.6996	2.8398	2.9860	3.1384	3.2973	3.4628	3.6352	3.8147	4.0015	4.1959	4.3980	4.6083	4.8268
7	2.8262	3.0012	3.1855	3.3793	3.5832	3.7975	4.0227	4.2593	4.5077	4.7684	5.0419	5.3288	5.6295	5.9447	6.2749
8	3.2784	3.5115	3.7589	4.0214	4.2998	4.5950	4.9077	5.2389	5.5895	5.9605	6.3528	6.7675	7.2058	7.6686	8.1573
9	3.8030	4.1084	4.4355	4.7854	5.1598	5.5599	5.9874	6.4439	6.9310	7.4506	8.0045	8.5948	9.2234	9.8925	10.6045
10	4.4114	4.8068	5.2338	5.6947	6.1917	6.7275	7.3046	7.9259	8.5944	9.3132	10.0857	10.9153	11.8059	12.7614	13.7858
11	5.1173	5.6240	6.1759	6.7767	7.4301	8.1403	8.9117	9.7489	10.6571	11.6415	12.7080	13.8625	15.1116	16.4622	17.9216
12	5.9360	6.5801	7.2876	8.0642	8.9161	9.8497	10.8722	11.9912	13.2148	14.5519	16.0120	17.6053	19.3428	21.2362	23.2981
13	6.8858	7.6987	8.5994	9.5964	10.6993	11.9182	13.2641	14.7491	16.3863	18.1899	20.1752	22.3588	24.7588	27.3947	30.2875
14	7.9875	9.0075	10.1472	11.4198	12.8392	14.4210	16.1822	18.1414	20.3191	22.7374	25.4207	28.3957	31.6913	35.3391	39.3738
15	9.2655	10.5387	11.9737	13.5895	15.4070	17.4494	19.7423	22.3140	25.1956	28.4217	32.0301	36.0625	40.5648	45.5875	51.1859
16	10.7480	12.3303	14.1290	16.1715	18.4884	21.1138	24.0856	27.4462	31.2426	35.5271	40.3579	45.7994	51.9230	58.8079	66.5417
17	12.4677	14.4265	16.6722	19.2441	22.1861	25.5477	29.3844	33.7588	38.7408	44.4089	50.8510	58.1652	66.4614	75.8621	86.5042
18	14.4625	16.8790	19.6733	22.9005	26.6233	30.9127	35.8490	41.5233	48.0386	55.5112	64.0722	73.8698	85.0706	97.8622	112.4554
19	16.7765	19.7484	23.2144	27.2516	31.9480	37.4043	43.7358	51.0737	59.5679	69.3889	80.7310	93.8147	108.8904	126.2422	146.1920
20	19.4608	23.1056	27.3930	32.4294	38.3376	45.2593	53.3576	62.8206	73.8641	86.7362	101.7211	119.1446	139.3797	162.8524	190.0496
25	40.8742	50.6578	62.6686	77.3881	95.3962	117.3909	144.2101	176.8593	216.5420	264.6978	323.0454	393.6344	478.9049	581.7585	705.6410

Appendix 3

Present value of an annuity of £1: $\dfrac{1-(1+r)^{-n}}{r} = \sum_{t=1}^{n} (1+r)^{-t}$

Years (n)	Interest Rates (r) 1	2	3	4	5	6	7	8	9	10	11	12	13	14	15	
1	0.9901	0.9804	0.9709	0.9615	0.9524	0.9434	0.9346	0.9259	0.9174	0.9091	0.9009	0.8929	0.8850	0.8772	0.8696	1
2	1.9704	1.9416	1.9135	1.8861	1.8594	1.8334	1.8080	1.7833	1.7591	1.7355	1.7125	1.6901	1.6681	1.6467	1.6257	2
3	2.9410	2.8839	2.8286	2.7751	2.7232	2.6730	2.6243	2.5771	2.5313	2.4869	2.4437	2.4018	2.3612	2.3216	2.2832	3
4	3.9020	3.8077	3.7171	3.6299	3.5460	3.4651	3.3872	3.3121	3.2397	3.1699	3.1024	3.0373	2.9745	2.9137	2.8550	4
5	4.8534	4.7135	4.5797	4.4518	4.3295	4.2124	4.1002	3.9927	3.8897	3.7908	3.6959	3.6048	3.5172	3.4331	3.3522	5
6	5.7955	5.6014	5.4172	5.2421	5.0757	4.9173	4.7665	4.6229	4.4859	4.3553	4.2305	4.1114	3.9975	3.8887	3.7845	6
7	6.7282	6.4720	6.2303	6.0021	5.7864	5.5824	5.3893	5.2064	5.0330	4.8684	4.7122	4.5638	4.4226	4.2883	4.1604	7
8	7.6517	7.3255	7.0197	6.7327	6.4632	6.2098	5.9713	5.7466	5.5348	5.3349	5.1461	4.9676	4.7988	4.6389	4.4873	8
9	8.5660	8.1622	7.7861	7.4353	7.1078	6.8017	6.5152	6.2469	5.9952	5.7590	5.5370	5.3282	5.1317	4.9464	4.7716	9
10	9.4713	8.9826	8.5302	8.1109	7.7217	7.3601	7.0236	6.7101	6.4177	6.1446	5.8892	5.6502	5.4262	5.2161	5.0188	10
11	10.3676	9.7868	9.2526	8.7605	8.3064	7.8869	7.4987	7.1390	6.8052	6.4951	6.2065	5.9377	5.6869	5.4527	5.2337	11
12	11.2551	10.5753	9.9540	9.3851	8.8633	8.3838	7.9427	7.5361	7.1607	6.8137	6.4924	6.1844	5.9176	5.6603	5.4206	12
13	12.1337	11.3484	10.6350	9.9856	9.3936	8.8527	8.3577	7.9038	7.4869	7.1034	6.7499	6.4235	6.1218	5.8424	5.5831	13
14	13.0037	12.1062	11.2961	10.5631	9.8986	9.2950	8.7455	8.2442	7.7862	7.3667	6.9819	6.6282	6.3025	6.0021	5.7245	14
15	13.8651	12.8493	11.9379	11.1184	10.3797	9.7122	9.1079	8.5595	8.0607	7.6061	7.1909	6.8109	6.4624	6.1422	5.8474	15
16	14.7179	13.5777	12.5611	11.6523	10.8378	10.1059	9.4466	8.8514	8.3126	7.8237	7.3792	6.9740	6.6039	6.2651	5.9542	16
17	15.5623	14.2919	13.1661	12.1657	11.2741	10.4773	9.7632	9.1216	8.5436	8.0216	7.5488	7.1196	6.7291	6.3729	6.0472	17
18	16.3983	14.9920	13.7535	12.6593	11.6896	10.8276	10.0591	9.3719	8.7556	8.2014	7.7016	7.2497	6.8399	6.4674	6.1280	18
19	17.2260	15.6785	14.3238	13.1339	12.0853	11.1581	10.3356	9.6036	8.9501	8.3649	7.8393	7.3658	6.9380	6.5504	6.1982	19
20	18.0456	16.3514	14.8775	13.5903	12.4622	11.4699	10.5940	9.8181	9.1285	8.5136	7.9633	7.4694	7.0248	6.6231	6.2593	20
25	22.0232	19.5235	17.4131	15.6221	14.0939	12.7834	11.6536	10.6748	9.8226	9.0770	8.4217	7.8431	7.3300	6.8729	6.4641	25
30	25.8077	22.3965	19.6004	17.2920	15.3725	13.7648	12.4090	11.2578	10.2737	9.4269	8.6938	8.0552	7.4957	7.0027	6.5660	30
35	29.4086	24.9986	21.4872	18.6646	16.3742	14.4982	12.9477	11.6546	10.5668	9.6442	8.8552	8.1755	7.5856	7.0700	6.6166	35
40	32.8347	27.3555	23.1148	19.7928	17.1591	15.0463	13.3317	11.9246	10.7574	9.7791	8.9511	6.2438	7.6344	7.1050	6.6418	40
45	36.0945	29.4902	24.5187	20.7200	17.7741	15.4558	13.6055	12.1084	10.8812	9.8628	9.0079	8.2825	7.6609	7.1232	6.6543	45
50	39.1961	31.4236	25.7298	21.4822	18.2559	15.7619	13.8007	12.2335	10.9617	9.9148	9.0417	8.3045	7.6752	7.1327	6.6605	50

Years (n)	Interest rates (r) 16	17	18	19	20	21	22	23	24	25	26	27	28	29	30	
1	0.8621	0.8547	0.8475	0.8403	0.8333	0.8264	0.8197	0.8130	0.8065	0.8000	0.7337	0.7874	0.7812	0.7752	0.7692	1
2	1.6052	1.5852	1.5656	1.5465	1.5278	1.5095	1.4915	1.4740	1.4568	1.4400	1.4235	1.4074	1.3916	1.3761	1.3609	2
3	2.2459	2.2096	2.1743	2.1399	2.1065	2.0739	2.0422	2.0114	1.9813	1.9570	1.9234	1.8956	1.8684	1.8420	1.8161	3
4	2.7982	2.7432	2.6901	2.6386	2.5887	2.5404	2.4936	2.4483	2.4043	2.3616	2.3202	2.2800	2.2410	2.2031	2.1662	4
5	3.2743	3.1993	3.1272	3.0576	2.9906	2.9260	2.8636	2.8035	2.7454	2.6893	2.6351	2.5827	2.5320	2.4830	2.4356	5
6	3.6847	3.5892	3.4976	3.4098	3.3255	3.2446	3.1669	3.0923	3.0205	2.9514	2.8850	2.8210	2.7594	2.7000	2.6427	6
7	4.0386	3.9224	3.8115	3.7057	3.6046	3.5079	3.4155	3.3270	3.2423	3.1611	3.0833	3.0087	2.9370	2.8682	2.8021	7
8	4.3436	4.2072	4.0776	3.9544	3.8372	3.7256	3.6193	3.5179	3.4212	3.3289	3.2407	3.1564	3.0758	2.9986	2.9247	8
9	4.6065	4.4506	4.3030	4.1633	4.0310	3.9054	3.7863	3.6731	3.5655	3.4631	3.3657	3.2728	3.1842	3.0997	3.0190	9
10	4.8332	4.6586	4.4941	4.3389	4.1925	4.0541	3.9232	3.7993	3.6819	3.5705	3.4648	3.3644	3.2689	3.1781	3.0915	10
11	5.0286	4.8364	4.6560	4.4865	4.3271	3.1769	4.0354	3.9018	3.7757	3.6564	3.5435	3.4365	3.3351	3.2388	3.1417	11
12	5.1971	4.9884	4.7932	4.6105	4.4392	4.2784	4.1274	3.9852	3.8514	3.7251	3.6059	3.4933	3.3868	3.2859	3.1903	12
13	5.3423	5.1183	4.9095	4.7147	4.5327	4.3624	4.2028	4.0530	3.9124	3.7801	3.6555	3.5381	3.4272	3.3224	3.2233	13
14	5.4675	5.2293	5.0081	4.8023	4.6106	4.4317	4.2646	4.1082	3.9616	3.8241	3.6949	3.5733	3.4587	3.3507	3.2487	14
15	5.5755	5.3242	5.0916	4.8759	4.6755	4.4890	4.3152	4.1530	4.0013	3.8593	3.7261	3.6010	3.4834	3.3726	3.2682	15
16	5.6685	5.4053	5.1624	4.9377	4.7296	4.5364	4.3567	4.1894	4.0333	3.8874	3.7509	3.6228	3.5026	3.3896	3.2832	16
17	5.7487	5.4746	5.2223	4.9897	4.7746	4.5755	4.3908	4.2190	4.0591	3.9099	3.7705	3.6400	3.5177	3.4028	3.2948	17
18	5.8178	5.5339	5.2732	5.0333	4.8122	4.6079	4.4187	4.2431	4.0799	3.9279	3.7861	3.6536	3.5294	3.4130	3.3037	18
19	5.8775	5.5845	5.3162	5.0700	4.8435	4.6346	4.4415	4.2627	4.0967	3.9424	3.7985	3.6642	3.5386	3.4210	3.3105	19
20	5.9288	5.6278	5.3527	5.1009	4.8696	4.6567	4.4603	4.2786	4.1103	3.9539	3.8083	3.6726	3.5458	3.4271	3.3158	20
25	6.0971	5.7662	5.4669	5.1951	4.9476	4.7213	4.5139	4.3232	4.1474	3.9849	3.8342	3.6943	3.5640	3.4423	3.3286	25
30	6.1772	5.8294	5.5168	5.2347	4.9789	4.7463	4.5338	4.3391	4.1601	3.9950	3.8424	3.7009	3.5693	3.4466	3.3321	30
35	6.2153	5.8582	5.5386	5.2512	4.9915	4.7559	4.5411	4.3447	4.1644	3.9984	3.8450	3.7028	3.5708	3.4478	3.3330	35
40	6.2335	5.8713	5.5482	5.2582	4.9966	4.7596	4.5439	4.3467	4.1659	3.9995	3.8458	3.7034	3.5712	3.4481	3.3332	40
45	6.2421	5.8773	5.5523	5.2611	4.9986	4.7610	4.5449	4.3474	4.1664	3.9998	3.8460	3.7036	3.5714	3.4482	3.3333	45
50	6.2463	5.8801	5.5541	5.2623	4.9995	4.7616	4.5452	4.3477	4.1666	3.9999	3.8461	3.7037	3.5714	3.4483	3.3333	50

Author Index

Subject Index